BENEFIT PLANS IN HIGHER EDUCATION

BENEFIT PLANS
IN
HIGHER EDUCATION

by
FRANCIS P. KING
and
THOMAS J. COOK

Columbia University Press
New York 1980

Library of Congress Cataloging in Publication Data

King, Francis Paul, 1922–
Benefit plans in higher education.

Includes bibliographical references and index.
1. College teachers—United States—Salaries,
pensions, etc.   2. College administrators—United
States—Salaries, pensions, etc.   I. Cook, Thomas J.,
1946–   joint author.   II. Title.
LB2334.K54   331.25′5   79-28751
ISBN 0-231-04914-5

Columbia University Press
New York   Guildford, Surrey

Contents

Foreword

INCREDIBLE! Ninety-nine point nine percent of America's faculty members and administrators are at colleges and universities with retirement plans. Nearly as many institutions have pensions for all staff members. Yet in business and industry, fewer than half of the employees have any employer pensions other than Social Security.

Coverages for the other great threats to income—medical expenses, disability, and death—are almost as widespread as are retirement plans in the college world. This also is a record well ahead of business and industry.

When I first joined TIAA, in 1941, Dr. Rainard B. Robbins had just made the first study of benefit plans. It covered only retirement—there were no major medical or disability and only a few life insurance plans available. In 1939 there were 350 college retirement plans, and only 1,500 plans in all of business and industry. The current study traces these developments for forty years, back through Robbins' work and the three volumes I prepared—in 1948, and with Dr. King in 1959 and 1969. The significant fact is the growth in coverage and improvement in plans that occurred in each of the decades, leading to near-universal protection now.

This data-packed volume covers, for the first time in one book, both senior and junior colleges. It analyzes all the plan provisions—participation, contributions, benefits, retirement ages, and types of plans. It also contains two exceptionally useful new sections—costs and regulation—and an analytical discussion of the Social Security program.

1. *Costs.* The authors have given us important new data regarding expenditures for benefit programs, both in absolute terms and as percentages of total payroll. Those interested can now examine the cost of benefits provided by public and by private institutions, by four- and two-year institutions, and in other classifications.

As the authors demonstrate, health and pension benefits have become a large portion of the total compensation package. This highlights the continuing challenge to college decision-makers in efficiently allocating resources among salary, benefits, and various other institutional needs.

2. *Government Regulation.* This caption is not to be found in the indexes of the previous volumes; it is the entire concluding chapter of this one. Government regulation has grown pervasively, and now includes such factors as ERISA, legislation affecting compulsory retirement, and mandated health benefit provisions that differ from state to state throughout the nation.

3. *Social Security.* Previous studies traced the basic federal plan and its impact upon college benefit programming. In the light of recent changes in the law that have altered the dynamics of the system, the authors provide a philosophical discussion of the impact the changes could have on benefits for all college staff members, and give a useful analysis of the structure of the benefits themselves.

The data in this study, drawn from a survey of over two thousand colleges and universities, are so extensive that a college faculty benefits committee, trustee study group, labor union or other decision-making body can find within it the information to help them design effective, efficient, and attractive benefit plans. Coverage may be well-nigh universal, but there is much work yet to be done on types and provisions of plans at many institutions. And this book will help get it done.

Dr. Francis P. King has studied and written about all phases of college benefit planning for over a quarter century, and he and Thomas J. Cook are superbly qualified to present this study. It is a scholarly contribution to pension literature and a "must" handbook for improving the security of college staff members during the decade of the 1980s.

New York, N.Y.   WILLIAM C. GREENOUGH
October 1979

Acknowledgments

THIS STUDY has depended in great measure on the cooperation of many people in higher education—college business officers, financial officers, personnel specialists, institutional researchers, and many others who took the time to gather the data we requested and to return the survey questionnaires. We gratefully acknowledge their assistance. Their conscientious work is all the more appreciated in an era awash with government forms and questionnaires that compete for the precious time of college administrators and that carry penalties, as ours did not, for failure to respond.

We are also grateful to the executive officers of the public retirement systems who supplied information regarding their plans and who very kindly checked our summary descriptions of the public plans.

We also wish to thank our many colleagues who gave valuable support. Donna M. Zucchi was responsible for the administration, editing, and liaison for data processing of the benefit cost survey. The administration of this newly introduced part of our regular survey required considerable direct contact with respondents. All of these duties were handled with great skill.

Peggy Eberhart carried the principal burden of the typing of draft chapters and the preparation of the final manuscript, as well as assisting with the questionnaires. We are deeply grateful for her patience and competence, and for the care with which each chapter draft was handled. We also appreciate the typing assistance of Betty Meyers and Anna Cerretani. Barry Hodes provided invaluable help in the preparation of the basic tapes incorporating the study universe and institutional classifications.

For their counsel and the calculation of many of the actuarial and other illustrations in the text, we are indebted to Thomas G. Walsh, Barry M. Black, Kirk L. Dorn, Robert C. Beetham, John Nader, and Roger Francisco. We benefited from comments by members of the TIAA legal staff on portions of several of the chapters, for which we thank JoAnn G. Sher, Louis R. Garcia, and William F. Heller II, for their advice and assistance. Russell E. Bone and Neil A. Bancroft provided comments on several parts of the manuscript, with substantial improvements as a result. Roy Hardiman, Mary Toulis, and Jill Arbuckle of T/C/A Associates managed the data processing of the returned questionnaires and we greatly appreciate their substantial contributions to this study.

In developing the test questionnaires for the study, we were assisted by the knowledge and expertise of D. Francis Finn, Executive Vice-President, and Abbott Wainwright, Associate Director for Information and Publication, of the National Association of College and University Business Officers. We also wish to acknowledge the help of Don Thiel, Manager, Office of Staff Benefits, University of Michigan, and Jack N. Ray, Director, Retirement and Insurance Plans, Indiana University, who, as members of the test panel of college business officers, provided valuable comments and assistance.

The final manuscript gained much from the work of those of our colleagues who read all of the chapters and offered many valuable comments and suggestions: William C. Greenough, Donald S. Willard, William T. Slater, and Bruce L. Boyd. We owe an immense debt of gratitude to the thoughtful hours they have given us.

New York, N.Y.   FRANCIS P. KING
October 1979   THOMAS J. COOK

1 Introduction and Summary

EMPLOYEE BENEFITS have come to occupy an important place as part of the total compensation of faculty, administrative officers, other professional personnel, and the supporting staff of clerical and service personnel in higher education. Need, convenience, efficiency, and the tax code have made employee benefit plans an emblem of the twentieth century. The growth of benefit plans in higher education is documented in a series of studies of these benefits published by the Columbia University Press, of which the present study is the fifth.

Prior Studies. The first of the study series, published in 1940, reviewed the development of plans for retirement income from the beginning of this century to the close of the year 1939.[1] In those early years, nearly all efforts were concentrated on introducing systematic means of providing pension income, an objective that took first priority. These efforts succeeded, for by 1940 the colleges and universities were well ahead of business and industry in providing pension plans for their employees. Some 350 institutions of higher education had formal retirement plans in 1940, while there were only about 1,700 such plans in all of business and industry.

The second survey of benefits in colleges and universities was published in 1948.[2] It documented further growth in retirement plan coverage and reported that although 40 percent of U.S. colleges and universities did not yet have a retirement plan, the institutions without plans employed only about 15 percent of college teachers.[3] With the postwar progress in pension coverage came greater attention to a second valuable employee benefit—life insurance. The 1948 study reported that "one out of four colleges now has group or collective life insurance plans in operation. The 225 United States institutions that have [life insurance] plans employ 44 percent of the college teachers, and about three out of four of the plans cover non-academic employees as well as faculty members and administrative officers."[4]

Between 1948 and 1959, a near-explosion of benefit protection took place. In the early 1950s, public and private colleges and universities were brought into the Social Security program on a voluntary basis. In addition, the growth of health insurance coverage under basic hospital-surgical-medical plans proceeded apace, with major medical coverage added in the latter part of the 1950s. Group long-term disability income insurance coverage also was made available to colleges and universities for the first time, through the joint efforts of the Ford Foundation and Teachers Insurance and Annuity Association (TIAA), which offered the first plans for educational institutions. As a result, the next study in the series, published in 1959, covered a

1

Table 1.1. Summary of Benefit Plans Reported by Four-Year Colleges and Universities in the 1969 Study (percent of institutions reporting plans and percent of employees in institutions reporting plans)

Type of Plan	Faculty		Administrative		Clerical-Service	
	Percent Insts	Percent EEs	Percent Insts	Percent EEs	Percent Insts	Percent EEs
	n = 1,232	n = 285,414	n = 1,232	n = 108,315	n = 1,232	n = 444,618
Retirement	95.0	99.5	92.6	99.4	74.8	94.7
Life insurance	70.1	87.4	69.6	90.4	62.7	85.1
Basic health insurance	90.0	91.6	89.8	92.8	89.8	90.3
Major medical	81.6	93.6	81.4	94.9	73.2	84.6
Short-term disability income	71.8	81.0	71.9	83.3	72.2	82.6
Long-term disability income	50.9	71.2	51.1	71.8	38.1	58.4

SOURCE: William C. Greenough and Francis P. King, *Benefit Plans in American Colleges* (New York: Columbia University Press, 1969).

broad range of benefits: retirement, life insurance, basic hospital-surgical-medical insurance, major medical, and short- and long-term disability insurance plans.[5]

The fourth study in the Columbia University Press series was published in 1969.[6] It spanned a period of continuing growth in the educational sector and a comparable growth in the extent of employee benefit plans. Table 1.1 summarizes the benefit plan coverage reported by the four-year colleges and universities in the 1969 study. Retirement plan coverage was virtually complete, with only a small gap in the coverage of clerical-service employees; about 25 percent of institutions employing 5 percent of clerical-service employees did not have a plan for this group. Between 85 and 90 percent of all employees were in educational institutions reporting a life insurance plan. Basic hospital-surgical-medical insurance was available in 90 percent of the institutions, which had about 90 percent of the employees in higher education. Major medical coverage had grown rapidly, so that by 1969 about 85 percent of clerical-service employees and nearly 95 percent of faculty and administrative groups were covered. Short-term sick pay or disability plans covered about 80 percent of employees. For faculty and administrative personnel, half the institutions, employing about 70 percent of the people, reported long-term disability income coverage, either as an insured plan or as part of a pension plan. Aside from retirement income protection, which had become almost universal a decade before, all of these figures represented rates of substantial growth over the period.

The 1960s also witnessed rapid growth in the junior and community college sector. A full-scale study of the benefit plans in these institutions was published in 1971.[7] The data from that study indicated that progress in benefit coverage comparable to the four-year institutions had been achieved in the two-year institutions. Table 1.2 summarizes the results of this 1971 study. Somewhat higher levels of short-term sick pay and disability coverage and long-term disability income plans were reported by the two-year colleges in 1971, compared with the four-year institutions in 1969. The major differences reflected the greater number of two-year institutions in the public

Table 1.2. Summary of Benefit Plans Reported by Two-Year Colleges in the 1971 Study (percent of institutions reporting plans and percent of employees in institutions reporting plans)

Type of Plan	Faculty		Administrative		Clerical-Service	
	Percent Insts	Percent EEs	Percent Insts	Percent EEs	Percent Insts	Percent EEs
	n = 893	n = 59,383	n = 893	n = 13,103	n = 893	n = 42,886
Retirement	94.3	98.4	94.1	97.6	88.1	94.6
Life insurance	70.2	78.3	70.2	76.7	66.5	74.3
Health insurance	95.5	98.6	95.5	98.1	95.2	98.6
Short-term disability income	90.9	95.4	91.0	93.9	91.5	95.3
Long-term disability income	86.9	94.6	87.0	91.4	82.1	90.2

SOURCE: Francis P. King, *Benefit Plans in Junior Colleges* (Washington, D.C.: American Association of Junior Colleges, 1971).

sector, with more formalized sick pay plans, and more long-term disability income coverage provided through public employee and teacher retirement systems.

Current Extent of Plans. The overall findings of the current study are presented in table 1.3. The first section combines responses of four-year colleges and universities and two-year institutions, thus giving a comprehensive view of the benefit plans in effect in all institutions of higher education. The other two sections of the table permit comparisons between the current study results and the results of the 1971

Table 1.3. Summary of Benefit Plans Reported by the Current Survey (percent of institutions reporting plans and percent of employees in institutions reporting plans)

Type of Plan	Faculty		Administrative		Clerical-Service	
	Percent Insts	Percent EEs	Percent Insts	Percent EEs	Percent Insts	Percent EEs
All Institutions	n = 2,092	n = 432,402	n = 2,092	n = 233,511	n = 2,092	n = 670,941
Retirement	97.3	99.6	97.0	99.6	92.2	98.9
Life insurance	85.7	92.8	85.9	94.4	83.6	93.5
Health insurance	98.7	99.8	98.8	99.8	98.5	99.9
Short-term disability income[a]	100.0	100.0	100.0	100.0	100.0	100.0
Long-term disability income	82.2	93.6	81.8	93.9	71.6	86.3
Four-Year Institutions	n = 1,407	n = 363,203	n = 1,407	n = 211,647	n = 1,407	n = 601,711
Retirement	97.0	99.7	96.4	99.7	90.2	98.9
Life insurance	85.5	93.7	85.6	95.0	83.3	94.3
Health insurance	98.8	99.9	99.0	99.9	98.6	99.9
Short-term disability income[a]	100.0	100.0	100.0	100.0	100.0	100.0
Long-term disability income	81.7	94.4	81.2	94.4	67.2	86.1
Two-Year Institutions	n = 685	n = 69,199	n = 685	n = 21,864	n = 685	n = 69,230
Retirement	97.8	99.2	98.0	99.3	95.9	98.8
Life Insurance	86.0	88.4	86.4	88.1	84.5	86.7
Health insurance	98.2	99.5	98.4	99.3	98.2	99.8
Short-term disability income[a]	100.0	100.0	100.0	100.0	100.0	100.0
Long-term disability income	83.3	89.6	83.1	88.6	80.6	88.2

[a] Includes Workers' Compensation.

two-year college study and the 1969 study of the four-year institutions. Each of the tables gives results according to numbers and percentages of institutions reporting plan coverages and numbers and percentages of educational employees represented by these institutions. The latter can be taken as weighted measurements of the coverages.

Generally, the current study results suggest that the last decade can be characterized as one in which modest remaining gaps in coverages have been nearly closed. In the four-year institutions, the proportion of employees covered reaches well into the 90th percentile, ranging (depending on the plan and the employee classification) from 93.7 percent to 100 percent, with only one exception. Long-term disability income coverage for clerical-service employees is reported by 67.2 percent of institutions employing 86.1 percent of these employees. Among the two-year institutions there is a somewhat lower proportion of life insurance coverage than in the four-year group, but in other areas the extent of coverage in the two-year group is comparable to that in the four-year colleges and universities. Taken all together, the data indicate that retirement plans, health insurance coverage, and short-term disability benefits (including Workers' Compensation) are almost universally available to employees in higher education, and that life insurance plans and long-term disability income coverages are not far behind.

With the vast majority of faculty and other employees in higher education covered by the major employee benefit plans, it becomes all the more important to inquire into the nature of the benefit protection that is offered under the plans. Assessments of quality are called for, including examination of eligibility provisions, waiting periods, the sharing of plan costs, the benefit provisions themselves—services provided or cash paid, and the various conditions under which the benefits become available. Also to be considered is the overall determination of benefit plan objectives and the relationships between the various benefit plans.

Study Purpose. The purpose of the present study is to describe the current status of benefit planning in higher education, to provide information on the types of retirement and insurance plans in effect, and to outline the principal provisions of the plans. This includes the presentation of the quantitative information reported by the 2,092 educational institutions that participated in the survey. In addition, the study offers qualitative and background information designed to be helpful in the understanding of the various benefit provisions and their alternatives, including brief discussions of annuity and insurance principles and practices. Consideration of pension and insurance principles can help advance understanding of how specific benefit plans work, how plans that appear similar may differ in their effects, or how alternative approaches may produce more (or less) advantageous cost-benefit relationships. It is hoped that this volume will be used as a handbook, a working paper, and not just as a collection of statistics to be glanced at and put on a shelf.

The report has attempted to avoid the technical and legalistic language that is often used in describing benefit plans. However, when dealing with theoretical and operating aspects of benefit plans, it is sometimes difficult to avoid technical language altogether, although the aim has been a report as free as possible of jargon.

This report is by no means solely designed for the use of policy makers and administrators. Understanding of college benefit plans is important to each individual faculty and staff member. Benefit plans are (or should be) designed to dovetail with an employee's own savings for old age, life insurance, and other economic planning, and of course with the Social Security benefits of employees covered under the federal program. Simply from the standpoint of effective individual money management, a review of the way a benefit plan operates can often lead to more intelligent individual use of the plan. At times, participants may not feel qualified to ask the right questions about the operation of their benefit plans. This study, it is hoped, will lead to a greater degree of knowledge and interest on the part of benefit plan participants.

Some benefit plans do a better job than others. Individual staff members can assist their employers by advising them as to the effectiveness of existing plans in meeting real needs and on whether the plans are meeting their stated objectives. Employers are aided by listening to informed feedback when the time comes to review or revise benefit plans.

Scope of Study. The report covers the four principal staff benefit areas: (1) retirement benefits; (2) benefits for survivors in the event of the death of the employee; (3) benefits to cover medical expenses resulting from illness or injury of employees or their dependents; and (4) income benefits payable during periods an employee is unable to work due to disability, however caused, for short or long periods.

The 2,955 educational institutions comprising the study universe include all United States colleges and universities, public and private, offering postsecondary education, including junior and community colleges and four-year colleges and universities. The only institutions of higher education excluded from the survey were proprietary institutions and nondegree-granting institutions, and institutions outside the fifty states. The listing of institutions and their classifications was obtained from tapes supplied by the Center for Higher Education Statistics of the U.S. Office of Education.

The study questionnaire, reprinted in Appendix A, was mailed January 9, 1978, to the president of each institution. Information in questionnaires returned after June 8, 1978 is not included in the study.

The study data were collected for three major personnel categories: (1) faculty—instruction/research; (2) administrative/managerial/other professional; and (3) other employees. Faculty is defined as persons employed for the primary purpose of performing instruction and/or research, including chairpersons of academic departments if they have no other administrative title. Administrative includes all employees whose primary responsibility is for the administration and management of the institution or its subdivisions, as well as all nonteaching professionals. The third category comprises all employees not included in the first two categories, including those subject to the provision of the Fair Labor Standards Act and persons engaged in activities categorized as technical, office/clerical, crafts and trades, service, etc., excluding student employees. In the table headings in the chapters and in Appendix C the three employee categories are abbreviated as follows: (1) faculty; (2) administrative; and (3) clerical-service.

Survey Response. A total of 2,092 institutions, representing 71 percent of the study group, responded to the benefit plan survey. These institutions employ (full time) 432,402 faculty, 233,511 administrative officers and other professionals, and 670,941 clerical-service employees, totaling 1,336,854 persons.

By type, 96 percent of universities and 79 percent of four-year liberal arts colleges responded. The response rate dropped to 60 percent for what are classified in the study as "other" four-year institutions—mainly professional schools, seminaries, and institutions devoted exclusively to teacher training. By control, 88 percent of public four-year colleges and universities and 72 percent of private four-year colleges and universities responded. Among the institutions offering less than four years of educational training, generally designated as two-year institutions in this study, 66 percent of the publicly supported institutions and 45 percent of the private institutions responded.[8]

HIGHLIGHTS OF SURVEY FINDINGS

RETIREMENT PLANS

• Virtually all institutions of higher education report a retirement plan. The few exceptions are mainly in the private sector of higher education. The 56 reporting institutions that said they do not have a retirement plan for faculty employed an average of thirty faculty members per institution. The 164 institutions that reported no retirement plan for clerical-service employees employed an average of forty-five of this employee group per institution.

• TIAA-CREF retirement plans and public retirement systems for teachers or other public employees constitute the main type of retirement plans in higher education. Taking all the responding institutions together, for faculty TIAA-CREF is reported by 67.7 percent, public employee systems by 20.1 percent, and state or local teacher systems by 35.4 percent. The percentages add to more than 100 because more than one plan may be in effect at an institution, including optional and supplemental plans. Throughout the study, the data for administrative/managerial/professional personnel are approximately the same as those cited for faculty.

• For clerical-service employees, TIAA-CREF plans are reported by 42.6 percent of all institutions, public employee retirement systems by 35.1 percent, and state or local teacher systems by 20.9 percent.

• For all four-year colleges and universities, faculty retirement coverage under TIAA-CREF is reported by 78.3 percent of institutions, public employee systems by 12.5 percent, and state or local teacher retirement systems by 21.5 percent. For their clerical-service employees, 52.8 percent of the four-year institutions report TIAA-CREF coverage, 22.2 percent report public employee systems, and 13.6 percent report state or local teacher systems.

• Among all private four-year colleges and universities, TIAA-CREF retirement plans are reported for faculty by 86.7 percent of institutions, church pension plans by 15.6 percent, insurance company plans by 10.4 percent, and self-funded retirement plans by 5.1 percent. For clerical-service employees in private four-year institutions, TIAA-CREF plans are reported by 69.4 percent, insurance company plans by 17.2 percent, church pension plans by 11 percent, and self-funded plans by 13.7 percent. Church pension plan coverage is usually available as an alternative to a TIAA-CREF plan in the same institution.

• Among all public four-year colleges and universities, TIAA-CREF retirement plans are reported for faculty by 62.8 percent of institutions, public employee retirement systems by 35.1 percent, and state or local teacher retirement systems by 57.1 percent. For their clerical-service employees, 25.4 percent of the public four-year institutions report TIAA-CREF plans, 58.9 percent public employee systems, and 35.8 percent state or local teacher systems.

• Among public two-year institutions (junior and community colleges), 71.3 percent report faculty coverage under a public teacher retirement system, 40.1 percent report a public employee retirement system for faculty, and 42.4 percent report faculty coverage under TIAA-CREF (sometimes as a supplementary or alternative plan).

• Among the private two-year colleges, 75.7 percent report a TIAA-CREF plan for faculty, 14.9 percent report an insurance company plan, and 10.8 percent report a self-funded plan.

• The great majority of faculty retirement plans in higher education are contributory, that is, employer and employees share in the cost of the plans.

• Noncontributory retirement plans (employer-pay-all) are reported by 6.9 percent of public four-year institutions employing 8.4 percent of faculty in the public four-year group, and by 15.4 percent of private four-year institutions, employing 16.6 percent of faculty in the private four-year colleges and universities.

• Among the private four-year institutions, the proportion of noncontributory plans is significantly higher for clerical-service personnel than for faculty or administrative and other professional personnel. Noncontributory retirement plans for clerical-service employees are reported by 25.3 percent of the private four-year colleges and universities employing 41.1 percent of this personnel class in the group.

• Flexibility has characterized the retirement age provisions of retirement plans in higher education. About 90 percent of the institutions report for all employee classes that employment could be extended beyond the stated normal retirement age.

• The most frequently stated normal retirement age for all institutions combined was age 65, with 81.0 percent of the four-year colleges and universities and 73.0 percent of the two-year colleges reporting a normal retirement age of 65.

• Publicly supported institutions tend to state earlier normal retirement ages than do the private institutions. Among the four-year public colleges and universities, a normal age under 65 was reported by 18.6 percent of institutions, compared with 0.5 percent of the private colleges and universities.

• A normal retirement age of 65 was reported by 61.8 percent of public four-year colleges and universities and by 91.3 percent of private colleges and universities.

• A normal retirement age of 65 was reported by 70.0 percent of public junior and community colleges and by 97.2 percent of private two-year colleges.

• Institutions providing for extensions of service beyond the normal retirement age generally state age 70 as the age beyond which extensions are not permitted.

GROUP LIFE INSURANCE

• Group life insurance plans are reported for faculty by 85.7 percent of all institutions of higher education, two-year and four-year, employing 92.8 percent of faculty. For clerical-service personnel, 83.6 percent of the institutions, employing 93.5 percent of all such personnel in all the responding institutions, provide a life insurance plan.

• Among the four-year colleges and universities, 90.6 percent of public institutions, employing 93.1 percent of faculty, and 82.8 percent of the private institutions, employing 94.7 percent of faculty, report a life insurance plan for the faculty group.

• For clerical-service personnel in the four-year institutions of higher education, 90.0 percent of public institutions, employing 94 percent of clerical-service personnel in the public sector, report a life insurance plan, as do 79.8 percent of the private four-year institutions, employing 94.7 percent of clerical-service personnel in the private sector.

• The full cost of basic group life insurance amounts for faculty is paid by 60.6 percent of the private four-year colleges and universities and by 40.9 percent of public four-year colleges and universities. The percentages are almost exactly the same for clerical-service employees as for faculty in these two types of institutions.

• In the two-year colleges, the life insurance plans covering faculty are paid for wholly by the employer in 62.3 percent of the private colleges and in 60.6 percent of the public colleges, with similar percentages also reported for clerical-service employees.

• The cost of basic group life insurance coverage for faculty is shared between employer and employee in 37.3 percent of the private four-year colleges and universities and by 44.1 percent of public four-year colleges and universities. The percentages are similar for clerical-service employees.

• In the two-year colleges, the cost of life insurance plans for faculty is shared between employer and employee in 36.1 percent of the private colleges and in 34.8 percent of the public colleges, with comparable percentages also reported for clerical-service employees.

• In addition to a group life insurance plan's basic insurance amount, paid for in full by about 60 percent of all the institutions combined, 43 percent of all colleges and universities make it possible for employees to elect additional insurance amounts. This ranges from 27.0 percent of the private four-year institutions to 59.6 percent of the public four-year group, and from 36 percent of the private two-year institutions to 55 percent of the public two-year group.

• Waiting periods before eligible employees can participate in a group life insurance plan in two-year and four-year colleges and universities are reported by about four-fifths of the institutions as being one month or less in duration.

• Group life insurance amounts may be assigned to employees in a variety of ways. Among all institutions, 44.4 percent assign it as a multiple of the employee's salary and 22.8 percent assign insurance according to job or salary category. The same amount of insurance for all employees is reported by 24 percent of the institutions.

• Taking all institutions together, 27.5 percent reported that the amount of group insurance of employees does not change as age or salary increases. Fifty-seven percent reported that the insurance amount increases as salary increases, and 26.6 percent reported that the amount decreases as age advances.

• Four-fifths of the responding institutions report that the insurance amount of the group life insurance program, however assigned, is the same for equally situated faculty employees regardless of dependents. Five percent indicate that employees with dependents could elect higher coverage amounts. Two percent indicated that the basic insurance amount was higher for employees with dependents than for those without. These percentages are approximately the same for clerical-service personnel. (As noted previously, 43 percent of all the institutions permit employee election of additional life insurance amounts regardless of dependents.)

• Slightly more than a third of all the responding institutions, employing between 55 and 60 percent of faculty, administrative, and clerical-service personnel, provide for some amounts of life insurance coverage during retirement. In the plans with retirement insurance amounts, the face value is usually less for retirees than for active employees.

• When life insurance is continued for retired faculty, 15.6 percent of the public four-year institutions and 24.6 percent of the public two-year institutions pay the whole cost, as do 45.6 percent of the private four-year institutions and 44.5 percent of the private two-year institutions. The employer and retired employee share the cost in 20 percent of the public four-year institutions, 23.6 percent of the public two-year institutions, 18 percent of the private four-year institutions, and 11.1 percent of the private two-year institutions.

• The retired faculty employee pays the full cost of continued group life insurance coverage in 45.1 percent of the public four-year institutions, in 18.3 percent of the private four-year institutions, in 27.2 percent of the public two-year institutions, and in 33.3 percent of the private two-year institutions.

• When group life insurance is continued for retired clerical-service employees, 30.3 percent of the public four-year institutions and 13.5 percent of the public two-year institutions pay the whole cost, as do 13.6 percent of the private four-year institutions and 25 percent of the private two-year institutions. The employer and retired employee share the cost in 28.7 percent of the public four-year institutions, 27.2 percent of the public two-year institutions, and in 55.5 percent of the private four-year institutions and 37.5 percent of private two-year institutions.

• The retired clerical-service employee pays the full cost of continued group life insurance coverage in 8 percent of the public four-year institutions, in 10.3 percent of the private four-year institutions, in 24.5 percent of the public two-year institutions, and in 12.5 percent of the private two-year institutions.

HEALTH INSURANCE

• Health insurance plans (basic hospital-surgical-medical, major medical, comprehensive basic and major medical, and/or health maintenance organizations—HMOs) are reported for faculty by 98.7 percent of all the responding institutions, employing 99.8 percent of faculty. The percentages of coverage are nearly identical for the other employee groups, administrative, other professional, and clerical-service employees.

• Basic and major medical insurance coverages are the predominant form of health insurance coverage for all employee groups in all reporting institutions. Basic hospital-surgical-medical coverage is reported for health insurance coverage in institutions employing between 97 and 98 percent of each employee classification, faculty, administrative and other professional, and clerical-service.

• Health insurance coverage under a medical service organization (health maintenance organization) was reported as available for faculty and other employee groups by slightly over 20 percent of all responding institutions.

• Dental care plans for faculty were reported by 30.1 percent of public four-year institutions and 9.2 percent of private four-year colleges and universities, and by 36.8 percent of public two-year institutions and 9.0 percent of private two-year institutions. These percentages are similar for the other employee classifications.

• Vision care plans were reported for faculty by 14.6 percent of the public four-year colleges and universities and by 2 percent of the private four-year institutions, by 11.6 percent of the public two-year colleges and by none of the private two-year colleges. The percentages are similar for the other employee classifications.

• Institutions having major medical insurance reported on whether the coverage is part of a single, comprehensive health insurance plan that includes basic coverage, or whether it is a separate plan. For faculty, among the public four-year colleges and universities, 88.4 percent reported a comprehensive plan and among private four-year colleges and universities, 70.9 percent reported a comprehensive plan. Two-year institutions reported comparable figures. Major medical as a separate plan was reported by 11.2 percent of public four-year institutions and 28.9 percent of private four-year institutions, by 10.1 percent of public two-year institutions and by 18.3 percent of private two-year institutions. The percentages are similar for nonfaculty employee groups.

• Blue Cross and Blue Shield predominate as the most frequently reported types of insurers for health insurance plans in the colleges, with insurance companies, including TIAA, reported next most frequently.

• For faculty in public four-year colleges and universities, 68.6 percent of these institutions reported Blue Cross, 62.3 percent reported Blue Shield, 42.7 percent reported insurance company coverage (basic and/or major medical), 13.6 percent reported other coverage, mainly HMOs, and 9.4 percent reported a self-insurance arrangement. Due to alternative choice arrangements, the percentages add to more than 100.

• For faculty, 60.3 percent of private four-year colleges and universities reported Blue Cross, 54.5 percent reported Blue Shield, 54.7 percent reported an insurance company plan, 14.1 percent reported other coverage (HMOs), and 2.7 percent reported a self-insurance arrangement. These proportions are similar for the other employee classes.

• For faculty and other employee classes, 70.4 percent of public two-year colleges reported Blue Cross, 56.8 percent reported Blue Shield, 40.0 percent reported an insurance company plan, 15.8 percent reported an HMO-type organization, and 5 percent reported self-insurance. For faculty and other employees of private two-year colleges, 67.9 percent reported Blue Cross, 65.4 percent reported Blue Shield, 37.2 percent reported an insurance company plan, 6.4 percent reported an HMO and 2.6 percent reported a self-insurance arrangement.

• Overall, about half of the institutions, public and private, two-year and four-year, pay the full cost of the health insurance coverage of the employee. With few exceptions, the cost is shared by employer and employee in the remaining plans.

• For employee health insurance coverage, the employer pays the full cost in 46.7 percent of the public four-year institutions and in 49 percent of the private four-year institutions. The cost of the employee's health insurance is shared in 53.3 percent of the public four-year institutions and in 46.6 percent of the private four-year institutions. In none of the public four-year institutions does the employee pay the full cost of his or her health insurance coverage, but the employee does pay this cost in 3.9 percent of the private four-year institutions. The figures given are for faculty but there is no significant difference between these figures and the figures for the other employee groups.

• For dependents' health insurance, the predominant overall pattern is the sharing of costs between employer and employee, closely followed by payment of the full cost of dependent coverage by the employee. The employer pays the full cost of dependent coverage in about 20 percent of the plans.

• For dependents' health insurance coverage, 15.9 percent of the public four-year institutions of higher education report that the employer pays the full cost, as do 17.4 percent of the private four-year group. The employer and employee share the cost of dependent coverage in 52.1 percent of the public four-year institutions and in 41.1 percent of the private four-year institutions. The employee pays the full cost of dependent coverage in 31.6 percent of the public four-year institutions and in 40.8 percent of the private.

• In the two-year colleges, the employer pays the full cost of employee health insurance coverage in 69.7 percent of public and 52.6 percent of private colleges. The employer and employee share the cost of employee coverage in 29.2 percent of the public two-year colleges and 41.0 percent of the private two-year institutions. The employee pays the full cost of employee coverage in 0.7 percent of the public two-year colleges and in 6.4 percent of the private. The figures given are for faculty, with other employee groups similar.

• For dependents' health insurance coverage in the two-year colleges, the employer pays the full cost in 31.8 percent of the public institutions and in 17.9 percent of the private. The employee pays the full cost of dependents' coverage in 30.4 percent of the public two-year colleges and in 44.9 percent of the private. The cost of dependents' coverage is shared by employer and employee in 37.1 percent of public two-year institutions and in 35.9 percent of private two-year colleges. The figures are for faculty, with other employee groups similar.

• Waiting periods for the start of participation in health insurance plans by new employees are generally short. About 90 percent of all institutions report a waiting period of one month or less.

• Overall, about 10 percent of the colleges and universities pay the full cost of Medicare (Part B) for their retired employees, and about 6 percent share the cost with the retired employees.

• Sharing of Medicare (Part B) costs, or employer payment of the full cost, is not extensive, but it is reported more frequently in the publicly supported institutions than in the private colleges and universities. In the four-year public colleges and universities, 17.4 percent report that the employer pays the full cost of Medicare (Part B) and shares the cost with the retired employee in 10.9 percent of the institutions. In the private four-year institutions, 8.2 percent report paying the full cost and 3.2 percent report sharing the cost with the retired employee. The reported percentages are essentially the same for faculty and other employee classes.

• In the two-year institutions, 10.8 percent of the public colleges and 7.7 percent of the private report that the employer pays the full cost of retirees' Medicare (Part B) coverage, 7.7 percent of the public and 5.1 percent of the private report a sharing of the cost, and 80.7 and 85.9 percent, respectively, report that the retired employee pays the full cost. The figures are for faculty but other classes are similar.

● About 85 percent of the public four-year institutions report that participation in the group health insurance plan is provided for retired employees, as do about 46 percent of the private four-year colleges and universities.

● When retired employees may continue participation in the institution's health insurance plan, about half the institutions provide for an eligibility requirement incorporating provisions for age and service.

● When retired group health insurance coverage is provided, about a third of all institutions report that the employer pays the full cost for the retired employee's coverage. About a quarter of the institutions report a sharing of cost between the employer and retired employee. The employee pays the full cost in the remaining plans, or about 43 percent. The figures are for faculty, but do not differ substantially for other employee groups.

● For coverage of dependents of retired employees for whom continued participation in the health insurance plan is provided, 9.3 percent of the public four-year colleges and universities report that the employer pays the full cost, as do 19.2 percent of the private four-year institutions. Sharing of dependent coverage cost is reported by 36.6 percent of public four-year institutions and by 17.7 percent of the private group. The retired employee pays the full cost of dependent coverage in 52.4 percent of the public four-year institutions and 58.8 percent of the private institutions. The figures are for faculty but do not differ substantially for other employee groups.

SHORT-TERM DISABILITY AND SICK PAY PLANS

● Plans providing employees with income during short-term periods of absence due to sickness or injury are reported by the great majority of the two-year colleges and four-year colleges and universities. Formal plans are reported by 68.7 percent of the institutions overall, informal plans by 22.2 percent, and group insurance plans by 14.3 percent. There is considerable overlapping among these plans. In addition, all of the institutions provide for Workers' Compensation benefits for work-connected illness and injury.

● Sick pay and other short-term disability plans are usually paid for in full by the employer. In only about 10 percent of the institutions, overall, is it reported that the employer and employee share the cost, usually for plans including group insurance benefits for short-term disabilities.

● Waiting periods for eligibility to participate in short-term disability or sick pay plans tend to be short for faculty. Overall, 73.5 percent of the institutions report a waiting period of one month or less. About 15 percent report a waiting period of between two and six months. Public institutions generally report shorter waiting periods than private institutions. Among public four-year institutions, 81.2 percent report a waiting period of one month or less for faculty, while among private four-year institutions 66.5 percent have a similar waiting period, with the remainder reporting a longer waiting period.

• Waiting periods for short-term sick pay and disability benefits tend to be longer for nonfaculty (clerical-service) than for faculty in both public and private educational institutions. Overall, 63.3 percent of the institutions report a waiting period of one month or less for clerical-service employees. Nearly 25 percent report a period of between two and six months. Distinguishing between public and private four-year colleges and universities, 73.9 percent of the public and 50.6 percent of the private state a waiting period of one month or less. Two to six months is stated by 18 percent of the public and 33.5 percent of the private four-year colleges and universities.

• The duration of sick pay benefits is usually geared to some requirements based on length of employee service. For clerical-service employees in public four-year institutions, 76.2 percent of the employers report that duration of benefits depends on length of service, as do 57.2 percent of private four-year institutions. For faculty, 70 percent of public and 48 percent of private institutions relate short-term benefit duration to length of service.

LONG-TERM DISABILITY INCOME PLANS

• Pension or group insurance plans providing long-term disability income benefits for faculty are reported by 92.3 percent of public four-year colleges and universities, by 76.3 percent of private four-year institutions, by 87.3 percent of public two-year colleges, and by 54.1 percent of private two-year colleges.

• Pension or group insurance plans providing long-term disability income benefits for clerical-service employees are reported by 88.9 percent of public four-year colleges and universities, by 56.1 percent of private four-year institutions, by 86 percent of public two-year colleges, and by 42.4 percent of private two-year colleges.

• The long-term disability income coverage in private institutions is achieved mainly through group insurance plans. For faculty, 91.5 percent of the private four-year colleges reporting long-term disability benefits report a group insurance plan; 2.7 percent report a self-insured plan.

• The long-term disability coverage among publicly supported institutions is achieved partly through the provisions of public employee and state teacher retirement systems and partly through the use of group insurance plans. Among the public four-year colleges and universities, 68.0 percent report benefits provided for faculty through a public employee or state teacher retirement system and 70.7 percent report a group insurance plan. For clerical-service employees, 76.0 percent of the public four-year institutions report coverage through a pension plan and 57.9 percent report a group insurance plan. The extensive overlapping of the two types of plans usually represents situations in which the insurance and retirement plans are integrated, often when lengthy waiting periods for benefit eligibility or low benefit levels may be incorporated in the public retirement system.

• For group insurance plans for long-term disability, the employer pays the full cost for faculty coverage in 40.9 percent of the plans in public four-year colleges and universities and in 67.9 percent of the plans in the private four-year colleges and universities. The cost is shared by employer and employee in approximately a quarter of the plans in both the public and private institutions. The employee pays the full cost in 30.7 percent of the public four-year group and in 5.7 percent of the private four-year group.

• For faculty group long-term disability insurance coverage in the two-year institutions, the employer pays the full cost in 54.7 percent of the plans in the public colleges and in 71.4 percent of the plans in the private. The cost of long-term disability coverage is shared by employer and employee in 23.2 percent of the public and in 14.3 percent of the private two-year colleges. The employee pays the full cost in 20.5 percent of the public two-year group and in 11.9 percent of the private two-year group.

• For clerical-service employees, the cost-sharing figures for long-term disability group insurance in the private four-year institutions are comparable to those for faculty. For clerical-service employees in the public four-year group, the percentage of employer-pay-all plans is smaller, 29.3 percent versus 40.9 percent for faculty, and the joint sharing and employee-pay-all categories are correspondingly larger.

• The length of time a total disability must last before the employee becomes eligible to receive monthly disability income benefits under a group insurance plan concentrates at six months (benefit waiting period). For faculty, half of the public four-year colleges and 71.7 percent of the private reported a six-month benefit waiting period. Three-month periods were reported by 17.7 percent of public four-year institutions and 16.6 percent of private. Periods of less than three months were reported by about a fifth of the public four-year institutions, and by 6.1 percent of private four-year institutions. The proportions of institutions reporting these benefit waiting periods for clerical-service employees are roughly the same as for faculty.

• The great majority of long-term disability group insurance plans provide their benefits for both work-connected and nonwork-connected disabilities. Only about 4 percent of the plans in the public and private four-year colleges and universities report that the long-term income benefits are payable for work-connected disabilities only.

• Continuation during periods of long-term disability of contributions to the retirement plan, so that retirement benefits may begin later, when the disabled employee reaches the employer's normal retirement age, were reported for faculty by slightly less than half of the public four-year colleges and universities and by about three-fourths of the private four-year institutions. For clerical-service employees, continuation of retirement plan contributions or credits were reported by a third of the public four-year institutions and by two-thirds of the private institutions.

• Waiting periods for participation in group insurance plans for long-term disability tend to be longer than waiting periods for other employee benefits. For faculty coverage among the public four-year institutions, half of the group insurance plans provided a waiting period of one month or less, a fifth provided for one year, and 15 percent for more than one year, with another 6 percent specifying a period between two and eleven months. Among the private four-year institutions the waiting period for faculty participation was set at one year by a third of the institutions with group insurance plans; one-half specified one year, with 8.4 percent having two to eleven months and 6.3 percent more than one year waiting periods. A short waiting period usually incorporates a "preexisting conditions" clause, while a long one usually does not. The provisions were roughly the same for the waiting periods specified for clerical-service employees' participation in group insurance plans for long-term disability.

• The period during which long-term disability benefits continue, provided disability continues, is mainly to age 65, as reported by 75 percent of public four-year institutions and 88.2 percent of private four-year institutions, and is similar for faculty, administrative, and clerical-service employees, and for both two-year and four-year institutions.

EMPLOYEE BENEFITS COST SURVEY

For the first time in the survey series, the current survey includes information on what employers in higher education are spending for specified employee benefits, including retirement and insurance plans. The benefit cost questionnaire is reproduced as Appendix B.

The benefit cost survey offers two principal measurements of college expenditures for each included benefit category: (1) expenditures as a percentage of gross payroll; and (2) expenditures per employee. Since no prior or comparable cost survey data are available, the current survey provides only initial benchmark information against which future surveys of the same type can be compared. Each institution, if it wishes, can measure its own expenditures in terms of those reported by the current respondents.

The benefit cost survey questionnaire was mailed to four-year colleges and universities with a full-time enrollment of 500 or more students, a total of 1,236 institutions (a smaller universe than for the questionnaire covering retirement and insurance benefit plan provisions, which went to all institutions of higher education). The questionnaire was sent out on March 30, 1978 and by September 18, 1978, the closing date of the survey, 574 institutions, or 46 percent, had responded.

The information from the benefit cost survey reported in this chapter covers the data collected for retirement, Social Security, life insurance, health insurance, and short- and long-term disability income plans.

Table 1.4 shows the average employer benefit plan expenditure for each type of benefit as a percentage of gross payroll for the fiscal or calendar year 1977. The averages are based on the number of institutions reporting in each category. The highest reported averages generally relate to retirement plan expenditures and Social Security. The highest average percent of payroll expenditure reported is for public employee retirement systems, 5.6 percent, a figure that presumably reflects both the benefit levels of the plans and amounts of employer contributions (including contributions of local or state governments) that represent programs for amortization of unfunded prior service liabilities. An average employer expenditure of 4 percent of total payroll is reported for insured pension plans, including TIAA-CREF plans. For the lesser numbers of institutions reporting expenditures for noninsured (self-insured) pension plans, 1.5 percent of payroll is reported, including informal and supplemental pension arrangements. Social Security taxes represent an average of 4.6 percent of total payroll for the reporting fiscal or calendar year of 1977. (The employer's share of the Social Security tax was 5.85 percent of the taxable earnings base of $15,300 in 1976 and $16,500 in 1977.)

Following Social Security and retirement plan expenditures, health insurance plans represent the next highest category of employer expenditures. An average of 2.2 percent of gross payroll was contributed by employers to health insurance plan premiums. Relatively few institutions reported expenditures for dental insurance plans; those that did averaged 0.4 percent of payroll for these expenses.

Table 1.4. Average Employer Benefit Plan Expenditures as a Percentage of Gross Payroll in 1977[a]

Type of Benefit	All Institutions	
	n	Percent of Payroll
Social Security	562	4.6%
Workers' Compensation	519	0.5
Insured pension plans	497	4.0
Noninsured pension plans	105	1.5
Public pension plans	124	5.6
Life insurance plans[b]	466	0.4
Health insurance plans[c]	519	2.2
Dental insurance plans	21	0.4
Sick leave pay	233	1.7
State sickness benefits insurance	63	0.7
Long-term disability plans	369	0.3

NOTE: n = number of institutions reporting expenditure.
[a]Fiscal or calendar year.
[b]Excludes travel accident insurance and death benefits not provided by insurance plans.
[c]Excludes self-insured plans and HMOs.

The average employer expenditure for group life insurance was 0.4 percent of gross payroll. When the lesser employer expenditures for travel accident insurance and for death benefits other than those under a group life insurance or pension plan are added to employer expenditures for group life insurance plans, the average employer life insurance expenditure is reduced to 0.3 percent of gross payroll, due to the relatively larger increase in the denominator (gross payroll) compared with the smaller increase in the numerator (expenditures) in the calculation of the average.

Workers' Compensation program taxes or other payments were reported as 0.5 percent of gross payroll. Sick leave pay plans, for absences of work due to short-term disabilities, involved average employer expenditures of 1.7 percent of payroll. Institutions in states requiring state sickness benefits insurance or direct pay equivalents reported expenditures in this category of 0.7 percent of gross payroll. Payments for long-term disability income plans, including insured and self-insured

Table 1.5. Average Employer Benefit Plan Expenditure by Type and Control of Institution as a Percentage of Gross Payroll in 1977[a]

Type of Benefit	Universities			Liberal Arts Colleges			Other 4-Year
	Total	Pubic	Private	Total	Pubic	Private	Private
Social Security	4.5%	4.5%	4.6%	4.9%	4.7%	5.0%	4.7%
	n = 80	n = 43	n = 37	n = 453	n = 90	n = 363	n = 29
Workers' Compensation	0.5	0.5	0.5	0.5	0.4	0.5	0.5
	n = 77	n = 40	n = 37	n = 413	n = 68	n = 345	n = 29
Insured pension plans	4.0	4.0	4.0	4.1	3.1	4.6	3.6
	n = 71	n = 35	n = 36	n = 399	n = 48	n = 351	n = 27
Noninsured pension plans	1.6	1.9	1.4	1.1	1.3	1.0	1.3
	n = 23	n = 6	n = 17	n = 75	n = 5	n = 70	n = 7
Public pension plans	5.2	5.2	—	7.1	7.1	6.3	—
	n = 38	n = 38	—	n = 86	n = 85	n = 1	—
Life insurance plans[b]	0.4	0.4	0.3	0.4	0.4	0.4	0.4
	n = 75	n = 40	n = 35	n = 371	n = 71	n = 300	n = 20
Health insurance plans[c]	2.2	2.4	1.8	2.2	2.3	2.1	1.9
	n = 75	n = 41	n = 34	n = 418	n = 84	n = 334	n = 26
Dental insurance plans	0.3	0.4	*	0.7	0.7	0.7	0.1
	n = 7	n = 5	n = 2	n = 12	n = 5	n = 7	n = 2
Sick leave pay	1.9	2.1	1.1	1.4	1.5	1.3	1.2
	n = 32	n = 20	n = 12	n = 190	n = 44	n = 146	n = 11
State sickness benefits	0.8	1.4	0.2	0.6	1.0	0.3	1.0
	n = 8	n = 4	n = 4	n = 51	n = 7	n = 44	n = 2
Long-term disability plans	0.2	0.2	0.2	0.3	0.3	0.3	0.3
	n = 57	n = 30	n = 27	n = 293	n = 36	n = 257	n = 19

NOTE: n = number of institutions reporting expenditure.
[a]Fiscal or calendar year.
[b]Excludes travel accident insurance and death benefits not provided by insurance plans.
[c]Excludes self-insured plans and HMOs.
*Less than 0.1%.

plans but excluding disability benefits under a pension plan, represented 0.3 percent of gross payroll.

Table 1.5 presents the information just summarized for all reporting institutions according to type of institution and by control, public or private. In most categories, there are no wide variations in proportionate expenditures among types of institutions in fiscal or calendar 1977, with some exceptions. Public universities report somewhat higher proportionate employer contributions toward health insurance plans (2.4 percent) than do private universities (1.8 percent). Public institutions report somewhat higher proportionate expenditures for sick leave pay plans than do private institutions. Public universities report a lower percentage going to public employee pension plans (5.2 percent) than do public colleges (7.1 percent). Colleges are spending slightly more for their long-term disability plans than are universities, with a 1/10 of 1 percent difference. Private colleges report Social Security contributions of 5 percent of gross payroll compared with 4.7 percent for public colleges, 4.6 percent for private universities, and 4.5 percent for public universities, with the differences due partly, at least, to differences in reporting periods and collection methods, as well as to salary level differences.

Dollars per Employee. Tables 1.6 and 1.7 give another measure of employer expenditures for employee benefit plan coverage—average numbers of dollars spent per employee. In these tables the employee count is based on a total of all full-time employees plus the full-time equivalent of all part-time employees, excluding student employees. Table 1.6 gives the expenditures per employee for all institutions and table 1.7 breaks the expenditures down according to type and control of institution.

Table 1.6. Average Employer Benefit Plan Expenditures Per Employee in 1977[a]

Type of Benefit	All Institutions	
	n	Dollars per employee
Social Security	562	$581
Workers' Compensation	519	$ 59
Insured pension plans	497	$502
Noninsured pension plans	105	$204
Public pension plans	124	$734
Life insurance plans[b]	466	$ 50
Health insurance plans[c]	519	$283
Dental insurance plans	21	$ 55
Sick leave pay	233	$229
State sickness benefits insurance	63	$ 87
Long-term disability plans	369	$ 34

NOTE: n = number of institutions reporting expenditure.
[a]Fiscal or calendar year; includes all full-time employees and full-time equivalent of part-time employees.
[b]Excludes travel accident insurance and death benefits not provided by insurance plans.
[c]Excludes self-insured plans and HMOs.

Table 1.7. Average Employer Benefit Plan Expenditures per Employee in 1977[a] by Type and Control of Institution

Type of Benefit	Universities			Liberal Arts Colleges			Other 4-Year
	Total	Public	Private	Total	Public	Private	Private
Social Security	$585	$571	$622	$568	$570	$566	$636
	n = 80	n = 43	n = 37	n = 453	n = 90	n = 363	n = 29
Workers' Compensation	61	64	53	54	44	61	64
	n = 77	n = 40	n = 37	n = 413	n = 68	n = 345	n = 29
Insured pension plans	511	495	546	484	401	522	460
	n = 71	n = 35	n = 36	n = 399	n = 48	n = 351	n = 27
Noninsured pension plans	227	276	196	116	118	115	198
	n = 23	n = 6	n = 17	n = 75	n = 5	n = 70	n = 7
Public pension plans	681	681	—	915	914	955	—
	n = 38	n = 38	—	n = 86	n = 85	n = 1	—
Life insurance plans[b]	50	53	43	49	52	47	53
	n = 75	n = 40	n = 35	n = 371	n = 71	n = 300	n = 20
Health insurance plans[c]	295	316	243	258	288	234	263
	n = 75	n = 41	n = 34	n = 418	n = 84	n = 334	n = 26
Dental insurance plans	47	55	2	98	115	85	9
	n = 7	n = 5	n = 2	n = 12	n = 5	n = 7	n = 7
Sick leave pay	264	284	164	168	196	147	165
	n = 32	n = 20	n = 12	n = 190	n = 44	n = 146	n = 11
State sickness benefits	113	176	32	68	106	32	27
	n = 8	n = 4	n = 4	n = 51	n = 7	n = 44	n = 4
Long-term disability plans	32	33	28	39	40	39	46
	n = 57	n = 30	n = 27	n = 293	n = 36	n = 257	n = 19

NOTE: n = number of institutions reporting expenditure.
[a] Fiscal or calendar year.
[b] Excludes travel accident insurance and death benefits not provided by insurance plans.
[c] Excludes self-insured plans and HMOs.

Table 1.6 generally reflects the benefit plan expenditures in prior tables shown as percentages of payroll. The highest per capita employer expenditure is for public employee pension plans ($734), followed by Social Security ($581), followed by insured pension plans ($502). Note that the pension figures are per employee, not per participant. Health insurance premiums come next ($283 per employee), followed by sick leave pay ($229) and noninsured pension plan expenditures ($204). It should be emphasized that different sets of institutions, as well as different numbers reporting, are involved in each of the table entries. Workers' Compensation works out to $59 per employee among the 519 institutions reporting; among the 21 institutions reporting dental insurance plans, the per capita expenditure is $55. Long-term disability income plans are reported by 369 institutions at a $34 per employee annual employer cost. All figures are for the 1977 year, either fiscal or calendar.

By type and control, the expenditures per employee shown in table 1.7 show general consistency within plan categories. Private universities spend slightly more per employee for Social Security taxes than do public universities, a difference that may be due to differences in calendar or fiscal year reporting and tax collection methods over the period, as well as to wage and salary levels. Workers' Compensation payments are somewhat lower in the colleges than in universities, $54 versus $61, and for insured pension plans, $484 in colleges versus $511 in universities. Public colleges with employee groups participating in public pension plans report significantly higher per capita expenditures for public employee pension plans than do public universities, $914 versus $681, a difference that may at least in part be due to a higher proportion of TIAA-CREF insured plans as regular, optional, or alternative plans in public universities.

Public institutions tend to spend somewhat more for health insurance plans than private institutions, with public universities reporting $316, private universities $243, public colleges reporting $288, and private colleges $234. State sickness benefit expenditures are substantially higher for public than private institutions among the relatively few institutions reporting this type of mandatory coverage. Expenditures per employee for long-term disability insurance benefit programs range from $28 in private universities to $40 in public colleges. Again, it should be emphasized that the figures for each benefit category are not expenditures per plan participant but for all institutional employees, including the full-time equivalent of part-time employees, many of whom may not be eligible for most of the programs.

Self-Comparison. An institution can locate itself in relation to the averages reported in tables 1.4 through 1.11 by entering the following figures from its own accounting records and making the indicated divisions:

Fiscal or Calendar Year Ending in 1977

1. Total gross payroll
   (salaries and wages) $ _____

2. Number of employees at start of year
   Full-time   _____
   Full-time equivalent of part-time   _____
   Total   _____

3. Number of employees at end of year
   Full-time   _____
   Full-time equivalent of part-time   _____
   Total   _____

4. $\dfrac{\text{Item 2 + item 3}}{2}$ _____

5. Employer Social Security contributions (FICA tax) $ _____

6. Worker's Compensation
   (estimate or actual if self-insured) $ _____

7. Premiums to insured pension plans
   (including TIAA-CREF) $ _____

8. Payments to noninsured self-administered or trusteed pension plans $ _____

9. Payments to public employee pension
   plans (by institution and/or unit of
   government) $ _____

10. Life insurance premiums (net) (exclud-
    ing survivor benefits provided under
    a pension plan) $ _____

11. Hospital, accident, surgical, medical,
    and major medical insurance pre-
    miums (net) and Medicare (Part B) $ _____

12. Dental insurance premiums $ _____

13. Sick leave pay $ _____

14. State sickness benefits insurance (esti-
    mate or actual if self-insured) $ _____

15. Payments for long-term disability in-
    come plans (including insured and
    self-insured plans but excluding dis-
    ability benefits under a pension plan) $ _____

Items 5 through 15 may then be entered successively in the following calculation:

$$\frac{\text{Benefit items 5 to 15, each}}{\text{Item 1 (gross payroll)}} \times 100 = \text{Employer benefit expenditure as \% of gross payroll}$$

$$\frac{\text{Benefit items 5 to 15, each}}{\text{Item 4}} = \text{Employer benefit expenditure per employee}$$

Expenditures by Size of Institution. Tables 1.8 and 1.9 summarize the cost study results for pensions, life, and health insurance according to size of institution. In these tables, size is based on student enrollment (fall 1975), including full- and part-time students, graduate and undergraduate. The three size categories are: small—500 to 1,000 enrollment; medium—1,000 to 5,000 enrollment; and large—over 5,000 enrollment.

Table 1.8 gives employer pension expenditures for insured, noninsured, and public employee pension plans by size and control. For all types of pension expenditures combined, average employer pension expenditures are 6.5 percent of gross payroll, or 4.3 percent for small, 5.2 percent for medium, and 6.9 percent for large institutions. By control, it is indicated that public institutions report higher total pension expenditures as a percent of payroll than do the private institutions. This is the case for all three size categories. For insured pension plans, the private institutions report higher percentages of total payroll expenditures than do the public institutions, presumably because in many of the public institutions the insured plan is an alternative or supplemental plan, so that total pension expenditures are divided between a public employee plan and an insured plan.

Table 1.8. Employer Pension Expenditures as Percentage of Gross Payroll in 1977[a] by Size and Control of Institution

Pension Expenditures as % of payroll:	Total All Institutions	Small			Medium			Large		
		Total	Public	Private	Total	Public	Private	Total	Public	Private
Insured pension plans	4.0 n = 497	4.2 n = 132	3.9 n = 003	4.2 n = 129	4.5 n = 252	3.0 n = 016	4.6 n = 236	3.9 n = 113	3.9 n = 064	4.0 n = 049
Noninsured pension plans	1.5 n = 105	1.3 n = 024	—	1.3 n = 024	1.1 n = 056	5.0 n = 003	1.0 n = 053	1.6 n = 025	1.8 n = 008	1.5 n = 017
Public pension plans	5.6 n = 124	5.5 n = 005	5.5 n = 005	—	6.6 n = 033	6.6 n = 032	6.3 n = 001	5.6 n = 086	5.6 n = 086	—
Average pension expenditures as % of payroll for institutions having pensions	6.5 n = 570	4.3 n = 141	6.7 n = 006	4.2 n = 135	5.2 n = 278	6.8 n = 038	4.9 n = 240	6.9 n = 151	7.6 n = 101	4.8 n = 050

NOTE: n = number of institutions reporting expenditure.
[a]Fiscal or calendar year.

Table 1.9. Average Employer Life and Health Insurance Expenditures as a Percentage of Gross Payroll in 1977[a] by Size and Control of Institution

	Total All Institutions	Small			Medium			Large		
		Total	Public	Private	Total	Public	Private	Total	Public	Private
Average Employer Insurance Premiums as % of Payroll										
Total	2.6	2.3	1.2	2.3	2.4	2.3	2.4	2.6	2.7	2.4
	n = 574	n = 143	n = 006	n = 137	n = 280	n = 038	n = 242	n = 151	n = 101	n = 050
Life[b]	.3	.3	.1	.3	.4	.3	.4	.3	.3	.3
	n = 485	n = 115	n = 004	n = 111	n = 239	n = 028	n = 211	n = 131	n = 081	n = 050
Health[c]	2.3	2.0	1.2	2.0	2.0	2.0	2.0	2.3	2.4	2.1
	n = 535	n = 129	n = 004	n = 125	n = 264	n = 035	n = 229	n = 142	n = 093	n = 049
Percent of Institutions Reporting Insurance Expenditures										
Life[b]	84.5	80.4	66.7	81.0	85.4	73.7	87.2	86.8	80.2	100.0
Health[c]	93.2	90.2	66.7	91.2	94.3	92.1	94.6	94.0	92.1	98.0

NOTE: n = number of institutions reporting expenditure.
[a]Fiscal or calendar year.
[b]Life includes net group life insurance premiums, net travel accident insurance premiums, and death benefits not covered by insurance or pension plans.
[c]Health includes hospital, accident, surgical, medical and major medical insurance premiums and Medicare (Part B), self-insured payments, and HMO premiums.

Table 1.9 gives employer expenditures for life and health insurance by size of institution and by control. In this table, the average employer expenditure for life insurance is 0.3 percent of total payroll, an average that includes a somewhat larger number of institutions than in the previous tables by incorporating the relatively small amounts reported by some institutions as premiums for travel accident insurance and for noninsured death benefit payments. Health insurance in table 1.9 includes premiums for health insurance plans and for self-insured payments and health maintenance organizations. With these categories of life and health insurance combined, employer expenditures average 2.6 percent of gross payroll. The largest institutions report a 2.6 percent average, while the small and medium ones report averages of 2.3 and 2.4 percent. A total of 93.2 percent of the responding institutions reported employer health insurance expenditures and 84.5 percent reported employer life insurance plan contributions. The range for the latter was from 66.7 percent of small public institutions (representing only four institutions, however) to 100 percent of large private institutions. Generally, a somewhat smaller proportion of public institutions reports employer life insurance expenditures than private ones. For health insurance contributions there is a similar relationship, but the difference between public and private is not quite as great.

Expenditure Range. As noted above, the average employer expenditure for all types of pensions—insured, noninsured, and public employee—is 6.5 percent of gross payroll. Table 1.10 shows the range of expenditures for pensions and for life and health insurance combined. In the lowest contribution category for pensions (0.1 to 1.9 percent of payroll), fifty-five out of the sixty-five reporting are private

Table 1.10. Distribution of Employer Pension and Combined Life and Health Insurance Expenditures as a Percentage of Gross Payroll in 1977[a]

Percent of Gross Payroll	Pensions[b]		Life[c] and Health[d]	
	Number	Percent	Number	Percent
0.0%	4	—	21	—
0.1–1.9	65	11.4	209	37.8
2.0–3.9	178	31.2	271	49.0
4.0–5.9	154	27.0	61	11.0
6.0–7.9	109	19.1	12	2.2
8.0–9.9	38	6.6	1	—
10% and over	26	4.6	1	—
Total Institutions	574	100.0%	574	100.0%
Average employer expenditure as percent of payroll:	6.5%		2.6%	

[a]Fiscal or calendar year.
[b]Pensions include insured, noninsured, and public employee retirement systems.
[c]Life insurance includes net group life insurance premiums, net travel accident insurance premiums, and death benefits not provided by insurance plans.
[d]Health insurance includes hospital, accident, surgical, medical and major medical insurance premiums and medicare (Part B), self-insured payments, and HMO premiums.

colleges. The majority of the institutions report between 2 and 6 percent of payroll as pension contributions. Thirty percent of the institutions report pension contributions in excess of 6 percent of gross payroll.

For life and health insurance expenditures, the combined average for these costs is 2.6 percent of gross payroll. About seven-eighths of the institutions report total employer contributions of 3.9 percent or less of payroll. About half of institutions with life and health plans report an employer expenditure of between 2 and 4 percent of gross payroll.

Employee Contributions. Not all benefit plans require an employee contribution, nor do contributory plans necessarily involve equal sharing of plan costs between employer and employee. But employee contributions to benefit plans are common among educational institutions, as indicated in the reports of institutions on benefit plan provisions in the later chapters. Table 1.11 summarizes the responses of the institutions participating in the benefit cost survey on the amounts of employee payroll deductions involved in the following benefit plans: Social Security, pension plans, life insurance plans, health insurance plans, and long-term disability income insurance plans. The table also gives the percent of payroll represented by employer contributions to the same benefit plans.

Table 1.11 indicates that employer and employee contributions to Social Security represent equal percentages of gross payroll, and that average employee pension contributions amount to about half of employer contributions expressed as a percentage of gross payroll, 6.5 percent for employers and 3.5 percent for employees. Life insurance plans show, on the average, an equal sharing of the total cost between employers and employees. For health insurance, employers on the average pay two-thirds of the cost and the employees one-third, or 2.2 percent of gross payroll by employers and 1.1 percent by employees. Long-term disability income insurance is shared on a three-to-two basis, with employers reporting 0.3 percent of gross pay-

Table 1.11. Average Employer and Employee Benefit Plan Contributions as a Percentage of Gross Payroll in 1977[a]

Type of Benefit	Employer		Employee	
	Number of institutions	Percent of payroll	Number of institutions	Percent of payroll
Social Security	562	4.6%	562	4.6%
Pension	570	6.5	478	3.5[b]
Life insurance[c]	466	0.4	297	0.4
Health insurance[d]	519	2.2	486	1.1
Long-term disability[e]	369	0.3	165	0.2

[a]Fiscal or calendar year.
[b]Required contributions.
[c]Excludes travel accident insurance and death benefits not provided by insurance plans.
[d]Excludes self-insured and HMOs.
[e]Excludes sick pay and other short-term disability plans, paid for mainly by employers.

roll as their cost of this coverage, and with employees' deductions for the coverage amounting to 0.2 percent of gross payroll.

Tables 1.4 through 1.11 state costs as a percentage of all wage and salary expenditures and not as percentages of the wages and salaries of just those employees covered by the benefit plan in question. Thus, the figures may be useful for comparative purposes, but do not indicate the cost of benefit plans as related to the particular segments of faculty or staff that participate on a voluntary or required basis in a specific benefit plan. In making comparisons, it should be noted that higher or lower costs of specific benefit plans as a percentage of gross payroll may represent either broader employee coverage or higher employer contributions, or both. Basically, the measurements provided by the cost survey indicate the size of the employer benefit package expressed in dollars in relation to the salary and wage portion of the package, but do not extend to measurements of extent of coverage of employees or of benefit plan provisions. Chapters 2 through 8 are devoted to the description and discussion of the benefit provisions themselves.

2 Retirement Systems in Higher Education

O F ALL the employee benefit plans, the retirement plan involves the largest expenditures and the greatest time spans of participation. An employee will probably enter a retirement plan by age 30, perhaps sooner. Participation may continue through thirty or forty years of a working lifetime. After retirement benefits start, participation may continue for another twenty years or more, a period that may be as long as half a working lifetime. Average annuitant life expectancies at age 65, for example, are now about seventeen years for men and twenty-one years for women. There will be those who outlive the statistical averages and receive annuity checks well into their nineties or beyond. Retirement can last a long time and most retirees hope that it will.

A retirement plan is a large investment for the future. At today's interest and mortality rates, for each $1,000 a month of lifetime annuity income beginning at age 65 (single life annuity with ten years certain), there must be on hand an annuity accumulation of about $100,000 for a man and $110,000 for a woman. A financing responsibility of this magnitude must be started early if it is to be achieved in an orderly manner at minimum cost.

If retirement benefits are to be adequate, each successive employer must do his part. No employer can be expected to compensate for the failure of some previous employer to provide employees with a pension plan, to require employees to participate in it, or to vest benefits without delay.

The long-term nature of a retirement plan not only affects individual participants but employing institutions. The retirement policies of an institution are comparable to its salary compensation policies. Attracting a capable faculty and staff is, at least in part, a function of the competitive position that has been established by the employer. Like the salary levels that have been established, the retirement plan will influence the capacity of the institution to attract the talent it needs to attain its educational objectives and to maintain its standards of quality. The quality of the retirement plan can affect the morale of the faculty and staff and the institution's reputation as a good place to work. Responsible college officials are well aware of the value of a good institutional retirement plan.

What kinds of retirement plans are provided by institutions of higher education? This chapter and the next aim at answering this question. This chapter reports on the extent of retirement plan coverage in higher education, the types of plans, the basic approaches used in accumulating retirement funds and in determining retirement benefits, and reviews the investment policies of pension plans. Chapter 3 offers a discussion of the objectives of retirement plans and describes the specific plan provisions employed in achieving stated goals.

EXTENT OF RETIREMENT PLANS IN HIGHER EDUCATION

For faculty, 97 percent of responding institutions reported a retirement plan; these institutions employed 99.7 percent of full-time faculty members in the responding institutions.* Comparable coverage was reported for administrative staff. For clerical-service personnel, 90.2 percent of the responding institutions reported a retirement plan; these institutions employed 98.9 percent of full-time clerical-service personnel. Table 2.1 summarizes the extent of retirement plans in the four-year institutions of higher education responding to the current survey. The table also includes the data from the previous (1968) survey. The major change reflected by the 1968 and 1978 data is the increase in the proportion of institutions reporting a pension plan covering clerical-service employees. In 1968, 74.8 percent of responding institutions, employing 94.7 percent of clerical-service personnel, reported a retirement plan for this group. By 1978, the proportion of institutions with plans had risen to 90.2 percent, representing 98.9 percent of full-time clerical-service employees in the four-year institutions.

Where are the remaining (very small) gaps in retirement coverage in the four-year institutions? Analysis of the more detailed tables in Appendix C indicates that for faculty, all of the forty-one four-year institutions reporting no retirement plan are private colleges. They represent 4.4 percent of private four-year institutions employing 0.9 percent of full-time faculty. The figures are comparable for administrators. All reporting public four-year institutions have a retirement plan for faculty and administrative officers. For clerical-service employees, the coverage gap is somewhat wider but is still concentrated in the private colleges: 14.5 percent of the private four-year institutions, employing 3.5 percent of employees in these institutions, report not having a retirement plan. (One public liberal arts college employing ninety-two clerical-service employees reported no retirement plan for the group.)

Institutions offering less than a four-year educational program (designated in this study as two-year institutions) report levels of retirement plan coverage comparable to the four-year institutions (table 2.2). In the current survey, for faculty and

*The numbers of employees shown in the tables in this chapter are full-time employees reported by the responding institutions in the survey questionnaire. The employee categories were defined as follows:

Faculty—Instruction/Research: persons employed for the primary purpose of performing instruction and/or research. Chairpersons of academic departments are included in this category if they have no other administrative title.

Administrative/Managerial/Other Professional: all employees whose primary responsibility is for the administration and management of the institution or its subdivisions. Also included are all nonteaching professionals.

Other Employees: all employees not included in the two prior groups, including those subject to the provisions of the Fair Labor Standards Act. Includes persons engaged in activities categorized as technical, office-clerical, crafts and trades, service, etc. (Excludes student employees.)

Table 2.1. Retirement Plans in Four-Year Institutions of Higher Education (percent of respondents reporting plans)

Employee Class Covered	Percent Institutions		Percent Employees	
	1968[a]	1978	1968[a]	1978
Faculty	n = 1,232	n = 1,407	n = 285,414	n = 363,203
	95.0	97.0	99.5	99.7
Administrative	n = 1,232	n = 1,407	n = 108,315	n = 211,647
	92.6	96.4	99.4	99.7
Clerical-Service	n = 1,232	n = 1,407	n = 444,618	n = 601,711
	74.8	90.2	94.7	98.9

NOTE: n = total responding institutions.
[a]William C. Greenough and Francis P. King, *Benefit Plans in American Colleges* (New York: Columbia University Press, 1969), p. 21, table 2.1.

administrative officers, 98 percent of the responding two-year institutions reported retirement plans; these institutions employed 99.3 percent of faculty and administrative employees in the two-year group. For clerical-service employees, 95.9 percent of the two-year institutions reported a retirement plan, and they employed 98.8 percent of such employees in two-year institutions. These institutions report a somewhat higher percentage of retirement plan coverage for clerical-service employees than do four-year institutions because the two-year group is composed largely of publicly supported junior and community colleges. Public employees are more likely to have retirement coverage than private employees since coverage is generally mandated by law. Twenty out of the twenty-eight two-year colleges reporting no retirement plan were private institutions. These twenty institutions represented 23.5 percent of the private two-year colleges and employed 443 clerical-service employees, or 17.8 percent of the clerical-service employees in the private two-year group. To put a further perspective on the coverage of clerical-service employees

Table 2.2. Retirement Plans in Two-Year Institutions of Higher Education (percent of respondents reporting plans)

Employee Class Covered	Percent Institutions		Percent Employees	
	1970[a]	1978	1970[a]	1978
Faculty	n = 893	n = 685	n = 59,383	n = 69,199
	94.3	98.0	98.4	99.2
Administrative	n = 893	n = 685	n = 13,103	n = 21,864
	94.1	98.0	97.6	99.3
Clerical-Service	n = 893	n = 685	n = 42,886	n = 69,230
	88.1	95.9	94.6	98.8

NOTE: n = total number of responding institutions.
[a]Francis P. King, *Benefit Plans in Junior Colleges*. (Washington, D.C.: American Association of Junior Colleges, 1971), p. 7, table 1.2.

in the two-year institutions, of the 69,230 full-time clerical-service employees reported by two-year institutions, all but 813 were employed by institutions reporting a retirement plan for the group.

TYPES OF RETIREMENT PLANS IN HIGHER EDUCATION

The retirement plans reported by institutions of higher education fall into six major categories:

1. State and local (city, county, district) systems set up exclusively for teachers.

2. Public employee retirement systems (state or local).

3. Teachers Insurance and Annuity Association and College Retirement Equities Fund (TIAA-CREF) plans.

4. Self-funded or trusteed (noninsured) plans.

5. Commercial insurance company plans.

6. Church pension plans.

Table 2.3 summarizes the types of retirement plans reported by four-year institutions of higher education in the current survey and in the prior 1968 survey.

A good deal of overlapping in types of reported pension coverage characterizes institutions of higher education; not infrequently a single institution will report more than one type of retirement plan. Depending on the institution, this is accounted for by the presence of (1) an optional alternative retirement plan; (2) concurrent participation in more than one plan by members of the employee group; or (3) different plans for different employee subgroups. Examples of the last category are often found in public institutions where a new employee who is already a participant in another state or local retirement system within the state is allowed to continue the original plan membership rather than changing plans. An example of optional alternative retirement plans is represented by the State University of New York, which reports three retirement plans for faculty, administrative, and professional employees. Newly hired personnel in any of these categories have the option of joining either the New York State Teachers' Retirement System, the New York State Employees' Retirement System, or TIAA-CREF. Although the New York institutions thus report three retirement systems, an employee would normally belong to just one. Concurrent participation is illustrated by the plans in effect at the University of Oklahoma and Oklahoma State University. In these institutions, employees who participate in the Oklahoma Teachers' Retirement System also participate in TIAA-CREF. Public institutions in Wyoming also provide an example of concurrent participation in both TIAA-CREF and a state system covering public employees. Table 2.3 indicates that public retirement systems and the TIAA-CREF system covering both public and private institutions constitute the main sources of

Table 2.3. Types of Retirement Plans Reported by Four-Year Institutions of Higher Education

Type of Plan	1978 Survey					
	Faculty		Administrative		Clerical-Service	
	Percent Insts	Percent EEs	Percent Insts	Percent EEs	Percent Insts	Percen EEs
	n = 1,365	n = 362,076	n = 1,357	n = 210,903	n = 1,270	n = 595,(
State or local teacher retire-tirement system	21.5	34.4	19.7	26.8	13.6	20.2
Public employee retirement system	12.5	22.0	16.5	32.3	22.2	41.1
TIAA-CREF	78.3	71.5	73.9	62.2	52.8	33.2
Self-funded or trusteed plan	4.8	7.1	5.6	17.0	10.9	21.2
Insurance company plan	9.7	8.8	10.4	7.6	12.6	10.6
Church pension plan	10.2	3.9	9.1	2.7	6.9	1.8
	1968 Survey					
	n = 1,170	n = 283,986	n = 1,141	n = 107,705	n = 921	n = 420,9
State teacher retirement system	17.9	32.0	16.7	17.4	8.9	9.3
State employee retirement system	8.4	15.2	12.9	21.8	22.8	32.6
Single state system for teachers and others	6.7	12.6	6.8	11.7	8.5	11.2
TIAA-CREF	63.8	53.3	61.3	59.1	39.2	24.3
Self-administered or trusteed	7.3	8.8	8.2	20.9	13.2	27.3
Church pension plan	13.8	3.7	12.3	3.0	8.1	1.5
Insurance company	9.6	5.0	10.2	5.0	10.2	7.1
Other	2.4	3.5	2.3	4.0	2.5	3.0

NOTE: Percentages add to over 100 because more than one plan may be reported by an institution (concurrent or alternative coverag

retirement coverage in the four-year institutions of higher education. Percentages in table 2.3 add up to more than 100 because of the institutional reporting of more than one plan for a particular employee group.

FOUR-YEAR INSTITUTIONS

TIAA-CREF plans for faculty are reported by slightly more than 78 percent of the responding four-year institutions, employing 71.5 percent of total faculty in these institutions. State or local teacher retirement systems are reported by 21.5 percent of the institutions, employing just over a third of faculty. Public employee retirement systems are reported by 12.5 percent of the four-year institutions, and these institutions employ 22 percent of the faculty. For administrative personnel, the figures are generally comparable, except that the proportion of institutions reporting public employee retirement systems for administrators is somewhat higher than for faculty.

Noninsured (self-funded or trusteed) plans for faculty are reported by nearly 5 percent of the four-year institutions, employing about 7 percent of total faculty in the four-year group. For administrative personnel, noninsured plans are reported by a slightly higher percentage of institutions (5.6 percent), representing 17 percent of employees in the administrative classification. The plans of commercial insurance companies are reported for faculty by 9.7 percent of institutions, employing 8.8 percent of faculty, and for administrative personnel by 10.4 percent of institutions, employing 7.6 percent of administrative employees.

Church pension plans for faculty or administrative personnel are reported by about 10 percent of the four-year institutions. As expected, these institutions are relatively small and are all privately supported. Almost all of them, except some seminaries, also report a TIAA-CREF plan concurrently with a church plan.

For clerical-service personnel, 13.6 percent of the four-year institutions report a state or local teacher system, 22.2 percent a public employee retirement system, and 52.8 percent a TIAA-CREF plan. When weighted according to percent of total employees in the clerical-service group in higher education, state or local teacher systems represent institutions employing 20.2 percent of clerical-service employees, the public employee systems represent 41.1 percent, and the TIAA-CREF plans 33.2 percent.

A higher proportion of noninsured plans is reported for clerical-service employees than for other groups. Noninsured plans are found mainly in private institutions; of the 139 noninsured plans reported for clerical-service employees, 109 were in the private sector of four-year higher education. Insurance company plans, like noninsured plans, play a slightly greater role for clerical-service employees than they do for faculty or administrative personnel. Insurance company plans for clerical-service employees were reported by 12.6 percent of the four-year institutions, employing 10.6 percent of clerical-service personnel in such institutions.

By control of institution, 57.1 percent of publicly supported four-year institutions report faculty coverage under a state or local teacher retirement system; they employ 48.7 percent of faculty members in public four-year institutions. A public employee retirement system covering faculty was reported by 35.1 percent of public four-year institutions, employing 32.8 percent of faculty in the public four-year sector. TIAA-CREF plans were reported for faculty by 62.8 percent of the four-year public institutions, employing 62.8 percent of faculty in the public four-year group.

Among the privately supported four-year institutions, 86.7 percent reported a TIAA-CREF retirement plan for faculty; these institutions employ 89.1 percent of faculty of private four-year institutions. A small number of privately supported institutions (twenty-three) reported coverage of some faculty members under a public retirement system, reflecting, usually, the presence of a unit of a state or local educational division associated with the private college or university. Cornell University, for example, operates several New York State educational units as a part of the university; employees in these units may choose a public plan or TIAA-CREF. Insurance company plans for faculty are reported by 10.4 percent of private four-year institutions, employing 4.9 percent of faculty. A church pension plan is reported by 15.6 percent, employing 11.3 percent of faculty. The types of retirement plans reported by private four-year institutions for administrative and professional personnel correspond closely to the types reported for faculty.

For clerical-service personnel, 35.8 percent of the publicly supported four-year institutions report a state or local teacher retirement system; these institutions employed 29.1 percent of clerical personnel in public four-year institutions. Public employee retirement system coverage for clerical-service employees was reported by 58.9 percent of public four-year institutions, employing 59.6 percent of such employees in the public four-year sector. TIAA-CREF retirement plans for clerical-service employees were reported by 25.4 percent of publicly supported four-year institutions, employing 23.6 percent of these employees. A self-funded retirement plan for clerical-service employees was reported by 6.3 percent of public four-year institutions, employing 14.8 percent of clerical-service employees, and insurance company plans were reported by 5 percent of public four-year institutions, employing 7.5 percent of clerical-service employees.

Among the privately supported four-year institutions, 69.4 percent reported a TIAA-CREF retirement plan for clerical-service employees; these institutions employ 54.9 percent of such employees in the private four-year sector. A noninsured pension plan (self-funded or trusteed) was reported for clerical-service employees by 13.7 percent of private four-year institutions, employing 35.8 percent of these employees in the private four-year sector. Insurance company plans for clerical-service employees were reported by 17.2 percent of private four-year institutions, employing 17.5 percent of clerical-service employees.

TWO-YEAR INSTITUTIONS

In the two-year colleges (see table 2.4), public retirement systems were reported most frequently for all employee categories, with state or local teacher systems predominating for faculty and administrative/professional personnel and public employee retirement systems for clerical-service personnel. For all two-year institutions combined, public and private, TIAA-CREF plans are reported by about 45 percent for faculty and administrative/professional staff and by about a fifth of the institutions for clerical-service personnel.

For faculty of publicly supported two-year institutions of higher education, 71.3 percent of the institutions reported a state or local teacher retirement system; they employed 74.6 percent of faculty in the public two-year group. Forty percent of the public two-year colleges reported a public employee retirement system for faculty; these institutions employed 42.2 percent of faculty. TIAA-CREF plans were reported by 42.4 percent of public two-year colleges, employing 40.4 percent of faculty.

Table 2.4. Types of Retirement Plans Reported by Two-Year Institutions of Higher Education

Type of Plan	1978 Survey					
	Faculty		Administrative		Clerical-Service	
	Percent Insts	Percent EEs	Percent Insts	Percent EEs	Percent Insts	Percent EEs
	n = 670	n = 68,654	n = 671	n = 21,710	n = 657	n = 68,417
State or local teacher retirement system	63.7	72.4	59.3	63.7	34.9	33.4
Public employee retirement system	35.7	40.9	45.9	53.3	60.1	66.6
TIAA-CREF	46.1	41.4	44.6	43.7	22.7	16.5
Self-funded or trusteed plan	2.1	0.9	2.2	1.6	2.1	1.0
Insurance company plan	9.1	8.5	9.1	8.0	4.7	3.1
Church pension plan	2.2	0.6	2.1	0.8	1.5	0.5
	1970 Survey					
	n = 842	n = 58,427	n = 840	n = 12,790	n = 787	n = 40,583
Single state system for teachers and other employees	24.5	19.7	24.5	20.0	26.3	15.3
State teacher retirement system	49.8	62.5	46.3	51.9	19.4	17.6
State employee retirement system	16.5	18.2	21.7	27.0	42.7	56.3
City, county, or district system	2.4	7.5	2.1	4.0	1.4	3.9
TIAA-CREF	25.7	27.8	24.3	33.2	10.2	8.7
Self-administered or trusteed	2.5	1.5	4.4	2.8	5.2	4.0
Church pension plan	3.4	1.3	3.7	2.2	3.0	1.3
Insurance company plan	6.2	5.4	6.0	5.6	4.1	3.4

NOTE: Percentages add to over 100 because more than one plan may be reported by an institution (concurrent or alternative coverage).

Among the small number of private two-year institutions, 75.7 percent reported a TIAA-CREF plan for faculty, and these employed 74.2 percent of faculty in the private two-year colleges.

DEVELOPMENT OF RETIREMENT PLANS IN HIGHER EDUCATION

Public Retirement Systems. State and local governments have established over 6,600 separate retirement systems with over 10 million active members, excluding beneficiaries. At the end of 1975, total assets of state and local retirement systems amounted to $115 billion.[1] A relatively small proportion of the public employees covered by these pension plans are employed by educational institutions at the postsecondary level. Sixty-eight public retirement systems provide the retirement benefits reported for the public colleges and universities participating in the current survey.

At present, the public retirement systems covering employees in higher education normally state their benefits in terms of a formula that relates the pension to salary and service. Accrued benefits may vest (become nonforfeitable) after five years or ten years of plan participation. The plans are generally supported by employee contributions and by contributions of the employing entity or unit of government that has established the plan. The legal obligation to meet the benefit commitment made is through statutes under which the state or local government binds itself to meet the obligations undertaken through the use of employee contributions, present and future tax revenue, and net investment earnings on pension fund reserves.

The earliest benefit plans for public employees were started by municipalities on behalf of police officers and school teachers. The predecessor plans for the public teacher retirement systems were voluntary employee associations. The earliest known was founded in New York City in 1869 to make lump-sum payments to survivors of deceased teachers from assessments levied on association members as needs arose. This forerunner of a later pension plan had no legislative sanction and no support from the employing municipality or school board. Pension legislation was sought by the public school teachers of New York City and Brooklyn as early as 1879, but while these efforts were repeated from time to time, it was not until 1894 that they were successful. It was in this year that the New York state legislature established the first teachers' pension fund in the country. It provided for the establishment of a fund to be built up from deductions made from the pay of teachers because of absence.[2]

In 1895 and 1896, voluntary associations were formed by public school teachers in seven other large cities, but none of these received support from the employing governments until 1907.[3] In 1895 compulsory teacher retirement funds were established in Brooklyn, Detroit, and Chicago, and voluntary funds in St. Louis and San Francisco. In 1896 compulsory plans were established in Buffalo and Cincinnati, and a voluntary plan was started on a statewide basis in New Jersey.[4]

These early public retirement plans for teachers initially focused on benefits and paid only modest attention to the question of revenue and to the long-term nature of the obligations being undertaken. Many began with no regular source of support other than contributions from members, mostly about 1 percent of salary. Since benefit projections usually indicated that the contributions would not go all the way toward meeting future obligations, the plans often provided that the benefits could be decreased if funds were not sufficient. While it was contended that these saving clauses made the plans financially sound, they also made them unstable and the benefits unpredictable.

The question of upgrading the early pension plans, both in terms of benefits and funding methods, soon became pressing. Especially concerned with the problem was the Carnegie Foundation for the Advancement of Teaching. The studies and reports of this foundation, issued over a number of years, did much to advance public understanding of the importance of sound financing methods in pension planning.

As the result of the work of a legislative commission, Massachusetts in 1911 became the first state to establish a statewide retirement plan for nonteaching employees. A system for teachers was enacted in 1913.[5]

The work of the Massachusetts legislative commission and the studies in New York by the Carnegie Foundation and by municipal study groups signified a growing realization of the importance of sounder funding methods than were currently being employed and of better methods of assessing the potential costs of retirement systems. The pension studies of the time regularly exposed both the temptations and the dangers of establishing liberal pension benefits without paying attention to adequate levels of employer and employee contributions. A five-year study of New York City pension plans by the New York Bureau of Research (1913–1918) is described by Professor Paul Studenski as having "brought to light the essential unsoundness of the pension arrangements maintained by the city and the actual bankrupt condition of most of the city's various departmental pension funds."[6]

During the 1920s, retirement plans for groups of public employees grew in numbers and coverage. The search for a sound financial base continued. Generally, the plans tended to follow the early pattern of separate coverage for special employee groups such as police officers, firefighters, and teachers, on the one hand, and for general state or municipal employees on the other. In some states, consolidations of plans brought teachers and other employees into the same plan; in others, teacher plans remained separate. The evolution of plans included the addition of provisions for nondisability retirements under stated age and/or service requirements, and compulsory membership. The principle of joint contributions by both employees and employers gained wide acceptance. By the early 1940s, about half of all state and local employees had some type of coverage under a public retirement system. By 1962 it was estimated that three out of four public employees had such protection.[7] At present about 90 percent of all full-time public employees are covered.[8] During the years of plan growth and expansion, employees of state-supported institutions of higher education, often starting with teacher-training institutions, were gradually brought into either the state plan for schoolteachers or the general plan for state employees. Much of this expansion occurred in the 30s and 40s.

The specific provisions of the public systems covering employees in higher education are described in chapter 3, including provisions for participation, vesting, contribution rates, the benefit formulas, retirement ages, and relation to Social Security. Most of the public retirement plans incorporate disability retirement benefits and survivor benefits payable in the event of the employee's death before retirement. All of the systems now provide survivor income options that make possible a continuation of life income to the spouse of a retired employee who dies after retiring.

TIAA-CREF System. The Teachers Insurance and Annuity Association (TIAA) was established as a funded successor to a free pension system inaugurated in 1906 by retired steel magnate Andrew Carnegie and administered by the trustees of the Carnegie Foundation for the Advancement of Teaching. Prior to 1906, very few institutions of higher education in the United States had established pension plans. By 1915, seventy-three colleges and universities had become members of the "associated" institutions for whose faculty retiring allowances would be paid by the foundation.[9] But as institutions of higher education grew in number and in enrollment, it soon became clear that the resources of the foundation would be insufficient to carry the burden of a free pension system. Accordingly, a review of the system was inaugurated by the foundation in 1915 with the cooperation of the Commission on Insurance and Annuities, composed of representatives from the American Association of University Professors, the Association of American Universities, the National Association of State Universities, and the Association of American Colleges. The commission submitted its report on April 27, 1917.

The commission confirmed the trustees' conclusion that the foundation's resources were insufficient to carry the burden of a free pension system for American higher education. It noted that the annual income of the foundation would need to be more than doubled within a generation to carry the estimated financial load just for the limited number of associated institutions, without providing "for much of any growth" or for increased salary levels. "It is clear," the commission concluded, "that no solution of this matter can be regarded as permanent or as satisfactory for the general body of teachers in the United States and Canada which involves a constantly growing obligation dependent on a limited source."

Another aspect of the free pension system was observed by the commission. A system for a limited number of institutions, although seemingly sound at its initiation, had led to the creation of an "educational tariff" favoring a small group, excluding a larger group, and tending "to restrict the healthy migration of teachers from one college to another." In its consideration of this matter, the commission underlined the importance of providing pensions broadly and on a contractual basis: the successor system should be able to "furnish to the teacher the security of a contract, so that the man who enters upon the accumulation of an annuity at thirty may have a contract for its fulfillment . . . ; [and] to afford these forms of protection in such manner as to leave to the teacher the utmost freedom of action, and to make his migration from one institution to another easy."[10]

Unquestionably the greatest single contribution to pension philosophy by the Carnegie free pensions was the concept of transferability. To qualify for a retiring allowance under the foundation's rules it was not necessary that a teacher spend any specified length of time at any particular one of the associated institutions, thus giving academic talent mobility. In 1918 this concept of mobility was carried over to the much broader TIAA plan, operating within the college world.

The proposed new retirement system, which became the Teachers Insurance and Annuity Association (TIAA), was approved by the commission in its 1917 report. The new organization was to be established by the Carnegie Foundation as a separately organized association to provide insurance and deferred annuities for college staff members, with the annuity contract being issued to the individual and based on month-by-month contributions by the staff member and the employer. The contributions and earnings on them would establish fully funded reserves. The contract would be the property of the staff member, who would be able to follow the teaching profession in an educational world free of pension barriers. Teachers entering the associated free pension institutions after November 1915, and teachers in the other institutions of higher education, were to be eligible for the new contributory system. Teachers already associated with the free pension group continued to be qualified for retiring allowances from the foundation under its established rules.

The Carnegie Foundation's 1918 report noted that Mr. Carnegie had been in the habit of quoting to his trustees from Robert Burns, one of his favorite poets: "Nae man can tether time or tide." Time had moved fast, the report concluded, between the creation of the foundation in 1905 and the emergence of the association in 1918. The trustees had been called on to solve a problem of far-reaching importance. In their study of it they came in time to a conception of a pension system widely different from that with which they had started. "The pension system no longer faces toward the group of teachers grown old in service," said the 1918 report, "but toward the men entering the profession, and offers to them the machinery thru [Carnegie's simplified spelling] which protection against dependence for themselves and for their families may be had upon terms that are secure, that make for a larger freedom of the individual, and that are within the reach of men on modest salary. The change is not merely one of details; the underlying philosophy of the pension problem has been transformed and its point of view oriented to conform to this philosophy."[11]

The College Retirement Equities Fund (CREF) was established in 1952 as a companion organization to TIAA, with the same nonprofit status and limited eligibility. CREF provides a variable annuity, organized by TIAA as a means of broadening the investment base of participants through participation in optional separate annuity contracts with benefits based on the long-term investment experience of common stocks.

Each educational institution's plan in the TIAA-CREF system is established by resolution of the institution's governing authority. In the case of public institutions, the plan is first authorized through enabling legislation and is established by subsequent action by the institution's governing board or by the state board of higher education. The retirement resolution is the basic plan document—the formal agreement between the institution, the participants in the plan, and the TIAA-CREF pension system. In the resolution the institution or a group of related institutions determines for itself (within statutory limits) the provisions governing employee eligibility, waiting periods for plan participation, employer and employee contribution rates, contributions during leaves of absence, prior service benefits, if any, normal retirement age, mandatory retirement age, and extensions of service beyond the mandatory age, if any. The provisions of TIAA-CREF plans differ among institutions and are described in more detail in chapter 3. While the provisions of an institution's TIAA-CREF plan as stated in its plan document will differ from institution to institution, system-wide uniformity is provided by the contractual relationship between each plan participant and TIAA and CREF. With common provisions throughout the system, the individual contracts detail the vesting of employer and employee contributions, payment of annuity benefits, preretirement death benefits, annuity income options, the right to pay additional premiums, and certain other provisions. Investment of funds, fund accounting, actuarial functions, and payment of benefits are carried out by TIAA and CREF.

The provision of immediate full vesting of premium payments in each participating staff member is an essential element of the retirement plans using TIAA and CREF annuities. (A few institutions provide for institutional ownership of the contract for up to the first five years of participation.) Under immediate full vesting, the staff member gains full ownership of all retirement and survivor benefits purchased by the employer and employee retirement contributions and their investment earnings.

As a corollary to immediate full vesting, the TIAA and CREF annuity contracts do not provide for a cash (single sum) or loan value. If accumulated funds could be turned in for cash or mortgaged at the staff member's request, either prior to or on termination of employment, neither the employer nor the employee would achieve the objective of lifetime income protection during retirement. Furthermore, the insuring organization would then require a degree of asset liquidity that could be expected to have an adverse effect on investment yield. By noncashability, full assurance is provided that contributed funds will be available solely for their intended purpose—retirement income or preretirement death benefits.

The TIAA-CREF preretirement death benefit builds up as the annuity accumulation grows, so that if the annuity policyholder dies before beginning to receive annuity payments, the full accumulation in the contract is payable to the named beneficiary or to the estate. The policyholder may choose in advance among several joint and survivor income payment methods or may leave the choice to the beneficiary.

The choice of annuity starting date is exercised by the TIAA-CREF annuity owner. Income is usually started, but need not be, at the time the individual retires from work. TIAA-CREF annuity contracts provide for the choice by the employee of various income options. All options provide a lifetime income for the retiring participant. All but the single life annuity and the installment refund make provision for a lifetime income for a survivor in the event of the primary annuitant's death. Selection from among the income options may be made at any time before income payments begin.

Church Plans. Retirement plans sponsored and operated by church organizations were reported by five private universities (8 percent), by ninety-three private four-year liberal arts colleges (14 percent), and by forty other four-year institutions (24 percent). Fifteen private two-year institutions (20 percent) reported a church plan covering some faculty employees.[12] In most instances, participants in church-sponsored plans are ministers serving as chaplains or as professors in a department of religion or theology, or as faculty members in seminaries. Normally the church plans are operated concurrently with a TIAA-CREF plan covering other faculty members and nonacademic employees. In seminaries, the church plan may be the exclusive plan for the institution. In universities and liberal arts colleges the proportion of employees participating in the church plan is likely to be quite small.

Retirement plans whose membership includes employees of seminaries, colleges, or universities, are reported by the following church bodies:

LUTHERAN CHURCH IN AMERICA, BOARD OF PENSIONS. Eight seminaries and eighteen colleges. This plan offers defined contribution retirement plans with optional fixed and variable annuity components.

ANNUITY BOARD OF THE SOUTHERN BAPTIST CONVENTION. Fifty-two institutions of higher education, including eight universities, and seven seminaries. The Annuity Board offers defined benefit plans and defined contribution plans using fixed and variable annuities.

THE MINISTERS AND MISSIONARIES BENEFIT BOARD OF THE AMERICAN BAPTIST CHURCHES. Covers approximately one hundred ministers and forty lay employees serving on the staff of colleges or seminaries. The program provides for a defined contribution variable annuity benefit with a guaranteed fixed-dollar minimum annuity for life.

PENSION FUND OF THE CHRISTIAN CHURCH. Twenty institutions of higher education, including fifteen colleges and five universities, plus eight seminaries. The Christian Church plan (Disciples of Christ) provides a benefit at age 65 equal to one-seventieth of the total lifetime salary upon which required dues have been paid.

THE LUTHERAN CHURCH—MISSOURI SYNOD. Available to full-time employees in thirteen colleges and two seminaries. A defined benefit plan providing 1.5 percent of final average salary (high five out of last fifteen) for each year of plan participation (maximum: 50 percent of salary), payable at age 65.

BOARD OF PENSIONS OF THE AMERICAN LUTHERAN CHURCH. Lay workers or clergy in twelve colleges and three seminaries. Provides a defined contribution annuity benefit based on contributions of 3 percent from participants and 10.5 percent from employers.

BOARD OF PENSIONS OF THE CHURCHES OF GOD. One college and one seminary. Defined contribution annuity based on 12 percent contributions by employee and employer, or by employer alone.

CHURCH OF THE BRETHREN. One seminary and six colleges. Plan details not available.

JOINT RETIREMENT BOARD OF THE RABBINICAL ASSEMBLY, THE UNITED SYNAGOGUE OF AMERICA, THE JEWISH THEOLOGICAL SEMINARY OF AMERICA. One seminary and one college. Defined contribution plan providing fixed and variable annuities.

CHRISTIAN REFORMED CHURCH IN NORTH AMERICA, MINISTERS' PENSION FUND. Defined benefit plan providing benefit of one-twelfth of a stated amount per year of service, gradual vesting to 100 percent after fifteen years.

Generally, church-related pension plans play a relatively small role in higher education. The main purpose of their use in higher education is to provide a continuity of coverage for ministerial employees as they move among employers, most of which are churches. Only among seminaries would it be likely that the majority of educational employees would be included in the church plan.

ANNUITY PRINCIPLES

Under every retirement plan, the application of annuity principles makes it possible to finance, in advance, a specified retirement income for life even though it cannot be known how long any particular plan member, or surviving spouse, will actually live. Providing—on a financially sound basis—an income that cannot be outlived is the single most important responsibility of a retirement system.

The implementation of annuity principles begins early, with the determination of the contributions needed to fund benefit payments that are, in many cases, to be made far in the future. During an employee's working years, funds are gradually accumulated by setting aside and investing employer and employee contributions. This is the "funding" process. At retirement, the contributions and their investment earnings become the basis for the retirement annuity, the payment mechanism that assures the maximum possible income for life. The accumulated funds constitute the "present value" (based on assumptions regarding future interest earnings of the funds and expected survival rates) of the lifetime income to be paid to the retired employee and, possibly, to a designated survivor. This present value is translated into monthly lifetime retirement income payments.

A monthly income for life can be assured because, although it is not possible to predict the life span of any particular individual, it is possible to establish probabilities of survival based on the mortality experience of large groups: large numbers of men of any given age or large numbers of women of any given age. Knowledge of the probability that an individual alive at one given age will survive to another makes possible the calculation of periodic annuity income payments assured for life, the result of a pooling of mortality risks among large numbers of men or women of the same age, each of whom at the outset has an equal chance with the others to be one of those who dies early or lives a long time. It allows the maximum monthly income payment, combining return of capital and investment earnings, that can be made to all annuitants in the pool throughout their retired lifetimes, however long or short any individual life may be. Application of the same principles to joint lives makes possible the survivor options that permit a retiring employee to make sure that an income will continue for life to a surviving spouse.

The practical difficulties of trying to manage funds in retirement without the help of the annuity mechanism are illustrated by the situation of a person without pension coverage but with some personal savings. A retired person might try to live on just the interest earned by accumulated savings, keeping the principal intact. But for most people this would produce a very small and probably inadequate monthly amount. Or a retiree might try a somewhat more sophisticated approach and plan on drawing on both principal and interest. Here, of course, the riddle is what rate to use, since a guess is required as to how long the income will be needed. Unfortunately, the matter is too important to be left to guessing.

A life annuity covers the financial risk of "living too long." An annuitant who dies early (soon after retiring) would have been better off (in hindsight) by taking the present value of the annuity at retirement, if it were available, and spending it faster than the statistical averages would suggest. But the risk of using up all the principal prematurely is too great, for no one can know in advance when death will occur. Accordingly, assurance of retirement security requires the financial mechanism of life annuities, the spreading of the risk of living too long among many thousands of annuitants. The use of the annuity principle eliminates the gamble of whether or not one will outlive financial resources and replaces it with the certainty of a lifetime monthly income, regardless of the length of that lifetime.

It is sometimes suggested that other factors in addition to age and sex could be used in annuity calculations. Suggested categories include smokers and nonsmokers, the thin and the fat, the adventurous and the conservative, various occupational hazard groups, hereditary health characteristics, and so on. But while these factors may affect accident rates or describe health conditions variously related to mortality, they are frequently voluntary, are nearly impossible to document with accuracy and are often subject to change. Since their impact on life expectancy cannot be quantified, they are lacking in reliabilty as statistical bases for the determination of pension liabilities. On the other hand, age and gender are universally and accurately documented as valid and reliable factors in measuring survival rates among large groups. (Actuarial criteria for annuitant risk classification require that the data utilized exhibit (1) significance; (2) stability; and (3) practicality in terms of measurement. The data must be significant to the risk of mortality of the group, stable in that they incorporate permanent characteristics and are not within the control of the annuitants, and practicable for the insurer to measure and to monitor at reasonable cost.)

In recent years, following the passage of the Equal Pay Act of 1963 and the Civil Rights Act of 1964, questions of discrimination have been raised regarding the use by private pensions of data-based tables reflecting sex differences in mortality, specifically the fact that, on the average, women live longer than men and therefore will have a longer period of time over which to collect benefits. The use of an age classification has not yet been disputed. At the present writing, three out of four federal agencies charged with administering laws banning sex discrimination in employment have guidelines that permit employers under defined benefit plans to make extra plan contributions for females in order to provide monthly amounts under a single life annuity formula benefit that are the same as for similarly situated males, with actuarially equivalent benefits for survivors. The agencies' guidelines also provide that employers with defined contribution plans may set aside an equal percentage of the salaries of male and female employees as premiums for annuities providing *actuarially* equal benefits under all annuity income options for similarly situated males and females. Actuarial equivalency means that identical accumulations for equally situated males and females will provide lower monthly benefits under a single life annuity for women than for men of the same age.

The two approaches encompassed by the federal guidelines have come to be known as the "either/or" approach: either equal contributions for men and women with actuarially equal benefits, or higher contributions for women with equal monthly benefits resulting under the single life annuity. It should be noted that two federal agencies (one of which administers the Equal Pay Act) have recently issued proposed new "equal in/equal out" guidelines that would appear to require equal contributions and equal monthly benefits for men and women in all pension plans. No final action on the proposed guidelines has been taken at the present writing.

A 1978 Supreme Court decision (City of Los Angeles Department of Water and Power v. Manhart et al.) ruled that under an employer-operated defined benefit plan it was a violation of Title VII of the Civil Rights Act of 1964 for the employer (a municipality) to require female employees to make greater pension plan contributions than male employees and thus have lower take-home pay than men in order to fund the extra cost of providing monthly (formula) single-life benefits for women that are the same as for equally situated men. In the lower federal courts in 1979, the defined contribution approach of "equal in/actuarially equal out" in private plans was being challenged on the grounds of sex discrimination under the Equal Pay Act and the Civil Rights Act.

DEFINED CONTRIBUTION AND DEFINED BENEFIT PLANS

The purpose of a pension plan, of course, is to pay benefits to participants who become eligible to receive them. The inflow of funds, the establishment of reserves, and the pension checks are all organized around this vital goal. All retirement plans incorporate a systematic means for the determination of benefits for participants. As mentioned briefly earlier in this chapter, two main approaches to the making of pension commitments are used: defined contribution (or money purchase) and defined benefit (or formula) plans. The *defined benefit* approach fixes benefits in advance as a percentage of salary for each year of service or, as in some industrial plans, a flat dollar amount per month or year of service. The *defined contribution* approach fixes contributions in advance as a percentage of each employee's salary, allocates these contributions to individual accounts, and pays benefits based on the funds credited to each participant.

Defined Contribution Plans. Nearly all TIAA-CREF plans in higher education use the defined contribution approach, as do many of the church pension systems and insurance company plans. In defined contribution plans the pension obligation is specified in terms of input to the plan. The regular contribution to the pension plan is stated as a percentage of the current compensation of the plan participant. This amount is credited to an individual account on behalf of the participant.

As an example, a defined contribution pension plan might call for a contribution rate of 10 percent of each participant's salary, paid each month to an annuity contract. At retirement the benefit is the monthly annuity that can be purchased by the total of employer and employee net contributions and the compound investment earnings credited to the individual's accumulating reserves. If the contributions are to a common-stock variable annuity, the annuity benefits will vary according to the number of annuity units purchased and the investment experience of the fund.

The contribution rate (percentage of earnings) established under a defined contribution pension plan is the same for each participant, with the exception of a few age-graded plans. The rate is set at a level estimated to be sufficient to achieve a stated pension goal, assuming a career of service of thirty or thirty-five years. The pension goal might be generally stated as half or more of the average of salary over the last three to five years of service, or even of the final year's service. A contribution rate is then selected that will enable an accumulation of funds sufficient to meet the stated general goal, given certain assumptions regarding interest earnings, mortality rates, and salary growth rates. Defined contribution plans are favored by small employers and the nonprofit sector. The largest of the defined contribution plans is the TIAA-CREF system. Some public employee and teacher retirement systems use the defined contribution approach for the determination of benefits from employee contributions.

The development of defined contribution plans was encouraged by passage of the Employee Retirement Income Security Act of 1974, due to its simplified treatment of the direct and uncomplicated funding method of these types of plans. Under this method, the salary of each participant is multiplied by the percentage contribution rate and the net dollar amount is credited directly to the individual's deferred annuity contract. Each such credit earns its pro rata investment share. Through regular reports the participant can easily determine how much the employer has contributed, how much (if anything) he or she has contributed, and the total fund credited, including investment earnings. The benefit itself is not precisely stated in advance, but is whatever pension can be purchased at retirement by the funds that have been accumulated on behalf of each plan participant. If contribution rates are increased or investment earnings are larger, the benefit is larger; the older the age of retirement, the larger the benefit; if a survivor income for a spouse is elected, the periodic income is less because it must continue throughout two lives. All benefits are actuarially established in order to achieve lifetime equivalency among all participants.

For the employer, budgeting and forecasting of operating costs are simple under defined contribution plans; the total employer cost is the employer's contribution rate multiplied by the salaries of plan participants. A specified and known amount of employer money becomes a clearly identified part of an employee's total compensation. Salary increases do not raise pension costs for service rendered prior to the increase, as is automatically the case under final-average defined benefit arrangements. Full funding of current service benefits under defined contribution plans occurs at the time service is rendered.

Defined Benefit Plans. Under defined benefit plans the pension commitment is defined in terms of plan output, i.e., a definition of the benefit. The amount of the benefit is stated by formula, and the formula is applied for each plan participant when he or she retires. The present and prospective pension obligation created by the formula for all participants combined also becomes the base for the actuarial calculation of the plan liabilities and for its funding requirements.

Defined benefit formulas (also termed "fixed formula" or "fixed benefit") are of two types: "unit benefit" and "flat benefit." The unit benefit percentage formula is the type most frequently encountered in defined benefit plans. It is the usual approach in the single-employer plans that cover about 70 percent of workers under private pension plans. It is also the approach used in government-sponsored plans for public employees and public school teachers. The unit benefit approach establishes benefits as a predetermined percentage of salary for each year of service. The salary factor can be expressed either as the average salary over the period of plan participation (the career average) or as the average salary over a designated period of service just preceding retirement, usually called the "final or highest average," such as the highest five years of average salary. Sometimes shorter averaging periods are used, three years or two years, for example, or the formula may provide for the use of the final year's salary if it is higher than alternatively stated longer averaging periods.

Under the defined benefit approach, the participant can determine an expected ratio of future retirement benefits to final average salary by multiplying the percentage factor in the benefit formula by an estimated service factor. The exact number of dollars of annuity income to be received during retirement cannot be predicted unless the salary factor as defined by the formula is known. The investment experience of defined benefit plans affects the employer's costs, but does not normally affect the amount of the individual's benefit.

Nearly all defined benefit plans covering employees in higher education are contributory, with employee contributions (a fixed percentage of current salary) withheld and deposited in the employee's pension account to help purchase the formula benefit. Employer contributions for current service benefits are made in whatever amounts are considered necessary, usually on recommendation of the plan's actuary, to purchase the portion of the prospective formula benefits not purchased by employee contributions. In calculating the amounts required to support future benefits in plans that do not vest retirement benefits immediately, discounts are incorporated for turnover, deaths, and for voluntary forfeitures of vested benefits (in plans that permit such forfeitures and that do not have to meet applicable ERISA requirements protecting such benefits). Since the price of a given amount of deferred annuity benefit increases as the period remaining until retirement shortens, the employer's contributions on behalf of each individual increase as the employee's age increases.

In any particular year under defined benefit plans, the total employer contribution required for current service is the sum of the dollar amounts (less any employee contributions) that are necessary to purchase the retirement benefits that the participants as a group are to be credited for that year's service. In some plans, mainly public retirement plans not subject to the funding requirements of ERISA, amounts required of the employer to support future benefits may not be currently funded, leading to increasing accrued unfunded liabilities.

When the pension benefit is expressed as a percentage of final or highest average salary, as in most defined benefit plans, additional employer input may be necessary in each successive year to pay for the increases in deferred benefits resulting from inflation and rising salaries, unless future salaries have been accurately forecast and appropriate level funding methods are being used. The total employer contribution is usually stated as a percentage of payroll, but this represents an average cost per employee rather than an actual credit to each pension account. The employer contribution may also include amounts applicable to the amortization of unfunded prior service benefits or interest payments on such unfunded liabilities. Taken as a percentage of payroll, then, the employer contribution to a defined benefit plan is easily subject to misinterpretation. It does not represent an amount added to each employee's compensation. It may be based on total payroll or covered payroll. It will vary with the age composition of the group. It may not represent the plan's full costs, for it may not be sufficient to cover current costs or include adequate contributions toward past service liabilities.

FINANCING DEFINED BENEFIT PLANS. Proper advance funding under the defined benefit approach requires the development of an actuarial cost method to inform the (public or private) employer of the rate at which the pension obligations that are accruing under the plan should be covered by the inflow of funds. The funding method chosen provides a scheme for spreading the aggregate costs over the working lifetime of those participants who are expected to remain in the plan long enough to acquire benefit eligibility. It also amortizes the supplemental liabilities represented by the credited prior service of employees who were at work before the plan was started or by benefit increases related to service rendered prior to the increase.

A number of actuarial cost-funding methods are available for the orderly accumulation of reserves to provide the benefits of defined benefit pension plans. In practice, the terminology employed to describe these methods is not wholly uniform, although the Committee on Pension and Profit-Sharing Terminology of the American Risk and Insurance Association has established recommended classifications.

Under the accrued benefit (unit credit) method, the cost of each dollar of current service benefit is met in the year in which it accrues. There is no attempt to anticipate or prefund benefits related to future wage or salary increases through the use of projections. In effect, a series of benefit purchases is made for each participant year by year. The annual total of these purchases is the employer's annual cost. The accrued benefit method is nearly always used in connection with group deferred annuity contracts.

Other funding methods incorporate projected benefit costs based on assumptions regarding rates of change in compensation, with the objective of leveling out the premiums and funding more evenly over time. The methods may use assumed ages of entry into the plan or actual ages. Several approaches to the treatment of initial past-service liabilities and of liabilities resulting from plan liberalizations are available under these standard cost methods.

THE DEFINED BENEFIT INPUT CURVE. Under defined benefit plans, the actual pattern of the input of contributions in the aggregate will depend on the actuarial cost method employed. In addition to the requirements of the cost method, relevant factors in the employer's aggregate annual outlay will be the age and sex composition of the covered group, the applicable mortality assumptions for active and retired employees, turnover rates in the various age categories, expected rates of future compensation, the benefit formula, any disability and survivor benefits associated with the plan, expected investment earnings, and administrative costs. The aggregate employer cost each year may be expressed as a percentage of covered payroll, of total payroll, or in other ways. The overall percentage measures the total employer cost, but, as noted earlier, it does not indicate to a given participant the amount of money that is being set aside to fund his or her particular benefit. Neither does it directly indicate how much it costs to employ men and women of various ages.

Level cost projected methods aid the employer in achieving funding adequacy and stability under a defined benefit plan, but a terminating vested participant is credited only with the benefit accrued to date, not with any additional funding based on projected future salary increments. The employee's departure effectively cancels the projected level contribution input pattern being followed on his or her behalf and fixes in its place the accrued benefit to termination with its lower associated accrued cost.

Comparing the Defined Benefit and Defined Contribution Approaches. The best way to illustrate the differences between these two basic approaches in their contribution patterns, funding, and levels of vested benefits at any given point for an individual employee is to take a stated retirement benefit and see how it is financed for individuals, rather than aggregates, under the two approaches during the working years.

Using an illustrative accrual (unit credit) approach for the defined benefit plan, table 2.5 compares costs and benefits under a defined benefit percentage formula plan and a defined contribution plan, each of which provides identical retirement benefits for a male worker who enters the plan at age 25 and retires at age 65. (For both types of plan, contribution rates for female workers would be higher in order to provide the same monthly single life annuity because of the greater female longevity.) The comparisons are based on a benefit formula of 1.5 percent of final five-year average salary per year of service for the defined benefit plan, and a contribution of 7.5 percent of each year's salary for the defined contribution plan. In addition, the following assumptions were made: immediate vesting of benefits, initial salary of $12,000 at age 25 increasing 3 percent per year to retirement at age 65, interest earnings assumed at 6 percent per year, with administrative expenses and annuity mortality factors as shown in the table.

Table 2.5 shows the yearly input, the accumulating funds, and the benefits payable beginning at age 65 that have accrued at the end of each year of participation in each type of plan. Under the "payment to fund" (columns 4-5 and 7-8) is shown the actual amount of annual contribution that is required to fund the plan's benefit liability to date for the individual employee described by the benefit illustration. For the defined benefit plan, the accrual method is used in the illustration in order to indicate the actual funding and vesting situation of an individual employee at any one time for any year between age 25 and age 65. A level funding method—not unit accrual—would be used in actual practice in a final-average defined benefit percentage formula plan, with the method based on the plan's liabilities for the covered group as a whole. However, comparison of the two approaches as they affect an individual employee requires analysis of individual situations rather than aggregates. On termination of an individual's employment, no matter what the funding method, the present value of the individual's own formula-determined benefit (column 6) is applied toward the deferred, vested benefit (column 10) under the defined benefit plan. Under the defined contribution plan, the annuity accumulation (column 9) purchases the deferred annuity shown in column 11.

CAREER PARTICIPATION. Comparing the two approaches on a career-long participation basis, the following characteristics may be observed:

• Under the defined benefit approach, the contribution is a low percentage of the entering employee's salary at younger ages, beginning at 1.52 percent of the salary of the 25-year-old participant, compared with a uniform 7.5 percent of salary contribution under the defined contribution plan for participants of all ages (columns 4 and 7, table 2.5).

• Not until the employee under a defined benefit plan reaches age 46 does the contribution as a percentage of current salary equal the uniform 7.5 percent of salary rate under the defined contribution approach.

• The steady annual rise in contributions as a percentage of salary under the defined benefit plan brings the annual cost up to a percentage of the employee's salary at the higher ages that far exceeds the defined contribution rate of 7.5 percent. By age 55, the defined benefit contribu-

Table 2.5. Comparison of Benefit Accrual and Employer Costs Under Defined Benefit and Defined Contribution Plans

| (1) | (2) | (3) | Defined Benefit Approach | | | Defined Contribution Approach | | | (10) Amount of Annuity Beginning at Age 65 Purchased to Age Shown in Column 2 | (11) |
| | | | Payment to fund | | | Payment to fund | | | | |
Years in plan	Age	Current salary	(4) % of current salary	(5) Amount in $	(6) Accumulation of principal + 6% interest	(7) % of current salary	(8) Amount in $	(9) Accumulation of principal + 6% interest	Defined benefit approach	Defined contribution approach
1	25	$12,000	1.52%	$ 182	$ 181	7.5%	$ 900	$ 898	$ 180	$ 891
2	26	12,360	1.61	199	390	7.5	927	1,877	365	1,757
3	27	12,731	1.70	216	629	7.5	955	2,942	556	2,599
4	28	13,113	1.81	237	903	7.5	983	4,100	753	3,417
5	29	13,505	1.92	259	1,215	7.5	1,013	5,357	955	4,212
6	30	13,911	2.19	305	1,592	7.5	1,043	6,720	1,181	4,985
7	31	14,329	2.38	341	2,028	7.5	1,075	8,196	1,419	5,735
8	32	14,758	2.59	382	2,530	7.5	1,107	9,792	1,670	6,464
9	33	15,201	2.81	427	3,108	7.5	1,140	11,518	1,936	7,173
10	34	15,657	3.05	478	3,771	7.5	1,175	13,381	2,215	7,862
11	35	16,127	3.31	534	4,528	7.5	1,210	15,391	2,510	8,531
12	36	16,611	3.59	596	5,394	7.5	1,246	17,557	2,820	9,181
13	37	17,109	3.89	666	6,380	7.5	1,283	19,891	3,147	9,813
14	38	17,622	4.21	743	7,501	7.5	1,325	22,404	3,491	10,427
15	39	18,151	4.56	828	8,775	7.5	1,361	25,107	3,852	11,023
16	40	18,696	4.93	922	10,219	7.5	1,403	28,013	4,233	11,603
17	41	19,256	5.33	1,027	11,855	7.5	1,445	31,135	4,632	12,166
18	42	19,834	5.76	1,142	13,704	7.5	1,487	34,487	5,052	12,713
19	43	20,429	6.23	1,273	15,794	7.5	1,532	38,086	5,492	13,245
20	44	21,042	6.73	1,416	18,151	7.5	1,578	41,946	5,955	13,762
21	45	21,673	7.26	1,573	20,809	7.5	1,625	46,085	6,440	14,264
22	46	22,324	7.84	1,750	23,801	7.5	1,674	50,521	6,949	14,752
23	47	22,993	8.46	1,945	27,167	7.5	1,724	55,273	7,483	15,226
24	48	23,683	9.13	2,162	30,950	7.5	1,776	60,362	8,043	15,686

25	49	24,394	9.85	2,402	35,200	7.5	1,829	65,810	8,629	16,134
26	50	25,125	10.62	2,669	39,968	7.5	1,885	71,639	9,244	16,569
27	51	25,879	11.44	2,961	45,316	7.5	1,941	77,875	9,887	16,992
28	52	26,655	12.33	3,287	51,308	7.5	2,000	84,542	10,561	17,402
29	53	27,455	13.28	3,645	58,019	7.5	2,059	91,670	11,267	17,801
30	54	28,279	14.30	4,044	65,529	7.5	2,121	99,286	12,005	18,189
31	55	29,127	15.40	4,486	73,930	7.5	2,185	107,424	12,777	18,566
32	56	30,001	16.58	4,974	83,320	7.5	2,250	116,115	13,585	18,932
33	57	30,901	17.84	5,513	93,811	7.5	2,318	125,394	14,430	19,288
34	58	31,828	19.20	6,111	105,527	7.5	2,387	135,300	15,313	19,634
35	59	32,783	20.65	6,769	118,603	7.5	2,459	145,872	16,236	19,970
36	60	33,766	22.21	7,500	133,190	7.5	2,533	157,151	17,201	20,296
37	61	34,779	23.89	8,309	149,457	7.5	2,609	169,184	18,210	20,613
38	62	35,823	25.68	9,199	167,587	7.5	2,687	182,016	19,263	20,921
39	63	36,898	27.60	10,184	187,786	7.5	2,768	195,698	20,363	21,221
40	64	38,004	29.66	11,271	210,285	7.5	2,850	210,285	21,512	21,512
Total					$112,927			$67,868		

SOURCE: William C. Greenough and Francis P. King, *Pension Plans and Public Policy*. (New York: Columbia University Press, 1976), pp. 184–85, table 8.2.
NOTE: Benefit objective for both plans: 1.5% of final 5-year average salary times years of service for a 40-year career under one employer.
Assumptions used in preparation of table: 6% interest factor; A-1949 Mortality Table (Projected Scale B); 3.5% of contribution administrative expense factor.

tion has risen to 15 percent. It is 22 percent of the even higher salary at age 60 and amounts to nearly 30 percent of salary at age 64.

• The heavy weighting of contributions under a defined benefit plan at the higher ages is even more startling when expressed in dollar terms. This is a result of the much higher percentage of contribution applied against a much higher salary. In the example, the cost of a person aged 30 under a defined benefit plan is $305, compared with $1,043 under a defined contribution plan. At age 64, the defined benefit plan cost is $11,271, compared with $2,850 under a defined contribution plan. The cost in dollars under a defined benefit plan in the illustration is thirty-seven times as high at age 64 as at age 30, even though salary is only three times as high. These relationships are shown graphically in chart 2.1. Under a defined contribution plan, the cost rises at the same rate as does the employee's salary.

• For the forty-year period of participation, the total amount contributed under the defined benefit approach is 66 percent higher than under the defined contribution approach: $112,900 under the defined benefit versus $67,900 under defined contribution. The $45,000 higher cost under the defined benefit approach is the consequence of its lower investment earnings capacity. Under a defined contribution plan, the higher contributions in earlier years result in higher investment earnings on the individually allocated basis illustrated. These earnings

Chart 2.1. Annual Employer Contributions—Noncontributory Defined Benefit and Defined Contribution Plans

(annual retirement income of $21,500 under both approaches)

Annual employer contribution

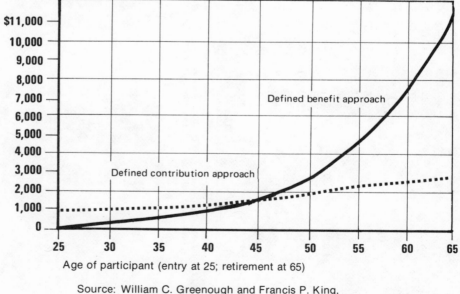

Age of participant (entry at 25; retirement at 65)

Source: William C. Greenough and Francis P. King,
Pension Plans and Public Policy.
(New York: Columbia University Press, 1976),
p. 186, chart 8.1.

alone amount to 68 percent of the $210,000 accumulation at age 65. Under defined benefit plans, total employer contributions for the entire forty-year period are higher, but are heaped up at the end of the employee's working career, so that their investment earnings represent only 46 percent of the total accumulation.

The combined effect of contributions and compound investment earnings on the growing accumulations under the two types of plan produces by age 65 exactly the same annuity accumulation amount under both plans. At all younger ages the accumulation is greater under the defined contribution plan. The accumulation at any age is equal under both plans to the single-sum value of the deferred benefits purchased by that age. For example, at age 35 the employee under a defined benefit plan has accumulated a single-sum (present) benefit value of $4,528 (column 6); under a defined contribution plan at the same age, it would be $15,391 (column 9).

At every age, on termination of employment prior to age 65, the deferred vested pension benefit under the defined contribution approach is substantially higher than under the defined benefit approach. This is the result of the higher contributions at the younger ages under the defined contribution plan and of the higher leverage of investment earnings on the larger input in the earlier years. The retirement benefit an employee would receive at age 65 on leaving the employer earlier than 65 is shown in table 2.6. After ten years of service (from ages 25 through 34), assuming vested status on termination, only $2,215 of the expected annual retirement benefit of $21,512 (on termination at age 65) has become vested under the defined benefit plan, against $7,862 under the defined contribution plan.

An employee may change jobs several times during a career and earn vested pension credits under several different employers. If all successive employers have had a defined contribution plan, at retirement age of 65 the benefits from all the plans will add up to the full $21,512 benefit (assuming no coverage gaps and based on the assumptions used in table 2.5). If all of the successive employers had defined benefit plans (also assuming no coverage gaps, full vesting under each plan, and the table

Table 2.6. Present Value and Annual Income Amount of Deferred Annuity Earned on Termination of Employment

Age	Years in plan	Defined Benefit Plan		Defined Contribution Plan	
		Present value at age shown	Annual annuity income at age 65[a]	Present value at age shown	Annual annuity income at age 65[a]
25	1	$ 181	$ 180	$ 898	$ 891
34	10	3,771	2,215	13,381	7,862
44	20	18,151	5,955	41,946	13,762
54	30	65,529	12,005	99,286	18,189
64	40	210,285	21,512	210,285	21,512

[a]Annuity income payable beginning at age 65. Assumptions same as for table 2.5.

Table 2.7. Effect of Job Changes on Retirement Benefits under Defined Benefit Plans—Continuous Participation under Successive Plans

Years of Service and Changes of Employers[a]	Annual annuity	Benefit percentage[b]
No change (full 40 years with one employer)	$21,500	100%
Change after 15 years (age 40)	17,300	80
Change after 25 years (age 50)	16,700	77
Change after 10 years (age 35) and again after 15 more years (age 50)	15,475	72

[a]Retirement plan entry at age 25, continuous participation thereafter in one or more plans, as shown.
[b]Percentages less than 100 show extent of benefit reduction due to successive job changes under defined benefit plans with identical provisions.

2.5 illustration), the total benefits will be less when added up at retirement than if the employee had participated in just one defined benefit plan throughout employment, a situation that has been described as "cold-storage vesting." Table 2.7 shows how one or two job changes with vested benefits under defined benefit plans can affect ultimate benefits, compared with the same number of years of participation in a plan of just one employer.

Employers who have chosen a defined benefit plan find costs so high for new participants in the upper age brackets that they feel almost forced to turn aside older job-seekers. In order to reduce this possibility and to moot the question of discrimination, ERISA allows employers with defined benefit plans to exclude employees from participation in the plan if they are initially employed within five years of the normal retirement age.

INVESTMENTS OF PUBLIC RETIREMENT SYSTEMS

The nature, diversification, and yield of a public pension plan's investments are important elements in the determination of the ultimate cost of the plan. The higher the yield, the lower can be the employer and/or employee contributions required to meet a particular benefit objective. An investment yield in excess of the assumed rate under a defined benefit plan can help control employer costs in a period of rising wages due to inflation or help reduce unfunded liabilities. In defined contribution plans, increases in the interest earnings rate of the pension fund provide increased annuity benefits.

Theoretically, all pension systems have the same investment opportunities. The investment results of a pension fund will be a function of investment policy and the expertise of the fund's managers. At times there may be specific internal limitations facing fund managers, items over which they have little or no control. For example, public retirement systems have been circumscribed in the past—and some still are—by legislative provisions restricting the range of permitted investments. As a result, some public systems have tended to hold substantially larger proportions of the lower-yield debt obligations of states, municipalities, other public bodies, and the federal government, than do private pension funds. A 1976 study of the finances of public employee retirement systems by Robert Tilove noted that "for a tax-exempt pension fund, investing in tax-exempt state or local obligations is, with rare exception, senseless."[13] Past approaches have adversely affected the investment performance of many public retirement systems, even though in recent years critical reaction to the restrictions has resulted in some changes. As late as 1967 the following comments could be made on the investment performance of public retirement systems, quoted from a report by Dr. Roger F. Murray for the National Bureau of Economic Research, submitted as part of a series of papers for the Subcommittee on Fiscal Policy of the Joint Economic Committee:

> The practice of seeking to secure competent investment advice by competitive bidding, the inability to pay adequate salaries for expert staff, and the apparent unwillingness to lay out even very modest sums for investment management are all factors conspiring to produce uninspired and mediocre portfolio management. Despite the great progress of recent years, few systems have adequate staffs, strong investment advisory arrangements, effective finance committees, and the capability of providing first-rate management. . . .

> Under the circumstances, it is doubtful that state and local retirement systems will soon break out of the statutory, accounting, and institutional restraints on their effective management of huge aggregations of capital. While the high cost of pension benefits will create increasing pressure to improve rates of return, it is not likely that the public systems will greatly accelerate the pace at which they follow private funds. Nor is it likely that they will be as flexible in approaching investment opportunities as they occur in the future of a dynamic capital market structure.[14]

The results of these earlier investment policies, and the changes that have taken place in more recent years, are shown in table 2.8, which summarizes the distribution of the investments of state and local retirement systems. As late as 1962 just over 26 percent of the assets of these funds were invested in federal obligations, and over 17 percent were invested in state and local securities. In 1976, the proportion of assets in federal obligations had declined to about 8.3 percent and only about 2.8 percent were invested in state and local obligations. Partly as a result of these changes, the proportion of nongovernmental securities rose dramatically over the same period. Investments in corporate bonds rose from 40.9 percent in 1962 to 51.5 percent in 1976; the proportion of investments in common stocks rose from 3 percent in 1962 to 22.1 percent in 1976. Mortgage investments represented 8.8 percent of assets in 1962 and 7.1 percent in 1976. Over the period, many of the systems changed from the exclusive use of in-house investment decisions made by staff to the use of outside professional investment counsel. Others augmented in-house professional staffs. In many of the systems former legal restrictions were repealed in order to give the fund managers an opportunity to use the conventional "prudent man rule" under which pension managers in private pension funds normally operate.

Table 2.8. Percentage of State and Local Retirement System Assets by Investment Category, 1962–1976

System category and fiscal year ending in	Cash and deposits (1)	Federal securities (2)	State and local government securities (3)	Corporate bonds (4)	Corporate stocks (5)	Mortgages (6)	Other securities (7)[a]	All other investments (8)[a]	Total
1961–62	1.2	26.2	17.4	40.9	3.0	8.8		2.4	100
1971–72	1.1	5.4	3.5	55.1	18.3	10.2		6.2	100
1972–73	1.4	4.4	1.9	55.3	21.7	8.7		6.5	100
1973–74	1.7	6.0	.9	54.8	22.3	7.6	5.4	1.1	100
1974–75	2.0	6.7	.7	54.6	22.2	7.5	5.5	.7	100
1975–76	1.3	8.3	2.8	51.5	22.1	7.1	5.7	1.3	100

SOURCE: U.S. Congress, House Committee on Education and Labor, *Pension Task Force Report on Public Employee Retirement Systems*, 95th Cong., 2d sess., Committee Print, March 15, 1978, p. 133, table F2.

[a]The categories "Other Securities" and "All Other Investments" were combined for the years 1961–62, 1971–72, and 1972–73.

While the percentage of total public pension fund assets invested in state and local government securities has substantially declined, such investments persist in the plans of a few states. The state-administered plans in twenty-eight states and locally-administered plans in seventeen states have no state and local government security investments. On the other hand, such investments exceed 5 percent of total assets for the locally-administered plans in six states and for the state-administered plans in one state. Reflecting the political pressures associated with New York's financial crisis, between the fiscal years 1974–75 and 1975–76, the percentage of plan assets invested in state and local government securities jumped from 4.6 percent to 19.7 percent for six New York City plans, and from 0.7 percent to 8.9 percent for two New York State plans.[15]

It takes time for changing investment policies to be reflected in a pension fund's overall portfolio. Many investment managers are reluctant to sustain a capital loss through the sale of low-yield publicly issued securities, even if that is desirable. While no new purchases of publicly issued securities may be made, many years or even decades may elapse before the maturity dates of existing public issues result in the disappearance of these issues from the fund's portfolio. In future years, it may be expected that the better-managed public pension systems will show an even lower proportion of lower-yield tax-exempt securities than at present.

MONITORING PERFORMANCE. Too often, individual members of public retirement systems and their employers fail to keep themselves informed about the financial policies, funding levels, and investment performance of their retirement systems. Yet these pension systems are public trustees of immense amounts of capital and are responsible for the promise of future income for millions of individuals and for the present income of millions of others. A pension system's policies and the ability of its management should be of as much concern to college administrators, faculty members, and staff as would be the case if the college were administering the plan itself. It is not necessary to be an actuary to ask intelligent questions about whether a system is providing for adequate advance funding of future obligations or is crediting reasonable interest rates to member contributions; nor is it necessary to be an investment expert to determine whether pension funds are being invested for reasonable yields. Although most public plans publish annual financial reports, some do not, and some do not include sufficient information to make them useful. One plan administrator informed the authors that "this system does not prepare any annual reports except for presentation to the general assembly and those are not in suitable form for publication."

FUNDING OF PUBLIC RETIREMENT SYSTEMS

Few state and local public retirement systems are fully funded. A pension system is fully funded only if reserves representing employee service already performed are sufficient to discharge completely all presently accrued benefit liabilities and if amounts being contributed currently to the fund on behalf of current service are sufficient, according to appropriate salary projections, interest expectations, turn-over and mortality rates, and expense calculations, to discharge currently accruing pension obligations as they mature. The employees' contributions are, of course, withheld from salary and paid directly to the system, and this provides for a partial funding of benefits promised. The degree of funding of earned benefits payable in the future varies considerably among public plans. The 1978 House Pension Task Force found that 17 percent of public retirement systems were on a pay-as-you-go basis, with appropriations covering only the actual benefits expected to be paid out during the following legislative period. The Task Force also stated that a realistic assessment of pension costs is unknown for the vast majority of public retirement systems, that one-third of the total public pension plans at all levels of government did not have actuarial valuations in the five-year period ending in 1975, and that most of the plans lacking actuarial valuations were financed on a pay-as-you-go or other nonactuarial basis. The report concluded that an outgrowth of the lack of actuarial standards applicable to public plans was the use of unrealistic actuarial assumptions by the public plans and that "there is a compelling need for public pen-sion plan actuarial valuations and for uniform actuarial measures and standards to enable plan participants, plan sponsors, and taxpayers to assess the present funding status and future funding needs of their systems."[16] Sometimes external proposals, as for earlier vesting or higher benefits, bring to public view the need for sounder financial support of the obligations already undertaken by a public pension plan.

Readers of the reports of auditors and of actuarial consultants to public pension plans will note the frequency of recommendations for more adequate levels of fund-ing. Year after year these reports emphasize the importance to long-range economy, to plan stability, and to benefit security of limiting, through sound financial prac-tice, the extent to which future legislatures may be asked to provide funds for bene-fits that were promised many years, perhaps many decades, before. The potential financial burdens resulting from delay in addressing the problem can mount with astonishing speed. For example, the State Universities Retirement System of Illi-nois (SURS) has been accumulating increasing levels of unfunded liabilities ever since it was established in 1941. The financial situation of this system may seem to involve large figures, but it is not unusual among public systems. A 1969 examina-tion of the SURS noted that "employer contributions provided from State appro-priations . . . were not sufficient to meet these requirements [current service costs] and the unfunded accrued liabilities increased from $167,000,000 as of August 31, 1968, to $193,990,000 as of August 31, 1969, according to computations by the Ac-tuary retained by the System."[17] Less than a decade later, in 1977, the unfunded li-ability had increased to $730,570,000. Here is the actuary's statement:

> The *Illinois Pension Code* provides that the State shall make contributions
> to the System each year which are at least equal to the State's share of the nor-
> mal cost of benefits earned by active employees during the year, plus interest on

the unfunded accrued liabilities. For the year ended August 31, 1977, the State should have appropriated 17.22 percent of payroll or about $109,744,000 to meet this minimum statutory requirement. Actual contributions by the State amounted to only $35,716,766, which was about $74,027,000 less than the minmum requirement.

During the year, the unfunded accrued liabilities of the System increased from $658,772,105 to $730,570,416. This increase was due mainly to the failure of the General Assembly to appropriate funds to meet the cost of pensions and other benefits earned by active employees. The State has been paying the System only enough money to meet the State's share of the benefit payments to persons already retired, and no appropriations are made to meet the future pension payment to persons who are still employed."[18]

If they can be found, the financial reports of most of the public employee and state teacher retirement systems in the country, and of local retirement systems, make gloomy and worrisome reading. Since the liabilities of a retirement system consist largely of obligations incurred on account of benefits that have not yet become payable, but that have already been promised, an annual statement of a system's receipts and disbursements or of its income and expenditures, however labeled, is not sufficient to indicate its true financial position. These statements give a picture of the current transactions of a retirement system and show what the present assets are, but since the measure of the system's obligations is in the cost of benefit promises made for many years in the future, balance sheets and income statements are not the place to look to judge the financial solvency of the system. Only the actuarial valuation can inform the plan member or the taxpayer of what the future benefits are likely to cost and whether the present assets together with reasonably expected future contributions will be sufficient to cover the cost. Not all reports give the actuarial valuation a prominent position, nor do all reports include an actuarial evaluation.

A few more examples of the gap between available assets and liabilities incurred to date will illustrate the financial soundness, or lack of it, of just a few of the public retirement systems covering employees in higher education. Because there has been a rapid growth in the number of public employees over the last few decades, the ratio of current income to current benefit payments tends to be relatively high. But benefit obligations are also accruing at a high rate. The absence of full current funding can ultimately be expected to result in a need for ever-increasing public appropriations in the future to make up for inadequate funding in the past.

EXAMPLE I: As reported in 1976, the California State Teachers' Retirement System currently requires a contribution of 8 percent of salary from employees and 8 percent of payroll from the district employers, plus $135 million per year from the state until the year 2002. The 1976 actuarial valuation reports that this funding level of 16 percent plus is insufficient. The minimum total rate from teachers and districts should be 21.19 percent, rather than 16 percent, composed of a normal cost of 17.18 percent of payroll plus 4.01 percent of payroll just to maintain future un-funded obligations in the same relation as at present to future payroll. The unfunded obligation in 1976 amounted to $7.65 billion. The actuarial report concluded with the following warning: "The concern is two-fold: (1) long range, that when all bene-fits now promised become due, funds to pay those benefits will not be on deposit; and (2) the continued growth in the unfunded accrued obligation."[19]

EXAMPLE II: As of March 31, 1977, the New York State Employees' Retirement System had assets of $7.8 billion and was committed to pay in future years benefits amounting to $16 billion.[20]

EXAMPLE III: As of June 30, 1976, the Pennsylvania Public School Employees' Retirement System held $3.4 billion in assets and had accrued benefit obligations of $5.7 billion, and was thus underfunded by $2.3 billion.[21]

EXAMPLE IV: In 1973, the New York State Teachers' Retirement System reported assets of $3.6 billion and liabilities of $8.6 billion.[22]

EXAMPLE V: The Massachusetts State Employees' Retirement System has, as a pay-as-you-go system, amassed unfunded liabilities of over $7 billion. In order to amortize this accumulated burden, the state will need to contribute more than 26 percent of payroll annually for forty years. The state now pays 13.5 percent of payroll.[23]

EXAMPLE VI: The Teachers' Retirement System of the State of Kentucky reported an actuarial deficiency of $799,279,900 (including an unfunded prior service liabil-ity of $50,007,571) as of July 1, 1976, increased from $442,556,691 just two years before.[24]

What will be the consequences of these heavy deficits? A *Wall Street Journal* article of November 24, 1977, concluded that little is being done about the sizable number of government pension plans that "are hurtling toward insolvency" and quoted pension expert Dan M. McGill of the Wharton School of the University of Pennsylvania, who said: "As a group, public employee retirement systems are in-adequately funded, poorly designed and subject to unsound political manipula-tion." The article noted that the traditional justification for underfunding, or failing to fund public pensions was that, unlike corporations, states and cities don't go bankrupt because they have the power to levy taxes to pay their debts. Lately, how-ever, the article added, that assumption has been demolished, as suggested by the fiscal situation of New York City and of Cleveland, Ohio, and by the so-called tax revolt of California citizens expressed in the passage of Proposition 13 in 1978, as a constitutional limitation of the taxing power of local authorities. Yet taxpayer resistance to increased taxation is one of the reasons why huge unfunded liabilities continue to accumulate. Although pensions represent a debt owed to public em-ployees by the taxpayer, the full amount of the debt does not come due until well into the future. These public unfunded liabilities measure the size of the financial obliga-tions—and the political problems—that are being shifted forward.

INVESTMENTS OF THE TIAA-CREF SYSTEM

TIAA-CREF investments differ substantially from those of public retirement systems. CREF invests all premiums allocated to it in common stocks and in securities convertible into common stocks. TIAA's investment portfolio emphasizes corporate securities, mainly direct placement loans, but also including purchases of publicly traded bonds, and it also places strong emphasis on mortgage loans. Mortgages, with their high yields and low liquidity, make attractive investments for pension funds investing for the long term. While mortgage investing requires skilled professional staff to handle the complex financial and legal aspects of this class of investments, the achievable rates of return demonstrate the value of a relatively heavy emphasis on these investments. In 1977, 48.1 percent of the total TIAA portfolio was invested in mortgages, including shopping centers, office buildings, and industrial centers. Of the *combined* TIAA-CREF portfolio in 1977, mortgages represented 27.8 percent. In contrast, among state and local government retirement systems in 1977, mortgages represented 6.7 percent of total assets. Among all private pension funds in 1976, mortgage investments represented 1.3 percent of assets (see table 2.10). Table 2.9 shows the distribution of investments by type for the combined TIAA-CREF system, from 1957 to 1977.

The net rate of return on total invested assets of TIAA after deductions of investment expenses was 8.71 percent for 1978, compared with 8.13 percent for 1976. For all U.S. life insurance companies, the before-tax average net rate of return on invested assets (excluding separate accounts) was 7.35 percent in 1978 and 6.68 percent in 1976. In practical terms, the leverage of superior investment performance is impressive and is of particular value to participants in defined contribution re-

Table 2.9. Investments of TIAA-CREF Retirement System by Type of Security, 1957–1977

Type of Security	Period: Calendar Years Ended in:				
	1957	1962	1967	1973	1977
Total Amount (millions)	$584.9	$1,106.9	$2,572.1	$5,947.4	$10,359.9
Percentage Distribution[a]					
Cash and demand deposits	0.5%	0.4%	0.5%	2.0%	1.1%
U.S. Gov't securities	0.6	0.6	0.2	0.3	0.1
Canadian obligations	1.1	1.7	0.9	0.9	0.1
Corporate bonds	37.9	30.5	22.2	20.3	24.1
Corporate equities[b]	9.1	22.4	38.9	43.5	42.8
Mortgages	47.4	40.6	32.8	30.0	27.8
Real estate	2.2	2.5	3.1	1.9	2.7
Other	0.8	0.9	1.1	0.7	0.9

[a]Percentages may not equal 100 due to rounding.
[b]Includes all corporate stock, preferred and common, owned by TIAA and CREF. The extent of participation by CREF in common stock ownership is dependent on policyholders' decisions as to allocation of premiums between TIAA and CREF.

Table 2.10. Investments of Private Pension Funds, 1957–1976

	1957	1962	1967	1973	1976
Total Amount (millions)	$21.108	$47.152	$89.417	$135.202	$175.5
Percentage Distribution					
Cash and demand deposits	1.9%	1.5%	1.4%	1.8%	2.2%
Corporate equities	33.4	46.4	57.1	66.9	62.5
U.S. Gov't securities	13.2	6.2	2.5	3.2	8.3
Corporate bonds	44.8	38.3	29.4	22.4	22.2
Mortgages	2.1	3.9	4.5	1.7	1.3
Miscellaneous	4.2	3.5	4.7	3.7	3.2

SOURCE: Board of Governors of the Federal Reserve System, Division of Research and Statistics, *Flow of Funds Accounts, 1946–1975* (Washington, D.C., December 1976), pp. 126–127, and *Flow of Funds Accounts, Assets and Liabilities Outstanding, 1965–76* (Washington, D.C., December 1977), p. 12.

tirement systems, in which extra investment earnings are credited to participants' annuity contracts. Over a forty-year period, a 1-percent difference in investment yield, for example the difference between 7 and 8 percent, could increase an annuity accumulation by 30 percent, while a 2-percent difference could increase the annuity accumulation by 70 percent.

Differences between the investment policies followed by the combined TIAA-CREF program and other types of private pension funds can be discerned by comparing tables 2.9 and 2.10.

3 Retirement Plan Provisions

THIS CHAPTER discusses pension benefit objectives and describes the specific provisions that affect participants in retirement plans in higher education: entry ages, waiting periods, contribution rates, vesting, retirement ages, and benefits.

THE COMPONENTS OF RETIREMENT INCOME

The Individual's Role. Individuals can and should make long-range economic decisions about the way they want to live in retirement, assuming that they foresee an end to full-time paid employment and some years of leisure to follow. The continuous process of deciding to spend now or to save for the future (sometimes called the lifetime allocation of resources) goes on constantly. But the more distant the savings goal, the more likely that disruptive emergencies and special needs will intervene. Consequently, the success of the longest term savings plans—saving for retirement—will be affected by many factors and the results will vary greatly among individuals. Over the years, some people will be better able than others to defer the use of current income. Some people will face emergency needs that others do not. Of those who save, not all will invest wisely. For many reasons, the possibility of accumulating significant personal savings for use in retirement lacks certainty. Yet, if personal savings plans are completed over the long term, they can make a difference in retirement living standards. Along with Social Security and a pension, savings can add a valuable third element to retirement security.

If each person were able to finance with certainty all expected retirement needs through a personal program of lifetime resource allocation, Social Security and private pension plans would not be needed and would not exist. But individual savings plans are often unsuccessful, as attested by the fact that income from assets and savings represent only about one dollar for every ten dollars of total income received by Social Security beneficiaries from all sources.[1] Since individual savings efforts are unreliable, institutionalized mechanisms are needed.

The Institutional Role. The institutionalized machinery used to assure retirement income for employees in higher education takes the form of participation in (1) the federal Social Security program; (2) public retirement systems established by units of government; and (3) private pension plans, primarily the nonprofit TIAA-CREF plans. The extent of coverage under the Social Security program of employees in higher education is discussed in chapter 4. Type and extent of coverage under employer-sponsored retirement plans, public and private, were discussed in chapter 2.

BENEFIT OBJECTIVES

Social Security and public retirement systems set system-wide benefit objectives determined as a matter of public policy by the Congress or by the respective state legislatures. Under TIAA-CREF plans the annuity contracts and funding methods are systemwide, but contribution rates and benefit objectives are determined by each participating institution. This section discusses benefit goals and the considerations that apply to them.

Social Security. The Social Security program provides benefits that for a career of service range from primary insurance amounts of 45 percent of final year's wages for lower-paid employees, to around 33 percent for employees whose average wages are near the top of the taxable earnings base, to less than 25 percent for persons with earnings well above the base. The benefit proportions are 50 percent higher for persons entitled to Social Security benefits on behalf of a spouse. Social Security has aimed at providing a basic floor of benefits upon which other pensions can build. Social Security benefits are based on a philosophy of social adequacy and presumed need that differs considerably from the individual equity philosophy of employer-sponsored pensions.

Pension plans in private industry are often integrated with the Social Security program, either by offsetting benefits by half of the Social Security primary insurance amount, or by use of a "step-rate" contribution or benefit formula. Benefit offsets are seldom if ever used in the field of higher education, where the prevailing practice is either not to integrate with Social Security or to integrate through step-rate contributions. The step-rate approach, described later in this chapter, takes into account the fact that Social Security benefits are weighted in favor of lower-paid persons, and it aims at a total replacement ratio (Social Security plus pension benefits) that is fairly uniform over all levels of salary. The step-rate approach is particularly appropriate where salaries span a wide range, as in many of the larger universities.

Employer Pension Plans. The benefit objectives of public retirement systems are normally stated as a percentage of "final average" salary per year of credited service, usually an average of the last or highest three years of salary. TIAA-CREF plans provide for benefit objectives that are determined by the contribution level that is set by each employer participating in the system; depending on the contribution rate selected, the objective for a career of service normally ranges from one-third to one-half of the salary level just prior to retirement, exclusive of Social Security.

Benefit Criteria. Pension plans seek to provide benefits in a systematic and even-handed way by the use of objective criteria related to employment. Consistency, uniformity, and equitable treatment of employees must characterize a pension plan's benefit goals and its methods of achieving them, despite the variety of individual situations that will be represented by the many participants in the plan. Thus, as a matter of policy and equity, pension plans do not vary benefit amounts according to different individuals' needs, personal wealth, amount of debt, marital status, extent of family burdens, or other personal or individual criteria, any more than salary varies by such criteria. An employee retirement plan cannot fairly make adjustments for each personal and family situation. Nor can it test for other income sources and amounts. To do so would introduce the equivalent of a needs test, appropriate for a welfare program but not for a pension plan in which benefits are earned as a matter of right and depend upon service to the employer.

Pension plans intentionally aim at less than 100 percent replacement of the wage or salary just prior to retirement. Thus, public retirement systems, whose benefit formulas are often relatively high compared with plans in private industry, sometimes specify that the retirement benefit amount cannot exceed a stated maximum percent of final average salary, for example 80 percent. Other such plans achieve a limit by stating a maximum number of years of credited service countable in the benefit formula.

Retiring employees should be able to choose an actuarially equivalent form of retirement income that will continue income benefits to a survivor (an income option). Under the Employee Retirement Income Security Act (ERISA), a private pension plan must automatically provide married persons with an actuarially equivalent joint and survivor annuity option if the employee does not specifically elect a single life annuity. All public retirement plans offer a survivor benefit option provided the survivor named is a spouse.

Replacement Ratios. The maximum proportion of preretirement wages or salary (the replacement ratio) that is to be the retirement benefit objective, including Social Security, is usually set by considering what the benefit should be at a stated normal retirement age following a full career under the retirement plan, that is, after thirty or thirty-five years of credited service. Shorter service would produce smaller benefits, longer service, greater benefits.

A retirement income goal may be stated (implicitly or explicitly) in graduated terms related to final pay. One such approach is a 60-50-40 goal, or a 70-60-50 goal. That is, a goal of 60 to 70 percent of final pay is set for employees whose earnings are at the lower end of the scale and well within the limits of the Social Security taxable earnings base, 50 to 60 percent for those whose earnings are in the middle ranges, and 40 to 50 percent for those with the highest pay levels provided by the employer.[2] A study funded by the National Science Foundation concluded that the needed percentage of preretirement income declines as salaries increase. The study gave a 69 percent replacement ratio as necessary to maintain the standard of living of an employee earning $7,500 at retirement, while only 42 percent would be required by someone earning $40,000 at retirement.[3] Workers at the very lowest end of the pay scale, however, may require nearly 100 percent of final pay in retirement, including Social Security, just in order to meet the necessary expenses of living. There are minimums below which food, clothing, shelter, and so on, cannot be purchased.

In educational institutions, the three-element benefit goal often appears as follows: A worker whose earnings have typically been below average national earnings rates would be entitled to Social Security benefits of about 45 percent of final pay. A pension benefit that provides about 30 percent of final salary would then produce a combined benefit of about 75 percent of final average pay. A worker whose salary has generally been at or near the maximum Social Security taxable earnings base might expect a primary insurance amount at age 65 of about a third of final average salary. When added to the pension benefit, the combined retirement income would be about 65 percent of final average salary. For employees whose salaries had typically been higher than the Social Security earnings base, the combined benefit might be higher in dollar amount but it would be lower as a percentage of final salary—nearer the 50-percent level.

Plan integration permits an employer to take into account the role of Social Security in providing a floor of benefits while at the same time providing benefit replacement ratios for all employees that are appropriate to a range of employee salary levels.

Inflation following retirement can erode initially adequate benefits. The Social Security portion of the benefit is scheduled to rise as living costs increase, so that purchasing power is retained. In recognition of the possible decline in the purchasing power of the pension portion, it may be desirable to set pension goals at a somewhat higher level than would be indicated under more stable economic conditions. There are some practical difficulties, however. Benefit goals cannot easily be altered to adjust to the behavior of secular economic indicators. Nor would retirees gain substantial protection from higher initial income amounts unless they saved a portion of the earlier years' benefits for use at a later time.

Disposable Income. Comparing disposable income before and after retirement allows a more realistic measurement of the actual "before and after" financial status of retirees than comparing pretax income amounts. Not only does the tax treatment of personal income differ in retirement, favoring retirees, but there are a number of deductions from pay that cease altogether at retirement. In addition, Social Security income, which may equal a fourth to a half of total retirement income, is not subject to federal or state income tax.

With Social Security benefits untaxed, additional annuity or pension income, and income from savings, will be taxed at a lower rate than if added on top of Social Security for tax purposes. In calculating the federal income tax, the personal exemption is doubled for each person over age 65. A husband and wife both aged 65 would thus have four personal exemptions of $1,000 for the 1979 taxable year, or $4,000. They would also benefit from the couple's standard deduction for 1979 of $3,400, which is part of the "zero bracket" calculation. Thus, it would be possible for a retired couple to receive an annual retirement income, including a maximum Social Security income for a couple of $9,000, of over $16,000 before starting to pay federal income taxes in the lowest tax bracket. In contrast, a preretirement $16,000 salary or wage would result in a federal income tax (joint return, two exemptions) of about $2,000, or a net after-tax income of $14,000.

The change in tax status in retirement is paralleled by the termination of a number of the payroll deductions that reduce take-home pay prior to retirement. Social Security taxes are no longer taken out. Employee contributions to pension and insurance plans are no longer made (although Medicare (Part B) and continuing health or life insurance premiums may still be payable). These deductions, taken together, may amount to from 12 to 15 percent of gross preretirement salary or wages.

There are also certain other types of expenditures that a person may have to make in connection with work but that are not incurred after retirement. Commuting expenses can be eliminated. Expenses for clothing appropriate to the job may be reduced on retirement. Housing expenses in retirement may be reduced. About three-fourths of retired married couples own their own homes and for about 80 percent of these the mortgage has been paid off. Only 37 percent of widows, widowers, and nonmarried persons age 65 or over own their own homes, however.[4] Some advantages of home ownership may be eroded by rising property taxes and upkeep expenses, both of which frequently prove to be a burden to the elderly. It is evident that costs of the education of children, items of considerable importance for younger families, are not so likely to figure in the expenses of people who are close to retirement or retired.

Table 3.1 compares both gross and disposable incomes before and after retirement. As the table shows, evaluating retirement income in disposable terms offers the more realistic perspective on the extent of the change of economic status that may be expected to take place in retirement.

AAUP-AAC Statement of Principles. The Statement of Principles on Academic Retirement and Insurance Plans was originally promulgated in 1950 by the governing bodies of the American Association of University Professors (AAUP) and the Association of American Colleges (AAC). Revised statements were endorsed by the associations in 1958 and 1969. At this writing the statement is being reviewed in order to bring its retirement age recommendations into accord with the changes in mandatory retirement ages enacted by the 1978 amendments to the Age Discrimination in Employment Act of 1967. The current AAUP statement opens with a comprehensive summary of the purpose of an institution's major benefit plan. "The purpose of an institution's retirement policy for faculty members and administrators and its program for their insurance benefits and retirement annuities should be to help educators and their families withstand the financial impacts of illness, old age, and death, and to increase the educational effectiveness of the college and university. The policy and program should be designed to attract individuals of the highest abilities to the faculty and administration, to sustain their morale, to permit

Table 3.1. Disposable Income Before and After Age 65 Retirement

Preretirement	Single	Married	Single	Married
Salary or wages (1978)	$20,000	$20,000	$30,000	$30,000
Deductions				
Federal tax	3,999	2,899	7,883	5,939
State tax	682	612	1,082	1,012
Social Security tax	1,071	1,071	1,071	1,071
Retirement contributions	1,000	1,000	1,500	1,500
Insurance contributions	200	200	300	300
Disposable income	$13,048	$14,218	$18,164	$20,178
Postretirement				
Social Security benefit (1979)	$ 6,336	$ 9,504	$ 6,336	$ 9,504
Annuity income	6,700	6,452	10,050	9,677
Deductions				
Federal tax	254	—	795	178
State tax	84	—	200	87
Medicare (Part B)	98	197	98	197
Disposable income	$12,600	$15,759	$15,293	$18,719
Gross postretirement income as % of gross preretirement income	65%	80%	55%	64%
Disposable (after-tax) postretirement income as % of disposable (after-tax) preretirement income	96%	111%	84%	93%

NOTE: Assumes age 65 retirement at the end of 1978, standard federal tax deductions, couple filing joint return, state income tax of 4 percent of federal taxable income. Single retiree's annuity income based on single life annuity of 33.5 percent of final salary, couple's annuity income based on joint and two-thirds to survivor income option, spouse same age. Postretirement federal tax on annuity income based on equal employer and employee annuity contributions.

them to devote their energies to the concerns of the institution and the profession, and to provide for their orderly retirement. . . . "

The statement sets forth certain recommended policies and practices in connection with an institution's retirement and insurance plans. The policies should be clearly defined. The plans should be coordinated with the Social Security program and permit mobility of faculty members and administrators among institutions without loss of accrued retirement benefits. There should be little or no gap in annuity and insurance plan coverage when moving from one institution to another. Institutions are urged to make available benefit plan information and to provide a preretirement counseling program.

The statement recommends that benefit plans be reviewed periodically to assure that they continue to meet the needs, resources, and objectives of the institution and the participants.

A central portion of the statement deals with recommendations for policies regarding normal and mandatory retirement age, currently the subject of review by a joint committee of the two associations.

The concluding part of the statement incorporates specific suggestions on the provisions of an institution's retirement and insurance plans. It recommends that participation in the retirement plan be required for all full-time faculty and administrators aged 30 and over and that the employer contribute at least as much as the employee to the retirement plan. As a retirement income objective, it advises that contributions be maintained at a level sufficient to provide, at the normal retirement age for those who have participated in the plan for at least thirty-five years, an after-tax income equivalent in purchasing power to approximately two-thirds of the yearly disposable salary during the last few years of full-time employment. The statement recommends to employers that they consent to the use of salary reduction agreements for the payment of regular or supplementary retirement plan contributions (See chapter 9.).

The full and immediate vesting of all annuity accumulations from employer and employee contributions, and the availability of the full accumulation as a survivor benefit in case of death before annuity payments begin, are recommended, as is that at retirement the bulk of the accumulated funds be made available only in the form of an annuity.

The statement suggests that employers provide a plan of group life insurance offering a benefit sufficient to sustain the standard of living of the family of a deceased staff member for at least one year following death. There should also be a health insurance plan, with emphasis upon protection against the major expenses of illness or injury, and long-term total disability insurance in amounts sufficient, with Social Security, to provide purchasing power equal to approximately two-thirds of the disposable income of the staff member just prior to disability. The disability income should continue throughout disability to the retirement age, with adequate provision for continuing income thereafter.

The Statement of Principles addresses itself to the main policies and practices involved in establishing and maintaining a retirement plan in an educational institution. The specific plan provisions that may be used to carry out the recommendations are discussed in the next section.

MAJOR PLAN PROVISIONS

A retirement plan document or summary plan description may take many pages. Among the items covered, four are of major importance to both employer and employee. These are: (1) eligibility and participation; (2) the vesting provisions; (3) the rates of contribution or the benefit formula; and (4) the point of retirement.

ELIGIBILITY AND PARTICIPATION

Year-by-year participation in the retirement plans of successive employers throughout an employee's working lifetime is important if benefits at retirement are going to meet reasonable objectives. The amount of money that must be put aside to support retirement income is too large to permit any extended gaps in coverage or any losses through forfeitures. Many retired persons who report low income from a pension plan do so because they failed to participate in a voluntary plan, or they participated in a pension plan for just a few years, or they did not meet the vesting requirements of one or more plans during their working career. If, at retirement, an employee's total vested membership period in one or more pension plans covers relatively few years, total retirement income must necessarily be small. It would be impractical and inequitable for a final employer to try to provide the same pension benefit for a retiring employee with only five or ten years of participation in the plan as for one with thirty-five or forty years of participation.

An early start in plan participation is therefore necessary. The 1974 ERISA legislation established participation requirements for private (but not public) pension plans. Prior to that law, no prescribed participation standards existed and long waiting periods plus long delays in vesting combined to exclude many employees from earning retirement credits. This was not true of TIAA-CREF plans, however, which have always provided for full and immediate vesting in the employee of employer and employee contributions. Congress specifically acknowledged the advantages of immediate vesting to employees in educational institutions by providing a special rule governing participation that may be used by educational institutions with a pension plan providing for 100 percent immediate vesting. Since benefits begin accruing at once under these plans, participation does not have to be offered an otherwise eligible employee until the attainment of age 30 or the completion of one year of service, whichever is later. Or educational institutions may use an alternative special ERISA provision, available to all private plans that vest pension benefits 100 percent after not more than three years of service, that permits a plan to require an employee to have reached age 25 and to have completed three years of service before commencing to participate.

Under private pension plans that delay vesting of benefits, as in some plans for clerical-service employees in higher education's private sector, the ERISA general rule must be observed. Under it, employees eligible for participation may not be excluded from the plan after the later of the attainment of age 25 or the completion of one year of service. Thus, for persons hired at age 25 or over, participation must be made available after one year of service. An employee who begins work well before age 25 will have more than a one-year waiting period (although service between ages 22 and 25 must be counted in determining where the employee stands on the vesting schedule).

The phrase "a year of service" is defined by ERISA as a twelve-month period during which the employee has not less than 1,000 hours of service. Alternative definitions of "hours of service" are provided under regulations prescribed by the Secretary of the Treasury.

The ERISA participation provisions for plans that delay vesting recognize that credit toward vesting benefits has to begin relatively early in such plans so that employees will have a chance to gain vested benefits. The one-year waiting period for new employees age 25 and over provides assurance that when a year of service has been completed, the employer may not exclude an eligible employee from the important lifetime process of accumulating vested pension credits. This helps new employees over age 25 get their credits toward eventual vesting started with only a one-year delay after each job change.

Following the completion of any ERISA-prescribed waiting periods, a private pension plan may not set an entry age limit beyond the normal retirement age of the plan unless it is a defined benefit plan. In this case, such exclusion is permitted if the plan specifies an age that is not more than five years before the normal retirement age under the plan. Thus, if the normal retirement age is 65, employees hired at age 60 and over may be completely excluded from the defined benefit plan. The rationale for this rule is that the cost of coverage under a defined benefit plan is extremely high for employees hired at the older ages. The result is that employers with a defined benefit plan have the choice of providing very costly benefits or none at all.

COMPULSORY VS. VOLUNTARY

ERISA provides only that an employer cannot exclude an employee in an eligible group from participating in a retirement plan following the completion of the prescribed waiting period. This does not settle the question of whether an employer should *require* employees to join the plan at some point, or whether it is enough just to provide that an employee can join the plan if he or she wishes to, i.e., provide for wholly voluntary participation.

A plan to which employees are required to contribute can be made wholly voluntary, wholly compulsory, or voluntary at first and compulsory after a prescribed age has been attained, a prescribed service period has been completed, or a combination of the two. In the case of a pension plan in which the employer pays the total cost (a noncontributory plan), employees are automatically brought into the plan following the prescribed waiting period, since there is little reason for an employee to refuse participation in a plan paid for wholly by the employer.

A pension plan that does not require employees to participate after some stated age and/or service point may be able to avoid the objections of employees who do not want to make the contributions required under a contributory retirement plan. These employees could choose not to join a plan if it were wholly voluntary. But administrators and trustees who sidestep the issue of compulsory participation by establishing or changing to a wholly voluntary plan should realize that by doing so they are bequeathing serious and perhaps insoluble problems to their successors, perhaps ten, twenty, or thirty years down the road. Only then is the seriousness of a failure to require early and steady plan participation revealed. At that point, because of the substantial cost involved, ERISA funding limitations, and in fairness to those who contributed to the plan, the chances are that little can be done by the employer to provide a pension for those employees who chose not to participate in the plan and thus find themselves facing retirement with inadequate income. If future retirement income is to be assured, participation in the retirement plan should be a condition of employment during a major portion of an individual's working years. An employing institution may appear to save money when employees eligible for pension plan participation on a voluntary basis do not join the plan. But it is only a short-term saving. In the longer run, employers have a strong interest in requiring staff members to participate in the retirement plan. Under a wholly voluntary plan a college will make annuity contributions for those who do join and yet ultimately will not meet the objective of retirement security for all, since under a voluntary plan some persons retiring from the college will end up with only the basic Social Security income.

The experience of colleges with voluntary plans (or no plan at all) has shown that it is wishful thinking to believe that very many college staff members can make adequate provisions for their old age on their own. Few people realize the large sums of money that must be accumulated during the working years in order to provide an adequate income during the retirement years. And there may be many retirement years to consider, as illustrated in table 3.2, which shows the expected number of persons retiring at age 65 who will still be living at various stated later ages. Out of every 1,000 men retiring at age 65, 431 can expect to be living at age 85, as can 630 out of every 1,000 women who retire at age 65. Social Security benefits alone would provide a decidedly lowered living standard for most college staff members, requiring drastic changes in housing and other living patterns.

Table 3.2. Survival Experience of Persons Retiring at Age 65

Age	Males Surviving (number)	Females Surviving (number)
65	1,000	1,000
70	909	955
75	786	892
80	625	790
85	431	630
90	237	411
95	83	188
100	13	57

SOURCE: The 1971 Individual Annuity Mortality Table with ages set back 1 year for males and 2½ years for females. *Transactions of the Society of Actuaries*, 23:496.

There was a time, if money could be found, when an ad hoc pension could be granted to a staff member who had not participated in an institution's plan over the years. Arrangements of this kind, although expensive, were sometimes made out of necessity to avoid the embarrassment and difficulties consequent to a voluntary retirement plan. Since the passage of ERISA, however, these kinds of arrangements are no longer practicable, since they raise a question under the nondiscrimination requirements of ERISA, nor can they easily meet the funding and vesting requirements, even if the money can be obtained. Additionally, free pensions were unfair to those who over the years shared the cost of their retirement protection. The alternative of requiring a signed waiver from those who failed to participate in a voluntary plan does little to protect the institution when a long-service staff member is facing retirement without an adequate income.

Wholly voluntary retirement plans also handicap both the individual and the institution in later years, when the desirability of *early* retirement may become evident. Not every employee is capable of, or wishes to, work as late as a normal retirement age of 65, let alone to a mandatory retirement age of 70. At the higher ages, there will be some who seek a change of pace, some who wish to pursue other interests, as well as employees whose quality of work has declined. It will be far easier for the employer to make early retirement possible for such employees when regular pension benefits are available. Employees may be as interested in ceasing work as the employer is to see them go, but unless there is a reasonable underlying benefit from the employer's pension plan to help replace earned income, the employee may feel the pressure to continue in service. Social Security retirement benefits payable as early as age 62 may help make early retirement easier, but these benefits alone will not be sufficient. Thus, an employer should consider the role a pension plan can play in helping employees choose between working to age 70 or beyond, or retiring earlier. Requiring younger employees to participate in the pension plan will help solve these problems when they come.

When the employer requires employee participation in the pension plan, at what point in the employee's career is the requirement to be set? With few exceptions, public retirement systems require immediate participation but delay vesting of benefits. In private educational institutions with plans vesting benefits immediately, ERISA requires that voluntary participation of eligible employees be available at least by attainment of age 30 and the completion of one year of service. Participation may then be required at some later point, such as age 30 and the completion of three years of service. The goal of a combination of voluntary and required participation provisions should be to assure thirty to thirty-five years of plan participation for a full career of service by the time the employee reaches age 65.

Of the sixty-eight public retirement systems covering institutions of higher education, sixty require participation immediately upon employment. The remaining eight systems require participation after a stated waiting period. One system states a three-year waiting period; two systems state a one-year waiting period, with one of these permitting voluntary participation immediately; four systems have a six-month waiting period, with one of these permitting voluntary participation immediately; one system state a five-month waiting period. One of the systems that require participation immediately makes participation optional for clerical-service employees and all employees hired at age 55 or older. It should be noted that such immediate participation is meaningless for all staff members who leave before becoming fully vested in the benefits, most frequently ten years under public retirement systems.

Among the 1,121 TIAA-CREF retirement plans covering faculty in four-year institutions of higher education, 68.5 percent report that participation is required either immediately or after a stated waiting period. Among the plans in which participation is required, participation is available on an earlier, voluntary basis in 312 plans, or 40.7 percent. Participation is wholly voluntary in 353 of the faculty retirement plans, or 31.5 percent, including plans at many of the smaller institutions. Among the 631 TIAA-CREF plans in four-year institutions of higher education covering clerical-service personnel, 293, or 46.4 percent, report that participation is required and 338, or 53.6 percent, report voluntary participation only. Table 3.3 summarizes the required and voluntary participation provisions for the two groups, faculty and clerical-service, in the four-year institutions.

Table 3.4 details the waiting periods stated for required plan participation in TIAA-CREF retirement plans in four-year institutions covering faculty and clerical-service employees. These are the provisions that determine the point at which the eligible employee must join the retirement plan. Table 3.4 indicates that for faculty, 267, or 34.8 percent of plans requiring participation, require immediate participation. A requirement in terms of service only (one to four years) is stated by 18.1 percent of plans. Most of the remaining plans state a requirement that combines age and service.

Table 3.3. Required and Voluntary Participation in TIAA-CREF Retirement Plans in Four-Year Institutions of Higher Education

	Faculty		Clerical-Service	
	No. of plans	% of plans	No. of plans	% of plans
Participation required	767	68.5	293	46.4
Number of above plans which permit voluntary participation before participation is required	(312)	(40.7)	(126)	(43.0)
Voluntary participation only	353	31.5	338	53.6
Subtotal	1,120	100.0	631	100.0
No information	1			
Total	1,121			

Table 3.4. Waiting Period for Required Plan Participation in TIAA-CREF Retirement Plans in Four-Year Institutions of Higher Education[a]

	Faculty		Clerical-Service Employees	
	No. of plans	% of plans	No. of plans	% of plans
Immediate participation	267	34.8	37	12.7
Years of service				
1 year	34		15	
2 years	49		5	
3 years	43		24	
4 years or more	13		13	
	139	18.1	57	19.6
Ages 25–29 only	3		2	
Ages 25–29 and/or one of the following				
1 year	12		11	
2 years	9		7	
3 years	35		37	
4 years or more	2		1	
	61	8.0	58	19.9
Age 30 only	23		4	
Age 30 and/or one of the following				
1 year	84		43	
2 years	42		24	
3 years	76		23	
4 years or more	9		14	
	234	30.5	108	37.1
Ages 31–35, with or without service requirement	34	4.4	24	8.3
Attainment of tenure	25	3.3	*	*
Other	7	0.9	7	2.4
Subtotal	767	100.0	291	100.0
Voluntary participation only	353		338	
No information	1		2	
Total	1,121		631	

[a]As of December 31, 1977.
*Not applicable.

Among the TIAA-CREF plans in four-year institutions that require participation for clerical-service personnel, 37, or 12.7 percent, state an immediate participation requirement. Nearly 20 percent of the plans state their waiting period in terms of years of service only, ranging from one to four years and concentrating at three years, and the balance of the plans combine an age and service requirement, as shown in table 3.4.

Among the 256 TIAA-CREF faculty retirement plans in two-year institutions of

Table 3.5. Required and Voluntary Participation in TIAA-CREF Retirement Plans in Two-Year Institutions of Higher Education

	Faculty		Clerical-Service	
	No. of plans	% of plans	No. of plans	% of plans
Participation required or automatic	204	79.7	45	56.2
Number of above plans which permit voluntary participation before participation is required	(28)	(13.7)	(17)	(37.8)
Voluntary participation only	52	20.3	35	43.8
Total	256	100.0	80	100.0

higher education, 79.7 percent report that participation is required either immediately or after a stated waiting period. Among these 204 plans, participation is available on an earlier, voluntary basis in 28. Faculty participation is on a wholly voluntary basis in 52 of the 256 plans, or 20.3 percent.

Among the 80 TIAA-CREF plans covering clerical-service personnel in two-year institutions of higher education, 45, or 56.2 percent, report that participation is required. Participation of these employees is wholly voluntary in 35, or 43.8 percent of the plans. Among the two-year college plans for clerical-service employees that require participation, 17, or 37.8 percent, permit earlier, voluntary participation. Table 3.5 summarizes the required and voluntary participation provisions for the faculty and clerical-service employees in the two-year colleges.

For the two-year institutions with TIAA-CREF plans, table 3.6 shows the waiting periods prescribed for plans requiring participation. For faculty, 161 plans, or 78.9 percent of these, bring participants into the plan immediately. Most of the rest of the plans state an age and service requirement combined, usually not more than three years and age 30. For clerical-service personnel in the two-year colleges, about two-thirds of the TIAA-CREF plans state a waiting period for required participation that combines age and service, usually not exceeding the attainment of age 30 and completion of three years of service.

VESTING

A vested pension benefit or annuity accumulation is one that is not forfeited by the employee when employment terminates. Although immediate full vesting of benefits is rarely found in pension plans in commerce and industry, it is well established in the field of higher education through the widespread use of the TIAA-CREF plans. Under TIAA-CREF plans, all contributions credited to each participant's individual annuity contracts, plus the individual's share of investment earnings arising from these contributions, are immediately nonforfeitable and remain to the individual's credit whether service with a particular employer con-

Table 3.6. Waiting Period for Required Plan Participation in TIAA-CREF Retirement Plans in Two-Year Institutions of Higher Education[a]

	Faculty		Clerical-Service	
	No. of plans	% of plans	No. of plans	% of plans
Immediate participation	161	78.9	17	37.8
Years of Service				
1 year	1		1	
2 years	5		3	
3 years	1		2	
4 years or more	0		1	
	7	3.4	7	15.5
Ages 25–29 only	3		1	
Ages 25–29 and/or one of the following				
1 year	1		0	
2 years	3		3	
3 years	5		3	
4 years or more	2		1	
	14	6.9	8	17.8
Age 30 only	4		4	
Age 30 and/or one of the following				
1 year	7		4	
2 years	1		0	
3 years	9		3	
4 years or more	1		2	
	22	10.8	13	28.9
Ages 31–35, with or without service requirement	0	0.0	0	0.0
Attainment of tenure	0	0.0	*	*
Other	0	0.0	0	0.0
Subtotal	204	100.0	45	100.0
Voluntary participation only	52		35	
Total	256		80	

[a]As of December 31, 1977.
*Not applicable.

tinues or not. When employment termination occurs prior to normal retirement age, receipt of the benefit earned is usually deferred until later.

The public retirement systems that cover employees in higher education, with few exceptions, incorporate delayed vesting. A participant who terminates employment prior to meeting the vesting requirement loses the pension credits or annuity accumulation attributable to the employer's contributions; employee contributions are returned to the employee. On forfeiture, the segment of employment history involved will of course have no deferred future pension benefits related to it.

When a pension plan provides only for gradual vesting (rare in higher education), a terminating employee retains only a stated fraction of the future retirement benefit if the service or age requirement for 100 percent vesting has not been met.

ERISA Requirement. ERISA introduced mandatory vesting requirements applicable to private pension plans. ERISA requires that each pension plan provide (1) that an employee's rights to retirement benefits become nonforfeitable (vested) on the attainment of normal retirement age; (2) that the employee's rights to accrued benefits from employee contributions are nonforfeitable; and (3) that an employee's right to accrued benefits derived from employer contributions become vested under one of the following three alternative minimum vesting schedules:*

1. Ten-year rule: 100 percent vesting of accrued benefits derived from employer contributions no later than the completion of ten years of service.

2. Five- to fifteen-year rule: 25 percent vesting of accrued benefits no later than completion of five years of service. Vesting must increase by at least 5 percent for each of the next five years of service, i.e., at least 50 percent vesting at ten years of service. Vesting must then increase by at least 10 percent for each year after ten so that 100 percent vesting occurs no later than completion of fifteen years of service.

3. Rule of forty-five: An employee with five or more years of service must be at least 50 percent vested in accrued benefits from employer contributions when the sum of his or her age and years of service total forty-five. Each year thereafter the employee's vested percentage must be at least in accordance with the following schedule:

If years of service equal or exceed:	and sum of age and service equals or exceeds:	nonforfeitable percentage is:
5	45	50
6	47	60
7	49	70
8	51	80
9	53	90
10	55	100

Notwithstanding the above schedule, the benefits of an employee with ten years of service under the rule of forty-five must be at least 50 percent vested and an additional 10 percent must vest for each additional year of service.

Vesting in the Colleges. Under the TIAA-CREF retirement plans in higher education, contract-holders can move freely among more than 3,000 employers (colleges, universities, independent schools, scientific and research organizations, and certain other employers) that have TIAA-CREF plans while continuing to build up future retirement benefits. If an employee moves to an institution that does not have a TIAA-CREF plan or leaves educational employment, the vested

*Generally, all of an employee's years of service (as defined in the act and computed according to regulations) with the employer must be taken into account for the purpose of determining vesting, with certain exceptions stated in the law, such as years of service before age 22, unless the plan adopts the rule of forty-five, in which case such years of service must be included.

benefits remain credited to the individual, as do continuing investment earnings on the accumulated amounts.

As a corollary to full vesting, the TIAA and CREF annuities do not provide for loan or cash redemption values. This is because a sound retirement plan must assure both individual and employer that funds will be available to finance the future retirement benefit. Employers are unwilling to contribute to a fully vested individual annuity contract that could be turned in for cash or mortgaged at the staff member's request. The no-cash-or-loan-value provision assures both employer and employee that the accumulation of contributed funds will be available solely for its intended purpose—providing retirement income or a preretirement death benefit.

The vesting provisions of TIAA-CREF contracts apply even if the employee dies before starting annuity benefits. In this event, the full accumulation in the contract is payable to a named beneficiary or to the estate; if the former, the policyholder may choose in advance among several income payment methods or may leave this choice to the beneficiary.

All but two of the sixty-eight public retirement systems covering employees in higher education provide for delay in the vesting of benefits. The range of vesting delays is wide, ranging from four years (four systems) to twenty years (one system). The most frequently stated vesting periods are ten years (thirty systems) and five years (twenty-four systems). During the delayed vesting period, unless the employee has met the retirement system's requirements for early or normal retirement, termination of service cancels the accrued retirement credit and the employee becomes entitled to receive only a return of the accumulated employee contributions plus interest credited at a stated rate. Table 3.7 shows the vesting provisions of the sixty-eight public retirement systems covering institutions of higher education.

During the last ten years, a number of the public retirement systems have reduced the vesting delays stated by their plan. In 1968, among the systems with vesting delays, fourteen reported vesting of four or five years; in 1978 the number of systems stating four or five years had increased to twenty-eight. And while sixteen systems reported vesting delays of fifteen years or more in 1968, in 1978 only six systems were in this category.

The Meaning of Vesting. In combination with early and sustained plan participation, early full vesting is an important factor in the attainment of adequate retirement benefits. Pension consultants to business and industry sometimes advise their clients that the ten-year vesting option of ERISA—that is, no vesting during the first ten years of plan participation and 100 percent vesting of all the previous ten-year credits on the tenth anniversary of employment—is the easiest to administer, the best understood by employees, and perhaps cheaper than the alternative minimum standards. But the larger question remains—how can plans providing delays in vesting of as long as ten years make their proper contribution to retirement security? For many workers, ten years is longer than any particular job will last.

Table 3.7. Vesting Provisions in Public Retirement Systems Covering Institutions of Higher Education[a]

		Number of Systems
Immediate Vesting		2
Completion of a Period of Credited Service[b]		65
4 years	4[c]	
5 years	24[d]	
8 years	1	
10 years	30	
15 years	5[e]	
20 years	1	
Qualification for Early or Normal Retirement		1
Total Systems		68[f]

[a]Vesting of deferred benefits on termination of employment.
[b]In some plans additional years of service permit starting a deferred benefit at an earlier age.
[c]One plan provides alternative vesting at age 55.
[d]One plan provides alternative vesting at age 50.
[e]Two plans provide alternative vesting with ten years of service: one at age 55, the other at age 35 or older.
[f]Five systems, in addition to the regular vesting requirements, do not permit withdrawal of EE contributions after specified age and/or service period.

Employees who shift jobs fairly often and forfeit benefits because of lengthy vesting requirements face a far leaner retirement than employees who make few or no shifts. Several job changes can mean that unless vesting is nearly immediate, a large part of a working life can go unrepresented in the process of building up future retirement income. Despite ERISA standards, just three or four job changes over a lifetime can leave a worker totally unprotected by all of the retirement plans in which he or she participated. It is this irony of coverage without protection that still concerns observers who recognize the otherwise substantial accomplishments of the 1974 pension reform legislation in setting sounder pension standards.

Early vesting of pension benefits can be advantageous to employers as well as employees. Delayed vesting can constitute a barrier to labor mobility that adversely affects institutions of higher education. As employers of highly trained professionals, it is important to educational institutions to compete in the broadest possible labor market, wider than the boundaries of a particular state. Barriers increase the cost of staffing and diminish the available choices. As noted by David G. Brown in his classic study of academic job changes, the labor market for professionals in higher education is defined by high training costs, high skill levels, and high experience levels. Thus, while "the local labor market concept has meaning for occupations where retraining workers is cheaper and faster than relocating, in the professions the cost of training and the benefits of experience dictate that employers draw boundaries that are related to what a man can do instead of how convenient it is for him to come."[5]

Many faculty and other staff members remain with one employer for an entire career. But free choice of employer is important, even for those who do not change jobs. Freedom to change can be as important as change itself. Whatever the present circumstances, no individual can be certain that he or she will not want to change jobs in the future. As for the idea that delays in vesting of retirement benefits hold people in their jobs, experience indicates that delayed vesting can actually encourage good staff members to "get out while the getting is good" and can encourage less productive staff members to stay on at least until vesting occurs.

During periods of declining enrollments and a shrinking academic job market, the retention of accrued pension benefits when changing jobs is also of significant value to professional staff members in higher education. Vesting of benefits is at least as important to those who have to find another job as to those who leave on their own initiative. In cutback situations, vested employee pension benefits can be helpful to institutions that have to make a difficult decision about shutting down schools or departments, since they will at least not be destroying pension credits already built up for those people who have to go.

In recent years, college teachers appear to have become more knowledgeable about vesting and its meaning and have shown increasing hesitancy to risk membership in retirement systems with long delays in vesting. This attitude is presumably involved in the trend toward opening up optional TIAA-CREF coverage in public institutions covered by public retirement systems, and in the introduction of shorter vesting delays in the public retirement systems themselves.

Forfeiture of Vested Benefits. TIAA-CREF annuity contracts are noncashable in order to make sure that the full value of the annuity accumulation is preserved in the form of a lifetime retirement income. Prior to ERISA, employees in many of the private plans outside of the educational world could obtain a refund of their own contributions if they chose to forfeit their vested retirement benefits on termination of service. ERISA introduced restrictions on these voluntary forfeitures. Under ERISA, a retirement plan may prohibit employee cash-outs as a matter of policy, but if it permits them, the benefits purchased by the employer's contributions must be either paid to the terminating employee who requests the cash-out of employee contributions, or maintained in vested status on the employee's behalf. If the value of the employee's benefit attributable to employer contributions is less than $1,750, however, the employee may receive a refund of employee contributions without the value of the employer's accrued obligation being credited to the employee.

Public retirement systems, not covered under ERISA, normally permit terminating vested employees to withdraw their own contributions in a lump sum; the price paid, as a rule, is the forfeiture of all future retirement benefits based on both employer and employee contributions, the value of which is likely to be many times the amount received in cash. Only five public retirement systems covering employees in higher education incorporate a degree of control over these costly (to the employee) voluntary forfeitures. The two Wisconsin plans and the Massachusetts

Teachers' Retirement System do not permit members terminating employment at age 55 or over to withdraw their own contributions and forfeit benefits. Two plans do not permit withdrawals after attainment of a specified age and service period: the Idaho Public Employees' Retirement System on attainment of age 55 and completion of five years of service, and the Indiana Public Employees' Retirement Fund on attainment of age 50 and completion of fifteen years of service. In each case, the age (and service) limits are also the qualifications for early retirement with actuarially reduced benefits.

CONTRIBUTIONS

Source of Contributions. The great majority of retirement plans in higher education are contributory, that is, the cost of the plan is shared by employer and employee. Table 3.8 shows the distribution of institutions according to whether the retirement plan is paid for wholly by the employer, by contributions of employer and employee, or by the employee alone. Among four-year institutions, 87.1 percent of plans covering faculty, 86.2 percent of plans covering administrative personnel, and 80 percent of plans covering clerical-service employees, are contributory. Noncontributory plans (employer contributions only) are reported for faculty by 12.5 percent of the institutions, for administrative personnel by 13.2 percent, and for clerical-service employees by 18.8 percent. Generally, the percentage distribution of employees in the responding institutions for each cost sharing category is about the same as the percentage distribution of institutions.

In the two-year institutions, contributory plans are reported by 90.6 percent of plans for faculty, 90.5 percent for administrative personnel, and 90.4 percent for

Table 3.8. Sharing of Retirement Plan Contributions in Institutions of Higher Education

	Faculty		Administrative		Clerical-Service	
	Percent Insts	Percent EEs	Percent Insts	Percent EEs	Percent Insts	Percent EEs
Four-Year Institutions	n = 1,365	n = 362,076	n = 1,357	n = 210,903	n = 1,270	n = 595,029
Employer pays full cost	12.5	11.1	13.2	10.5	18.8	18.6
Cost shared	87.1	88.8	86.2	89.5	80.0	79.9
Employee pays full cost	0.1	*	0.2	*	0.6	0.1
No response	0.3	0.1	0.4	*	0.6	1.4
Total	100.0	100.0	100.0	100.0	100.0	100.0
Two-Year Institutions	n = 670	n = 68,654	n = 671	n = 21,710	n = 657	n = 68,417
Employer pays full cost	9.4	8.4	9.5	10.7	9.6	10.0
Cost shared	90.6	91.6	90.5	89.3	90.4	90.0
Employee pays full cost	—	—	—	—	—	—
No response	—	—	—	—	—	—
Total	100.0	100.0	100.0	100.0	100.0	100.0

*Less than 0.1%.

clerical-service employees. In the plans of the remaining institutions (approximately 10 percent), the employer pays the full cost. Here also, the proportion of employees represented in each reporting category is similar to the proportion of institutions.

Overall, the proportion of employer-pay-all plans to contributory plans reported in 1978 does not differ substantially from the results of the 1968 survey of four-year institutions or the 1970 survey of two-year institutions.

When analyzed by institutional control, public and private, it appears that non-contributory retirement plans are reported more often by private institutions than by public institutions. And among the private institutions, noncontributory plans are reported more often for clerical-service employees than for faculty or administrative and other professional employees. Furthermore, it appears that private two-year institutions are more likely to report a noncontributory plan (both for faculty and for clerical-service employees) than private four-year institutions. Table 3.9 shows retirement plan contribution arrangements by institutional type and control. For faculty, 6.9 percent of public four-year institutions report a noncontributory plan, while 15.4 percent of private four-year institutions do so. The difference for faculty is even greater between public and private among the two-year institutions, with 7.6 percent of public two-year institutions and 24.3 percent of private institutions reporting a noncontributory plan. The number of such private institutions, however, is relatively small.

For clerical-service personnel, among both two- and four-year publicly supported institutions, the sharing arrangement for retirement plan contributions scarcely differs from that for faculty. Among private institutions, however, a noncontributory retirement plan is reported by 10 percent more four-year institutions for clerical-service employees than for faculty and by 6 percent more two-year institutions.

As tables 3.8 and 3.9 indicate, both public and private educational institutions generally follow a tradition of joint participation by employer and employee in the financing of retirement plan benefits. Prior surveys confirm that the joint contributory approach is one that has long been in place. This contrasts with the financing patterns of retirement plans of business and industrial employers, in which about 70 percent of plans neither require nor permit contributions by the employee.[6]

Contributory vs. Noncontributory. Although the policy of most institutions is to finance the retirement plan on a joint-contributory basis, a number of institutions have established noncontributory plans, particularly for clerical-service employees. A change from contributory to noncontributory status is sometimes urged as an indirect method of increasing employee compensation, especially in private institutions. In public plans the benefit formulas are often quite generous and employee contributions to them seem well justified.

The reasons frequently advanced for a noncontributory retirement plan are:

1. The tax treatment accorded employer (compared with employee) contributions. Under federal tax law, employer contributions to a pension plan are not treated as currently taxable income to the employee. Income tax is not avoided, however, but deferred; retirement income

Table 3.9. Sharing of Retirement Plan Contributions in Higher Education According to Institutional Type and Control

| | Four-Year Institutions | | | | Two-Year Institutions | | | |
| | Public | | Private | | Public | | Private | |
	Percent Insts	Percent EEs	Percent Insts	Percent EEs	Percent Insts	Percent EEs	Percent Insts	Percent EEs
Faculty	n = 478	n = 242,041	n = 887	n = 120,035	n = 596	n = 66,548	n = 74	n = 2,106
Employer pays full cost	6.9	8.4	15.4	16.6	7.6	7.6	24.3	32.2
Cost shared	92.9	91.5	84.1	83.2	92.4	92.4	75.7	67.8
Employee pays full cost	—	—	0.2	0.1	—	—	—	—
No response	0.2	0.1	0.3	0.1	—	—	—	—
Total	100.0	100.0	100.0	100.0	100.0	100.0	100.0	100.0
Clerical-Service	n = 477	n = 413,018	n = 793	n = 182,011	n = 592	n = 66,378	n = 65	n = 2,039
Employer pays full cost	8.0	8.7	25.3	41.1	7.3	9.3	30.8	32.6
Cost shared	91.6	91.2	72.9	54.3	92.7	90.7	69.2	67.4
Employee pays full cost	—	—	1.0	0.3	—	—	—	—
No response	0.4	0.1	0.8	4.3	—	—	—	—
Total	100.0	100.0	100.0	100.0	100.0	100.0	100.0	100.0

that is attributable to employer contributions and to all investment earnings is taxable as income to the employee when it is received. The public policy of excluding from taxable income such funds currently being put aside for retirement encourages saving for the future and lessens dependency in old age, while at the same time treating the ultimate retirement income as taxable, usually in a lower tax bracket. An employee's contributions, on the other hand, are included in taxable income currently if made by salary deduction, but are excluded if made under a salary reduction agreement in accordance with Section 403(b) of the Internal Revenue Code and related regulations. (See chapter 9.)

2. A noncontributory plan is simple to administer. No deductions from an employee's salary are required; no records are needed to distinguish employer from employee contributions for tax purposes. Record keeping costs are therefore lower.

3. Participation of all eligible employees in the retirement plan is assured under a noncontributory plan. While participation in the plan normally is required under contributory plans, some employees may object to the salary deduction. In voluntary plans, a required contribution will keep some people from joining the plan, to their ultimate disadvantage. Under a noncontributory plan, on the other hand, participation is automatic as soon as any waiting period requirement has been met.

4. Noncontributory plans avoid the situations in contributory plans in which terminating participants sometimes seek a cash-out of employee contributions.

5. There is a high degree of employee approval associated with noncontributory plans. Employees appreciate an employer's willingness to assume the full cost of a retirement plan as part of employee compensation.

Reasons advanced in favor of a contributory approach are:

1. Employee contributions play an important role in building future benefits. Unless the institution or retirement system is confident that it can maintain the necessary level of funding without employee money, it probably should remain contributory. Once a noncontributory plan has been established, it is not easy to change back. In some of the public retirement systems covering college employees, the employee contributions represent the only fully funded portion of the retirement plan's obligations; without the employee's contributions, unfunded accrued liabilities would be even higher than they are.

2. Particularly where benefits vest immediately in the individual participant and are nonforfeitable, it seems reasonable for an employee to share in the cost of such benefits.

3. Contributory retirement plans promote more interest in and understanding of the plan among participants. Employees feel that they have more of a voice in the provisions of the plan when they pay part of its cost.

4. An employer can retain the sharing principle of a contributory plan and yet give each participant's contributions the tax treatment of a noncontributory plan through the use of the salary reduction provisions of Section 403(b) of the Internal Revenue Code. (See chapter 9.)

As shown by tables 3.8 and 3.9, some employers provide a noncontributory plan for clerical and service employees, while the plan for faculty and other professional staff members requires an employee contribution. The rationale supporting the divergent approach is as follows:

1. At the lower salary levels every take-home dollar counts more. It is a relatively heavier burden for the lower-paid employees to have part of their earnings syphoned off as contributions to the retirement plan than it is for employees at the higher end of the pay scale. If plan

participation is voluntary, required contributions may be a particularly strong deterrent to enrolling in the plan.

2. Experience shows that when lower-paid employees contribute to a retirement plan, they are more likely to seek the return of their contributions on termination of employment. Plans that return employee contributions to terminating employees tend to encourage some employees to leave in order to obtain needed immediate cash. This question is not raised under a noncontributory plan.

3. Because of the relatively greater value of Social Security benefits to employees at the lower wage levels, a lower employer annuity contribution for lower-paid groups than for higher-paid staff can in itself support a good level of integrated total benefits and perhaps help justify a noncontributory plan.

CONTRIBUTION RATES

Public Retirement Systems. All but four of the sixty-eight public retirement systems covering institutions of higher education are contributory, that is, are based on joint contributions by employer and employee. In four systems the employer (the educational institution or the state or other unit of government) pays the whole cost. Employee contributions are normally expressed as a percentage of salary. Employer contributions for the normal plan costs and for the funding of prior service liabilities, if any, constitute the balance of funds going in to the defined benefit public retirement systems. These employer contributions vary according to plan benefit levels, the sex and age distribution of participants, assumed interest, mortality and turnover rates, changes in salaries of the covered group, and the extent of amortization of unfunded liabilities.

Employee contributions required by the public systems are provided for on either a level or step-rate basis. Level contributions are the same percentage on all of salary. Step-rate contributions usually apply one percentage to a lower portion of salary, usually related to a present or prior maximum Social Security taxable earnings base, and a higher percentage to salary above the stated step-rate point. The objective of a step-rate contribution and/or benefit formula is to integrate the pension plan with the Social Security program so that combined benefits will represent a fairly uniform replacement ratio (retirement income as a percentage of preretirement earnings) throughout the entire range of salary levels.

Table 3.10 shows the employee contribution rates reported by the public systems. Of the sixty-four that are contributory, fifty-six express the employee contribution as a single level percentage of salary; percentage rates range between 3.0 and 9.5, with the modal point between 5 and 6 percent. Fourteen systems state a rate below 5 percent and sixteen a rate of 7 percent or higher. The remaining seven contributory systems report a step-rate approach. Five of these systems apply a lower percentage rate to salary up to the current Social Security wage base with a higher percentage applied to the balance of salary, one applies a lower percentage to the prior Social Security wage base of $4,800, and one applies four increasing percentages to successive segments of salary.

Table 3.10. Employee Contribution Rates in Public Retirement Systems Covering Institutions of Higher Education

		Number of Systems
Noncontributory		4
Level Percentage of Salary[a]		
3.0%–3.9%	7[b]	56
4.0%–4.9%	7[c]	
5.0%–5.9%	16[d]	
6.0%–6.9%	10[e]	
7.0%–7.9%	9[f]	
8.0%–8.5%	5	
9.0%–9.5%	2	
Step-Rate		7[g]
2% on OASDHI base; 5% on balance		
3% on OASDHI base minus 1st $6,000; 5% on balance		
3% on OASDHI base; 5% on balance		
4% on 1st $4,800; 6% on balance		
4% on 1st $6,000; 5% on 2nd $6,000; 6% on 3rd $6,000; 7% on balance		
4.60% on OASDHI base; 9.20% on balance		
5% on OASDHI base; 5.50% on balance		
Unknown at time of publication		1[h]
Total Systems		68

[a]Includes four plans in which employer may elect to pay all or part of EE's required contribution and five plans in which EE may make additional contributions by salary deduction or reduction.

[b]Includes one plan which limits contributions to first $20,000 of salary.

[c]Includes one plan that requires an additional contribution of 5% on salary between $6,000 and $15,000 which is allocated to a Supplementary Retirement Fund.

[d]Includes two plans in which contributions are limited to a specified maximum salary: first $10,000 and first $35,000; one plan in which contribution rate is applied only to annual salary above $6,156; one plan in which an additional contribution of 0.8% required if Optional Spouse Survivor Protection selected.

[e]Includes one plan that limits contributions to first $25,000 of salary and one plan in which EE has the option of contributing on full salary or first $7,800 only.

[f]Includes one plan which requires an additional contribution of 1% if survivor benefit selected.

[g]Includes one plan in which step-rate percentages reduced for service between ages 62 and 65. One plan provides alternative of 5% of total annual salary with alternative benefit formula. In one plan minimum monthly contribution is $19.

[h]New contribution rates are currently being considered by state legislature.

TIAA-CREF Plans. Among the TIAA-CREF plans covering faculty, the employer pays the full cost in 16.6 percent of the TIAA-CREF plans in the four-year institutions and in 21.9 percent of the two-year institutions. In the remaining plans the contributions are shared by the employer and employees. The employer's share is larger than the employee's in 39.6 percent of the contributory plans in the four-year institutions and in 33.6 percent of the two-year institutions. Contributions to the plan are shared equally in 43.1 percent of the four-year group and 43.0 percent of the two-year group. A negligible number of employers pay a smaller share than the employee. Table 3.11 summarizes this information for the TIAA-CREF faculty retirement plans in the two-year and four-year institutions of higher education.

Table 3.11. Sharing of Faculty Retirement Plan Contributions under TIAA-CREF Plans in Higher Education[a]

	Four-Year Institutions				Two-Year Institutions			
	No. of plans	% of plans	No. of partic- ipants	% of partic- ipants	No. of plans	% of plans	No. of partic- ipants	% of partic- ipants
College pays smaller share	8	0.7	1,045	0.4	4	1.5	24	0.1
Contributions shared equally	483	43.1	76,072	27.1	110	43.0	5,229	28.1
College pays larger share	444	39.6	140,811	50.3	86	33.6	7,519	40.4
College pays entire premium	186	16.6	62,294	22.2	56	21.9	5,845	31.4
Total	1,121	100.0	280,222	100.0	256	100.0	18,617	100.0

[a]As of December 31, 1977.

TIAA-CREF retirement plans incorporate either a level or a step-rate contribution pattern. Under a level pattern, the combined employer and employee contribution is the same percentage of all of salary, for example, 10 percent, 12 percent, or 15 percent of the employee's full salary. Under the step-rate pattern, the combined employer-employee contribution rate is one percentage of salary up to a stated point and a higher percentage above. The traditional step-rate pattern has taken the Social Security wage base as the step-rate point: for example, contributions that are 10 percent of salary within the wage base and 15 percent of salary in excess of the base. At some institutions the step-rate point has been frozen at some prior year's maximum taxable wage base, but under most of the step-rate plans, as the wage base increased under Social Security, the step-rate point moved with it, thereby reducing contributions to TIAA-CREF annuities. Increases in the wage base produced increases in prospective Social Security benefits that for most participants were large enough to offset the decrease in prospective TIAA-CREF benefits.

These conditions were changed, however, by 1977 amendments to the Social Security Act, effective January 1, 1979. The amendments provided for a rapid and unprecedented increase in the Social Security earnings base from $17,700 in 1978 to $29,700 in 1981—68 percent over a three-year period. Thereafter, the wage base is to increase each year according to a formula established by prior law and related to increases in national average wages. Also under the 1977 amendments, the Social Security benefit calculation formula was changed in a way that lowered future Social Security benefits as a percent of final salary and, equally or more important, weighted the benefits even more heavily in favor of lower-paid persons. These changes affected step-rate plans using the Social Security wage base as the step-rate point, the vast majority of such plans. The traditional objective of the step-rate contribution pattern has been to bring persons of high, low, and middle salary levels to retirement with combined Social Security and TIAA-CREF benefits that represent a more uniform percentage, or replacement ratio, of final salaries than can be achieved with a level contribution plan when the range of salaries is quite wide from low to high. In order to continue meeting their objectives and to take into account the attenuation of future Social Security benefits for higher-paid employees under the new Social Security wage base and benefit formula, a recommended approach for step-rate plans, beginning in 1979, was to relate the step-rate point to the new Social Security benefit formula instead of to the rapidly rising wage base.

The benefit formula, which is discussed in chapter 4, is composed of three weighted brackets of Average Indexed Monthly Earnings under Social Security. The brackets will be changed each year according to figures released by the Social Security Administration. The new benefit formula will provide the lowest ratio of Social Security benefit replacement on earnings, if any, above the top of the second bracket. This "second formula bracket point" thus becomes an appropriate step-rate point for step-rate plans in 1979 and after. For 1979, the second formula bracket point was set at $13,020 on an annualized basis. It will increase each year and, according to Social Security Administration projections of national average wages, will catch up with the 1978 maximum taxable earnings base of $17,700 by 1984.

As the result of the significant 1977 Social Security amendments, it is expected at this writing that many, if not most, of the step-rate plans will change their step-point in 1979 or shortly thereafter. It is anticipated that a phasing-in method will be used, usually by freezing the plan's step-rate point at its 1978 level of $17,700 until the annually increasing second formula bracket point equals or exceeds $17,700. Thereafter, the second formula bracket point would become the step-rate point in the TIAA-CREF step-rate plans.

Table 3.12 indicates that in the level pattern TIAA-CREF plans, about half of the plans in both the two-year and the four-year institutions provide for an equal sharing of the contributions between employee and employer. Colleges that pay the smaller share are very few in number. Among two-year institutions with TIAA-CREF faculty plans, 5 percent have noncontributory plans; among the four-year group, 11.4 percent of plans are noncontributory. The college pays the larger share, but not the whole cost, in about 37 percent of both two- and four-year level TIAA-CREF plans.

Among the 59 step-rate TIAA-CREF plans in the two-year institutions, 46 are noncontributory. In all but one of the remaining plans, the college pays the larger share of the contributions. In the 213 step-rate plans in the four-year institutions, 80, or 37.5 percent, provide for the payment of the entire cost by the college. Under the contributory plans for this group, in 50.2 percent the college pays the larger share and in 11.7 percent the cost is shared equally by the employer and employee. Only one of the TIAA-CREF step-rate plans provides for a contribution from the employer that is smaller than that required of the employee.

Tables 3.13 and 3.14 show the contribution rates (percent of salary) provided for under TIAA-CREF level and step-rate plans in the four-year institutions of higher education. Under the level pattern plans, the contribution rates concentrate at 10

Table 3.12. Sharing of Faculty Retirement Plan Contributions According to Contribution Pattern (Level or Step-Rate) under TIAA-CREF Plans in Higher Education[a]

| | Four-Year Institutions[b] | | | | | | | | Two-Year Institutions | | | | | | | |
| | Level Plans | | | | Step-Rate Plans | | | | Level Plans | | | | Step-Rate Plans | | | |
	No. of plans	% of plans	No. of partic- ipants	% of partic- ipants	No. of plans	% of plans	No. of partic- ipants	% of partic- ipants	No. of plans	% of plans	No. of partic- ipants	% of partic- ipants	No. of plans	% of plans	No. of partic- ipants	% of partic- ipants
College pays smaller share	7	0.7	992	0.5	1	0.4	53	*	4	2.0	24	0.1	0	0.0	0	0.0
Contributions shared equally	449	50.5	65,981	37.4	25	11.7	8,637	8.8	109	55.3	5,226	42.8	1	1.6	3	*
College pays larger share	331	37.2	85,097	48.2	107	50.2	52,513	53.6	74	37.5	5,725	46.9	12	20.3	1,794	27.8
College pays entire premium	102	11.4	24,136	13.6	80	37.5	36,653	37.4	10	5.0	1,209	9.9	46	77.9	4,636	72.0
Total	889	100.0	176,206	100.0	213	100.0	97,856	100.0	197	100.0	12,184	100.0	59	100.0	6,433	100.0

NOTE: Percentages may not add to 100 because of rounding.
[a] As of December 31, 1977.
[b] Nineteen TIAA-CREF plans in four-year institutions, with 6,160 participants, are not classified in this table.
* Less than 0.1 percent.

Table 3.13. Contribution Rates under Level Pattern TIAA-CREF Faculty Retirement Plans in Four-Year Institutions of Higher Education

Level Contribution Rate	Total Level Plans	% of Level Plans	Total Participants Level Plans	% of Participants Level Plans
Under 10%	71	8.0	11,370	6.4
10%	391	44.0	41,540	23.6
10.1–11.9%	57	6.4	11,446	6.5
12–12.9%	167	18.8	42,536	24.1
13–13.9%	21	2.4	5,788	3.3
14–14.9%	50	5.6	11,217	6.4
15%	113	12.7	45,139	25.6
Above 15%	19	2.1	7,170	4.1
Total	889	100.0	176,206	100.0

Table 3.14. Contribution Rates under Step-Rate Pattern TIAA-CREF Faculty Retirement Plans in Four-Year Institutions of Higher Education

Step-Rate Contributions

Contributions on the lower portion of salary	Contributions on the balance of salary	Total Step-Rate Plans	% of Step-Rate Plans	Total Participants Step-Rate Plans	% of Participants Step-Rate Plans
Under 10%	10–12.9%	15	7.0	3,183	3.3
Under 10%	13–14.9%	3	1.4	1,001	1.0
Under 10%	15%	6	2.8	20,339	20.8
Under 10%	above 15%	5	2.4	3,023	3.1
Total under 10% on the lower portion		29	13.6	27,556	28.2
10%	10–12.9%	8	3.8	5,437	5.6
10%	13–14.9%	6	2.8	2,159	2.2
10%	15%	78	36.6	18,839	19.2
10%	above 15%	14	6.6	4,872	5.0
Total 10% on the lower portion		106	49.8	31,307	32.0
10.1–12.5%	10–12.9%	3	1.4	775	0.8
10.1–12.5%	13–14.9%	3	1.4	1,782	1.8
10.1–12.5%	15%	48	22.5	22,751	23.2
10.1–12.5%	above 15%	24	11.3	13,685	14.0
Total 10.1–12.5% on the lower portion		78	36.6	38,993	39.8
Total		213	100.0	97,856	100.0

percent, 12 percent, and 15 percent, with about a fourth of total participants in the level plans covered at each of these modes. Among the step-rate plans, there are a considerable number of combinations of contributions on the lower and upper portions of salary, although the most frequently stated rates are in the neighborhood of

10 percent on the lower portion and 15 percent or above on the upper portion of salary.

Contributions after Normal Retirement Age. Regulations that have been prepared by the Department of Labor for administration of the 1978 amendments to the Age Discrimination in Employment Act of 1967 permit discontinuation of employer contributions to defined contribution retirement plans that are not "supplemental plans" upon the participant's attainment of normal retirement age. A plan is considered supplemental only if it covers the same employees that are covered under another plan. For example, if an employer maintains a defined benefit plan for clerical-service employees and a defined contribution plan for faculty members, neither should be considered supplemental, because no employee participates in both plans.

A defined contribution plan that is supplemental to another retirement plan may not provide for termination of employer contributions during employment between normal retirement age and age 70, under the Labor Department interpretations. When an employer maintains both a defined contribution retirement plan and a tax-deferred annuity (TDA) plan for additional voluntary contributions, with some of the same employees participating in both plans, it is reasonable to designate the TDA plan as supplemental, since the TDA contributions are made by voluntary salary reductions, an arrangement which in any case an institution would not want to terminate at the normal retirement age.

Under the same regulations, defined benefit retirement plans are not required (1) to credit, for purposes of determining benefits, any service which occurs after the plan's normal retirement age; or (2) to pay the actuarial equivalent of normal retirement benefits if employment continues beyond normal retirement age. Under defined contribution plans, employees who retire at an age later than the normal retirement age are credited for the full resulting actuarial increase in benefits.

BENEFITS

Public Retirement Systems. Public retirement systems normally define their benefits by a formula that incorporates (1) a specified percentage factor or factors; (2) years of credited service; and (3) a final average of the participant's salary over a stated period of time, usually encompassing the years of highest earnings. These three items are multiplied together at the time of the employee's retirement. The dollar amount derived from the calculation is the annual single life annuity payable to the retiring employee. For example, the retirement benefit might be derived as follows: 1.5 percent × 30 years of service × $20,000 = $9,000, the annual single life annuity. An income option providing continuing lifetime benefits to a surviving spouse may be selected instead of the single life annuity. In the case of a survivor option, conversion tables are provided by the retirement system to determine by age and sex the actuarially adjusted income amounts available under the options offered. Where early retirement with actuarially reduced benefits is provided for, conversion tables are also utilized to determine the income payable.

Formula Percentage Factor. The percentage factor or factors of a defined benefit formula are applied as a single level percentage or under a graded or step-rate approach. Of the sixty-eight systems, fifty-five define their benefits by use of a single percentage of final average salary, three use a single percentage to provide a portion of the benefit, the balance of which is a defined contribution annuity purchased by employee contributions, and ten use two or more percentage factors. Table 3.15 shows the specific formula percentages used by the sixty-eight systems.

Among the fifty-five public retirement systems that base the entire benefit on a single percentage, the percentage factors range from 1 to 2.5 percent. The most frequently stated factor is 2 percent (twenty-five systems). The next most frequent is 1.66 percent (six systems).

The three systems that provide a formula benefit plus a defined contribution annuity state a percentage factor for the formula benefit of 1 percent (one system) and 1.1 percent (two systems).

In three of the public retirement systems, different formula percentage points are related to successive levels of salary, with a prior Social Security earnings base as the dividing point in two systems. In these three systems the percentage factors on the lower and higher portions of average salary are: 1.5 and 1.75 percent, 1.25 and 1.65 percent, and 1 and 2 percent. Another approach, unrelated to Social Security integration, provides for different percentage factors on different segments of service. For example, one benefit formula appears as 2.5 percent of final average salary times the first twenty years of service and 1 percent of final average salary times service exceeding twenty years. In a somewhat different approach, another system provides 1.5 percent of final average salary for the first five years of service, 1.75 percent for the next five years, and 2 percent for each year of service after ten years.

In the 1968 survey, seventeen out of sixty-seven defined benefit plans were reported by public retirement systems as having step-rate or graded formula percentage factors, compared with ten out of sixty-eight in the current survey. Concurrently, there has been an increase over the decade in the single percentage factor plans reported. In 1968, thirty-seven out of sixty-seven plans indicated a single percentage factor; in 1978, fifty-five out of sixty-eight plans stated a single percentage. In 1968, among the single percentage factor plans, ten of the thirty-seven plans (27 percent) reported a factor of 2 percent or above; in 1978, twenty-nine of the fifty-five single percentage plans (51 percent) reported a factor of 2 percent or higher.

Other changes in the public retirement plans took place over the ten-year period. The number of public plans stating benefits as a defined benefit pension purchased by employer contributions plus defined contribution benefits from employee contributions declined from thirteen in 1968 to three in 1978. In 1968, five plans provided

Table 3.15. Formula Percentage Factors in Public Retirement Systems Covering Institutions of Higher Education

Entire Benefit Based on Defined Benefit Calculation	Number of Systems
Single percentage of final average salary	55
2.50%	3[a]
2.01%	1
2.00%	25[b]
1.90%	2[c]
1.80–1.89%	3
1.66%	6
1.60–1.63%	4[d]
1.50–1.59%	4[e]
1.47%	1
1.30%	2[f]
1.25%	1
1.00–1.09%	3[g]
Two percentage factors applied to steps of final average salary	3
1.50% × 1st $8,400 + 1.75% × balance:	1
1.25% × 1st $4,800 + 1.65% × balance:	1
1.00% × 1st $4,800 + 2.00% × balance:	1[h]
Two or more percentage factors applied to successive periods of service	7
successive 10-year periods	
1.70%, 1.90%, 2.40%:	1
1.67%, 1.90%, 2.10%, 2.30%:	1[i]
first 10 years, followed by subsequent service	
1.00%, 1.50%:	2
first 20 years, followed by subsequent service	
2.50%, 1.00%:	1
two 5-year periods, followed by successive service	
1.50%, 1.75%, 2.00%:	1[j]
all service to age 62 followed by service to age 65	
1.60%, 1.25%:	1[k]
Benefit Composed of Defined (EE) Contribution Annuity Plus Defined Benefit Pension, Single Percentage Factor of Final Average Salary	3
1.10%:	2
1.00%:	1
Total Systems	68

[a]One plan provides an additional annual benefit of $300.

[b]Includes five plans in which retirement benefit is integrated with Social Security benefit and four plans with alternate formula percentage of one-sixtieth of final average salary for EEs with less than 20 years of service. In one plan, a defined contribution annuity is an alternative. In one plan with normal retirement age 60, benefit increased for each year of delayed retirement to age 63.

[c]In one plan with normal retirement age 62, benefit increased for each year of delayed retirement to age 65.

[d]In one plan with normal retirement age 62, benefit increased for each year of delayed retirement to age 65.

[e]If larger benefit results one plan provides 1.65% × (final average salary minus $1,200) if final average salary $13,200 or more. In one plan, formula applied to first $7,800 only if EE elected to limit contributions to that amount.

[f]In both plans, a defined contribution annuity is an alternative.

[g]One plan provides alternative formula percentage of 2% if benefit derived less all other public benefits (including primary Social Security benefit) is greater. The other plan provides an additional unfunded 0.25% on a year-to-year basis.

[h]Formula effective at age 65; prior to age 65, 2% of final average salary.

[i]A defined contribution annuity is an alternative.

[j]Formula percentage of 1%, plus $25 times years of service if a larger benefit results.

[k]Contribution rate reduced after age 62. Benefits coordinated with Social Security at age 65.

defined contribution benefits based on both employer and employee contributions. In 1978, four defined contribution plans were reported, with each offering a defined benefit as an alternative.

Formula Service Factor. In fifty-seven of the sixty-eight public retirement systems, no limit is imposed on the number of years of service that may be used in calculating the benefit. Eleven of the sixty-eight systems state a limit on the service factor, nine in terms of a maximum number of years that may be used in the formula and two by excluding years of service performed after a stated age, one 70, one 65 years of age. Table 3.16 shows the service limits stated by systems that have such limits. Five systems state a thirty-year limit, one thirty-eight years, two forty years, and one states forty-five years.

Table 3.16 also shows the other limits on benefits that are stated by the public retirement systems covering institutions of higher education. Seventeen systems (in addition to the eleven stating a credited service limit) specify a maximum percentage of final average salary that may be received as a benefit under the defined benefit formula. Retirement benefit maximums tend to be stated by systems incorporating benefit formula percentage factors higher than 1.5 percent, and often extending up into the 2-percent and 2.5-percent range. Limits are appropriate in these systems because of the possibility of retirement benefits that are in excess of wages or salary just prior to retirement. As a matter of personnel policy, it is considered undesirable to provide more in retirement benefits than for paid work.

Formula Salary Factor. As noted, the formula salary factor relates the defined benefit to the retiring employee's earnings level, usually the years of highest earnings. The prescribed salary-averaging periods in the sixty-eight public systems covering employees in higher education range between three and five years, as shown in table 3.17. The most frequently stated period is three years (thirty-seven systems). Of these thirty-seven systems, four specify that the highest three years must be selected from the last ten years of service. Seventeen of the thirty-seven systems require that the three years selected be consecutive years.

Of the twenty-nine systems stating a five-year salary-averaging period, twelve require that the years selected be consecutive, four require that they be selected from the last ten years of service, and one requires that the period be selected from the last fifteen years of service. Two of the sixty-eight systems state the highest four consecutive years of salary as the averaging period.

The salary averaging periods in the defined benefit public retirement systems have been reduced over the last decade. In 1968, a majority of forty-seven of the sixty-seven defined benefit public systems surveyed stated a highest five-year period. Five systems stated a career-average salary, ten stated a highest three-year period, and five a highest ten-year period.

Benefits Under TIAA-CREF Plans. Defined contribution plans, including virtually all of the TIAA-CREF plans and many of the insurance company and church plans providing retirement benefits in higher education, fix contributions in ad-

Table 3.16. Limits on Benefits Under Public Retirement Systems Covering Institutions of Higher Education

		Number of Systems
No Limit Imposed		40
Limit Stated		28
Specified maximum number of countable years	Formula percentage	
45 years	1.10% + annuity	1[a]
40 years	1.84%	2
	1.00% × 1st 10 yrs. + 1.50% × balance	
38 years	1.70% × 1st 10 yrs. + 1.90% × 2d 10 yrs. + 2.40% × yrs. over 20	1
30 years	2.00%	4
	1.60%	1
Specified percentage of final average salary as maximum annual benefit		
100%	2.00%	3[b]
	2.00% + Social Security PIA	
	1.625% + Social Security PIA	
90%	2.00%	2[c]
80%	2.50%	6
	2.00%	
	1.90%	
	1.50% × 1st 5 yrs. + 1.75% × 2d 5 yrs. + 2.00% × balance	
	1.30%	
	1.30% + Social Security PIA	
75%	2.50%	5[d]
	2.00%	
	1.67% × 1st 10 yrs. + 1.90% × 2d 10 yrs. + 2.10% × 3d 10 yrs. + 2.30% × 4th 10 yrs.	
	1.66% + 80% of PIA	
	1.50% × 1st $8,400 + 1.75% × balance	
70%	2.50% × 1st 20 yrs. + 1.00% × balance	1
Specified age after which service credit not countable		2
70	1.47%	
65	1.90%	—
Total Systems		68

[a]Maximum of all service to age 70 if more service would result.
[b]In one plan alternative formula of 2.5% with specified age and service requirements.
[c]One plan permits alternative of flat amount ($86) times years of service.
[d]In 2.5% formula plan, EE with thirty years' credit prior to age 55 continues to accrue 2.5% per year until age 55 or, if earlier, 90% of final average salary.

Table 3.17. Salary Averaging Periods in Public Retirement Systems Covering Institutions of Higher Education

Salary Averaging Period in Benefit Formula[a]		Number of Systems
Highest 3 years		37
highest 3 consecutive:	16[b]	
highest 3:	17	
highest 3 out of last 10:	3	
highest 3 consecutive out of last 10:	1	
Highest 4 consecutive years		2
Highest 5 years		29
highest 5 consecutive:	10	
highest 5:	14	
highest 5 out of last ten:	2	
highest 5 consecutive out of last 10:	2	
highest 5 out of last fifteen:	1	
Total Systems		68

[a]Includes three plans in which part of the benefit is based on a defined contribution approach and four plans in which a defined benefit is an alternative to a defined contribution option.
[b]In four plans, salary in any one year may not exceed average of previous two years by more than 10%.

vance as a percentage of salary, as described earlier in this chapter. A number of factors determine the size of the annuity income, including: (1) the age at which contributions begin; (2) the number of years over which contributions are made: (3) the level of salary and contributions (contribution rate as a percentage of salary); (4) the investment earnings of the accumulating contributions; (5) the resulting annuity accumulation; (6) the age at which annuity payments begin; (7) the type of income option selected at retirement (single life annuity, joint and survivor annuity, etc.); and (8) the applicable annuity purchase rates, by age and sex, and any extra credited investment earnings rates during the annuity payout period.

Table 3.18 illustrates the benefits of a defined contribution retirement plan based on a 10 percent level contribution rate. The table shows the retirement benefits from TIAA and from Social Security at age 65 as a percentage of the final year's salary for employees who entered the retirement plan at age 30 with three different assumed starting salaries: $10,000, $14,000, and $18,000 per year. The illustration assumes salary increases of 7 percent per year, including promotional increases, and retirement under both a single-life annuity and for couples under a survivor income option. The Social Security benefit projection is based on 1978 Social Security Administration assumptions of annual growth rates in average wages and in the Consumer Price Index (CPI).

Table 3.18 shows that for a career of service under a 10 percent defined contribution TIAA plan, the retirement benefit starting at age 65, under the stated assump-

Table 3.18. Illustrative Retirement Benefit as a Percentage of Final Year's Salary, Entry Age 30 in 1979, and Retirement at Age 65—10% Level TIAA Contribution Rate Plan

	Replacement Ratios: Retirement Income at Age 65 as a Percentage of Final Year's Salary							
	Individuals[a]					*Couples[b]*		
Salary at Entry Age 30	Social Security	TIAA Plan		Total		Social Security	TIAA Plan	Total
		Male	Female	Male	Female			
$10,000	33%	34%	31%	67%	64%	50%	32%	82%
14,000	29	34	31	63	60	44	32	76
18,000	25	34	31	59	56	38	32	70

NOTE: Institutions with level contributions of more than 10% will have proportionately higher benefits. For example, to determine the benefits produced by a plan with a 12% contribution multiply the TIAA figures by 1.2.

Assumes payment of all premiums to a TIAA annuity. TIAA benefits based on 1978 deferred annuity rates and dividends (excluding the extra dividend); not guaranteed for the future.

[a]TIAA life annuity option with payments guaranteed for a minimum of ten years, and the Social Security Primary Insurance Amount.

[b]TIAA joint and two-thirds to survivor option with payments guaranteed for a minimum of ten years, and Social Security retired employee and spouse benefits, with husband and wife assumed to be age 65.

tions, will be approximately a third of the final year's salary under the single-life option. With Social Security added, the total becomes about two-thirds of final salary at the lower salary range, and somewhat less for higher salaries. For couples, as illustrated, the benefits are from 21 to 25 percent higher, due mainly to the addition of the spouse's benefit under Social Security.

A 10 percent contribution rate is exceeded in many of the TIAA-CREF level contribution rate plans (see Table 3.13), as well as in the upper portion of the step-rate plans. Using the 10 percent contribution rate illustration of table 3.18 as a starting point, it is relatively easy to estimate benefits under other level contribution rates, since benefits are increased under defined contribution plans in direct proportion to increases in the contribution rate. For example, a 15 percent contribution, instead of 10 percent, would raise the illustrated TIAA replacement ratio from 34 percent of final salary by one-half, or to a benefit of 51 percent of final salary.

In addition to the rate of contribution, the age of retirement is another factor that affects defined contribution plan benefits. Even if annuity contributions do not continue after a stated normal retirement age, 65, for example, each year of delay in retirement after 65 can increase the annuity benefit by as much as 10 percent, depending on plan entry age. Thus, retirement at age 68 instead of 65 could raise benefits by some 30 percent. In terms of dollar amounts, the effect of a delay in the start of retirement benefits from age 65 to a later age is shown in table 3.19. The table shows how much a $100 per month TIAA annuity benefit payable at age 65 is increased (without further annuity contributions) by delaying the start of annuity benefits, the actuarial increase.

The increase in annuity benefits payable (the actuarial increase) is due to the shortening of life expectancy as age advances and therefore the shorter average period over which the benefit is expected to be paid, and to the increased time over which

**Table 3.19. Effect of Delaying to Later Ages the Start
of a TIAA Monthly Annuity Benefit**

Starting Age	TIAA Monthly Benefit Amount[a]
65	$100
66	109
67	119
68	130
69	142
70	155

[a]Assumes 1978 TIAA dividend and annuity rates, single
life annuity with ten-years certain. Contributions cease at
age 65, when a $100 monthly annuity becomes payable.

interest is credited to the full amount of the annuity accumulation. This actuarial increase in benefits under defined contribution plans adds an element of flexibility in financial planning for retirement that is not provided for under defined benefit formula plans. Under the latter, delayed retirement can increase benefits only if benefit accruals after age 65 are permitted and even then only to the extent of any increases in final average salary and in the formula service factor; the actuarial gains due to late retirement under formula plans normally accrue to the plan rather than to the plan participant.

RETIREMENT AGE

Mandatory Retirement. With the signing into law in 1978 of amendments to the Age Discrimination in Employment Act of 1967 (ADEA), employers—private, state, and local—were prohibited after January 1, 1979, from mandating retirement for age earlier than 70. Application of the age 70 provision was delayed until July 1, 1982, for tenured employees of institutions of higher education. A second exception—without a time limit—was made for persons employed in a "bona fide" executive or high policy-making position for a period of at least two years immediately before retirement and who are entitled to an immediate nonforfeitable annual retirement income equivalent to a $27,000 single life annuity, excluding Social Security benefits, based on contributions of the employer who effects the retirement.[7] Thus, retirement at age 65 may be mandated for top executives who meet these conditions.

The ADEA of 1967 had set ages 40 to 65 as the perimeters of its prohibition of age discrimination, but that act appeared to provide some exceptions with respect to retirement ages incorporated in a "bona fide" retirement plan or seniority system. The result was a lack of clarity as to whether a retirement plan could mandate retirement at an age under 65. Several lower federal court cases gave conflicting answers and a 1977 Supreme Court decision had let stand an age 62 provision that was established in a plan prior to the passage of the 1967 ADEA.[8] But Congress in the

1978 ADEA amendments specifically clarified the 1967 act to prohibit the mandatory retirement of an employee within the extended age group (40 to 70, with stated exceptions) under a "bona fide" employee benefit plan or seniority system. The conference committee report went to the trouble of saying that "the conferees specifically disagree with the Supreme Court's holdings and reasoning in the [age 62 provision] case."[9] Now, the only exceptions under the federal age 70 rule, other than those mentioned above, are those relating to an established "bona fide *occupational* qualification" as defined by the Department of Labor.

Although Congress's interest in mandatory retirement legislation seemed to emerge suddenly (it was less than a year between the introduction of H.R. 5383 by Claude Pepper of Florida and the passage of the act), the forces behind the change had been gathering for at least two decades. The ADEA of 1967 had been the first formal step in age discrimination legislation. However, much earlier, in the mid-1950s, Dr. Ethel Percy Andrus, a retired California schoolteacher and founder of the National Retired Teachers Association and the American Association of Retired Persons, began to speak against mandatory retirement. In 1959 Dr. Andrus declared that "it would be difficult to conceive a more vast waste of manpower and/ or production than that caused by compulsory retirement."[10] This subject was a lively topic of discussion at two White House Conferences on the Aging, in 1960 and 1970. Meanwhile, the momentum of the social and civil rights concerns and legislation of the 1960s, the women's rights movement, and growth in the activism of older people drew more attention to various types of discrimination, including age discrimination by employers in hiring and firing.

In addition to the federal government, certain states have passed laws that prohibit certain types of employers from requiring employee retirement because of age. The State of California abolished mandatory retirement (effective January 1, 1980) at any age for both public and private employees (excluding public law enforcement and firefighting employees). The State of Connecticut has passed similar legislation for private employees. Maine, Florida, and Montana have passed age discrimination laws abolishing mandatory retirement for state and local government employees. Other states may be expected to abolish mandatory retirement either for employees in the private sector and/or for public employees. The federal age discrimination legislation does not preempt state laws where state law sets a mandatory age later than federal law, or abolishes mandatory retirement.

Prior to the 1978 ADEA amendments, age 65 had become a commonly accepted age for uniform mandatory retirement of employees in many types of organizations, including institutions of higher education. Age 65 also had gained a benchmark status because it was established by the Social Security program in 1935 as the age at which Social Security old-age benefits were to become available and that age continues to be the first age for full Social Security retirement benefits.

Whatever the particular retirement age that is established by an employer—age 65 in the past, age 70 or later now, or none at all—it has long been recognized that, as in other matters of human relations, there is no single retirement rule that can deal in perfect equity with all employed persons. Individual capacities and abilities change at different rates. Particularly in professional fields, there are few yardsticks to measure changes in physiological age as easily as chronological age, or to measure the intangibles of mental agility and elasticity, artistic and scientific awareness, sensitivity to the problems and interests of youth, and the other mental and personal capacities that make educators effective. In view of the difficulties of individual testing, it has seemed reasonable to set mandatory retirement ages that affect all employees uniformly, even though there are exceptional men and women who still retain striking intellectual vigor and other desirable capacities well beyond any arbitrarily determined and uniform retirement age. The present age 70 provision of the federal age discrimination act is as arbitrary as age 65 formerly was, but higher. It may well be that future legislation at the federal level will go as far as some state legislation does now and eliminate mandatory retirement. Bills were introduced into Congress to this effect shortly after the ADEA amendments of 1978 were signed into law. And Congress did eliminate by the 1978 amendments any mandatory age for most federal Civil Service employees.

Age discrimination laws, however, are not intended to assure continuance on the job for incompetent workers or to interfere with regular employer personnel procedures for the evaluation of job performance and the fair discharge of employees who fail to meet prescribed work standards. As the amended age discrimination law went into effect, objective and uniformly applied methods for the evaluation of job performance were expected to become more widely used by educational employers. To be nondiscriminatory, personnel appraisal procedures must, of course, be applied uniformly at all ages.

During the discussion and debate on raising the ADEA limit from 65 to 70, it was repeatedly emphasized that the purpose of the change was to give employees expanded options to continue or to discontinue work. There was no legislative intention to make it necessary for employees to work longer unless they wished to do so. It was expected that most employers would retain their existing "normal" retirement ages and the benefit goals associated with them. Thus, a full pension benefit would still be available at age 65 to become payable then, or later upon voluntary retirement, or later still at a compulsory age.

The present survey was made just prior to the ADEA amendments, so that the responses in the next section reflect preamendment retirement ages. However, it appears at the present writing that the normal retirement ages reported will generally be maintained as such for the future, except that when under age 70 the normal age can no longer also serve as a mandatory age.

Retirement Ages Reported. The 1978 survey questionnaire asked each responding institution to designate its normal retirement age, that is, the first stated age at which retirement would not be considered early. Table 3.20 gives the distribution of stated normal retirement ages in four-year institutions by institutional type and

Table 3.20. Stated Normal Retirement Age, Four-Year Institutions of Higher Education, by Type and Control

Stated Normal Age	Faculty[a]				Clerical-Service			
	Public		Private		Public		Private	
	Percent Insts	Percent EEs	Percent Insts	Percent EEs	Percent Insts	Percent EEs	Percent Insts	Percent EEs
	n = 478	n = 242,041	n = 887	n = 120,035	n = 477	n = 413,018	n = 793	n = 182,011
Under 62	13.0	11.8	0.1	*	13.6	11.4	0.3	0.1
62	5.6	6.4	0.3	0.4	8.6	7.9	0.4	0.2
63	—	—	0.1	*	—	—	0.1	*
64	—	—	—	—	—	—	—	—
65	61.8	58.0	91.3	85.2	59.8	56.1	93.5	93.1
66	0.6	0.7	0.8	4.1	0.6	0.5	0.8	2.9
67	5.9	8.6	0.8	0.5	5.0	12.2	0.6	0.2
68	3.3	6.0	3.2	6.3	1.7	3.1	1.8	2.5
69	—	—	—	—	—	—	—	—
70	9.4	8.2	2.4	3.2	10.3	8.5	1.5	0.8
Over 70	—	—	—	—	—	—	—	—
No response	0.4	0.3	1.0	0.3	0.4	0.3	1.0	0.2

[a] Administrative and other professional personnel similar to faculty.
*Less than 0.1 percent.

by institutional control (public and private). Table 3.21 gives the normal retirement age distributions for the two-year institutions.

Tables 3.20 and 3.21 indicate that publicly supported institutions generally state earlier normal retirement ages than do private institutions. In the latter, the stated normal retirement age tends to be concentrated more at age 65, while in the public institutions, although there is also a concentration at age 65, there is a greater dispersion of normal ages from 62 to 70. And just as public institutions report normal retirement ages under 65 to a greater extent than their private counterparts, they also report age 70 more frequently. Thus, for faculty in four-year institutions, 9.4 percent of public employers reported a normal retirement age of 70, while only 2.4 percent of private four-year institutions stated age 70 as their normal age for faculty.

Considerable flexibility in the age of retirement was a tradition in higher education for many years. In the previous (1968) survey, 88 percent of the four-year institutions reported provisions for extensions of faculty service beyond the stated normal retirement age, and 83 percent of institutions reported similar flexibility for retirement of clerical-service employees. Similarly, in the 1970 study of two-year institutions, 77 percent and 83 percent of public and private colleges, respectively, reported flexible-age plans for faculty, as did 70 percent and 76 percent of public and private institutions, respectively, for clerical-service personnel. The flexible-age retirement plans were useful to colleges by helping them respond to changes in supply and demand for teaching and other personnel. During periods of rapidly rising enrollments, more extensions of service could be approved. During periods of retrenchment, a tighter extension policy could be followed. However, this degree of flexibility, which usually spanned the five-year period between ages 65 and 70, is no longer possible under the ADEA legislation, except for tenured college and university employees until July 1, 1982.

However, other flexibilities will remain. This may include the development of early retirement programs that are attractive financially to staff at the higher age and salary ranges. Over the past two decades there has been a general trend toward earlier retirement. Voluntary tapering-off or phased-retirement arrangements can provide for reductions in work load and commensurate pay, perhaps accompanied by the start of a portion of retirement income. Private institutions usually have more options in developing special early retirement arrangements than do many public colleges and universities, whose retirement arrangements frequently must be provided on a uniform basis along with all other departments of state government. The retirement plans of public institutions often provide for a full-formula retirement benefit at an age earlier than 65 for faculty and staff who have met a stated years of service requirement, a provision that helps make early retirement feasible at least for longer-service employees.

The federal law prohibiting mandatory retirement before age 70, and the likelihood that more states will pass legislation eliminating mandatory retirement at any age, suggest that the next few years, probably well into the decade of the eighties,

Table 3.21. Stated Normal Retirement Age, Two-Year Institutions of Higher Education, by Type and Control

| | Faculty[a] | | | | Clerical-Service | | | |
| | Public | | Private | | Public | | Private | |
Stated Normal Age	Percent Insts	Percent EEs	Percent Insts	Percent EEs	Percent Insts	Percent EEs	Percent Insts	Percent. EEs
	n = 596	n = 66,548	n = 74	n = 2,106	n = 592	n = 66,378	n = 65	n = 2,039
Under 62	17.6	14.8	—	—	17.4	13.5	—	—
62	5.0	5.9	—	—	5.9	8.4	—	—
63	—	—	—	—	0.3	0.5	—	—
64	—	—	—	—	—	—	—	—
65	70.0	70.7	97.2	99.0	63.9	59.3	95.4	97.5
66	0.8	0.9	—	—	—	—	—	—
67	1.2	1.2	—	—	5.1	10.8	—	—
68	—	—	—	—	1.0	1.0	—	—
69	—	—	—	—	—	—	—	—
70	3.9	5.1	1.4	0.5	4.7	4.8	—	—
Over 70	—	—	—	—	—	—	1.5	1.7
No response	1.5	1.4	1.4	0.5	1.7	1.7	3.1	0.8

[a] Administrative and other professional personnel similar to faculty.

will witness further changes in retirement rules and practices. One question is whether educational institutions will continue to follow patterns of flexibility in allowing extensions of service beyond age 70 similar to those formerly used for extensions beyond age 65. Another is whether many individuals will want to work until reaching the higher mandatory age, or will retire at ages earlier than 70, continuing the current trend toward earlier retirements. Yet another is whether educational institutions will be able to work out arrangements that encourage voluntary early retirement, or to establish practices that make possible mutually satisfactory phased retirements. The answers to these questions will depend partly on external economic conditions and on the adaptability of the educational institutions themselves, including how they define and differentiate early, normal, and mandatory retirement ages.

Normal Retirement Age. Whatever an institution's mandatory retirement age, if any, there should also be a "normal" age—an age at which an institution's retirement benefit objective is targeted and at which an employee may reasonably elect to retire. Unless retirement benefits plus Social Security have reached an adequate level prior to an age 70 mandatory retirement, the individual will not really have the choice of retiring until the later compulsory age. Social Security plays a major role in influencing the normal retirement age, since its unreduced old-age benefit is first available at 65. Age 65 is the most frequently stated normal retirement age in the public retirement systems covering institutions of higher education (although there are earlier normal ages that have an accompanying service requirement). The TIAA-CREF plans also generally set their contribution based on a benefit objective that incorporates age 65 normal retirement.

In the past, the normal retirement age was frequently the mandatory age as well. Extensions of service, however, often liberally granted, gave great flexibility both to employers and employees in higher education. With the new age 70 provision, it seems likely that the stated normal age and the stated mandatory age will be different more often than they will coincide. A difference will in fact become necessary if employees are to have a viable option to retire prior to age 70. Consequently, a normal age will continue its role as a measuring point for benefit adequacy as a career of service comes to a close. The normal ages currently reported by the public plans and under TIAA-CREF plans covering institutions of higher education are described below.

Public Retirement Systems. In many public retirement systems, the full formula benefit (actuarially unreduced) may become available at different ages under the same system, depending on length of service. Consequently, one system may, in effect, state several different normal retirement ages. In these systems, as the tables show, the required service periods are usually associated with ages under 65. The longer the service, therefore, the more likely it is that an employee will be entitled to a full formula benefit at a relatively early age. Age 65 tends to be associated more often than the other ages with the entitlement to a full formula benefit without an accompanying service requirement.

Some examples of retirement age statements in public plans will illustrate how a single public plan may have several different normal retirement ages. Thus, more than one table is required to classify the various ages stated and the service requirements that may be associated with them. In the State Universities' Retirement System of Illinois, full-formula benefits are available at age 60 with eight years of service, at age 62 with five years of service, and at any age with thirty-five years of service. In the Louisiana State Employees' Retirement System the normal ages are age 60 with ten years of service; age 55 with twenty-five years of service; or any age with thirty years or more of service. The Ohio State Teachers Retirement System states 65 as a normal retirement age or any age with thirty years of service.

In many of the public retirement systems with alternative normal retirement ages, the longer the required service period, the earlier the age entitlement to a full-formula benefit. Table 3.22 shows the *longest* service requirements and therefore the *earliest* ages at which full-formula benefits are payable on the completion of the stated service requirements. Table 3.23 shows the alternative provisions that incorporate the *highest* ages and the *shortest* service requirements, or no service requirements.

Table 3.22. Earliest Normal Retirement Ages as Determined by Longest Stated Service Requirements—Public Retirement Systems Covering Institutions of Higher Education

		Number of Systems
Age 62		3
Plus 20 years of service	1	
Plus 30 years of service	2	
Age 60		4
Plus 15 years of service	1	
Plus 25 years of service	1	
Plus 30 years of service	2	
Age 55		5
Plus 30 years of service	4	
Plus 40 years of service	1	
Age 50		1
Plus 25 years of service	1	
No specified age		31
Plus 20 years of service	2	
Plus 30 years of service	19	
Plus 35 years of service	10	
No alternate requirement[a]		24
Total Systems		68

[a]Provisions of plans stating only one normal retirement age, with or without service requirements, are included in table 3.23.

Table 3.23. Normal Retirement Age as Determined by Shortest Stated Service Requirement, if Any, in Public Retirement Systems Covering Institutions of Higher Education

		Number of Systems
Age 65		30
No service requirement	16	
Plus 4 years of service	2	
Plus 5 years of service	6	
Plus 10 years of service	6	
Age 62		11
No service requirement	3	
Plus 5 years of service	2	
Plus 10 years of service	6	
Age 60		24
No service requirement	9	
Plus 3 years of service	1	
Plus 4 years of service	1	
Plus 5 years of service	5	
Plus 10 years of service	7	
Plus 20 years of service	1	
Age 55		3
Plus 5 years of service	2	
Plus 8 years of service	1	
Total Systems		68

NOTE: Forty-four plans have more than one age and service requirement for normal retirement (actuarially unreduced benefits).

As table 3.22 indicates, forty-four of the sixty-eight public employee systems incorporate alternative normal retirement provisions. Thirteen of the forty-four plans with alternatives specify an attained age plus a service requirement, with the ages specified ranging from 50 to 62. The remaining thirty-one systems do not state a specific normal retirement age, but rather permit full-formula normal retirement on the completion of service periods ranging from twenty years (one system), to thirty years (nineteen systems), to thirty-five years (ten systems). For employees with long service, the normal retirement age can be quite low. Twenty-four systems do not state an alternative normal age provision.

Table 3.23 shows the normal retirement ages for public retirement systems where there are no service requirements or where, if specified, the service requirements are the shortest. In twenty-eight of the sixty-eight plans, no service requirement for full-formula normal retirement is stated. Note that the normal retirement ages shown without service requirements or with short service requirements are higher than those shown in table 3.22 in connection with longer-service requirements. Among the twenty-eight systems stating a normal age without a service requirement, sixteen state a normal age of 65, three a normal age of 62, and nine a normal age of 60.

Table 3.24. Normal Faculty Retirement Age in TIAA-CREF Retirement Plans in Four-Year Colleges and Universities

Normal Retirement Age	Total Plans	% Distribution of Plans According to Normal Retirement Age	No. of Participants Represented by Plans According to Normal Retirement Age	% Distribution of Participants According to Normal Retirement Age
Under 65	12	1.1	2,723	1.0
65	932	84.4	180,669	65.0
66	10	0.9	4,601	1.7
67	17	1.5	8,777	3.2
68	47	4.3	29,020	10.4
69	0	0.0	000	0.0
70	84	7.6	51,807	18.7
Over 70 or none	2	0.2	129	*
Subtotal	1,104	100.0	277,726	100.0
Not classified or no information	17		2,496	
Total	1,121		280,222	

*Less than 0.1 percent.

TIAA-CREF Plans. Under TIAA-CREF retirement plans, as shown in table 3.24, the normal faculty retirement age is determined by the employing institution as the age at which the plan's benefit goal (a function of the contribution rate) is set for an employee after thirty or thirty-five years of plan participation. The normal age is usually set at 65 and corresponds with the earliest age of eligibility for unreduced Social Security old-age benefits. A TIAA-CREF plan participant may begin to receive annuity income at any time after retiring, which may be earlier or later than the plan's stated normal retirement age, but not after age 71. (Persons who continue employment may delay the start of benefits to as late as age 80.) The benefit is always the actuarial equivalent of the amount of annuity accumulation credited to the participant's annuity contracts. Retirement earlier than the normal age results in lower benefits due to the cessation of plan contributions, a shorter period of interest earnings on the full annuity accumulation, and the longer life expectancy involved in determining the level of annuity payments.

Later retirement results in higher TIAA-CREF benefits (even though plan contributions may cease at the normal retirement age). The option to delay the start of benefits can be useful to persons with other sources of income who choose to tap those sources first and leave their annuity benefits paid up until a later date to take advantage of the actuarial increases that will result in higher benefits when the annuity income is ultimately commenced.

Early Retirement. Early retirement generally describes retirements that take place at an age prior to a plan's stated normal retirement age, keeping in mind that some public retirement systems have more than one normal age. If retirement is not at or later than a stated normal age, it may be associated with any of the combined service and age provisions that under public systems entitle a retiree to an actuarially reduced formula benefit (defined benefit plans). Defined contribution plans provide an actuarial equivalent at any and all retirement ages, so that retirement before a stated normal age automatically results in actuarially reduced benefits.

Table 3.25 shows the early retirement provisions for age and service in public re-

Table 3.25. Early Retirement Age With Actuarially Reduced Benefits According to Age and Service Requirements—Public Retirement Systems Covering Institutions of Higher Education

		Number of Systems
Age 60		5
No service requirement	1	
Plus 10 years of service	3	
Plus 20 years of service	1	
Age 58		1
Plus 20 years of service	1	
Age 55		31
No service requirement	5	
Plus 5 years of service	9	
Plus 8 years of service	1	
Plus 10 years of service	7	
Plus 15 years of service	3	
Plus 20 years of service	2	
Plus 25 years of service	4	
Age 50		8
Plus 5 years of service	2	
Plus 8 years of service	1	
Plus 10 years of service	1	
Plus 15 years of service	2	
Plus 20 years of service	2	
No Specified Age		19
Plus 10 years of service	2	
Plus 25 years of service	10	
Plus 30 years of service	6	
Years of service plus age equal 75	1	
No provisions		4
Total Systems		68

NOTE: Seventeen plans have more than one age and service requirement for early retirement (reduced benefits).

tirement systems providing for retirements with actuarial reductions in benefits. Table 3.26 summarizes the reductions that are applied.

For most employees, actuarially reduced pension benefits discourage early retirement. The reason for the reduction, of course, is that retirements at early ages require pension funds to pay benefits over a longer period because of the greater life expectancies of persons at younger ages. Without an actuarial reduction, the cost of the plan could be materially affected. Yet, despite the higher cost, some employers encourage early retirements, as for example under the public retirement systems that incorporate full-formula benefits at ages under 65.

Employers with defined contribution plans can encourage early retirements by supplementing actuarially reduced benefits, either through additional premiums

Table 3.26. Actuarial Reduction Factors Applied to Early Retirement Benefits—Public Retirement Systems Covering Institutions of Higher Education

		Number of Systems
Actuarial reduction[a]		30[b]
Single factor: per year percentage reduction[c]		23
0.10% below age 65	1	
2.00% below age 55	1	
3.00% below age 55	1	
3.00% below age 65	3	
4.80% below age 60	2	
5.00% below age 60	1	
5.00% below age 65	1	
5.50% below age 65	2	
6.00% below age 60	5	
6.00% below age 65	4	
6.60% below age 60	1	
8.00% below age 60	1	
Multiple factors: per year percentage reduction		11
1.20% below age 65; 5.00% below age 60	2	
3.00% below age 65; 5.00% below age 60	1	
3.00% below age 65; actuarial reduction below age 60	1	
5.00% below age 65; 4.00% below age 60	1	
6.00% below age 65; 3.00% below age 60	1	
6.00% below age 65; 4.80% below age 60	1[d]	
6.66% below age 62; 3.33% below age 60	4	
No provision		4
Total Systems		68

[a]Payments that are actuarially equivalent to unreduced payments for normal age retirement, taking into account a given interest rate and mortality according to a given table.
[b]One plan provides alternate 3% reduction with specified age and service requirement.
[c]Five plans applying percentage reduction below age 60 and one plan below age 65 instead apply percentage reduction to number of years short of completing thirty years of service if a smaller reduction amount results.
[d]With thirty years of service, percentage reduction is 6% below age 60; 4.8% below age 55.

to the retirement annuities, separate deferred compensation agreements, sponsoring tax-deferred annuity programs, or through combinations of continued salary and retirement benefits under a phased-retirement arrangement. Early retirement schemes, except for deferred compensation agreements, maintained by private employers must meet all the requirements for pension plans as prescribed by ERISA, including reporting and disclosure, participation, vesting, and funding. A severance pay program may also be of some interest to employers. Under Department of Labor proposals, a severance pay plan may provide as much as two years' salary payable over a period not to exceed two years and need not be classified as a pension plan subject to ERISA.

Informality characterizes some early retirement arrangements. Since interest in voluntary early retirement may vary greatly among individual employees, employers may hesitate to develop a rigid and formally-stated plan. Some arrangements involve continuation of service by the early retiree in a consulting capacity. The services required may be nominal. The retiree's total income may then consist of the arranged consulting salary plus the benefits resulting from the early start of annuity income.

Employee benefits other than retirement income should also be considered in the development of an early retirement program. Continuation of group health insurance is important to early retirees, and it may also be considered desirable to continue a small amount of group life insurance protection.

The start of Social Security benefits before age 65 results in a reduction of the Primary Insurance Amount by 5/9ths of 1 percent per month for each month under age 65 that the benefit is started. The earliest age at which Social Security old-age benefits may commence is 62, with a 20 percent reduction. If an employee is receiving an early retirement income that combines continued salary (for a reduced workload or in a consulting capacity, for example), that part of income from "earnings in covered employment" is subject to the Social Security tax and, in addition, such earned income is also counted in the "retirement test" to determine if the retiree is to lose Social Security benefits. The individual on a reduced salary arrangement may therefore lose all of his or her Social Security benefits during the period of continued employment, since benefits will be reduced or discontinued in any year in which a working beneficiary under age 72 (under age 70 starting in 1981) earns more than a specified annual amount.

POST-RETIREMENT YEARS

During the retirement years, the real value of retirement income will be related to price changes. Annual rates of price inflation vary, with average rates varying greatly according to the length of the periods over which they are measured. Seldom, if ever, have inflation rates been forecast accurately. Neither economists nor retirees, therefore, can be very sure about the rates of price change in the future. Although past rates are no sure guide, they do suggest two considerations: (1) changes are not always just in one direction; and (2) inflation rates, plus or minus, can be quite different over different periods. For instance, between 1925 and 1950, the compound annual rate of inflation, as measured by the U.S. Consumer Price Index, was 1.3 per cent. Over the following quarter century, the compound annual rate (between 1951 and 1975) was 3.1 percent. More recently, the average annual compound rate, from 1969 to 1978, was 6.6 percent.

There were also lengthy periods of downward change in price levels. Over the period 1882 to 1899, the annual average change was minus 0.9 percent. Between 1920 and 1933 the Consumer Price Index declined at a compound annual rate of minus 3.3 percent. Under current economic conditions, continued inflation at the relatively recent high current rates may be reasonably expected. Over the longer term, however, it is apparent that rates of change have varied in both positive and negative directions, and the future may be no great exception to the past. Table 3.27 reviews the course of the U.S. Consumer Price Index over the last twenty years.

A retired person should be aware of the possibilities of diminished purchasing power due to inflation. A look at what future income dollars will buy under different anticipated rates of inflation will help illuminate the problem. Then, available

Table 3.27. U.S. Consumer Price Index (All Items) 1959–1978

Year	Consumer Price Index (annual average)	Percent Change
1959	87.3	0.8
1960	88.7	1.6
1961	89.6	1.0
1962	90.6	1.1
1963	91.7	1.2
1964	92.9	1.3
1965	94.5	1.7
1966	97.2	2.9
1967	100.0	2.9
1968	104.2	4.2
1969	109.8	5.4
1970	116.3	5.9
1971	121.3	4.3
1972	125.3	3.3
1973	133.3	6.2
1974	147.7	11.0
1975	161.2	9.1
1976	170.5	5.8
1977	181.5	6.4
1978	195.3	7.6

SOURCE: Department of Labor, Bureau of Labor Statistics.

Table 3.28. Amount of Income Needed to Maintain Initial Purchasing Power in Retirement Under Annual Inflation Rates of 3, 5, and 8 Percent

Years Following Retirement	Amount of Income Needed to Maintain Purchasing Power at Stated Inflation Rate		
	3 Percent	5 Percent	8 Percent
0	$100	$100	$100
5	116	128	147
10	134	163	216
15	156	208	317
20	181	265	466

means to help cope with the problem can be examined. This approach is equally valid for benefit plan administrators in the process of reviewing the experience of a retirement plan's beneficiaries. Feedback from retirees can help in the consideration of the effectiveness of the retirement plan's current provisions and income objectives, which should be reviewed periodically.

Table 3.28 shows, at successive five-year points, the amount of income that would be needed to keep up with three different annual rates of inflation: 3 percent, 5 percent and 8 percent. At a relatively low 3 percent annual rate of inflation (the average annual rate between 1951 and 1972, for example), a retiree after ten years would need $134 for each $100 of income in the initial year of retirement. The most recent year in which the U.S. inflation rate was no more than 3 percent was 1967. After twenty years (at the same rate) the retiree's income would have had to increase to $181 to retain its initial purchasing power.

At a 5 percent inflation rate (5 percent was exceeded in eight of the eleven years between 1967 and 1978), after just five years each $100 of starting income would have had to increase to $128 to retain constant purchasing power. After ten years of retirement at a 5 percent inflation rate, a retiree would have to have $163 for each $100 initially, and after twenty years, $265.

Active workers can expect wage and salary adjustments to accommodate wholly or partially for inflation rates, even though some economic sectors respond more rapidly than others. And inflation rates can decline as well as rise. How do retirees, who are no longer a part of the labor force and who no longer have the connection with the economy that workers have, gain protection against the effects of inflation? A number of protective devices, formal and informal, are in use.

Social Security Escalator. Social Security provides for an automatic cost-of-living increase in benefits when there has been a "significant" increase in the Consumer Price Index. (See chapter 4 for a more detailed description of the escalator provision.) The first automatic escalator benefit increase was 8 percent, effective in June of 1975; thereafter, there were benefit increases of 6.4, 5.9, and 6.5 percent, in June of 1976, 1977 and 1978, respectively. The inflation protection that a person's retirement income has is thus related, at least in part, to the proportion of the total income, often substantial, that comes from Social Security. Because Social Security benefits are weighted in favor of people at the lower wage levels, they will normally represent a larger proportion of income for low- and average-paid workers, compared with higher-paid workers.

A benefit escalator provision equal to each year's full change in the CPI is costly and open-ended. The Social Security escalator requires increasing amounts of OASDHI taxes—withheld from employees and matched by employers—to be sent to the Treasury for virtually immediate disbursement to beneficiaries. Pension plans, on the other hand, rarely offer and can ill afford automatic annual increases in benefits equal to or even near current rates of inflation. The potential cost can be gauged by the actuarial rule of thumb that pension plan costs would be increased by about 10 percent for each 1 percent of annual postretirement benefit increase. Thus, provision for retirement benefit increases of 5 percent each year would increase plan costs by about 50 percent.

Automatic Increases in Public Retirement Systems. Forty-three of the sixty-eight public retirement systems covering institutions of higher education have adopted formal provisions for increasing benefits being received by retired members. (See table 3.29.) In thirty-four of the systems, a benefit increase is triggered by a rise

Table 3.29. Types of Retirement Benefit Increase Provisions in Public Retirement Systems Covering Institutions of Higher Education

	Number of Systems
Change equal to full increase in U.S. CPI	4
Change related to change in U.S. CPI, with stated limits	30[a]
Automatic annual percentage increase not related to CPI	9[b]
Variable annuity	6[c]
Change related to investment experience of the retirement system	4
No provision	15
Total Systems	68[d]

[a]In four plans, CPI-related increase depends on favorable investment experience.

[b]Includes three plans with mandatory EE contributions (1.8%, 0.5% and 0.5%) allocated for funding of cost-of-living adjustment.

[c]Includes two plans in which the variable annuity is funded by voluntary supplementary contributions, one plan in which EE may allocate a percentage of required contributions to the variable fund which is part of the regular benefit and two plans in which 50% of required contributions and 100% of any voluntary supplementary contributions may be allocated to the variable fund. In one plan an EE makes contributions for a variable annuity on salary between $6,000 and $15,000, which is in addition to the regular EE contribution. Three plans provide additional cost-of-living adjustments based on change in the CPI to specified maximums and one plan provides an additional adjustment based on the investment experience of the fund.

[d]Eighteen systems report having made adjustments in retirement benefits through occasional benefit supplements, usually on an ad hoc basis.

in the Consumer Price Index. The benefit increase in four of these thirty-four systems is equal to the full percentage increase in the CPI (two systems in Maryland, one in Massachusetts, and the Federal Civil Service Retirement System). In the remaining thirty systems in this group, a limit is placed on the benefit increase, under which the increase cannot exceed a stated percentage or the increase in the CPI, whichever is less. The CPI-related systems are summarized in table 3.30.

Nine of the forty-three systems with automatic annual increase provisions simply state a percentage by which the benefit is increased each year. These percentages are: 1 percent (one plan); 1.5 percent (two plans); 2 percent (one plan); 2.5 percent (one plan); 3 percent (two plans); 4 percent (one plan); 2 to 5 percent, depending on investment experience (one plan).

In four systems, a benefit increase may be granted if the investment experience of the fund permits.

The increase percentages are normally applied to the original retirement benefit rather than compounded.

Six of the sixty-eight public retirement systems provide variable annuity benefits, either as part of the regular benefit plan or as supplementary annuity benefits.

Twenty-two of the sixty-eight plans do not report any stated formal benefit increase provisions. Of these, eighteen report that ad hoc increases have been made in the past, in some cases limited to employees who had retired under earlier, less generous benefit formulas.

Variable Annuities. The variable annuity, in which pension contributions are invested in a widely diversified portfolio of common stocks, is a means of accumulating funds so as to permit both the accumulation and pay-out of annuity income to reflect the investment experience of the economy. Variable annuities are usually offered along with fixed-income annuities that are based on fixed-return investments— long-term mortgages, publicly issued corporate bonds, and directly placed loans to corporations.

In higher education, the College Retirement Equities Fund (CREF) provides a variable annuity that is an optional companion to the standard fixed-income TIAA annuity. In addition, variable annuities are provided by six of the public retirement systems covering institutions of higher education: the Wisconsin Retirement Fund, the Wisconsin State Teachers' Retirement System, the New Jersey Public Employees Retirement System, the Oregon Public Employees' Retirement System, the University of California Retirement System, and the Minnesota State Teachers' Retirement System. Under the New Jersey and California systems, variable annuity participation is limited to voluntary employee contributions.

Participation in the variable annuity components of the public systems is optional except for employees under the Minnesota State Teachers' Retirement System. In this plan, in addition to the regular employee contribution of 4 percent of total salary, required employee contributions of 5 percent of salary between $6,000 and $15,000 are matched by the employer and paid into the separate Minnesota Supplementary Retirement Fund. Employees may elect to place these additional required

Table 3.30. Summary of CPI-Related Retirement Benefit Escalator Provisions in Public Retirement Systems Covering Institutions of Higher Education

Name of System	Frequency of Increase	Based on	Maximum Increase	Remarks
Alaska Public Employees' Retirement System[a]	Annual	CPI	4%	Based on financial experience of fund
Alaska Teachers' Retirement System[a]	Annual	CPI	4%	Based on financial experience of fund
Arkansas Public Employees' Retirement System	Annual after CPI increases at least 3%	CPI	3%	Automatic
California Public Employees' Retirement System	Annual	CPI	2%	Automatic
University of California Retirement System	Annual	CPI	2%	Automatic
Colorado Public Employees' Retirement Association	Annual	CPI	3%	Automatic; increases over 3% accumulated for following years
Connecticut State Employees' Retirement Association	Annual after 9 months of retirement	CPI	5%	Automatic
Connecticut Teachers' Retirement System	Annual	CPI	3%	Automatic
Florida Retirement System	Annual	CPI	3%	Automatic
Georgia Teachers' Retirement System	Every 6 months	CPI	1.5%	Automatic
Idaho Public Employees' Retirement System	Annual	CPI	6%	Based on financial experience of fund
Louisiana State Employees' Retirement System	Annual	Difference between CPI of preceding 2 years	3%	Automatic
Maine State Retirement System	Annual	CPI	4%	Automatic
Maryland State Employees' Retirement System	Annual	CPI	CPI	Automatic
Maryland State Teachers' Retirement System	Annual	CPI	CPI	Automatic
Massachusetts Teachers' Retirement System	After CPI rises more than 3% from previous increase	CPI	CPI	Automatic
Missouri Public School Retirement System	Annual after CPI increases by 2%	CPI	2%	Commences 4th January 1 after retirement, for a maximum of five times
New Jersey Public Employees' Retirement System	Annual after 24 months of benefit payments	CPI	60% of CPI	Automatic

System

System	Frequency	Basis	%	Type
New York City Teachers' Retirement System	Annual	CPI	3%	Automatic
New York State Teachers' Retirement System	Annual	CPI	3%	Automatic
New York State Employees' Retirement System	Annual	CPI	3%	Automatic
North Carolina Teachers' and State Employees' Retirement System	Annual	CPI	6.5%	Subject to financial experience of fund and general statutes of N.C.
Ohio Public Employees' Retirement System	Annual starting with 2d year of retirement	CPI	2%	Automatic. CPI increase over 2% accumulated for following years
Ohio State Teachers' Retirement System	Annual starting with 2d year of retirement after CPI increase by 2%	CPI	2%	Automatic. CPI increase over 2% accumulated for following years
Oregon Public Employees' Retirement System	Annual	Portland CPI	2%	Automatic
South Carolina Retirement System	Annual	CPI increase of 3% or more in one year	4%	Automatic
South Dakota Retirement System	Annual	½ annual CPI	2%	Automatic
Tennessee Consolidated Retirement System	Annual after 1 year of retirement	CPI when it rises 1% or more	3%	Automatic
United States Civil Service Retirement System	Every 6 months in which CPI rises	CPI	CPI	Automatic
Utah State Retirement System	Annual starting with 2d year of retirement	CPI	4%	Automatic
Vermont State Retirement System	Annual	CPI to nearest 1/10 of 1% when CPI rises 1% or more	5%	Automatic
Virginia Supplemental Retirement System	Annual starting with 2d year of retirement	Full CPI up to 3%; ½ CPI from 3% to 7%	5%	Automatic
Washington Public Employees' Retirement System	Annual	Washington CPI 1 yr. prior to retirement divided by Washington CPI 1 yr. prior to increase	3%	Automatic

aFor retired EEs who remain Alaska residents, adjustment of 10% of the original benefit granted automatically in addition to the cost-of-living provision.

contributions in either an "income share" account (up to 50 percent of which is invested in common stocks) or a "growth share" account (up to 100 percent of which is invested in common stocks).

Variable annuities are also reported by three of the church plans covering groups of employees in institutions of higher education: the American Baptist Churches Retirement Plan, the Ministerial Pension Plan of the Lutheran Church in America, and the plan administered by the annuity board of the Southern Baptist Convention.

Since variable annuities generally work the same way except for minor variations, the operation of CREF can serve as a general illustration. Premiums paid to CREF buy accumulation units, that is, units of participation. Each unit represents a share in a broadly diversified common stock fund. Prior to retirement, dividend income received from the common stock investments is prorated to participants in the form of additional accumulation units. A given amount of premium (or dividend credit) buys fewer new accumulation units as the accumulation unit value rises, and more new units as the unit value falls. This permits dollar-cost-averaging over long periods of time. As common stock prices rise and fall over the premium-paying years, so also do the value of accumulation units and therefore, of each participant's share in the fund.

When a pension plan participant elects to begin receiving the variable annuity income, the accumulation units that have been purchased over the working years are converted into a monthly annuity income expressed in terms of a fixed number of annuity units. This fixed number is payable monthly for life, but the dollar value of each unit changes annually, primarily as a result of the investment experience of the fund. In the transition from the accumulation stage to the pay-out stage, the particular level of common stock market prices at the time of conversion does not have a significant effect, either up or down, on the number of annuity units payable.

Throughout retirement, the dollar amount of the CREF annuity income changes on May 1 of each year and remains constant for the next twelve months. This annual revaluation reflects total fund experience for the fiscal year ending March 31. The most important factors in the revaluation are the change in market prices of the components of the investment portfolio and the level of dividend income received on investments. Variations in annuitant mortality and in expenses of administration have caused relatively minor changes in the annuity unit.

Variations in common stock values and dividends do not match cost-of-living changes year by year, and they sometimes move in opposite directions. But over reasonably long periods of time, economic studies have shown that a combined annuity income based on retirement plan contributions invested partly in debt obligations and partly in common stocks through the mechanism of the variable annuity has offered greater promise of weathering long-term economic changes than either a fixed-dollar annuity alone or a variable annuity alone.[11]

For equity investments, recent years have included periods of sharp rises and steep declines in common stock prices, accompanied by extremes in optimism and pessimism regarding equity markets. While total returns on common stocks have usually exceeded interest rate returns over extended periods, at times, over shorter periods, the reverse has been true. As a result, variable annuity participation has declined somewhat as rising interest rates on fixed-dollar investments have made fixed-dollar annuity funds more attractive. Variations in the performance levels of both fixed-dollar and variable annuities may be expected to continue. The economy and the securities markets react not only to fundamental shifts in population, productivity, resource availability, and international payment balances, but also to significant swings in the nation's political and social outlook and to major historical events.

Fixed-Dollar Annuity Dividends. Under fixed-dollar defined contribution retirement plans, such as TIAA, increasing earnings due to rising interest rates on fixed-dollar investments are credited as dividends to annuity policyholders. The extra dividends can result in increased monthly income for retirees. For example, a TIAA annuitant who retired in 1970 with a contractual annuity income of $10,000 yearly would in 1970 have received a total TIAA income in that year of $13,770, including dividend additions. In 1978, the income for the same annuitant, due to increased dividends, was $16,510, or an increase of 20 percent over the 1970 income.

Table 3.31 shows the annual net total investment returns for TIAA and for CREF for the calendar years 1952 through 1978, a twenty-seven-year period. The table reflects gradually rising earnings rates for the fixed-dollar annuity fund and also shows the varying annual net rates of return experienced by the common stock fund.

Table 3.31. Annual Net Rates of Return TIAA and CREF

Year	TIAA Net Rate Earned on Total Invested Assets	CREF Total Net Rate of Return on Equity Portfolio	Year	TIAA Net Rate Earned on Total Invested Assets	CREF Total Net Rate of Return on Equity Portfolio
1952	3.33%	+1.96% (6 mos.)	1966	5.11%	− 4.66%
1953	3.48	+ 2.53	1967	5.24	+23.42
1954	3.51	+48.83	1968	5.45	+ 6.12
1955	3.58	+25.48	1969	5.72	− 5.51
1956	3.70	+ 9.49	1970	5.95	− 3.22
1957	3.78	− 4.71	1971	6.28	+20.25
1958	3.95	+41.22	1972	6.58	+17.07
1959	4.14	+13.89	1973	7.16	−18.14
1960	4.35	+ 3.36	1974	7.59	−30.96
1961	4.52	+18.60	1975	7.82	+32.06
1962	4.68	−14.36	1976	8.13	+21.19
1963	4.79	+18.34	1977	8.39	− 6.44
1964	4.88	+12.66	1978	8.71	+ 8.68
1965	4.99	+17.75			

NOTE: This table shows past TIAA and CREF investment experience and should not be considered a prediction of TIAA or CREF performance for the years ahead.

Benefit Supplements. Another source of benefit adjustments in retirement is through occasional benefit supplements, usually on an ad hoc basis, made by employers or by public retirement systems. Eighteen of the sixty-eight public retirement systems covering higher education have from time to time raised pension benefits for already-retired members. In some cases these increases have been limited to persons whose benefits began many years ago or who are being paid under prior benefit formulas. Since ERISA, the provision of ad hoc benefits under private retirement plans has been severely restricted, since various participation, vesting, funding, and other requirements have made the supplementation of benefits more difficult.

Personal Planning. Individuals themselves are sometimes able to compensate for increases in the cost of living by reserving existing savings for later use in retirement. Holding available savings for future use in recognition of possible future increases in the cost of living is a form of prudent financial management. It is usually possible to reduce housing costs by the sale of a home that may be too large for retirees and by relocating in a suitable apartment or smaller home.

Another way of planning for the management of higher living costs in later years is to delay the start of annuities that may have been accumulated separately from the regular retirement plan. Many educational employees, for example, have accumulated extra tax-deferred annuity savings (under Section 403(b) of the Internal Revenue Code). The monthly pay-out of these annuities can be increased by delaying their start until several years of retirement have passed.

Under the regular TIAA-CREF annuities used in TIAA-CREF retirement plans, as well as under TIAA Supplemental Retirement Annuities for extra tax-deferred annuity savings, part of the annuity income can be started at the time of retirement, and part later, thus providing a second or even a third layer of annuity benefits to help offset increases in the cost of living. Again, continued interest earnings and reduced life expectancy for the part of the annuity not started at retirement helps increase the income amounts available later on.

4 Social Security

THE SOCIAL SECURITY program is by a wide margin the largest benefit plan in the country. As a program incorporating both a wage-related benefit and elements of a social transfer system, it is also, perhaps, the least understood. This lack of understanding has often resulted in unreasonable and conflicting demands on the program, including expectations that it perform like an employer-sponsored, actuarially sound pension plan while simultaneously acting as a social program, in proposals for added benefits without adequate consideration of long-term costs, and in proposals for "improvements" that would unwittingly alter the program's intent.

ORIGIN

Social Security legislation was a product of the Great Depression. The original act was passed by Congress in 1935 (years after most other nations had established social insurance programs). Tax collections under the program began in 1937, and the first benefits were paid beginning in 1940. Passage of the Social Security Act reflected a belief in the need for a method of systematically assuring at least a minimum income in old age that would not be an assistance program based on a means test. Benefits would be paid as a matter of earned right. Eligibility for benefits would be based on the number of years in covered employment and the benefit amount on an individual's covered earnings history. To achieve stated social goals, however, the amount and duration of benefits would also be related to a set of "presumed needs" as defined in the law.

One of the principal figures in the design of the original legislation, Professor Edwin E. Witte, noted in an article written twenty years later that the act would probably not have passed had it been offered to Congress any later than 1935, after which point the economy appeared to be recovering. This is not to say that a broad-based social insurance program would never have developed in this country, but it does suggest that the program might have assumed a different form had it been in other hands at another time.

COVERAGE

The program provided for compulsory but initially limited coverage. Only workers in commerce and industry, except for the railroads, were originally included.

Many employee groups were omitted at the outset: agricultural workers, federal employees, state and local employees, the military, self-employed people, and employees in nonprofit organizations. President Roosevelt wanted to start the program small as an aid to its acceptance by the public and the Congress. Even so, large firms with pension plans opposed the program and recommended (unsuccessfully) that workers covered under private pension plans be excluded.

Coverage under Social Security was expanded gradually. Thirteen years after the first collection of taxes, regularly employed farm and domestic workers were brought under compulsory coverage, plus nonfarm self-employed workers (except professionals) on a voluntary basis. In the same year (1950), state and local employees not covered under a retirement system and employees (other than ministers) of nonprofit organizations were permitted to be covered at the employer's option. In 1954, nonfarm self-employed workers and all self-employed professionals except lawyers and doctors were required to participate. Also in 1954, coverage was made elective by employers and current employees for state and local government employees under retirement systems. These groups were given further attention in 1956, when certain designated states were permitted to divide their employees into two groups, one for employees not desiring coverage, and the other for those who elected Social Security coverage, plus all new employees. These arrangements are the basis on which a few public institutions in the present survey indicate that some but not all of their employees are covered under Social Security.

In 1967, ministers and members of religious orders not under a vow of poverty (unless exemption is claimed on the grounds of conscience or religious principles) were brought under compulsory coverage, as were self-employed doctors. In the present survey of colleges and universities, a number of church-related institutions have reported that some but not all faculty are covered under Social Security. In these instances, such clergy may be covered as self-employed persons, and others may have claimed exemptions on the grounds of conscience. While clergy or other staff under a vow of poverty are not required to participate in Social Security, under 1972 legislation an employer may elect to bring this group under coverage.

Federal civil service employees are not covered under Social Security. State and local public employers and nonprofit organizations may participate at their own choice and, unlike other employers, have the option of dropping the program. Today, about 90 percent of the employees of all types of nonprofit organizations (roughly 3.6 out of 4 million) and 70 percent of the employees of state and local governments (some 8.4 million out of approximately 12 million) have elected to be covered.[1]

Table 4.1 shows the extent of participation in the federal Social Security program among two- and four-year educational institutions. Virtually all of the privately supported colleges participate in Social Security, and the program applies about equally to all employee classes.

Table 4.1. Social Security Coverage of College and University Employees (percent of institutions reporting plans and percent of employees in institutions reporting plans)

	Four-Year Institutions				Two-Year Institutions			
	Public		Private		Public		Private	
	Percent Insts	Percent EEs	Percent Insts	Percent EEs	Percent Insts	Percent EEs	Percent Insts	Percent EEs
Faculty[a]	n = 478	n = 242,041	n = 929	n = 121,162	n = 600	n = 66,915	n = 85	n = 2,284
Covered under Social Security	88.2	87.6	98.4	99.8	70.8	67.6	98.8	99.5
All	71.0	67.1	88.8	94.5	58.5	52.3	87.0	89.4
Some	17.2	20.5	9.6	5.3	12.3	15.3	11.8	10.1
Not covered	10.3	11.7	1.5	0.2	29.0	32.3	1.2	0.5
No response	1.5	0.7	0.1	—	0.2	0.1	—	—
Clerical-Service	n = 478	n = 413,110	n = 929	n = 188,601	n = 600	n = 66,748	n = 85	n = 2,482
Covered under Social Security	89.3	88.3	99.3	99.9	79.8	82.4	98.8	99.8
All	72.6	66.6	95.5	97.1	68.8	69.9	94.1	96.5
Some	16.7	21.7	3.8	2.8	11.0	12.5	4.7	3.3
Not covered	10.7	11.7	0.6	0.1	20.2	17.6	1.2	0.2
No response	—	—	0.1	—	—	—	—	—

[a]Administrative and other professional personnel similar to faculty.

While the publicly supported institutions do not match the nearly 100 percent coverage level of the private institutions, the extent of participation in Social Security among public institutions reflects a very high degree of support for the program. Nearly 90 percent of all public four-year institutions employing nearly 90 percent of employees report coverage under Social Security for all employee classes. Between 70 and 80 percent of the public two-year institutions provide coverage under Social Security. These public two-year institutions employ well over two-thirds of all such employees. As a class, clerical-service employees are more likely to be in the program than are faculty or administrative personnel.

Colleges in the "some covered" group are those at which new employees are brought under Social Security but at which one or more groups of longer-service employees elected not to participate in the program when the coverage started at the institution.

Colleges whose employees do not participate in Social Security face the problem of compensating, at least in part, for the absence of the federal program. Compensatory attempts are normally made through public employee or state teacher retirement systems, since it is mainly the public colleges in which groups of employees are outside of Social Security. The benefits to be augmented are: retirement, survivor, disability, and health insurance for persons aged 65 and over.

For retirement, the public systems whose participants are not covered by Social Security must incorporate a formula benefit higher than that necessary under public plans covered by Social Security if they are to compensate for the absent Social Security benefit. Employees in twelve of the sixty-eight public retirement systems surveyed are not covered by Social Security. In these twelve systems the retirement benefit is 2 percent or higher of final average salary for each year of membership. Among the systems covered by the program, nineteen also provide a benefit formula of 2 percent or more; only five of these nineteen, however, attempt to integrate the combined benefits. One of the serious cost problems of the public plans derives from the fact that when Social Security was made available optionally to public employees, instead of integrating the benefits to provide a uniform total benefit from both Social Security and the public retirement plans, many states simply added the benefits to existing coverage. In the State of New York, for example, because of this and other liberal benefit provisions, some long-service employees can retire earlier than age 65 with total retirement benefits exceeding 100 percent of final salary.[2]

The survivor benefits under the public retirement systems whose employees are not covered by Social Security do not, as a rule, come up to the level of the maximum benefits provided for under Social Security. Generally speaking, the state systems outside Social Security have not moved to increase survivor benefits when Social Security benefits have been increased.

Perhaps the least satisfactory substitute arrangements have been the provisions for long-term total disability. Service requirements of five, ten, or fifteen years leave a substantial number of employees outside the scope of the coverage (see chapter 8).

In contrast, under Social Security, work in covered employment for as short a period as a year and a half (if disabled at age 24) can bring entitlement to maximum disability benefits. An employee who leaves a state teacher or public employee retirement system, whether or not the retirement benefits have vested, loses entitlement to the survivor and disability benefits of the system. Social Security, on the other hand, offers a valuable continuity of survivor and disability coverage.

The addition to Social Security of hospital insurance for the aged posed a new problem for employees outside the federal program. The public retirement systems, including those whose participating employers provide some continued major medical coverage for retirees, have not attempted to match this benefit. Employees 65 or over under these systems currently have to depend on having become fully insured for Social Security benefits under other employment in order to be eligible without a monthly premium charge for hospital insurance (Part A), or have to look to their employers for provision of health insurance, at whatever level, through private insurance companies.

CONTRIBUTORY FINANCING

Except for a part of Medicare, the Old-Age, Survivors, Disability, and Health Insurance (OASDHI) program is supported by taxes paid by employees and employers and by self-employed persons, plus interest earnings on the relatively small Social Security trust funds. Any excess of income to the system over administrative costs and benefits is credited to the trust funds and invested in government bonds.

The reserve accumulation of these government trust funds is not at all comparable, either in function or in the ratio to accrued benefits, to the reserve funds necessary for fully funded retirement plans. The Social Security trust funds constitute only a small contingency reserve to even out year-to-year benefit payments, rather than a traditional insurance reserve, since the program is largely a "pay-as-you-go" (unfunded) system.

Increases in the payroll tax rate and wage base are designed to cover estimated future costs of the old-age, survivors, and disability benefits, and of the hospital insurance portion of Medicare. A wide spectrum of people and organizations—labor unions, management, economists, sociologists, government officials, and politicians—has always strongly supported the contributory feature of Social Security. Past increases in benefits have been accompanied by increases in the scheduled tax rates and wage base. Thus it is reasonable to assume that the maximum level of payroll tax that is generally acceptable will be an important factor determining the general future benefit levels of Social Security.

Earnings Base. Employers and employees are required to pay OASDHI taxes based on the legislated percentage rate applied to earned income up to a designated amount. The amount of income used in the calculation of payable taxes is described as the taxable wage base. Annual earnings in excess of the base are not subject to the tax, and there are no benefits related to such earnings. The wage base started out at $3,000 in 1937, was increased five times up to 1971, and since 1972 has increased annually to its 1979 level of $22,900.

Significant changes were voted by Congress in 1972 and 1977. Compared to the previous thirty-five years of gradual increases, these changes resulted in sharply higher increases in the wage base and in the tax rates of the program. Increases in the wage base under the 1972 law raised the amount in stages from $9,000 in 1972 to $14,000 in 1975, at which time a provision became effective that automatically increases the wage base each year by essentially the same rate as the increase in average national wages.[3] The 1977 legislative changes again stipulated ad hoc increases in the wage base, rising from the 1977 level of $16,500 to $29,700 in 1981, an increase of 80 percent in just four years. As of 1982, the automatic wage base increase provision again takes over. It is estimated that if the automatic provision in the 1972 law had been allowed to continue to operate, the base in 1981 would likely have been $21,900, as against the 35 percent higher figure of $29,700 actually enacted. Expressed in another way, the wage base in 1977 of $16,500 covered the full wages of about 86 percent of all workers in covered employment, while the 1981 base of $29,700 is expected to cover the full wages of about 94 percent of all workers, or 91 percent of all earnings in covered employment. By contrast, from the original $3,000 in 1937 through the subsequent increases to $9,000 in 1972, the taxable wage bases covered the full wages of about half the regularly employed male workers or about 80 percent of all earnings in covered employment. Table 4.2 compares the pre- and postamendment wage base changes from 1977 through 1987.

Taxes. The legislated tax rate paid by employer and employee each as a percentage of covered wages within the wage base rose from 1.0 percent (of $3,000) in 1937 to 5.2 percent (of $9,000) in 1972. For a person paying the tax on the maximum covered amount, this represented a nearly fifteen-fold increase in the actual dollar amount payable. Effective January 1, 1973, the tax rate applicable to income cov-

Table 4.2. Social Security Taxable Wage Bases, Actual and Estimated, Before and After 1977 Amendments

Calendar Year	Preamendment	Postamendment
1977	$16,500	$16,500
1978	17,700	17,700
1979	18,900[a]	22,900
1980	20,400[a]	25,900
1981	21,900[a]	29,700
1982	23,400[a]	31,800[a]
1983	24,900[a]	33,900[a]
1984	26,400[a]	36,000[a]
1985	27,900[a]	38,100[a]
1986	29,400[a]	40,200[a]
1987	31,200[a]	42,600[a]

[a]Estimate.

Table 4.3. Social Security Tax Rate Changes Before and After 1977 Amendments (rates for employer and employee, each)

Year	Preamendment			Postamendment		
	OASDI	HI	Total	OASDI	HI	Total
1977	4.95%	0.90%	5.85%	4.95%	0.90%	5.85%
1978	4.95	1.10	6.05	5.05	1.00	6.05
1979–80	4.95	1.10	6.05	5.08	1.05	6.13
1981	4.95	1.35	6.30	5.35	1.30	6.65
1982–84	4.95	1.35	6.30	5.40	1.30	6.70
1985	4.95	1.35	6.30	5.70	1.35	7.05
1986–89	4.95	1.50	6.45	5.70	1.45	7.15
1990–2010	4.95	1.50	6.45	6.20	1.45	7.65
2011	5.95	1.50	7.45	6.20	1.45	7.65

ered by the earnings base was increased from 5.2 percent to 5.85 percent (of $10,800) for employer and employee each. The new rate, applied to the increased wage base, raised maximum Social Security taxes for each from $468 in 1972 to $819 in 1975, nearly doubling in three years.

On the benefit side of the picture, from January 1940 to June 1977, the OASDI benefit increased 510 percent, while the CPI rose 333 percent. From September 1950 to June 1977, the benefit increase was 245 percent, while the CPI rose 147 percent.[4]

The 1977 legislative amendments established tax rates through the year 2011. Table 4.3 shows the pre- and postamendment scheduled rates for employer and employee each through 2011. The OASDHI tax rate scheduled for 1980 is 6.13 percent, composed of 5.08 percent for OASDI and 1.05 percent for HI. Looking ahead ten years, the maximum tax payable by employer and employee each will increase from $965 to an estimated $3,046 in 1987, a 215 percent increase.

ELIGIBILITY FOR BENEFITS

The monthly cash benefits under Social Security are paid as a matter of earned right to workers who gain insured status and to eligible dependents and survivors of such workers. *Fully insured* status qualifies a worker and his or her family for most types of benefits on the basis of the worker's Social Security earnings credits. To be fully insured, a person must have at least one quarter of coverage for each calendar year (four quarters) elapsing after 1950, or if later, after the year in which the person attained age 21. A person who has earned forty quarters of coverage, whether consecutively in ten years or not, is fully insured for life. For some types of benefits, either fully insured or *currently insured* status is required. A person is currently insured who has at least six quarters of coverage during the full thirteen-quarter period ending with the calendar quarter in which he or she died, most recently became entitled to disability benefits, or became entitled to retirement benefits.

In addition to fully insured status, eligibility for disability benefits is dependent on a special *disability insured* status. This status is attained if the worker has not less than twenty quarters coverage during the forty-quarter period ending with the quarter in which disability began. Special eligibility provisions apply to persons disabled because of blindness or prior to attaining age 31.

Precise definitions of the insured status required for a particular type of benefit are stated in the Social Security Act as amended. In addition, a small lump sum payment is payable on the death of a fully or currently insured worker.

CALCULATING THE BENEFIT

PIA. An insured individual's *primary insurance amount* (PIA) is determined by a formula established under Social Security law in conjunction with the individual's covered earnings record. For a worker retiring at age 65, the actual benefit payable would be the same as the PIA; in other cases, the benefit payable is expressed as a fraction of the PIA. For example, a worker retiring at age 62 would receive a reduced benefit equal to 80 percent of the PIA otherwise payable at age 65; a spouse age 65 is eligible for a benefit that is 50 percent of the insured worker's PIA (spouse benefit actuarially reduced if claimed by spouses between ages 62 and 64).

AIME. As a result of the 1977 amendments to the Social Security law, an individual's average covered earnings are converted to *average indexed monthly earnings* (AIME) before the benefit formula is applied. Under this new method, a worker's covered earnings are updated (indexed) to the period two years prior to the year the worker reaches age 62, becomes disabled, or dies, to reflect increases in average national wages that have occurred since the earnings were paid. The worker's covered earnings are indexed by multiplying them by the ratio of average national wages in the second year before he or she reaches age 62, becomes disabled, or dies, to the average national wages in each year being updated.[5]

This process is carried out for each year of covered employment credited to the worker except that covered earnings after age 60 or disablement are counted at actual dollar value—that is, unindexed—and substituted for earlier years of indexed covered earnings if they are larger. Then the prescribed number of benefit computation years is selected, i.e., all of the individual's working years between 1950 (or year of attainment of age 21, if later) and the year of first entitlement to benefits, less the five years of lowest covered earnings, and the dollar amounts are added together and divided by the number of months in those years. The result is the worker's average indexed monthly earnings.

Benefit Formula. A worker's PIA is then calculated by applying the benefit formula to the AIME. The formula for those reaching age 62 in 1979 consists of three brackets, as follows:

90 percent of the first $180 of AIME, plus

32 percent of AIME from $180 to $1,085, plus

15 percent of any additional AIME

The benefit formula will be changed for each future year's attainment of age 62, death, and disability. The dollar bands will be adjusted (either upward or downward) according to changes in the general wage level of the country.

Automatic Cost-of-Living Adjustment. The automatic cost-of-living escalator was added to the program by the 1972 amendments. The automatic benefit increase takes place in June of any year when the Consumer Price Index of the Department of Labor shows an increase of 3 percent or more as measured from the first quarter of the preceding year (or from any other quarter of the previous year for which Congress legislated a benefit increase) to the first quarter of the year in question. The cost-of-living provision is open-ended, i.e., there is no imposed maximum percentage of annual increase. The first increase under this provision was 8 percent, effective in June of 1975; thereafter, benefits increased 6.4 percent, 5.9 percent, 6.5 percent and 9.9 percent in June of 1976 through 1979, respectively.

RETIREMENT EARNINGS TEST

Social Security was designed to counter economic insecurity from loss of earnings in retirement by providing income for those who had substantially withdrawn from the labor force. There was no intent under the provisions of the program to tax younger *working* people in order to pay benefits to older *working* people. Consequently, Social Security law provides for an earnings test under which loss of earned income or very low earnings (and the attainment of age 62 or 65) is a condition for eligibility for old-age retirement benefits.

Under the 1939 amendments, no benefit payments were made when a beneficiary had earnings in covered employment of more than $14.99 per month, regardless of the beneficiary's age. The concept of an age beyond which the retirement test would not apply was first introduced under the 1950 amendments which made the test inapplicable at age 75 or over; the 1954 amendments lowered this age to 72. In both cases the inclusion of an upper age was designed as a political compromise to make the program more attractive to a newly covered group of employees—the self-employed in 1950 and the self-employed farmers in 1954—who claimed that their members rarely "retired" and thus would never draw benefits if the retirement test applied without limit as to age. Under pressure from those who would abolish the earnings test entirely, Congress further lowered the age to 70 (after 1981) as part of the 1977 amendments.

Beginning with the 1950 amendments, the $14.99 monthly amount of exempt earnings was gradually increased and was established under the 1977 amendments at the annual level of $4,000 in 1978, increasing by $500 units each year until reaching $6,000 in 1982. Thereafter, the amount will be automatically adjusted according to changes in the general level of wages. The 1977 amendments also eliminated the provision for applying the earnings test on a monthly basis except during the first year of retirement; now, the total earnings for any year after the first must be "tested" against the annual exempt amount regardless of the pattern of earnings. For example, a man or woman who retired at age 65 in 1979, but who earned $9,000 in 1980, would have earned $4,000 over the 1980 exempt amount of $5,000. This individual would be subject to the annual test and would lose $2,000 in Social Security benefits—$1 for each $2 earned over the exempted $5,000.

A SYSTEM OF SOCIAL EQUITY

Social Security should not attempt to provide the full benefits needed and desired by all people at various income levels in this country. A substantial part of that job is best done in the private sector, where the individual's and the employer's extra efforts can be directly reflected in the size of the individual's benefits. Social Security is primarily a system of "social equity." It is a transfer system, different in its treatment of people from the "individual equity" of insurance in the private sector, under which each dollar of premium purchases a specified right to retirement, death, disability, or health benefits. To some degree, Social Security benefits are related to the taxes paid on behalf of an individual, but the emphasis is on income redistribution and on the individual's presumed needs, appropriate criteria for a national social program.[6]

Several provisions implement the social equity aspects of the system. The Social Security tax rate, representing the total cost of the benefit for covered employees, is applied uniformly to the taxable wage base. Provision of retirement income for persons with earnings above the wage base is thus left to individual efforts through personal savings and to private pension coverage. Social Security benefits, although related to the average monthly wage on which taxes have been paid, are heavily weighted in favor of those who earn less than the full wage base. The weighting in favor of lower-paid workers through the graduated benefit formula is the means by which one of the main social redistributions of the system is engineered—that is, the transfer from middle-income earners to lower-income earners. The benefits produced under the new (1979) formula are more heavily weighted in favor of lower salaries than in the past. The benefits on earnings at the high end of the formula are only one-sixth of those at the low end and less than one-half of those in the middle range. At retirement, therefore, a lower-paid worker could receive Social Security benefits representing as much as 45 percent of final year's salary, while a worker whose earnings have always been equal to or exceeded the maximum taxable amount would receive a benefit representing approximately one-third to one-quarter or less of final average earnings. Chart 4.1 shows graphically the relative weight of the various segments of AIME in the benefit formula. If all earners were treated the same, the line descending in steps would instead be a level line from left to right.

A social transfer designed to meet presumed needs also occurs between single and married beneficiaries. When a worker retires and begins old-age benefits, the monthly amount is automatically increased by 50 percent if the retired worker has a spouse age

Chart 4.1. Relative Weight In The Social Security Benefit Formula of Average (Indexed) Monthly Earnings

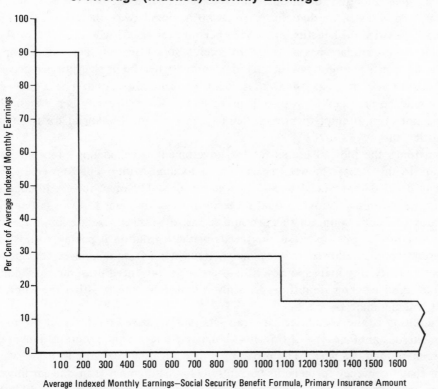

Average Indexed Monthly Earnings—Social Security Benefit Formula, Primary Insurance Amount

65 or over (reduced spouse's benefits available at age 62) unless the spouse is entitled on his or her own to more than 50 percent of the retired worker's PIA. When either husband or wife dies, the initial PIA becomes the benefit amount for the survivor.

Transfers are also made from small families to large. The program's survivor benefits provide monthly income for children up to age 18 and to the surviving spouse caring for them. Thus all families are equally protected from loss of income in the event of death of the breadwinner in spite of the fact that the real cost of survivor benefits is higher for large families than for small families or childless workers.

At any given point in its history, Social Security has been attacked as being unfair to some groups—the young, the single, the working elderly, families with both husband and wife working, or women compared with men, or men compared with women. The question generally hinges on the objective of social equity compared with individual equity. Under Social Security, social equity of benefits is a most useful and important consideration, but it is impossible for any system to provide social equity and full individual equity at the same time. The primary job of Social Security is to provide socially adequate benefits, i.e., livable benefits for typical family compositions. It cannot do this and concurrently accept the idea that the single person has "paid for" and should therefore receive the same size benefits as a married person (and spouse), or that the person who has paid twice the taxes of another should have twice the benefits, or that the person over age 62 who keeps on working full-time at high salary has a "right" to receive Social Security benefits on top of wages, or that a younger worker of today should when he or she retires receive as generous an actuarial bargain as those who have already retired. These goals can and should be provided by private pension plans; Social Security is a system that should not even attempt to provide "equal and equitable" financial treatment for its participants.

Sometimes the judicial branch of the government is called upon to contribute answers to this debate between social and individual equity. The Supreme Court recently decided that Social Security's test for eligibility of widowers for old-age benefits was unconstitutional (equal protection) when the same test was not applied to widows.[7] The meaning of this decision seems to be that there are limitations on the power of Congress in presuming needs in the legislation it passes. In this case Congress was not allowed to presume that surviving female spouses had greater needs than surviving male spouses. Still, there are many "need presumptions" in the program, and it seems doubtful—certainly it would be unwise—that the Supreme Court will eliminate them all.

In addition to the Social Security transfers that are based on different presumed needs, there is another type of transfer—a massive one—in the program. This is the "intergenerational transfer." The program is paid for on a current cost basis, which means that the money for benefits currently being paid comes from the earnings of workers currently paying Social Security taxes. Under these transfers, in 1976 for example, $70.7 billion went from workers to beneficiaries; since outgo exceeded income that year, an additional $3.2 billion was taken out of the small (relatively) trust fund to cover the difference. These transfers were from current workers to retirees and their survivors (the largest part of the program), to the currently disabled, to the survivors of deceased workers, and to beneficiaries of the hospital insurance program.

Given a specified set of benefits, the cost level of the program at any given time, then, depends largely on the number of persons receiving benefit payments; the tax rate depends on the number and willingness of workers available to support these payments through their tax withholdings. The fewer the workers, the higher the tax. As the number of workers relative to the number of retirees declines, the burden on workers grows. When Social Security started out, there were about ten workers for each person 65 or over. The total cost of the program was low as a percentage of taxable payroll, as little as 1.17 percent in 1950. At present the ratio has changed to three workers per person over 65. By the year 2030, the ratio is expected to move close to two to 1 and the program's cost is expected to rise to between 15 and 20 percent of taxable payroll, compared to about 11 percent in 1978.[8]

OASDHI ADMINISTRATION

The Old-Age, Survivors, Disability, and Health Insurance program provides monthly cash benefits to retired and disabled workers and their dependents and to survivors of insured workers. It also provides health insurance benefits for persons aged 65 and over and for the disabled under age 65. Old-age retirement benefits were provided by the original Social Security Act of 1935, benefits for dependents and survivors by the 1939 amendments, benefits for the disabled by the 1956 amendments, and benefits for the dependents of disabled workers by the 1958 amendments. The 1965 amendments initiated the health insurance program generally known as Medicare.

Separate trust funds are maintained in the United States Treasury for the four component parts of OASDHI: (1) the Old-Age and Survivors Insurance program (OASI); (2) the Disability Insurance program (DI); and, for Medicare, (3) the Hospital Insurance program (HI), and (4) the Supplementary Medical Insurance program (SMI). These trust funds are managed by a board of trustees consisting of the Secretary of the Treasury, the Secretary of Labor, and the Secretary of Health, Education, and Welfare. Once each year the trustees issue a report on the financial condition of each trust account.

The trust funds receive monies as follows: taxes paid under the Federal Insurance Contributions Act and Self-Employment Contributions Act and contributions under section 218 of the Social Security Act dealing with the coverage of state and local government employees; any sums received under the financial interchange with the Railroad Retirement account; voluntary hospital and medical insurance premiums; and transfers of general federal revenues to finance military and other gratuitous wage credits, "special age 72" benefits, and matching payments under Supplementary Medical Insurance—Part B of Medicare. Funds not withdrawn for current cash or service benefits and administrative expenses are invested in interest-bearing federal securities, as required by law. The interest earned by the invested funds is also deposited in the trust accounts.

OASI Program. The old-age and survivors portion of the program provides retirement benefits for retired workers, benefits for a retired worker's wife or husband aged 62 or over, and benefits for the dependent children of a retired worker. Under the survivor portion of the program, benefits are provided for a retired worker's widow or widower, for dependent children in the care of such a person, for the surviving spouse of a deceased worker if the survivor has dependent children in his or her care or if the survivor is aged 60 or over, and for a dependent parent age 62 or over who received at least one half of his or her support from the deceased child and who has not remarried. The basic benefit, and the one from which other benefits are calculated, is the Primary Insurance Amount (PIA).

DI Program. A monthly disability income benefit is paid to workers who become disabled and are insured for disability purposes. Disability is defined as the inability to engage in a gainful activity by reason of any medically determinable physical or mental impairment that can be expected to result in death or to last for a continuous period of not less than twelve months. Inability to engage in a gainful activity means:

1. For a nonblind disabled worker, a blind worker under age 55, or a disabled child, the inability to engage in any substantial gainful activity.

2. For a blind worker age 55 or over, inability to engage in any substantial gainful activity requiring skills comparable to those in any gainful activity in which he or she previously engaged.

Monthly disability benefits are payable to a disabled worker under age 65 after six months of continuous disability. The benefit amount is the PIA computed as if the worker were age 62 and had applied for retirement benefits. The dependents of a disabled worker entitled to benefits are: the husband, wife or divorced wife age 62 or older, a wife (any age) caring for a child entitled to benefits, unmarried child or grandchild if the child is (a) under age 18; (b) age 18 to 22 and a full-time student; (c) age 18 or older and suffering a disability that began before the child reached age 22.

Disabled widows, widowers and surviving divorced wives age 50 or over who can meet a special, more stringent definition of disability are entitled to disability benefits based on the deceased worker's fully insured status.

The program provides for a "disability freeze" for a disabled worker which protects against loss or reduction of disability or retirement benefits, or benefits for survivors, by providing that the period of disability will not be counted in any future determinations of his or her insured status or the amount of benefits payable. Vocational rehabilitation services are provided the disabled worker at no cost in those cases where it appears likely that savings will result to the program from such rehabilitation.

Under an offset provision a reduction in disability income benefits is made when the employee's combined monthly Social Security benefits and any Workers' Compensation benefits that are payable exceed 80 percent of his or her average monthly earnings prior to the onset of disability.

As an incentive to rehabilitation, the disability program provides for continuation of benefits for a trial employment period of up to nine months, plus an additional three months applicable to any recovery case.

Medicare. The Medicare program consists of two separate but coordinated programs: Part A, Hospital Insurance (HI); and Part B, Supplementary Medical Insurance (SMI). The program is officially described as "health insurance for the aged and disabled."

The Hospital Insurance program enrolls for benefits all persons age 65 and over who are entitled to monthly cash benefits under the OASDHI or railroad retirement programs (whether retired or not), as well as disabled persons under age 65 who have been entitled to disability cash benefits for at least twenty-four consecutive months. In addition, persons with chronic renal disease who require renal dialysis or kidney transplant were added through legislation effective July 1, 1973. Persons age 65 or over who are not eligible by virtue of their work in covered employment for cash benefits under the OASDHI or railroad retirement program may enroll for hospital insurance by paying the full monthly premium for HI protection (Part A) if they are also enrolled for voluntary SMI (Part B) protection.

The HI program includes, in addition to hospital benefits, part of the cost of in-patient and related health care provided by skilled-nursing facilities and home health agencies following a period of hospitalization. The first 60 days of covered services in a benefit period in a participating hospital are essentially paid for in full after the patient pays a specified deductible. For each of the next 30 covered days in a benefit period the patient pays a specified amount (equal to one-fourth of the deductible). Each HI beneficiary also has a "lifetime reserve" of 60 additional hospital days that can be used at his or her option when the covered 90 days within a benefit period have been exhausted. HI benefits include reimbursement for inpatient tuberculosis and psychiatric hospital services, with a lifetime limit of 190 days of care in a psychiatric hospital. In addition, HI pays for emergency services in a non-participating hospital.

The HI program pays for part of the cost of all covered inpatient services in participating skilled-nursing facilities for up to 100 days in a benefit period after a hospital stay of 3 or more consecutive days. The cost of the first 20 days is covered in full. The patient pays a specified amount of the daily cost for each of the remaining 80 covered days. Also covered under HI is the reasonable cost of up to one hundred home health visits during the year, after at least 3 days of hospitalization or a stay of any duration in a skilled-nursing facility.

Under the Supplementary Medical Insurance program, all persons entitled to coverage under HI by virtue of their work in covered employment are eligible to enroll on a voluntary basis by paying a monthly premium. It is also possible for a person upon reaching age 65 to enroll in SMI without being entitled to monthly Social Security or railroad retirement benefits or to Hospital Insurance protection. The program is financed by the premium payments from enrollees and by funds appropriated by the federal government. The monthly premium rate for enrollees has increased from $3.00 in July 1966 to $8.20 through June 1979, as shown in table 4.4.

The SMI program pays 80 percent of the charges allowed for a variety of medical services and supplies furnished by physicians and others in connection with physicians' services, outpatient hospital services, and home health services after the beneficiary has met an established deductible amount. Radiology and pathology services furnished by physicians to hospital inpatients are covered without any deductible or coinsurance payments. Up to one hundred home health visits each year are covered in full after the deductible is met.

**Table 4.4. Standard Monthly Premium
Rates under SMI Program**

Period	Rate
July 1966–March 1968	$3.00
April 1968–June 1970	4.00
July 1970–June 1971	5.30
July 1971–June 1972	5.60
July 1972–June 1973	5.80
July 1973	5.80[a]
Aug. 1973	6.10[a]
Sept. 1973–June 1974	6.30
July 1974–June 1976	6.70
July 1976–June 1977	7.20
July 1977–June 1978	7.20
July 1978–June 1979	8.20

[a]Reflects freeze under Economic Sta-
bilization Program.

VOLUNTARY WITHDRAWAL FROM SOCIAL SECURITY

When voluntary participation in the OASDHI system was extended to private nonprofit organizations and units of state and local government in the 1950s, they were also given the option of dropping out after a minimum period of participation (five years for public employers or eight for private nonprofit organizations) and a two-year waiting period preceded by a notice of intent to withdraw. While only a small number of employers in these categories have exercised their option to terminate participation (about 0.5 percent), recent debate focusing on the funding problems of the system prior to enactment of the 1977 amendments, and the subsequent higher tax and wage base schedules, have spurred interest in the withdrawal option.

There is no doubt that the cost of Social Security is increasing, but in considering the question of dropping out it is important to weigh carefully the cost element in context with the special features of the program.

Tax-free Benefits. One feature of the Social Security program is that benefits are received tax-free. Employer-sponsored retirement benefits, on the other hand, are taxed upon receipt to the extent that they reflect previously untaxed employer contributions, employee contributions made on a tax-deferred basis, and investment earnings on both employer and employee contributions. (See chapter 9.) One of the problems with trying to replace or equal the old-age benefits, such as through annuity contracts or a state retirement system, is that new benefits would have to be high enough to provide an *after*-tax benefit equal to the tax-free Social Security benefit. It would also be very expensive for a private pension plan to attempt to match the Social Security cost-of-living escalator for retirement benefits.

Effect on Insured Status and Benefits. Employers who drop out may face difficulties in hiring new employees when Social Security is not a part of the benefit program. Because earned quarters of coverage are fully vested and portable, a younger job applicant with dependents who has partially but not fully insured status might hesitate to consider a prospective employer who does not participate in the program.

Some employers consider dropping out because most of their employees are already fully insured under the program, that is, have ten or more years (40 quarters) of covered employment. However, employees with fully insured status would still suffer reductions in benefit amounts because fully insured status determines only benefit entitlement, and even then not to all benefits. Benefit amounts are based on average indexed earnings representing an entire working lifetime, and years of noncoverage are counted in the benefit calculation as years of zero earnings, thus lowering the average. For persons already fully insured, years of noncoverage would reduce their survivor's income protection as well.

Employees not yet fully insured—generally younger staff members with the greatest need for family protection—would not be eligible for any survivor benefits within two years of the date their participation was terminated, owing to the concurrent "currently insured" requirement. Individuals who had already met the eligibility requirements for Social Security disability income would lose this coverage entirely in five years from the time their participation terminated. Once lost, eligibility for the disability benefits could not be regained by employees who shifted jobs to another employer covered under the program until they had again participated for a continuous five-year period.

No Reentry. Once an institution has filed an intent to withdraw, passed the two-year waiting period and officially dropped out, there is no provision under present law for reentry. If Congress decides at some future time to use general revenue funds in financing Social Security benefits, the employees of such an institution would be placed in the position of contributing to the support of the system through their income taxes without receiving any benefits.

FINANCIAL PROSPECTS OF THE SOCIAL SECURITY SYSTEM

The Social Security Amendments of 1977, the most significant Social Security legislation since 1972—and possibly since 1950—reflected an effort by Congress to deal with the serious financial problems confronting the program. In 1972, Congress had legislated the greatest expansion in Social Security benefits to date. The 1977 amendments represented the first attempt to legislate any sort of cutback in benefits. The OASDI Trustee's Report for 1975 indicated that outgo exceeded income by $2.9 billion in that year and predicted steadily increasing deficits for succeeding years, growing to as much as $6.7 billion by 1979.[9] Clearly the 1977 amendments reflected a need for legislative action.

Both short- and longer-range causes can be cited for the OASDI deficits detailed in the 1975 report. There were three main immediate causes: (1) higher than anticipated inflation, resulting in a cash flow situation in which income from taxes rose less rapidly than the price-indexed benefit outgo; (2) unemployment rates that were greater than expected, resulting in more retirements and somewhat lower tax income; and (3) higher than expected disability insurance expenditures (which traditionally have accompanied periods of depressed economic activity). The longer-range expected deficits, also projected in recent OASDI trustee reports, were due in part to two additional reasons: (1) the technically faulty 1972 automatic adjustment provisions that would have caused future benefit levels to grow at a faster rate than wages, eventually providing new beneficiaries with initial benefits that would in many cases have been higher than any earnings during their working careers; and (2) demographic developments that shortly after the turn of the century are expected to show a ratio of only about two workers for each beneficiary, compared with the current ratio of about three to one.

Considering only the OASDI program, changes under the 1977 amendments in the calculation of the benefit formula, wage base and tax rates averaged over a seventy-five-year period reduce the projected deficit—average annual expenditures compared to average scheduled tax income—to 1.46 percent of taxable payroll. This contrasts with an 8.20 percent projected deficit before the amendments. Considering the entire seventy-five-year period, however, provides a somewhat distorted picture. Total income and outgo are projected after the 1977 amendments to be in approximate balance during the next fifty years (1977–2026). During the succeeding twenty-five-year period (2027–2051), expenditures are projected to be 16.69 percent of taxable payroll, while scheduled income is projected at only 12.40 percent of taxable payroll, a deficit of 4.29 percent. The deficit in the last third of the seventy-five-year period remains unresolved by the 1977 amendments and will have to be dealt with eventually by Congress.

As mentioned, the above figures do not include projected costs and tax receipts for Hospital Insurance and Supplementary Medical Insurance. The anticipated rise in the cost of SMI beyond the required premiums will necessitate greater infusions of general revenues, which by current law must pay the difference between actual costs and total income. Adding projected costs for HI to those for OASDI advances to the mid-1990s the date when expenditures will once again exceed tax income. Congressional proposals for hospital cost containment legislation limiting future increases in the cost of health care and the possibility that the HI program will be absorbed by some form of national health insurance within the next decade have tended to reduce the emphasis and the interest in the program's imminent financing problems.

One proposal to deal with anticipated deficits in the next century is to raise from 65 to 68 the earliest age at which full Social Security old-age benefits can be achieved, as well as from 62 to 65 for earliest reduced benefits and from 70 (after 1981) to 75 for exemption from the retirement earnings test.[10] The increases would be carried out gradually over a period of years starting in the year 2005, so that in the early part of the twenty-first century age 68 would become the normal retirement age for (actuarially unreduced) benefits. Raising the age to 68 would cut the costs and increase the revenues of the program because the workers would continue to pay Social Security taxes longer and would draw benefits for fewer years. More workers would mean fewer retirees, so that the cost per worker of supporting retirees would not rise as high as otherwise will be the case when the members of the "baby boom" generation will be significantly increasing the ranks of retirees to be supported by the members of the "baby bust" generation. Also, this proposal fits in with the 1978 amendments to the Age Discrimination in Employment Act, which raised to 70 the first age at which employers can mandate employee retirement. Lifting the normal Social Security retirement age to 68 could be viewed as consistent with public policy embodied in the ADEA amendments.

From its narrow, experimental beginning, Social Security has become a mature social insurance program, one of the most successful "social engineering" experiments ever tried in this country. Over its lifetime—now more than four decades—Social Security has reduced the national welfare burden by helping to alleviate want and worry of millions of elderly and disabled people and of survivors of covered workers. Through its broad coverage and comprehensive benefits, it has provided a floor of benefit protection to which private pensions and personal savings can be added. The overly generous benefit increases and escalator provisions legislated in 1972 introduced wholly new cost levels into this pay-as-you-go system, while the sharply higher wage bases and tax rates legislated in 1977 made the new (and necessary) cost levels both highly visible and controversial. The fact that even at a higher level of support, substantial deficits are still anticipated early in the next century makes it apparent that this pay-as-you-go system has its own imperatives—the support capacity of the economy and the continuing willingness of the taxpayers to pay. Congress must continue to face the task of keeping taxes and benefit payments in balance, weighing both the interests of those who pay the taxes and the interests of those who receive the benefits.

5 Group Life Insurance Plans

G ROUP LIFE insurance plans for faculty, administrative personnel, and other professionals were reported by 86 percent of the institutions covered by the current survey. These institutions employ about 93 percent of faculty, administrative, and other professionals in higher education. For clerical-service personnel, the proportion of employees in institutions reporting a group life plan is about the same, 93 percent, although slightly fewer institutions report group life plans for this group than for faculty (83.6 percent for clerical-service employees compared with 85.7 for faculty).

Among responding four-year institutions of higher education, those reporting a group life insurance plan employ between 93 and 95 percent of all employees. Among private four-year colleges and universities, the institutions without plans for faculty (17 percent) employ only 5.2 percent of faculty in four-year private institutions. The public four-year institutions indicating that they have no group life coverage (9.4 percent of institutions) employ about 7 percent of faculty in public four-year institutions. For clerical-service employees, the proportions of group life coverage are not significantly different: 6 percent of publicly employed clerical-service personnel and 5.2 percent of privately employed are in institutions reporting no group life coverage.

Two-year colleges do not report as high a proportion of group life plans as the four-year colleges and universities. The difference is most noticeable among private junior colleges, but it also extends to the public ones. For faculty, 88 percent of public two-year colleges (employing 88.6 percent of faculty) and 71.8 percent of the private two-year institutions (employing 78.6 percent of faculty) report a group life plan. The coverage proportions for administrative and other professionals, and for clerical-service employees in two-year institutions, are similar to those reported for faculty, including the same differences between public and private, except that about 30 percent of clerical-service employees in the private two-year colleges do not have group life coverage, compared with about 20 percent for faculty.

Table 5.1 shows the extent of group life insurance plans for faculty and for clerical-service employees. The plan coverage for administrative and other professional employees is similar to that reported for faculty. The table gives the data for all institutions, two-year and four-year, and also gives responses for the institutions according to control, public and private.

Table 5.1. Group Life Insurance Plans In Institutions of Higher Education (percent of institutions reporting plans and percent of employees in institutions reporting plans)

	Faculty[a]		Clerical-Service	
	Percent Insts	Percent EEs	Percent Insts	Percent EEs
All Institutions	n = 2,092	n = 432,402	n = 2,092	n = 670,941
Group life plan	85.7	92.8	83.6	93.5
No plan	14.1	7.1	16.1	6.5
No response	0.2	0.1	0.3	*
All Four-Year Institutions	n = 1,407	n = 363,203	n = 1,407	n = 601,711
Group life plan	85.5	93.7	83.3	94.3
No plan	14.4	6.3	16.6	5.7
No response	0.1	*	0.1	*
All Two-Year Institutions	n = 685	n = 69,199	n = 685	n = 69,230
Group life plan	86.0	88.4	84.5	86.7
No plan	13.6	11.4	14.9	13.1
No response	0.4	0.2	0.6	0.2
All Four-Year Institutions				
Public	n = 478	n = 242,041	n = 478	n = 413,110
Group life plan	90.6	93.1	90.0	94.0
No plan	9.4	6.9	10.0	6.0
No response	—	—	—	—
Private	n = 929	n = 121,162	n = 929	n = 188,601
Group life plan	82.8	94.7	79.8	94.7
No plan	17.0	5.2	20.0	5.2
No response	0.2	0.1	0.2	0.1
All Two-Year Institutions				
Public	n = 600	n = 66,915	n = 600	n = 66,748
Group life plan	88.0	88.6	87.0	87.3
No plan	11.5	11.1	12.3	12.5
No response	0.5	0.3	0.7	0.2
Private	n = 85	n = 1,795	n = 85	n = 2,482
Group life plan	71.8	78.6	67.1	70.8
No plan	28.2	21.4	32.9	29.2
No response	—	—	—	—

[a]Administrative and other professional similar to faculty.
*Less than 0.1 percent.

Over the last decade, the proportion of institutions reporting group life insurance has risen, along with the proportion of employees in institutions reporting coverage. In 1968, 70 percent of four-year colleges and universities, employing about 90 percent of faculty and administrative personnel, reported a group life plan.[1] In 1978, as indicated by table 5.1, these percentages had risen to 85.5 and 93.7, respectively. For clerical-service personnel, the growth rate was somewhat greater than for faculty between 1968 and 1978, due to a lower 1968 base. For clerical-service personnel, 63 percent of four-year institutions, employing 85 percent of employees in this category, reported group life plans in 1968. In 1978 these figures had risen to 83 percent and 94 percent, respectively. Growth in coverage is also evident in the two-year colleges. In the previous survey (in 1970), 70 percent of the two-year institutions reported a group life plan for faculty and administrators and they employed about 80 percent of this employee group.[2] In the current survey, 86 percent of the institutions reported a plan for faculty and administrators, and they employed over 88 percent of employees in this category. For clerical-service employees in 1970, two-thirds of the two-year colleges, employing about three-fourths of this employee category, reported a group life plan. By 1978, these proportions of coverage for clerical-service employees had risen to 84.5 and 86.7 percent, respectively.

PURPOSE OF GROUP LIFE INSURANCE

The main purpose of life insurance is to provide cash and income benefits to dependent survivors of persons who, when living, were a source of support. Occasionally, other purposes are achieved through life insurance, such as "key-man" insurance, designed to help a business firm finance a loss sustained by the death of a principal officer, or credit insurance, which assures repayment of a personal installment loan on the death of the borrower. Overall, 54 percent of life insurance in force in the United States in 1976 was obtained through individually-purchased policies and 46 percent was through group life insurance plans.[3]

As table 5.1 shows, group life insurance plans are widely used by educational employers. An employer-sponsored plan makes it possible to provide every employee with at least a basic amount of life insurance protection. While many employees of an educational institution will have individual life insurance protection under policies purchased on their own, additional protection under a group plan is usually desirable. The average amount of individual life insurance coverage per insured family in 1976 was approximately $30,100, not a large amount.[4] For employees who have no individual insurance, coverage under a group plan can be an incentive to seek additional protection through individual policies. A 1967 survey of insurance coverage among newly hired university faculty members indicated that the faculty group did provide more adequately for their insurance needs than any comparable group on which data are available, but also found that approximately one-half of the group was inadequately insured according to criteria supplied by the respondents themselves.[5]

In addition to the provision of basic life insurance protection for all eligible employees, group life insurance offers other advantages. More insurance can be purchased per premium dollar on a group basis than under most individual life insurance policies. The lower cost is due in part to lower administrative expenses and to the elimination of the expense of physical examinations for the determination of insurability, a process necessary under individual insurance policies to control selection against the insurer by persons in ill health. The fact that group insurance normally does not require evidence of insurability (except on late enrollment), makes the availability of group life insurance of considerable value to staff members who, because of their health, cannot obtain individual insurance at a standard rate, or cannot obtain it at all.

OTHER SURVIVOR BENEFITS

An employer-sponsored group life plan does not usually work alone as a means of replacing lost income. Two other benefit plans also play a part: (1) the survivor benefits of the Social Security program; and (2) the death or survivor benefits of the retirement plan. A life insurance plan that has been designed with these two other programs in mind stands the best chance of providing an appropriate pattern of benefits at reasonable cost.

Social Security. The survivor benefits under the Social Security program consist of a regular monthly income for widows with children under age 18 in their care, and a regular monthly income for children under 18 (under 22, if students). Survivor benefits are provided for widows age 60 and over, whether or not they have children in their care. There is also a small lump sum death benefit of $255 payable to a widow or widower who has been living in the same household as the deceased at the time of death, or, if no widow or widower is entitled to the lump sum amount, to a funeral home at which burial expenses were incurred. The family survivor benefits have a potential value that is far higher than is generally realized. Table 5.2 illustrates the magnitude of Social Security survivor benefits for young families by

Table 5.2. Social Security Income Benefits for Survivors—Illustration of Monthly Income Amounts and Cumulative Totals

Workers' Average Indexed Monthly Earnings[a]	Survivors' Monthly Income (widow and 1 child)	Cumulative Total if Payable for		
		5 Years	10 Years	15 Years
$ 400	$362	$23,574	$ 52,267	$ 87,187
900	612	39,793	88,218	147,150
1,425	784	50,976	113,013	188,506

Worker's Average Indexed Monthly Earnings[a]	Survivors' Monthly Income— Maximum Family Benefit	Cumulative Total if Payable for		
		5 Years	10 Years	15 Years
$ 400	$365	$23,778	$ 52,729	$ 87,967
900	734	47,737	105,829	176,527
1,425	914	59,461	131,822	219,871

[a]Assumes death of worker in 1979 and 4% annual increase in benefits.

Table 5.3. Illustrative Death Benefits under TIAA-CREF Retirement Plans

Plan Entry Age: 30 Attained Age	Retirement Plan Contribution Rate as a Percentage of Salary					
	10 Percent		10-15 Percent Step-Rate		15 Percent	
	death benefit	multiple of salary[a]	death benefit	multiple of salary[a]	death benefit	multiple of salary[a]
40	$ 23,839	1.04	$ 23,842	1.04	$ 35,759	1.55
50	97,182	2.15	98,687	2.18	145,773	3.22
60	297,249	3.34	308,159	3.46	445,874	5.01

NOTE: Assumptions: All premiums paid to TIAA, 1978 annuity dividend rates (not guaranteed for the future). Starting salary of $12,500 at entry age 30 in 1979, salary increasing at 7% per year. Step-rate plan illustration based on step-point at second bracket point of Social Security benefit computation formula, 4% annual increase in Consumer Price Index, and 5.75% increase in average national wages.
[a]Death benefit as a multiple of salary in year of attained age.

showing the cumulative totals of such benefits when payable over five-, ten-, and fifteen-year periods. The total amounts can reach into six figures.

TIAA-CREF Annuities. Under TIAA-CREF retirement plans, the full annuity accumulation is payable as a survivor benefit to any named beneficiary if the retirement plan participant (the annuity contractholder) dies before beginning to receive the annuity income. Such death benefits are small in the early years of plan participation, but they can build up to substantial amounts. Table 5.3 illustrates the TIAA-CREF death benefits at ages 40, 50, and 60 under various contribution rates, assuming a starting salary of $12,500 a year at age 30, increasing at 7 percent a year, including promotional and living-cost increases.

Public Retirement Systems. Forty-five of the sixty-eight public retirement systems covering employees in higher education provide specific income benefits for survivors having a stated family relationship to the deceased employee if nonservice-connected death occurs prior to eligibility for early or normal retirement benefits. Eligible beneficiaries are usually limited to spouses with minor children in their care, and to children. Dependent parents are sometimes included. The survivor benefits are usually paid in lieu of any lump sum benefits or return of employee contributions, the latter usually being provided for on behalf of employees who die with no survivors in the categories named by the retirement plan. Eligibility for survivor income benefits is often based on employee service requirements, sometimes of some length, and occasionally an age requirement as well. In addition to these special provisions, survivor annuities are normally available to spouses of employees who die after becoming eligible for retirement benefits but prior to retiring. Gaps in survivor coverage, where present, suggest that a group life insurance plan can be of special value to younger employees who have not yet met a retirement plan's survivor benefit eligibility requirements, may have young families, and are likely to be in greater need of insurance protection. Table 5.4 shows the eligibility requirements stated for spe-

Table 5.4. Survivor Benefits in Case of Death Prior to Eligibility for Retirement under Public Retirement Systems— Nonservice-Connected Death Benefits[a]

		Number of Systems
Monthly Survivor Benefits—Eligibility Based on Specified Service Requirement:		45[b]
None	5	
1 year	3	
1½ years	4	
2 years	4	
5 years	10	
10 years	8	
15 years	5	
15 years and age 55	2	
20 years	2	
25 years	1	
25 years and age 50	1	
Lump Sum Payment		16[c]
Return of Employee Contributions		7[d]
Total Systems		68

[a]All plans provide for return of EE contributions when no other death benefit is payable.

[b]Includes eleven plans which provide a lump sum payment in case of death prior to attainment of specified service requirement. Four plans provide lump sum payment in addition to survivor annuity. Three plans permit election of lump sum amount in lieu of survivor annuity. In four plans, additional specified years of service prior to eligibility for retirement qualify survivors for payments at a higher level.

[c]Includes one plan with provision for survivor benefits after one year of service if EE made optional 1% survivor contribution. In three plans, spouse, if designated beneficiary, may elect payment of annuity that could be purchased with lump sum amount. In three plans, beneficiary may elect payment of annuity that could be purchased with lump sum amount if lump sum payment is $5,000 or more. Thirteen plans provide for return of EE contributions in addition to lump sum payment.

[d]Includes two plans in which beneficiary may elect payment of annuity based on amount of EE contributions and one plan in which annuity payment may be elected if monthly amount purchasable by EE contributions is $25 or more.

cific nonservice-connected survivor benefits prior to eligibility for retirement under the public retirement systems covering employees in higher education.

BENEFIT OBJECTIVES

The benefit of a group life insurance plan cannot reasonably be expected to replace regular family income for any significant period, but it can meet an objective of providing needed funds during a difficult period of transition. A modest plan can meet this limited objective. More generous plans can be designed to meet income needs of young and growing families, perhaps for several years following the death of the principal breadwinner.

The Statement of Principles of the American Association of University Professors and the Association of American Colleges has recommended that educational institutions have a life insurance program that provides a benefit sufficient to sustain the standard of living of a deceased staff member's family for at least one year following death. Where additional protection is contemplated, the statement recommends that the special financial needs of families of younger faculty members receive particular consideration.[6]

Basic Readjustment Benefit. A flat insurance amount or an insurance amount directly keyed to salary is frequently used to provide a basic readjustment benefit. A flat amount provides the same insurance for everyone, or for all covered persons in a stated employee classification. In a salary-related plan, each employee's insurance amount may be specified as a multiple of salary ($1 \times$ salary or $1.5 \times$ salary, for example), or insurance may be assigned according to salary brackets. Other methods of assigning a basic insurance amount include determining the amount by rank or by job classification. The commonly used methods of assigning basic insurance amounts are described in this chapter.

Additional Protection. A college insurance program that provides more than a basic insurance amount may reasonably provide larger benefits for the younger staff members. Typically, the insurance needs of younger staff members are high because they are more likely to have young children and their salaries are at the lower levels. Their accumulated death benefits under a defined contribution retirement plan are not likely to have built up to substantial amounts. Under defined benefit retirement plans it may be many years before they are eligible for survivor benefits. The lower cost of life insurance for younger staff members aids the institution desiring to apply its available funds economically at the point where there is the greatest need. For example, an appropriate program might incorporate insurance of three or four times salary at the younger ages, decreasing to more modest amounts at later ages.

If the life insurance program has properly taken family needs into account, its benefits plus the basic Social Security survivor benefits, any death or survivor benefits from a retirement plan, and individual insurance proceeds, can be of enormous help in relieving financial pressure on the surviving parent while children are young and require care.

TYPES OF LIFE INSURANCE PLANS

Three general types of life insurance coverage are available for groups of employees: group term, collective, and group permanent. Group accidental death and dismemberment insurance is a subsidiary feature that is often added to a group life plan at extra cost.

Group Term Insurance. The form of insurance used most frequently in group life plans is one-year renewable term insurance. The group contract is issued to the employer (or to an employee association); each insured employee receives a certificate summarizing his or her coverage. The group contract sets forth all the provisions of the plan, including the full schedule of benefits, the classes of employees to be covered, and the effective date of insurance.

Group life insurance incorporates a "conversion privilege" that may be exercised by the employee who terminates employment. Under this provision the terminating employee may convert the group term insurance to an individual policy without evidence of insurability. Because insurers normally require that a person convert to a permanent form of individual life insurance with premium rates based on age at the time of conversion, the new premium cost to the individual will be substantially higher than under the former group plan. For this reason the conversion privilege is seldom used except by persons with impaired health; only about 1.25 percent of all terminating employees in the United States with group insurance exercise the conversion right.[7] A physical examination is required on conversion if the disability waiver of premium provision is desired as a part of the individual policy.

Collective Life Insurance. Collective insurance, a quasi-group insurance developed by TIAA, provides decreasing term insurance which automatically concentrates a greater amount of protection at the younger ages. TIAA collective life insurance coordinates well with the growing death benefit under TIAA-CREF retirement plans. The death benefits of the retirement plan are small at first but accumulate to substantial amounts in later years.

Under a collective insurance plan, each covered staff member receives an individual life insurance policy defining the coverage. The same administrative economies are provided as under group term insurance, but unlike group term, the premium for each participant's insurance remains the same from year to year. The protection provided is the amount of one-year term insurance the premium will purchase at the participant's age. The insurance is issued in units; one unit of protection is the amount that can be purchased at each age by a premium of one dollar per month. Dividends as declared are applied as additional insurance protection. If the employee leaves the institution, the individual policy may be continued in force, including the disability waiver of premium provision, at the same premium.

Group Permanent Insurance. Group paid-up life insurance and level premium group permanent life insurance plans have been adopted by relatively few colleges.

Under a group paid-up plan the employee's contributions are applied each month to purchase increments of paid-up, as distinguished from term, insurance. The employer's contributions are applied to purchase term insurance; employer contributions are not used for the paid-up insurance coverage because they would then be taxable to the employee as income. As the paid-up insurance accumulates from successive employee contributions, the term insurance purchased by employer contributions decreases by corresponding amounts. The amount of each purchased segment of paid-up insurance depends on the employee's age and the size of the employee's contribution. The paid-up insurance is retained by the employee on termination of employment, or it may be surrendered for its cash value. On the term portion, the standard conversion privilege is available.

Level premium group permanent life insurance also provides for paid-up insurance, but with separate certificates, as a rule, for the original amount of permanent insurance and for any subsequent increases. It is frequently used to provide supplemental life insurance for pension plans of business and industrial organizations.

Several characteristics of group paid-up or permanent insurance account for its infrequent use for group coverage. For a given expenditure, much higher levels of protection can be obtained with group term insurance or collective insurance. The paid-up insurance has a high cash value component; compared with term insurance it is more of a savings plan. Many regard this as an expensive way to save since the employee can do as much or more on his or her own. Furthermore, administration is more complex under paid-up or permanent plans because much individual record-keeping is required, and it is sometimes difficult to give the covered employees a clear understanding of the plan.

Group Accidental Death and Dismemberment Insurance. Accidental death and dismemberment insurance (AD&D) pays specified indemnity amounts if the individual dies as the result of an accident, or sustains the accidental loss of certain parts of the body. When provided, AD&D is usually written in conjunction with group term life insurance. The "principal amount" of AD&D insurance is normally equal to the individual's group term benefit and is paid for loss of life or the loss of both hands, both feet, sight of both eyes, one hand and one foot, one hand and the sight of one eye, or one foot and the sight of one eye. Half of the principal amount is paid for the loss of one hand, one foot, or the sight of one eye. Not more than the principal amount is paid for all losses sustained by an employee in any one accident. Most insurers do not pay AD&D benefits for death caused by suicide or intentionally self-inflicted injury, war or acts of war, disease or bodily or mental infirmity, ptomaine or bacterial infections (except for infection of accidental cuts or wounds), or participation in the commission of a felony. AD&D sometimes goes by other names; one insurer calls it personal accident insurance.

About 60 percent of the four-year colleges and universities report that accidental death and dismemberment provisions are included in their life insurance plans, as do about 75 percent of two-year institutions, with no significant difference between faculty, administrative, and clerical-service employee groups. By control, public institutions are somewhat more likely to include the AD&D coverage than the private educational employers. For example, in the four-year colleges and universities, 66.1 percent of the public institutions reported AD&D coverage for faculty, while 57.9 percent of the private four-year institutions reported the coverage.

Although AD&D provisions are found in a slight majority of plans, college administrators and staff members sometimes question the appropriateness of providing insurance benefits that are paid in connection with accidental death or dismemberments, but that are not paid for death from other causes. On the other hand, the considerable amount of faculty and staff travel called for by many college activities leads some to feel that AD&D, within its benefit limits, can serve as low-cost travel accident insurance. According to insurance company and census figures, only about 6 percent of deaths are caused by accidents each year.[8]

INSURANCE ADMINISTRATION

Group Underwriting. Some of the common underwriting standards for group life insurance are written into state insurance laws; others are set forth by the insurer. The principal requirements for group life insurance, which also apply to group health and disability insurance, are:

1. A cohesive group, usually with a minimum of ten people. The group must be based on a strong and continuing common relationship other than the desire for insurance, normally the employer-employee relationship. New entrants should continually be entering the group as others leave.

2. A central administrative unit for enrollment, record-keeping, and for collection of participants' contributions, normally by payroll deduction, when the employees share in the cost of the plan.

3. Precision in the definition of the employees eligible and of the amounts of insurance provided. Eligibility should be based on factors pertaining to employment. There should be no doubt about which employee categories are eligible for the plan, when, and for how much insurance.

4. A high percentage of enrollment of the eligible group in order to assure a reasonable distribution between healthy and impaired lives. When the employer pays the entire cost of the insurance (noncontributory), all members of the eligible classes are automatically insured. When the employees share in the cost, an initial enrollment of at least 75 percent of the eligible employees is normally required.

5. Benefits for each participant that are reasonable in relation to the benefits provided other participants.

Premiums and Experience Rating. In determining the total monthly premium for an insured group, the amount of insurance in force at the respective ages of all insured employees (nearest birthday) is first multiplied by the premium per $1,000 of insurance for males of each age and for females of each age, and the results are totaled. This total is commonly adjusted to reflect the proportionately smaller administrative expense for larger plans. It is then divided by one-thousandth of the total insurance in force to obtain the average monthly premium rate per $1,000 of insurance for the group as a whole. The college's total monthly premium is then determined by applying the average premium rate for the plan to the total amount of insurance in force that month. The insurance in force may vary each month according to additions and terminations of employees under the plan, and according to any changes in the amounts for which individual participants are insured. The average monthly premium rate per $1,000 is recalculated periodically.

After a plan has gone into operation, its claim experience may influence the level of rates. Whether or not it does will depend on several factors, such as the size of the group, the volume of insurance in force, and the practices of the insurer. In general, the experience of a relatively small group (this varies, but may involve groups with up to a few hundred employees) is pooled with the experience of groups of similar size and, under some methods, with part of the experience of larger groups.

Pooling among many groups is the basic insurance or risk-sharing function. Premium rates can be maintained at a fairly constant level for all institutions to the extent they participate in the pool, despite periods of high claim experience for some groups in the pool. For example, the yearly premium might be $700 for a group of ten participants in which each member is insured for $10,000. The death of just one staff member—resulting in a $10,000 benefit expenditure—would thus equal about fifteen years of premium payments. One employer alone could not afford to assume so great a risk; without pooling there could be no risk sharing to make insurance possible at reasonable cost.

Large institutions having many hundreds or thousands of employees tend to have a more predictable number of deaths in their group over the years and are thus often "self-rated" or "experience-rated." The net cost (premiums less dividends) of a self-rated plan is based on the experience of the plan, although, depending on the practice of the insurer, a portion of even a large group's claim experience may be pooled with other groups' experience.

Insurers are willing to provide self-rating for groups that are sufficiently large to produce a reasonably predictable level of claims. The relative weight assigned to a group's own experience and to the pool differs among insurers. If there are few claims, self-rating is advantageous to a large institution, since dividends or retroactive rate adjustments reflect this experience, reducing the cost of the plan. Numerous claims produce the opposite effect in a self-rated plan.

When a group is large enough to have its plan self-rated to some extent, the rates of the insurers competing to underwrite the plan are usually compared on the basis of "retention" illustrations. The retention is the insurer's charge for the plan, and it includes administrative expenses, contingency reserves, commissions, taxes, and, for commercial stock insurance companies, a margin for profit. The balance of gross premium is applied to pay claims, establish claim reserves, and provide dividends or premium refunds.

Special Contract Provisions. To continue insurance for employees who become disabled, a waiver of premium provision is usually incorporated in the master contract. Under a typical waiver benefit, a participant under age 60 who becomes totally disabled for a period of more than six months has his or her life insurance coverage continued under the group policy without further premium payments during such disability. The charge for the benefit is included in the group life premium rate.

A group life insurance contract may provide a disability pay-out, that is, in the event of a total disability before age 60 that has continued for six months, the death benefit of the policy may be paid out to the insured as monthly income, usually over a five-year period. Serious side effects of the provision are readily apparent: (1) the benefit pay-out reduces the amount of life insurance at a time when the breadwinner has become uninsurable and needs insurance protection as never before; and (2) since the benefit can continue only for a limited time, it does not provide satisfactory long-term disability income.

The beneficiary of a group insurance policy may choose to take group insurance proceeds as a lump sum or as monthly income under several different options. The options usually include: (1) a life annuity with income ceasing at death; (2) a life annuity for the original payee with income continuing to a second payee for the balance of a stated period if death occurs within that period (usually the first ten or twenty years); (3) an income of a specified monthly amount, as selected, for as long as proceeds plus interest permit; (4) an income for a fixed period of years, usually from one to thirty, as selected; or (5) a monthly income consisting of interest earned on the proceeds, with the principal remaining intact to be paid at a later date.

LIFE INSURANCE PLAN PROVISIONS

An employer's decisions with respect to the provisions of a group life insurance plan cover five main points: (1) the classes of employees to be eligible for coverage; (2) the waiting period, if any, that eligible employees must complete before becoming covered by the plan; (3) the amounts of insurance to be provided; (4) the relative roles of employer and employee in paying for the insurance coverage; and (5) whether an amount of insurance coverage is to be continued for retiring employees.

Eligibility. Broad eligibility for coverage is a characteristic of almost all group life insurance plans. Results of the current and previous surveys of group life plans in higher education reveal that there is little significant difference in eligibility for coverage between faculty, administrative officers and other professional staff, and clerical-service employees. Most institutions include all permanent, full-time employees in their life insurance plan.

Eligibility rules must normally be based on conditions pertaining to employment, such as employee job classification or salary. In instances where group insurance is provided through an employee association, eligibility is based on association membership.

In assigning amounts to eligible employees, there is sufficient flexibility within which to recognize various broad categories of need. This is done by assigning insurance amounts by age, marital status, job category, rank, salary level, or combinations of these factors.

Each employee's eligibility for the plan will be covered in the definition of eligibility in the group insurance policy; the institution should use its own specific personnel terminology.

When the employer pays the entire premium, all eligible staff members automatically participate. If the employee pays a part or all of the premium, participation in the plan may be required, but it usually is made voluntary. Medical evidence of insurability is required by insurers for individuals who elect coverage more than 31 days after they become eligible.

Table 5.5. Waiting Period Before Employee Is Eligible to Participate in Group Life Insurance Plan, by Type and Control

| | Faculty[a] | | | | Clerical-Service | | | |
| | Public | | Private | | Public | | Private | |
	Percent Insts	Percent EEs	Percent Insts	Percent EEs	Percent Insts	Percent EEs	Percent Insts	Percent EEs
Four-Year Institutions	n = 433	n = 225,459	n = 769	n = 114,807	n = 430	n = 388,434	n = 741	n = 178,775
1 month or less	84.1	87.8	79.5	81.3	81.2	88.3	60.4	62.0
2 to 6 months	12.0	8.3	11.8	8.9	14.2	7.8	28.1	27.9
To plan anniversary date	3.0	2.3	3.1	1.6	2.8	1.5	1.8	0.7
Other	0.9	1.6	5.2	7.3	1.6	2.3	9.2	8.8
No response	—	—	0.4	0.4	0.2	0.1	0.5	0.6
Two-Year Institutions	n = 528	n = 59,332	n = 61	n = 1,795	n = 522	n = 58,282	n = 57	n = 1,758
1 month or less	86.9	82.8	72.2	73.9	85.8	84.9	63.2	55.1
2 to 6 months	10.2	11.9	8.2	7.9	11.5	10.8	17.5	27.4
To plan anniversary date	1.5	2.8	4.9	3.6	1.5	2.3	3.5	2.1
Other	0.6	0.6	13.1	13.9	0.8	0.8	14.0	15.2
No response	0.8	1.9	1.6	0.7	0.4	1.2	1.8	0.2

[a]Administrative and other professional personnel similar to faculty.

Waiting Period. Early plan coverage is advantageous for both employer and employee. Some delay in the coverage of newly-hired employees in an eligible category may be desired, however, in order to provide reasonable administrative time for the enrollment of the employee in the plan and for making provision for salary deductions, if any. High-turnover employee groups may be assigned a longer waiting period than other groups in order to reduce the cost of administration.

Table 5.5 shows the waiting periods for group life insurance coverage reported for faculty and for clerical-service employees in the two-year and four-year institutions, public and private.

For faculty in four-year institutions (administrative officers and other professional personnel have similar waiting periods), about four-fifths of the institutions report the relatively short waiting period of one month or less. It is frequently specified that the eligible employee may join the plan on the first of the month next following the date of employment. The proportion reporting one month or less is slightly higher among public four-year colleges and universities (84.1 percent of institutions employing 87.8 percent of faculty) than among the private institutions (79.5 percent of institutions employing 81.3 percent of faculty). A faculty waiting period of from two to six months is reported by about 12 percent of the public and private four-year institutions, representing between 8 and 9 percent of faculty. About 3 percent of plans report a waiting period that spans the period from date of employment to the next anniversary date of the plan.

While the waiting periods for clerical-service employees in four-year public institutions do not differ greatly from faculty in such institutions, waiting periods for clerical-service employees in private four-year colleges and universities tend to be longer than for faculty. Thus, a clerical-service waiting period of one month or less is reported by 60.4 percent of private four-year institutions and waiting periods of from two to six months are reported by 28 percent.

In the two-year colleges, the pattern of waiting period provisions is similar to that exhibited by four-year institutions: relatively short waiting periods for all employee classes, but with private institutions prescribing somewhat longer waiting periods for clerical-service employees than for faculty and administrative officers and professionals.

Since the previous surveys in 1968 and 1970 of the four-year and two-year institutions, respectively, there has been no significant change in length of waiting periods for faculty, but there has been an increase in the proportion of four-year institutions reporting a month or less waiting period for clerical-service personnel, from 59 percent of all four-year institutions in 1968 to 68 percent in 1978.[9] As today, waiting periods for group life coverage in four-year institutions in 1968 were somewhat longer in private institutions than in public institutions.

Waiting period and plan eligibility provisions are often combined in the same plan statement. Various approaches are illustrated in the provisions for existing plans shown below:

All active full-time permanent employees are eligible for the plan on the first day of the month coinciding with or next following the date of employment.

All active full-time permanent faculty, administrative officers and administrative staff are eligible for the plan on the first day of the month coinciding with or next following the date of entry into such class. All active full-time permanent clerical and service employees are eligible for the plan on the first day of the month coinciding with or next following three months of service in such class.

Each person employed full time (i.e., on a regular working schedule of twenty hours or more per week and not designated as temporary by the Board of Education) will become eligible to participate on the first day of the month following that in which such employment begins and will become a participant if application is made within thirty-one days after becoming eligible.

INSURANCE PATTERNS

Table 5.6 summarizes the principal methods of stating amounts of insurance in group life plans in the four-year colleges and universities, public and private. Table 5.7 gives the same information for the two-year institutions.

Among the four-year institutions there is no substantial difference between insurance allocation methods for faculty as compared with clerical-service personnel, with the exception that flat-amount allocations are reported more often for clerical-service employees by private colleges and universities than for faculty. Table 5.6 indicates that about three-quarters of the four-year institutions report insurance schedules related to salary. Consequently, they also report that insurance increases as salary increases. At the same time, some institutions provide for insurance amounts that are related to salary but decrease, after some stated point, as age advances, so that from about a quarter to a third of the institutions, according to type of institution reporting, indicate that insurance amounts decrease with age. About 90 percent of the respondents report that the insurance amount is the same for equally situated employees; these institutions include those providing insurance schedules of a level insurance amount for all employees regardless of differences in salary, or about 20 percent of the respondents. About 6 percent of the public four-year institutions and about 2 percent of the private make provision in their group life plans for the election of additional optional insurance amounts by both faculty and clerical-service employees, usually paid for by the employee, to meet additional insurance needs, if desired.

Table 5.7 shows a slightly different emphasis of insurance patterns among the two-year institutions. A higher proportion of both the public and private two-year group allocate the same insurance amount for all employees (faculty and clerical-service) than the four-year institutions, about 30 percent of the public two-year colleges and about 40 percent of the private two-year colleges. Correspondingly, a lesser proportion of the two-year than the four-year institutions report scheduling insurance as a multiple of salary. Nevertheless, among the public two-year institutions, the most frequently reported insurance pattern is a multiple of salary. Among

Table 5.6. Methods of Allocating Insurance Amounts in Group Life Insurance Plans—Four-Year Colleges and Universities

Insurance Pattern	Faculty[a]				Clerical-Service			
	Public		Private		Public		Private	
	Percent Insts	Percent EEs	Percent Insts	Percent EEs	Percent Insts	Percent EEs	Percent Insts	Percent EEs
	n = 433	n = 225,459	n = 769	n = 114,807	n = 430	n = 388,434	n = 741	n = 178,755
A.								
1. Multiple of salary	57.3	62.2	39.9	54.3	55.1	66.1	36.7	53.3
2. Job or salary category	23.6	20.1	23.0	20.8	23.7	17.6	23.2	22.6
3. Same for all EEs	18.9	17.2	21.6	11.8	20.9	17.0	28.1	16.1
4. Collective insurance	2.3	2.8	15.7	12.1	2.1	1.7	12.1	7.3
5. Other	5.8	7.0	5.7	7.9	6.5	6.2	5.3	6.1
B.								
1. Decreases with age	29.1	36.0	32.8	38.7	28.8	37.4	28.1	29.0
2. Increases with salary	73.2	74.7	50.6	61.0	71.2	76.9	47.8	63.3
3. No change—age/salary	21.9	21.4	24.6	15.9	24.7	23.1	31.3	21.1
C.								
1. Basic amount same for all equally situated EEs	92.1	93.5	88.4	89.2	91.9	93.4	88.8	86.9
2. Amount greater with dependents	0.2	0.3	3.1	2.4	0.5	0.3	3.0	2.6
3. Optional added amounts for EEs with dependents	6.7	7.7	1.8	2.4	6.7	6.5	1.8	5.8
4. Includes AD&D provision	66.1	69.9	57.9	54.2	65.8	70.4	59.1	56.7

[a]Administrative and other professional personnel similar to faculty.

Table 5.7. Methods of Allocating Insurance Amounts in Group Life Insurance Plans—Two-Year Institutions of Higher Education

Insurance Pattern	Faculty[a]				Clerical-Service			
	Public		Private		Public		Private	
	Percent Insts	Percent EEs	Percent Insts	Percent EEs	Percent Insts	Percent EEs	Percent Insts	Percent EEs
	n = 528	n = 59,332	n = 61	n = 1,795	n = 522	n = 58,282	n = 57	n = 1,758
A.								
1. Multiple of salary	42.4	43.9	26.2	39.7	40.2	41.7	28.1	37.4
2. Job or salary category	21.8	15.6	24.6	25.3	21.6	15.6	26.3	28.6
3. Same for all EEs	29.5	31.7	41.0	27.9	30.8	31.4	38.6	26.6
4. Collective insurance	2.7	4.1	9.8	10.4	2.7	6.0	8.8	10.0
5. Other	5.5	6.8	3.3	2.0	6.1	7.2	3.5	4.7
B.								
1. Decreases with age	15.5	17.1	26.2	23.2	15.7	17.9	24.6	22.0
2. Increases with salary	55.1	51.6	37.7	50.4	53.4	51.7	40.4	53.0
3. No change—age/salary	34.5	36.5	44.3	32.8	35.6	38.1	43.9	31.3
C.								
1. Basic amount same for all equally situated EEs	88.8	89.1	82.0	84.8	88.7	87.2	80.7	81.7
2. Amount greater with dependents	0.9	0.9	1.6	1.2	1.0	0.8	1.8	0.5
3. Optional added amounts for EEs with dependents	5.3	3.8	4.9	5.0	5.6	3.9	5.3	5.3
4. Includes AD&D provision	76.5	72.7	63.9	70.0	77.0	72.3	63.2	65.5

[a]Administrative and other professional personnel similar to faculty.

the private two-year institutions the most frequent pattern is the scheduling of the same amount of insurance for all employees. However, by numbers of total faculty and clerical-service employees employed by the private two-year institutions, the most frequently reported approach is the multiple of salary method, 39.7 percent of private two-year college faculty and 37.4 percent of clerical-service employees.

Four states and the District of Columbia set statutory limits on the amounts of group insurance that may be provided an employee under a group life insurance plan. Arizona and Wisconsin limit the group insurance amount to $100,000. Colorado limits it to the greater of $21,000 or 300 percent of the employee's salary. Texas limits the group insurance amount to the greater of $50,000 or 200 percent of the employee's compensation up to $100,000.[10]

Illustrations of Insurance Schedules. Illustrations of a variety of life insurance plans are offered in the following extracts from the allocation provisions of group life insurance plans in institutions of higher education. The specific provisions are not necessarily to be regarded as typical or average plans, although they include most of the major approaches.

MULTIPLE OF SALARY

The amount of your Life Insurance at any date will be equal to two times your Annual Salary as of such date. If the amount of Life Insurance is not a multiple of $1,000, such amount will be raised to the next higher multiple of $1,000. In no event will the amount of Life Insurance be less than $10,000 nor more than $100,000.

The term Annual Salary will mean your basic annual salary rate exclusive of over-time, bonuses and other forms of additional compensation.

Your amount of Life Insurance will be one and a half times your annual compensation, adjusted to the nearest $1,000. Any amount ending in $500 will be increased by $500. The insurance amount is subject to a maximum of $40,000.

For all employees who work full time or at least twenty hours per week, the life insurance amount for those who participate in the retirement plan is two times annual salary up to a maximum of $75,000, rounded upward to the nearest $500, and for those who do not participate in the retirement plan is one times annual salary up to a maximum of $37,500, rounded upward to the nearest $500.

The life insurance coverage for all employees of the College District is as follows:

Age under 50	150 percent of salary
Age 50–59	100 percent of salary
Age 60–64	50 percent of salary
Age 65 to retirement	25 percent of salary

SALARY BRACKET

Employees with Basic Annual Earnings of:	Life Insurance:
$20,000 or over	$25,000
$15,000 but less than $20,000	$20,000
$10,000 but less than $15,000	$15,000
Less than $10,000	$10,000

Basic annual earnings means annual earnings exclusive of overtime pay or any other extra compensation.

Amounts 50 percent of the above if age 65 or over when insured, or reduced 50 percent on the July 1st coinciding with or next following 65th birthday.

Schedule of Life Insurance

Employees with Base Annual Earnings of:	Life Insurance		
	Under age 65	Age 65 but under 70	Age 70 or over
Less than $5,000	$ 5,000	$ 2,500	$2,000
$5,000 but less than $6,000	7,500	3,750	2,000
$6,000 but less than $7,000	9,000	4,500	2,000
$7,000 but less than $8,000	10,500	5,250	2,000
$8,000 but less than $9,000	12,000	6,000	2,000
$9,000 but less than $10,000	13,500	6,750	2,000
$10,000 but less than $12,500	16,000	8,000	2,000
$12,500 but less than $15,000	19,000	9,500	2,000
$15,000 but less than $17,500	22,000	11,000	2,000
$17,500 but less than $20,000	25,000	12,500	2,000
$20,000 but less than $25,000	30,000	15,000	2,000
$25,000 but less than $30,000	35,000	17,500	2,000
$30,000 and over	40,000	20,000	2,000

Decreasing Insurance. A decreasing group insurance pattern coordinates well with a fully vested defined contribution retirement plan by providing the largest insurance amounts during the years when the annuity accumulation is still relatively small. A decreasing pattern also permits the insurance schedule to maximize benefits for the staff members most likely to have a financial responsibility for a young family, but who at the same time may also be at the lower end of the salary scale. And decreasing insurance patterns can concentrate these larger amounts of insurance on the younger staff at a cost that is substantially lower than if the same amounts were scheduled for the older, senior staff. This is mainly due to the steeply rising cost of term insurance at the higher ages. For example, each $1,000 of group term insurance costs about five times as much at age 55, and twelve times as much at age 65, as it does at age 35. (See table 5.10.)

As the following examples show, decreasing insurance may be scheduled by age alone, by age and salary multiples, or by units of insurance. The decreasing insurance schedules of collective life insurance are illustrated in the next section of this chapter.

Age Classification	Amount of Life Insurance
Under age 25	$50,000
25 but less than 30	45,000
30 but less than 35	40,000
35 but less than 40	35,000

Age Classification	Amount of Life Insurance
40 but less than 45	30,000
45 but less than 50	25,000
50 but less than 55	20,000
55 but less than 60	15,000
60 but less than 65	10,000
65 and over	5,000

The amount of life insurance for employees with dependents is determined by multiplying annual salary by the factor opposite the attained age according to the schedule below. For employees without dependents, the life insurance amount is one times salary at any age. Any portion of annual salary in excess of $50,000 is excluded in determining insurance amounts.

Age	Salary Multiple
Less than 35	4.0
35 but less than 40	3.5
40 but less than 45	3.0
45 but less than 50	2.5
50 but less than 55	2.0
55 but less than 60	1.5
60 and over	1.0

The amount of life insurance for all eligible employees with dependents (spouse and/or dependent children under age 19) is eight units of insurance. For all other eligible employees the amount of life insurance is four units of insurance. Insurance amounts are according to the following schedule:

Age Nearest Birthday	Amount of Insurance
Ages through 50	$40,000
51	38,000
52	36,000
53	34,000
54	32,000
55	30,000
56	28,000
57	26,000
58	24,000
59	22,000
60	20,000
61	18,000
62	16,000
63	14,000
64	12,000
65	10,000
66	8,000
67	6,000
68 and over	4,000

COLLECTIVE LIFE INSURANCE. Collective life insurance establishes another pattern of decreasing insurance by providing substantial amounts of protection at the younger ages and decreasing each year as age advances. A five-unit TIAA collective plan is illustrated. Dividends are credited as extra insurance.

**Insurance Amounts under a Five-Unit Collective
Life Insurance Plan**

Age[a]		Monthly Premium[b]	Guaranteed Death Benefit	Benefits Including 1979 Dividend[c]
Male	Female			
20	25	$5	$31,650	$63,300
25	30	5	29,300	58,600
30	35	5	26,650	53,300
35	40	5	22,400	44,800
40	45	5	15,200	30,400
45	50	5	9,550	19,100
50	55	5	6,100	12,200
55	60	5	3,850	7,700
60	65	5	2,550	5,100

[a]Insurance amounts shown only at quinquennial ages. Insurance ceases at age 70.
[b]Five units of collective life insurance at $1.00 per month per unit.
[c]1979 dividend scale for TIAA collective life insurance, not guaranteed for future years.

FLAT AMOUNTS (WITH OR WITHOUT OPTIONAL ADDITIONAL COVERAGE)

The scheduled amount of insurance for all noncontract employees, excluding administrative personnel, less than age 65, is $4,000. For all employees age 65 or more the amount of life insurance is $1,000. The principal amount of Accidental Death and Dismemberment Insurance is equal to the amount of life insurance.

The group life insurance plan provides $10,000 of coverage free of cost to each staff member. In addition, each staff member has the option of purchasing additional coverage of one and a half times gross annual compensation.

The basic benefit of the Life Insurance plan is $15,000. You may elect additional Life Insurance equal to your annual salary. The insurance amount is rounded to the lower $1,000. In no event will the overall amount of insurance exceed $100,000.

All full-time employees are provided the following group life insurance benefits:

Employee Classification	Life Insurance
Faculty and Administrative staff	$20,000
All other employees	$10,000

The plan provides the following amounts of group life insurance:

Employee Classification	Amounts
I. Academic and administrative	$20,000
II. Supervisory and clerical	$10,000
III. All other personnel	$ 5,000

Amounts of life insurance are reduced 50 percent at age 65 and reduced a further 50 percent at age 70. Life insurance terminates at retirement.

Dependent Life Insurance. Until recent years, most state insurance laws did not permit group life insurance plans to include insurance on the lives of dependents of insured employees. At present, thirty-nine states permit their insurers to write group dependent life insurance within specified limits.[11] The usual limit on the insurance amount for a spouse is the lesser of 50 percent of the employee insurance amount or a stated dollar amount, varying by state from $5,000 to $20,000. For children, the insurance amount is usually limited to $5,000, with lesser amounts provided for in some states for children under stated ages. Dependent coverage for the spouse ceases in some plans at a specified age of the spouse.

The following examples illustrate the provision of dependent insurance benefits:

Insurance for active employees is scheduled by salary bracket, ranging from $12,000 of insurance for persons earning less than $6,000 to $24,000 of insurance for persons earning $12,000 and over.

Insurance for dependents:	Amount
Spouse	$2,000
Life insurance benefits shall terminate on the date the spouse attains age 65.	
Each child under age 19*	$1,000

*To 21 years if child is dependent, unmarried, and attending school or college.

Life insurance for active employees:
A. Noncontributory—$6,000 for all nontemporary employees except those normally working less than thirty hours per week.
B. Contributory— One and one-half times annual compensation raised to the
  · $.66 per $1,000   next higher $1,000 multiple if not a $1,000 multiple.
C. Contributory— Life insurance for dependents:
    $.66 per $1,000   Spouse—$5,000
        Each child—$1,000

Life insurance amount reduced by 75 percent on attainment of age 70 or date of retirement, whichever is earlier. Insurance may not exceed $75,000. Dependents' insurance may be no greater than 50 percent of total amount of employee's life insurance, and for retired employees no more than $2,000 for spouse or $500 for child.

Coverage During Retirement. Table 5.8 indicates the extent of group life plans that continue coverage for retired employees. As the preceding illustrations show, when such coverage is continued for retirees, the insurance is normally reduced, often to a nominal amount. Table 5.8 shows that about 60 percent of four-year public institutions report some group insurance coverage for retired faculty and clerical-service employees, and that about 30 percent of private four-year institutions report this continued coverage. These private colleges and universities employ about 44 percent of faculty and 51 percent of clerical-service employees in the private four-year institutions.

Among two-year institutions, 38 percent of the public colleges and about 14 percent of the private institutions report insurance continuation for retirees.

Table 5.8. Coverage of Retired Employees under Group Life Insurance Plans

| | Faculty[a] | | | | Clerical-Service | | | |
| | Public | | Private | | Public | | Private | |
	Percent Insts	Percent EEs	Percent Insts	Percent EEs	Percent Insts	Percent EEs	Percent Insts	Percent EEs
Four-Year Institutions	n = 433	n = 225,459	n = 769	n = 114,807	n = 430	n = 388,434	n = 741	n = 178,775
Retired coverage	60.5	65.3	28.5	43.7	60.7	65.0	28.7	50.9
No retired coverage	39.3	34.6	71.4	56.3	38.8	34.5	71.2	49.0
No response	0.2	0.1	0.1	*	0.5	0.5	0.1	0.1
Two-Year Institutions	n = 528	n = 59,332	n = 61	n = 1,795	n = 522	n = 58,282	n = 57	n = 1,758
Retired coverage	38.4	38.4	14.8	13.8	38.3	35.1	14.0	8.0
No retired coverage	61.2	61.3	85.2	86.2	61.3	64.7	86.0	92.0
No response	0.4	0.3	—	—	0.4	0.2	—	—

[a]Administrative and other professional similar to faculty.
*Less than 0.1 percent.

The cost of group life insurance for retired staff members is dramatically high. For example, the cost of group life at age 70 is about eighteen times the cost at age 35 and about double the cost at age 60. As age advances, the yearly premium moves closer to the face amount of insurance. Under a noncontributory plan, an institution will spend a substantial amount if it wishes to provide even a modest program of life insurance during retirement. Unlike the insurance coverage for the active staff, every dollar of group insurance for the retired staff must inevitably be paid, perhaps only to an estate or to distant relatives. Fortunately, the need for insurance declines as insurance costs increase. By the time a person attains retirement age, dependent children have become self-supporting adults. When retirement income is begun, the individual will usually select an income option that will take the place of insurance by continuing an income for life to a spouse in the event the retired employee dies first. ERISA requires that such an income option be made available at the time the employee retires. In addition, Social Security provides for continuation of income to the widow or widower after the death of the primary beneficiary.

With respect to group life coverage for retired employees, the following questions may be considered: (1) Do retired staff members really need the insurance? (2) Is insurance protection during retirement worth its high cost? (3) If money is available, might it be more appropriately applied toward improvements in the retirement plan, greater life insurance protection for the active staff, or perhaps improvements in the health insurance plan for both active and retired employees?

CONTRIBUTIONS

Thirty-eight states require that private employers pay at least a part of the cost of a group life insurance plan. Thirty-two states require that a public employer pay a part of the cost.[12] Group life of association groups (such as state educational associations or professional organizations) may be paid for wholly by the plan participants. It is likely that some of the life insurance plans reported by a few of the institutions in the current study as paid for wholly by the employee are in fact not employer-sponsored plans but association plans to which substantial numbers of employees subscribe.

Table 5.9 shows the patterns of employer and employee contributions to the cost of group life insurance plans. In the four-year institutions, noncontributory plans are reported more frequently in the private colleges and universities than in the public institutions for both faculty and clerical-service employee groups. As in most of the other data in this survey, figures for administrative officers and other professional personnel are similar to those reported for faculty. About 40 percent of the public four-year institutions report a noncontributory plan, compared with slightly over 60 percent of the private institutions. The public group employs 38.6 percent of faculty in public four-year institutions; the private group employs just over half of total four-year private faculty. These percentages of employees repre-

Table 5.9 Employer and Employee Contributions to the Cost of Group Life Insurance Plans

| | Faculty[a] | | | | Clerical-Service | | | |
| | Public | | Private | | Public | | Private | |
	Percent Insts	Percent EEs	Percent Insts	Percent EEs	Percent Insts	Percent EEs	Percent Insts	Percent EEs
Four-Year Institutions	n = 433	n = 225,459	n = 769	n = 114,807	n = 430	n = 388,434	n = 741	n = 178,775
Employer pays full cost	40.9	38.6	60.6	51.5	40.5	34.0	62.5	53.8
Cost shared	44.1	48.3	37.3	47.8	44.3	54.8	35.2	45.6
Employee pays full cost	14.3	12.9	2.1	0.7	14.7	11.0	0.1	0.5
No response	0.7	0.2	—	—	0.5	0.2	0.1	0.1
Two-Year Institutions	n = 528	n = 59,332	n = 61	n = 1,795	n = 522	n = 58,282	n = 57	n = 1,785
Employer pays full cost	60.6	67.1	62.3	59.5	59.4	67.9	61.4	63.3
Cost shared	34.8	29.2	36.1	37.4	35.8	28.9	38.6	36.7
Employee pays full cost	4.4	3.3	—	—	4.6	2.9	—	—
No response	0.2	0.4	1.6	3.1	0.2	0.3	—	—

[a]Administrative and other professional similar to faculty.

sented by noncontributory plans for faculty are very similar to those for clerical-service personnel.

Life insurance plans for which the institution reports that the employees pay the full cost are mainly in the public sector. Between 14 and 15 percent of public four-year institutions report an employee-pay-all plan, compared with about 2 percent of private four-year institutions (employing less than 1 percent of faculty and clerical-service employees).

Sharing of group life plan costs between employer and employee is reported in four-year institutions by 44 percent of public institutions and about 35 percent of private institutions (which employ between 45 and 48 percent of faculty and clerical-service personnel).

Among the two-year educational institutions, about 60 percent of all institutions—approximately the same percentage for both public and private—pay the full group life insurance cost for faculty, administrative, and clerical-service employee groups. All the remaining plans provide for sharing of contributions by employer and employee, except for a few employee-pay-all plans reported by public institutions employing about 3 percent of faculty and clerical-service employees in the two-year public sector.

The maximum group life insurance contribution that may be made by the employee is frequently limited by statute or state insurance regulation to no more than 60 cents per month per $1,000 of insurance. Under the minimum standard monthly rate shown for the State of New York in table 5.10, a 60-cent-per-month-per-$1,000 charge is more than the group insurance premium for persons up to about age 43 and less than the premium for persons above that age. (The minimum standard rate is that required during the first policy year of a plan, except for groups transferring from one insurer to another; lower premium rates may be and usually are applied in subsequent policy years.) The 60-cent limit may be exceeded as long as the employer pays 25 percent or more of the total premium for the plan.

When the employee shares in the cost of a group life plan, care should be taken to avoid overcharging the younger employees, for whom the cost of group life is relatively low. To avoid overcharging, graded employee contributions may be established, for example, 20 cents a month per $1,000 for persons under age 30, 30 cents for persons from 30 to 39 years of age, 40 cents for persons from ages 40 to 44, and 50 cents for those aged 45 or more. In any event, the employee contribution should not be set at an amount per $1,000 of insurance that is higher than the net cost for which the individual on his own can buy TIAA or other individual life insurance.

Under contributory group life plans, the employee contribution is usually expressed as a monthly amount per $1,000 of insurance. If insurance is expressed in units, the employee contribution is normally set at an amount *per unit* of insurance; the employer pays the balance. Another contribution pattern is the payment by the employer of the same fixed amount per employee. Under collective life insurance a

Table 5.10. Monthly Premium per $1,000 of Group Life Insurance

Age Nearest Birthday[a]	Monthly Premium[b]		Age Nearest Birthday[a]	Monthly Premium[b]	
	Male	Female		Male	Female
20	$ .23	.14	60	$ 2.51	1.51
25	.25	.15	65	3.78	2.27
30	.27	.16	70	5.81	3.49
35	.32	.19	75	8.56	5.14
40	.45	.27	80	12.83	7.70
45	.68	.41	85	18.80	11.28
50	1.06	.64	90	26.62	15.97
55	1.65	.99	95	40.98	24.59

[a]Shown for quinquennial ages only.

[b]State of New York minimum first year group life renewable term insurance gross premiums, Commissioner's Standard Group Mortality Table with interest at 3 percent, effective August 1, 1961, exclusive of adjustments based on premium or insurance volume. N.Y. State Insurance Regulation No. 32, September 26, 1961. The minimum premium is not applicable to a group that is transferring its coverage from one insurer to another.

common sharing arrangement is for the college and the employee each to pay 50 cents per month toward the $1 per unit cost.

Contributory versus Noncontributory. The employer should pay at least a part of the cost of a group life insurance plan. As to the extent of employer participation in the cost, good arguments can be advanced for either an employer-pay-all plan or a plan in which the cost is shared with the employees.

Advantages frequently cited for a plan in which the employee shares the cost with the employer are: (1) benefits are larger than the employer could finance alone; (2) more effective application of employer contributions to expressed economic needs, if it is assumed that the employees who elect participation in a contributory plan are most often those with large insurance needs; (3) greater control by the employees over plan provisions and amendments, assuming that those who pay part of the cost generally expect a greater voice in plan changes and improvements; (4) greater employee awareness of the plan; employees may be more aware of the value and provisions of a benefit plan when they contribute each month to a part of the cost.

Advantages frequently cited for employer-pay-all (noncontributory) plans include: (1) certainty that all eligible employees are covered; this may be achieved, for instance, by providing a base of noncontributory insurance along with a plan of voluntary additional contributory insurance; (2) economy of installation and simplicity of administration; there are fewer accounting operations and no payroll deductions; (3) employee good will and approval of the employer's willingness to finance the whole cost; (4) employer contributions toward the first $50,000 of group life insurance are not includable in the employee's taxable income, whereas employee contributions are made from after-tax income.

A plan that provides for a modest basic amount of employer-pay-all insurance and an additional optional amount, to which the employer may make no contribution, results in an effective overall sharing of contributions with employees whose dependent situation makes the optional amount a wise investment.

PLAN OPERATION

When a plan is installed, the insurer normally makes available to the college an administration manual outlining the procedures necessary to keep the plan running smoothly. The manual includes the procedures for enrolling newly eligible employees, applying for benefit payments, premium remittance, maintenance of records, reporting individual changes in insurance amounts, and terminations of employees leaving the institution. Group life insurance plans are subject to the reporting, disclosure, and other requirements of ERISA, including the preparation of a summary plan description and annual reports.

The value of any benefit plan is enhanced by full employee understanding of the benefits provided. Newly hired or newly eligible employees should be thoroughly informed about the plan and how it coordinates with the individual's own life insurance protection. Those who have participated in the plan for some time should periodically be reminded of the protection provided. In addition to plan documents, the summary plan description, and annual reporting, employee information booklets, the faculty handbook, and the personnel policy manual offer means of presenting plan information. Staff meetings offer added opportunities for review of plan provisions and for question-and-answer sessions.

6 Health Insurance

THIS CHAPTER discusses the types of group health insurance plans reported in 1978 at colleges and universities. It is divided into two main sections: (1) basic plans, including prepaid group practice plans (HMOs) and dental insurance; and (2) major medical expense insurance plans.

Health insurance is the general term applied to insurance and prepayment plans that provide medical services or that indemnify or reimburse for the cost of hospital care, physicians' services, and other items such as prescribed medicine. The term may also include disability income insurance; in this study it is confined to plans relating directly to medical care, either insured plans or those actually involved in the delivery of services.

Health insurance protection has expanded rapidly during the last twenty-five years. The number of people who had hospital expense insurance has increased from some 77 million in 1950 to about 177 million in 1976. Health insurance may be obtained by individuals through the purchase of an individual contract or by employers through employee group coverage. Group coverage has grown at a far greater rate than individual coverage, largely through the lower cost of mass-marketing this product, the tax advantages associated with group as opposed to individual insurance, and economies of scale. Group premiums earned by insurance companies in 1976 accounted for about 80 percent of annual health insurance premiums in the United States.[1]

The purpose of health insurance is to substitute a known, moderate, regular payment (e.g., a monthly premium) for an unknown and potentially large expense. Up to a certain level it seems reasonable to assume that an individual should pay the cost of routine items of medical care out of regular family income. But in cases requiring hospitalization, surgery, or prolonged or complex medical treatment, costs may quickly exceed the "routine" and put a strain on a family's financial resources. Basic health insurance provides a mechanism for meeting some of these nonroutine medical costs, especially those involving hospitalization. In the case of a serious illness or accident, the costs of medical treatment can easily exceed the levels of coverage under a basic plan. At this point the supplementary benefits of major medical coverage become increasingly important.

Nearly 100 percent of four-year institutions—both public and private—provide some type of health insurance. At two-year institutions, coverage is provided by over 99 percent of public and about 91 percent of private institutions. Considering all institutions included in the current study, 99.8 percent of all employees are covered by some type of health insurance.

Group health insurance is usually provided in one or more of the following forms: (1) a basic hospital-surgical-medical plan; (2) a basic plan plus a supplementary major medical expense plan; (3) a single comprehensive plan combining features of both basic and major medical plans; or (4) independent prepaid medical service plans with accompanying provisions for hospital coverage. Table 6.1 summarizes the overall reporting of health insurance plans.

TYPES OF HEALTH INSURANCE COVERAGE

Many institutions have more than one health plan. One reason is that about a fifth of the colleges and universities reporting a basic hospital-surgical-medical plan report a separate supplementary major medical expense insurance plan. Also, in a number of institutions the employees may select coverage under one or more alternative plans, such as prepaid community group practice plans, generally described as health maintenance organizations. The result is that in some of the following tables the number of health insurance plans exceeds the number of reporting institutions.

The *types* of health insurance coverage available to employees of colleges and universities are summarized in table 6.2. For faculty, the types of coverage may be summarized as follows: at four-year institutions, nearly 99 percent of public and 95 percent of private institutions provide a basic hospital-surgical-medical plan. Major medical insurance is reported by 99 percent of public and 96 percent of private institutions. Health maintenance organizations are reported by 25 percent of public and 21 percent of private institutions. Thirty percent of public and 9 percent of private institutions report dental care insurance; 15 percent of public and 2 percent of private have a vision care insurance option. These percentages for coverage of faculty differ only slightly for the coverage of administrators and clerical-service employees at four-year institutions.

For two-year institutions, the types of health insurance coverage available follow very closely the percentages described above for faculty at four-year institutions. The only exception occurs in the availability of an HMO option; in the private sector, two-year institutions are far less likely to provide this type of coverage than four-year institutions.

A large majority of all institutions, around 80 percent, report that their basic hospital-surgical-medical plan is part of a comprehensive health plan that includes major medical insurance protection. At the remaining institutions there is usually a basic hospital-surgical-medical plan supplemented by a major medical plan.

Dental insurance was envisioned by organized dentistry as a means of encourag-

Table 6.1. Group Health Insurance Plan Coverage in Institutions of Higher Education (percent of institutions reporting plans and percent of employees in institutions reporting plans)

| | Faculty[a] | | | | Clerical-Service | | | |
| | Public | | Private | | Public | | Private | |
	Percent Insts	Percent EEs	Percent Insts	Percent EEs	Percent Insts	Percent EEs	Percent Insts	Percent EEs
Four-Year Institutions	n = 478	n = 242,041	n = 929	n = 121,162	n = 478	n = 413,110	n = 929	n = 188,601
Health Ins. plan in effect	100.0	100.0	98.2	99.6	100.0	100.0	98.0	99.8
No plan	—	—	1.7	0.4	—	—	2.0	0.2
No response	—	—	0.1	*	—	—	—	—
Two-Year Institutions	n = 600	n = 66,915	n = 85	n = 2,284	n = 600	n = 66,748	n = 85	n = 2,482
Health ins. plan in effect	99.1	99.6	91.7	96.2	99.3	99.8	90.6	97.3
No plan	0.7	0.3	7.1	3.0	0.5	0.2	8.2	2.3
No response	0.2	0.1	1.2	0.8	0.2	*	1.2	0.4

[a] Administrative and other professional personnel similar to faculty.
* Less than 0.1%.

Table 6.2. Types of Health Insurance Coverage Reported by Institutions of Higher Education

| | Faculty[a] | | | | Clerical-Service | | | |
| | Public | | Private | | Public | | Private | |
	Percent Insts	Percent EEs	Percent Insts	Percent EEs	Percent Insts	Percent EEs	Percent Insts	Percent EEs
Four-Year Institutions	n = 478	n = 242,041	n = 912	n = 120,620	n = 478	n = 413,110	n = 910	n = 188,185
Basic hospital-surgical-medical	98.3	97.9	94.8	96.7	99.0	99.2	95.2	97.3
Major medical	99.2	99.2	95.9	97.5	99.0	97.5	94.1	95.9
HMO	24.9	32.3	21.4	46.6	27.4	38.6	21.1	50.1
Dental care	30.1	27.7	9.2	5.9	30.1	24.3	10.2	7.7
Vision care	14.6	14.5	2.0	2.4	14.4	19.3	2.7	5.6
Two-Year Institutions	n = 595	n = 66,689	n = 78	n = 2,197	n = 596	n = 66,620	n = 77	n = 2,415
Basic hospital-surgical-medical	97.3	97.1	94.9	95.4	98.2	97.9	96.1	97.3
Major medical	97.8	98.1	91.0	92.9	97.5	97.4	89.6	91.0
HMO	21.5	34.6	2.6	3.0	22.0	37.2	2.6	3.1
Dental care	36.8	49.4	9.0	11.5	35.7	47.4	9.1	10.4
Vision care	11.6	19.4	—	—	10.2	18.1	—	—

[a]Administrative and other professional personnel similar to faculty.

ing regular examinations and treatment for the maintenance of good oral health. Unlike medical insurance, which is geared to treatment after illness strikes, dental insurance attempts to promote regular preventive treatment as a way to minimize serious and expensive problems later. In 1968, only about 6 million Americans were receiving dental care under prepayment programs. In 1978, more than 48 million workers, their spouses, and their families had dental coverage under 170 insurance and service plans.[2] Among colleges and universities surveyed in 1978, dental insurance is reported more often by public than by private institutions. At four-year institutions, dental insurance is provided by 30 percent of public and 9 percent of private institutions; at two-year institutions, it is available at 37 percent of public and 9 percent of private.

Vision plans for regular vision care, a relatively new development in group health insurance, are more likely to be available at public institutions, either four-year or two-year, than at private institutions. The percentages for faculty range from 12 percent at two-year public to 15 percent at four-year public and from zero at two-year private to 2 percent at four-year private.

Maternity benefit coverage was made mandatory on October 31, 1978, when President Carter signed into law amendments to the 1964 Civil Rights Act. The act prohibits employers of fifteen or more full-time employees from discriminating against any individual because of, among other reasons, the individual's sex. The 1978 amendments incorporated pregnancy and childbirth within the meaning of the term "sex" as areas in which discrimination is prohibited.[3] Employers must now treat pregnant women like any other employee. The same fringe benefits, including medical and disability benefits, that are provided to others must also be provided to pregnant employees. In the past, benefits for pregnancy were usually either excluded or eliminated from medical and disability plans.

Insurers are responding to the new law by adding benefits for pregnancy and childbirth to medical and disability plans. The law does not require employers to provide health insurance for abortion, except where the life of the mother would be otherwise endangered or where medical complications have arisen from an abortion. Employers are thereby given the choice of providing benefits in such a situation or not.

TYPES OF HEALTH INSURERS

The types of insurers reported by the colleges and universities for their health insurance coverage are shown in table 6.3.

Among four-year institutions, health insurance plans underwritten by insurance companies, including TIAA, are reported for faculty by 43 percent of public and 55 percent of private institutions; for clerical-service employees, the comparable figures are 42 percent for public and 52 percent for private institutions. Among two-year institutions, health insurance is underwritten by an insurance company at 40

Table 6.3. Types of Insurers Reported for Health Insurance Coverage by Institutions of Higher Education

| | Faculty[a] | | | | Clerical-Service | | | |
| | Public | | Private | | Public | | Private | |
	Percent Insts	Percent EEs	Percent Insts	Percent EEs	Percent Insts	Percent EEs	Percent Insts	Percent EEs
Four-Year Institutions	n = 478	n = 242,041	n = 912	n = 120,620	n = 478	n = 413,110	n = 910	n = 188,185
Blue Cross	68.6	69.4	60.3	72.7	68.8	75.5	61.4	76.3
Blue Shield	62.3	62.8	54.5	65.8	62.6	69.8	55.3	68.9
Insurance co.[b]	42.7	42.3	54.7	54.4	42.1	42.7	51.9	51.3
Self-insured	9.4	8.9	2.7	2.4	9.4	7.5	2.6	2.3
Other	13.6	19.6	14.1	17.7	13.4	24.5	14.1	17.8
No response	—		—		—		—	
Two-Year Institutions	n = 595	n = 66,689	n = 78	n = 2,197	n = 596	n = 66,620	n = 77	n = 2,415
Blue Cross	70.4	75.1	67.9	74.6	70.6	74.1	67.5	72.7
Blue Shield	56.8	55.5	65.4	72.0	57.2	54.5	64.9	68.7
Insurance co.[b]	40.0	41.6	37.2	33.1	38.3	42.6	35.1	37.0
Self-insured	5.0	4.2	2.6	1.2	5.0	4.4	2.6	0.5
Other	15.8	26.3	6.4	7.9	15.8	27.8	6.5	5.6
No response	—		—		—		—	

[a] Administrative and other professional personnel similar to faculty.
[b] Includes TIAA plans.

percent of public and 37 percent of private institutions for faculty, and at 38 percent of public and 35 percent of private institutions for clerical-service employees.

At four-year institutions, Blue Cross coverage is reported by 69 percent of public and 60 percent of private institutions for faculty, and is nearly identical for clerical-service employees. The percentage of two-year institutions providing Blue Cross coverage for both faculty and clerical-service employees is about 70 percent for public and 68 percent for private institutions.

At four-year institutions, Blue Shield base plans are reported for faculty by 62 percent of public and 54 percent of private institutions, and for clerical-service employees, by 63 percent of public and 55 percent of private institutions. At two-year institutions, a Blue Shield plan is in effect for both faculty and clerical-service employees at around 57 percent of public and 65 percent of private institutions.

Among all institutions participating in the survey of higher education, prepaid group medical practice plans, or HMOs, are available at 22 percent of institutions.

BASIC HOSPITAL-SURGICAL-MEDICAL PLANS

Basic health insurance protection insures against the costs of ordinary hospital expense, surgical expense and, to a lesser extent, other medical costs. Covered expenses incurred in a hospital generally include semi-private room and board and miscellaneous hospital services and supplies, such as laboratory services, X-ray examinations, drugs, medicines, and use of an operating room. Surgical expense coverage helps pay the physician's charges for surgery performed either in a hospital or doctor's office. Medical expense coverage provides benefits toward physicians' fees for nonsurgical care given in a hospital, home, or doctor's office, although coverage for home or office visits is generally available only under HMOs.

Origin of Basic Plans. Health insurance as we now define it was not developed until the early 1930s. Earlier, such protection was available only in the form of replacement of lost income for a time or payment of a lump sum amount. The emphasis on income replacement insurance continued until 1929. The economic hardships worked by the Great Depression of the thirties gave rise to the need to distinguish between loss of earned income due to disability and the extra demands made on income by medical expenses, specifically hospital bills. This led to the development of the nonprofit Blue Cross hospital service plans, which foreshadowed the development of insurance company reimbursement policies for hospital and surgical care. (The predecessor of the Blue Cross organizations was a group hospital plan for a local teachers' association established in 1929 by Baylor University Hospital, Dallas, Texas.) Nonprofit Blue Shield plans were added to the health care landscape in 1939 to help pay for specified physicians' services rendered principally in hospitals. These developments met two pressing needs: hospitals faced empty beds and declining revenues in a period of economic depression. Individuals faced the virtual impossibility of financing hospital and medical care without a systematic means of prepayment or insurance. The changes that took place met the needs of the times and continue as the broad base of today's approaches. Group health plans increased rapidly during World War II; with industrial wages frozen, they became an important element in collective bargaining for employee benefits. The postwar role of group health insurance was established in part by the U.S. Supreme Court decision that employee benefits, including health insurance, were a legitimate part of the bargaining process by which labor negotiated its contracts with management.[4]

Types of Basic Benefits. Group health insurance plans provide employees and their dependents with either an *indemnity* or a *service* benefit for the care specified. The Blue Cross hospital plans are by far the most numerous service plan arrangements. Here the benefit is in the form of the care or service rendered. Most Blue Cross plans compensate participating hospitals for their services on the basis of reimbursement contracts with the hospitals. When a covered individual is hospitalized, designated services are provided without charge to him or her; costs for non-designated services are billed to the individual directly. In some geographical areas full services for hospital and medical care are provided under prepaid community group practice plans, either in association with Blue Cross hospital plans or through their own closely related hospital service units.

Indemnity plans provide for a cash payment to the insured when the individual or his or her dependents incur a covered expense. Insurance company hospital-surgical-medical plans and Blue Shield or medical society surgical-medical plans are generally of the indemnity type.

Role of Base Plans in Medical Protection. Allocations from regular family income and savings may be reasonably expected to meet needs for routine items of medical care. But when medical expenses begin to accumulate, most people need financial help. Hospitalization is one point of presumed need, and this is the point at which basic plans commonly step in.

Although base plans meet real needs, a serious illness or accident can result in expenses considerably in excess of their limits. Hence, basic health insurance plans are not the total answer to the need for protection; they are almost always accompanied by major medical expense insurance.

Insurance Company Plans. The basic plans of commercial insurance companies differ from one another much more than do the Blue Cross and Blue Shield plans. The particular array of benefits and dollar levels under a plan depend on the choice of the individual employer.

Under insurance company basic plans, hospital costs, usually divided between charges for room and board and charges for necessary services, drugs, and supplies, are reimbursed to the individual on the basis of the providers' stated charge (the indemnity-type benefit). Reimbursement for room and board is generally based on the cost of a semiprivate room in the geographic area where the group is located up to a specified daily limit, such as $80. (Ninety percent of newly issued plans now provide daily room and board benefits of $50 or more.) A weakness of the daily maximum approach is that in periods of rapidly rising hospital costs, the stated daily maximum benefit may soon be much lower than the average local semiprivate room and board charge. A maximum is also set on the number of days for which the benefit will be paid, typically from 70 to 120 days, although longer periods are not uncommon. If a private room is used, the individual pays the difference between the average cost of a semiprivate room and the cost of the private room.

Surgical expense benefits under insurance company plans are usually offered in combination with a hospital expense policy, and include charges for surgery, whether performed in a hospital or a doctor's office. Benefit payments under surgical expense insurance are usually made according to a schedule of surgical procedures in the policy that lists the maximum amount of benefits for each type of operation covered. Among recently issued plans, eight in ten employees with basic surgical expense coverage had plans with maximum benefits of $1,000 or more.[5] Sometimes the benefit limit is stated in the form of reimbursement up to the "usual and customary" charges, in which case surgical schedules are not used. Usual and customary charge is defined as not more than the amount normally charged by most providers of a comparable service in the locality where the service is received.

At the close of 1976, some 163 million persons had regular medical expense insurance which helps pay physician's fees for nonsurgical care in a hospital, home or doctor's office. There are usually maximum benefits for specific services, which sometimes include diagnostic X-ray and laboratory expenses.[6]

A category of necessary services and supplies typically covers charges for drugs, medicines, use of the operating room, and ambulance service (whether charged by the hospital or other party). Reimbursement for these charges is usually expressed in terms of either a *multiple* of the room and board daily benefit and/or a specified dollar maximum, with charges in excess of the maximum subject to coinsurance, the insurer paying a percentage of the excess charges and the individual insured paying the balance. In either case, an overall maximum may or may not be applied.

Other types of benefits that may be provided under an insurance company group health contract are benefits for diagnostic X-ray and laboratory examination expenses—covering costs of such treatment when the individual is not confined to a hospital; radiotherapy—providing payment toward the cost of radiological treatment; home health care—reimbursing the cost of skilled nursing care in order to avoid prolonged institutional confinement when care could be provided at a lower cost at home; extended care facility—providing reimbursement for the cost of skilled nursing care in an institution specializing in such care. This last type of benefit helps hold down total costs by covering the transferral of patients from the more expensive care provided in a hospital, but it is not intended to provide for care that is primarily custodial.

Many insurance company plans incorporate supplemental accident expense insurance for reimbursement of medical expenses that exceed, or are not covered under, other parts of the base plan and which are incurred within ninety days after an accident. Benefits are payable for accidents only and often cover the costs of hospital care, treatment by a physician, registered graduate nursing care, and X-ray and laboratory examinations. Benefits, subject to an overall maximum such as $300, may be applied to the difference between the base plan's daily room and board maximum and a hospital's higher regular semiprivate charge, or to charges above the plan's overall maximum benefit, or to fees for services of special nurses, physicians or surgeons, or to the cost of medical supplies.

Blue Cross. There are currently sixty-nine regional Blue Cross insurance plans. In 1976 they paid hospitals over $26 billion.[7] Some 20 percent of the total U.S. population is covered by a Blue Cross plan.

A group contract between Blue Cross and the employer sets forth all the details of the benefit coverage of the employees and their dependents. Employees receive an individual or family certificate describing benefits. Employee contributions toward the cost are made by salary deduction. Blue Cross participants who are cared for in a noncontracting hospital usually receive a cash benefit instead of a service benefit.

Most Blue Cross service benefits provide for a specified number of days of care per hospital confinement in semiprivate accommodations. Periods of full benefit vary among plans and are sometimes followed by periods of half benefit in which the plan pays 50 percent of the hospital's regular daily semiprivate charge. Typical periods of coverage per confinement are 21 days of full benefit followed by 90 days of half benefit, or from 30 to 365 days of full care per confinement.

Blue Cross service benefits in semiprivate accommodations typically include room and board, special diets, general nursing service, use of equipment, use of operating and treatment rooms, and drugs and medicines required during hospitalization. The following services are also included when rendered as a regular service provided by the hospital: laboratory examinations, X-ray examinations, electrocardiograms, basal metabolism tests, physical therapy, oxygen and its administration, anesthesia and its administration, administration of blood and plasma (but not the cost of the blood or plasma itself), and intravenous injections.

When a hospital patient uses private instead of semiprivate accommodations, Blue Cross plans provide an allowance toward the cost of the private room and board. In some plans the allowance is a specified daily dollar amount. In others it is an allowance equal to the hospital's minimum, average, or most common semiprivate rate. The difference between the room and board allowance and the charge is billed to the patient.

Maternity benefits have normally been available under Blue Cross plans after nine or ten months of participation. Maternity benefits were usually limited to a specified dollar amount of hospital charges for such care, or to a specified number of days of care, including use of the delivery room, ordinary nursery care, and diaper service during the in-hospital period. With the recent amendments to the 1964 Civil Rights Act, we can expect to see Blue Cross provide the same level of benefits for maternity as for sickness or surgery.

For hospital emergency outpatient treatment, Blue Cross generally provides full service in contracting hospitals for emergency accident care within twenty-four hours, or sometimes seventy-two hours, of the accident.

Normally excluded from Blue Cross basic coverage is hospitalization primarily for diagnostic studies, physical therapy, X-ray therapy, radium therapy, or convalescence. For a small number of health conditions Blue Cross benefits are either excluded or limited; these include chronic alcoholism, drug addiction, mental disorders, and pulmonary tuberculosis.

Enrollment of new employees in Blue Cross plans is normally made at times specified in the group contract. Enrollment of new employees may be monthly, quarterly, or during a specified period following employment, such as thirty or sixty days. To be covered as a dependent, a new spouse must be enrolled within a specified number of days after marriage. In most states children are covered as dependents from birth to the end of the year in which the child reaches age 19. After age 19, children may obtain individual direct-pay contracts. Unmarried children between the ages of 19 and 23 are also often considered eligible dependents if they are full-time students.

A stated percentage of enrollment of eligible employees must be maintained in Blue Cross plans. Typically, a higher percentage enrollment is required of smaller groups. The requirements, which differ among plans, may range from 40 or 50 percent for groups of five hundred or more, to 100 percent for groups of less than ten.

Blue Shield. These plans offer basic surgical-medical insurance coverage. As with the nonprofit hospital plans, various regional names are used to identify the Blue Shield plan.

Most Blue Shield plans operate in coordination with the local Blue Cross plan, with premium billing, enrollment, and other business carried on through consolidated procedures. As under Blue Cross, employee contributions, if any, are paid by salary deduction, and an employee who leaves a group may continue Blue Shield coverage by paying the premium directly.

Blue Shield plans cover specified surgical procedures performed in the hospital, the doctor's office or on home visits, and doctor's visits to a hospitalized patient. The level of benefit provided is based on a schedule listing maximum dollar amounts that will be paid for specific procedures.

Many Blue Shield plans provide a choice among surgical fee schedules at the time of each individual's enrollment, with a higher premium charged for the higher schedule. For example, one scale might range from $5 for minor to $200 for major surgery, another from $5 to $550. For doctors' visits in the hospital, one schedule might provide $10 for the first visit and lesser amounts for the remainder of the period up to a total dollar limit. Some Blue Shield plans include certain additional benefits, such as specified amounts for X-ray diagnosis (sometimes limited to fractures and dislocations), pathological analysis, treatment by radiation therapy in lieu of surgery, and general anesthesia services by a doctor in a hospital. Surgical policies usually impose a waiting period for some common surgical procedures to minimize "adverse selection" by the insured.

Because of the variation in charges in different areas of the United States, both Blue Cross and Blue Shield have developed indexes that indicate the value of one procedure in relation to another rather than in terms of absolute dollar amounts. More recently, Blue Shield has begun offering surgical benefits without specific schedules, limiting reimbursement instead to "usual, customary, and reasonable" charges.

Prepaid Group Medical Practice Plans. Prepaid group medical practice plans developed in part out of a belief that they could provide greater cost control through emphasis on preventive medicine in keeping patients healthy and through a peer review process that would be more likely to be effective in a group practice setting. The plans usually emphasize broad, comprehensive coverage, with physicians paid on a salary rather than a fee-for-service basis. These plans, originally known as community group plans, are now frequently described as health maintenance organizations (HMOs).

To help provide an alternative system of health care delivery and reduce and eliminate some of the problems of the existing delivery systems, Congress passed the Health Maintenance Organization Act of 1973. The act was intended to spur development of HMOs through provision of federal grants, contracts, and loan guarantees for their planning and development. Certain requirements under the legislation that actually impeded the development of HMOs were modified in amendments to the act in 1976. Section 1310 of the act mandated a dual choice option whereby an employer having twenty-five employees living in a federally qualified HMO geographic service area must if approached offer participation in the HMO as an alternative to the existing group medical coverage.

HMOs may be sponsored by insurance companies, Blue Cross-Blue Shield plans, government hospitals, medical schools, medical societies, consumer groups, universities, unions, and other organizations. The Kaiser Foundation Health Plan, a comprehensive group community medical practice founded in 1938, is usually referred to as the prototype of today's HMO. As of August 1978, there were 199 federally qualified HMOs, a 21-percent increase over the previous year.[8]

HMOs provide doctors' services for home, office, and hospital visits, and for surgery. Their coverage includes preventive medicine, diagnosis, regular medical treatment, specialists' care, physical examinations, pediatric checkups for children, immunization, eye examinations for glasses, laboratory tests, X-ray, and radiation and physiotherapy treatments. Under some plans the individual can elect to pay a lower premium rate in exchange for agreeing to pay a small charge for each visit to the doctor.

Some of the HMOs provide their hospital benefits under a Blue Cross plan. Where the group operates its own hospital, as does the Kaiser plan, hospital care is usually provided as a stated number of days of full care per illness, such as 365, or days of full care followed by days of half care, such as 125 days of full care for each illness, followed by 240 days at half the prevailing semiprivate rate. Full coverage of the following is normally included: drugs in the hospital, X-ray, laboratory tests, physical therapy, general nursing, use of equipment, use of operating and treatment rooms. Provision is usually made for low-cost purchase of prescription drugs out of the hospital.

For persons who require emergency hospital care when temporarily away from the group service area, the service plans normally will pay up to $1,000, or in some plans $2,000, for the cost of such care. In addition, provision is usually made for reimbursement of related emergency physicians' fees.

GROUP MAJOR MEDICAL EXPENSE INSURANCE

Group major medical expense insurance is designed to provide coverage for large, unpredictable expenses—the higher costs associated with prolonged illness or serious injury that can easily amount to thousands or tens of thousands of dollars. Lesser medical expenses are usually handled through base plan coverage or through regular family budgeting.

Major medical plans were introduced nationally by insurance companies in 1951; until that time coverage had concentrated on first-dollar protection for basic medical expenses, with the upper limits of protection largely oriented toward acute, short-term protection. A 1956 Ford Foundation grant to Teachers Insurance and Annuity Association (TIAA), following a TIAA study of medical insurance needs in the colleges, provided developmental expenses and contingency reserves for the introduction of major medical expense insurance specifically designed for educational institutions. Today, provision of some form of major medical coverage at colleges and universities is nearly universal. Table 6.2, earlier in this chapter, summarizes the extent of major medical coverage currently reported.

Since its introduction, the growth of major medical has been more rapid than that of any other form of health insurance. Its rapid development has coincided with continued dramatic increases in medical care costs, a socioeconomic problem that continues to defy solution. Table 6.4 shows that except for the cost of prescriptions and drugs, price indexes of medical care items have continued to rise more rapidly than the Consumer Price Index for all consumer items.

Major medical protection is usually offered either as a supplemental major medical expense insurance plan added on top of a separate base plan, or as a comprehensive plan in which one insurer provides both types of coverage under a single plan. A majority of institutions offer a single comprehensive insurance plan and/or an HMO which includes hospitalization benefits and covers a full range of health care.

Major medical benefits are paid toward virtually all kinds of health care costs prescribed by a physician, including the cost of treatment given in and out of the hospital, special nursing care, X-rays, prescriptions, medical appliances, nursing home care, and many other health care needs.

In establishing or revising major medical coverage, careful thought should be given to the features of the plan that determine when medical expenses become "ma-

Table 6.4. Consumer Price Indices for Medical Care Items in the United States (1967 = 100.0)

Year	CPI All Items	All Medical Care Items	Physicians' Fees	Dentists' Fees	Semiprivate Hospital Room Rates	Prescriptions and Drugs
1950	72.1	53.7	55.2	63.9	30.3	88.5
1955	80.2	64.8	65.4	73.0	42.3	94.7
1960	88.7	79.1	77.0	82.1	57.3	104.5
1965	94.5	89.5	88.3	92.2	75.9	100.2
1966	97.2	93.4	93.4	95.2	83.5	100.5
1967	100.0	100.0	100.0	100.0	100.0	100.0
1968	104.2	106.1	105.6	105.5	113.6	100.2
1969	109.8	113.4	112.9	112.9	128.8	101.3
1970	116.3	120.6	121.4	119.4	145.4	103.6
1971	121.3	128.4	129.8	127.0	163.1	105.4
1972	125.3	132.5	133.8	132.3	173.9	105.6
1973	133.1	137.7	138.2	136.4	182.1	105.9
1974	147.7	150.5	150.9	146.8	201.5	109.6
1975	161.2	168.6	169.4	161.9	236.1	118.8
1976	170.5	184.7	188.5	172.2	268.6	126.0
1977	181.5	202.4	206.0	185.1	299.5	134.1
1978	195.3	219.4	223.3	199.3	331.6	132.1

SOURCE: U.S. Department of Labor, Bureau of Labor Statistics.

jor" and to the provisions that govern reimbursement. These considerations will include the amount of the cash deductible and the accumulation period, a coinsurance percentage, the benefit period, and the maximum level of benefits.

Cash Deductible Amount. The cash deductible amount is the out-of-pocket amount (not reimbursed by a basic hospital-surgical-medical plan) paid by the individual for covered medical expenses before reimbursement begins under the major medical plan. Use of a cash deductible helps hold down the insurer's cost by eliminating small, routine expenses. In most major medical plans all covered expenses incurred by an individual, regardless of cause, are combined for the purpose of satisfying the cash deductible. The period of time during which the cash deductible must be satisfied by the insured is the *deductible accumulation period*. When stated in months, the usual period is three months, and the deductible must be satisfied in a period of three consecutive months or less. More commonly, the deductible accumulation period is defined as the calendar year, January 1 to December 31.

Coinsurance. This feature, like the deductible amount, aims at helping to keep overall plan costs reasonable by giving the individual a personal stake in the size of his or her medical bills. The coinsurance percentage, usually 20 percent, is the percentage of covered medical expenses above the cash deductible amount that the insured individual must pay and for which there is no reimbursement under the major medical plan. A comprehensive major medical expense plan (not supplementary to a base plan) may provide an area of full reimbursement (no coinsurance) for a stated amount of covered charges, such as the first $1,000; other charges are then reimbursed, after the cash deductible, on a regular coinsurance basis. Recently, because of the burden imposed by the rapidly rising cost of medical care, some plans have set a dollar limit on the amount of out-of-pocket expenses that must be borne by the insured by eliminating coinsurance for the expenses within an insured period above a specified amount, such as $5,000.

The Benefit Period. Once the deductible has been satisfied within the prescribed period, a benefit period begins and major medical benefits are paid for covered expenses. The benefit period runs for a prescribed length of time. When the benefit period has terminated, the insured individual must again pay the cash deductible amount in order to establish another benefit period.

The benefit period may be based on a calendar year, continuing through December 31, or on a benefit year, continuing for a period of twelve consecutive months starting from the date of the first covered expense used to satisfy the deductible.

Under calendar or benefit year plans the individual has to satisfy a new deductible each year even though major medical expenses continue, and benefits are continued until the end of the calendar or benefit year even when covered expenses become very light. To prevent an individual from having to satisfy two deductibles in quick succession, calendar year plans generally provide that any part of the deductible that applies to expenses occurring in the last three months of a year will be credited toward the deductible payable in the following year.

The two- or three-year benefit period plans provide longer maximum benefit periods than either the calendar or benefit year methods. Under a "continued expense" plan, the benefit period, which is figured from the date of the first expense used to satisfy the deductible amount, continues until whichever occurs first: (a) the end of three years, or (b) the end of any three consecutive months during which covered expenses, exclusive of any paid by a base plan, have not exceeded a certain amount, such as $50. This is a "continued expense" test.

The continued expense plan is designed to continue uninterrupted benefits during a period that will normally be long enough to meet the major needs of a serious illness or accident. The three-month continued expense test helps keep plan costs down by eliminating payments for lesser medical expenses once the period of major expenses has ended.

The deductible and the benefit periods are normally applied separately to each member of a family. Where charges are incurred as a result of a common accident sustained by two or more insured members of a family, expenses are usually combined to satisfy only one deductible amount, which then establishes a benefit period for each injured person. Each person continues to have his or her own separate maximum benefit amount.

A *reinstatement provision* is usually included to avoid penalizing insured persons who may have exhausted their benefits but have recovered to the extent of again being acceptable insurance risks. Reinstatement may be based on submitting evidence of insurability or may be more automatic in its operation. An example of the latter is a plan that restores some or all of the maximum if the insured does not incur medical expenses of more than a specified amount, such as $1,000 or $5,000, during a given period, such as six months. Since it is common today to find lifetime (all cause) maximums as high as $1,000,000, and even plans with unlimited benefits, the reinstatement provision does not have the significance it had in the past.

Maximum Benefits. These may range from $10,000 to $250,000 per person and higher, and in some cases are unlimited, subject to deductibles and coinsurance. A 1977 survey of new group insurance coverage by the Health Insurance Association of America showed that 90 percent of those with comprehensive major medical expense plans had maximum benefits of $100,000 or more available to them, and 57 percent had available to them benefits which could go up to $1 million or had no limit.[9]

All Cause Approach. In most major medical plans all covered expenses incurred by an individual, regardless of cause, are combined for the purpose of the deductible, benefit period, and maximum benefit amount. After a person has paid the deductible amount, he or she receives the benefits for any and all subsequent covered expenses incurred during the remainder of the benefit period up to the maximum benefit amount. This *all cause* approach recognizes that a person's budget is hit just as hard by medical expenses whether they arise from one or from several causes.

An alternative approach, rarely used today, is the per cause method, in which each illness or accident is treated separately for the purpose of the deductible, the benefit period, and usually the maximum benefit amount.

Scope of Coverage. Group major medical plans normally insure employees and their eligible dependents, including unmarried children to age 19 and unmarried children age 19 to 23 who are full-time students and dependent on the employee for support. Relatively few expense limitations are placed on major medical coverage. The full cost of semiprivate hospital accommodations is normally a covered medical expense under major medical plans. However, a maximum is placed on the daily hospital charges allowable for private accommodations. There are no "inside limits," such as scheduled allowances for specified surgical charges or doctors' visits, or numbers of days of hospitalization allowed, as under basic health insurance plans. The broad "reasonable and customary" rule governs the level of doctors' fees that are reimbursable.

A few expenses are generally not covered by major medical insurance, such as eye examinations, glasses, hearing aids, expenses incurred in a government hospital, sickness or injury resulting from war, and dental treatment except for treatment of injuries sustained in an accident. Covered expenses under major medical do not include expenses incurred on account of sickness or injury arising out of or in the course of employment to the extent that benefits are payable under applicable Workers' Compensation laws or similar statutes.

Expenses for treatment of mental or nervous disorders while confined in a hospital are usually covered on the same basis as other expenses incurred in a hospital, although some plans place a limit on days of care, or on maximum applicable benefits, or both, and some change the 80-20 coinsurance to 50-50 after a stated number of days in the hospital. Treatment of mental or nervous disorders when an individual is not confined in the hospital is frequently not covered or, if covered, is limited; limits may be placed on numbers of visits to the doctor that will be covered and on the dollar amount of covered charges per visit. The coinsurance percentage is usually set at 50-50.

Some provision is usually made for continuation of major medical coverage for employees who become disabled. Generally, if an employee is disabled when employment terminates, the employer has the option of continuing major medical expense insurance coverage.

In some instances, when a major medical plan supplements a base plan, employees are required to participate in the base plan in order to be eligible for major medical. In other instances, the employee may choose either combined major medical and base plan coverage, or one plan without the other. When the major medical deductible is the same for all participants, the cost of major medical coverage for those who do not participate in the base plan will be higher than if they also had base plan coverage. This is the case because major medical benefits begin sooner in the absence of base plan benefits; consequently, a higher premium contribution is usually required for persons not participating in the base plan.

On the other hand, some major medical plans require the same contribution for major medical coverage regardless of each employee's decision as to basic coverage, but incorporate deductibles that differ according to the extent of employee participation in a base plan. For example, persons with neither basic hospital nor surgical-medical coverage would have a deductible of $1,000 under the major medical plan, with the deductible amount declining for employees with only surgical-medical coverage or only hospital coverage.

OPERATION OF HEALTH INSURANCE PLANS

The master contract between the insurer and the employer sets forth the type of health insurance plan in effect and states in contract language the benefits provided. Where separate basic and major medical plans are in operation, there will be two master contracts. Where a health insurance plan is offered by a state teacher or employee association, the contract is between the association and the insurer.

The insurer administers the benefits as determined by the contract. Once the type of plan and the extent of coverage have been decided, the employer's responsibility includes determination of the following: (1) the employees to be covered; (2) the waiting period, if any, before new employees are eligible to participate; (3) the sharing of the cost of the plan between employer and employee; (4) the participation of retired employees and their dependents.

Classes of Employees Covered. Everyone is subject to accidents and illness and to the hospital and doctor bills that result; broad opportunity for protection is important to both the college as an employer and to the faculty and staff. If the institution has a health insurance plan, there is good reason to make it available to all full-time employees and to regular employees working half-time or more as well. Virtually all of the institutions reporting basic plans make all employee classes eligible; table 6.2 shows no significant differences among employee classes in eligibility for basic coverage.

Most colleges and universities recognize that extraordinary medical expenses create serious problems for any employee by extending group major medical coverage to all categories of permanent full-time employees. Table 6.2 indicates that the percentage of colleges and universities reporting a major medical plan for faculty is nearly identical to the percentage reporting a plan for clerical-service employees.

As with other group insurance plans, a precise definition of those who are eligible is important. Two examples of the classifications used by colleges and universities are the following:

> Eligible classes for major medical coverage: You are in an eligible class if you are a full-time employee, a regular part-time employee who works a minimum of twenty hours a week in an academic year, or a graduate assistant. Your eligibility date, if you are in an eligible class, is the effective date of the plan if you are then working for your employer; otherwise it is the date you commence active work for your employer.

> You become eligible for these benefits on the date you commence to work, if you are a full-time employee. You will be insured for employee benefits and, if you have signed a dependents' benefit enrollment card, for dependents' benefits on the date you become eligible provided you are at work. If you are away from work, your insurance will be postponed until the date you return to work.

When a health insurance plan is being installed, all eligible employees are covered automatically if the entire premium for employee coverage is paid by the college. If employee contributions are required, at least 75 percent of the eligible group must elect coverage before a plan can become effective, as provided under most insurance statutes.

The dependents of eligible employees are normally covered when the employee enrolls and requests dependent coverage. An employee who has no dependents may add such coverage, as a rule, at any time within thirty-one days of a change in dependent status.

Waiting Periods. For new employees and their dependents, coverage is usually effective on the first day of the month coinciding with or following employment. Some colleges have set up short waiting periods for classes of employees that experience a relatively high turnover rate in the early months of employment.

In the majority of the health insurance plans reported by colleges and universities, the waiting period is one month or less, which includes the many plans with no waiting period.

Table 6.5 shows the health insurance waiting periods reported by the colleges and universities. The table covers waiting periods for all types of health insurance plans; if the waiting period is different for basic and major medical insurance, the minimum time period is shown. For faculty, participation is permitted within one month or less (or immediately) at about 90 percent of public and about 88 percent of private two- and four-year institutions. The percentage of institutions permitting participation within one month or less for clerical-service employees is slightly lower than for faculty, about 88 percent of public two- and four-year institutions, 83 percent of private two-year institutions and 76 percent of private four-year institutions. The next most frequently cited waiting period, a "stated number of months," is reported by less than 10 percent of institutions for any category except for clerical-service employees at private four-year institutions (15 percent). The waiting period, "until stated date during first year of employment, but after one month of service," was reported mainly for clerical-service employees at private two- and four-year institutions (about 7 percent of institutions).

When the employer pays the entire health insurance premium, eligible employees are covered automatically as soon as they have completed any waiting period, provided the staff members meet the "actively at work" requirement of the group policy. When the employee is to pay part or all of the premium (and is not required to participate in the plan as a condition of employment), the group contract states a period within which the newly eligible employee can elect coverage. Provisions for subsequent enrollment are stated for those who did not elect coverage when they initially became eligible. The later enrollment opportunities are often offered during periodic "open enrollment" periods. An individual may join the plan at any time, as a rule, by providing medical evidence of insurability.

Dependent Coverage. Dependent coverage, like employee coverage, becomes effective automatically for the eligible dependents of insured employees if the employer pays the full premium for dependents. If the employee pays part or all of the premium for dependent coverage, he or she can elect dependent coverage (a family certificate) at the time of joining the plan. If a dependent is hospitalized when first eligible, coverage begins after confinement ends. Coverage for a new spouse must usually be applied for within a specified period after the date of marriage; otherwise the addition may be made only at specified times or by furnishing evidence of insurability. In most plans, newborn children are covered automatically under a family certificate. Under other plans, coverage for a newborn child must be applied for within a specified period after birth.

The coverage of an employee's dependents normally can include the spouse of an eligible employee, unmarried children under age 19, and unmarried children from age 19 to 23 or 25 who are full-time students and dependent on the employee for support.

Sharing the Cost. The last ten years have seen an increase in the proportion of colleges and universities which pay the entire cost of their staff members' own group

Table 6.5. Group Health Insurance Plans in Higher Education, Waiting Period Before Employee is Eligible to Participate

| | Faculty[a] | | | | Clerical-Service | | | |
| | Public | | Private | | Public | | Private | |
	Percent Insts	Percent EEs	Percent Insts	Percent EEs	Percent Insts	Percent EEs	Percent Insts	Percent EEs
Four-Year Institutions	n = 478	n = 242,041	n = 912	n = 120,620	n = 478	n = 413,110	n = 910	n = 188,185
One month or less	90.6	92.2	88.8	87.8	89.1	91.5	76.3	73.2
Until stated date(s) during first year employment, but after one month of service	2.5	2.2	4.2	3.9	2.7	2.1	6.3	4.1
Stated number of months	4.6	3.5	5.4	3.3	6.9	4.4	14.9	17.8
Other	2.1	1.9	1.9	6.0	1.7	2.2	3.1	5.8
No response	0.2	0.2	0.3	*	—	—	0.4	*
Two-Year Institutions	n = 595	n = 66,689	n = 78	n = 2,197	n = 596	n = 66,620	n = 77	n = 2,415
One month or less	89.1	89.3	87.2	86.9	87.4	87.5	83.1	81.7
Until stated date(s) during first year employment, but after one month of service	2.0	1.3	6.4	4.9	2.2	1.1	7.8	6.6
Stated number of months	8.1	9.8	3.8	1.9	9.7	11.0	6.5	6.6
Other	0.7	0.5	2.6	6.3	0.7	0.4	2.6	5.1
No response	0.3	0.3	—	—	—	—	—	—

[a]Administrative and other professional personnel similar to faculty.
*Less than 0.1%.

health insurance coverage and a marked decline in the proportion of institutions requiring the employee to pay the full cost. Overall, for faculty at four-year institutions in 1968, the employer paid the entire cost of basic coverage at 24 percent and the entire cost of major medical coverage at 38 percent of institutions. In 1978, 48 percent of all four-year institutions paid the entire cost of group health insurance coverage. For faculty at two-year institutions in 1970, the employer paid the entire cost of basic and major medical coverage at about 47 percent of institutions; in 1978, the proportion of all two-year institutions paying the entire cost was 68 percent. Percentages for administrative and clerical-service personnel are comparable.

A significant change has taken place among plans reporting that the employee pays the full cost of group health insurance. At all four-year institutions in 1968, faculty paid the entire cost of basic coverage at 35 percent and the entire cost of major medical coverage at 19 percent of institutions. In 1978, faculty paid the entire cost of their group health coverage at only 2 percent of four-year institutions. At all two-year institutions in 1970, faculty paid the entire cost of basic coverage at 24 percent and the entire cost of major medical at 22 percent of institutions. In 1978, faculty paid the entire cost of group health insurance at 1 percent of all two-year institutions. Again, figures for administrative and clerical-service personnel are comparable.

Table 6.6 outlines the current premium-sharing arrangements for group health insurance coverage reported by the colleges and universities. The table indicates that there is little difference between four-year public and private institutions as to the proportion with employer-pay-all and those with sharing arrangements; at two-year institutions, the public are more likely to provide an employer-pay-all plan than the private institutions, but both public and private ones are more likely to have an employer-pay-all plan than any other arrangement.

The proportion of colleges contributing to the cost of dependents' coverage under group health insurance is significantly lower than the proportion contributing to the cost of employee coverage. Sixty-one percent of all four-year and 67 percent of all two-year institutions contributed to the cost of dependent coverage for faculty. This includes the 17 percent of all four-year and 30 percent of all two-year institutions which pay the full cost of dependent coverage. In contrast, 97 percent of all four-year and 98 percent of all two-year institutions contribute toward the cost of employee coverage, including the 48 percent of all four-year and the 68 percent of all two-year institutions paying the full cost. The employee pays the full cost of dependent coverage in about 37 percent of all four-year and 32 percent of all two-year institutions. Table 6.7 details the sharing of premiums for basic coverage of dependents. Statistics for other employee groups are similar.

Generally speaking, where the cost of health insurance is shared between employer and employee, the lower the required employee contribution, the easier it is to achieve a higher level of participation in the plan. Of course, where the employer pays the full cost, 100 percent employee participation is attained. It should also be

Table 6.6. Group Health Insurance Plans in Higher Education, Employer-Employee Sharing of Cost of Health Insurance—Employee Coverage

| | Faculty[a] | | | | Clerical-Service | | | |
| | Public | | Private | | Public | | Private | |
	Percent Insts	Percent EEs	Percent Insts	Percent EEs	Percent Insts	Percent EEs	Percent Insts	Percent EEs
Four-Year Institutions	n = 478	n = 242,041	n = 912	n = 120,620	n = 478	n = 413,110	n = 910	n = 188,185
Employer pays full cost	46.7	45.8	49.0	39.8	46.2	44.2	47.4	37.8
Cost shared	53.3	54.2	46.6	56.3	53.6	55.6	48.5	60.0
Employee pays full cost	—	—	3.9	3.6	0.2	0.2	4.2	2.2
No response	—	—	0.5	0.3	0.2	—	4.2	—
Two-Year Institutions	n = 595	n = 66,689	n = 78	n = 2,197	n = 596	n = 66,620	n = 77	n = 2,415
Employer pays full cost	69.7	68.3	52.6	52.9	70.0	69.5	50.6	52.1
Cost shared	29.2	30.9	41.0	42.4	29.4	30.2	41.6	41.1
Employee pays full cost	0.7	0.6	6.4	4.7	0.5	0.3	7.8	6.7
No response	0.4	0.2	—	—	0.1	*	—	—

[a] Administrative and other professional personnel similar to faculty.
* Less than 0.1%.

Table 6.7. Group Health Insurance Plans in Higher Education, Employer-Employee Sharing of Cost of Health Insurance—Dependent Coverage

	Faculty[a]				Clerical-Service			
	Public		Private		Public		Private	
	Percent Insts	Percent EEs	Percent Insts	Percent EEs	Percent Insts	Percent EEs	Percent Insts	Percent EEs
Four-Year Institutions	n = 478	n = 242,041	n = 912	n = 120,620	n = 478	n = 413,110	n = 910	n = 188,185
Employer pays full cost	15.9	18.0	17.4	14.4	16.3	18.0	15.5	12.6
Cost shared	52.1	53.1	41.1	55.7	51.9	53.0	41.8	61.5
Employee pays full cost	31.6	28.6	40.8	29.6	31.4	28.7	42.1	25.6
No response	0.4	0.3	0.7	0.3	0.4	0.3	0.6	0.3
Two-Year Institutions	n = 595	n = 66,689	n = 78	n = 2,197	n = 596	n = 66,620	n = 77	n = 2,415
Employer pays full cost	31.8	35.0	17.9	17.4	32.9	37,9	14.3	12.1
Cost shared	37.1	34.2	35.9	34.8	35.6	28.7	37.7	29.1
Employee pays full cost	30.4	30.6	44.9	47.3	30.9	33.3	46.8	58.6
No response	0.7	0.2	1.3	0.5	0.6	0.1	1.2	0.2

[a]Administrative and other professional personnel similar to faculty.

kept in mind that employee contributions are generally paid in after-tax dollars. Under federal income tax law, one-half of the amount paid by a taxpayer for medical care insurance for the taxpayer and dependents, but not more than $150, is allowed as a deduction from taxable income. The remaining one-half, plus any excess over the $150 limit, is deductible along with any unreimbursed medical expenses only if such medical expenses exceed 3 percent of adjusted gross income.[10]

CONTINUATION OF COVERAGE

Upon Termination. The right of a terminating employee to convert to an individual basic health insurance policy depends on the provisions written into the group contract or the requirements of state law. Under Blue Cross and Blue Shield, terminating employees may normally convert their group coverage to an individual "direct-pay" contract. Some insurance company plans make no such provision; under others, the conversion is limited to persons who are under 65 years of age. In fifteen states the right of a terminating employee to convert to an individual basic health insurance policy is mandated by law.[11] Generally, direct-pay plans do not provide the same level of benefits available under the group policy.

Health Insurance While on Leave of Absence. Most plans state that coverage under group health insurance ceases upon termination of employment. In certain cases, coverage is continued for employees not actively at work. Plans at a few colleges and universities incorporate provisions applicable to employees on sabbatical leaves with full or part pay, and leaves with or without pay for study, research, and special service projects. Some plans simply state that during an approved leave of absence, the individual's coverage continues. In other plans, coverage for both the employee and dependents is continued during approved leave only if the employee pays the entire premium directly to the insurer. In this case, if the employee chooses not to continue coverage, insurance is usually reinstituted without evidence of insurability if reapplication is made within the first pay period following return to work.

Where the employer pays the entire health insurance premium, continuation of coverage during an approved leave of absence presents no special problem. The institution simply continues premiums as before. Under contributory plans the employer may make a special arrangement for continuation of the employee's share of the premium by accepting a lump-sum payment in advance from the employee out of which premiums can be paid as they fall due, or leave the responsibility for continuation of premium payments and coverage to the employee dealing directly with the insurer.

Under TIAA major medical plans, a faculty or staff member's insurance may be continued for twenty-four months of leave with at least one-quarter pay. Insurance may also be continued for twenty-four months of leave without pay if the individual is engaged in education or research, such as under a foundation grant, Fulbright grant or government project, or full-time study for an advanced degree. Most other insurers make similar arrangements on request.

Health Insurance in Retirement. For most retired persons aged 65 and over, Medicare provides needed continuing health insurance after employment ceases. All persons aged 65 and over who are eligible for Social Security retirement benefits are automatically eligible for Part A (Hospital Insurance) without additional cost, whether they are retired from work or not. (Since 1972, persons 65 and over who are not eligible for Social Security benefits are permitted to enroll in Medicare (Part A) if they also enroll in Part B, by voluntarily paying a monthly premium. The Part A premium was $69 per month through June, 1980). All persons upon reaching age 65 become eligible for Part B, supplementary medical insurance, which helps pay for physicians' services and some medical services and supplies not covered by Part A. Part B enrollment is totally voluntary and is financed by monthly premiums shared equally by those who choose this protection and by the federal government. (As of 1976, approximately 96.4 percent of those persons enrolled under the hospitalization portion of Medicare (Part A) were also enrolled in the Part B portion. The monthly premium rate for individuals electing Part B was $8.70 through June 1980.)[12] Part B of Medicare provides benefits covering 80 percent of medical-surgical charges once the insured individual has paid a $60 deductible on these charges. Of all two- and four-year institutions participating in this survey, 11 percent of institutions paid all of the monthly premium for a retired employee's coverage under Medicare (Part B), and 6 percent of the institutions paid for part of the coverage.

Group health insurance, if continued into retirement, is designed to supplement but not duplicate Medicare. If group health insurance is provided for persons who have retired at an age earlier than 65, before Medicare benefits are available, the coverage either changes to the supplementary form when age 65 is reached, or terminates. Basic insurance to supplement Medicare consists mainly in filling in the deductible and coinsurance amounts of the federal program. In deciding to terminate regular coverage at retirement, some colleges have questioned the need for basic group coverage *and* Medicare. Continuation of major medical coverage, along with Medicare, is more important. Where major medical benefits for retired persons are integrated with Medicare, the maximum benefit amount available is usually somewhat lower than the maximum provided for active employees. A maximum of $250,000, for example, might be reduced to $50,000 in retirement.

Among four-year institutions, 84 percent of public and 46 percent of private colleges and universities permit continued participation in the institution's group health insurance plan after retirement for all categories of employees. Among two-year institutions, 52 percent of public and 32 percent of private colleges extend such coverage to all employees.

Coverage for dependents is an important part of the group health insurance protection at all ages. The relatively greater level of medical need at the higher ages affirms the continued importance of full family protection, particularly for those not yet eligible for Medicare. Practically all institutions that continue health insurance coverage for retired staff members also continue it for dependents.

Where retired employee health insurance coverage is provided, slightly more than half of all institutions require an employee to meet a years of service and/or age requirement in order to be eligible for continued coverage; the remaining institutions have no special requirements. The employer pays the full cost of continued health insurance for retired employees at 30 percent of all four-year and 37 percent of all two-year institutions providing such coverage. The employer and retired employee share the cost of continued coverage at 25 percent of all four-year and 21 percent of all two-year institutions. At the remainder of institutions, the employee, if he or she desires the coverage, pays the entire cost.

For the coverage of dependents of retired employees, about the same percentages of institutions as cited above for continuation of retired employee coverage share the cost with the employee; about half as many institutions assume the full cost, and an additional 10 percent of institutions require the employee to pay the full cost.

A group health insurance plan for retired employees that is not wholly paid for by the employer raises the question of how to find a dependable method of collecting contributions from persons no longer with the institution. Salary withholding is not possible, and address changes, delays in premium payments or notices of changes in premium rates, and other communications problems create administrative difficulties and raise administrative expenses.

COORDINATION OF BENEFITS

The rapid extension of group health insurance coverage in recent years, combined with the fact that there are many more working couples than formerly, has resulted in many instances in which an employee may be covered under one plan while being covered as a dependent under a second plan. Total benefits payable can thus exceed the actual medical expenses incurred by the insured individual. This overutilization of insurance leads ultimately to higher insurance costs.

In order to keep the cost of insurance as reasonable as possible while at the same time providing needed benefits, most group insurance plans now incorporate a "coordination of benefits" provision designed to meet the problem of overinsurance and excess benefits. Under this provision, an insured person receives from all applicable benefit plans combined no more than 100 percent of the covered medical expenses incurred.

Under the coordination procedure, benefits are paid under a primary-secondary plan method when duplicate coverage is involved. When two plans contain the coordination of benefits provision, the plan that insures the person incurring the expense as an employee is the primary plan. The primary plan pays its normal benefits first and the secondary plan pays either the balance of the expenses or its contractual benefits second. If an individual is insured under two plans through two jobs, the plan that covered the individual for the longer time would pay first. With respect to children, the plan that insures the father as an employee is primary, although this provision is sometimes a source of controversy, particularly where divorced parents are involved. A plan whose group contract does not contain a coordination of benefits provision or other antiduplication provision is always considered as the primary plan.

CONTROLLING HEALTH CARE COSTS

The cost of health care and the annual rate of increase in costs have been spiraling dramatically in recent years. According to government officials, the nation's total spending on health services in 1979 will approach $200 billion, about one-tenth of the nation's total output of goods and services. This represents a threefold increase since 1970. Government expenditures to provide health care for the elderly (Medicare) and the poor (Medicaid) amount to $64 billion, or nearly $1 in $10 of the federal budget. Between 1965 and 1975, when the Consumer Price Index rose 71 percent, the cost of the average hospital stay more than tripled, from $311 to $1,017; over that same period of time, the average length of stay in the hospital actually declined. Currently, hospital charges are increasing at an annual rate of 15 percent, a precipitous rate of increase that in itself is one of the major forces in pushing up the CPI. All of these increases are reflected in the cost to employers and employees of their health insurance protection.

Increasing health care costs have sparked a national debate over causes and methods of control. A number of causes have been identified. On the side of providers—hospitals and medical personnel—there has been a rapid advance in technology, including highly sophisticated equipment that carries an equally high price tag, and a vast expansion of knowledge and of specialization. While the health care thus available is at an advanced level, the ability to pay directly for this care has surpassed the means of most individuals. The result today is that 92 percent of all hospital bills are paid by a third party, either the government or private insurers, thereby removing the critical element of cost from most individual decisions about how much care to consume and what price level to select.

Efforts to bring some order to and control over the rising cost of health care led to the introduction of eighteen national health insurance bills in the 1977 Congress, a somewhat chaotic situation in itself. The most radical of these bills, the Kennedy-Corman bill, calls for health care as a right provided by the government to everyone on a zero-cost basis to the individual. Such a bill would vest complete control of health care in the federal government, and new regulatory agencies would fix physicians' fees and set hospital budgets. Studies ranging from the optimistic to the pessimistic place the increased cost that would result from increased demand under a national health insurance program in the range of $180 to $230 billion in 1976 dollars.[13]

Government has taken an active role in attempting to hold down health care costs. A Professional Standards Review Organization program has been established to monitor and attempt to reduce the length of time spent in the hospital by patients covered under Medicare and Medicaid. The program is staffed by doctors who function as a peer review group. The Health Maintenance Organization (HMO) Act of 1973 and amendments in 1976 encouraged the development of fixed-fee health care organizations in an attempt to counter the predominating practice of fee for service payments to doctors and cost reimbursement of hospitals—two factors considered major contributors to spiraling health costs. HMOs have an incentive to minimize unnecessary procedures, because their revenues are paid in advance, and their profits are a function of how efficiently they do their job. Thus their emphasis is on preventive care and the maintenance of good health. From these developments we may expect that, regardless of the fate of the various national health insurance proposals and programs to control costs, government will continue to move toward increased control and regulation of the health care industry.

For their part, major hospital and medical associations have instituted voluntary efforts to reduce costs with the aim of warding off mandatory government controls. Virtually all of the large health insurance companies are instituting programs designed to encourage cutting costs. Many companies are offering second opinion programs under which the insurer will pay a second doctor to check whether a patient really needs the surgery recommended by the first doctor—in the expectation that enough operations will be ruled out to more than cover the cost of the extra consultation expense. Companies are attempting to cut the length of hospital stays by setting up programs similar to the Professional Standards Review Organizations. Some companies are also trying to identify doctors who charge fees substantially above average and to encourage patients to question such fees. In addition, both commercial insurance companies and Blue Cross/Blue Shield are encouraging the formation and expansion of health maintenance organizations.

The most potent method, however, of making consumers aware of the high cost of insurance—and the need to exercise restraint in health care utilization—is through the traditional means of cost sharing, the use of deductibles and coinsurance. Some insurers, however, have departed from this practice by offering 100 percent first dollar coverage, often with premiums paid entirely by the employer. Patients in this situation have no incentive to keep costs in check, and, in fact, are often totally unaware of what the final bill might be. For insurers then, there must necessarily be attempts in the future to educate the insurance-buying public regarding the relation of health care costs and health care insurance provisions.

7 Short-Term Disability Income and Sick Pay Plans

MOST INDIVIDUALS and their families rely on current income for their daily maintenance. Any interruption in the steady flow of income can cause financial hardship, so that even minor disabilities resulting in absence from work for a few days to a few weeks need to be accompanied by some means of continuation of wage or salary. This chapter deals with the provision of short-term disability income covering brief absences from work; the next chapter discusses long-term disability, the continuation of income during extended absence from work.

Disability income (or loss of income) protection is designed to provide people with regular weekly or monthly cash payments or continuation of amounts equal to their wage or salary if they are absent from work because of illness or accident. Employer-administered short-term sick pay plans are often informal and may provide benefits for an indefinite duration. Insured short-term plans commonly provide for up to ten, thirteen, or twenty-six weeks. While some short-term disability income plans may provide benefits for as long as two years, six months has become a conventional dividing line between short- and long-term disability and is used by many employers, insurers, and by the Social Security disability program.

TYPES OF SHORT-TERM SICK PAY AND SICK LEAVE PLANS

Four principal methods are used by institutions of higher education to provide short-term disability income (Table 7.1): formal sick pay or salary continuation plans, informal plans with each case judged on its merits, Workers' Compensation insurance, and group insurance plans. In addition to Workers' Compensation, a majority of both four-year and two-year institutions report a formal plan arrangement for the provision of short-term sick pay or salary continuation. Among public institutions, the number reporting a formal plan for either faculty or clerical-service employees ranges between 80 and 90 percent. Among private institutions the number reporting a formal plan for either category ranges between 45 and 64 percent.

Informal arrangements, under which short-term disability income is handled "on the merits," that is, through ad hoc arrangements depending on individual circumstances, are reported more frequently by private than public institutions. About one-third of private institutions offer an informal arrangement to all employees. At public institutions, about 12 percent provide an informal arrangement for faculty and about 5 percent for clerical-service employees.

196

Table 7.1. Short-Term Sick Pay and Sick Leave Plans (percent of institutions reporting plans and percent of employees in institutions reporting plans)

| | Faculty[a] | | | | Clerical-Service | | | |
| | Public | | Private | | Public | | Private | |
	Percent Insts	Percent EEs	Percent Insts	Percent EEs	Percent Insts	Percent EEs	Percent Insts	Percent EEs
Four-Year Institutions	n = 478	n = 242,041	n = 929	n = 121,162	n = 478	n = 413,110	n = 929	n = 188,601
Formal	83.3	81.4	54.4	62.9	91.6	93.0	64.4	86.2
Informal	14.4	17.0	32.8	33.7	5.0	3.7	21.7	9.6
Workers' Compensation	100.0	100.0	100.0	100.0	100.0	100.0	100.0	100.0
Group insurance	17.2	20.0	12.1	9.0	19.0	25.9	13.9	13.9
Other	2.9	3.4	4.0	4.8	2.9	2.6	5.3	6.7
Two-Year Institutions	n = 600	n = 66,915	n = 85	n = 2,284	n = 600	n = 66,748	n = 85	n = 2,482
Formal	82.5	85.4	47.1	57.1	86.8	86.8	45.9	47.2
Informal	10.5	8.5	31.8	32.1	6.5	5.3	30.6	28.9
Workers' Compensation	100.0	100.0	100.0	100.0	100.0	100.0	100.0	100.0
Group insurance	16.3	18.7	9.4	11.4	16.5	20.3	9.4	11.1
Other	3.3	5.5	1.2	1.8	3.3	5.4	1.2	1.4

NOTE: Percentages total more than 100 due to the presence of more than one program at some institutions.
[a] Administrative and other professional personnel similar to faculty.

A relatively small proportion of employers provide short-term disability income coverage through group insurance, and these occur more frequently at public than at private institutions. Between 16 and 19 percent of public institutions provide an insured plan for all employees; the number of private institutions providing an insured plan for all employees is about 9 percent (two-year institutions) and 13 percent (four-year institutions).

For service-connected disabilities, state Workers' Compensation insurance is available to all employees.

FORMAL SALARY CONTINUATION OR SICK PAY PLANS

A formal plan for salary continuation or sick pay (sick leave) sets forth the duration of salary continuation during disability, the portion of salary that is continued, and the conditions under which the income is paid. The full statement normally appears in the college's personnel policy manual with a shortened description included in employee booklets. Staff members thus know in advance just how much they may expect in terms of income when illness or injury forces them to be absent and the specified number of days, weeks, or months for which regular pay, or a portion of it, will be continued.

In contrast with insured short-term disability income programs, noninsured salary continuation or sick pay plans do not incorporate exclusion or waiting periods before benefits begin. Salary continuation benefits are paid directly from the salary budget, from current operating funds, or from designated reserves. An auxiliary budget may provide for the compensation of substitutes for teachers or other employees on temporary sick leave.

Taxation of Short-Term Disability Income. The Internal Revenue Code provides that disability income benefits paid for by employee contributions are excludable from taxable income, as are amounts received under Workers' Compensation as compensation for personal injuries or sickness. Amendments to the code effective for taxable years beginning after December 31, 1976, eliminated comparable provisions applicable to short-term disability income benefits paid for by the employer, including salary or wage continuation plans, payment in lieu of salary or wages, or accident and health insurance benefits. As a result of the amendments, employer-provided disability income is taxed as income to the individual except (within limits) in the case of employees who have retired under a permanent, totally disabling condition.[1]

Payments made to an employee on account of sickness or accident disability, including those made under a noninsured sick pay or salary continuation plan, are excludable from wages for the purpose of calculating taxable earnings under Social Security provided they are made under a plan or system established by the employer that applies to all employees generally or a class or classes of employees.[2]

Duration of Sick Leave. Formal paid sick leave plans normally provide for the accrual of a stated amount of sick leave time, commonly one day per month. While some institutions make substantially different provisions for teaching versus non-academic personnel, generally the sick leave allocations do not differ greatly between these two groups.

Unless otherwise stated, sick leave benefits normally provide full pay for each day of allowable sick leave. Days of unused sick leave may normally be accumulated and transferred to subsequent years, although the majority of plans place a limit on the total days that may be accumulated, for example, 180 days. A few plans grant extra service-related short-term sick leave credit to long-service employees who may have used up substantial units of accumulated leave, as illustrated in the following provision of a plan which provides 15 days of sick leave annually without an accumulation limit:

> After fifteen years' service an employee shall begin each successive year with a minimum of fifteen days' sick leave plus one day for each year of service; after twenty-five years' service, an employee shall begin each successive year with a minimum of fifteen days plus two days for each year of service.

Uses of Sick Leave. Sick leave is used most commonly for time lost because of personal illness. Sick leave may also be authorized in the case of an employee's personal medical and dental appointments, or serious illness or death in the immediate family. Where reference is made to illness or death in the employee's immediate family, the definition of "immediate family" may vary from the relatively limited "spouse, children, or parents residing in the same household," to the broader "father, mother, brother, sister, wife, husband, child, grandparents, near relatives residing in the household, or immediate in-laws."

PROVISIONS OF SHORT-TERM DISABILITY AND SICK PAY PLANS

Statements as to the amount of sick leave provided vary from the brief to the elaborate, depending on the college. The excerpts below are offered as examples of policies in effect, although they do not necessarily represent "average" or "typical" provisions.

Provisions Covering All Employees

All full-time employees are entitled to sick leave with pay, accruing one-half day per month. Accumulation of sick leave will begin after six months of employment. Up to forty days of sick leave with pay may be accumulated. No compensation is made for unused sick leave upon separation or retirement from the college.

An employee is eligible for one and a quarter days' sick leave upon completion of a minimum of sixteen working days per month. There is no limit on the number of days accumulated.

The sick leave plan for short-term disability pays all or part of basic salary for an eligible individual who is absent from work for a period of days, weeks, or months due to disability that is not related to the job. The benefit varies (the maximum is a full year) and is determined by the individual's position and length of service.

Sick leave accrues one full day each full month of employment, inclusive but beginning after the first full month of employment. After twelve months of employment and subsequent years of employment, all unused sick days may be carried over, up to a maximum of twenty-four working days, excluding days accrued in the current fiscal year. Sick leave does not accrue during a leave of absence without pay or any other non-active duty without pay. Any time spent in the hospital will not be counted in the normal accumulation of sick leave days.

Sick leave is earned at the rate of six hours and forty minutes each month or eighty hours each year. Sick leave may be accumulated indefinitely and may be used to extend an employee's creditable service upon retirement. The employee will not be paid for unused sick leave.

Sick leave may be used for personal illnesses, for necessary time off in the event of a death in the employee's immediate family, or for medical appointments. It may not be used for illness of a member of an employee's immediate family.

The supervisor may, if circumstances so dictate, require a doctor's certificate to cover absences charged to sick leave. In any event, the supervisor must be notified as soon as possible if an employee is ill and unable to report for work.

Provisions Covering Faculty and Administrators

The university has no fixed policy on faculty and administrative sick leave. Individuals will be dealt with generously and fairly when extended illness is involved. These are treated as separate cases, with recommendations coming from department heads and deans to the appropriate vice-president.

Faculty and administrators receive full pay for the first two months of disability, then sixty percent of the first $1,000 and forty percent of each $1,000 thereafter for the next four months, at which time long-term disability coverage begins.

Salary continuation for faculty and administrators is equal to one month at full pay for each year of service, to a maximum of six months. If the employee has less than six years of service, he/she receives benefits for one month at full pay for each year of service and the remaining months at half pay up to six months of short-term disability payments.

For regular full-time and part-time faculty (including faculty with visiting appointments) and professional, administrative, and supervisory staff, full salary is continued during sick leave.

For up to	If length of university service at beginning of disability is:
2 months	less than 2 years
4 months	2 but less than 4 years
6 months	4 but less than 6 years
8 months	6 but less than 8 years
10 months	8 but less than 10 years
12 months	10 years or more

Successive periods of disability caused by the same or a related injury or sickness are considered a single period of disability if separated by less than three months.

Provisions Covering Clerical-Service Employees

For full-time and part-time staff members in clerical and service positions, ten days of sick pay protection are available immediately upon appointment and at the start of each anniversary year, up to a maximum accumulation of twenty days.

Leave for illness or temporary disability at full pay is provided for a continuous period of sixty working days, provided that following one or more days of illness or temporary disability, a request for leave shall be submitted and filed in the area personnel office. After three or more consecutive days of illness, the request must be accompanied by an attending physician's report explaining extent of illness or temporary disability and recommendation for continuing recuperation time or the return to work. If illness or temporary disability continues for the sixty-working-day period, and the attending physician does not recommend the return to work, the personnel officer should be so informed in order to get proper applications filed for long-term disability insurance benefits.

During the sixty-working-day period, a physician's report will be requested at ten-day intervals regarding the employee's ability to return to work.

Personal Necessity. More than half of the institutions make a distinction between sick leave and other types of leave with pay. The latter are allocated under their own separate provisions and include family death, family illness, personal necessity, personal business, and jury duty or other court appearances, for example:

Funeral leave: An employee is eligible for up to five working days for funeral leave due to a death in the immediate family.

Military leave: Up to fifteen calendar days of paid leave are granted for annual military leave.

Court and jury duty: Full pay is allowed for authorized duty. Any compensation for actual service on the jury must be turned back to the employer.

Sick Leave for New Employees. Some formal sick leave plans do not result in sufficient sick leave protection for newly hired employees for whom a period of illness, even though brief in duration, exceeds their limited sick leave accumulation. This problem usually arises in plans providing for accruals on a days per month of service basis, or which express the leave allowance simply as "twelve days per year," for example, without further elaboration.

Most plans, however, take this problem into account. Some plans specifically make available on initial employment the full allocation of sick days for the first year of service, or make available an extra allocation:

If an eligible employee has no sick leave credit he/she will still be allowed sick leave pay in the event of any one illness up to one month during any one academic year from September through June in the case of faculty members, and during any one fiscal year in the case of staff and maintenance personnel.

Other plans provide for either a borrowing of leave yet to be earned or a combination of both approaches:

> Fifteen days per college year, credited at the beginning of service each year, will be granted to each member of the faculty annually. An additional fifteen days will be allowed as a loaned benefit which must be repaid to the college out of the second year's credited days, or should service terminate after this banked credit is used and before it is repaid, it will be considered a debt to the college and deducted from salary.

An informal approach, covering the needs of both new and established employees, is the following:

> The department head, director or administrator concerned shall have authority to grant sick leave up to a maximum of ten working days per fiscal year to the professional or administrative employee who incurs absences from work because of illness, injury, or hospitalization. The dean or vice-president concerned, upon the recommendation of the employee's supervisor, may grant up to ten additional days of sick leave to the employee during a given fiscal year. In those cases where an employee's absence due to sickness, injury, or hospitalization necessarily may exceed twenty working days per fiscal year, the dean or vice-president concerned may recommend to the Vice-President for Administrative Services an additional period of sick leave. Approval of the president is necessary to grant a further extension.

Part-Time Personnel. Most colleges provide a pro-rata form of sick leave for part-time personnel who perform work on a regular schedule over substantial periods of time.

Examples of sick leave statements for part-time employees are the following:

> A pro-rata share of the benefit available to regular full-time staff is available to regular part-time staff. Rate of accrual is determined by the percentage of full-time you work.

> A part-time certificated employee is entitled to sick leave on the basis of one hour of leave for each eighteen hours of service. The amount accrued but not taken is cumulative from year to year. Leave accumulated for part-time service may be taken only for absence from such part-time service.

> When a clerical or service employee is employed less than five days per week, he/she shall be entitled, for a fiscal year of service, to that proportion of twelve days of sick leave that the number of days he/she is employed per week bears to five.

Termination of Employment. Sick leave is usually cancelled upon termination of employment, or on termination due to retirement or death. Some institutions, however, provide for the payment of a cash value of unused sick leave. The following statements illustrate these approaches:

> The sick leave policy is established for the protection of employees during active employment with the college. An employee will not be paid for unused sick leave beyond resignation or termination. Sick leave is provided for those who need it and is not convertible to cash.

Accrued days of sick leave shall be given one-half value for terminal leave benefits (accrued to one hundred days), based on the average per diem salary paid the employees during their full term of employment. Sick leave terminal pay benefits will be paid only to employees who resign in good standing and have been in the service of the college for one consecutive year or more.

One month of credit is allowed for each twenty days, or any portion thereof, of sick leave outstanding to your credit upon retirement. However, sick leave shall not be counted in computing creditable service for the purpose of determining eligibility for service retirement, disability retirement, early retirement or for a vested deferred allowance. Sick leave may be used to complete thirty years of service for an unreduced benefit provided the member is at least age 50.

An argument sometimes advanced on behalf of a provision of cash value for unused sick leave on retirement or death, but not necessarily for termination of employment for other reasons, is that sick leave may be subject to less abuse if the employee knows that restraint in its utilization will ultimately result in a cash benefit for the employee or beneficiary.

Verification of Sickness. As a means of monitoring the use of sick leave time, many institutions require a statement from an attending physician for absences of more than a few days. This helps limit the use of sick leave to its intended purpose and aids in the equitable administration of the plan. The submission of a doctor's statement may either be required or be left to the discretion of the employer, as circumstances suggest. Typical statements are as follows:

An eligible employee whose illness incapacitates him or her for more than a week at any time during the academic year shall present to the proper authority a written statement by a physician concerning the nature of the illness.

Sick leave, in excess of three consecutive days, shall be substantiated by a statement from the attending physician. At the president's discretion, a physician's statement for illness of less than three days duration may be required.

Accumulation During Leave with Pay. It is usually provided that an employee on paid sick leave, or on sabbatical or other leave with pay, continues to earn sick leave and vacation credit. Provision is sometimes made for the use of sick leave when sickness interrupts a vacation, although many plans do not refer to this contingency.

INSURED PLANS PROVIDING SHORT-TERM DISABILITY INCOME

As shown in Table 7.1, about 11 percent (private institutions) and 17 percent (public institutions) of the short-term disability income plans for college employees are carried with insurance companies. Clearly, most employers in higher education prefer to self-insure their short-term disability income plans through the use of salary continuation sick leave arrangements.

Insured plans, variously called "accident and sickness," "weekly indemnity," or "wage replacement" insurance, usually pay a stated weekly income for a maximum period of thirteen or twenty-six weeks, or occasionally longer. The weekly benefit may be a level amount for all covered employees, but usually it varies according to the employee's salary or job classification. Benefits provided may replace half to two-thirds of the employee's take-home earnings.

Benefits usually begin after four to eight days of disability; during an exclusion period the institution normally continues regular salary or wages. The exclusion period is designed to cut the costs of the insured plan, including administrative costs, by excluding the one- or two-day illnesses which are most common. The exclusion for a disability due to accident is sometimes shorter than for sickness. Coverage often begins immediately upon hospital confinement if that occurs earlier than the expiration of the exclusion period. Also, some plans will retroactively pay benefits for the exclusion period if the disability lasts for a specified period, such as three weeks.

Insured plans often specify certain conditions under which benefits are not payable under the policy. Typical limitations which preclude the payment of benefits include:

1. Any period of disability during which the employee is not under the direct care of a physician.
2. Disability due to self-inflicted injuries.
3. Disability due to accidental bodily injuries arising out of and in the course of employment by an employer.
4. Disability due to disease with respect to which benefits are payable under any Workers' Compensation, occupational disease or similar law.

WORKERS' COMPENSATION BENEFITS

Occupational Illness and Injury. State Workers' Compensation laws provide mandatory benefits for employees suffering work-connected injuries and occupational illnesses. Benefits include temporary disability income for stated periods, medical care costs, rehabilitation services, death benefits, and benefits for dependents of recipients of disability income who die. Temporary disability income payments may approximate one-half to two-thirds of an employees' average weekly wages. For permanent disabilities, partial or total, specific awards or indemnities are paid.

Workers' Compensation laws are usually administered by state commissions responsible for compliance and procedures. All states except Louisiana require that compensation liability be secured. The employer is required to secure the insurance through one of three prescribed sources: private insurance, state-funded insurance, and self-insurance. Three states (Nevada, North Dakota, and Wyoming) require the insurance to be provided through an exclusive state fund. Three states (Ohio,

Washington, and West Virginia) require use of either an exclusive state fund or self-insurance. Use of self-insurance is not permitted in Texas. All other states permit the use of either private insurance, self-insurance, or state-fund insurance.[3]

Twelve states specifically exempt colleges, universities, and other nonprofit employers from Workers' Compensation legislation, but provide for their voluntary participation. Where no specific language includes or excludes nonprofit employers, the courts have usually held them to be subject to Workers' Compensation statutes.

Compulsory Nonoccupational Disability Benefits. In addition to statutory requirements for Workers' Compensation coverage of work-connected illness and injury, five states require employers to provide benefits during temporary nonoccupational disability: California, Hawaii, New Jersey, New York, and Rhode Island. The jurisdiction of Puerto Rico also requires the provision of such benefits.

Benefit amounts are normally expressed as a percentage of the disabled employee's weekly wage, such as 50 or 55 percent, subject to a maximum weekly benefit. Maximum benefits, depending on the state, generally range from $60 to $85 per week. Nonprofit educational organizations, public and private, are not required to participate but may do so voluntarily.

Sequence of Benefits. Most temporary absences from work in educational institutions are the result of nonoccupational illnesses or injuries to which regular nonoccupational sick leave provisions apply. In the five states providing for compulsory nonoccupational temporary disability benefits, nonoccupational sick leave benefits must meet the standards prescribed by state legislation; benefits may be paid at a higher level and higher benefits are usually provided under the full-salary sick pay plans of the colleges.

For temporary absences caused by a job-related injury or illness, colleges normally provide that the payments from Workers' Compensation will take precedence over payments under the sick leave program. The sick leave program normally makes up any difference between the Workers' Compensation benefits and the continuation of wage or salary as provided for under the sick leave plan. The following excerpt from a short-term disability income plan illustrates this kind of provision:

> Your disability benefit will be reduced by Workers' Compensation or occupational disease payments for an on-the-job accident or occupational illness and by disability income insurance payments under a policy which is financed wholly or in part by your employer.

GAPS IN SHORT-TERM PROTECTION

With the majority of salary continuation plans in colleges based on the gradual accumulation of annual sick leave, long-service employees with average or below-average temporary absences can accumulate substantial sick leave reserves. With ten years of service, an employee under a plan providing twelve days of sick leave a year, who has had five days of absence annually, will still have a reserve of seventy days of leave (fourteen weeks). Although adequate for most of the longer temporary absences, fourteen weeks' accumulation still leaves twelve weeks without benefits before completing the six-month Social Security elimination period for disability benefits or the start of benefits under many insured long-term total disability benefit programs. Short-term disability income protection of younger employees may incorporate even greater gaps if an illness lasts a month or longer.

Accumulated sick leave may be insufficient to encompass an absence, or too short to cover the period elapsing before benefits begin under a long-term plan. Long-term plans generally begin benefits after three or, more often, six months of continuous disability. Short-term plans should measure their adequacy in terms of filling the gap between inception of a serious disability and the point at which long-term benefits commence.

Now that insured long-term plans have become available at reasonable cost, it is practicable to consider the revision of short-term sick leave policies to provide full coordination with long-term benefits. However, it appears that some institutions adopting long-term total disability plans have not made needed changes in their temporary disability plans. Short-term disability plans will, no doubt, become subject to reexamination as more attention is paid to long-term protection.

 Long-Term Disability
Income Plans

UNTIL THE late 1950s, except for Workers' Compensation programs, long-term disabilities due to illness or severe injury and resulting in total incapacity to work were threats to loss of income against which there was virtually no adequate protection through employee benefit plans. Employers could offer life insurance plans, health insurance plans, temporary disability or sick pay plans, and perhaps early retirement for disabled employees, but there was no group insurance protection against loss of earning power because of a long-term physical or mental disability. Consequently, nearly every employee was vulnerable to the effect on earned income of a total, prolonged disability. Then in 1956 the Social Security program added total disability benefits for covered workers aged 50 through 64, and in 1960 the disability protection of Social Security was extended to all covered workers.

Social Security and Workers' Compensation provide long-term disability benefits, but for many disabled individuals these benefits alone cannot be relied upon to maintain a predisability standard of living. Also, not all disabled employees are eligible for Workers' Compensation benefits. Some workers will not have been in covered employment long enough to be eligible for Social Security benefits, and in some states groups of public employees are not covered under Social Security.

The development of group insurance plans to provide long-term disability income benefits for employees in institutions of higher education grew out of the concern of the Ford Foundation and TIAA about the absence of disability protection other than that provided by Social Security. A survey by TIAA in 1956 found that many colleges had been faced with long-term disabilities among their staff members, but had been unable to provide needed benefits. With the exception of a few self-administered programs, the only regular employer-sponsored provisions for disability income were early- or disability-retirement arrangements under public employee retirement systems. The benefits were usually available only to employees having long periods of service at the onset of disability and were sometimes restricted to employees whose disability was due to accidents incurred on the job.

TIAA introduced its group insurance plan for long-term total disability (LTD) in 1957. From this point on there began a period of rapid growth in long-term disability income protection. Following the TIAA plan, other insurers also began to enter the group long-term disability field. By 1968, 450 insured group long-term disability plans had been installed in colleges and universities, or about a third of the institutions surveyed in that year.[1]

208   LONG-TERM DISABILITY PLANS

THE DISABILITY RISK

The loss of earned income due to a lengthy and total disability involves not only the disabled person's health and economic status, but the well-being of his or her family. Studies indicate that the entire social environment of the individual and family can be negatively affected when a wage earner is disabled.[2] In the economic sense, a long-term disability may affect a worker's family more severely than would the worker's death. A breadwinner who becomes disabled becomes a dependent member of the household and may require prolonged medical care and special nursing. Under these circumstances, the sustaining value of a continuing income can be of overriding importance in the maintenance of living standards and of human and family values.

The risk of incurring a long-term total disability is only slightly less than the risk of death, a risk that is commonly covered through individual or group life insurance. This perhaps surprising fact is disclosed by actuarial data. Table 8.1 shows that the chances of becoming *totally disabled* before age 65 for a period of six months or more is on the average nearly one out of five for men aged 25 to 45, somewhat less at higher ages, while the probability of *dying* before age 65 is not substantially different. For women, the probability of a total disability is substantially greater than the probability of dying before age 65. These figures are worth pondering, for they bring into focus the unwanted and unpredictable human event whose financial consequences can be insured against at a rate well below the cost of insuring automobiles.

Relation to Short-Term Sick Pay Plans.   Most disability absences are short and fall well within the scope of sick pay, sick leave, and other short-term salary continuation plans (see chapter 7). Relatively few disabilities last as long as six months, a period that has therefore become a customary dividing line between temporary and

Table 8.1. Probability of Becoming Disabled for Six Months or More Before Attaining Age 65 Compared with Probability of Dying Before Age 65

AGE	Probability of Becoming Disabled		Probability of Dying	
	Male	Female	Male	Female
25	19.2%	16.7%	20.9%	9.8%
30	18.8%	16.3%	20.5%	9.6%
35	18.5%	15.9%	20.0%	9.3%
40	18.1%	15.4%	19.4%	8.9%
45	17.2%	13.8%	18.3%	8.2%
50	15.8%	11.8%	16.5%	7.2%
55	13.0%	9.0%	13.6%	5.8%
60	7.9%	4.9%	8.6%	3.6%

SOURCE: The table is derived from data contained in intercompany studies of the Society of Actuaries, Committee on Life and Health Insurance, "Reports of Mortality and Morbidity Experience, Group and Self-Administered Life Insurance." *Transactions:* 1975 Reports (1975), pp. 200, 201, 255.

long-term disabilities. Thus, it has become traditional to start insured LTD benefits after a six-month period of disability, although some LTD plans start their benefits as early as ninety days after the onset of the disability or as late as one year thereafter. The span between the onset of the disability and the beginning of LTD benefits is usually called the benefit waiting period; it is during this time that disabled persons who recover are eliminated from the immediate prospect of becoming LTD beneficiaries.

Total disabilities that cross the six-month line are likely to last at least a year; they may last five, ten, twenty years, or a lifetime. With these lengthy periods in prospect, few if any employees could expect temporary sick leave plans to meet their needs or could themselves be sure of having enough personal resources to protect against long earnings gaps.

EXTENT OF LONG-TERM DISABILITY COVERAGE

In seeking a measurement of the extent of long-term disability income coverage, the survey used a fairly broad definition. Respondents were asked to report "insurance and/or pension plans (insured or noninsured) providing income benefits to totally disabled employees following a specified period of total disability (usually six months) and continuing throughout disability for life, for a specified period of years, or to a stated age when retirement benefits begin." Table 8.2 shows the overall response on the extent of long-term disability income arrangements for faculty and for clerical-service employees in the two-year and four-year institutions according to institutional control, public or private. Responses covering administrative and other professional employees were similar to those shown in table 8.2 for the faculty.

Table 8.2 indicates that among the publicly supported institutions somewhat higher percentages of institutions report an LTD plan than do private institutions. This is partly due to the inclusion of some form of long-term disability benefit in most of the public employee retirement systems. Among the private institutions, LTD coverage is reported more frequently for faculty and administrative and other professional employees than for clerical-service groups. Private four-year institutions are more likely to report LTD coverage than are private two-year institutions.

The qualitative differences in long-term disability income plans are the subject of much of this chapter. The key to the differences, for the most part, is in the type of plan reported and the specific provisions for plan eligibility, benefit amounts, and duration of benefit payments.

TYPES OF LONG-TERM DISABILITY INCOME PLANS

There are three basic types of long-term disability programs: (1) long-term disability benefits may be payable under the provisions of an insured group LTD plan; (2) the benefits may be payable under the provisions of a pension plan; disability

Table 8.2. Extent of Long-Term Total Disability Income Coverage (percent of institutions reporting plans and percent of employees in institutions reporting plans)

| | Faculty[a] | | | | Clerical-Service | | | |
| | Public | | Private | | Public | | Private | |
	Percent Insts	Percent EEs	Percent Insts	Percent EEs	Percent Insts	Percent EEs	Percent Insts	Percent EEs
Four-Year Institutions	n = 478	n = 242,041	n = 929	n = 121,162	n = 478	n = 413,110	n = 929	n = 188,601
Plan in effect	92.3	95.8	76.3	91.5	88.9	92.7	56.1	71.5
No plan	7.7	4.2	23.6	8.5	11.1	7.3	43.5	28.4
No response	—	—	0.1	*	—	—	0.4	0.1
Two-Year Institutions	n = 600	n = 66,915	n = 85	n = 2,284	n = 600	n = 66,748	n = 85	n = 2,482
Plan in effect	87.3	90.4	54.1	63.8	86.0	90.0	42.4	40.5
No plan	12.5	9.5	45.9	36.2	13.8	9.9	57.6	59.5
No response	0.2	0.1	—	—	0.2	0.1	—	—

[a]Administrative and other professional personnel similar to faculty.
*Less than 0.1%.

benefits are frequently provided as part of the public retirement systems covering employees in higher education; an insured group LTD program may be used to fill in the gaps of the long-term benefits provided under a public retirement sytem; or (3) an employer may establish a noninsured (self-insured) program.

Table 8.3 shows the types of long-term disability plans in effect among the institutions reporting one or more such plans. The table indicates that group insurance plans for LTD are the predominant method of providing long-term disability income protection. Group plans are reported for faculty by 70.7 percent of public four-year institutions and by 91.5 percent of private four-year institutions, with comparable percentages reported by the two-year institutions. About 68 percent of the public institutions, both four-year and two-year, report faculty disability protection under the provisions of a public retirement system. A sizeable proportion of the public institutions report a combination of disability income protection that includes coverage under both a public retirement system and a group LTD insurance plan: 42.6 percent of the four-year institutions and 38.7 of the two-year group. The types of LTD coverage reported for administrative and other professional personnel are comparable to those reported for faculty.

For clerical-service employees, a somewhat higher proportion of LTD coverage under public retirement systems is reported than for faculty, and somewhat lower percentages of group insurance plans are reported, although for the clerical-service employee group these two methods of providing the coverage are the predominant ones, as they are also for faculty. About a third of the public institutions, both two-year and four-year, report coverage for clerical-service employees under both a public employee pension plan and a group insurance plan.

Self-insured plans are reported by relatively small proportions of both public and private institutions, that is, by approximately 10 percent of the public four-year institutions for both faculty and clerical-service employees, and by about 2.5 percent of private four-year institutions. For the public two-year institutions, self-insured plans are reported even less frequently than by their public four-year counterparts, or by only about 3.5 percent; the figures for private two-year institutions are similar to those for private four-year institutions. No specific information details the type of coverages included under the "other" category, but it may be assumed that some relatively informal arrangements are entered into this group.

Over the last decade, long-term disability income protection has experienced substantial growth among the four-year institutions. (Two-year institutions, on the other hand, do not exhibit comparable change; the great majority are public and were already extensively covered for long-term benefits under public pension plans as reported in the 1970 study.) Table 8.4 compares the extent of overall long-term disability income coverage reported by the four-year institutions in 1968 compared with the coverage reported in the current survey. Included in the table are all types of long-term disability benefit programs, disability pension as well as group insurance benefits.

Table 8.3. Types of Long-Term Disability Income Plans in Effect

| | Four-Year Institutions | | | | Two-Year Institutions | | | |
| | Public | | Private | | Public | | Private | |
	Percent Insts	Percent EEs	Percent Insts	Percent EEs	Percent Insts	Percent EEs	Percent Insts	Percent EEs
Faculty[a]	n = 441	n = 231,840	n = 709	n = 110,905	n = 524	n = 60,542	n = 46	n = 1,457
Public retirement system	68.0	63.5	3.2	1.6	68.1	72.1	2.2	0.3
Group insurance	70.7	75.6	91.5	84.7	68.5	68.1	89.1	89.1
Self-insured	11.1	13.7	2.7	11.4	3.4	4.9	2.2	0.8
Other	4.5	6.4	3.4	4.1	1.3	1.8	8.7	10.1
Public retirement system and group insurance	42.6	44.0	0.4	0.1	38.7	41.5	2.2	0.3
No response	—	—	0.1	*	—	—	—	—
Clerical-Service	n = 425	n = 383,005	n = 521	n = 134,794	n = 516	n = 60,038	n = 36	n = 1,005
Public retirement system	76.0	75.4	2.9	0.8	68.6	71.9	2.8	0.6
Group insurance	57.9	71.6	92.7	85.8	62.2	59.9	86.1	89.9
Self-insured	10.1	10.8	2.5	9.5	3.5	7.4	2.8	0.3
Other	4.2	12.1	2.9	4.2	1.6	2.2	11.1	9.9
Public retirement system and group insurance	35.8	50.2	0.6	0.1	32.8	33.0	2.8	0.6
No response	—	—	0.2	0.1	—	—	—	—

[a]Administrative and other professional personnel similar to faculty.
*Less than 0.1%.

Table 8.4. Growth of Long-Term Disability Income Programs in Four-Year Institutions of Higher Education, 1968 to 1978

	Faculty[a]		Clerical-Service	
	Percent Insts	Percent EEs	Percent Insts	Percent EEs
1968	n = 1,232	n = 285,414	n = 1,232	n = 444,618
Plan in effect	50.9	71.2	38.1	58.4
No plan	49.1	28.8	61.9	41.6
1978	n = 1,407	n = 363,203	n = 1,407	n = 601,711
Plan in effect	81.7	94.4	67.2	86.1
No plan	18.2	5.6	32.5	13.9

[a]Administrative and other professional personnel similar to faculty.

INSURED LTD PLAN OBJECTIVES AND PROVISIONS

The basic purpose of an insured LTD plan is to provide eligible employees who become totally disabled with an adequate income replacement at reasonable cost. To do so, an LTD plan incorporates certain basic objectives and specific provisions. (Disability provisions of public retirement systems that cover employees in higher education are described later in this chapter.)

A Definition of Disability. A precise and complete definition of disability is a crucial element of any LTD plan. In defining the contingencies covered by a long-term disability insurance plan, a distinction may be made between a disability that prevents an individual from carrying out his or her regular occupation and one that prevents an individual from pursuing *any* occupation. Combinations of these two basic definitions may be used in a single plan, i.e., a dual definition. In group LTD plans utilizing the any occupation approach, disability is normally defined as "the inability of the employee, by reason of sickness or bodily injury, to engage in any occupation for which the employee is reasonably fitted by education, training or experience."

When a dual definition of disability is used, a time sequence is usually introduced: "During the first thirty months of disability (two years plus a six month benefit waiting period), the complete inability of the employee, by reason of sickness or bodily injury, to engage in his or her regular occupation. Thereafter it will mean the inability of the employee, by reason of sickness or bodily injury, to engage in any occupation for which he or she is reasonably fitted by education, training or experience."

Under Social Security, disability is defined as "the inability to engage in a gainful activity by reason of any medically determinable physical or mental impairment that can be expected to result in death or to last for a continuous period of not less than twelve months." The "inability to engage in a gainful activity" is further defined as one of the following, each applicable under different circumstances: (1) the inability to engage in a substantial gainful activity; (2) the inability to engage in any substantial gainful activity requiring skills comparable with those in any gainful activity in which he or she previously engaged; or (3) the inability to engage in any gainful activity. Substantial gainful activity is defined under Social Security as any work generally performed for gain or profit, even if part-time, and even if less demanding or less responsible than the individual's prior work. Any of these disabilities must not only be total, but must be expected to last at least twelve months.

Excluded Disabilities. There are a few categories of disability for which benefits are not normally payable under insured LTD plans. These are: (1) injury or sickness resulting from war, declared or undeclared; (2) intentional self-inflicted injury or sickness; (3) disabilities incurred while committing a crime; and (4) disabilities during the first year of the contract resulting from any condition existing prior to the beginning of coverage.

Some plans add other exclusions: (1) disabilities resulting from insurrection, rebellion, or participation in a riot; (2) any disability lasting longer than twenty-four months if such disability is due to neuroses, psychoneuroses, psychopathies, psychoses, and other mental and emotional diseases or disorders of any type; and (3) aviation speed contests and air travel other than as a passenger in any aircraft having a current and valid air-worthiness certificate.

Eligibility. A seriously disabling accident or illness can strike anyone; continuing total disabilities are no respecters of job category. In considering a long-term disability plan, the employer normally opens plan participation as broadly as possible. If the plan requires an employee contribution, efforts must be made to sign up the required percentage of enrollees, usually 75 percent of the eligible group. An active program of staff meetings and distribution of descriptive material is important. If the required enrollment percentage cannot be obtained, eligibility may be redefined to take into account the broad employee groups that have expressed the most interest in the coverage.

As with other group insurance plans, the definition of eligible classes of employees requires language that is precise as to who is and who is not covered. Since the insurance is issued without medical examination (except for late applicants), group underwriting rules require the use of clearly defined and automatic eligibility factors such as job category, length of service, or salary category. Often a work test stating a required number of hours of work per week also governs eligibility. Temporary employees are not normally made eligible for the coverage; eligibility usually requires a "permanent" employment status. Where eligibility is limited to staff members earning more than a certain minimum, there may be other disability benefits available for the nonparticipants which, as a percentage of salary, meet a desired disability income goal; these income sources may include Social Security and occupational and mandated nonoccupational Workers' Compensation benefits in certain states.

Some examples of statements of eligibility for group long-term disability coverage are as follows:

Full-time teachers and administrative employees become eligible immediately.
Other full-time employees become eligible when they have been in continuous active service for three months.

All active full-time salaried academic, nonclassified and certain classified employees whose pay scale maximum exceeds $400 per month and who are under 70 years of age are eligible to join the plan. Your coverage will commence after you report to work and your application is received, provided your application is received not later than thirty days after you report to work.

This program is effective on the first day of employment for staff on regular academic or annual contractual salary base and assigned as professors, associate professors, assistant professors, or instructors, and executives with administrative-faculty status. The program is effective on the first day of the calendar month following the month of employment for all other staff employed on a regular annual salary base and normally working thirty hours or more per week.

Early Plan Entry. Early participation of eligible employees generally characterizes insured and self-insured LTD plans. Overall, insured group LTD plans in both the public and private institutions reflect a general aim to bring eligible employees under the protection of the plan either immediately upon employment or within at least a period of one year. Table 8.5 outlines the waiting periods reported by insured and self-insured plans.

For the four-year public institutions, table 8.5 indicates that about half of the plans for faculty, and about 60 percent of plans for clerical-service employees, state a waiting period of one month or less. The private four-year institutions generally report longer waiting periods. For faculty, a third of the private four-year institutions report a waiting period of one month or less, and they employ 22.3 percent of faculty in the private four-year group. For clerical-service employee coverage under LTD plans, 27.5 percent of the private four-year institutions report a one-month-or-less waiting period, and they employ just under 11 percent of clerical-service employees in the private four-year colleges and universities.

One-year waiting periods are reported more frequently by private four-year institutions for both faculty and for other personnel (about one-half of the institutions) than by public four-year institutions (about one-fifth). The weighting of responses by numbers of employees reduces these proportions slightly in the clerical-service category for private institutions, which report greater use of two through eleven month waiting periods for clerical-service personnel.

Waiting periods in excess of one year are reported less frequently than one-month or one-year waiting periods. For faculty, when weighted by numbers of employees, the frequency of reported periods over one year is about the same for public and private four-year institutions, 13.3 percent and 14.8 percent, respectively. For clerical-service employees, the weighted proportions of "over one year" waiting periods are 14.8 percent for public four-year institutions and 22.4 percent for private.

Generally, two-year institutions report shorter waiting periods than the four-year colleges and universities; there is a higher concentration of two-year institutions re-

Table 8.5. Waiting Periods for Participation of Eligible Employees in Insured and Self-Insured Group LTD Plans by Type and Control

| | Faculty[a] | | | | Clerical-Service | | | |
| | Public | | Private | | Public | | Private | |
	Percent Insts	Percent EEs	Percent Insts	Percent EEs	Percent Insts	Percent EEs	Percent Insts	Percent EEs
Four-Year Institutions	n = 345	n = 195,304	n = 667	n = 106,512	n = 273	n = 298,019	n = 494	n = 128,206
1 month or less	50.8	52.7	33.0	22.3	59.3	52.0	27.5	10.9
2-11 months	6.1	6.1	8.4	7.4	9.2	6.9	14.6	17.3
One year	22.3	23.0	49.2	46.9	19.0	27.5	43.1	37.7
Over 1 year	14.8	13.3	6.3	14.8	4.8	7.8	9.9	22.4
Other	4.3	3.5	2.8	8.4	5.1	4.5	4.5	11.5
No response	1.7	1.4	0.3	0.2	2.6	1.3	0.4	0.2
Two-Year Institutions	n = 370	n = 42,266	n = 42	n = 1,310	n = 332	n = 37,004	n = 32	n = 906
1 month or less	69.4	67.3	40.5	36.7	72.3	65.2	37.5	46.6
2-11 months	8.1	8.6	19.0	16.4	9.9	16.0	25.0	27.2
One year	15.7	16.8	33.3	33.5	13.3	16.0	31.3	19.6
Over 1 year	5.1	6.3	4.8	11.8	3.0	2.0	3.1	3.8
Other	1.4	0.9	2.4	1.6	1.2	0.8	3.1	2.8
No response	0.3	0.1	—	—	0.3	*	—	—

[a] Administrative and other professional personnel similar to faculty.
*Less than 0.1%.

porting one month or less, about 70 percent of the public and about 40 percent of the private ones, both for faculty and clerical-service employees.

In LTD plans in which the waiting period is less than one year, a "preexisting condition exclusion" is normally made a part of the group contract. This excludes from coverage disabilities commencing during the first year of participation if the disability results from injuries that occurred or sickness that commenced prior to the date the employee became insured under the group policy. Other disabilities are fully covered during the initial year of plan participation, as are all covered disabilities, preexisting or not, thereafter.

If the waiting period for LTD plan participation is one year or longer, a preexisting condition clause is not normally included in the group contract except for employees being covered initially when a plan first goes into effect.

Here are two examples of preexisting condition clauses:

> You are not insured against a period of disability (including all separate periods considered as one) which commences during the first twelve months you are insured, if the disability is caused, directly or indirectly, by a disease or injury for which you received treatment or services or took drugs or medicines which were prescribed or recommended by a physician during the three-month period just before your insurance went into effect.

> Benefits will not be payable if total disability results from injuries sustained in an accident which occurred or sickness which commenced prior to the date the employee becomes insured under this policy, but this exclusion will not apply to a period of total disability commencing after a period of at least one year during which the employee is continuously insured under this policy.

Benefit Waiting Period. The benefit waiting period is a part of every LTD plan and, as mentioned earlier, is the stated initial period of continuous total disability during which the long-term benefits are not yet payable. Usually set at six months, it will sometimes be three months, or, occasionally, twelve months. Sometimes it depends on the duration of the employer's sick leave or sick pay arrangements that provide benefits prior to the completion of the LTD benefit waiting period. Ideally, an accompanying short-term disability plan is structured so that there is often little or no gap in the stream of income for eligible persons between the time benefits cease under the short-term plan and the time they begin under the long-term plan. Most disabilities, of course, are short-term in nature and terminate well within a six-month period.

Typical statements of the benefit waiting period are as follows:

> Benefits begin on the first of the month after an insured staff member has been totally disabled for a period of six consecutive months; with respect to disabilities which occur at age 60 or less, benefits cease at age 65; with respect to disabilities which occur after age 60, benefits cease five years after disablement or at age 70, whichever occurs first.

> The benefits will be paid starting at the end of the 90-day qualifying disability period, or the date your sick-leave benefits expire, whichever is later, and will continue until the disability ceases, or until you reach age 70.

Table 8.6 shows the benefit waiting periods currently reported by institutions with insured, self-insured, or pension plans providing long-term disability benefits. The benefit waiting period helps distinguish long-term disabilties from disabilities that will turn out to be short-term in nature and cuts down the cost of initiating and then perhaps terminating benefits that do not ultimately qualify as long-term. Short-term sick pay and sick leave plans are normally designed to handle the disability absences that last six months or less.

As table 8.6 shows, in the four-year colleges and universities a benefit waiting period of six months is most frequently reported for both faculty and clerical-service employees. In the public four-year group, 49.4 percent, employing 54.5 percent of faculty in that category, indicate a six-month benefit waiting period, while for the private institutions, 71.7 percent, employing 77.2 percent of faculty in private institutions, reported the six-month period. For clerical-service employees in the four-year institutions, 36.3 percent of public institutions, employing 47.4 percent of clerical-service employees in the public group, and 65.6 percent of the private institutions, employing 76.3 percent of people in this category, report a six-month benefit waiting period. A three-month period is reported by about 18 percent of the public four-year institutions for both faculty and clerical-service employees, and by about 17 percent of private institutions for faculty and 20 percent for clerical-service employees. Periods of less than three months are reported by about three times as many public four-year institutions as by private institutions. Generally, this appears to reflect the more frequent use of disability benefit provisions under public retirement systems, with shorter benefit waiting periods, by publicly supported colleges and universities. Relatively few insured LTD programs state benefit waiting periods of less than three months.

In the two-year colleges, benefit waiting periods of less than three months are reported more frequently than in the four-year institutions. Over 37 percent of the public two-year institutions report under-three-month waiting periods for both faculty and clerical-service employees. Also, the public two-year colleges report three-month benefit waiting periods more frequently than their four-year counterparts. Consequently, they report six-month periods less frequently, with generally about 25 percent indicating the six-month period. The private two-year colleges, on the other hand, concentrate their benefit waiting periods at six months, with 60.9 percent reporting a six-month period for faculty and 55.5 percent for clerical-service employees. Again, for the two-year group, twelve-month periods are reported quite infrequently, as with the four-year institutions.

Cause of Disability. In the current survey, over 86 percent of the institutions reporting insured, self-insured, or pension disability plans, and employing over 90 percent of employees (all categories) in the reporting two-year and four-year institutions, indicated that their disability plans provided benefits for both work-connected and nonwork-connected disabilities.

Table 8.6. Benefit Waiting Periods Reported by Institutions with Insured, Self-Insured, or Pension Plans Providing Long-Term Disability Income Benefits, by Type and Control

| | Faculty[a] | | | | Clerical-Service | | | |
| | Public | | Private | | Public | | Private | |
	Percent Insts	Percent EEs	Percent Insts	Percent EEs	Percent Insts	Percent EEs	Percent Insts	Percent EEs
Four-Year Institutions	n = 441	n = 231,840	n = 709	n = 110,905	n = 425	n = 383,005	n = 521	n = 134,794
Less than 3 months	22.0	20.4	6.1	2.3	26.4	23.8	7.5	2.3
3 months	17.7	16.8	16.6	12.9	18.1	17.4	20.0	14.1
6 months	49.4	54.5	71.7	77.2	36.3	47.4	65.6	76.3
12 months or more	2.5	1.8	2.0	1.6	3.5	3.3	1.7	0.3
No response	8.4	6.5	3.6	6.0	15.7	8.1	5.2	7.0
Two-Year Institutions	n = 524	n = 60,542	n = 46	n = 1,457	n = 516	n = 60,038	n = 36	n = 1,005
Less than 3 months	37.2	35.6	10.9	7.3	37.5	32.6	13.9	11.1
3 months	26.3	24.7	19.6	15.9	25.0	22.6	19.4	22.1
6 months	27.7	29.5	60.9	68.1	24.0	26.9	55.5	51.8
12 months or more	1.9	2.7	4.3	5.4	2.5	4.8	5.6	6.1
No response	6.9	7.5	4.3	3.3	11.0	13.1	5.6	8.9

[a]Administrative and other professional personnel similar to faculty.

A few insured disability benefit plans and quite a few disability plans provided under public retirement systems distinguish between disabilities due to illness and those due to accident, or those due to physical and those due to mental illnesses, and pay benefits for one type longer than the other. In addition, quite a few of the total disability provisions under public retirement systems provide higher income benefits for disabilities that occur on the job than for disabilities unrelated to the job, or provide the benefits sooner by prescribing shorter waiting periods for benefits when the injury or illness was job-related. Such distinctions may have been thought appropriate at one time, but they now seem anachronistic. If the purpose of a disability plan is to meet income needs when they occur regardless of whether the cause of the need was injury or illness, physical or mental, a disability plan should not make such distinctions. A plan may reasonably offset, though, for benefits concurrently receivable from other types of disability programs.

Income Continuing Throughout Disability. Once it becomes evident that a disability is so severe as to prevent an individual from working for a long but indefinite period, an income should be assured as long as the disability lasts—whether two years, twenty years, or longer—until the individual reaches the normal retirement age and can begin retirement benefits. The continuation of disability income throughout the period of disability would seem to be a self-evident aspect of a sound disability insurance plan, but it must be noted that some disability plans described as long-term actually continue their benefits for just two or perhaps five years, even though the total disability of some individuals will last longer.

Distinction Between Disability and Retirement Benefits. The income benefits of insured group LTD plans normally continue during the period the individual is fully disabled and unable to work. The disability income ceases when disability ends, or at the normal retirement age stated by the employing institution in its pension plan, whichever occurs first. Under certain circumstances, Department of Labor interpretations to the Age Discrimination in Employment Act require continuation of benefits beyond the normal retirement age. (See chapter 9.) At retirement, however, there need be no break in the income stream, since the retirement plan's benefits can take over. This is made possible by the annuity premium benefit, a feature of the insured LTD plan (optional but often adopted as part of the plan) that insures continued contributions to the retirement plan throughout the period of disability.

Annuity Premium Benefit. It was noted earlier that disability plans that provide benefits for just two to five years merely lead a disabled individual to a point where he or she is out of sight and forgotten. The same thing can be said of plans that bring disabled persons up to a normal retirement age of 65 or 70 and then drop them completely and leave them with an inadequate level of benefits under a retirement plan. This can occur when there has been no provision for continuing payment of annuity premiums concurrently with the payment of a disability income benefit, or when the individual became disabled early on and was required under a public retirement system to begin benefits in the form of relatively low "early" or "disability" retirement income. Whenever a college is considering the protection of income during a period of continuing total disability, it should also be thinking about the collateral benefit—the annuity premium benefit—that continues regular contributions to the retirement plan throughout the period of disability.

As a rule, the amount of the annuity premium benefit is the percentage of salary (employer plus employee contributions) being applied to a person's annuity in the regular operation of the institution's retirement plan at the time total disability begins. If, for legal, technical, or other reasons, payments cannot be continued to the individual's regular retirement plan (for example, under a defined benefit public retirement system), the annuity premium benefit may be applied to newly issued individual annuity contracts or group annuities providing retirement income or death benefits, but no cash withdrawal options. The annuity is normally provided by the insurer of the disability income plan. The annuity premium benefit as part of a long-term disability plan was originally developed in the late 1950s as a part of the TIAA plan for educational institutions. More recently, the annuity premium benefit has also been offered by commercial insurance companies as a component of their own insured disability income plans.

Premium Factors. The cost of a group long-term total disability insurance plan is normally stated in terms of a composite monthly premium rate for each $100 of monthly benefit. Or it may be stated as a percent of covered payroll or as a dollar amount per employee. One rate is stated for the income benefit, another for the annuity premium benefit. The rate will differ from group to group on the basis of such factors as:

1. The benefits provided.
2. Age and sex distribution of insured employees.
3. Salary distribution of insured employees.
4. For the waiver benefit, the rate of contributions to the retirement plan.
5. Size of the insured group.
6. Whether the institution's staff members are covered by Social Security, Workers' Compensation, or other comparable benefits.

The relatively low cost of long-term total disability insurance benefits as compared with other staff benefit plans—usually from 0.75 percent to 1 percent of covered payroll—makes the benefit practicable for most colleges. The rapid growth of group long-term total disability insurance in the last decade reflects in part the need for the benefit and in part its relatively low cost.

Sharing the Cost. When the employer pays the whole cost of a long-term group disability insurance plan, all eligible employees are covered automatically and administrative procedures are at their simplest. There is no danger in a noncontributory plan that a total disability will strike an individual who did not sign up because the plan required an employee contribution. When balanced against potential benefits, the relatively low cost of a noncontributory plan as a percentage of payroll makes a persuasive argument for the employer-pay-all approach.

Table 8.7 shows the sharing of contributions to insured or self-insured LTD plans according to institutional type and control for faculty and for clerical-service employees. As with most of the other coverages, the pattern for administrative and other professional personnel is similar to that for faculty. The table indicates that noncontributory plans predominate in the private four-year and two-year institutions. In the four-year institutions, 67.3 percent of the institutions with insured or self-insured plans pay the full cost of the coverage for faculty, and 69.8 percent pay the full cost for clerical-service employees. Employer and employees share the cost of the LTD plan in about 25 percent of the private four-year institutions. The employee pays the full cost in about 5 percent.

The contribution patterns of the public institutions with insured or self-insured LTD plans differ to a considerable degree from their private counterparts. For faculty, 40.9 percent of the four-year public institutions reported a noncontributory plan, but only 29.3 percent reported such a plan for clerical-service employees. While employer and employees share the cost in about the same percentage of plans in the public as in the private institutions, the proportion of public four-year institutions reporting that the employee pays the full cost of the LTD plan was substantially higher, 30.7 percent for faculty (compared with 5.7 percent for private four-year institutions), and 39.9 percent for clerical-service employees (compared with 5.1 percent for private four-year institutions).

In the two-year colleges, a somewhat higher proportion of the public institutions reported noncontributory plans than in the public four-year institutions, with 54.7 percent of the two-year group reporting a noncontributory plan for faculty (representing 64.3 percent of faculty in reporting institutions) and 50.9 percent reporting a noncontributory plan for clerical-service employees (representing 63.0 percent of this employee class). Concurrently, somewhat lower percentages of employee-pay-all plans were reported by the two-year institutions, 20.5 percent for faculty and 23.2 for clerical-service employees.

Private two-year colleges report a relatively high percentage of noncontributory LTD plans, 71.4 percent for faculty and 65.6 percent for clerical-service employees. At the same time, they reported a little less sharing of contributions than their four-year equivalents, and a somewhat higher percentage of employee-pay-all plans than in the four-year private institutions.

When both employer and employee pay toward plan costs, the college determines the approximate share of the total premium it will pay, perhaps one-half, and then selects a method of relating employee contributions to salary. Since benefits are related to salary, a salary-related contribution produces a fair method of relating benefits to costs. The formula used should be simple to express, convenient to administer, not need frequent changes, and yet produce the desired sharing. The employee contribution can be stated as a simple percentage of monthly salary, as so much for each $100 of monthly salary, or as a specified dollar amount by salary bracket. A similar

Table 8.7. Employer and Employee Contributions to the Cost of Insured or Self-Insured Long-Term Disability Income Plans, by Type and Control

| | Faculty[a] | | | | Clerical-Service | | | |
| | Public | | Private | | Public | | Private | |
	Percent Insts	Percent EEs	Percent Insts	Percent EEs	Percent Insts	Percent EEs	Percent Insts	Percent EEs
Four-Year Institutions	n = 345	n = 195,304	n = 667	n = 106,512	n = 273	n = 298,019	n = 494	n = 128,206
ER pays full cost	40.9	39.7	67.9	63.3	29.3	24.7	69.8	66.9
ER-EE share cost	26.4	24.9	25.5	26.4	28.2	27.3	24.1	24.7
EE pays full cost	30.7	34.0	5.7	10.0	39.9	46.7	5.1	8.1
No response	2.0	1.4	0.9	0.3	2.6	1.3	1.0	0.3
Two-Year Institutions	n = 370	n = 42,266	n = 42	n = 1,310	n = 332	n = 37,004	n = 32	n = 906
ER pays full cost	54.7	64.3	71.4	75.9	50.9	63.0	65.6	62.1
ER-EE share cost	23.2	17.4	14.3	11.4	24.1	18.4	18.8	21.2
EE pays full cost	20.5	15.9	11.9	11.8	23.2	14.9	12.5	13.5
No response	1.6	2.4	2.4	0.9	1.8	3.7	3.1	3.2

[a]Administrative and other professional personnel similar to faculty.

approach is used when the employee pays the whole cost. Choice of the best formula for employee contributions at a particular college may depend in part on the college's own payroll and accounting procedures.

Leave of Absence. A college should make sure that the disability plan states provisions for coverage during leaves of absence, that such provisions are clear, and that they meet the needs of employees.

A leave of absence provision with sufficient latitude for most colleges' needs is one providing coverage for up to twenty-four months of sabbatical or other leave *with pay*, or for a similar period for leave *without pay* when the staff member is engaged in education or research, such as under a foundation grant, Fulbright grant or government project, or is engaged in full-time study for an advanced degree. During leaves of absence the level of coverage remains the same as immediately before the start of the leave.

During leaves with full or part pay, regular employer and/or employee contributions are normally continued as usual during the employee's absence. The same arrangement may be established for leaves without pay, or it may be arranged that the employee assume the full cost during his or her absence.

Termination of Insurance. Termination of a staff member's long-term disability insurance occurs if active service is terminated, if employee premium contributions cease under a contributory plan, if the employee ceases to be in a class of employees eligible for coverage, or if the group policy is discontinued. Termination of a staff member's insurance should not, and in most college plans does not, affect benefits being paid for a total disability existing on the date of such termination.

Amounts. Insured disability income plans generally aim to provide an adequate monthly income, with care taken to assure that the monthly benefit amount provides a level of take-home pay that is significantly less than the take-home pay that could be earned from work. Generally, the take-home disability benefits, including any Social Security or Workers' Compensation benefits, should amount to no more than 75 to 85 percent of take-home pay from former earnings. LTD benefits limited to 50 or 60 percent of gross income are frequently provided and usually result in take-home benefits that normally fall within this 75–85 percent range.

Many insured LTD plans incorporate an annual percentage increase in the income benefit, usually 3 percent per year, to provide a degree of protection against the erosive effects of inflation on a fixed income. The increase factor is also applied to the annuity premium benefit, mentioned earlier as that part of the insured LTD plan that continues annuity premiums during disability.

Examples of benefit levels provided for under insured LTD plans are illustrated in the following excerpts from plans currently in effect:

> The monthly income benefit which, including any income benefits payable from Social Security, Workers' Compensation and any disability benefits payable under any insurance or retirement plan for which contributions or payroll deductions are made

by the college, is equal to 60 percent of your covered monthly salary up to $2,000, plus 40 percent of covered monthly salary in excess of $2,000 as of the date the disability began, but not to exceed $2,500 monthly. In no event will the monthly income benefit be less than $50, even though this amount may bring your total disability income to more than 60 percent of salary.

Your benefit will be equal to 60 percent of your basic monthly salary or wage up to a maximum of $2,000 per month. This amount shall be subject to a reduction for any salary or wage received from the employer during that monthly period and for other income benefits as defined in this plan. In no instance will the amount of your benefits be less than $50.

If the employee becomes totally disabled as the result of an accident or sickness, either mental or physical, the plan will provide him with 50 percent of his monthly salary, to a maximum monthly benefit of $1,500, less any amount paid or payable under Workers' Compensation, occupational disease act or law, any statutory disability law and/or any benefits paid or payable to the employee, including dependent benefits, as a result of the employee's disability under the Social Security Act.

Each of the examples above incorporates a maximum benefit amount. The use of a maximum plus the expression of the disability benefit as a *percentage* of monthly salary at the time of disability assures that income from disability is lower than income from work and, presumably, provides an incentive for return to work where a disability is of the kind that might ultimately permit this.

Many insurers adjust the maximum LTD benefit available under an insured plan according to the size of the group involved. A lower maximum benefit amount applies if the size of the group is below certain stated limits. For example, one schedule of maximum benefits according to the size of the group is as follows:

Number of Eligible Employees	Maximum Covered Monthly (Annual) Salary	Maximum Monthly Income Benefit*
10 but less than 100	$2,750 ($33,000)	$1,500
100 but less than 500	[$4,000 ($48,000)]	$2,000
500 or more	$5,250 ($63,000)	$2,500

*Determined as 60 percent of the first $2,000 of covered monthly salary + 40 percent of additional covered monthly salary.

Benefit Offsets. Because of the multiple types of benefits that may become payable during total disability, including benefits from Social Security and from Workers' Compensation or similar laws, it would be possible to pile benefit on benefit, with the result that a disability income in its total amount could exceed the level of prior net or even gross earnings. Thus, insured LTD plans provide for benefit offsets so that the maximum benefit under an insured LTD plan usually *includes* any benefits that are payable from Social Security, Workers' Compensation, salary or wages from the employer, disability plans compulsory under state statutes, or pension plan benefits being provided by a private employer or through a public retirement system—federal, state, or local. Premium rates for LTD plans take into account the types and extent of offsets that may become applicable under the plan. Under some plans the primary benefit of Social Security is offset, but not the benefits payable on behalf of dependents. When an insured LTD plan is installed in a public educational institution participating in a public retirement system, it is desirable to provide for the deferment of early retirement benefits payable under the retirement plan so that they are not currently offset and may be built up for later use.

Taxation of Disability Benefits. Any portion of total disability income that is based on employee contributions is not currently taxable as income to the individual, nor is the disability benefit payable under Social Security. In addition, federal tax law provides individual taxpayers who are under age 65 and who are retired on disability and are permanently and totally disabled with a maximum annual exclusion of $5,200 ($100 per week) of disability income payable under an employer-sponsored plan. A disability test is part of the law. The taxpayer must be permanently and totally disabled and thereby unable to engage in any substantial gainful activity. The test is comparable to that used for Social Security purposes in that the disability must be expected to last for at least twelve months.

The $5,200 tax exclusion is phased out at a certain point, however, depending on the disabled individual's level of adjusted gross income. There is a dollar-for-dollar reduction from the $5,200 maximum exclusion for every dollar of adjusted gross income in excess of $15,000. An adjusted gross income of $20,200 would, therefore, entirely eliminate the $5,200 income exclusion amount. In the calculation, the amount of the employer-sponsored disability benefit itself is included in the adjusted gross income amount.[3]

As a result of the limited tax exclusion, a disability income comprised of both non-taxed Social Security benefits and LTD benefits totaling 60 percent of gross earnings prior to disability can, for middle-income people, amount to perhaps as much as three-quarters of the *take-home pay* from former earnings. In addition, there would no longer be deductions from income for Social Security taxes, pension plan contributions, or employee contributions for group life insurance, which are usually waived during total disability.

Rehabilitation. Rehabilitation and return to work are goals that are normally shared by the disabled employee, the employer, and the insurer. To encourage rehabilitation, most insurers provide for a continuation of some disability income during an initial period of return to work. Such a period usually involves increasing amounts of part-time work until full-time work is resumed. For example, if an employee returns to work and is able to earn 30 percent of previous salary, both the disability income benefit and the annuity premium benefit (if any) would be based on the 70 percent of predisability salary that is not being earned during rehabilitation.

If a recovered employee who has returned to work once again becomes disabled from the same cause within one year after the termination of benefits, many insurers waive reapplying the benefit waiting period before benefits resume.

DISABILITY BENEFITS UNDER PUBLIC RETIREMENT SYSTEMS

The disability benefits provided under public retirement systems normally take the form of retirement benefits begun early, often at a level that is lower than the retirement benefit that would have been payable had the employee continued at work until the stated normal retirement age. Thus, under many public retirement plans, the nearer the employee is to the retirement age at the time disability starts, the higher the monthly disability benefit is likely to be.

Generally, the types of disability benefits payable under public retirement systems suggest that a retirement plan functions best as a source of old-age retirement benefits, with disability benefits most effectively provided (until the retirement age) through a combination of group LTD insurance, Social Security, and Workers' Compensation. This approach enables the retirement benefit to be built up during both the working and the disability periods and enables both the disability benefits and the retirement benefits to be paid in more adequate amounts. Historically, most public systems first offered disability benefits only for job-connected disabilities. Later, nonservice-connected disabilities were added. Many of the plans continue to describe their benefits according to these two categories.

Nonservice-Connected Benefits. The public retirement systems provide nonservice-connected disability benefits to eligible participants under four basic approaches. The disability benefit may be:

1. The retirement benefit that would have been earned had the employee continued in service to the normal retirement age, either with the benefit not actuarially reduced because of the younger age at disability (eleven out of sixty-eight systems), or actuarially or otherwise reduced because of the younger age (six systems).

2. The retirement benefit that the employee has earned up to the date of disability, with this benefit amount not actuarially reduced for age (twenty-four systems), or actuarially or otherwise reduced for age (four systems).

3. A disability benefit stated as a percentage of final average salary preceding the onset of disability, sometimes a flat percentage without service component (thirteen systems), or sometimes a percentage that is multiplied by a service component (seven systems).

4. A flat benefit amount per month (one system).

Table 8.8 outlines the various benefit formulas for nonservice-connected long-term disability benefits under public retirement systems covering employees in higher education. Two of the sixty-eight retirement systems do not provide disability benefits.

The public retirement systems most likely to provide adequate disability income are the eleven systems in which service that would have been rendered after disability to the established normal retirement age is counted in the benefit formula and in which there is no actuarial reduction for age at disability. Also reasonably adequate are the thirteen systems in which the disability benefit is stated as a percentage of average salary over a stated period preceding disability. Other provisions may pro-

Table 8.8. Public Employee Retirement Systems—Benefit Formulas for Nonservice-Connected Long-Term Disability Benefits[a] (as applied to participants meeting eligibility requirements)

		Number of Systems
Retirement Benefit Which Would Have Been Earned Had Employee Continued in Service to Normal Retirement Age[b]		17
Not actuarially reduced	11[c]	
Actuarially reduced according to age at disability	1	
Reduced by a percentage applied to the benefit formula	5[d]	
Retirement Benefit Earned to Date of Disability		28
Not actuarially reduced	24[e]	
Actuarially reduced according to age at disability	2[f]	
Reduced by a percentage applied to the benefit formula	2[g]	
Percentage of Final Average Salary Preceding Disability Retirement		20
Flat percentage	13[h]	
Service component in formula	7[i]	
Flat Amount per Month		1[j]
No Provision		2
Total Systems		68

[a]Twelve plans offset disability benefit by amount of any disability benefit received from Social Security, Workers' Compensation or both.

[b]Two plans limit benefit to 50% of final average salary if a smaller benefit results.

[c]One plan limits creditable service to twice that actually earned if less than the number of years that would have been completed to EE's age 60. One plan limits years that may be borrowed, when added to actual years of service, to the sum total of twenty-five. One plan provides an additional 25% of disabilty benefit.

[d]One plan provides additional 1% for each year of service over twenty. One plan provides 50% of final full year's salary if a larger benefit results.

[e]Two plans provide an alternative as follows: for EEs under age 50, ER contributions that would have been made up to EE's age 50 are included; 25% of final average salary if a larger benefit results.

[f]One plan provides a money purchase annuity if a larger benefit results.

[g]One plan provides an alternative of 25% of final compensation if a larger benefit results.

[h]Four plans provide an alternate formula computation if a larger benefit. Three plans provide additional 10% of final average salary for each child to maximum of 40% (two plans) or 90% (one plan). One plan limits benefit to 50% of total earnings during membership service to age 68. One plan provides benefit based on regular retirement formula for EEs with fifteen years of service. One plan provides additional 1% for each year of service over 15.

[i]With ten years of service, one plan includes years that would have been earned had employee continued in service to age 60 subject to maximum of 33 1/3% of final average salary. In one plan, number of eligible dependents is a factor in determination of benefit. One plan limits benefit to 90% of allowance EE would have received if retirement occurred at age 60. One plan provides additional payment of $75 monthly.

[j]Plus $5 per month for each year of service in excess of five.

duce adequate benefits if disability occurs after a lengthy period of service under the system and near the normal retirement age but cannot do nearly as well for eligible persons who become disabled at younger ages.

Twelve of the public systems report offsetting disability benefits by other disability benefits received from Social Security (one plan), Workers' Compensation (five plans), or both (six plans). Under thirteen of the plans described in table 8.8, employees do not participate in Social Security; these plans are among those that provide the highest levels of disability benefits.

Table 8.9 summarizes the membership service periods required before public retirement plan participants become eligible for long-term disability benefits result-

Table 8.9. Public Retirement Systems—Eligibility Requirements for Nonservice-Connected Long-Term Disability Benefits

		Number of Systems
No Service Requirement		3[a]
Service Requirement		63
2 years	2	
3 years	1	
5 years	34[b]	
7 years	1	
8 years	1	
10 years	23[c]	
15 years	1[d]	
No Provision		2
Total Systems		68

[a]One plan requires five years of service if disability existed prior to latest date of employment.
[b]Four plans also require eligibility for Social Security disability benefits.
[c]Includes two plans with five-year requirement for EEs over age 50.
[d]Requirement reduced to ten years for veterans to age 70.

ing from nonservice-connected injuries and illnesses. All but three of the sixty-six public retirement systems that provide disability retirement benefits have established service requirements for benefit eligibility. The requirements range from two to fifteen years of membership service. Of the sixty-three systems stating service requirements, thirty-four systems (53 percent) specify five years of service and twenty-three systems (35 percent) specify ten years of service. The remaining 12 percent of the systems stating eligibility requirements are distributed as follows: two years of membership service (two systems), three years (one system), seven years (one system), eight years (one system), and fifteen years (one system). On attainment of eligibility, benefits are usually payable throughout disability, including postnormal retirement years. Some plans, however, state a maximum length of time for which benefits are payable.

By combining the provisions shown in tables 8.8 and 8.9, table 8.10 shows the nonservice-connected disability benefit formulas according to the service requirements associated with those benefits in the public plans. The relatively long service requirements shown indicate situations in which coordination with a group total disability insurance plan would result in increased benefit protection. In this connection, over 40 percent of the public institutions responding to the current survey indicated that they had both a group insurance plan for long-term disability income benefits and a provision for disability benefits under a public employee or teacher retirement system.

Coordination of Disabilty Insurance and Pension Plans. By coordinating an insured total disability plan with a public pension plan, the long membership service periods that often characterize the disability benefit eligibility provisions of the public systems can be compensated for. Much shorter waiting periods for plan participation can be established under the insured component of a two-plan combination. At the same time, the retirement benefits of the public pension system can be coordinated with the insured plan so as to defer payment of the system's benefits until the retirement age, with the result that retirement benefits for disabled persons under the plan can build up to more adequate levels. During disability, the insurance plan is responsible for the continuation of disability benefit payments. So as to continue contributions to the retirement plan during disability, the group insurance plan can incorporate an annuity premium benefit to provide for the continued payment of both the employer and employee retirement plan contributions during disability. This would be desirable where service credit is not given during disability absence under a public employee retirement system.

In public retirement systems not incorporating a coordinated method of providing disability benefits under both an insured plan and under the retirement system, the proper enmeshing of retirement benefits with a new insured long-term disability income plan may depend on making changes in certain provisions of the system and may require legislation. Necessary changes may include: (1) incorporation of a right to defer the start of the retirement plan's benefits until normal retirement age rather than beginning income immediately at the reduced level as disability benefits; (2) authorization for the installation of a group long-term disability insurance plan; (3) an arrangement for automatic continuation of the regular employer and employee contribution amounts to the public retirement system on behalf of disabled persons, or, if this cannot be done, the addition of an annuity premium benefit under the insured long-term disability income plan in order to provide adequate deferred retirement benefits under a supplementary insured retirement plan; and (4) coordination of the retirement system and the group insured disability plan so as to assure participants that benefits payable under the public retirement system but deferred to retirement age are offset only if the benefits are actually being received.

NONINSURED LTD PLANS

A few large educational institutions have established noninsured (self-insured) long-term disability benefit plans. Table 8.3 indicates about 11 percent of public four-year colleges and universities and about 3 percent of private colleges and universities report noninsured LTD plans. Among two-year colleges, 3.5 percent of the public institutions report noninsured LTD plans, as do about 3 percent of the private.

Noninsured plans are utilized by relatively few institutions (mainly the larger ones). Only large institutions with many employees stand a chance of experiencing a relatively stable rate of disability incidence and persistency under an arrangement

Table 8.10. Public Retirement Systems—Eligibility Requirements for Nonservice-Connected Long-Term Disability Benefits by Type of Disability Benefit Formula

	Number of Systems
Retirement Benefit Which Would Have Been Earned Had Employee Continued in Service to Normal Retirement Age	17
Not actuarially reduced	
5 years of service	7
10 years of service	4
Actuarially reduced according to age at disability	
5 years of service	1
Reduced by a percentage applied to the benefit formula	
5 years of service	3
8 years of service	1
10 years of service	1
Retirement Benefit Earned to Date of Disability	28
Not actuarially reduced	
5 years of service	12
10 years of service	12[a]
Actuarially reduced according to age at disability	
No service requirement	1
10 years of service	1
Reduced by a percentage applied to the benefit formula	
5 years of service	1
10 years of service	1
Percentage of Final Average Salary Preceding Disability Retirement	20
Flat percentage	
No service requirement	2[b]
2 years of service	1
3 years of service	1
5 years of service	7[c]
7 years of service	1
10 years of service	1
Service component in formula	
2 years of service	1
5 years of service	2
10 years of service	3
15 years of service	1[d]
Flat Amount per Month	
5 years of service	1
No Disability Income Provision	2
Total Systems	68

[a]Includes two plans with five-year requirement for employees over age 50.
[b]Includes one plan with five-year requirement if disability existed prior to latest date of employment.
[c]Includes four plans which also require Social Security eligibility.
[d]Requirement reduced to ten years for veterans to age 70.

in which there is no pooling of disability risks with other employers. Even in large institutions, however, there are real actuarial risks to self-insuring. In smaller educational institutions, self-insured plans are wholly impractical, since the incidence of total disabilities among covered employees is likely to vary widely from year to year. Small variations in numbers of disabled employees can result in relatively large changes in plan liabilities. Lack of cost predictability resulting from variations in plan experience are the principal reasons why both large and small employers generally prefer to pool their LTD risks through the use of insured plans that can take advantage of the laws of large numbers.

The benefit and eligibility provisions of noninsured LTD plans generally parallel those of insured plans. Typically, a plan booklet will be prepared and will describe eligibility rules and enrollment procedures, benefit amounts and maximums, offsets for Social Security, Workers' Compensation, and other employer-paid disability benefits, the benefit waiting period, duration of benefits, employee contributions, if any, and procedures for applying for benefits.

Like insured LTD plans, noninsured plans generally experience relatively higher claims rates for lower-paid staff members. For example, one large plan reported that nearly 9 percent of staff members earning $10,000 or less received disability income benefits under the plan, while among employees earning $24,000 or more, disabled beneficiaries represented less than 2/10 of 1 percent of employees. The absence of third-party administration can sometimes result in higher claims ratios for noninsured plans. Widely ranging and unpredictable experience can be tempered through advanced funding and the establishment of reserves as under insured plans. However, most educational institutions, as the survey results indicate, prefer not to get involved in such insurance functions as processing applications for benefits, predicting experience, setting up reserves, paying benefits, and monitoring disability status.

Regulation and Taxation
of Benefit Plans

Until 1974, federal government regulation of private pension plans was limited in scope and was exercised mainly through the Internal Revenue Code. The Employee Retirement Income Security Act of 1974 (ERISA) added a new dimension to federal regulation, however, and public policy regarding private pensions is now largely expressed by a combination of ERISA and the Internal Revenue Code. In addition, laws of the fifty states regulate insurance companies and, consequently, many provisions of the benefit plans they provide. Congress has the right to regulate insurance in interstate commerce, but the McCarran-Ferguson Act delegated the regulation function to the separate states, which may act in the absence of federal action.[1]

Public retirement systems were exempted from the standards set by ERISA, although that legislation did call for a study of public systems (published in March 1978) to assist the Congress in determining the appropriateness of extending comparable legislation to public plans.[2]

BACKGROUND OF FEDERAL REGULATION

Federal regulation of private pension plans started in a limited way in the early 1920s and was later consolidated in the Internal Revenue Code revisions of 1942. Colleges and universities, due to their nonprofit or public-support status, were not as closely affected by the federal measures as other employers, but in 1974 this situation was materially changed for the private educational institutions by the passage of ERISA. Following the congressional study of public plans that was called for by ERISA, several members of Congress announced plans to introduce legislation providing for state and local public retirement plans certain standards patterned after some of the previously enacted ERISA provisions.[3]

The earliest federal attention to private pension plans was related to taxation.[4] Most of the early industrial pension benefits were simply paid out of current company earnings, with costs treated as a current business expense. By the 1920s it became evident that there were advantages in establishing at least some reserves. As a result, many pay-as-you-go plans were transformed into trusts. Although they were by no means fully funded, separate trusts became a conventional mechanism of financing industrial pension plans.

The taxability of the income of pension trusts and the tax status of employer contributions to these trusts immediately became a question. In 1926, pension trusts created by private employers for the exclusive benefit of some or all employees were made exempt from federal income tax. Employer contributions to such trusts were to be treated as a deductible business expense. Nonprofit educational institutions received parallel treatment through their tax-exempt status. It was also provided that employer contributions to such trusts and the investment earnings from such contributions would not be taxable as income to the beneficiaries until actually distributed. These provisions had been applied earlier (in 1921) to trusts created by employers as a part of a stock-bonus or profit-sharing plan.

In 1928, to clear up an ambiguity in the 1926 law, employer contributions to an exempt trust on account of past service were specifically authorized as a deductible business expense. A decade later, a "no diversion—exclusive benefit" requirement was added. This law provided that under a pension trust instrument it must be impossible, at any time prior to the satisfaction of all liabilities due employees and their beneficiaries, for any part of the income to be used for or diverted to purposes other than the exclusive benefit of employees or their beneficiaries.

During these early years, pension protection in the educational world had been advancing under an insured system greatly different from the single-employer industrial pension trusts. The nonprofit TIAA system had been founded in 1918, and by 1940 its fully-vested plans covered a third of colleges and universities, including both privately and publicly supported institutions. In addition, employees of many publicly supported colleges, universities, and teachers' colleges were becoming covered under a wide variety of public retirement systems.

By the early 1940s it became apparent that the existing laws and regulations affecting business and industrial pension plans needed refinement. The tax treatment of pension trusts and contributions was simple and uncomplicated, but the trusts had often been established for relatively small groups of officers and favored key employees, apparently as a means of tax avoidance or deferment for persons in a position to create a trust in the first place. The challenge was to develop statutes that would be more effective in achieving a desired goal of broader employee welfare while preventing the use of employee trusts primarily for tax avoidance.

The Treasury Department submitted extensive proposals for revision of the federal tax laws relating to pension plans to the House Committee on Ways and Means early in 1942. It is interesting to note that the Treasury's proposals for the vesting of benefits under industrial plans had already become accepted practice in the plans of educational institutions. The Treasury recommended that pension plans of private employers, in order to retain their tax-exempt status, be required to meet the following three standards of vesting and nondiscrimination:

1. The right of the employee to his portion of the employer's contribution to the trust, and to its earnings, as well as to his own contributions, should be fully vested.

2. The trust should cover 70 percent or more of all employees, excluding employees who have been employed for less than a minimum period not exceeding five years, and casual, part-time, and seasonal employees, or such employees as qualify under a classification set up by

the employer and found by the commissioner not to be based upon any favoritism for employees who are officers, shareholders, supervising employees, or highly compensated employees.

3. The system of contributions and benefits under the trust should not discriminate in favor of officers, shareholders, supervising employees, or highly compensated employees.[5]

The original Treasury proposal calling for immediate vesting was later changed to gradual vesting, which in turn was dropped, so that a vesting standard was missing from the legislation by the time the 1942 revenue bill reached the floor of the Congress.[6] It was later confirmed that representatives of various groups had told the Treasury that a vesting requirement, however stated, would substantially increase the cost or reduce the retirement benefits under existing plans. Although employers took the initiative in bringing about the elimination of the vesting requirement, they were not solely responsible for its abandonment. Some union representatives favored collective bargaining as a basis for pension changes and expressed fear that plan terminations would occur if vesting was required and costs consequently rose.

While the 1942 code addressed the possibility of discrimination in favor of managers and other employees with comparable status, it ignored discrimination implicit in the absence of a standard for the vesting of accrued benefits. Thus, under many plans, employees who terminated service prior to eligibility for early or normal retirement could lose all the protection they thought they had. Another result was a continuing overstatement of the proportion of employees in the private sector with actual pension coverage, there being no distinction made between plan members who had attained vested status and those who had not. Consequently, a part of the apparent increase in pension protection over the next three decades was illusory in the sense that some portion of covered employees would not serve long enough to attain vested status in the plans to which they belonged. In addition, some employees who had attained vested status were not protected by adequate funding of the benefits promised.

Also missing from the 1942 legislation were funding standards for the pension obligations subject to the code's provisions. There was little or no discussion of this question during the hearings. The Internal Revenue Service seemed more concerned that a company might "overfund" its pension plan and exclude "too much" from taxable income. This was a significant factor in the subsequent underfunding of non-insured pension plans for several generations of workers.

It is interesting to speculate what the level of private pension protection would have become in the decades to follow had vesting and funding standards been incorporated in the 1942 law. It seems likely that more than thirty-five years of reasonable standards would have helped many workers and retirees over the years and made private pension plans as a whole much more significant as sources of income for retired workers.

The tax code adopted in 1942 did, however, incorporate the public policy principle that federal tax laws can and should be used as a means of requiring employers to meet express standards in voluntarily established private pension plans. Prior to 1942, the code had dealt narrowly with the tax status of pension contributions and trust earnings. The new code, without going very far, entered as a matter of public policy into the area of plan provisions. This was done through the code's requirements for plan "qualification" for tax-exempt status under Section 401(a). Under these provisions a plan was required to be: (1) for the exclusive benefit of the employer's employees or their beneficiaries; (2) for the purpose of distributing the corpus and income to the employees; (3) protected from use or diversion of funds by the employer before satisfying the plan's liabilities to the employees and their beneficiaries; and (4) nondiscriminatory as to extent of coverage, i.e., a large percentage of regular employees eligible to participate, and neither contributions nor benefits discriminating in favor of officers, stockholders, or highly compensated employees or supervisors. The provisions of Section 401(a) remained relatively unchanged for over thirty years.

Another area in which the 1942 code turned out to be weak related to the fiduciary aspects of fund management. The code provided for little or no real protection of pension plan participants against financial mismanagement on the part of trustees and officers of noninsured pension plans. While insured pension plans were protected by the insurance laws of the various states, the separate pension trusts that characterized the majority of pension plans in the private sector offered opportunities for self-dealing, and a number of examples of serious breaches of fiduciary responsibility reached public attention.

Outside of the tax area, another important piece of legislation generally affecting pension plans was the Labor Management Relations Act of 1947—the Taft-Hartley law. This act amended and supplemented the original basic labor relations law of 1935, the Wagner Act. Among the areas of collective bargaining covered by the Taft-Hartley law were "rates of pay, wages, hours of employment, or other conditions of employment. . . ." Within a year after the law was enacted a question arose between the Inland Steel Company and the Steelworkers' Union as to whether it imposed a duty on employers to bargain with the representatives of their employees on the subject of pensions. The National Labor Relations Board decided that companies were required to bargain on pension plans. The ruling was based on the dual grounds that the term "wages" as defined in the statute includes any emoluments of value such as pension or insurance benefits, and that the provisions of pension plans come within the definition of "conditions of employment." The Federal Court of Appeals (Seventh Circuit) affirmed the view of the NLRB that retirement plans were a proper subject for collective bargaining. The Court's opinion in the Inland Steel case read in part as follows:

While, as the company has demonstrated, a reasonable argument can be made that the benefits flowing from such a plan are not "wages," we think the better and more logical argument is on the other side, and certainly there is, in our opinion, no sound basis for an argument that such a plan is not clearly included in the phrase, "other conditions of employment." . . . It surely cannot be seriously disputed but that such a pledge [to provide pensions under a plan] on the part of the Company forms a part of the consideration for work performed. . . . In this view, the pension thus promised would appear to be as much a part of his "wages" as the money paid him at the time of the rendition of his services. But again we say that in any event such a plan is one of the "conditions of employment."[7]

With the introduction of the 1942 code, it became necessary for employers outside the nonprofit and public sectors to "qualify" their plans in order that their contributions to such plans could become deductible as a business expense, and in order for the investment earnings of such plans to be exempt from federal income tax. Since nonprofit organizations, including educational institutions, are not subject to federal income tax, the qualification procedures were unnecessary and were not required. One of the results of the "qualification" of a business or industrial plan was that employer payments to the pension fund on behalf of employees were not considered as taxable income to the employees until received as a pension benefit. By 1958, it appeared that a more precise parallel treatment should be provided for participants in the pension plans of nonprofit organizations. This was done in the Technical Amendments Act of 1958.

The new section of the code—Section 403(b)—established a limit on the amount of an educational employer's contributions that would not be taxable as current income to the employee, the "20-percent rule." Under this rule, employer contributions to a vested annuity contract would not constitute taxable income to the employee provided they did not exceed 20 percent of the employee's includable compensation, times years of service, less total contributions made to the employee's annuity in all prior years. Under Treasury Department regulations interpreting this provision, employee contributions to vested annuities could acquire the tax-deferral status accorded employer contributions through salary-reduction agreements made within the 20-percent rule limits. These provisions and subsequent modifications are described in more detail later in this chapter.

Pension plan participants are thus exempt from paying current income tax on employer contributions to their pension plan only if the plan is "qualified" under Section 401(a) of the Internal Revenue Code or operates under the parallel 403(b) limitations for nonprofit organizations. Publicly supported educational institutions are among those employers whose contributions to fully vested annuities are tax-deferred for employees under the limitations of Section 403(b). However, public employers have been in a gray area when it comes to the alternative application of Section 401(a) to their plans. In theory, employer contributions on behalf of public employees to public retirement systems would be taxable as income to those employees if the plan were not "qualified." In practice, however, the Internal Revenue

Service has considered public retirement plans as qualified and has thus disposed of the question as to whether the state and local plans meet the qualification requirements of the code, thus exempting participants from treating employer contributions as the equivalent of current income.

In other 1958 legislation, the Welfare and Pension Plans Disclosure Act of 1958, the Congress sought to strengthen the protection of pension plan participants from financial mismanagement by requiring plans qualified under Section 401(a) of the Internal Revenue Code to file with the Secretary of Labor each year a report, disclosing their financial operations. The act excluded the plans of nonprofit organizations and of public employers. The intent of the law was to utilize disclosure of financial practices as a means of informing participants of situations that might require corrective action. The act was amended in 1962 to make it possible for the Justice Department, as well as affected individuals, to bring legal action and designate as criminal offenses breaches of fiduciary responsibility. However, the reports required by the law were not sufficient to reveal questionable financial practices of plan operations, and audits were not provided for. Staffing by the Labor Department for examination of the required reports was never adequate, and the act did not achieve its intended purposes.

Although the 1942 revenue revisions had attempted to prevent discrimination in favor of certain employee groups, there was nothing to prevent a pension plan from being established, continued in operation for a fairly short time on behalf of long-service employees entitled to benefits under the plan (very often managers and highly compensated employees) and then terminated once these employees had retired. A "termination-vesting" provision, added in 1962 in Section 401(a)(7), sought to correct the abuse by providing that "a trust shall not constitute a qualified trust under this section unless . . . , upon its termination or upon complete discontinuance of contributions under the plan, the rights of all employees to benefits accrued to the date of such termination or discontinuance, to the extent then funded, or the amounts credited to the employees' accounts are nonforfeitable."[8]

By the early 1960s it was apparent that as a matter of public policy more attention would have to be given to the operation of private pension plans if they were ultimately to play a significant and reliable role in the provision of income in old age. The Social Security program had been developed to provide a "floor" of benefits upon which other pensions and private savings could be built. The potential role of private pensions in providing old-age security, and their significance to the economy in other ways, led President Kennedy to appoint, in March 1962, a committee to carry out a "review of the implications of the growing retirement and welfare funds for the financial structure of the economy, as well as a review of the role and character of the private pension and other retirement systems in the economic security system of the nation. . . ." This committee's report was released in 1965.[9] It concluded that there was a strong public interest in sound private pension plans and offered numerous recommendations for legislation setting standards for vesting, funding, plan termination provisions, and fiduciary protection.

Just prior to the report's appearance, a shutdown of the South Bend, Indiana, Studebaker Corporation plant revealed heavy losses in pension expectations, including those of vested senior employees, due to insufficient funding. In the same year (1964), Professor Merton C. Bernstein published a comprehensive and influential analysis of private pensions and their possible future directions. The report documented and described many of the principal weaknesses of private pension plans.[10] Three years later (1967), Senator Jacob K. Javits of New York introduced a bill that generally aimed at the implementation of the major recommendations of the president's committee. Later, Senator Harrison Williams of New Jersey joined with Senator Javits in introducing a series of related bills. In the House, Representative John H. Dent (Pennsylvania) introduced similar bills beginning in 1969. Subsequently, other pension bills were introduced in both chambers, further hearings were held, fact-finding studies were carried out by the Treasury and Labor departments, and on September 2, 1974 (Labor Day) a comprehensive new pension act, the Employee Retirement Income Security Act of 1974 (ERISA) was signed into law.[11]

EMPLOYEE RETIREMENT INCOME SECURITY ACT (ERISA)

One of the main features of this important legislation, the most significant for pension plans since the Revenue Act of 1942, was its provision for the vesting of pension benefits. A pension benefit is vested when the participant has a right, whether or not employment continues, to receive at normal or early retirement the pension benefits (deferred benefits) he or she has accumulated to date. Since immediate full vesting of benefits had long been provided for in higher education through the widespread use of TIAA-CREF plans, the new vesting standards did not require changes in the vesting provisions of these plans. But for pension plans in business and industry, the ERISA standards in many cases required substantial plan changes, since delays in vesting were common to almost all of the plans.

Prior to ERISA, the sole legal requirement for vesting under private pension plans was that all of a participant's accrued benefits had to vest in case a plan was terminated or in case employer contributions permanently ceased. Otherwise, there was no mandated vesting standard and virtually all private pension plans included delayed vesting provisions, with the exception of the TIAA-CREF plans in the education field. These long delays built up barriers to individual changes of employment and to labor mobility in general, and they resulted in low benefits for many workers, or in none at all. Overall, the widespread pattern of vesting delays limited the effectiveness of private pension plans.

Vesting. ERISA provided for three alternative minimum vesting standards. One permits the delay of any vesting until the completion of ten years of service, at which time all accrued benefits vest and benefits earned thereafter are fully and immediately vested. This is the provision now most frequently used in private pension plans. A second standard provides for gradual vesting, beginning after five years of service and continuing with full vesting after fifteen years. This alternative provides that at the end of five years a plan must vest at least 25 percent of the employee's accrued benefits. Over the next five years, benefits must vest 5 percent more each year, and over the last five-year period an additional 10 percent per year. The third available standard utilizes a combination of service and age: after five years of service accrued benefits must be 50 percent vested as soon as the employee's age and years of service add up to 45 (the "Rule of 45"). Each year thereafter, benefits must vest an additional 10 percent until full vesting takes place.

These minimum standards are recognized as far from ideal. A five-year vesting standard was discussed, but in the committee stage it was concluded that five-year minimum vesting would have to wait until some later time because the proposed standards would impose, along with the other requirements of the law, substantially increased costs. Given the value of a mobile labor force and the dynamics of the U.S. economy, plus the important human values involved in assuring adequate private pension protection, it would seem that a next step in pension reform would be to bring all plans to a five-year minimum standard, at least for all workers age 30 or over. Although a lower minimum would result in increased pension costs, this must be balanced against the ultimate test of a pension plan: its capacity to provide benefits reasonably commensurate with related employee service.

Funding. ERISA introduced new funding standards for defined benefit plans. One of the vulnerable spots of defined benefit retirement plans had been (and still is) the flexibility of available funding methods. While in some respects an advantage, flexibility often has resulted in understatement of plan costs and liabilities. In the process of averaging current costs over all employees, of whatever age and salary, and in spreading prior service liabilities out over future years, it seems to be that part of the financial burden of defined benefit plans has been continually thrust forward, with current costs understated. In part, this situation results from the many choices that are available in the selection of assumptions about future investment earnings and wage increases, both of which are keys to a proper and realistic statement of plan costs. The tendency is to emphasize a "conservative" approach, which usually means investment earnings assumptions that are somewhat higher than the wage increase assumptions, a relationship that is considered to be in a "conservative" balance. However, investment earnings assumptions that substantially exceed wage increase assumptions can result in understatement of current costs and in an unwelcome growth in unfunded liabilities. Any advantage is illusory, for over the long run it hardly seems desirable to operate a pension plan that may require future administrators to raise funds that should have been set aside earlier as a current expense. Educational employers, with their limited budgets and constraints on tuition charges, are especially aware of the dangers of underestimating pension costs.

ERISA sought to limit the latitude of the assumptions employed in the determination of normal costs for defined benefit plans. The law established requirements for actuarial certification of the "reasonableness" of the assumptions used. But reasonable is a flexible word, and only the future can tell whether real reform was achieved.

Prior to ERISA, there was no requirement for the amortization of past service liabilities of defined benefit pension plans, although it was required that the interest on such liabilities be paid as a part of current contributions to the plans. There was a limit on the maximum extent to which amortization could occur: 10 percent per year of the outstanding liability. ERISA changed the funding requirements for defined benefit pension plans so that the minimum amount that an employer must contribute to a defined benefit plan includes the normal costs of funding the plan *plus* amortization of past service costs, increases in liabilities and experience losses, *less* amortization of decreases in pension liabilities and experience gains. The amortization payments must be calculated on a level payment basis and the payments must include interest and principal (not interest only as in the past).

Payments of initial past service costs, that is, costs in recognition of an employee's service prior to the adoption of the defined benefit plan, must be amortized over a period not to exceed thirty years. For plans in existence on January 1, 1974, past service liabilities already in existence may be funded over an amortization period of forty years, except that past service liabilities arising after the first plan year to which ERISA applies must be amortized over a thirty-year period.

Under ERISA, the "normal cost" of funding a plan must be met each year, and an actuarial certification must be made with respect to the adequacy of the contributions and the cost method utilized under a defined benefit plan. As noted earlier, however, the addition of this standard in ERISA with respect to funding by no means eliminates the possibility of continued underfunding in defined benefit pension plans. Normal costs may be understated through selective use of interest, turnover, or mortality assumptions. Past service liabilities may increase, despite amortization schedules, if benefit improvements are introduced or if the effect of future wage increases on the benefit levels are being underestimated. ERISA requires that "experience losses" of this kind be continually monitored and that such losses be amortized over a period of fifteen years.

Pension Benefit Guaranty Corporation. In the past, when an employer ceased business operations, the presence of unfunded liabilities, large or small, led to many pension disappointments. Public attention was galvanized by the Studebaker Corporation's plan termination, but there had been many other plan terminations prior to the Studebaker announcement, and others occurred thereafter. Through its funding standards, ERISA sought to reduce the level of unfunded liabilities in pension plans. But in itself this would not eliminate the prospect or possibility of plan terminations. Consequently, the reform legislation incorporated a scheme of plan termination insurance. Under this provision, qualified defined benefit plans are required to participate in a plan termination insurance system to insure participants and beneficiaries against loss of benefits arising from a complete or partial plan termination. The insurance arrangement required is administered by a government agency within the Department of Labor, the Pension Benefit Guaranty Corporation (PBGC). Each covered plan is required to pay a per-employee premium. The insurance plan provides for benefit payments by the PBGC to vested participants of an insufficiently funded, terminated plan, up to certain stated limits on monthly benefits payable.

To protect the PBGC against deliberate termination of an underfunded plan in order to transfer the liabilities to the PBGC, the law provides that the PBGC may claim up to 30 percent of the employer's net worth in case of a pension fund failure. The claim has the high priority status of a tax lien. Prior to ERISA, pension benefits could not be paid if a pension trust's assets were insufficient to meet its obligations; there was no recourse to the employer. The PBGC provisions and premium charges do not apply to defined contribution plans.

Reporting and Disclosure. Congressional hearings prior to ERISA revealed that lack of employee understanding of employers' pension plans had created serious problems. For example, many employees had not realized that lengthy periods of plan membership did not necessarily guarantee a retirement income. In testimony, many former employees indicated that information about their pension plan's benefits had been disseminated, but that the vesting requirements for benefit entitlement had not been emphasized.[12] The result was what was described by a television documentary on pensions as "the broken promise."[13] In fact, relevant plan documents, had they been accessible and understandable to participating employees, would have revealed that no promises were made beyond those described in the pension plan provisions. But it seemed that descriptive booklets often glossed over negative aspects of coverage, and in visual form depicted happy retirees in attitudes of recreation, relaxation, and comfort.

If some of the important details of individual coverage under pension plans were neglected, full information about the financial condition of the plans was often even less available. This hiatus is still the case among many public retirement systems, not affected by ERISA legislation.

Not only was information unavailable to employees, it was lacking for regulatory purposes. The Welfare and Pension Plans Disclosure Act (1958) had aimed to provide the Department of Labor with information through which the condition of pension plans could be monitored. But the attempt failed in its purpose, largely because the information sought was not sufficient to enable a judgment of the soundness of the pension plan, and because the Department of Labor was not sufficiently staffed to examine the reports.

ERISA established new reporting and disclosure requirements for pension and other employee welfare plans. Basically, such reports and disclosures are made to plan participants and to the Department of Labor. All employee pension and welfare plans in the private sector are covered by the law, except that welfare plans (group life and health insurance plans) with fewer than one hundred participants are not required to file a description of their plan under certain stated conditions.

Form EBS-1. Under ERISA, each pension plan and each welfare plan with more than one hundred employees is required to file with the Department of Labor a plan description form EBS-1. New plans established after January 1976, are required to file their initial EBS-1 form within 120 days following the effective date of the plan. The form must be updated every five years to reflect any changes in a plan that has already filed an EBS-1 form. A copy of the current EBS-1 form must be provided within 30 days to participants and beneficiaries who request it. Since the Summary Plan Description (see below) contains essentially the same information, the Department of Labor had proposed, as of this writing, the elimination of the EBS-1 form.[14]

Summary of Material Plan Modifications. When plan provisions are modified through changes that are "most important to participants," as outlined in the form EBS-1 instructions, a summary of material plan modifications must be filed with the Department of Labor no later than 210 days after the close of the plan year (generally the calendar year or year ending with the anniversary date of the plan) in which the modification occurred. The summary must also be provided to participants and beneficiaries within the same time period. It must also be sent within 30 days upon written request of participants or beneficiaries.

Summary Plan Description. In addition to the EBS-1 form, a "summary plan description" (SPD) must also be filed with the Department of Labor. This summary, for which there is no officially prescribed form, must offer a description of all the principal elements of the plan and it must be written in a manner that permits an understanding of the plan by the average plan participant. The initial SPD must be filed within 120 days following the later of the effective date or the adoption of the plan. If changes in the plan are made, the summary plan description must be supplemented by the summary of material plan modifications, mentioned just above, as an amendment to the SPD. If a plan has been revised (with amendments to the original SPD having been sent to the Department of Labor), a completely new and updated SPD must be submitted five years after the original SPD was filed. In any event, even if no changes whatever have been made in the plan, an employer must nevertheless resubmit the SPD after a lapse of ten years.

Information for Employees. The EBS-1 form must be made available for the inspection of plan participants either during working hours on the work premises or on written request. The summary plan description must likewise be made available, but, in addition, it must be provided to each employee within 90 days of that employee's entitlement to eligibility for plan membership. For a newly established plan, the SPD must be provided automatically to plan participants within 120 days after the later of the effective date of the plan or the date of the plan's adoption. Automatic provision of information to participants is also required following any material modifications to the plan (such as are required for reports to the Department of

Labor). Every employee must be supplied with an updated SPD every ten years even if no material plan changes have been made, and every five years if the plan has been changed since the previous SPD distribution.

The plans and benefits described in form EBS-1 and the summary plan descriptions and amendments all are derived from an original plan document. The plan document is the basic legal instrument establishing the plan in all its details. For example, a college or university's retirement plan resolution, a group insurance policy, any relevant collective bargaining agreements, documents describing sick leave and sick pay plans, and so on, constitute the family of plan documents underlying pension and welfare plans. Plan documents do not, under ERISA, have to be filed with the Department of Labor. However, they must be available to plan participants on written request, and must be available for inspection on the premises during working hours by plan participants. Changes in these documents will, of course, trigger changes that must be filed with the Department of Labor.

Financial Information. The summary plan description and form EBS-1 do not provide sufficient ongoing information to enable the monitoring of the financial condition of pension and welfare plans. Consequently, an annual financial report is also required. The Internal Revenue Service provides annual report form 5500 for pension and welfare plans with one hundred or more participants, and form 5500-C for plans with less than one hundred participants. Annual report forms 5500 or 5500-C must be filed with the Internal Revenue Service each year by the end of the seventh month following the end of the plan year. The forms are forwarded to the Department of Labor by the Internal Revenue Service.

Copies of annual report form 5500 or 5500-C are not required to be distributed to plan members or to be made available to them for routine inspection. However, a copy must be supplied within 30 days to plan members who request a copy in writing. A summary annual (financial) report must be provided to plan members, however, for each plan year, no later than nine months following the end of the plan year. There is no prescribed form for this summary annual report, except that a copy of form 5500 or 5500-C must be included as a part of the summary annual report for those plans for which the form was filed.

Other Reports. In addition to the reports mentioned above, administrators of institutions having retirement plans may be required to provide some or all of the following reports, depending on the nature of the plan:

1. Schedule B, Annual Reporting Form—actuarial information for defined benefit plans subject to minimum funding standards.
2. Schedule SSA, Annual Reporting Form—information concerning plan participants who terminated employment during the year with deferred vested benefits, to be filed with the IRS.
3. Personal Accrued and Vested Pension Statement—must be sent to participants of pension plans within thirty days of written request but not more often than once a year.
4. PBGC-1—Premium Payment Form, to be filed with the Pension Benefit Guaranty Cor-

poration seven months after the beginning of the plan year, for plans covered by PBGC termination insurance.

5. Notice of Reportable Event—to be filed with PBGC thirty days after knowledge that such event has occurred.

6. Notice of Intent to Terminate—must be filed with PBGC at least ten days before proposed termination of those plans subject to PBGC insurance requirements.

AGE DISCRIMINATION IN EMPLOYMENT ACT (ADEA)

The purpose of age discrimination legislation, which affects such matters as hiring, job retention, compensation and other terms and conditions of employment, including retirement plans, is to protect employees from discriminatory employment practices. The Age Discrimination in Employment Act of 1967 (ADEA), with 1978 amendments, prohibits discrimination in employment practices against persons between the ages of 40 and 70 on the basis of their age.[15] The law applies to employers having twenty or more employees, including public employers, to employment agencies serving such employers, and to labor organizations with twenty-five or more members. Several states have gone beyond the requirements of the federal law by completely eliminating age-mandated retirement, either in the public sector, the private sector, or both. For federal civil service employees, the 1978 ADEA amendments completely eliminated a mandatory retirement age.

Two major exceptions were made by the 1978 amendments to the extension to age 70 of the earliest age for mandatory retirement. Colleges and universities were allowed to continue to require retirement of tenured employees as early as age 65 until July 1, 1982. The other exception is provided for employees in a "bona fide executive or high policymaking position," but only if they are entitled at age 65 to an immediate employer-purchased annual nonforfeitable retirement benefit, exclusive of Social Security, which is the equivalent of a single life annuity of at least $27,000, provided by the final employer's plan. For employees to whom this exemption applies, the lowest mandatory retirement age continues to be 65.

An employer may retain a stated "normal" retirement age below 70. (See chapter 3.) Short of termination for cause, an employee may wish to retire at the normal age or may decide to keep on working, perhaps until the mandatory age. For employees who remain employed after attainment of the plan's normal retirement age, Department of Labor regulations permit termination of retirement plan contributions or benefit accruals at the normal age.[16] Under defined contribution plans that are not "supplemental plans," the regulations permit discontinuation of employer contributions to retirement plans upon the participant's attainment of the normal retirement age. Defined benefit plans are not required to credit, for purposes of determining benefits, any service or salary increases which occur after the plan's normal retirement age, or to pay the actuarial equivalent of normal retirement benefits if employment continues beyond the normal retirement age. The Department of

Labor has stated that it will scrutinize carefully any pension plan providing for an unusually low normal retirement age.

A defined contribution plan is defined as "supplemental" if it is maintained by an employer in addition to a defined benefit plan. Where an employer has no defined benefit plan but two or more defined contribution plans covering the same employees, all but one of the defined contribution plans would be defined as supplemental. The one defined contribution plan which is not supplemental would not be required to provide for contributions after normal retirement age. The employer would determine which plan was not supplemental. When an employer has two or more defined contribution plans that cover different employees, there is no need to designate any of the plans as supplemental as long as there is no overlap in participation among the plans. (See chapter 3 for further discussion of supplemental plans.)

Department of Labor regulations permit an employer to exclude from a defined benefit retirement plan, on the basis of age, an employee hired within the five years preceding the plan's stated normal retirement age, or at any time after the normal retirement age. An individual hired five or more years prior to the normal retirement age could not be excluded on the basis of age under a defined benefit plan subject to ERISA. Under defined contribution plans, no employee hired prior to the normal retirement age may be excluded from the plan.

The extension to age 70 of the earliest age for mandatory retirement raised a number of questions regarding benefit levels and costs of life insurance, health insurance, sick pay, and disability income plans. Department of Labor regulations regarding these plans state in general that reductions in benefits for older workers are permitted where such reductions are based on actuarially significant cost considerations. Whether or not age is an actuarially significant cost factor in plan design depends on the actual cost data for the plan in question, or on reasonable actuarial data if the actual cost data are not statistically significant because of the size of the plan. For those benefits in which age is not an actuarially significant factor in plan design, such as paid vacations and paid sick leave, the regulations require that older workers be provided with the same benefits as younger workers.

For group life insurance, the Department of Labor regulations permit the continuation of the common practice of maintaining a constant amount of life insurance coverage until age 65 and then providing reduced amounts of insurance for those who remain employed, as long as the amount of reduction in insurance is no greater than is justified by the increased cost of the coverage. Coverage may be terminated upon the termination of employment or the attainment of age 70, whichever occurs first.

Under health insurance plans, the regulations permit plans to reduce benefits at age 65 to recognize the availability of Medicare. However, reductions in *total* medical benefits (that is, medical insurance plus Medicare) are not permitted for employees between ages 65 to 70. Thus, any age-based reduction in benefits provided under a medical insurance plan is not acceptable unless it occurs because of the availability of an identical benefit from Medicare. Employers must pay an employee's Medicare Part B premium to the extent it exceeds the employee's contribution to the pre-age 65 medical plan.

Insured long-term disability income plans have typically provided for disability benefits only until attainment of age 65, the usual normal retirement age, at which time benefits under the retirement plan begin. With the extension to age 70 of the protection of the Age Discrimination in Employment Act, the relevant regulations provide that benefit reductions on the basis of age before age 70 in the level or duration of benefits are justifiable only if they are based on age-related cost considerations. For example, the coverage and payments may continue to age 70, but the level of benefits can be reduced for older employees. Or, the benefit level can remain constant but the duration may vary with age, as follows: (a) LTD payments may cease at age 65 if an employee becomes disabled at or before age 60; (b) if disability occurs after age 60, LTD payments may be cut off after five years or when the individual reaches age 70, whichever is earlier.

FEDERAL TAXATION OF ANNUITIES

As applied to individuals, the basic principle of the federal taxation of annuity contributions and benefits is that employer contributions to a pension plan and the plan's investment earnings are not currently taxable as income to the employee, but are included in taxable income later, when received as pension or annuity benefits.

The part of annuity income attributable to employee contributions is treated differently. These contributions, made from the individual's income after current income tax is paid, become what is defined in the federal tax law as the individual's "investment in the contract."[17] Since the individual has already paid income taxes on these contributed amounts, under the tax law a retired annuitant receives as tax-free annuity income an amount equal to his or her investment in the contract. Consequently, during the retirement years the annuitant reports as taxable income only that part of annuity income (usually the larger part) that is considered to result from previously untaxed employer contributions and from the investment earnings on the annuity funds. When the employer has paid all the premiums (a noncontributory pension plan), the full annuity income is taxable as received.

Since an individual's annuity or pension income is payable for life, and may also continue as a life annuity to a designated survivor, federal tax law sets forth the way income taxes are applied to these benefits over the periods involved. The law specifies which of two rules—the *special* rule or the *general* rule—will be automatically applied to determine how the retiree (and the survivor, if a survivor option is elected) will receive the investment in the contract as tax-free income. The balance of the annuity is taxed as ordinary current income.

The special rule applies only if an employee contributed part of the premiums and the total annuity income over the first thirty-six months of benefit payments is expected to be equal to or greater than the investment in the contract. Under this special rule, contractual annuity payments are not taxable until the total of such payments received equals the investment in the contract. Thereafter, the full annuity income is taxable. Where extra annuity dividends become payable, the taxable income includes the full amount of additional dividends received.

The general rule applies to all annuities except those covered by the special rule. Under the general rule, the investment in the contract is distributed as tax-free income evenly over the number of years payments are *expected* to be made, as determined from actuarial tables published by the Internal Revenue Service. Once determined, the annual tax-free income remains fixed and any amount received in excess of it each year is taxable.

As an example of the use of the special rule and the general rule in determining the part of retirement income that is taxable, assume that Professor Roe retires at age 65 and begins to receive both a fixed and a variable single-life annuity. For the illustration, we assume that the contractual fixed-dollar payment is $100 per month. Let us also assume a variable annuity income, initially also $100 per month. In addition, it is assumed that both the employer and employee contributed to the cost of the pension benefits. During the first thirty-six months of retirement, the total payments expected to be paid from each annuity would be $100 × 36, or $3,600 from each of the annuities.

Special Rule. To illustrate this rule, let us say that the investment in the contract for each annuity is $3,000, the amount, that is, that the employee contributed towards the annuity during the working years. This is less than the $3,600 expected to be paid during the first thirty-six months of retirement. The special rule, therefore, applies. Professor Roe's fixed-dollar *contractual* payments will be tax-free through the thirtieth monthly payment, at which time the total contractual payments received will equal the investment in the contract. Beginning with the thirty-first monthly payment, the entire fixed-dollar annuity income will be fully taxable. Any annuity dividends paid to Professor Roe will be taxable in the year received, even though the contractual payments may not yet be taxable. Under a public retirement system, any increase in benefits due to a cost-of-living escalator, for example, would be treated the same way as annuity dividends.

Professor Roe's variable annuity income will be tax-free until the total received equals $3,000, the investment in the contract. Thereafter, the variable annuity income will be fully taxable. Since the income will vary in dollar amount from year to year, it is not possible to determine in advance exactly what date the variable income becomes taxable.

General Rule. The general rule is applied when the investment in the contract is greater than the amount of income that is expected to be received by the end of the first thirty-six months. Here we take the same annuity income, but this time assume that Professor Roe's investment in the contract for each annuity is $5,400, which is

Table 9.1. Taxable and Tax-Free Portions of Annuity Income—General Rule, Federal Income Tax

Item	TIAA Income		CREF Income	
1. Investment in the contract	$5,400		$5,400	
2. Annual contractual payments	$1,200		$1,200[a]	
	Male	*Female*	*Male*	*Female*
3. Number of years payments are expected to be made	15	18.2	15	18.2
4. Annual tax-free income (item 1 divided by item 3)	$360	$297	$360	$297
5. Annual taxable contractual payments (item 2 minus item 4)	$840[b]	$903[b]	$840[a]	$903[a]

[a]First year only; variable annuity income will change each year.
[b]Dividends payable under TIAA annuity contracts are taxed as received.

larger than the $3,600 that would be received during the first thirty-six months. According to the Internal Revenue Service actuarial tables, the number of years that single-life annuity payments are expected to be made (on the average) to a man aged 65 is 15 years (to a woman aged 65 it is 18.2 years). The resulting annual tax-free and taxable incomes are shown in table 9.1. The tax-free component of each contractual payment remains the same each year for life; of the total fixed-dollar income, about a third to a fourth is tax-free. As noted, income represented by annuity dividends is taxed separately and is fully taxable in the year received. The annual tax-free income from the variable annuity will remain the same each year for life, but since the income from this annuity will vary in dollar amount from year to year, the taxable income will vary, being the excess of the total amount received each year over the fixed annual tax-free amount.

Since many retirees select an income option to provide a continuing income for a spouse or other beneficiary, the calculation under the general rule for any option other than the single-life annuity (illustrated) requires adjustments to account for the provision for payments to a second annuitant. If the annuity provides for a lifetime income to a second annuitant, the IRS tables provide an appropriate actuarial factor to determine the number of years payments are expected to be made, taking into account the life expectancy of both individuals. After the death of one annuitant, the general rule continues to apply to the survivor's payments. If the survivor's payments are reduced to two-thirds or one-half of the original amount, the annual tax-free and taxable amounts are proportionately reduced.

Some annuity options provide for the continuation to a beneficiary of payments for a guaranteed period (a refund provision) in case the original annuitant dies before the end of that period. To account for this guaranteed period, a reduction in the amount of the investment in the contract is made before it is distributed as tax-free income to a beneficiary. After the death of the annuitant or of both a primary and secondary annuitant, but prior to the termination of a guaranteed period, the beneficiary's contractual payments are not taxable until the total received by the beneficiary, plus the tax-free income that was received by the annuitants, equals the full amount of the investment in the contract before it was adjusted. Thereafter, the payments are fully taxable.

Federal Taxation of Preretirement Death Benefits. Most or all preretirement death benefits may be subject to federal income tax. The taxable portion is the entire amount accumulated in the annuity except for the sum of any premiums that were paid from after-tax income.

If a single-sum payment is available to a deceased employee's beneficiary, the entire taxable portion is taxed as ordinary income in the year of the employee's death, unless the beneficiary elects within sixty days after the death to begin receiving benefits as an annuity income. When an annuity income is selected within the sixty-day period, income taxation is distributed over the years of actual payment. If an annuity income payment method is not elected within the sixty-day period, the beneficiary is taxed on the entire taxable portion in the year of the employee's death. When the entire benefit is taxed in one year, up to $5,000 of the taxable portion is excluded from taxable income if the employing institution was a school, college, or university not an integral part of state or local government (Sec. 101(b)).

If the single-sum method is not made available to the beneficiary, the sixty-day limit does not apply and the beneficiary may take longer to select an income method of payment without being taxed on the entire taxable portion in the year of death. The payment method selected may provide for income for the lifetime of the beneficiary, either with or without a minimum number of payments guaranteed in any event, or an income for a fixed period of years. Taxation is then spread over the years of actual payment of the benefits.

Some annuity owners prohibit the use of a single sum when designating their beneficiary in order to give a beneficiary more time to decide on how to receive the death benefit without the entire taxable portion being taxed in one year.

Tax-deferred annuities, described below, are taxed the same as annuities under employer pension plans in which all the contributions have been paid by the employer. Consequently, there is no tax-free portion.

Federal Estate Taxes. Any benefits payable after an annuity owner's death, either before or after retirement, are subject to federal estate taxes. The portion of the benefit attributable to the investment in the contract is included in the gross estate. The portion attributable to contributions made by a school, college, or university not an integral part of state or local government is excluded from estate taxes, provided the benefits are not paid to the decedent's estate.

TAX-DEFERRED ANNUITIES

Employees of public schools and of nonprofit organizations tax exempt under Section 501(c)(3) of the Internal Revenue Code may arrange with their employer to divert a portion of before-tax salary to purchase fully-vested retirement benefits under the provisions of Section 403(b) of the code. A nonprofit 501(c)(3) organization is one that is organized and operated exclusively for religious, charitable, scientific, literary, educational, or safety-testing purposes, or for the prevention of cruelty to children or animals. Employees of public schools and of public colleges and universities are eligible to purchase tax-deferred annuities, as are employees of private colleges, universities, and schools.

To purchase a tax-deferred annuity, the employee and employer enter into an agreement under which the employee authorizes a reduction in salary in order to release funds for the employer to pay to an annuity contract that is fully vested in the employee. This is sometimes described as the "salary-or-annuity" option. Within limits prescribed by the Internal Revenue Code, the amount of the reduction is not currently taxable as income to the employee. However, the tax comes later, when the resulting benefits are received.

The advantage of saving through tax-deferred annuities is partly due to the deferral of income tax on a portion of salary to a time when an individual will probably be in a lower tax bracket and partly to income tax deferral on the compounding investment earnings of the annuity contributions. Tables 9.2 and 9.3 compare the results from saving through a regular after-tax savings account and a tax-deferred annuity. Table 9.2 shows that for the same spendable income, a tax-deferred annuity contribution through salary reduction enables savings to be increased from $1,129 per year to $1,577 per year. In this illustration, the gross salary of $25,000 would normally leave an after-tax amount of $21,129. If living expenses take $20,000 $1,129 is available for after-tax savings. An alternative saving method, however, is through the tax-deferred annuity. While still having $20,000 to live on, a salary reduction amount of $1,577 per year can be paid into the tax-deferred annuity, or $448 more in savings each year.

Table 9.3 shows the result of the two accumulations. Under the savings account, the compound investment earnings reflect the smaller deposits and the income tax (at a 28 percent marginal rate) that must be paid currently out of these earnings.

Table 9.2. Amount Available for Savings in a Savings Account Compared with Amount Available through Salary Reduction for a Tax-Deferred Annuity

	For Savings Account	For Tax-Deferred Annuity
Gross salary	$25,000	$25,000
Less TDA savings (salary reduction)	—	1,577
Taxable salary[a]	$25,000	$23,423
Less federal income tax	3,871	3,423
After-tax salary	$21,129	$20,000
Less after-tax savings	1,129	—
Spendable income	$20,000	$20,000

[a]1978 federal tax only, joint return, four exemptions, standard deduction.

Table 9.3. Savings Account Accumulation Compared with Tax-Deferred Annuity Accumulation

End of Year	Amount Accumulated in Savings Account with Income Tax Deducted[ad]	Amount Accumulated in Tax-Deferred Annuity[ab]
1	$ 1,157	$ 1,567
5	6,462	9,147
10	14,919	22,432
15	25,986	41,728
20	40,467	69,752
Monthly income from purchase of annuity[c]:		
Before taxes	$351	$627
After taxes[d]	$304	$452

[a]Annual interest rate of 7.75 percent credited monthly.
[b]Expense charge of 4 percent deducted from each annuity premium, paid monthly, TIAA 1978 rates and dividends, not guaranteed for the future.
[c]Assumes purchase of TIAA joint and two-thirds benefit to survivor, 1978 rates and dividends, not guaranteed for the future, both annuitants age 65, 3.5 percent expense charge deducted from savings account accumulation for annuity purchase.
[d]28 percent marginal rate.

Under the TDA, the deposits are larger and the investment earnings are not currently taxable to the employee. As a result, at the end of twenty years the savings account has accumulated $40,467 and the TDA has accumulated $69,752, 72 percent more.

Table 9.3 also shows the annuity income at age 65 that can be purchased by the accumulated savings account as well as by the tax-deferred annuity accumulation. Even though the tax-deferred annuity is wholly taxable, on an after-tax basis it is still 49 percent larger than the annuity purchased with the savings account proceeds.

The amount that may be diverted to a tax-deferred annuity through salary reduction is the difference between the employer's regular contribution to the pension plan and the least of the following amounts established by the Internal Revenue Code: (a) the individual's "exclusion allowance" provided under Section 403(b) of the Internal Revenue Code; (b) 25 percent of "includable compensation" (salary less any reduction); or (c) a CPI-indexed dollar limit ($32,700 in 1979). Certain special alternative limitations are provided for employees of an educational institution, a hospital, or a home health service agency.

Each employee's exclusion allowance is figured individually. This is done by taking 20 percent of the employee's includable compensation for the current year (after any salary reduction). This figure (20 percent of includable compensation) is multiplied by the employee's total number of years of service. From this is subtracted the total contributions made by the employer in prior years (including any made under a salary reduction agreement) toward the tax-deferred annuity and any other retirement plan to the extent that such contributions were excludable from the employee's gross income. The remainder is the employee's exclusion allowance for the taxable year. In the calculation, only compensation, contributions, and years of service with the current employer can be taken into account. A long-term employee, consequently, will be likely to have a higher exclusion allowance than a short-term employee.

Only compensation which is includable in the employee's gross income is "includable compensation." Consequently, as noted earlier, if the employee takes a reduction in salary to finance the annuity, his exclusion allowance is based on 20 percent of his reduced salary. This means that the maximum reduction which will come within the exclusion allowance (assuming no past service and no employer contributions to other plans) is 16 2/3 percent of gross salary. For example, a gross salary of $12,000 reduced by 16 2/3 percent to $10,000 produces the maximum reduction of $2,000 (20 percent of the reduced salary of $10,000).

Employer contributions that were excludable from the employee's gross income in prior years include contributions to any qualified pension or annuity plan and contributions to a public retirement plan. Where employer contributions are not allocated to individual employees (as under public retirement systems), IRS regulations provide a formula for determining the applicable amounts.

Since an employee's maximum salary reduction is the least of the exclusion allowance just summarized, the reduction possibility under the 25 percent of compensation (reduced salary) limit, or the current CPI-indexed limit, all three determinations must be made. The 25 percent reduction possibility is determined by subtracting 80 percent of the employer's contributions for the year of determination from 20 percent of the employee's gross salary. For 1979, the CPI-indexed reduction possibility is determined by subtracting the institution's contributions for the year from $32,700, a figure which changes each year according to CPI changes.

SUMMARY

The extensive government regulation of employer benefit plans that are not themselves legally mandated, but have been established voluntarily or through negotiation, is relatively new in the United States. Such regulation as did exist in earlier decades was largely related to the tax treatment of employer contributions to the plans and of the earnings of invested plan reserves. More recently, however, public policy regarding benefit plans has emphasized greater protection of employee interests. Thus, the Employee Retirement Income Security Act of 1974 established standards of vesting in order to provide more workers with assured pension protection, and standards of funding were legislated in order to strengthen the capacity of pension plans to carry out their obligations. Changes in age discrimination legislation, described in this chapter, have affected pension and welfare benefit plans, again with the aim of providing increased protection for a wider range of employees.

Increased regulation results in higher administrative costs. Thus, increased reporting requirements, both to government offices and to plan participants, lead to higher expenses, as does any required extension of benefit protection or improvement in funding standard. In view of intensified regulation in recent years, it becomes all the more important for employers to pay close attention to the administration of their array of benefit plans, and to the benefit provisions themselves. As plan expenditures rise as a percentage of an institution's total payroll, and as administrative costs associated with the plans also rise, careful monitoring of this important and growing part of total employee compensation can help minimize potential costs and at the same time assure that employees are provided with the benefit protection they need.

APPENDIXES

APPENDIXES

Appendix A
Survey of Retirement and Insurance Plans in Higher Education

Instructions

1. Please answer the questions on this page and in the following benefit information sections, giving information as of January, 1978. Each section has at least one item to be answered even though your institution may not have the plan. Most answers require single check marks or short entries.

2. Each question seeks data for only three general employee categories. Although variations in coverage among subgroups may result in minor inaccuracies, please provide answers in a category if any subgroup is covered.

3. Public institutions: In questions asking whether employer contributions are made toward the cost of a plan, employer includes the institution itself or units of state or local government.

4. A reply envelope is enclosed for your convenience.

Survey Questionnaire

1. _____
   (Name of Institution)   (City and State)

2. _____
   (Name of Respondent)   (Title)   (Telephone Number)

3. Number of Full-Time Employees.

   Please report the number of full-time employees in each category below. (Current head count—give estimates if necessary.)

   Faculty—Instruction/Research

   Persons employed for the primary purpose of performing instruction and/or research. Chairpersons of academic departments should be included in this category if they have no other administrative title.

   CARD 6-1

   [ ]
   14-18

   Administrative/Managerial/Other Professional

   All employees whose primary responsibility is for the administration and management of the institution or its subdivisions. Also include all non-teaching professionals such as librarians, accountants, systems analysts, personnel specialists, counselors, recruiters, etc.

   [ ]
   19-23

   Other Employees

   All employees not included in the categories above, including those subject to the provisions of the Fair Labor Standards Act. Includes persons engaged in activities categorized as: technical, office/clerical, crafts and trades, service, etc. (Exclude student employees.)

   [ ]
   24-28

257

Section 1 **Retirement Plans**

Please answer for each employee category to the right.	**Faculty**	**Administrative/ Managerial/Other Professional**	**Other Employees**
4. Are your institution's employees covered under federal Social Security?	☐ Yes—All 29-1 ☐ Yes—Some -2 ☐ None -3	☐ Yes—All 31-1 ☐ Yes—Some -2 ☐ None -3	☐ Yes—All 33-1 ☐ Yes—Some -2 ☐ None -3
5. Does your institution have a retirement plan(s)? If your institution has no retirement plan for any employee group, please turn to question 11.	☐ Yes 30-1 ☐ No -2	☐ Yes 32-1 ☐ No -2	☐ Yes 34-1 ☐ No -2

Please complete the following questions for the columns checked YES in question 5.

6. Please check the retirement plan(s) available for each employee category. (*Check as many as apply.*) *Do not include plans now closed to new entrants.*			
a. State or Local Teacher Retirement System.	☐ 35-1	☐ 40-1	☐ 45-1
b. Public Employee Retirement System.	☐ -2	☐ -2	☐ -2
c. TIAA-CREF.	☐ -3	☐ -3	☐ -3
d. Self-Funded or Trusteed Plan.	☐ -4	☐ -4	☐ -4
e. Insurance Company Plan. (Specify: _____)	☐ -5	☐ -5	☐ -5
f. Church Pension Plan. (Specify: _____)	☐ -6	☐ -6	☐ -6
7. Does the employer pay toward the cost of the retirement plan?	☐ Yes 36-1 ☐ No -2	☐ Yes 41-1 ☐ No -2	☐ Yes 46-1 ☐ No -2
8. Does the employee pay toward the cost of the retirement plan? If YES, does your institution permit or require *regular employee contributions* to the retirement plan to be made through salary REDUCTION under Internal Revenue Code Sec. 403(b), the Salary-or-Annuity Option?	☐ Yes 37-1 ☐ No -2 ☐ Yes—Permits 38-1 ☐ Yes—Requires -2 ☐ No -3	☐ Yes 42-1 ☐ No -2 ☐ Yes—Permits 43-1 ☐ Yes—Requires -2 ☐ No -3	☐ Yes 47-1 ☐ No -2 ☐ Yes—Permits 48-1 ☐ Yes—Requires -2 ☐ No -3
9. Does your institution permit employees to make *extra* annuity contributions (over and above regular plan contributions) by salary REDUCTION under Internal Revenue Code Sec. 403(b) (the Salary-or-Annuity option)?	☐ Yes 39-1 ☐ No -2	☐ Yes 44-1 ☐ No -2	☐ Yes 49-1 ☐ No -2

Section 1 **Retirement Plans**

Please answer for each employee category to the right.	Faculty	Administrative/ Managerial/Other Professional	Other Employees

10. Retirement Age:

a. What does the retirement plan state as the "normal" retirement age? (A stated age at which retirement is not considered "early.")

	Faculty	Administrative	Other
	Age _____ 50-51	Age _____ 59-60	Age _____ 68-69

b. May an employee—at *his/her* own option—continue to work beyond this age?

	Faculty	Administrative	Other
	☐ Yes 52-1	☐ Yes 61-1	☐ Yes 70-1
	☐ No -2	☐ No -2	☐ No -2

If YES, at what age does this option end?

	Faculty	Administrative	Other
	Age _____ 53-54	Age _____ 62-63	Age _____ 71-72

May service beyond this age be extended at the *employer's* option?

	Faculty	Administrative	Other
	☐ Yes 55-1	☐ Yes 64-1	☐ Yes 73-1
	☐ No -2	☐ No -2	☐ No -2

c. Is there a retirement age beyond which neither employer nor employee has the option to continue employee service?

	Faculty	Administrative	Other
	☐ Yes 56-1	☐ Yes 65-1	☐ Yes 74-1
	☐ No -2	☐ No -2	☐ No -2

If YES, state the age:

	Faculty	Administrative	Other
	Age _____ 57-58	Age _____ 66-67	Age _____ 75-76

Remarks or explanations on retirement plans:

Section 2 **Life Insurance Plans**

Please answer for each employee category to the right. CARD 6-2	**Faculty**	**Administrative/ Managerial/Other Professional**	**Other Employees**
11. Does your institution have a group life insurance plan? (*Do not include as life insurance the death or survivor benefit provisions of a retirement plan.*) If your institution has no group life plan for any employee group, please turn to question 22.	☐ Yes 7-1 ☐ No -2	☐ Yes 18-1 ☐ No -2	☐ Yes 29-1 ☐ No -2
Please complete the following questions for the columns checked YES in Question 11.			
12. Does the employer pay toward the cost of the plan?	☐ Yes 8-1 ☐ No -2	☐ Yes 19-1 ☐ No -2	☐ Yes 30-1 ☐ No -2
13. Does the employee pay toward the cost of the plan?	☐ Yes 9-1 ☐ No -2	☐ Yes 20-1 ☐ No -2	☐ Yes 31-1 ☐ No -2
14. May a covered employee choose additional optional insurance coverage under the plan?	☐ Yes 10-1 ☐ No -2	☐ Yes 21-1 ☐ No -2	☐ Yes 32-1 ☐ No -2
If YES, check here if the employee's *only* contribution is for the extra optional insurance.	☐ 11-1	☐ 22-1	☐ 33-1
15. Please indicate the waiting period before a new employee is eligible to participate in the plan: (*Check one.*)			
1 month or less.	☐ 12-1	☐ 23-1	☐ 34-1
2 to 6 months.	☐ -2	☐ -2	☐ -2
Until next plan anniversary date.	☐ -3	☐ -3	☐ -3
Other. (Specify: _____)	☐ -4	☐ -4	☐ -4
16. Please check below and on following page the items that most nearly describe the way group life insurance amounts are determined: (*Check as many as apply.*)			
a. As a multiple of salary.	☐ _____ 13-1 State Multiple	☐ _____ 24-1 State Multiple	☐ _____ 35-1 State Multiple
According to job or salary category.	☐ -2	☐ -2	☐ -2
Same amount for all employees.	☐ $_____ -3 State amount	☐ $_____ -3 State amount	☐ $_____ -3 State amount
As assigned units of collective insurance.	☐ -4	☐ -4	☐ -4
Other. (Specify: _____)	☐ -5	☐ -5	☐ -5

Section 2 **Life Insurance Plans**

Please answer for each employee category to the right.	Faculty	Administrative/ Managerial/Other Professional	Other Employees
b. Amount decreases as age advances.	☐ 40-1	☐ 48-1	☐ 56-1
Amount increases as salary increases.	☐ -2	☐ -2	☐ -2
Amount does not change as age or salary increases.	☐ -3	☐ -3	☐ -3
c. Basic amount is same for equally situated employees regardless of dependents.	☐ 41-1	☐ 49-1	☐ 57-1
Basic amount is greater for employees with dependents.	☐ -2	☐ -2	☐ -2
Employees with dependents may elect higher coverage amounts.	☐ -3	☐ -3	☐ -3
d. Insurance plan includes accidental death and dismemberment provision (AD&D).	☐ 42-1	☐ 50-1	☐ 58-1
17. Are any *retired employees* covered under the group life insurance plan?	☐ Yes 43-1 ☐ No -2	☐ Yes 51-1 ☐ No -2	☐ Yes 59-1 ☐ No -2

If retired employees are not covered under the group life insurance plan, please turn to question 22.

For columns checked YES in question 17, please answer the following:

	Faculty	Administrative/ Managerial/Other Professional	Other Employees
18. Check the type of retired employee insurance in force. (*Check one.*)			
Paid-up insurance.	☐ 44-1	☐ 52-1	☐ 60-1
Term insurance (with continuing premiums).	☐ -2	☐ -2	☐ -2
19. Is amount of retired employee insurance less than that provided active employees?	☐ Yes 45-1 ☐ No -2	☐ Yes 53-1 ☐ No -2	☐ Yes 61-1 ☐ No -2
20. Does the employer pay toward the cost of retired employee coverage?	☐ Yes 46-1 ☐ No -2	☐ Yes 54-1 ☐ No -2	☐ Yes 62-1 ☐ No -2
21. Does the retired employee pay toward the cost of the coverage?	☐ Yes 47-1 ☐ No -2	☐ Yes 55-1 ☐ No -2	☐ Yes 63-1 ☐ No -2

Remarks or explanations on life insurance plans:

Section 3 **Health Insurance Plans**

Please answer for each employee category to the right. CARD 6-3	Faculty	Administrative/ Managerial/Other Professional	Other Employees
22. Does your institution have a health insurance plan? If your institution has no health insurance plan for any employee group, please turn to question 33.	☐ Yes 7-1 ☐ No -2	☐ Yes 15-1 ☐ No -2	☐ Yes 23-1 ☐ No -2
Please complete the following questions for the columns checked YES in question 22.			
23. Please check health insurance in effect. (*Check as many as apply.*)			
a. Basic hospital-surgical-medical (any one or more of these three basic coverages).	☐ 8-1	☐ 16-1	☐ 24-1
b. Major medical.	☐ -2	☐ -2	☐ -2
c. Health Maintenance Organization.	☐ -3	☐ -3	☐ -3
d. Dental.	☐ -4	☐ -4	☐ -4
e. Vision care.	☐ -5	☐ -5	☐ -5
24. If you have checked major medical insurance, is that coverage part of a single, comprehensive health insurance plan that includes basic coverage, or is it a separate plan? (*Check one*.)	☐ Single 9-1 comprehensive plan ☐ Separate plan -2	☐ Single 17-1 comprehensive plan ☐ Separate plan -2	☐ Single 25-1 comprehensive plan ☐ Separate plan -2
25. Type of insurer: (*Check as many as apply.*)			
Blue Cross.	☐ 10-1	☐ 18-1	☐ 26-1
Blue Shield.	☐ -2	☐ -2	☐ -2
Insurance Company (including TIAA).	☐ -3	☐ -3	☐ -3
Self-insured.	☐ -4	☐ -4	☐ -4
Other. (Specify: _____)	☐ -5	☐ -5	☐ -5
26. Cost of health insurance coverage:			
a. Employee coverage:			
1. Does *employer* pay toward the cost?	☐ Yes 11-1 ☐ No -2	☐ Yes 19-1 ☐ No -2	☐ Yes 27-1 ☐ No -2
2. Does *employee* pay toward the cost?	☐ Yes 12-1 ☐ No -2	☐ Yes 20-1 ☐ No -2	☐ Yes 28-1 ☐ No -2
b. Dependents' coverage:			
1. Does *employer* pay toward the cost?	☐ Yes 13-1 ☐ No -2	☐ Yes 21-1 ☐ No -2	☐ Yes 29-1 ☐ No -2
2. Does *employee* pay toward the cost?	☐ Yes 14-1 ☐ No -2	☐ Yes 22-1 ☐ No -2	☐ Yes 30-1 ☐ No -2

Section 3 **Health Insurance Plans**

Please answer for each employee category to the right.	Faculty	Administrative/ Managerial/Other Professional	Other Employees
27. Cost of Health Maintenance Organization (providing medical services) coverage: (*If not applicable, go to question 28.*)			
a. Employee coverage:			
1. Does the *employer* pay toward the cost?	☐ Yes 31-1 ☐ No -2	☐ Yes 37-1 ☐ No -2	☐ Yes 43-1 ☐ No -2
2. Does the *employee* pay toward the cost?	☐ Yes 32-1 ☐ No -2	☐ Yes 38-1 ☐ No -2	☐ Yes 44-1 ☐ No -2
b. Dependents' coverage:			
1. Does the *employer* pay toward the cost?	☐ Yes 33-1 ☐ No -2	☐ Yes 39-1 ☐ No -2	☐ Yes 45-1 ☐ No -2
2. Does the *employee* pay toward the cost?	☐ Yes 34-1 ☐ No -2	☐ Yes 40-1 ☐ No -2	☐ Yes 46-1 ☐ No -2
28. Plan participation: please indicate the minimum waiting period, if any, before a new employee is covered under your institution's health insurance plan(s). (*Check one.*)			
One month or less.	☐ 35-1	☐ 41-1	☐ 47-1
Until stated date(s) during first year of employment, but after one month of service.	☐ -2	☐ -2	☐ -2
Stated number of months.	☐ -3	☐ -3	☐ -3
Other. (Specify: _____)	☐ -4	☐ -4	☐ -4
29. *Medicare coverage for retired employees.*			
Does your institution pay all, part, or none of the monthly premium for a retired employee's coverage under Medicare Part B (Supplementary Medical Insurance) of Social Security?	☐ All 36-1 ☐ Part -2 ☐ None -3	☐ All 42-1 ☐ Part -2 ☐ None -3	☐ All 48-1 ☐ Part -2 ☐ None -3

Section 3 . Health Insurance Plans

Please answer for each employee category to the right.	Faculty	Administrative/ Managerial/Other Professional	Other Employees
30. *Retired employees' group health insurance coverage:* Are any employees eligible to continue participation in your institution's group health insurance plan(s) after retirement, e.g., as a supplement to Medicare? (*Do not include conversion to an individual policy or to "direct-pay" Blue Cross-Blue Shield*.) If retired employees may not continue as participants in your group health insurance plan(s), please turn to question 33.	☐ Yes 49-1 ☐ No -2	☐ Yes 55-1 ☐ No -2	☐ Yes 61-1 ☐ No -2
31. Must an employee meet a "years of service" and/or age requirement in order to be eligible for continued group health insurance coverage during retirement?	☐ Yes 50-1 ☐ No -2	☐ Yes 56-1 ☐ No -2	☐ Yes 62-1 ☐ No -2
32. Cost of continued coverage:			
a. Retired employee's coverage:			
1. Does the *employer* pay toward the cost?	☐ Yes 51-1 ☐ No -2	☐ Yes 57-1 ☐ No -2	☐ Yes 63-1 ☐ No -2
2. Does the *retired employee* pay toward the cost?	☐ Yes 52-1 ☐ No -2	☐ Yes 58-1 ☐ No -2	☐ Yes 64-1 ☐ No -2
b. Retirees' dependents' coverage:			
1. Does the *employer* pay toward the cost?	☐ Yes 53-1 ☐ No -2	☐ Yes 59-1 ☐ No -2	☐ Yes 65-1 ☐ No -2
2. Does the *retired employee* pay toward the cost?	☐ Yes 54-1 ☐ No -2	☐ Yes 60-1 ☐ No -2	☐ Yes 66-1 ☐ No -2

Remarks or explanations on health insurance plans:

Section 4 Short-Term Disability and Sick Pay Plans

This section covers plans that provide income during temporary absences from work caused by illness or injury and lasting from a few days to perhaps as long as six months or so.

Please answer for each employee category to the right. CARD 6-4	Faculty	Administrative/ Managerial/Other Professional	Other Employees
33. Does your institution have a short-term disability income or sick-pay plan?	☐ Yes 7-1 ☐ No -2	☐ Yes 13-1 ☐ No -2	☐ Yes 19-1 ☐ No -2
If your institution has no plan for any employee group, please turn to question 38.			

Please complete the following questions for the columns checked YES in question 33.

	Faculty	Administrative/ Managerial/Other Professional	Other Employees
34. Please check the short-term disability income plan(s) in effect. (*Check as many as apply.*)			
a. Formal sick pay or salary continuation plan (i.e., amounts, duration, and conditions stated in writing).	☐ 8-1	☐ 14-1	☐ 20-1
b. Informal plan.	☐ -2	☐ -2	☐ -2
c. State Workmen's Compensation insurance.	☐ -3	☐ -3	☐ -3
d. Group insurance plan (other than mandatory Workmen's Compensation) providing short-term disability income.	☐ -4	☐ -4	☐ -4
e. Other. (Specify: _____)	☐ -5	☐ -5	☐ -5
35. Cost of short-term sick-pay or salary continuation plan:			
a. Does the *employer* pay toward the cost?	☐ Yes 9-1 ☐ No -2	☐ Yes 15-1 ☐ No -2	☐ Yes 21-1 ☐ No -2
b. Does the *employee* pay toward the cost?	☐ Yes 10-1 ☐ No -2	☐ Yes 16-1 ☐ No -2	☐ Yes 22-1 ☐ No -2
36. Please indicate the waiting period before a new employee becomes eligible for sick-pay benefits (other than Workmen's Compensation) under your plan(s). (*Check one.*)			
1 month or less.	☐ 11-1	☐ 17-1	☐ 23-1
2 to 6 months.	☐ -2	☐ -2	☐ -2
Other. (Specify: _____)	☐ -3	☐ -3	☐ -3
37. Does the duration of sick-pay vary according to length of service?	☐ Yes 12-1 ☐ No -2	☐ Yes 18-1 ☐ No -2	☐ Yes 24-1 ☐ No -2

Remarks or explanations on short-term disability and sick-pay plans:

Section 5 Long-Term Total Disability Income Plans

This section covers insurance and/or pension plans providing income benefits to totally disabled employees following a specified period of total disability (usually six months) and continuing throughout disability for life, for a specified period of years, or to a stated age when retirement benefits begin.

Please answer for each employee category to the right.	Faculty	Administrative/ Managerial/Other Professional	Other Employees
38. Does your institution have a plan(s) providing income during periods of long-term total disability? (*Include benefits provided under the provisions of pension plans and under separate insured or noninsured plans.*)	☐ Yes 25-1 ☐ No -2	☐ Yes 32-1 ☐ No -2	☐ Yes 39-1 ☐ No -2

If your institution has no plan for any employee group, please turn to question 43.

Please complete the following questions for the columns checked YES in question 38.

	Faculty	Administrative/ Managerial/Other Professional	Other Employees
39. Please check the long-term total disability income plan(s) covering employees of your institution. (*Check as many as apply.*)			
a. Public employee or teacher retirement system.	☐ 26-1	☐ 33-1	☐ 40-1
b. Group insurance plan.	☐ -2	☐ -2	☐ -2
c. Self-insured (i.e., "noninsured") plan.	☐ -3	☐ -3	☐ -3
d. Other. (Specify: _____)	☐ -4	☐ -4	☐ -4
40. How long (in months) must an employee be totally disabled before long-term disability income benefits begin?	_____ months 27	_____ months 34	_____ months 41
41. Please check whether total disability income is payable for (1) work connected disabilities, (2) non-work connected disabilities, or both. (*Check one or both.*)			
Payable for work-connected disabilities.	☐ 28-1	☐ 35-1	☐ 42-1
Payable for non-work connected disabilities.	☐ -2	☐ -2	☐ -2
42. If the plan is insured or self-insured (and is not part of a public retirement system):			
a. Does the *employer* pay toward the cost?	☐ Yes 29-1 ☐ No -2	☐ Yes 36-1 ☐ No -2	☐ Yes 43-1 ☐ No -2
b. Does the *employee* pay toward the cost?	☐ Yes 30-1 ☐ No -2	☐ Yes 37-1 ☐ No -2	☐ Yes 44-1 ☐ No -2
c. Does the plan provide for continuation during disability of contributions or credited service toward the retirement annuity?	☐ Yes 31-1 ☐ No -2	☐ Yes 38-1 ☐ No -2	☐ Yes 45-1 ☐ No -2

Section 5 Long-Term Total Disability Income Plans

Please answer for each employee category to the right.	Faculty	Administrative/ Managerial/Other Professional	Other Employees

d. Please indicate the waiting period before a new employee is eligible to participate in the plan. (*Check one.*)

	Faculty	Administrative/ Managerial/Other Professional	Other Employees
One month or less.	☐ 46-1	☐ 48-1	☐ 50-1
Two to 11 months.	☐ -2	☐ -2	☐ -2
One year.	☐ -3	☐ -3	☐ -3
More than one year.	☐ -4	☐ -4	☐ -4
Other. (Specify: _____)	☐ -5	☐ -5	☐ -5

e. What is the maximum period during which total disability income is paid to a disabled employee?

	Faculty	Administrative/ Managerial/Other Professional	Other Employees
For a stated number of years. (Specify: _____)	☐ 47-1	☐ 49-1	☐ 51-1
To age 65.	☐ -2	☐ -2	☐ -2
For life.	☐ -3	☐ -3	☐ -3
Other. (Specify: _____)	☐ -4	☐ -4	☐ -4

Remarks or explanations on long-term disability income plans.

Section 6 **Other Benefit Plans**

Please answer for each employee category to the right.	Faculty	Administrative/ Managerial/Other Professional	Other Employees

43. Please check any of the following employee benefit plans that are in effect in your institution. (*Check as many as apply.*)

   a. Legal services.
   ☐ 52-1   ☐ 53-1   ☐ 54-1

   b. Business travel accident insurance.
   ☐ -2   ☐ -2   ☐ -2

   c. Key man insurance or other supplementary life insurance.
   ☐ -3   ☐ -3   ☐ -3

   d. Annual physical examinations.
   ☐ -4   ☐ -4   ☐ -4

   e. Other. (Specify: _____)
   ☐ -5   ☐ -5   ☐ -5

   Please enclose plan descriptions, if available.

Remarks or explanations on other benefit plans.

Appendix B
Employee Benefits
Cost Survey-1977

This is the first of a survey series that we plan to repeat every two years. We wish to invite your institution's participation.

The survey is made in response to growing interest on the part of financial officers of institutions of higher education in up-to-date information about expenditures for employee benefits. Such surveys in other sectors have been widely used in wage negotiations, government hearings, and employer-employee publications.

This survey is strictly confidential. Only persons handling the research will see your data. Your institution's name will not be divulged. Data will be published only in the form of totals for groups of institutions. Each participating college and university will receive a copy of the report when completed.

Would you please direct the questionnaire to the appropriate official for completion. If you have any questions about the survey, please write or telephone.

We greatly appreciate your participation in this survey.

INSTRUCTIONS   Identity of individual institutions will not be disclosed. Data furnished will be published only in the form of totals for groups of institutions. Only persons handling the research will see your report.

**THIS SURVEY
IS
CONFIDENTIAL**

1. **INSTITUTIONS COVERED.** If your data include other branches or campuses, please write in names or attach a list.

2. **EMPLOYEE GROUPS COVERED.** Please include all employees, including all hourly and salaried employees in all employee categories, full-time and part-time (but excluding student employees). If any employee groups are not included (part-time, temporary, etc.), please check box in Item A and specify groups excluded.

3. **APPROXIMATE OR INCOMPLETE DATA.** If you are unable to give exact data for the various items in the questionnaire, please give estimates—we would prefer a good estimate to a blank space. Give figures in whole dollar amounts (omit cents). If you are unable to break down the data or payments exactly as outlined, please give the data that are available; indicate the included items for which payments were made but for which you cannot give separate figures. Write in NA if the requested figures are not available.

4. **ITEM A. GROSS PAYROLL DATA.** For this item report actual wages and salaries paid (not take-home pay after deductions have been made).

5. **ITEMS C-1, C-4, C-5, C-7, C-9, C-10. PENSION AND INSURANCE PREMIUMS.** Report net payments after deducting any dividends or credits returned to the employer by the insurer (or expected to be returned based on experience during the reporting year).

6. **ITEM C-7. HEALTH INSURANCE.** Include premiums for insurance that supplements Medicare coverage of retirees, and any payments toward Medicare Part B.

7. **ITEM F. EMPLOYEE PAYROLL DEDUCTIONS.** For this question report deductions from employee pay. Employer contributions are reported in questions B, C, D, and E.

8. **ITEM G. NUMBER OF 1977 EMPLOYEES.** Report total number of full-time employees and total full-time equivalent of part-time employees at beginning and end of fiscal year or calendar year.

269

SURVEY QUESTIONNAIRE

_____   _____
         (Name of Institution)   **(Branches included—attach list if necessary)**

_____   _____
              (Address)   **(Zip)**

_____
        (Name of Respondent)   **(Title)**

CONFIDENTIAL

Show actual data or best estimate

**Total for Fiscal
or Calendar Year
Ending in 1977
(omit cents)**

A. TOTAL GROSS PAYROLL (check box if some employee groups, e.g., part-time, are not included ☐ , and specify: _____) $ _____ 7

B. LEGALLY MANDATED EXPENDITURES (employer's share only)

1. Social Security contributions (FICA tax) .... $ _____ 16

2. Unemployment Compensation (Federal and State taxes) .... $ _____ 25

3. Workmen's Compensation (estimate if self-insured) .... $ _____ 34

4. State sickness benefits insurance (including self-insured) .... $ _____ 43

5. Other (Specify: _____) $ _____ 52

6. Total .... $ _____ 61 - 80 ☐1

C. BENEFIT PLAN EXPENDITURES (employer's share only)

1. Premiums to insured pension plans (including TIAA-CREF) .... $ _____ 7

2. Payments to (uninsured) self-administered or trusteed pension plans ... $ _____ 15

3. Payments to public employee pension plans .... $ _____ 23

4. Life insurance premiums (net) (excluding life insurance provided under a pension plan) .... $ _____ 31

5. Travel accident insurance premiums (net) .... $ _____ 39

6. Death benefits not covered by insurance or pension plans .... $ _____ 47

7. Hospital, accident, surgical, medical and major medical _insurance premiums_ (net) and Medicare Part B .... $ _____ 55

8. Hospital, accident, surgical, and medical care payments _self-insured_ or _provided directly_ (including Health Maintenance Organizations) ...... $ _____ 63

9. Payments for long-term disability income plans (including insured and self-insured plans but excluding disability benefits under a pension plan) .... $ _____ 71 - 80 ☐2

10. Dental insurance premiums (check box if dental insurance is included in Items C-7 or C-8: ☐) .... $ _____ 7

11. Other (Specify: _____) $ _____ 15

12. Total .... $ _____ 23

**Total for Fiscal
or Calendar Year
Ending in 1977
(omit cents)**

D. OTHER EMPLOYER EXPENDITURES

1. Supplementary or other payments under unfunded pension programs $ _____ 31

2. Payments under deferred compensation agreements .... $ _____ 39

3. Payments to tax-deferred (403(b)) annuities under employee
   salary-reduction agreements .... $ _____ 47

4. Education expenditures for employees and dependents (tuition waivers,
   grants, refunds, etc.) .... $ _____ 55

5. Service awards, suggestion awards, good-teaching awards, etc. ...... $ _____ 63

6. Other (Specify: _____) $ _____ 71 - 80 [3]

7. Total .... $ _____ 7

E. PAYMENTS FOR TIME NOT WORKED

1. Payments for or in lieu of vacations .... $ _____ 15

2. Payments for holidays not worked .... $ _____ 23

3. Sick leave pay .... $ _____ 31

4. Payments required under guaranteed work-week or work-year .... $ _____ 39

5. Jury, witness, and voting pay allowances .... $ _____ 47

6. National Defense, State, or National Guard duty .... $ _____ 55

7. Payment for time taken due to death in family or other
   personal reasons .... $ _____ 63

8. Other (Specify: _____) $ _____ 71 - 80 [4]

9. Total .... $ _____ 7

F. EMPLOYEE PAYROLL DEDUCTIONS

1. Social Security contributions (FICA tax) .... $ _____ 15

2. Required pension and annuity plan premiums or contributions .... $ _____ 23

3. Life insurance premiums .... $ _____ 31

4. Hospital, accident, surgical, medical and major medical insurance
   premiums or contributions (including dental insurance and
   Blue Cross/Blue Shield) .... $ _____ 39

5. State sickness benefits insurance tax .... $ _____ 47

6. Long-term disability income insurance (excluding disability benefits
   under a pension plan) .... $ _____ 55

7. Other (Specify: _____) $ _____ 63

8. Total .... $ _____ 71 - 80 [5]

G. NUMBER OF 1977 EMPLOYEES

	Full-time Employees	Full-time Equivalent of Part-time Employees	Total
1. Number of employees at start of year	_____ 7	_____ 15	_____ 23	
2. Number of employees at end of year	_____ 31	_____ 39	_____ 47	80 [6]

Please return the filled-out questionnaire to:
BENEFIT PLAN ANALYSIS AND STUDY GROUP/TIAA-CREF/730 THIRD AVENUE/NEW YORK, N.Y. 10017

Appendix C Tables

The following tables present in detail
information derived from the survey questionnaire.

In the tables the responding institutions are classified by
type as universities, four-year liberal arts colleges, other four-year
colleges (including teachers' colleges, technical institutes, independent
professional schools, and theological and religious schools) and
two-year institutions. By control the institutions are classified as
public or private. The responses are given by numbers of institutions
and numbers of full-time employees reported, which in effect weights
responses by size of institution. Each table is divided into subsections
showing the responses for faculty and for clerical-service employees.
Responses for administrative and other professional
personnel were similar to those for faculty.

Limited space prevents publication of all the tables prepared from
the questionnaire. Questionnaire information not found in this appendix
is generally summarized in the text.

Percentages are rounded to the nearest tenth; an asterisk indicates
a percentage of less than one tenth of a percent.

FEDERAL SOCIAL SECURITY COVERAGE OF COLLEGE AND UNIVERSITY EMPLOYEES

TABLE 1A

FACULTY

	ALL INSTITUTIONS		ALL 4-YEAR INSTITUTIONS		ALL 4-YEAR INSTITUTIONS PUBLIC		ALL 4-YEAR INSTITUTIONS PRIVATE		UNIVERSITIES PUBLIC		UNIVERSITIES PRIVATE	
	INSTS	EES	INSTS	EES	INSTS	EES	INSTS	EES	INSTS	EES	INSTS	EES
TOTAL	2092	432402	1407	363203	478	242041	929	121162	93	121628	61	54258
	100.0	100.0	100.0	100.0	100.0	100.0	100.0	100.0	100.0	100.0	100.0	100.0
NO RESPONSE	9	1848	8	1805	7	1795	1	10	-	-	-	-
	.4	.4	.6	.5	1.5	.7	.1	☆	-	-	-	-
EMPLOYEES COVERED UNDER SOCIAL SECURITY	1845	380366	1336	332868	422	211952	914	120916	79	105759	61	54258
	88.2	88.0	94.9	91.6	88.2	87.6	98.4	99.8	84.9	87.0	100.0	100.0
ALL EMPLOYEES	1590	313696	1165	276693	340	162223	825	114470	63	82913	57	52044
	76.0	72.6	82.7	76.1	71.0	67.1	88.8	94.5	67.7	68.2	93.4	95.9
SOME EMPLOYEES	255	66670	171	56175	82	49729	89	6446	16	22846	4	2214
	12.2	15.4	12.2	15.5	17.2	20.5	9.6	5.3	17.2	18.8	6.6	4.1
EMPLOYEES NOT COVERED UNDER SOCIAL SECURITY	238	50188	63	28530	49	28294	14	236	14	15869	-	-
	11.4	11.6	4.5	7.9	10.3	11.7	1.5	.2	15.1	13.0	-	-

FEDERAL SOCIAL SECURITY COVERAGE OF COLLEGE AND UNIVERSITY EMPLOYEES

TABLE 1B

CLERICAL SERVICE

	ALL INSTITUTIONS		ALL 4-YEAR INSTITUTIONS		ALL 4-YEAR INSTITUTIONS PUBLIC		ALL 4-YEAR INSTITUTIONS PRIVATE		UNIVERSITIES PUBLIC		UNIVERSITIES PRIVATE	
	INSTS	EES	INSTS	EES	INSTS	EES	INSTS	EES	INSTS	EES	INSTS	EES
TOTAL	2092	670941	1407	601711	478	413110	929	188601	93	231299	61	94679
	100.0	100.0	100.0	100.0	100.0	100.0	100.0	100.0	100.0	100.0	100.0	100.0
NO RESPONSE	1	55	1	55	-	-	1	55	-	-	-	-
	☆	☆	.1	☆	-	-	.1	☆	-	-	-	-
EMPLOYEES COVERED UNDER SOCIAL SECURITY	1912	610829	1349	553359	427	364952	922	188407	79	201716	61	94679
	91.4	91.0	95.8	92.0	89.3	88.3	99.3	99.9	84.9	87.2	100.0	100.0
ALL EMPLOYEES	1727	507464	1234	458404	347	275285	887	183119	66	159864	58	90826
	82.6	75.6	87.6	76.2	72.6	66.6	95.5	97.1	70.9	69.1	95.1	95.9
SOME EMPLOYEES	185	103365	115	94955	80	89667	35	5288	13	41852	3	3853
	8.8	15.4	8.2	15.8	16.7	21.7	3.8	2.8	14.0	18.1	4.9	4.1
EMPLOYEES NOT COVERED UNDER SOCIAL SECURITY	179	60057	57	48297	51	48158	6	139	14	29583	-	-
	8.6	9.0	4.1	8.0	10.7	11.7	.6	.1	15.1	12.8	-	-

| 4-YEAR LIBERAL ARTS COLLEGES | | | | OTHER 4-YEAR COLLEGES | | | | ALL 2-YEAR INSTITUTIONS | | 2-YEAR INSTITUTIONS | | | |
| PUBLIC | | PRIVATE | | PUBLIC | | PRIVATE | | | | PUBLIC | | PRIVATE | |
INSTS	EES	INSTS	EES	INSTS	EES	INSTS	EES	INSTS	EES	INSTS	EES	INSTS	EES
341	109911	686	57084	44	10502	182	9820	685	69199	600	66915	85	2284
100.0	100.0	100.0	100.0	100.0	100.0	100.0	100.0	100.0	100.0	100.0	100.0	100.0	100.0
7	1795	-	-	-	-	1	10	1	43	1	43	-	-
2.1	1.6	-	-	-	-	.5	.1	.1	.1	.2	.1	-	-
304	96189	681	56988	39	10004	172	9670	509	47498	425	45225	84	2273
89.1	87.5	99.3	99.8	88.6	95.3	94.6	98.5	74.4	68.6	70.8	67.6	98.8	99.5
248	71500	622	53435	29	7810	146	8991	425	37003	351	34961	74	2042
72.7	65.0	90.7	93.6	65.9	74.4	80.3	91.6	62.1	53.4	58.5	52.3	87.0	89.4
56	24689	59	3553	10	2194	26	679	84	10495	74	10264	10	231
16.4	22.5	8.6	6.2	22.7	20.9	14.3	6.9	12.3	15.2	12.3	15.3	11.8	10.1
30	11927	5	96	5	498	9	140	175	21658	174	21647	1	11
8.8	10.9	.7	.2	11.4	4.7	4.9	1.4	25.5	31.3	29.0	32.3	1.2	.5

| 4-YEAR LIBERAL ARTS COLLEGES | | | | OTHER 4-YEAR COLLEGES | | | | ALL 2-YEAR INSTITUTIONS | | 2-YEAR INSTITUTIONS | | | |
| PUBLIC | | PRIVATE | | PUBLIC | | PRIVATE | | | | PUBLIC | | PRIVATE | |
INSTS	EES	INSTS	EES	INSTS	EES	INSTS	EES	INSTS	EES	INSTS	EES	INSTS	EES
341	153051	686	76960	44	28760	182	16962	685	69230	600	66748	85	2482
100.0	100.0	100.0	100.0	100.0	100.0	100.0	100.0	100.0	100.0	100.0	100.0	100.0	100.0
-	-	1	55	-	-	-	-	-	-	-	-	-	-
-	-	.1	.1	-	-	-	-	-	-	-	-	-	-
310	138752	681	76801	38	24484	180	16927	563	57470	479	54993	84	2477
90.9	90.7	99.3	99.8	86.4	85.1	98.9	99.8	82.2	83.0	79.8	82.4	98.8	99.8
255	97700	660	75890	26	17721	169	16403	493	49060	413	46664	80	2396
74.8	63.9	96.2	98.6	59.1	61.6	92.9	96.7	72.0	70.9	68.8	69.9	94.1	96.5
55	41052	21	911	12	6763	11	524	70	8410	66	8329	4	81
16.1	26.8	3.1	1.2	27.3	23.5	6.0	3.1	10.2	12.1	11.0	12.5	4.7	3.3
31	14299	4	104	6	4276	2	35	122	11760	121	11755	1	5
9.1	9.3	.6	.1	13.6	14.9	1.1	.2	17.8	17.0	20.2	17.6	1.2	.2

RETIREMENT PLANS IN COLLEGES AND UNIVERSITIES

TABLE 2A

FACULTY

	ALL INSTITUTIONS		ALL 4-YEAR INSTITUTIONS		ALL 4-YEAR INSTITUTIONS PUBLIC		PRIVATE		UNIVERSITIES PUBLIC		PRIVATE	
	INSTS	EES	INSTS	EES	INSTS	EES	INSTS	EES	INSTS	EES	INSTS	EES
TOTAL	2092	432402	1407	363203	478	242041	929	121162	93	121628	61	5425
	100.0	100.0	100.0	100.0	100.0	100.0	100.0	100.0	100.0	100.0	100.0	100.
NO RESPONSE	1	10	1	10	-	-	1	10	-	-	-	
	✧	✧	.1	✧	-	-	.1	✧	-	-	-	
RETIREMENT PLAN IN EFFECT	2035	430730	1365	362076	478	242041	887	120035	93	121628	61	5425
	97.3	99.6	97.0	99.7	100.0	100.0	95.5	99.1	100.0	100.0	100.0	100.
NO RETIREMENT PLAN	56	1662	41	1117	-	-	41	1117	-	-	-	
	2.7	.4	2.9	.3	-	-	4.4	.9	-	-	-	

RETIREMENT PLANS IN COLLEGES AND UNIVERSITIES

TABLE 2B

CLERICAL SERVICE

	ALL INSTITUTIONS		ALL 4-YEAR INSTITUTIONS		ALL 4-YEAR INSTITUTIONS PUBLIC		PRIVATE		UNIVERSITIES PUBLIC		PRIVATE	
	INSTS	EES	INSTS	EES	INSTS	EES	INSTS	EES	INSTS	EES	INSTS	EE
TOTAL	2092	670941	1407	601711	478	413110	929	188601	93	231299	61	9467
	100.0	100.0	100.0	100.0	100.0	100.0	100.0	100.0	100.0	100.0	100.0	100.
NO RESPONSE	1	75	1	75	-	-	1	75	-	-	-	
	✧	✧	.1	✧	-	-	.1	✧	-	-	-	
RETIREMENT PLAN IN EFFECT	1927	663446	1270	595029	477	413018	793	182011	93	231299	61	9467
	92.2	98.9	90.2	98.9	99.8	100.0	85.4	96.5	100.0	100.0	100.0	100.
NO RETIREMENT PLAN	164	7420	136	6607	1	92	135	6515	-	-	-	
	7.8	1.1	9.7	1.1	.2	✧	14.5	3.5	-	-	-	

| 4-YEAR LIBERAL ARTS COLLEGES | | | | OTHER 4-YEAR COLLEGES | | | | ALL 2-YEAR INSTITUTIONS | | 2-YEAR INSTITUTIONS | | | |
| PUBLIC | | PRIVATE | | PUBLIC | | PRIVATE | | | | PUBLIC | | PRIVATE | |
INSTS	EES	INSTS	EES	INSTS	EES	INSTS	EES	INSTS	EES	INSTS	EES	INSTS	EES
341	109911	686	57084	44	10502	182	9820	685	69199	600	66915	85	2284
100.0	100.0	100.0	100.0	100.0	100.0	100.0	100.0	100.0	100.0	100.0	100.0	100.0	100.0
-	-	-	-	-	-	1	10	-	-	-	-	-	-
-	-	-	-	-	-	.5	.1	-	-	-	-	-	-
341	109911	664	56364	44	10502	162	9413	670	68654	596	66548	74	2106
100.0	100.0	96.8	98.7	100.0	100.0	89.1	95.9	97.8	99.2	99.3	99.5	87.1	92.2
-	-	22	720	-	-	19	397	15	545	4	367	11	178
-	-	3.2	1.3	-	-	10.4	4.0	2.2	.8	.7	.5	12.9	7.8

| 4-YEAR LIBERAL ARTS COLLEGES | | | | OTHER 4-YEAR COLLEGES | | | | ALL 2-YEAR INSTITUTIONS | | 2-YEAR INSTITUTIONS | | | |
| PUBLIC | | PRIVATE | | PUBLIC | | PRIVATE | | | | PUBLIC | | PRIVATE | |
INSTS	EES	INSTS	EES	INSTS	EES	INSTS	EES	INSTS	EES	INSTS	EES	INSTS	EES
341	153051	686	76960	44	28760	182	16962	685	69230	600	66748	85	2482
100.0	100.0	100.0	100.0	100.0	100.0	100.0	100.0	100.0	100.0	100.0	100.0	100.0	100.0
-	-	1	75	-	-	-	-	-	-	-	-	-	-
-	-	.1	.1	-	-	-	-	-	-	-	-	-	-
340	152959	582	70910	44	28760	150	16422	657	68417	592	66378	65	2039
99.7	99.9	84.9	92.1	100.0	100.0	82.4	96.8	95.9	98.8	98.7	99.4	76.5	82.2
1	92	103	5975	-	-	32	540	28	813	8	370	20	443
.3	.1	15.0	7.8	-	-	17.6	3.2	4.1	1.2	1.3	.6	23.5	17.8

TYPES OF RETIREMENT PLANS COVERING COLLEGE AND UNIVERSITY STAFF MEMBERS

TABLE 3A

FACULTY	ALL INSTITUTIONS		ALL 4-YEAR INSTITUTIONS		ALL 4-YEAR INSTITUTIONS: PUBLIC		ALL 4-YEAR INSTITUTIONS: PRIVATE		UNIVERSITIES: PUBLIC		UNIVERSITIES: PRIVATE	
	INSTS	EES	INSTS	EES	INSTS	EES	INSTS	EES	INSTS	EES	INSTS	EES
TOTAL	2035	430730	1365	362076	478	242041	887	120035	93	121628	61	54258
	100.0	100.0	100.0	100.0	100.0	100.0	100.0	100.0	100.0	100.0	100.0	100.0
NO RESPONSE	3	111	3	111	-	-	3	111	-	-	-	-
	.1	*	.2	*	-	-	.3	.1	-	-	-	-
STATE OR LOCAL TEACHER RETIREMENT SYSTEM	720	174142	293	124446	273	117799	20	6647	39	47409	4	5318
	35.4	40.4	21.5	34.4	57.1	48.7	2.3	5.5	41.9	39.0	6.6	9.8
PUBLIC EMPLOYEE RETIREMENT SYSTEM	410	107831	171	79727	168	79456	3	271	29	32299	-	-
	20.1	25.0	12.5	22.0	35.1	32.8	.3	.2	31.2	26.6	-	-
TIAA-CREF	1378	287403	1069	258953	300	151955	769	106998	60	81448	55	46834
	67.7	66.7	78.3	71.5	62.8	62.8	86.7	89.1	64.5	67.0	90.2	86.3
SELF-FUNDED OR TRUSTEED PLAN	80	26262	66	25651	21	16918	45	8733	4	7732	5	5965
	3.9	6.1	4.8	7.1	4.4	7.0	5.1	7.3	4.3	6.4	8.2	11.0
INSURANCY COMPANY PLAN	194	37684	133	31825	41	26000	92	5825	9	17139	2	420
	9.5	8.7	9.7	8.8	8.6	10.7	10.4	4.9	9.7	14.1	3.3	.8
CHURCH PENSION PLAN	154	14593	139	14159	1	541	138	13618	-	-	5	6401
	7.6	3.4	10.2	3.9	.2	.2	15.6	11.3	-	-	8.2	11.8

TYPES OF RETIREMENT PLANS COVERING COLLEGE AND UNIVERSITY STAFF MEMBERS

TABLE 3B

CLERICAL SERVICE	ALL INSTITUTIONS		ALL 4-YEAR INSTITUTIONS		ALL 4-YEAR INSTITUTIONS: PUBLIC		ALL 4-YEAR INSTITUTIONS: PRIVATE		UNIVERSITIES: PUBLIC		UNIVERSITIES: PRIVATE	
	INSTS	EES	INSTS	EES	INSTS	EES	INSTS	EES	INSTS	EES	INSTS	EES
TOTAL	1927	663446	1270	595029	477	413018	793	182011	93	231299	61	94679
	100.0	100.0	100.0	100.0	100.0	100.0	100.0	100.0	100.0	100.0	100.0	100.0
NO RESPONSE	8	1211	6	1119	1	763	5	356	1	763	1	130
	.4	.2	.5	.2	.2	.2	.6	.2	1.1	.3	1.6	.1
STATE OR LOCAL TEACHER RETIREMENT SYSTEM	402	143270	173	120429	171	120318	2	111	28	66134	-	-
	20.9	21.6	13.6	20.2	35.8	29.1	.3	.1	30.1	28.6	-	-
PUBLIC EMPLOYEE RETIREMENT SYSTEM	677	291753	282	246171	281	246079	1	92	52	127887	-	-
	35.1	44.0	22.2	41.4	58.9	59.6	.1	.1	55.9	55.3	-	-
TIAA-CREF	820	208747	671	197478	121	97547	550	99931	23	60187	36	43206
	42.6	31.5	52.8	33.2	25.4	23.6	69.4	54.9	24.7	26.0	59.0	45.6
SELF-FUNDED OR TRUSTEED PLAN	153	127113	139	126434	30	61297	109	65137	7	35266	19	45864
	7.9	19.2	10.9	21.2	6.3	14.8	13.7	35.8	7.5	15.2	31.1	48.4
INSURANCY COMPANY PLAN	191	65165	160	63043	24	31121	136	31922	4	20384	10	14424
	9.9	9.8	12.6	10.6	5.0	7.5	17.2	17.5	4.3	8.8	16.4	15.2
CHURCH PENSION PLAN	98	11265	88	10944	1	3187	87	7757	-	-	3	2050
	5.1	1.7	6.9	1.8	.2	.8	11.0	4.3	-	-	4.9	2.2

4-YEAR LIBERAL ARTS COLLEGES				OTHER 4-YEAR COLLEGES				ALL 2-YEAR INSTITUTIONS		2-YEAR INSTITUTIONS			
PUBLIC		PRIVATE		PUBLIC		PRIVATE				PUBLIC		PRIVATE	
INSTS	EES	INSTS	EES	INSTS	EES	INSTS	EES	INSTS	EES	INSTS	EES	INSTS	EES
341	109911	664	56364	44	10502	162	9413	670	68654	596	66548	74	2106
100.0	100.0	100.0	100.0	100.0	100.0	100.0	100.0	100.0	100.0	100.0	100.0	100.0	100.0
-	-	2	81	-	-	1	30	-	-	-	-	-	-
-	-	.3	.1	-	-	.6	.3	-	-	-	-	-	-
211	65986	14	1223	23	4404	2	106	427	49696	425	49671	2	25
61.9	60.0	2.1	2.2	52.3	41.9	1.2	1.1	63.7	72.4	71.3	74.6	2.7	1.2
119	42597	1	20	20	4560	2	251	239	28104	239	28104	-	-
34.9	38.8	.2	☆	45.5	43.4	1.2	2.7	35.7	40.9	40.1	42.2	-	-
209	62748	589	51752	31	7759	125	8412	309	28450	253	26888	56	1562
61.3	57.1	88.7	91.8	70.5	73.9	77.2	89.4	46.1	41.4	42.4	40.4	75.7	74.2
12	6595	27	1566	5	2591	13	1202	14	611	6	425	8	186
3.5	6.0	4.1	2.8	11.4	24.7	8.0	12.8	2.1	.9	1.0	.6	10.8	8.8
26	8282	65	4257	6	579	25	1148	61	5859	50	5578	11	281
7.6	7.5	9.8	7.6	13.6	5.5	15.4	12.2	9.1	8.5	8.4	8.4	14.9	13.3
-	-	93	6546	1	541	40	671	15	434	-	-	15	434
-	-	14.0	11.6	2.3	5.2	24.7	7.1	2.2	.6	-	-	20.3	20.6

4-YEAR LIBERAL ARTS COLLEGES				OTHER 4-YEAR COLLEGES				ALL 2-YEAR INSTITUTIONS		2-YEAR INSTITUTIONS			
PUBLIC		PRIVATE		PUBLIC		PRIVATE				PUBLIC		PRIVATE	
INSTS	EES	INSTS	EES	INSTS	EES	INSTS	EES	INSTS	EES	INSTS	EES	INSTS	EES
340	152959	582	70910	44	28760	150	16422	657	68417	592	66378	65	2039
100.0	100.0	100.0	100.0	100.0	100.0	100.0	100.0	100.0	100.0	100.0	100.0	100.0	100.0
-	-	4	226	-	-	-	-	2	92	1	67	1	25
-	-	.7	.3	-	-	-	-	.3	.1	.2	.1	1.5	1.2
127	49188	2	111	16	4996	-	-	229	22841	228	22835	1	6
37.4	32.2	.3	.2	36.4	17.4	-	-	34.9	33.4	38.5	34.4	1.5	.3
204	97345	-	-	25	20847	1	92	395	45582	394	45533	1	49
60.0	63.6	-	-	56.8	72.5	.7	.6	60.1	66.6	66.6	68.6	1.5	2.4
86	31493	426	47540	12	5867	88	9185	149	11269	106	9925	43	1344
25.3	20.6	73.2	67.0	27.3	20.4	58.7	55.9	22.7	16.5	17.9	15.0	66.2	65.9
18	23617	67	13331	5	2414	23	5942	14	679	6	392	8	287
5.3	15.4	11.5	18.8	11.4	8.4	15.3	36.2	2.1	1.0	1.0	.6	12.3	14.1
15	8923	95	12413	5	1814	31	5085	31	2122	20	1908	11	214
4.4	5.8	16.3	17.5	11.4	6.3	20.7	31.0	4.7	3.1	3.4	2.9	16.9	10.5
-	-	64	5161	1	3187	20	546	10	321	-	-	10	321
-	-	11.0	7.3	2.3	11.1	13.3	3.3	1.5	.5	-	-	15.4	15.7

EMPLOYER-EMPLOYEE CONTRIBUTION TOWARD THE COST OF THE RETIREMENT PLAN

TABLE 4A

FACULTY

	ALL INSTITUTIONS		ALL 4-YEAR INSTITUTIONS		ALL 4-YEAR INSTITUTIONS				UNIVERSITIES			
					PUBLIC		PRIVATE		PUBLIC		PRIVATE	
	INSTS	EES	INSTS	EES	INSTS	EES	INSTS	EES	INSTS	EES	INSTS	EES
TOTAL	2035	430730	1365	362076	478	242041	887	120035	93	121628	61	54258
	100.0	100.0	100.0	100.0	100.0	100.0	100.0	100.0	100.0	100.0	100.0	100.0
NO RESPONSE	4	275	4	275	1	203	3	72	-	-	-	-
	.2	.1	.3	.1	.2	.1	.3	.1	-	-	-	-
EMPLOYER PAYS FULL COST	233	46088	170	40331	33	20375	137	19956	6	9085	7	9730
	11.4	10.7	12.5	11.1	6.9	8.4	15.4	16.6	6.5	7.5	11.5	17.9
EMPLOYER AND EMPLOYEE SHARE COST	1796	384239	1189	321342	444	221463	745	99879	87	112543	54	44528
	88.3	89.2	87.1	88.8	92.9	91.5	84.1	83.2	93.5	92.5	88.5	82.1
EMPLOYEE PAYS FULL COST	2	128	2	128	-	-	2	128	-	-	-	-
	.1	✲	.1	✲	-	-	.2	.1	-	-	-	-

EMPLOYER-EMPLOYEE CONTRIBUTION TOWARD THE COST OF THE RETIREMENT PLAN

TABLE 4B

CLERICAL SERVICE

	ALL INSTITUTIONS		ALL 4-YEAR INSTITUTIONS		ALL 4-YEAR INSTITUTIONS				UNIVERSITIES			
					PUBLIC		PRIVATE		PUBLIC		PRIVATE	
	INSTS	EES	INSTS	EES	INSTS	EES	INSTS	EES	INSTS	EES	INSTS	EES
TOTAL	1927	663446	1270	595029	477	413018	793	182011	93	231299	61	94679
	100.0	100.0	100.0	100.0	100.0	100.0	100.0	100.0	100.0	100.0	100.0	100.0
NO RESPONSE	8	8040	8	8040	2	267	6	7773	-	-	2	7651
	.4	1.2	.6	1.4	.4	.1	.8	4.3	-	-	3.3	8.1
EMPLOYER PAYS FULL COST	302	117566	239	110728	38	35921	201	74807	9	22145	20	41493
	15.7	17.7	18.8	18.6	8.0	8.7	25.3	41.1	9.7	9.6	32.8	43.8
EMPLOYER AND EMPLOYEE SHARE COST	1609	537320	1015	475741	437	376830	578	98911	84	209154	39	45535
	83.5	81.0	80.0	79.9	91.6	91.2	72.9	54.3	90.3	90.4	63.9	48.1
EMPLOYEE PAYS FULL COST	8	520	8	520	-	-	8	520	-	-	-	-
	.4	.1	.6	.1	-	-	1.0	.3	-	-	-	-

| 4-YEAR LIBERAL ARTS COLLEGES | | | | OTHER 4-YEAR COLLEGES | | | | ALL 2-YEAR INSTITUTIONS | | 2-YEAR INSTITUTIONS | | | |
| PUBLIC | | PRIVATE | | PUBLIC | | PRIVATE | | | | PUBLIC | | PRIVATE | |
INSTS	EES	INSTS	EES	INSTS	EES	INSTS	EES	INSTS	EES	INSTS	EES	INSTS	EES
341	109911	664	56364	44	10502	162	9413	670	68654	596	66548	74	2106
100.0	100.0	100.0	100.0	100.0	100.0	100.0	100.0	100.0	100.0	100.0	100.0	100.0	100.0
-	-	2	42	1	203	1	30	-	-	-	-	-	-
-	-	.3	.1	2.3	1.9	.6	.3	-	-	-	-	-	-
27	11290	79	7631	-	-	51	2595	63	5757	45	5078	18	679
7.9	10.3	11.9	13.5	-	-	31.5	27.6	9.4	8.4	7.6	7.6	24.3	32.2
314	98621	581	48563	43	10299	110	6788	607	62897	551	61470	56	1427
92.1	89.7	87.5	86.2	97.7	98.1	67.9	72.1	90.6	91.6	92.4	92.4	75.7	67.8
-	-	2	128	-	-	-	-	-	-	-	-	-	-
-	-	.3	.2	-	-	-	-	-	-	-	-	-	-

| 4-YEAR LIBERAL ARTS COLLEGES | | | | OTHER 4-YEAR COLLEGES | | | | ALL 2-YEAR INSTITUTIONS | | 2-YEAR INSTITUTIONS | | | |
| PUBLIC | | PRIVATE | | PUBLIC | | PRIVATE | | | | PUBLIC | | PRIVATE | |
INSTS	EES	INSTS	EES	INSTS	EES	INSTS	EES	INSTS	EES	INSTS	EES	INSTS	EES
340	152959	582	70910	44	28760	150	16422	657	68417	592	66378	65	2039
100.0	100.0	100.0	100.0	100.0	100.0	100.0	100.0	100.0	100.0	100.0	100.0	100.0	100.0
-	-	3	116	2	267	1	6	-	-	-	-	-	-
-	-	.5	.2	4.5	.9	.7	*	-	-	-	-	-	-
28	13745	127	23479	1	31	54	9835	63	6838	43	6173	20	665
8.2	9.0	21.8	33.1	2.3	.1	36.0	60.0	9.6	10.0	7.3	9.3	30.8	32.6
312	139214	445	46832	41	28462	94	6544	594	61579	549	60205	45	1374
91.8	91.0	76.5	66.0	93.2	99.0	62.6	39.8	90.4	90.0	92.7	90.7	69.2	67.4
-	-	7	483	-	-	1	37	-	-	-	-	-	-
-	-	1.2	.7	-	-	.7	.2	-	-	-	-	-	-

PAYMENT OF REGULAR EMPLOYEE CONTRIBUTIONS TO RETIREMENT PLAN BY SALARY REDUCTION UNDER SECTION 403(B) INTERNAL REVENUE CODE ("SALARY OR ANNUITY" OPTION)

TABLE 5A

FACULTY

	ALL INSTITUTIONS		ALL 4-YEAR INSTITUTIONS		ALL 4-YEAR INSTITUTIONS				UNIVERSITIES			
					PUBLIC		PRIVATE		PUBLIC		PRIVATE	
	INSTS	EES	INSTS	EES	INSTS	EES	INSTS	EES	INSTS	EES	INSTS	EES
TOTAL	1798	384367	1191	321470	444	221463	747	100007	87	112543	54	44528
	100.0	100.0	100.0	100.0	100.0	100.0	100.0	100.0	100.0	100.0	100.0	100.0
NO RESPONSE	54	7927	30	5967	11	4530	19	1437	3	1927	1	428
	3.0	2.1	2.5	1.9	2.5	2.0	2.5	1.4	3.4	1.7	1.9	1.0
NOT PERMITTED BY INSTITUTION	355	105832	201	86682	155	77205	46	9477	28	35098	4	7004
	19.7	27.5	16.9	27.0	34.9	34.9	6.2	9.5	32.2	31.2	7.4	15.7
REQUIRED FOR REGULAR EMPLOYEE CONTRIBUTIONS	474	87528	252	64465	85	36634	167	27831	11	12721	15	15291
	26.4	22.8	21.2	20.1	19.1	16.5	22.4	27.8	12.6	11.3	27.8	34.3
OPTIONAL FOR REGULAR EMPLOYEE CONTRIBUTIONS	915	183080	708	164356	193	103094	515	61262	45	62797	34	21805
	50.9	47.6	59.4	51.0	43.5	46.6	68.9	61.3	51.8	55.8	62.9	49.0

PAYMENT OF REGULAR EMPLOYEE CONTRIBUTIONS TO RETIREMENT PLAN BY SALARY REDUCTION UNDER SECTION 403(B) INTERNAL REVENUE CODE ("SALARY OR ANNUITY" OPTION)

TABLE 5B

CLERICAL SERVICE

	ALL INSTITUTIONS		ALL 4-YEAR INSTITUTIONS		ALL 4-YEAR INSTITUTIONS				UNIVERSITIES			
					PUBLIC		PRIVATE		PUBLIC		PRIVATE	
	INSTS	EES	INSTS	EES	INSTS	EES	INSTS	EES	INSTS	EES	INSTS	EES
TOTAL	1618	537911	1024	476332	438	376901	586	99431	84	209154	39	45535
	100.0	100.0	100.0	100.0	100.0	100.0	100.0	100.0	100.0	100.0	100.0	100.0
NO RESPONSE	52	9024	28	7467	15	5938	13	1529	3	2715	2	686
	3.2	1.7	2.7	1.6	3.4	1.6	2.2	1.5	3.6	1.3	5.1	1.5
NOT PERMITTED BY INSTITUTION	455	250067	268	228391	216	213724	52	14667	45	113258	6	10361
	28.1	46.5	26.2	47.9	49.4	56.7	8.9	14.8	53.6	54.1	15.4	22.8
REQUIRED FOR REGULAR EMPLOYEE CONTRIBUTIONS	406	78543	188	55851	72	42626	116	13225	8	19768	6	3472
	25.1	14.6	18.4	11.7	16.4	11.3	19.8	13.3	9.5	9.5	15.4	7.6
OPTIONAL FOR REGULAR EMPLOYEE CONTRIBUTIONS	705	200277	540	184623	135	114613	405	70010	28	73413	25	31016
	43.6	37.2	52.7	38.8	30.8	30.4	69.1	70.4	33.3	35.1	64.1	68.1

| 4-YEAR LIBERAL ARTS COLLEGES | | | | OTHER 4-YEAR COLLEGES | | | | ALL 2-YEAR INSTITUTIONS | | 2-YEAR INSTITUTIONS | | | |
| PUBLIC | | PRIVATE | | PUBLIC | | PRIVATE | | | | PUBLIC | | PRIVATE | |
INSTS	EES	INSTS	EES	INSTS	EES	INSTS	EES	INSTS	EES	INSTS	EES	INSTS	EES
314	98621	583	48691	43	10299	110	6788	607	62897	551	61470	56	1427
100.0	100.0	100.0	100.0	100.0	100.0	100.0	100.0	100.0	100.0	100.0	100.0	100.0	100.0
8	2603	13	894	-	-	5	115	24	1960	18	1804	6	156
2.5	2.6	2.2	1.8	-	-	4.5	1.7	4.0	3.1	3.3	2.9	10.7	10.9
111	39571	35	2199	16	2536	7	274	154	19150	150	19063	4	87
35.4	40.1	6.0	4.5	37.2	24.6	6.4	4.0	25.4	30.4	27.2	31.0	7.1	6.1
67	22264	120	9702	7	1649	32	2838	222	23063	209	22695	13	368
21.3	22.6	20.6	19.9	16.3	16.0	29.1	41.8	36.5	36.7	37.9	37.0	23.2	25.8
128	34183	415	35896	20	6114	66	3561	207	18724	174	17908	33	816
40.8	34.7	71.2	73.8	46.5	59.4	60.0	52.5	34.1	29.8	31.6	29.1	59.0	57.2

| 4-YEAR LIBERAL ARTS COLLEGES | | | | OTHER 4-YEAR COLLEGES | | | | ALL 2-YEAR INSTITUTIONS | | 2-YEAR INSTITUTIONS | | | |
| PUBLIC | | PRIVATE | | PUBLIC | | PRIVATE | | | | PUBLIC | | PRIVATE | |
INSTS	EES	INSTS	EES	INSTS	EES	INSTS	EES	INSTS	EES	INSTS	EES	INSTS	EES
312	139214	452	47315	42	28533	95	6581	594	61579	549	60205	45	1374
100.0	100.0	100.0	100.0	100.0	100.0	100.0	100.0	100.0	100.0	100.0	100.0	100.0	100.0
12	3223	8	780	-	-	3	63	24	1557	19	1436	5	121
3.8	2.3	1.8	1.6	-	-	3.2	1.0	4.0	2.5	3.5	2.4	11.1	8.8
150	85463	38	3958	21	15003	8	348	187	21676	185	21631	2	45
48.1	61.4	8.4	8.4	50.0	52.6	8.4	5.3	31.5	35.2	33.7	35.9	4.4	3.3
59	19804	86	7809	5	3054	24	1944	218	22692	208	22291	10	401
18.9	14.2	19.0	16.5	11.9	10.7	25.3	29.5	36.7	36.9	37.8	37.0	22.2	29.2
91	30724	320	34768	16	10476	60	4226	165	15654	137	14847	28	807
29.2	22.1	70.8	73.5	38.1	36.7	63.1	64.2	27.8	25.4	25.0	24.7	62.3	58.7

EXTRA ANNUITY CONTRIBUTIONS TO RETIREMENT PLAN
BY EMPLOYEES UNDER "SALARY OR ANNUITY" OPTION OF SECTION 403(B)
INTERNAL REVENUE CODE

TABLE 6A

FACULTY

				ALL 4-YEAR INSTITUTIONS				UNIVERSITIES			
	ALL INSTITUTIONS		ALL 4-YEAR INSTITUTIONS		PUBLIC		PRIVATE		PUBLIC		PRIVATE	
	INSTS	EES	INSTS	EES	INSTS	EES	INSTS	EES	INSTS	EES	INSTS	EE
TOTAL	2035	430730	1365	362076	478	242041	887	120035	93	121628	61	5425
	100.0	100.0	100.0	100.0	100.0	100.0	100.0	100.0	100.0	100.0	100.0	100.
NO RESPONSE	6	499	4	183	-	-	4	183	-	-	-	
	.3	.1	.3	.1	-	-	.5	.2	-	-	-	
EXTRA CONTRIBUTIONS PERMITTED	1784	399343	1232	342278	423	225893	809	116385	87	116491	61	5425
	87.7	92.7	90.2	94.5	88.5	93.3	91.2	96.9	93.5	95.8	100.0	100.
EXTRA CONTRIBUTIONS NOT PERMITTED	245	30888	129	19615	55	16148	74	3467	6	5137	-	
	12.0	7.2	9.5	5.4	11.5	6.7	8.3	2.9	6.5	4.2	-	

EXTRA ANNUITY CONTRIBUTIONS TO RETIREMENT PLAN
BY EMPLOYEES UNDER "SALARY OR ANNUITY" OPTION OF SECTION 403(B)
INTERNAL REVENUE CODE

TABLE 6B

CLERICAL SERVICE

				ALL 4-YEAR INSTITUTIONS				UNIVERSITIES			
	ALL INSTITUTIONS		ALL 4-YEAR INSTITUTIONS		PUBLIC		PRIVATE		PUBLIC		PRIVATE	
	INSTS	EES	INSTS	EES	INSTS	EES	INSTS	EES	INSTS	EES	INSTS	EE
TOTAL	1927	663446	1270	595029	477	413018	793	182011	93	231299	61	9467
	100.0	100.0	100.0	100.0	100.0	100.0	100.0	100.0	100.0	100.0	100.0	100.
NO RESPONSE	16	4312	11	3355	-	-	11	3355	-	-	3	211
	.8	.6	.9	.6	-	-	1.4	1.8	-	-	4.9	2.
EXTRA CONTRIBUTIONS PERMITTED	1526	546448	1025	494291	383	354953	642	139338	79	199907	46	6883
	79.2	82.4	80.7	83.0	80.3	85.9	80.9	76.6	84.9	86.4	75.4	72.
EXTRA CONTRIBUTIONS NOT PERMITTED	385	112686	234	97383	94	58065	140	39318	14	31392	12	2373
	20.0	17.0	18.4	16.4	19.7	14.1	17.7	21.6	15.1	13.6	19.7	25.

4-YEAR LIBERAL ARTS COLLEGES				OTHER 4-YEAR COLLEGES				ALL 2-YEAR INSTITUTIONS		2-YEAR INSTITUTIONS			
PUBLIC		PRIVATE		PUBLIC		PRIVATE				PUBLIC		PRIVATE	
INSTS	EES	INSTS	EES	INSTS	EES	INSTS	EES	INSTS	EES	INSTS	EES	INSTS	EES
341	109911	664	56364	44	10502	162	9413	670	68654	596	66548	74	2106
100.0	100.0	100.0	100.0	100.0	100.0	100.0	100.0	100.0	100.0	100.0	100.0	100.0	100.0
-	-	1	41	-	-	3	142	2	316	2	316	-	-
-	-	.2	.1	-	-	1.9	1.5	.3	.5	.3	.5	-	-
297	99229	606	53331	39	10173	142	8796	552	57065	489	55182	63	1883
87.1	90.3	91.2	94.6	88.6	96.9	87.6	93.5	82.4	83.1	82.1	82.9	85.1	89.4
44	10682	57	2992	5	329	17	475	116	11273	105	11050	11	223
12.9	9.7	8.6	5.3	11.4	3.1	10.5	5.0	17.3	16.4	17.6	16.6	14.9	10.6

4-YEAR LIBERAL ARTS COLLEGES				OTHER 4-YEAR COLLEGES				ALL 2-YEAR INSTITUTIONS		2-YEAR INSTITUTIONS			
PUBLIC		PRIVATE		PUBLIC		PRIVATE				PUBLIC		PRIVATE	
INSTS	EES	INSTS	EES	INSTS	EES	INSTS	EES	INSTS	EES	INSTS	EES	INSTS	EES
340	152959	582	70910	44	28760	150	16422	657	68417	592	66378	65	2039
100.0	100.0	100.0	100.0	100.0	100.0	100.0	100.0	100.0	100.0	100.0	100.0	100.0	100.0
-	-	6	365	-	-	2	874	5	957	5	957	-	-
-	-	1.0	.5	-	-	1.3	5.3	.8	1.4	.8	1.4	-	-
266	126620	474	59148	38	28426	122	11357	501	52157	447	50420	54	1737
78.2	82.8	81.5	83.4	86.4	98.8	81.4	69.2	76.2	76.2	75.6	76.0	83.1	85.2
74	26339	102	11397	6	334	26	4191	151	15303	140	15001	11	302
21.8	17.2	17.5	16.1	13.6	1.2	17.3	25.5	23.0	22.4	23.6	22.6	16.9	14.8

SUMMARY OF PROVISIONS FOR FIXED AND FLEXIBLE RETIREMENT AGE COLLEGE AND UNIVERSITY RETIREMENT PLANS

TABLE 7A

FACULTY

	ALL INSTITUTIONS		ALL 4-YEAR INSTITUTIONS		ALL 4-YEAR INSTITUTIONS				UNIVERSITIES			
					PUBLIC		PRIVATE		PUBLIC		PRIVATE	
	INSTS	EES	INSTS	EES	INSTS	EES	INSTS	EES	INSTS	EES	INSTS	EES
TOTAL	2035	430730	1365	362076	478	242041	887	120035	93	121628	61	54258
	100.0	100.0	100.0	100.0	100.0	100.0	100.0	100.0	100.0	100.0	100.0	100.0
NO RESPONSE	20	2002	10	1181	2	837	8	344	1	694	-	-
	1.0	.5	.7	.3	.4	.3	.9	.3	1.1	.6	-	-
SERVICE MAY BE EXTENDED BEYOND AGE STATED	1828	383625	1221	321539	407	210486	814	111053	81	106917	57	50646
	89.9	89.0	89.5	88.9	85.2	87.0	91.8	92.5	87.1	87.9	93.4	93.3
RETIREMENT AGE FIXED AT AGE STATED	182	44769	131	39277	69	30718	62	8559	11	14017	4	3612
	8.9	10.4	9.6	10.8	14.4	12.7	7.0	7.1	11.8	11.5	6.6	6.7
NO RETIREMENT AGE STATED	5	334	3	79	-	-	3	79	-	-	-	-
	.2	.1	.2	☆	-	-	.3	.1	-	-	-	-

SUMMARY OF PROVISIONS FOR FIXED AND FLEXIBLE RETIREMENT AGE COLLEGE AND UNIVERSITY RETIREMENT PLANS

TABLE 7B

CLERICAL SERVICE

	ALL INSTITUTIONS		ALL 4-YEAR INSTITUTIONS		ALL 4-YEAR INSTITUTIONS				UNIVERSITIES			
					PUBLIC		PRIVATE		PUBLIC		PRIVATE	
	INSTS	EES	INSTS	EES	INSTS	EES	INSTS	EES	INSTS	EES	INSTS	EES
TOTAL	1927	663446	1270	595029	477	413018	793	182011	93	231299	61	94679
	100.0	100.0	100.0	100.0	100.0	100.0	100.0	100.0	100.0	100.0	100.0	100.0
NO RESPONSE	19	2546	9	1805	2	1249	7	556	1	949	1	130
	1.0	.4	.7	.3	.4	.3	.9	.3	1.1	.4	1.6	.1
SERVICE MAY BE EXTENDED BEYOND AGE STATED	1667	581454	1090	520972	384	358098	706	162874	77	199424	53	83031
	86.5	87.7	85.8	87.6	80.5	86.7	89.0	89.5	82.8	86.2	86.9	87.7
RETIREMENT AGE FIXED AT AGE STATED	237	79130	169	72205	91	53671	78	18534	15	30926	7	11518
	12.3	11.9	13.3	12.1	19.1	13.0	9.8	10.2	16.1	13.4	11.5	12.2
NO RETIREMENT AGE STATED	4	316	2	47	-	-	2	47	-	-	-	-
	.2	☆	.2	☆	-	-	.3	☆	-	-	-	-

4-YEAR LIBERAL ARTS COLLEGES				OTHER 4-YEAR COLLEGES				ALL 2-YEAR INSTITUTIONS		2-YEAR INSTITUTIONS			
PUBLIC		PRIVATE		PUBLIC		PRIVATE				PUBLIC		PRIVATE	
INSTS	EES	INSTS	EES	INSTS	EES	INSTS	EES	INSTS	EES	INSTS	EES	INSTS	EES
341	109911	664	56364	44	10502	162	9413	670	68654	596	66548	74	2106
100.0	100.0	100.0	100.0	100.0	100.0	100.0	100.0	100.0	100.0	100.0	100.0	100.0	100.0
1	143	6	291	-	-	2	53	10	821	9	810	1	11
.3	.1	.9	.5	-	-	1.2	.6	1.5	1.2	1.5	1.2	1.4	.5
288	93655	608	51513	38	9914	149	8894	607	62086	537	60045	70	2041
84.5	85.2	91.6	91.4	86.4	94.4	92.0	94.4	90.6	90.4	90.1	90.2	94.5	96.9
52	16113	48	4489	6	588	10	458	51	5492	48	5438	3	54
15.2	14.7	7.2	8.0	13.6	5.6	6.2	4.9	7.6	8.0	8.1	8.2	4.1	2.6
-	-	2	71	-	-	1	8	2	255	2	255	-	-
-	-	.3	.1	-	-	.6	.1	.3	.4	.3	.4	-	-

4-YEAR LIBERAL ARTS COLLEGES				OTHER 4-YEAR COLLEGES				ALL 2-YEAR INSTITUTIONS		2-YEAR INSTITUTIONS			
PUBLIC		PRIVATE		PUBLIC		PRIVATE				PUBLIC		PRIVATE	
INSTS	EES	INSTS	EES	INSTS	EES	INSTS	EES	INSTS	EES	INSTS	EES	INSTS	EES
340	152959	582	70910	44	28760	150	16422	657	68417	592	66378	65	2039
100.0	100.0	100.0	100.0	100.0	100.0	100.0	100.0	100.0	100.0	100.0	100.0	100.0	100.0
1	300	5	388	-	-	1	38	10	741	9	736	1	5
.3	.2	.9	.5	-	-	.7	.2	1.5	1.1	1.5	1.1	1.5	.2
271	134267	522	64502	36	24407	131	15341	577	60482	516	58513	61	1969
79.7	87.8	89.6	91.0	81.8	84.9	87.3	93.5	87.8	88.4	87.2	88.2	93.9	96.6
68	18392	54	5981	8	4353	17	1035	68	6925	65	6860	3	65
20.0	12.0	9.3	8.4	18.2	15.1	11.3	6.3	10.4	10.1	11.0	10.3	4.6	3.2
-	-	1	39	-	-	1	8	2	269	2	269	-	-
-	-	.2	.1	-	-	.7	*	.3	.4	.3	.4	-	-

DISTRIBUTION OF "NORMAL" RETIREMENT AGE

TABLE 8A

FACULTY

	ALL INSTITUTIONS		ALL 4-YEAR INSTITUTIONS		ALL 4-YEAR INSTITUTIONS				UNIVERSITIES			
					PUBLIC		PRIVATE		PUBLIC		PRIVATE	
	INSTS	EES	INSTS	EES	INSTS	EES	INSTS	EES	INSTS	EES	INSTS	EES
TOTAL	2035	430730	1365	362076	478	242041	887	120035	93	121628	61	54258
	100.0	100.0	100.0	100.0	100.0	100.0	100.0	100.0	100.0	100.0	100.0	100.0
NO RESPONSE	21	2150	11	1209	2	837	9	372	1	694	-	-
	1.0	.5	.8	.3	.4	.3	1.0	.3	1.1	.6	-	-
UNDER AGE 62	168	38285	63	28459	62	28441	1	18	6	7719	-	-
	8.3	8.9	4.6	7.9	13.0	11.8	.1	✽	6.5	6.3	-	-
62	60	19926	30	15987	27	15515	3	472	5	7298	1	315
	2.9	4.6	2.2	4.4	5.6	6.4	.3	.4	5.4	6.0	1.6	.6
63	1	17	1	17	-	-	1	17	-	-	-	-
	✽	✽	.1	✽	-	-	.1	✽	-	-	-	-
64	-	-	-	-	-	-	-	-	-	-	-	-
	-	-	-	-	-	-	-	-	-	-	-	-
65	1594	291673	1105	242541	295	140311	810	102230	62	77162	50	41835
	78.4	67.8	81.0	67.1	61.8	58.0	91.3	85.2	66.5	63.5	82.1	77.1
66	10	6650	10	6650	3	1712	7	4938	2	1616	1	4429
	.5	1.5	.7	1.8	.6	.7	.8	4.1	2.2	1.3	1.6	8.2
67	40	21977	35	21393	28	20814	7	579	4	7527	-	-
	2.0	5.1	2.6	5.9	5.9	8.6	.8	.5	4.3	6.2	-	-
68	51	22925	44	22122	16	14585	28	7537	5	9626	6	5321
	2.5	5.3	3.2	6.1	3.3	6.0	3.2	6.3	5.4	7.9	9.8	9.8
69	-	-	-	-	-	-	-	-	-	-	-	-
	-	-	-	-	-	-	-	-	-	-	-	-
70	90	27127	66	23698	45	19826	21	3872	8	9986	3	2358
	4.4	6.3	4.8	6.5	9.4	8.2	2.4	3.2	8.6	8.2	4.9	4.3
OVER 70	-	-	-	-	-	-	-	-	-	-	-	-
	-	-	-	-	-	-	-	-	-	-	-	-

	4-YEAR LIBERAL ARTS COLLEGES				OTHER 4-YEAR COLLEGES				ALL 2-YEAR INSTITUTIONS		2-YEAR INSTITUTIONS			
	PUBLIC		PRIVATE		PUBLIC		PRIVATE				PUBLIC		PRIVATE	
	INSTS	EES	INSTS	EES	INSTS	EES	INSTS	EES	INSTS	EES	INSTS	EES	INSTS	EES
	341	109911	664	56364	44	10502	162	9413	670	68654	596	66548	74	2106
	100.0	100.0	100.0	100.0	100.0	100.0	100.0	100.0	100.0	100.0	100.0	100.0	100.0	100.0
	1	143	6	326	-	-	3	46	10	941	9	930	1	11
	.3	.1	.9	.6	-	-	1.9	.5	1.5	1.4	1.5	1.4	1.4	.5
	50	20103	-	-	6	619	1	18	105	9826	105	9826	-	-
	14.7	18.3	-	-	13.6	5.9	.6	.2	15.7	14.3	17.6	14.8	-	-
	18	6857	1	41	4	1360	1	116	30	3939	30	3939	-	-
	5.3	6.2	.2	.1	9.1	12.9	.6	1.2	4.5	5.7	5.0	5.9	-	-
	-	-	1	17	-	-	-	-	-	-	-	-	-	-
	-	-	.2	✳	-	-	-	-	-	-	-	-	-	-
	-	-	-	-	-	-	-	-	-	-	-	-	-	-
	-	-	-	-	-	-	-	-	-	-	-	-	-	-
	208	56269	614	51643	25	6880	146	8752	489	49132	417	47047	72	2085
	60.9	51.2	92.3	91.5	56.9	65.5	90.0	93.0	73.0	71.5	70.0	70.7	97.2	99.0
	1	96	3	369	-	-	3	140	-	-	-	-	-	-
	.3	.1	.5	.7	-	-	1.9	1.5	-	-	-	-	-	-
	22	12710	6	548	2	577	1	31	5	584	5	584	-	-
	6.5	11.6	.9	1.0	4.5	5.5	.6	.3	.7	.9	.8	.9	-	-
	10	4259	18	1924	1	700	4	292	7	803	7	803	-	-
	2.9	3.9	2.7	3.4	2.3	6.7	2.5	3.1	1.0	1.2	1.2	1.2	-	-
	-	-	-	-	-	-	-	-	-	-	-	-	-	-
	-	-	-	-	-	-	-	-	-	-	-	-	-	-
	31	9474	15	1496	6	366	3	18	24	3429	23	3419	1	10
	9.1	8.6	2.3	2.7	13.6	3.5	1.9	.2	3.6	5.0	3.9	5.1	1.4	.5
	-	-	-	-	-	-	-	-	-	-	-	-	-	-
	-	-	-	-	-	-	-	-	-	-	-	-	-	-

DISTRIBUTION OF "NORMAL" RETIREMENT AGE

TABLE 8B

CLERICAL SERVICE

	ALL INSTITUTIONS		ALL 4-YEAR INSTITUTIONS		ALL 4-YEAR INSTITUTIONS				UNIVERSITIES			
					PUBLIC		PRIVATE		PUBLIC		PRIVATE	
	INSTS	EES	INSTS	EES	INSTS	EES	INSTS	EES	INSTS	EES	INSTS	EES
TOTAL	1927	663446	1270	595029	477	413018	793	182011	93	231299	61	94679
	100.0	100.0	100.0	100.0	100.0	100.0	100.0	100.0	100.0	100.0	100.0	100.0
NO RESPONSE	22	2838	10	1698	2	1249	8	449	1	949	1	130
	1.1	.4	.8	.3	.4	.3	1.0	.2	1.1	.4	1.6	.1
UNDER AGE 62	170	56284	67	47338	65	47186	2	152	7	15559	-	-
	8.8	8.5	5.3	8.0	13.6	11.4	.3	.1	7.5	6.7	-	-
62	79	38682	44	33101	41	32797	3	304	6	15275	1	261
	4.1	5.8	3.5	5.6	8.6	7.9	.4	.2	6.5	6.6	1.6	.3
63	3	323	1	23	-	-	1	23	-	-	-	-
	.2	＊	.1	＊	-	-	.1	＊	-	-	-	-
64	-	-	-	-	-	-	-	-	-	-	-	-
	-	-	-	-	-	-	-	-	-	-	-	-
65	1467	441986	1027	400628	285	231394	742	169234	60	142856	54	85370
	76.0	66.8	80.8	67.3	59.8	56.1	93.5	93.1	64.3	61.8	88.7	90.2
66	9	7528	9	7528	3	2201	6	5327	2	2085	1	4822
	.5	1.1	.7	1.3	.6	.5	.8	2.9	2.2	.9	1.6	5.1
67	59	58017	29	50825	24	50427	5	398	2	21232	-	-
	3.1	8.7	2.3	8.5	5.0	12.2	.6	.2	2.2	9.2	-	-
68	28	18082	22	17432	8	12826	14	4606	2	9094	3	3704
	1.5	2.7	1.7	2.9	1.7	3.1	1.8	2.5	2.2	3.9	4.9	3.9
69	-	-	-	-	-	-	-	-	-	-	-	-
	-	-	-	-	-	-	-	-	-	-	-	-
70	90	39706	61	36456	49	34938	12	1518	13	24249	1	392
	4.7	6.0	4.8	6.1	10.3	8.5	1.5	.8	14.0	10.5	1.6	.4
OVER 70	-	-	-	-	-	-	-	-	-	-	-	-
	-	-	-	-	-	-	-	-	-	-	-	-

	4-YEAR LIBERAL ARTS COLLEGES				OTHER 4-YEAR COLLEGES				ALL 2-YEAR INSTITUTIONS		2-YEAR INSTITUTIONS			
	PUBLIC		PRIVATE		PUBLIC		PRIVATE				PUBLIC		PRIVATE	
	INSTS	EES	INSTS	EES	INSTS	EES	INSTS	EES	INSTS	EES	INSTS	EES	INSTS	EES
	340	152959	582	70910	44	28760	150	16422	657	68417	592	66378	65	2039
	100.0	100.0	100.0	100.0	100.0	100.0	100.0	100.0	100.0	100.0	100.0	100.0	100.0	100.0
	1	300	5	298	-	-	2	21	12	1140	10	1123	2	17
	.3	.2	.9	.4	-	-	1.3	.1	1.8	1.7	1.7	1.7	3.1	.8
	50	25985	-	-	8	5642	2	152	103	8946	103	8946	-	-
	14.7	17.0	-	-	18.2	19.6	1.3	.9	15.7	13.1	17.4	13.5	-	-
	29	11279	1	21	6	6243	1	22	35	5581	35	5581	-	-
	8.5	7.4	.2	*	13.6	21.7	.7	.1	5.3	8.2	5.9	8.4	-	-
	-	-	1	23	-	-	-	-	2	300	2	300	-	-
	-	-	.2	*	-	-	-	-	.3	.4	.3	.5	-	-
	-	-	-	-	-	-	-	-	-	-	-	-	-	-
	-	-	-	-	-	-	-	-	-	-	-	-	-	-
	202	74859	549	67935	23	13679	139	15929	440	41358	378	39371	62	1987
	59.4	48.9	94.3	95.8	52.3	47.6	92.7	97.1	67.0	60.3	63.9	59.3	95.4	97.5
	1	116	3	435	-	-	2	70	-	-	-	-	-	-
	.3	.1	.5	.6	-	-	1.3	.4	-	-	-	-	-	-
	20	26498	4	340	2	2697	1	58	30	7192	30	7192	-	-
	5.9	17.3	.7	.5	4.5	9.4	.7	.4	4.6	10.5	5.1	10.8	-	-
	6	3732	9	755	-	-	2	147	6	650	6	650	-	-
	1.8	2.4	1.5	1.1	-	-	1.3	.9	.9	1.0	1.0	1.0	-	-
	-	-	-	-	-	-	-	-	-	-	-	-	-	-
	-	-	-	-	-	-	-	-	-	-	-	-	-	-
	31	10190	10	1103	5	499	1	23	29	3250	28	3215	1	35
	9.1	6.7	1.7	1.6	11.4	1.7	.7	.1	4.4	4.8	4.7	4.8	1.5	1.7
	-	-	-	-	-	-	-	-	-	-	-	-	-	-
	-	-	-	-	-	-	-	-	-	-	-	-	-	-

DISTRIBUTION OF STATED "NORMAL" RETIREMENT AGES UNDER PLANS PROVIDING FOR EXTENSIONS OF SERVICE BEYOND "NORMAL" RETIREMENT AGE

TABLE 9A

FACULTY

	ALL INSTITUTIONS		ALL 4-YEAR INSTITUTIONS		ALL 4-YEAR INSTITUTIONS PUBLIC		PRIVATE		UNIVERSITIES PUBLIC		PRIVATE	
	INSTS	EES	INSTS	EES	INSTS	EES	INSTS	EES	INSTS	EES	INSTS	EES
TOTAL	1828	383625	1221	321539	407	210486	814	111053	81	106917	57	50646
	100.0	100.0	100.0	100.0	100.0	100.0	100.0	100.0	100.0	100.0	100.0	100.0
NO RESPONSE	2	385	1	8	-	-	1	8	-	-	-	-
	.1	.1	.1	✧	-	-	.1	✧	-	-	-	-
UNDER AGE 62	168	38285	63	28459	62	28441	1	18	6	7719	-	-
	9.2	10.0	5.2	8.9	15.2	13.5	.1	✧	7.4	7.2	-	-
62	60	19926	30	15987	27	15515	3	472	5	7298	1	315
	3.3	5.2	2.5	5.0	6.6	7.4	.4	.4	6.2	6.8	1.8	.6
63	1	17	1	17	-	-	1	17	-	-	-	-
	.1	✧	.1	✧	-	-	.1	✧	-	-	-	-
64	-	-	-	-	-	-	-	-	-	-	-	-
	-	-	-	-	-	-	-	-	-	-	-	-
65	1472	272749	1027	227614	267	131957	760	95657	58	73716	48	38897
	80.5	71.1	83.9	70.7	65.6	62.6	93.4	86.1	71.6	69.1	84.1	76.9
66	8	5469	8	5469	2	779	6	4690	1	683	1	4429
	.4	1.4	.7	1.7	.5	.4	.7	4.2	1.2	.6	1.8	8.7
67	26	11104	22	10617	17	10222	5	395	1	1332	-	-
	1.4	2.9	1.8	3.3	4.2	4.9	.6	.4	1.2	1.2	-	-
68	46	21819	40	21208	15	14135	25	7073	5	9626	5	4921
	2.5	5.7	3.3	6.6	3.7	6.7	3.1	6.4	6.2	9.0	8.8	9.7
69	-	-	-	-	-	-	-	-	-	-	-	-
	-	-	-	-	-	-	-	-	-	-	-	-
70	45	13871	29	12160	17	9437	12	2723	5	6543	2	2084
	2.5	3.6	2.4	3.8	4.2	4.5	1.5	2.5	6.2	6.1	3.5	4.1
OVER 70	-	-	-	-	-	-	-	-	-	-	-	-
	-	-	-	-	-	-	-	-	-	-	-	-

4-YEAR LIBERAL ARTS COLLEGES				OTHER 4-YEAR COLLEGES				ALL 2-YEAR INSTITUTIONS		2-YEAR INSTITUTIONS			
PUBLIC		PRIVATE		PUBLIC		PRIVATE				PUBLIC		PRIVATE	
INSTS	EES	INSTS	EES	INSTS	EES	INSTS	EES	INSTS	EES	INSTS	EES	INSTS	EES
288	93655	608	51513	38	9914	149	8894	607	62086	537	60045	70	2041
100.0	100.0	100.0	100.0	100.0	100.0	100.0	100.0	100.0	100.0	100.0	100.0	100.0	100.0
-	-	-	-	-	-	1	8	1	377	1	377	-	-
-	-	-	-	-	-	.7	.1	.2	.6	.2	.6	-	-
50	20103	-	-	6	619	1	18	105	9826	105	9826	-	-
17.4	21.5	-	-	15.8	6.2	.7	.2	17.3	15.8	19.6	16.4	-	-
18	6857	1	41	4	1360	1	116	30	3939	30	3939	-	-
6.3	7.3	.2	.1	10.5	13.7	.7	1.3	4.9	6.3	5.6	6.6	-	-
-	-	1	17	-	-	-	-	-	-	-	-	-	-
-	-	.2	*	-	-	-	-	-	-	-	-	-	-
-	-	-	-	-	-	-	-	-	-	-	-	-	-
-	-	-	-	-	-	-	-	-	-	-	-	-	-
185	51433	575	48469	24	6808	137	8291	445	45135	376	43104	69	2031
64.2	54.8	94.5	94.2	63.2	68.7	91.9	93.2	73.3	72.7	70.0	71.8	98.6	99.5
1	96	2	121	-	-	3	140	-	-	-	-	-	-
.3	.1	.3	.2	-	-	2.0	1.6	-	-	-	-	-	-
15	8571	4	364	1	319	1	31	4	487	4	487	-	-
5.2	9.2	.7	.7	2.6	3.2	.7	.3	.7	.8	.7	.8	-	-
9	3809	17	1871	1	700	3	281	6	611	6	611	-	-
3.1	4.1	2.8	3.6	2.6	7.1	2.0	3.2	1.0	1.0	1.1	1.0	-	-
-	-	-	-	-	-	-	-	-	-	-	-	-	-
-	-	-	-	-	-	-	-	-	-	-	-	-	-
10	2786	8	630	2	108	2	9	16	1711	15	1701	1	10
3.5	3.0	1.3	1.2	5.3	1.1	1.3	.1	2.6	2.8	2.8	2.8	1.4	.5
-	-	-	-	-	-	-	-	-	-	-	-	-	-
-	-	-	-	-	-	-	-	-	-	-	-	-	-

DISTRIBUTION OF STATED "NORMAL" RETIREMENT AGES UNDER PLANS PROVIDING FOR EXTENSIONS OF SERVICE BEYOND "NORMAL" RETIREMENT AGE

TABLE 9B

CLERICAL SERVICE					ALL 4-YEAR INSTITUTIONS				UNIVERSITIES			
	ALL INSTITUTIONS		ALL 4-YEAR INSTITUTIONS		PUBLIC		PRIVATE		PUBLIC		PRIVATE	
	INSTS	EES	INSTS	EES	INSTS	EES	INSTS	EES	INSTS	EES	INSTS	EES
TOTAL	1139	370751	809	337055	237	192176	572	144879	55	124669	51	80714
	100.0	100.0	100.0	100.0	100.0	100.0	100.0	100.0	100.0	100.0	100.0	100.0
NO RESPONSE	-	-	-	-	-	-	-	-	-	-	-	-
	-	-	-	-	-	-	-	-	-	-	-	-
UNDER AGE 62	5	9793	4	9640	3	9500	1	140	1	5510	-	-
	.4	2.6	.5	2.9	1.3	4.9	.2	.1	1.8	4.4	-	-
62	2	66	1	22	-	-	1	22	-	-	-	-
	.2	✿	.1	✿	-	-	.2	✿	-	-	-	-
63	-	-	-	-	-	-	-	-	-	-	-	-
	-	-	-	-	-	-	-	-	-	-	-	-
64	-	-	-	-	-	-	-	-	-	-	-	-
	-	-	-	-	-	-	-	-	-	-	-	-
65	998	294794	714	268012	176	134882	538	133130	39	86824	46	71796
	87.7	79.6	88.2	79.4	74.1	70.2	94.0	91.8	71.0	69.6	90.1	88.9
66	8	7503	8	7503	3	2201	5	5302	2	2085	1	4822
	.7	2.0	1.0	2.2	1.3	1.1	.9	3.7	3.6	1.7	2.0	6.0
67	23	5587	7	2217	3	1877	4	340	-	-	-	-
	2.0	1.5	.9	.7	1.3	1.0	.7	.2	-	-	-	-
68	24	17663	21	17394	8	12826	13	4568	2	9094	3	3704
	2.1	4.8	2.6	5.2	3.4	6.7	2.3	3.2	3.6	7.3	5.9	4.6
69	-	-	-	-	-	-	-	-	-	-	-	-
	-	-	-	-	-	-	-	-	-	-	-	-
70	79	35345	54	32267	44	30890	10	1377	11	21156	1	392
	6.9	9.5	6.7	9.6	18.6	16.1	1.7	1.0	20.0	17.0	2.0	.5
OVER 70	-	-	-	-	-	-	-	-	-	-	-	-
	-	-	-	-	-	-	-	-	-	-	-	-

4-YEAR LIBERAL ARTS COLLEGES				OTHER 4-YEAR COLLEGES				ALL 2-YEAR INSTITUTIONS		2-YEAR INSTITUTIONS			
PUBLIC		PRIVATE		PUBLIC		PRIVATE				PUBLIC		PRIVATE	
INSTS	EES	INSTS	EES	INSTS	EES	INSTS	EES	INSTS	EES	INSTS	EES	INSTS	EES
163	55880	421	52465	19	11627	100	11700	330	33696	293	32483	37	1213
100.0	100.0	100.0	100.0	100.0	100.0	100.0	100.0	100.0	100.0	100.0	100.0	100.0	100.0
-	-	-	-	-	-	-	-	-	-	-	-	-	-
-	-	-	-	-	-	-	-	-	-	-	-	-	-
2	3990	-	-	-	-	1	140	1	153	1	153	-	-
1.2	7.1	-	-	-	-	1.0	1.2	.3	.5	.3	.5	-	-
-	-	-	-	-	-	1	22	1	44	1	44	-	-
-	-	-	-	-	-	1.0	.2	.3	.1	.3	.1	-	-
-	-	-	-	-	-	-	-	-	-	-	-	-	-
-	-	-	-	-	-	-	-	-	-	-	-	-	-
-	-	-	-	-	-	-	-	-	-	-	-	-	-
-	-	-	-	-	-	-	-	-	-	-	-	-	-
123	38370	398	50011	14	9688	94	11323	284	26782	247	25569	37	1213
75.5	68.7	94.5	95.4	73.6	83.3	94.0	96.7	86.1	79.5	84.4	78.7	100.0	100.0
1	116	3	435	-	-	1	45	-	-	-	-	-	-
.6	.2	.7	.8	-	-	1.0	.4	-	-	-	-	-	-
2	405	4	340	1	1472	-	-	16	3370	16	3370	-	-
1.2	.7	1.0	.6	5.3	12.7	-	-	4.8	10.0	5.5	10.4	-	-
6	3732	8	717	-	-	2	147	3	269	3	269	-	-
3.7	6.7	1.9	1.4	-	-	2.0	1.3	.9	.8	1.0	.8	-	-
-	-	-	-	-	-	-	-	-	-	-	-	-	-
-	-	-	-	-	-	-	-	-	-	-	-	-	-
29	9267	8	962	4	467	1	23	25	3078	25	3078	-	-
17.8	16.6	1.9	1.8	21.1	4.0	1.0	.2	7.6	9.1	8.5	9.5	-	-
-	-	-	-	-	-	-	-	-	-	-	-	-	-
-	-	-	-	-	-	-	-	-	-	-	-	-	-

GROUP LIFE INSURANCE PLANS IN COLLEGES AND UNIVERSITIES
TABLE 10A

FACULTY

	ALL INSTITUTIONS		ALL 4-YEAR INSTITUTIONS		ALL 4-YEAR INSTITUTIONS PUBLIC		ALL 4-YEAR INSTITUTIONS PRIVATE		UNIVERSITIES PUBLIC		UNIVERSITIES PRIVATE	
	INSTS	EES	INSTS	EES	INSTS	EES	INSTS	EES	INSTS	EES	INSTS	EES
TOTAL	2092 100.0	432402 100.0	1407 100.0	363203 100.0	478 100.0	242041 100.0	929 100.0	121162 100.0	93 100.0	121628 100.0	61 100.0	54258 100.0
NO RESPONSE	5 .2	245 .1	2 .1	75 *	- -	- -	2 .2	75 .1	- -	- -	- -	- -
GROUP PLAN IN EFFECT	1791 85.7	401393 92.8	1202 85.5	340266 93.7	433 90.6	225459 93.1	769 82.8	114807 94.7	89 95.7	117169 96.3	61 100.0	54258 100.0
NO GROUP LIFE PLAN	296 14.1	30764 7.1	203 14.4	22862 6.3	45 9.4	16582 6.9	158 17.0	6280 5.2	4 4.3	4459 3.7	- -	- -

GROUP LIFE INSURANCE PLANS IN COLLEGES AND UNIVERSITIES
TABLE 10B

CLERICAL SERVICE

	ALL INSTITUTIONS		ALL 4-YEAR INSTITUTIONS		ALL 4-YEAR INSTITUTIONS PUBLIC		ALL 4-YEAR INSTITUTIONS PRIVATE		UNIVERSITIES PUBLIC		UNIVERSITIES PRIVATE	
	INSTS	EES	INSTS	EES	INSTS	EES	INSTS	EES	INSTS	EES	INSTS	EES
TOTAL	2092 100.0	670941 100.0	1407 100.0	601711 100.0	478 100.0	413110 100.0	929 100.0	188601 100.0	93 100.0	231299 100.0	61 100.0	94679 100.0
NO RESPONSE	6 .3	234 *	2 .1	109 *	- -	- -	2 .2	109 .1	- -	- -	- -	- -
GROUP PLAN IN EFFECT	1750 83.6	627249 93.5	1171 83.3	567209 94.3	430 90.0	388434 94.0	741 79.8	178775 94.7	89 95.7	224238 96.9	60 98.4	94549 99.9
NO GROUP LIFE PLAN	336 16.1	43458 6.5	234 16.6	34393 5.7	48 10.0	24676 6.0	186 20.0	9717 5.2	4 4.3	7061 3.1	1 1.6	130 .1

4-YEAR LIBERAL ARTS COLLEGES				OTHER 4-YEAR COLLEGES				ALL 2-YEAR INSTITUTIONS		2-YEAR INSTITUTIONS			
PUBLIC		PRIVATE		PUBLIC		PRIVATE				PUBLIC		PRIVATE	
INSTS	EES	INSTS	EES	INSTS	EES	INSTS	EES	INSTS	EES	INSTS	EES	INSTS	EES
341	109911	686	57084	44	10502	182	9820	685	69199	600	66915	85	2284
100.0	100.0	100.0	100.0	100.0	100.0	100.0	100.0	100.0	100.0	100.0	100.0	100.0	100.0
-	-	1	65	-	-	1	10	3	170	3	170	-	-
-	-	.1	.1	-	-	.5	.1	.4	.2	.5	.3	-	-
308	99608	571	51671	36	8682	137	8878	589	61127	528	59332	61	1795
90.3	90.6	83.3	90.5	81.8	82.7	75.3	90.4	86.0	88.4	88.0	88.6	71.8	78.6
33	10303	114	5348	8	1820	44	932	93	7902	69	7413	24	489
9.7	9.4	16.6	9.4	18.2	17.3	24.2	9.5	13.6	11.4	11.5	11.1	28.2	21.4

4-YEAR LIBERAL ARTS COLLEGES				OTHER 4-YEAR COLLEGES				ALL 2-YEAR INSTITUTIONS		2-YEAR INSTITUTIONS			
PUBLIC		PRIVATE		PUBLIC		PRIVATE				PUBLIC		PRIVATE	
INSTS	EES	INSTS	EES	INSTS	EES	INSTS	EES	INSTS	EES	INSTS	EES	INSTS	EES
341	153051	686	76960	44	28760	182	16962	685	69230	600	66748	85	2482
100.0	100.0	100.0	100.0	100.0	100.0	100.0	100.0	100.0	100.0	100.0	100.0	100.0	100.0
-	-	2	109	-	-	-	-	4	125	4	125	-	-
-	-	.3	.1	-	-	-	-	.6	.2	.7	.2	-	-
306	140829	544	68349	35	23367	137	15877	579	60040	522	58282	57	1758
89.7	92.0	79.3	88.9	79.5	81.2	75.3	93.6	84.5	86.7	87.0	87.3	67.1	70.8
35	12222	140	8502	9	5393	45	1085	102	9065	74	8341	28	724
10.3	8.0	20.4	11.0	20.5	18.8	24.7	6.4	14.9	13.1	12.3	12.5	32.9	29.2

EMPLOYER-EMPLOYEE CONTRIBUTION TOWARD COST OF GROUP LIFE INSURANCE PLAN

TABLE 11A

FACULTY

	ALL INSTITUTIONS		ALL 4-YEAR INSTITUTIONS		ALL 4-YEAR INSTITUTIONS PUBLIC		ALL 4-YEAR INSTITUTIONS PRIVATE		UNIVERSITIES PUBLIC		UNIVERSITIES PRIVATE	
	INSTS	EES	INSTS	EES	INSTS	EES	INSTS	EES	INSTS	EES	INSTS	EES
TOTAL	1791	401393	1202	340266	433	225459	769	114807	89	117169	61	54258
	100.0	100.0	100.0	100.0	100.0	100.0	100.0	100.0	100.0	100.0	100.0	100.0
NO RESPONSE	5	782	3	511	3	511	-	-	-	-	-	-
	.3	.2	.2	.2	.7	.2	-	-	-	-	-	-
EMPLOYER PAYS FULL COST	1001	186988	643	146089	177	86953	466	59136	31	43220	28	23396
	55.9	46.5	53.5	42.9	40.9	38.6	60.6	51.5	34.8	36.9	45.9	43.1
EMPLOYER AND EMPLOYEE SHARE COST	684	181696	478	163686	191	108862	287	54824	47	63034	32	30712
	38.2	45.3	39.8	48.1	44.1	48.3	37.3	47.8	52.8	53.8	52.5	56.6
EMPLOYEE PAYS FULL COST	101	31927	78	29980	62	29133	16	847	11	10915	1	150
	5.6	8.0	6.5	8.8	14.3	12.9	2.1	.7	12.4	9.3	1.6	.3

EMPLOYER-EMPLOYEE CONTRIBUTION TOWARD COST OF GROUP LIFE INSURANCE PLAN

TABLE 11B

CLERICAL SERVICE

	ALL INSTITUTIONS		ALL 4-YEAR INSTITUTIONS		ALL 4-YEAR INSTITUTIONS PUBLIC		ALL 4-YEAR INSTITUTIONS PRIVATE		UNIVERSITIES PUBLIC		UNIVERSITIES PRIVATE	
	INSTS	EES	INSTS	EES	INSTS	EES	INSTS	EES	INSTS	EES	INSTS	EES
TOTAL	1750	*627249	1171	567209	430	388434	741	178775	89	224238	60	94549
	100.0	100.0	100.0	100.0	100.0	100.0	100.0	100.0	100.0	100.0	100.0	100.0
NO RESPONSE	4	944	3	788	2	620	1	168	-	-	-	-
	.2	.2	.3	.1	.5	.2	.1	.1	-	-	-	-
EMPLOYER PAYS FULL COST	982	269100	637	228415	174	132154	463	96261	32	77591	30	42772
	56.1	42.9	54.4	40.3	40.5	34.0	62.5	53.8	36.0	34.6	50.0	45.2
EMPLOYER AND EMPLOYEE SHARE COST	661	311927	452	294427	191	212993	261	81434	46	131450	29	51499
	37.8	49.7	38.6	51.9	44.3	54.8	35.2	45.6	51.6	58.6	48.3	54.5
EMPLOYEE PAYS FULL COST	103	45278	79	43579	63	42667	16	912	11	15197	1	278
	5.9	7.2	6.7	7.7	14.7	11.0	2.2	.5	12.4	6.8	1.7	.3

4-YEAR LIBERAL ARTS COLLEGES				OTHER 4-YEAR COLLEGES				ALL 2-YEAR INSTITUTIONS		2-YEAR INSTITUTIONS			
PUBLIC		PRIVATE		PUBLIC		PRIVATE				PUBLIC		PRIVATE	
INSTS	EES	INSTS	EES	INSTS	EES	INSTS	EES	INSTS	EES	INSTS	EES	INSTS	EES
308	99608	571	51671	36	8682	137	8878	589	61127	528	59332	61	1795
100.0	100.0	100.0	100.0	100.0	100.0	100.0	100.0	100.0	100.0	100.0	100.0	100.0	100.0
3	511	-	-	-	-	-	-	2	271	1	216	1	55
1.0	.5	-	-	-	-	-	-	.3	.4	.2	.4	1.6	3.1
134	40930	345	30171	12	2803	93	5569	358	40899	320	39831	38	1068
43.5	41.1	60.4	58.4	33.3	32.3	67.9	62.7	60.8	66.9	60.6	67.1	62.3	59.5
126	41389	214	20840	18	4439	41	3272	206	18010	184	17338	22	672
40.9	41.6	37.5	40.3	50.0	51.1	29.9	36.9	35.0	29.5	34.8	29.2	36.1	37.4
45	16778	12	660	6	1440	3	37	23	1947	23	1947	-	-
14.6	16.8	2.1	1.3	16.7	16.6	2.2	.4	3.9	3.2	4.4	3.3	-	-

4-YEAR LIBERAL ARTS COLLEGES				OTHER 4-YEAR COLLEGES				ALL 2-YEAR INSTITUTIONS		2-YEAR INSTITUTIONS			
PUBLIC		PRIVATE		PUBLIC		PRIVATE				PUBLIC		PRIVATE	
INSTS	EES	INSTS	EES	INSTS	EES	INSTS	EES	INSTS	EES	INSTS	EES	INSTS	EES
306	140829	544	68349	35	23367	137	15877	579	60040	522	58282	57	1758
100.0	100.0	100.0	100.0	100.0	100.0	100.0	100.0	100.0	100.0	100.0	100.0	100.0	100.0
2	620	1	168	-	-	-	-	1	156	1	156	-	-
.7	.4	.2	.2	-	-	-	-	.2	.3	.2	.3	-	-
131	46466	336	42540	11	8097	97	10949	345	40685	310	39572	35	1113
42.8	33.0	61.8	62.3	31.4	34.7	70.8	68.9	59.6	67.8	59.4	67.9	61.4	63.3
127	71902	195	25080	18	9641	37	4855	209	17500	187	16855	22	645
41.5	51.1	35.8	36.7	51.5	41.2	27.0	30.6	36.1	29.1	35.8	28.9	38.6	36.7
46	21841	12	561	6	5629	3	73	24	1699	24	1699	-	-
15.0	15.5	2.2	.8	17.1	24.1	2.2	.5	4.1	2.8	4.6	2.9	-	-

GROUP LIFE INSURANCE PLANS:
PROVISION OF ADDITIONAL OPTIONAL AMOUNTS OF INSURANCE COVERAGE
TABLE 12A

FACULTY

	ALL INSTITUTIONS		ALL 4-YEAR INSTITUTIONS		ALL 4-YEAR INSTITUTIONS PUBLIC		ALL 4-YEAR INSTITUTIONS PRIVATE		UNIVERSITIES PUBLIC		UNIVERSITIES PRIVATE	
	INSTS	EES	INSTS	EES	INSTS	EES	INSTS	EES	INSTS	EES	INSTS	EES
TOTAL	1791	401393	1202	340266	433	225459	769	114807	89	117169	61	54258
	100.0	100.0	100.0	100.0	100.0	100.0	100.0	100.0	100.0	100.0	100.0	100.0
NO RESPONSE	7	569	2	126	-	-	2	126	-	-	-	-
	.4	.1	.2	✿	-	-	.3	.1	-	-	-	-
ADDITIONAL OPTIONAL COVERAGE AVAILABLE	770	217351	466	184081	258	137265	208	46816	47	68355	28	29612
	43.0	54.2	38.8	54.1	59.6	60.9	27.0	40.8	52.8	58.3	45.9	54.6
ADDITIONAL OPTIONAL COVERAGE NOT AVAILABLE	1014	183473	734	156059	175	88194	559	67865	42	48814	33	24646
	56.6	45.7	61.0	45.9	40.4	39.1	72.7	59.1	47.2	41.7	54.1	45.4

GROUP LIFE INSURANCE PLANS:
PROVISION OF ADDITIONAL OPTIONAL AMOUNTS OF INSURANCE COVERAGE
TABLE 12B

CLERICAL SERVICE

	ALL INSTITUTIONS		ALL 4-YEAR INSTITUTIONS		ALL 4-YEAR INSTITUTIONS PUBLIC		ALL 4-YEAR INSTITUTIONS PRIVATE		UNIVERSITIES PUBLIC		UNIVERSITIES PRIVATE	
	INSTS	EES	INSTS	EES	INSTS	EES	INSTS	EES	INSTS	EES	INSTS	EES
TOTAL	1750	627249	1171	567209	430	388434	741	178775	89	224238	60	94549
	100.0	100.0	100.0	100.0	100.0	100.0	100.0	100.0	100.0	100.0	100.0	100.0
NO RESPONSE	9	755	4	353	-	-	4	353	-	-	-	-
	.5	.1	.3	.1	-	-	.5	.2	-	-	-	-
ADDITIONAL OPTIONAL COVERAGE AVAILABLE	737	356225	438	321079	254	243375	184	77704	49	137711	29	57558
	42.1	56.8	37.4	56.6	59.1	62.7	24.8	43.5	55.1	61.4	48.3	60.9
ADDITIONAL OPTIONAL COVERAGE NOT AVAILABLE	1004	270269	729	245777	176	145059	553	100718	40	86527	31	36991
	57.4	43.1	62.3	43.3	40.9	37.3	74.7	56.3	44.9	38.6	51.7	39.1

4-YEAR LIBERAL ARTS COLLEGES				OTHER 4-YEAR COLLEGES				ALL 2-YEAR INSTITUTIONS		2-YEAR INSTITUTIONS			
PUBLIC		PRIVATE		PUBLIC		PRIVATE				PUBLIC		PRIVATE	
INSTS	EES	INSTS	EES	INSTS	EES	INSTS	EES	INSTS	EES	INSTS	EES	INSTS	EES
308	99608	571	51671	36	8682	137	8878	589	61127	528	59332	61	1795
100.0	100.0	100.0	100.0	100.0	100.0	100.0	100.0	100.0	100.0	100.0	100.0	100.0	100.0
-	-	2	126	-	-	-	-	5	443	4	388	1	55
-	-	.4	.2	-	-	-	-	.8	.7	.8	.7	1.6	3.1
186	62785	145	13687	25	6125	35	3517	304	33270	282	32697	22	573
60.4	63.0	25.4	26.5	69.4	70.5	25.5	39.6	51.7	54.5	53.4	55.1	36.1	31.9
122	36823	424	37858	11	2557	102	5361	280	27414	242	26247	38	1167
39.6	37.0	74.2	73.3	30.6	29.5	74.5	60.4	47.5	44.8	45.8	44.2	62.3	65.0

4-YEAR LIBERAL ARTS COLLEGES				OTHER 4-YEAR COLLEGES				ALL 2-YEAR INSTITUTIONS		2-YEAR INSTITUTIONS			
PUBLIC		PRIVATE		PUBLIC		PRIVATE				PUBLIC		PRIVATE	
INSTS	EES	INSTS	EES	INSTS	EES	INSTS	EES	INSTS	EES	INSTS	EES	INSTS	EES
306	140829	544	68349	35	23367	137	15877	579	60040	522	58282	57	1758
100.0	100.0	100.0	100.0	100.0	100.0	100.0	100.0	100.0	100.0	100.0	100.0	100.0	100.0
-	-	4	353	-	-	-	-	5	402	5	402	-	-
-	-	.7	.5	-	-	-	-	.9	.7	1.0	.7	-	-
181	91691	128	15582	24	13973	27	4564	299	35146	279	34677	20	469
59.2	65.1	23.5	22.8	68.6	59.8	19.7	28.7	51.6	58.5	53.4	59.5	35.1	26.7
125	49138	412	52414	11	9394	110	11313	275	24492	238	23203	37	1289
40.8	34.9	75.8	76.7	31.4	40.2	80.3	71.3	47.5	40.8	45.6	39.8	64.9	73.3

GROUP LIFE INSURANCE PLANS:
WAITING PERIOD BEFORE NEW EMPLOYEE IS ELIGIBLE TO PARTICIPATE IN PLAN

TABLE 13A

FACULTY

| | ALL INSTITUTIONS | | ALL 4-YEAR INSTITUTIONS | | ALL 4-YEAR INSTITUTIONS | | | | UNIVERSITIES | | | |
| | | | | | PUBLIC | | PRIVATE | | PUBLIC | | PRIVATE | |
	INSTS	EES	INSTS	EES	INSTS	EES	INSTS	EES	INSTS	EES	INSTS	EES
TOTAL	1791	401393	1202	340266	433	225459	769	114807	89	117169	61	54258
	100.0	100.0	100.0	100.0	100.0	100.0	100.0	100.0	100.0	100.0	100.0	100.0
NO RESPONSE	8	1532	3	410	-	-	3	410	-	-	-	-
	.4	.4	.2	.1	-	-	.4	.4	-	-	-	-
1 MONTH OR LESS	1478	342401	975	291908	364	197943	611	93965	83	109939	49	44708
	82.5	85.2	81.1	85.8	84.1	87.8	79.5	81.8	93.3	93.8	80.3	82.4
2 TO 6 MONTHS	202	36069	143	28878	52	18659	91	10219	3	4165	9	4121
	11.3	9.0	11.9	8.5	12.0	8.3	11.8	8.9	3.4	3.6	14.8	7.6
UNTIL NEXT PLAN ANNIVERSARY DATE	48	8736	37	6997	13	5149	24	1848	2	1565	-	-
	2.7	2.2	3.1	2.1	3.0	2.3	3.1	1.6	2.2	1.3	-	-
OTHER	55	12655	44	12073	4	3708	40	8365	1	1500	3	5429
	3.1	3.2	3.7	3.5	.9	1.6	5.2	7.3	1.1	1.3	4.9	10.0

GROUP LIFE INSURANCE PLANS:
WAITING PERIOD BEFORE NEW EMPLOYEE IS ELIGIBLE TO PARTICIPATE IN PLAN

TABLE 13B

CLERICAL SERVICE

| | ALL INSTITUTIONS | | ALL 4-YEAR INSTITUTIONS | | ALL 4-YEAR INSTITUTIONS | | | | UNIVERSITIES | | | |
| | | | | | PUBLIC | | PRIVATE | | PUBLIC | | PRIVATE | |
	INSTS	EES	INSTS	EES	INSTS	EES	INSTS	EES	INSTS	EES	INSTS	EES
TOTAL	1750	627249	1171	567209	430	388434	741	178775	89	224238	60	94549
	100.0	100.0	100.0	100.0	100.0	100.0	100.0	100.0	100.0	100.0	100.0	100.0
NO RESPONSE	8	2003	5	1320	1	273	4	1047	-	-	-	-
	.5	.3	.4	.2	.2	.1	.5	.6	-	-	-	-
1 MONTH OR LESS	1281	504222	797	453753	349	342843	448	110910	78	203625	32	69858
	73.1	80.3	68.1	80.0	81.2	88.3	60.4	62.0	87.7	90.8	53.3	73.9
2 TO 6 MONTHS	339	87034	269	80243	61	30330	208	49913	7	10778	24	18724
	19.4	13.9	23.0	14.1	14.2	7.8	28.1	27.9	7.9	4.8	40.0	19.8
UNTIL NEXT PLAN ANNIVERSARY DATE	35	8583	25	7211	12	5985	13	1226	2	3368	-	-
	2.0	1.4	2.1	1.3	2.8	1.5	1.8	.7	2.2	1.5	-	-
OTHER	87	25407	75	24682	7	9003	68	15679	2	6467	4	5967
	5.0	4.1	6.4	4.4	1.6	2.3	9.2	8.8	2.2	2.9	6.7	6.3

4-YEAR LIBERAL ARTS COLLEGES				OTHER 4-YEAR COLLEGES				ALL 2-YEAR INSTITUTIONS		2-YEAR INSTITUTIONS			
PUBLIC		PRIVATE		PUBLIC		PRIVATE				PUBLIC		PRIVATE	
INSTS	EES	INSTS	EES	INSTS	EES	INSTS	EES	INSTS	EES	INSTS	EES	INSTS	EES
308	99608	571	51671	36	8682	137	8878	589	61127	528	59332	61	1795
100.0	100.0	100.0	100.0	100.0	100.0	100.0	100.0	100.0	100.0	100.0	100.0	100.0	100.0
-	-	2	400	-	-	1	10	5	1122	4	1109	1	13
-	-	.4	.8	-	-	.7	.1	.8	1.8	.8	1.9	1.6	.7
252	81492	461	42380	29	6512	101	6877	503	50493	459	49165	44	1328
81.9	81.8	80.6	82.0	80.5	75.0	73.8	77.5	85.4	82.6	86.9	82.8	72.2	73.9
44	13833	58	4552	5	661	24	1546	59	7191	54	7050	5	141
14.3	13.9	10.2	8.8	13.9	7.6	17.5	17.4	10.0	11.8	10.2	11.9	8.2	7.9
10	3575	21	1664	1	9	3	184	11	1739	8	1675	3	64
3.2	3.6	3.7	3.2	2.8	.1	2.2	2.1	1.9	2.8	1.5	2.8	4.9	3.6
2	708	29	2675	1	1500	8	261	11	582	3	333	8	249
.6	.7	5.1	5.2	2.8	17.3	5.8	2.9	1.9	1.0	.6	.6	13.1	13.9

4-YEAR LIBERAL ARTS COLLEGES				OTHER 4-YEAR COLLEGES				ALL 2-YEAR INSTITUTIONS		2-YEAR INSTITUTIONS			
PUBLIC		PRIVATE		PUBLIC		PRIVATE				PUBLIC		PRIVATE	
INSTS	EES	INSTS	EES	INSTS	EES	INSTS	EES	INSTS	EES	INSTS	EES	INSTS	EES
306	140829	544	68349	35	23367	137	15877	579	60040	522	58282	57	1758
100.0	100.0	100.0	100.0	100.0	100.0	100.0	100.0	100.0	100.0	100.0	100.0	100.0	100.0
1	273	3	1039	-	-	1	8	3	683	2	679	1	4
.3	.2	.6	1.5	-	-	.7	.1	.5	1.1	.4	1.2	1.8	.2
244	120131	333	32224	27	19087	83	8828	484	50469	448	49501	36	968
79.8	85.2	61.2	47.1	77.1	81.7	60.6	55.5	83.6	84.1	85.8	84.9	63.2	55.1
48	16179	144	25155	6	3373	40	6034	70	6791	60	6310	10	481
15.7	11.5	26.5	36.8	17.1	14.4	29.2	38.0	12.1	11.3	11.5	10.8	17.5	27.4
9	2610	11	1201	1	7	2	25	10	1372	8	1335	2	37
2.9	1.9	2.0	1.8	2.9	☼	1.5	.2	1.7	2.3	1.5	2.3	3.5	2.1
4	1636	53	8730	1	900	11	982	12	725	4	457	8	268
1.3	1.2	9.7	12.8	2.9	3.9	8.0	6.2	2.1	1.2	.8	.8	14.0	15.2

GROUP LIFE INSURANCE PLANS:
SUMMARY OF INSURANCE AMOUNTS PROVIDED

TABLE 14A

FACULTY	ALL INSTITUTIONS		ALL 4-YEAR INSTITUTIONS		ALL 4-YEAR INSTITUTIONS				UNIVERSITIES			
					PUBLIC		PRIVATE		PUBLIC		PRIVATE	
	INSTS	EES	INSTS	EES	INSTS	EES	INSTS	EES	INSTS	EES	INSTS	EES
TOTAL	1791	401393	1202	340266	433	225459	769	114807	89	117169	61	54258
	100.0	100.0	100.0	100.0	100.0	100.0	100.0	100.0	100.0	100.0	100.0	100.0
NO RESPONSE	2	211	1	115	-	-	1	115	-	-	-	-
	.1	.1	.1	☆	-	-	.1	.1	-	-	-	-
AS A MULTIPLE OF SALARY	795	229337	555	202579	248	140247	307	62332	60	78711	38	36880
	44.4	57.1	46.2	59.5	57.3	62.2	39.9	54.3	67.4	67.2	62.3	68.0
ACCORDING TO JOB OR SALARY CATEGORY	409	78909	279	69174	102	45289	177	23885	14	15702	12	10621
	22.8	19.7	23.2	20.3	23.6	20.1	23.0	20.8	15.7	13.4	19.7	19.6
SAME AMOUNT FOR ALL EMPLOYEES	429	71495	248	52209	82	38692	166	13517	11	19477	5	1560
	24.0	17.8	20.6	15.3	18.9	17.2	21.6	11.8	12.4	16.6	8.2	2.9
AS ASSIGNED UNITS OF COLLECTIVE INSURANCE	151	22739	131	20119	10	6283	121	13836	4	4847	4	2646
	8.4	5.7	10.9	5.9	2.3	2.8	15.7	12.1	4.5	4.1	6.6	4.9
OTHER	100	28976	69	24902	25	15871	44	9031	8	10727	5	4140
	5.6	7.2	5.7	7.3	5.8	7.0	5.7	7.9	9.0	9.2	8.2	7.6
AMOUNT DECREASES AS AGE ADVANCES	476	136065	378	125492	126	81103	252	44389	29	44350	21	21809
	26.6	33.9	31.4	36.9	29.1	36.0	32.8	38.7	32.6	37.9	34.4	40.2
AMOUNT INCREASES AS SALARY INCREASES	1020	269907	706	238358	317	168327	389	70031	68	86186	45	38861
	57.0	67.2	58.7	70.1	73.2	74.7	50.6	61.0	76.4	73.6	73.8	71.6
AMOUNT DOES NOT CHANGE AS AGE OR SALARY INCREASES	493	88830	284	66556	95	48255	189	18301	19	26547	8	4555
	27.5	22.1	23.6	19.6	21.9	21.4	24.6	15.9	21.3	22.7	13.1	8.4
BASIC AMOUNT SAME FOR EQUALLY SITUATED EMPLOYEES REGARDLESS OF DEPENDENTS	1598	367686	1079	313270	399	210870	680	102400	81	108798	57	50193
	89.2	91.6	89.8	92.1	92.1	93.5	88.4	89.2	91.0	92.9	93.4	92.5
BASIC AMOUNT GREATER FOR EMPLOYEES WITH DEPENDENTS	31	3974	25	3431	1	713	24	2718	1	713	-	-
	1.7	1.0	2.1	1.0	.2	.3	3.1	2.4	1.1	.6	-	-
EMPLOYEES WITH DEPENDENTS MAY ELECT HIGHER COVERAGE AMOUNTS	74	22430	43	20057	29	17248	14	2809	5	6425	2	2050
	4.1	5.6	3.6	5.9	6.7	7.7	1.8	2.4	5.6	5.5	3.3	3.8
INSURANCE PLAN INCLUDES ACCIDENTAL DEATH AND DISMEMBERMENT PROVISION	1174	264187	731	219800	286	157622	445	62178	66	88057	28	29849
	65.5	65.8	60.8	64.6	66.1	69.9	57.9	54.2	74.2	75.2	45.9	55.0

4-YEAR LIBERAL ARTS COLLEGES				OTHER 4-YEAR COLLEGES				ALL 2-YEAR INSTITUTIONS		2-YEAR INSTITUTIONS			
PUBLIC		PRIVATE		PUBLIC		PRIVATE				PUBLIC		PRIVATE	
INSTS	EES	INSTS	EES	INSTS	EES	INSTS	EES	INSTS	EES	INSTS	EES	INSTS	EES
308	99608	571	51671	36	8682	137	8878	589	61127	528	59332	61	1795
100.0	100.0	100.0	100.0	100.0	100.0	100.0	100.0	100.0	100.0	100.0	100.0	100.0	100.0
-	-	1	115	-	-	-	-	1	96	1	96	-	-
-	-	.2	.2	-	-	-	-	.2	.2	.2	.2	-	-
166	56160	212	20823	22	5376	57	4629	240	26758	224	26045	16	713
53.9	56.4	37.1	40.3	61.1	61.9	41.6	52.1	40.7	43.8	42.4	43.9	26.2	39.7
81	27865	129	11701	7	1722	36	1563	130	9735	115	9281	15	454
26.3	28.0	22.6	22.6	19.4	19.8	26.3	17.6	22.1	15.9	21.8	15.6	24.6	25.3
65	17682	128	10444	6	1533	33	1513	181	19286	156	18785	25	501
21.1	17.8	22.4	20.2	16.7	17.7	24.1	17.0	30.7	31.6	29.5	31.7	41.0	27.9
6	1436	105	10334	-	-	12	856	20	2620	14	2433	6	187
1.9	1.4	18.4	20.0	-	-	8.8	9.6	3.4	4.3	2.7	4.1	9.8	10.4
16	5093	30	3736	1	51	9	1155	31	4074	29	4038	2	36
5.2	5.1	5.3	7.2	2.8	.6	6.6	13.0	5.3	6.7	5.5	6.8	3.3	2.0
92	35383	193	19974	5	1370	38	2606	98	10573	82	10157	16	416
29.9	35.5	33.8	38.7	13.9	15.8	27.7	29.4	16.6	17.3	15.5	17.1	26.2	23.2
220	75925	269	26257	29	6216	75	4913	314	31549	291	30644	23	905
71.4	76.2	47.1	50.8	80.6	71.6	54.7	55.3	53.3	51.6	55.1	51.6	37.7	50.4
70	20146	144	11040	6	1562	37	2706	209	22274	182	21685	27	589
22.7	20.2	25.2	21.4	16.7	18.0	27.0	30.5	35.5	36.4	34.5	36.5	44.3	32.8
286	94135	500	44405	32	7937	123	7802	519	54416	469	52894	50	1522
92.9	94.5	87.6	85.9	88.9	91.4	89.8	87.9	88.1	89.0	88.8	89.1	82.0	84.8
-	-	22	2684	-	-	2	34	6	543	5	521	1	22
-	-	3.9	5.2	-	-	1.5	.4	1.0	.9	.9	.9	1.6	1.2
21	10728	10	729	3	95	2	30	31	2373	28	2284	3	89
6.8	10.8	1.8	1.4	8.3	1.1	1.5	.3	5.3	3.9	5.3	3.8	4.9	5.0
196	63062	332	28088	24	6503	85	4241	443	44387	404	43131	39	1256
63.6	63.3	58.1	54.4	66.7	74.9	62.0	47.8	75.2	72.6	76.5	72.7	63.9	70.0

GROUP LIFE INSURANCE PLANS:
SUMMARY OF INSURANCE AMOUNTS PROVIDED

TABLE 14B

CLERICAL SERVICE					ALL 4-YEAR INSTITUTIONS						UNIVERSITIES			
	ALL INSTITUTIONS		ALL 4-YEAR INSTITUTIONS		PUBLIC		PRIVATE		PUBLIC		PRIVATE	
	INSTS	EES	INSTS	EES	INSTS	EES	INSTS	EES	INSTS	EES	INSTS	EES
TOTAL	1750	627249	1171	567209	430	388434	741	178775	89	224238	60	94549
	100.0	100.0	100.0	100.0	100.0	100.0	100.0	100.0	100.0	100.0	100.0	100.0
NO RESPONSE	1	291	-	-	-	-	-	-	-	-	-	-
	.1	※	-	-	-	-	-	-	-	-	-	-
AS A MULTIPLE OF SALARY	735	376836	509	351862	237	256662	272	95200	57	152460	32	57843
	42.0	60.1	43.5	62.0	55.1	66.1	36.7	53.3	64.0	68.0	53.3	61.2
ACCORDING TO JOB OR SALARY CATEGORY	402	118442	274	108868	102	68490	172	40378	15	27391	10	22727
	23.0	18.9	23.4	19.2	23.7	17.6	23.2	22.6	16.9	12.2	16.7	24.0
SAME AMOUNT FOR ALL EMPLOYEES	481	113514	298	94771	90	65912	208	28859	13	41343	12	7457
	27.5	18.1	25.4	16.7	20.9	17.0	28.1	16.1	14.6	18.4	20.0	7.9
AS ASSIGNED UNITS OF COLLECTIVE INSURANCE	118	23556	99	19882	9	6755	90	13127	4	5817	4	2409
	6.7	3.8	8.5	3.5	2.1	1.7	12.1	7.3	4.5	2.6	6.7	2.5
OTHER	101	39222	67	34941	28	23982	39	10959	9	15244	3	4592
	5.8	6.3	5.7	6.2	6.5	6.2	5.3	6.1	10.1	6.8	5.0	4.9
AMOUNT DECREASES AS AGE ADVANCES	428	208096	332	197260	124	145387	208	51873	29	78951	17	25969
	24.5	33.2	28.4	34.8	28.8	37.4	28.1	29.0	32.6	35.2	28.3	27.5
AMOUNT INCREASES AS SALARY INCREASES	962	442870	660	411793	306	298651	354	113142	67	170586	39	66448
	55.0	70.6	56.4	72.6	71.2	76.9	47.8	63.3	75.3	76.1	65.0	70.3
AMOUNT DOES NOT CHANGE AS AGE OR SALARY INCREASES	549	150300	338	127540	106	89830	232	37710	22	60699	16	16465
	31.4	24.0	28.9	22.5	24.7	23.1	31.3	21.1	24.7	27.1	26.7	17.4
BASIC AMOUNT SAME FOR EQUALLY SITUATED EMPLOYEES REGARDLESS OF DEPENDENTS	1562	570509	1053	518234	395	362834	658	155400	80	205669	55	82843
	89.3	91.0	89.9	91.4	91.9	93.4	88.8	86.9	89.9	91.7	91.7	87.6
BASIC AMOUNT GREATER FOR EMPLOYEES WITH DEPENDENTS	30	6148	24	5698	2	1100	22	4598	1	1016	-	-
	1.7	1.0	2.0	1.0	.5	.3	3.0	2.6	1.1	.5	-	-
EMPLOYEES WITH DEPENDENTS MAY ELECT HIGHER COVERAGE AMOUNTS	74	38002	42	35632	29	25335	13	10297	5	12250	3	9248
	4.2	6.1	3.6	6.3	6.7	6.5	1.8	5.8	5.6	5.5	5.0	9.8
INSURANCE PLAN INCLUDES ACCIDENTAL DEATH AND DISMEMBERMENT PROVISION	1159	418352	721	375035	283	273636	438	101399	68	163115	28	53939
	66.2	66.7	61.6	66.1	65.8	70.4	59.1	56.7	76.4	72.7	46.7	57.0

4-YEAR LIBERAL ARTS COLLEGES				OTHER 4-YEAR COLLEGES				ALL 2-YEAR INSTITUTIONS		2-YEAR INSTITUTIONS			
PUBLIC		PRIVATE		PUBLIC		PRIVATE				PUBLIC		PRIVATE	
INSTS	EES	INSTS	EES	INSTS	EES	INSTS	EES	INSTS	EES	INSTS	EES	INSTS	EES
306	140829	544	68349	35	23367	137	15877	579	60040	522	58282	57	1758
100.0	100.0	100.0	100.0	100.0	100.0	100.0	100.0	100.0	100.0	100.0	100.0	100.0	100.0
-	-	-	-	-	-	-	-	1	291	1	291	-	-
-	-	-	-	-	-	-	-	.2	.5	.2	.5	-	-
161	90276	186	27078	19	13926	54	10279	226	24974	210	24317	16	657
52.6	64.1	34.2	39.6	54.3	59.6	39.4	64.7	39.0	41.6	40.2	41.7	28.1	37.4
80	36013	125	15586	7	5086	37	2065	128	9574	113	9071	15	503
26.1	25.6	23.0	22.8	20.0	21.8	27.0	13.0	22.1	15.9	21.6	15.6	26.3	28.6
69	20316	159	19388	8	4253	37	2014	183	18743	161	18276	22	467
22.5	14.4	29.2	28.4	22.9	18.2	27.0	12.7	31.6	31.2	30.8	31.4	38.6	26.6
5	938	77	9782	-	-	9	936	19	3674	14	3498	5	176
1.6	.7	14.2	14.3	-	-	6.6	5.9	3.3	6.1	2.7	6.0	8.8	10.0
18	8636	29	5505	1	102	7	862	34	4281	32	4198	2	83
5.9	6.1	5.3	8.1	2.9	.4	5.1	5.4	5.9	7.1	6.1	7.2	3.5	4.7
90	60554	156	21498	5	5882	35	4406	96	10836	82	10449	14	387
29.4	43.0	28.7	31.5	14.3	25.2	25.5	27.8	16.6	18.0	15.7	17.9	24.6	22.0
212	113299	238	35362	27	14766	77	11332	302	31077	279	30145	23	932
69.3	80.5	43.8	51.7	77.1	63.2	56.2	71.4	52.2	51.8	53.4	51.7	40.4	53.0
77	24921	178	18217	7	4210	38	3028	211	22760	186	22209	25	551
25.2	17.7	32.7	26.7	20.0	18.0	27.7	19.1	36.4	37.9	35.6	38.1	43.9	31.3
284	135091	478	57946	31	22074	125	14611	509	52275	463	50838	46	1437
92.8	95.9	87.9	84.8	88.6	94.5	91.2	92.0	87.9	87.1	88.7	87.2	80.7	81.7
1	84	21	4577	-	-	1	21	6	450	5	442	1	8
.3	.1	3.9	6.7	-	-	.7	.1	1.0	.7	1.0	.8	1.8	.5
21	12919	9	1035	3	166	1	14	32	2370	29	2276	3	94
6.9	9.2	1.7	1.5	8.6	.7	.7	.1	5.5	3.9	5.6	3.9	5.3	5.3
193	92939	324	39431	22	17582	86	8029	438	43317	402	42165	36	1152
63.1	66.0	59.6	57.7	62.9	75.2	62.8	50.6	75.6	72.1	77.0	72.3	63.2	65.5

TABLE 15A

GROUP LIFE INSURANCE PLANS: COVERAGE OF RETIRED EMPLOYEES

FACULTY

	ALL INSTITUTIONS		ALL 4-YEAR INSTITUTIONS		ALL 4-YEAR INSTITUTIONS PUBLIC		ALL 4-YEAR INSTITUTIONS PRIVATE		UNIVERSITIES PUBLIC		UNIVERSITIES PRIVATE	
	INSTS	EES	INSTS	EES	INSTS	EES	INSTS	EES	INSTS	EES	INSTS	EES
TOTAL	1791	401393	1202	340266	433	225459	769	114807	89	117169	61	54258
	100.0	100.0	100.0	100.0	100.0	100.0	100.0	100.0	100.0	100.0	100.0	100.0
NO RESPONSE	4	381	2	200	1	152	1	48	-	-	-	-
	.2	.1	.2	.1	.2	.1	.1	*	-	-	-	-
PLAN COVERS RETIRED EMPLOYEES	693	220600	481	197568	262	147358	219	50210	57	76190	31	29325
	38.7	55.0	40.0	58.0	60.5	65.3	28.5	43.7	64.0	65.0	50.8	54.0
PLAN DOES NOT COVER RETIRED EMPLOYEES	1094	180412	719	142498	170	77949	549	64549	32	40979	30	24933
	61.1	44.9	59.8	41.9	39.3	34.6	71.4	56.3	36.0	35.0	49.2	46.0

TABLE 15B

GROUP LIFE INSURANCE PLANS: COVERAGE OF RETIRED EMPLOYEES

CLERICAL SERVICE

	ALL INSTITUTIONS		ALL 4-YEAR INSTITUTIONS		ALL 4-YEAR INSTITUTIONS PUBLIC		ALL 4-YEAR INSTITUTIONS PRIVATE		UNIVERSITIES PUBLIC		UNIVERSITIES PRIVATE	
	INSTS	EES	INSTS	EES	INSTS	EES	INSTS	EES	INSTS	EES	INSTS	EES
TOTAL	1750	627249	1171	567209	430	388434	741	178775	89	224238	60	94549
	100.0	100.0	100.0	100.0	100.0	100.0	100.0	100.0	100.0	100.0	100.0	100.0
NO RESPONSE	5	1958	3	1848	2	1751	1	97	1	1600	-	-
	.3	.3	.3	.3	.5	.5	.1	.1	1.1	.7	-	-
PLAN COVERS RETIRED EMPLOYEES	682	364401	474	343826	261	252679	213	91147	57	145220	35	57008
	39.0	58.1	40.5	60.6	60.7	65.0	28.7	50.9	64.1	64.8	58.3	60.3
PLAN DOES NOT COVER RETIRED EMPLOYEES	1063	260890	694	221535	167	134004	527	87531	31	77418	25	37541
	60.7	41.6	59.2	39.1	38.8	34.5	71.2	49.0	34.8	34.5	41.7	39.7

4-YEAR LIBERAL ARTS COLLEGES				OTHER 4-YEAR COLLEGES				ALL 2-YEAR INSTITUTIONS		2-YEAR INSTITUTIONS			
PUBLIC		PRIVATE		PUBLIC		PRIVATE				PUBLIC		PRIVATE	
INSTS	EES	INSTS	EES	INSTS	EES	INSTS	EES	INSTS	EES	INSTS	EES	INSTS	EES
308	99608	571	51671	36	8682	137	8878	589	61127	528	59332	61	1795
100.0	100.0	100.0	100.0	100.0	100.0	100.0	100.0	100.0	100.0	100.0	100.0	100.0	100.0
1	152	1	48	-	-	-	-	2	181	2	181	-	-
.3	.2	.2	.1	-	-	-	-	.3	.3	.4	.3	-	-
181	64122	151	16968	24	7046	37	3917	212	23032	203	22784	9	248
58.8	64.3	26.4	32.8	66.7	81.2	27.0	44.1	36.0	37.7	38.4	38.4	14.8	13.8
126	35334	419	34655	12	1636	100	4961	375	37914	323	36367	52	1547
40.9	35.5	73.4	67.1	33.3	18.8	73.0	55.9	63.7	62.0	61.2	61.3	85.2	86.2

4-YEAR LIBERAL ARTS COLLEGES				OTHER 4-YEAR COLLEGES				ALL 2-YEAR INSTITUTIONS		2-YEAR INSTITUTIONS			
PUBLIC		PRIVATE		PUBLIC		PRIVATE				PUBLIC		PRIVATE	
INSTS	EES	INSTS	EES	INSTS	EES	INSTS	EES	INSTS	EES	INSTS	EES	INSTS	EES
306	140829	544	68349	35	23367	137	15877	579	60040	522	58282	57	1758
100.0	100.0	100.0	100.0	100.0	100.0	100.0	100.0	100.0	100.0	100.0	100.0	100.0	100.0
1	151	1	97	-	-	-	-	2	110	2	110	-	-
.3	.1	.2	.1	-	-	-	-	.3	.2	.4	.2	-	-
180	88493	142	24639	24	18966	36	9500	208	20575	200	20434	8	141
58.9	62.8	26.1	36.0	68.6	81.2	26.3	59.8	35.9	34.3	38.3	35.1	14.0	8.0
125	52185	401	43613	11	4401	101	6377	369	39355	320	37738	49	1617
40.8	37.1	73.7	63.9	31.4	18.8	73.7	40.2	63.8	65.5	61.3	64.7	86.0	92.0

GROUP LIFE INSURANCE PLANS:
TYPE OF RETIRED EMPLOYEE INSURANCE IN FORCE

TABLE 16A

FACULTY

	ALL INSTITUTIONS		ALL 4-YEAR INSTITUTIONS		ALL 4-YEAR INSTITUTIONS PUBLIC		ALL 4-YEAR INSTITUTIONS PRIVATE		UNIVERSITIES PUBLIC		UNIVERSITIES PRIVATE	
	INSTS	EES	INSTS	EES	INSTS	EES	INSTS	EES	INSTS	EES	INSTS	EES
TOTAL	693	220600	481	197568	262	147358	219	50210	57	76190	31	29325
	100.0	100.0	100.0	100.0	100.0	100.0	100.0	100.0	100.0	100.0	100.0	100.0
NO RESPONSE	26	9958	25	9156	22	8987	3	169	3	3576	-	
	3.8	4.5	5.2	4.6	8.4	6.1	1.4	.3	5.3	4.7	-	
PAID-UP INSURANCE	137	44277	88	39368	50	28595	38	10773	8	12572	11	7672
	19.8	20.1	18.3	19.9	19.1	19.4	17.4	21.5	14.0	16.5	35.5	26.2
TERM INSURANCE (WITH CONTINUING PREMIUMS)	530	166365	368	149044	190	109776	178	39268	46	60042	20	21653
	76.4	75.4	76.5	75.5	72.5	74.5	81.2	78.2	80.7	78.8	64.5	73.8

GROUP LIFE INSURANCE PLANS:
TYPE OF RETIRED EMPLOYEE INSURANCE IN FORCE

TABLE 16B

CLERICAL SERVICE

	ALL INSTITUTIONS		ALL 4-YEAR INSTITUTIONS		ALL 4-YEAR INSTITUTIONS PUBLIC		ALL 4-YEAR INSTITUTIONS PRIVATE		UNIVERSITIES PUBLIC		UNIVERSITIES PRIVATE	
	INSTS	EES	INSTS	EES	INSTS	EES	INSTS	EES	INSTS	EES	INSTS	EES
TOTAL	682	364401	474	343826	261	252679	213	91147	57	145220	35	57008
	100.0	100.0	100.0	100.0	100.0	100.0	100.0	100.0	100.0	100.0	100.0	100.0
NO RESPONSE	25	14283	25	14283	23	14205	2	78	3	6220	-	
	3.7	3.9	5.3	4.2	8.8	5.6	.9	.1	5.3	4.3	-	
PAID-UP INSURANCE	133	82291	83	76859	48	51331	35	25528	8	27627	12	20580
	19.5	22.6	17.5	22.4	18.4	20.3	16.4	28.0	14.0	19.0	34.3	36.1
TERM INSURANCE (WITH CONTINUING PREMIUMS)	524	267827	366	252684	190	187143	176	65541	46	111373	23	36428
	76.8	73.5	77.2	73.4	72.8	74.1	82.7	71.9	80.7	76.7	65.7	63.9

4-YEAR LIBERAL ARTS COLLEGES				OTHER 4-YEAR COLLEGES				ALL 2-YEAR INSTITUTIONS		2-YEAR INSTITUTIONS			
PUBLIC		PRIVATE		PUBLIC		PRIVATE				PUBLIC		PRIVATE	
INSTS	EES	INSTS	EES	INSTS	EES	INSTS	EES	INSTS	EES	INSTS	EES	INSTS	EES
181	64122	151	16968	24	7046	37	3917	212	23032	203	22784	9	248
100.0	100.0	100.0	100.0	100.0	100.0	100.0	100.0	100.0	100.0	100.0	100.0	100.0	100.0
19	5411	1	115	-	-	2	54	1	802	1	802	-	-
10.5	8.4	.7	.7	-	-	5.4	1.4	.5	3.5	.5	3.5	-	-
38	14488	14	1411	4	1535	13	1690	49	4909	48	4891	1	18
21.0	22.6	9.3	8.3	16.7	21.8	35.1	43.1	23.1	21.3	23.6	21.5	11.1	7.3
124	44223	136	15442	20	5511	22	2173	162	17321	154	17091	8	230
68.5	69.0	90.0	91.0	83.3	78.2	59.5	55.5	76.4	75.2	75.9	75.0	88.9	92.7

4-YEAR LIBERAL ARTS COLLEGES				OTHER 4-YEAR COLLEGES				ALL 2-YEAR INSTITUTIONS		2-YEAR INSTITUTIONS			
PUBLIC		PRIVATE		PUBLIC		PRIVATE				PUBLIC		PRIVATE	
INSTS	EES	INSTS	EES	INSTS	EES	INSTS	EES	INSTS	EES	INSTS	EES	INSTS	EES
180	88493	142	24639	24	18966	36	9500	208	20575	200	20434	8	141
100.0	100.0	100.0	100.0	100.0	100.0	100.0	100.0	100.0	100.0	100.0	100.0	100.0	100.0
20	7985	-	-	-	-	2	78	-	-	-	-	-	-
11.1	9.0	-	-	-	-	5.6	.8	-	-	-	-	-	-
36	19048	13	1410	4	4656	10	3538	50	5432	49	5423	1	9
20.0	21.5	9.2	5.7	16.7	24.5	27.8	37.2	24.0	26.4	24.5	26.5	12.5	6.4
124	61460	129	23229	20	14310	24	5884	158	15143	151	15011	7	132
68.9	69.5	90.8	94.3	83.3	75.5	66.6	62.0	76.0	73.6	75.5	73.5	87.5	93.6

AMOUNT OF RETIRED EMPLOYEE INSURANCE COMPARED WITH ACTIVE EMPLOYEES

TABLE 17A

FACULTY

	ALL INSTITUTIONS		ALL 4-YEAR INSTITUTIONS		ALL 4-YEAR INSTITUTIONS PUBLIC		PRIVATE		UNIVERSITIES PUBLIC		PRIVATE	
	INSTS	EES	INSTS	EES	INSTS	EES	INSTS	EES	INSTS	EES	INSTS	EES
TOTAL	693	220600	481	197568	262	147358	219	50210	57	76190	31	2932?
	100.0	100.0	100.0	100.0	100.0	100.0	100.0	100.0	100.0	100.0	100.0	100.(
NO RESPONSE	5	1031	2	152	-	-	2	152	-	-	-	
	.7	.5	.4	.1	-	-	.9	.3	-	-	-	
AMOUNT IS LESS THAN THAT PROVIDED ACTIVE EMPLOYEES	538	177121	379	161334	199	117468	180	43866	47	62932	28	2733?
	77.7	80.3	78.8	81.6	76.0	79.7	82.2	87.4	82.5	82.6	90.3	93.2
AMOUNT NOT LESS	150	42448	100	36082	63	29890	37	6192	10	13258	3	1994
	21.6	19.2	20.8	18.3	24.0	20.3	16.9	12.3	17.5	17.4	9.7	6.8

AMOUNT OF RETIRED EMPLOYEE INSURANCE COMPARED WITH ACTIVE EMPLOYEES

TABLE 17B

CLERICAL SERVICE

	ALL INSTITUTIONS		ALL 4-YEAR INSTITUTIONS		ALL 4-YEAR INSTITUTIONS PUBLIC		PRIVATE		UNIVERSITIES PUBLIC		PRIVATE	
	INSTS	EES	INSTS	EES	INSTS	EES	INSTS	EES	INSTS	EES	INSTS	EES
TOTAL	682	364401	474	343826	261	252679	213	91147	57	145220	35	57008
	100.0	100.0	100.0	100.0	100.0	100.0	100.0	100.0	100.0	100.0	100.0	100.0
NO RESPONSE	3	128	1	30	-	-	1	30	-	-	-	-
	.4	✻	.2	✻	-	-	.5	✻	-	-	-	-
AMOUNT IS LESS THAN THAT PROVIDED ACTIVE EMPLOYEES	528	294649	374	280800	197	200494	177	80306	46	117110	31	50773
	77.5	80.9	78.9	81.7	75.5	79.3	83.1	88.1	80.7	80.6	88.6	89.1
AMOUNT NOT LESS	151	69624	99	62996	64	52185	35	10811	11	28110	4	6235
	22.1	19.1	20.9	18.3	24.5	20.7	16.4	11.9	19.3	19.4	11.4	10.9

4-YEAR LIBERAL ARTS COLLEGES				OTHER 4-YEAR COLLEGES				ALL 2-YEAR INSTITUTIONS		2-YEAR INSTITUTIONS			
PUBLIC		PRIVATE		PUBLIC		PRIVATE				PUBLIC		PRIVATE	
INSTS	EES	INSTS	EES	INSTS	EES	INSTS	EES	INSTS	EES	INSTS	EES	INSTS	EES
181	64122	151	16968	24	7046	37	3917	212	23032	203	22784	9	248
100.0	100.0	100.0	100.0	100.0	100.0	100.0	100.0	100.0	100.0	100.0	100.0	100.0	100.0
-	-	2	152	-	-	-	-	3	879	3	879	-	-
-	-	1.3	.9	-	-	-	-	1.4	3.8	1.5	3.9	-	-
135	49239	121	13782	17	5297	31	2753	159	15787	153	15637	6	150
74.6	76.8	80.2	81.2	70.8	75.2	83.8	70.3	75.0	68.6	75.3	68.6	66.7	60.5
46	14883	28	3034	7	1749	6	1164	50	6366	47	6268	3	98
25.4	23.2	18.5	17.9	29.2	24.8	16.2	29.7	23.6	27.6	23.2	27.5	33.3	39.5

4-YEAR LIBERAL ARTS COLLEGES				OTHER 4-YEAR COLLEGES				ALL 2-YEAR INSTITUTIONS		2-YEAR INSTITUTIONS			
PUBLIC		PRIVATE		PUBLIC		PRIVATE				PUBLIC		PRIVATE	
INSTS	EES	INSTS	EES	INSTS	EES	INSTS	EES	INSTS	EES	INSTS	EES	INSTS	EES
180	88493	142	24639	24	18966	36	9500	208	20575	200	20434	8	141
100.0	100.0	100.0	100.0	100.0	100.0	100.0	100.0	100.0	100.0	100.0	100.0	100.0	100.0
-	-	1	30	-	-	-	-	2	98	2	98	-	-
-	-	.7	.1	-	-	-	-	1.0	.5	1.0	.5	-	-
134	70271	117	21989	17	13113	29	7544	154	13849	149	13763	5	86
74.4	79.4	82.4	89.3	70.8	69.1	80.6	79.4	74.0	67.3	74.5	67.3	62.5	61.0
46	18222	24	2620	7	5853	7	1956	52	6628	49	6573	3	55
25.6	20.6	16.9	10.6	29.2	30.9	19.4	20.6	25.0	32.2	24.5	32.2	37.5	39.0

EMPLOYER-EMPLOYEE CONTRIBUTION TOWARD COST OF GROUP LIFE INSURANCE RETIRED COVERAGE

TABLE 18A

FACULTY

	ALL INSTITUTIONS		ALL 4-YEAR INSTITUTIONS		ALL 4-YEAR INSTITUTIONS — PUBLIC		ALL 4-YEAR INSTITUTIONS — PRIVATE		UNIVERSITIES — PUBLIC		UNIVERSITIES — PRIVATE	
	INSTS	EES	INSTS	EES	INSTS	EES	INSTS	EES	INSTS	EES	INSTS	EES
TOTAL	693	220600	481	197568	262	147358	219	50210	57	76190	31	29325
	100.0	100.0	100.0	100.0	100.0	100.0	100.0	100.0	100.0	100.0	100.0	100.0
NO RESPONSE	3	1014	1	165	1	165	-	-	-	-	-	-
	.4	.5	.2	.1	.4	.1	-	-	-	-	-	-
EMPLOYER PAYS FULL COST	195	55356	141	49883	41	25141	100	24742	11	15393	12	14251
	28.1	25.1	29.3	25.2	15.6	17.1	45.6	49.3	19.3	20.2	38.7	48.5
EMPLOYER AND EMPLOYEE SHARE COST	142	48536	93	44197	52	33084	41	11113	17	20174	7	7087
	20.5	22.0	19.3	22.4	19.8	22.5	18.7	22.1	29.8	26.5	22.6	24.2
EMPLOYEE PAYS FULL COST	216	71417	158	63955	118	60373	40	3582	21	28051	1	315
	31.2	32.3	32.9	32.4	45.1	40.9	18.3	7.1	36.9	36.8	3.2	1.1
NO CONTRIBUTION (PAID UP)	137	44277	88	39368	50	28595	38	10773	8	12572	11	7672
	19.8	20.1	18.3	19.9	19.1	19.4	17.4	21.5	14.0	16.5	35.5	26.2

EMPLOYER-EMPLOYEE CONTRIBUTION TOWARD COST OF GROUP LIFE INSURANCE RETIRED COVERAGE

TABLE 18B

CLERICAL SERVICE

	ALL INSTITUTIONS		ALL 4-YEAR INSTITUTIONS		ALL 4-YEAR INSTITUTIONS — PUBLIC		ALL 4-YEAR INSTITUTIONS — PRIVATE		UNIVERSITIES — PUBLIC		UNIVERSITIES — PRIVATE	
	INSTS	EES	INSTS	EES	INSTS	EES	INSTS	EES	INSTS	EES	INSTS	EES
TOTAL	682	364401	474	343826	261	252679	213	91147	57	145220	35	57008
	100.0	100.0	100.0	100.0	100.0	100.0	100.0	100.0	100.0	100.0	100.0	100.0
NO RESPONSE	71	30633	47	28055	38	27313	9	742	5	14302	-	-
	10.4	8.4	9.9	8.2	14.6	10.8	4.2	.8	8.8	9.8	-	-
EMPLOYER PAYS FULL COST	137	83155	108	79209	79	74741	29	4468	16	40829	1	261
	20.1	22.8	22.8	23.0	30.3	29.6	13.6	4.9	28.1	28.1	2.9	.5
EMPLOYER AND EMPLOYEE SHARE COST	271	137559	193	131929	75	79990	118	51939	23	52432	19	30357
	39.7	37.8	40.7	38.3	28.7	31.7	55.5	57.0	40.3	36.2	54.2	53.2
EMPLOYEE PAYS FULL COST	70	30763	43	27774	21	19304	22	8470	5	10030	3	5810
	10.3	8.4	9.1	8.1	8.0	7.6	10.3	9.3	8.8	6.9	8.6	10.2
NO CONTRIBUTION (PAID UP)	133	82291	83	76859	48	51331	35	25528	8	27627	12	20580
	19.5	22.6	17.5	22.4	18.4	20.3	16.4	28.0	14.0	19.0	34.3	36.1

4-YEAR LIBERAL ARTS COLLEGES				OTHER 4-YEAR COLLEGES				ALL 2-YEAR INSTITUTIONS		2-YEAR INSTITUTIONS			
PUBLIC		PRIVATE		PUBLIC		PRIVATE				PUBLIC		PRIVATE	
INSTS	EES	INSTS	EES	INSTS	EES	INSTS	EES	INSTS	EES	INSTS	EES	INSTS	EES
181	64122	151	16968	24	7046	37	3917	212	23032	203	22784	9	248
100.0	100.0	100.0	100.0	100.0	100.0	100.0	100.0	100.0	100.0	100.0	100.0	100.0	100.0
1	165	-	-	-	-	-	-	2	849	2	849	-	-
.6	.3	-	-	-	-	-	-	.9	3.7	1.0	3.7	-	-
29	9705	74	9180	1	43	14	1311	54	5473	50	5353	4	120
16.0	15.1	49.0	54.1	4.2	.6	37.9	33.5	25.5	23.8	24.6	23.5	44.5	48.3
27	9829	31	3370	8	3081	3	656	49	4339	48	4281	1	58
14.9	15.3	20.5	19.9	33.3	43.7	8.1	16.7	23.1	18.8	23.6	18.8	11.1	23.4
86	29935	32	3007	11	2387	7	260	58	7462	55	7410	3	52
47.5	46.7	21.2	17.7	45.8	33.9	18.9	6.6	27.4	32.4	27.2	32.5	33.3	21.0
38	14488	14	1411	4	1535	13	1690	49	4909	48	4891	1	18
21.0	22.6	9.3	8.3	16.7	21.8	35.1	43.2	23.1	21.3	23.6	21.5	11.1	7.3

4-YEAR LIBERAL ARTS COLLEGES				OTHER 4-YEAR COLLEGES				ALL 2-YEAR INSTITUTIONS		2-YEAR INSTITUTIONS			
PUBLIC		PRIVATE		PUBLIC		PRIVATE				PUBLIC		PRIVATE	
INSTS	EES	INSTS	EES	INSTS	EES	INSTS	EES	INSTS	EES	INSTS	EES	INSTS	EES
180	88493	142	24639	24	18966	36	9500	208	20575	200	20434	8	141
100.0	100.0	100.0	100.0	100.0	100.0	100.0	100.0	100.0	100.0	100.0	100.0	100.0	100.0
28	8314	7	697	5	4697	2	45	24	2578	24	2578	-	-
15.6	9.4	4.9	2.8	20.8	24.8	5.6	.5	11.5	12.5	12.0	12.6	-	-
57	31744	23	3430	6	2168	5	777	29	3946	27	3939	2	7
31.7	35.9	16.2	13.9	25.0	11.4	13.9	8.2	13.9	19.2	13.5	19.3	25.0	5.0
44	20145	82	17179	8	7413	17	4403	78	5630	75	5551	3	79
24.4	22.8	57.7	69.8	33.3	39.1	47.1	46.3	37.6	27.4	37.5	27.2	37.5	56.0
15	9242	17	1923	1	32	2	737	27	2989	25	2943	2	46
8.3	10.4	12.0	7.8	4.2	.2	5.6	7.8	13.0	14.5	12.5	14.4	25.0	32.6
36	19048	13	1410	4	4656	10	3538	50	5432	49	5423	1	9
20.0	21.5	9.2	5.7	16.7	24.5	27.8	37.2	24.0	26.4	24.5	26.5	12.5	6.4

HEALTH INSURANCE PLANS IN COLLEGES AND UNIVERSITIES
TABLE 19A

FACULTY

	ALL INSTITUTIONS		ALL 4-YEAR INSTITUTIONS		ALL 4-YEAR INSTITUTIONS				UNIVERSITIES			
					PUBLIC		PRIVATE		PUBLIC		PRIVATE	
	INSTS	EES	INSTS	EES	INSTS	EES	INSTS	EES	INSTS	EES	INSTS	EES
TOTAL	2092	432402	1407	363203	478	242041	929	121162	93	121628	61	54258
	100.0	100.0	100.0	100.0	100.0	100.0	100.0	100.0	100.0	100.0	100.0	100.0
NO RESPONSE	3	78	1	10	-	-	1	10	-	-	-	-
	.1	✻	.1	✻	-	-	.1	✻	-	-	-	-
HEALTH INSURANCE PLAN IN EFFECT	2063	431547	1390	362661	478	242041	912	120620	93	121628	61	54258
	98.7	99.8	98.8	99.9	100.0	100.0	98.2	99.6	100.0	100.0	100.0	100.0
NO HEALTH INSURANCE PLAN IN EFFECT	26	777	16	532	-	-	16	532	-	-	-	-
	1.2	.2	1.1	.1	-	-	1.7	.4	-	-	-	-

HEALTH INSURANCE PLANS IN COLLEGES AND UNIVERSITIES
TABLE 19B

CLERICAL SERVICE

	ALL INSTITUTIONS		ALL 4-YEAR INSTITUTIONS		ALL 4-YEAR INSTITUTIONS				UNIVERSITIES			
					PUBLIC		PRIVATE		PUBLIC		PRIVATE	
	INSTS	EES	INSTS	EES	INSTS	EES	INSTS	EES	INSTS	EES	INSTS	EES
TOTAL	2092	670941	1407	601711	478	413110	929	188601	93	231299	61	94679
	100.0	100.0	100.0	100.0	100.0	100.0	100.0	100.0	100.0	100.0	100.0	100.0
NO RESPONSE	2	29	-	-	-	-	-	-	-	-	-	-
	.1	✻	-	-	-	-	-	-	-	-	-	-
HEALTH INSURANCE PLAN IN EFFECT	2061	670330	1388	601295	478	413110	910	188185	93	231299	61	94679
	98.5	99.9	98.6	99.9	100.0	100.0	98.0	99.8	100.0	100.0	100.0	100.0
NO HEALTH INSURANCE PLAN IN EFFECT	29	582	19	416	-	-	19	416	-	-	-	-
	1.4	.1	1.4	.1	-	-	2.0	.2	-	-	-	-

4-YEAR LIBERAL ARTS COLLEGES				OTHER 4-YEAR COLLEGES				ALL 2-YEAR INSTITUTIONS		2-YEAR INSTITUTIONS			
PUBLIC		PRIVATE		PUBLIC		PRIVATE				PUBLIC		PRIVATE	
INSTS	EES	INSTS	EES	INSTS	EES	INSTS	EES	INSTS	EES	INSTS	EES	INSTS	EES
341	109911	686	57084	44	10502	182	9820	685	69199	600	66915	85	2284
100.0	100.0	100.0	100.0	100.0	100.0	100.0	100.0	100.0	100.0	100.0	100.0	100.0	100.0
-	-	-	-	-	-	1	10	2	68	1	50	1	18
-	-	-	.-	-	-	.5	.1	.3	.1	.2	.1	1.2	.8
341	109911	678	56658	44	10502	173	9704	673	68886	595	66689	78	2197
100.0	100.0	98.8	99.3	100.0	100.0	95.1	98.8	98.2	99.5	99.1	99.6	91.7	96.2
-	-	8	426	-	-	8	106	10	245	4	176	6	69
-	-	1.2	.7	-	-	4.4	1.1	1.5	.4	.7	.3	7.1	3.0

4-YEAR LIBERAL ARTS COLLEGES				OTHER 4-YEAR COLLEGES				ALL 2-YEAR INSTITUTIONS		2-YEAR INSTITUTIONS			
PUBLIC		PRIVATE		PUBLIC		PRIVATE				PUBLIC		PRIVATE	
INSTS	EES	INSTS	EES	INSTS	EES	INSTS	EES	INSTS	EES	INSTS	EES	INSTS	EES
341	153051	686	76960	44	28760	182	16962	685	69230	600	66748	85	2482
100.0	100.0	100.0	100.0	100.0	100.0	100.0	100.0	100.0	100.0	100.0	100.0	100.0	100.0
-	-	-	-	-	-	-	-	2	29	1	20	1	9
-	-	-	-	-	-	-	-	.3	✧	.2	✧	1.2	.4
341	153051	677	76615	44	28760	172	16891	673	69035	596	66620	77	2415
100.0	100.0	98.7	99.6	100.0	100.0	94.5	99.6	98.2	99.8	99.3	99.8	90.6	97.3
-	-	9	345	-	-	10	71	10	166	3	108	7	58
-	-	1.3	.4	-	-	5.5	.4	1.5	.2	.5	.2	8.2	2.3

TYPE OF HEALTH INSURANCE PLAN IN EFFECT

TABLE 20A

FACULTY

	ALL INSTITUTIONS		ALL 4-YEAR INSTITUTIONS		ALL 4-YEAR INSTITUTIONS				UNIVERSITIES			
					PUBLIC		PRIVATE		PUBLIC		PRIVATE	
	INSTS	EES	INSTS	EES	INSTS	EES	INSTS	EES	INSTS	EES	INSTS	EES
TOTAL	2063	431547	1390	362661	478	242041	912	120620	93	121628	61	54258
	100.0	100.0	100.0	100.0	100.0	100.0	100.0	100.0	100.0	100.0	100.0	100.0
NO RESPONSE	-	-	-	-	-	-	-	-	-	-	-	-
	-	-	-	-	-	-	-	-	-	-	-	-
BASIC HOSPITAL-SURGICAL-MEDICAL	1988	420466	1335	353598	470	236952	865	116646	89	117230	59	53370
	96.4	97.4	96.0	97.5	98.3	97.9	94.8	96.7	95.7	96.4	96.7	98.4
MAJOR MEDICAL	2002	425236	1349	357795	474	240183	875	117612	92	120686	59	53509
	97.0	98.5	97.1	98.7	99.2	99.2	95.9	97.5	98.9	99.2	96.7	98.6
HEALTH MAINTENANCE ORGANIZATION	444	157574	314	134416	119	78150	195	56266	27	44171	37	39231
	21.5	36.5	22.6	37.1	24.9	32.3	21.4	46.6	29.0	36.3	60.7	72.3
DENTAL	454	107337	228	74163	144	67085	84	7078	22	28697	2	590
	22.0	24.9	16.4	20.4	30.1	27.7	9.2	5.9	23.7	23.6	3.3	1.1
VISION CARE	157	50977	88	38017	70	35179	18	2838	8	15165	1	1297
	7.6	11.8	6.3	10.5	14.6	14.5	2.0	2.4	8.6	12.5	1.6	2.4

TYPE OF HEALTH INSURANCE PLAN IN EFFECT

TABLE 20B

CLERICAL SERVICE

	ALL INSTITUTIONS		ALL 4-YEAR INSTITUTIONS		ALL 4-YEAR INSTITUTIONS				UNIVERSITIES			
					PUBLIC		PRIVATE		PUBLIC		PRIVATE	
	INSTS	EES	INSTS	EES	INSTS	EES	INSTS	EES	INSTS	EES	INSTS	EES
TOTAL	2061	670330	1388	601295	478	413110	910	188185	93	231299	61	94679
	100.0	100.0	100.0	100.0	100.0	100.0	100.0	100.0	100.0	100.0	100.0	100.0
NO RESPONSE	-	-	-	-	-	-	-	-	-	-	-	-
	-	-	-	-	-	-	-	-	-	-	-	-
BASIC HOSPITAL-SURGICAL-MEDICAL	1998	660608	1339	593027	473	409973	866	183054	92	228924	59	93227
	96.9	98.5	96.5	98.6	99.0	99.2	95.2	97.3	98.9	99.0	96.7	98.5
MAJOR MEDICAL	1979	650397	1329	583303	473	402800	856	180503	91	221432	58	93284
	96.0	97.0	95.7	97.0	99.0	97.5	94.1	95.9	97.8	95.7	95.1	98.5
HEALTH MAINTENANCE ORGANIZATION	456	278514	323	253650	131	159441	192	94209	28	91245	37	65433
	22.1	41.5	23.3	42.2	27.4	38.6	21.1	50.1	30.1	39.4	60.7	69.1
DENTAL	457	146774	237	114918	144	100346	93	14572	23	50654	6	2576
	22.2	21.9	17.1	19.1	30.1	24.3	10.2	7.7	24.7	21.9	9.8	2.7
VISION CARE	155	102344	94	90264	69	79655	25	10609	9	43972	4	4588
	7.5	15.3	6.8	15.0	14.4	19.3	2.7	5.6	9.7	19.0	6.6	4.8

	4-YEAR LIBERAL ARTS COLLEGES				OTHER 4-YEAR COLLEGES				ALL 2-YEAR INSTITUTIONS		2-YEAR INSTITUTIONS			
	PUBLIC		PRIVATE		PUBLIC		PRIVATE				PUBLIC		PRIVATE	
	INSTS	EES	INSTS	EES	INSTS	EES	INSTS	EES	INSTS	EES	INSTS	EES	INSTS	EES
	341	109911	678	56658	44	10502	173	9704	673	68886	595	66689	78	2197
	100.0	100.0	100.0	100.0	100.0	100.0	100.0	100.0	100.0	100.0	100.0	100.0	100.0	100.0
	-	-	-	-	-	-	-	-	-	-	-	-	-	-
	-	-	-	-	-	-	-	-	-	-	-	-	-	-
	337	109220	643	53881	44	10502	163	9395	653	66868	579	64771	74	2097
	98.8	99.4	94.8	95.1	100.0	100.0	94.2	96.8	97.0	97.1	97.3	97.1	94.9	95.4
	338	108995	651	54867	44	10502	165	9236	653	67441	582	65399	71	2042
	99.1	99.2	96.0	96.8	100.0	100.0	95.4	95.2	97.0	97.9	97.8	98.1	91.0	92.9
	81	30597	110	12643	11	3382	48	4392	130	23158	128	23091	2	67
	23.8	27.8	16.2	22.3	25.0	32.2	27.7	45.3	19.3	33.6	21.5	34.6	2.6	3.0
	106	33870	58	5418	16	4518	24	1070	226	33174	219	32922	7	252
	31.1	30.8	8.6	9.6	36.4	43.0	13.9	11.0	33.6	48.2	36.8	49.4	9.0	11.5
	51	18343	14	1459	11	1671	3	82	69	12960	69	12960	-	-
	15.0	16.7	2.1	2.6	25.0	15.9	1.7	.8	10.3	18.8	11.6	19.4	-	-

	4-YEAR LIBERAL ARTS COLLEGES				OTHER 4-YEAR COLLEGES				ALL 2-YEAR INSTITUTIONS		2-YEAR INSTITUTIONS			
	PUBLIC		PRIVATE		PUBLIC		PRIVATE				PUBLIC		PRIVATE	
	INSTS	EES	INSTS	EES	INSTS	EES	INSTS	EES	INSTS	EES	INSTS	EES	INSTS	EES
	341	153051	677	76615	44	28760	172	16891	673	69035	596	66620	77	2415
	100.0	100.0	100.0	100.0	100.0	100.0	100.0	100.0	100.0	100.0	100.0	100.0	100.0	100.0
	-	-	-	-	-	-	-	-	-	-	-	-	-	-
	-	-	-	-	-	-	-	-	-	-	-	-	-	-
	337	152289	643	73174	44	28760	164	16653	659	67581	585	65231	74	2350
	98.8	99.5	95.0	95.5	100.0	100.0	95.3	98.6	97.9	97.9	98.2	97.9	96.1	97.3
	338	152608	637	72482	44	28760	161	14737	650	67094	581	64896	69	2198
	99.1	99.7	94.1	94.6	100.0	100.0	93.6	87.2	96.6	97.2	97.5	97.4	89.6	91.0
	90	54916	108	21876	13	13280	47	6900	133	24864	131	24788	2	76
	26.4	35.9	16.0	28.6	29.5	46.2	27.3	40.9	19.8	36.0	22.0	37.2	2.6	3.1
	105	39134	62	10692	16	10558	25	1304	220	31856	213	31605	7	251
	30.8	25.6	9.2	14.0	36.4	36.7	14.5	7.7	32.7	46.1	35.7	47.4	9.1	10.4
	49	29421	17	5901	11	6262	4	120	61	12080	61	12080	-	-
	14.4	19.2	2.5	7.7	25.0	21.8	2.3	.7	9.1	17.5	10.2	18.1	-	-

TYPE OF MAJOR MEDICAL INSURANCE

TABLE 21A

FACULTY

| | ALL INSTITUTIONS | | ALL 4-YEAR INSTITUTIONS | | ALL 4-YEAR INSTITUTIONS | | | | UNIVERSITIES | | | |
| | | | | | PUBLIC | | PRIVATE | | PUBLIC | | PRIVATE | |
	INSTS	EES	INSTS	EES	INSTS	EES	INSTS	EES	INSTS	EES	INSTS	EES
TOTAL	2002	425236	1349	357795	474	240183	875	117612	92	120686	59	53509
	100.0	100.0	100.0	100.0	100.0	100.0	100.0	100.0	100.0	100.0	100.0	100.0
NO RESPONSE	10	1193	4	199	2	86	2	113	-	-	-	-
	.5	.3	.3	.1	.4	☆	.2	.1	-	-	-	-
SINGLE COMPREHENSIVE PLAN	1614	339485	1039	279532	419	206341	620	73191	71	94822	31	31497
	80.6	79.8	77.0	78.1	88.4	85.9	70.9	62.2	77.2	78.6	52.5	58.9
SEPARATE PLAN	378	84558	306	78064	53	33756	253	44308	21	25864	28	22012
	18.9	19.9	22.7	21.8	11.2	14.1	28.9	37.7	22.8	21.4	47.5	41.1

TYPE OF MAJOR MEDICAL INSURANCE

TABLE 21B

CLERICAL SERVICE

| | ALL INSTITUTIONS | | ALL 4-YEAR INSTITUTIONS | | ALL 4-YEAR INSTITUTIONS | | | | UNIVERSITIES | | | |
| | | | | | PUBLIC | | PRIVATE | | PUBLIC | | PRIVATE | |
	INSTS	EES	INSTS	EES	INSTS	EES	INSTS	EES	INSTS	EES	INSTS	EES
TOTAL	1979	650397	1329	583303	473	402800	856	180503	91	221432	58	93284
	100.0	100.0	100.0	100.0	100.0	100.0	100.0	100.0	100.0	100.0	100.0	100.0
NO RESPONSE	9	765	3	109	2	106	1	3	-	-	-	-
	.5	.1	.2	☆	.4	☆	.1	☆	-	-	-	-
SINGLE COMPREHENSIVE PLAN	1619	524442	1039	465263	421	350192	618	115071	73	181477	31	53043
	81.8	80.7	78.2	79.8	89.0	87.0	72.2	63.8	80.2	82.0	53.4	56.9
SEPARATE PLAN	351	125190	287	117931	50	52502	237	65429	18	39955	27	40241
	17.7	19.2	21.6	20.2	10.6	13.0	27.7	36.2	19.8	18.0	46.6	43.1

4-YEAR LIBERAL ARTS COLLEGES				OTHER 4-YEAR COLLEGES				ALL 2-YEAR INSTITUTIONS		2-YEAR INSTITUTIONS			
PUBLIC		PRIVATE		PUBLIC		PRIVATE				PUBLIC		PRIVATE	
INSTS	EES	INSTS	EES	INSTS	EES	INSTS	EES	INSTS	EES	INSTS	EES	INSTS	EES
338	108995	651	54867	44	10502	165	9236	653	67441	582	65399	71	2042
100.0	100.0	100.0	100.0	100.0	100.0	100.0	100.0	100.0	100.0	100.0	100.0	100.0	100.0
1	65	2	113	1	21	-	-	6	994	5	960	1	34
.3	.1	.3	.2	2.3	.2	-	-	.9	1.5	.9	1.5	1.4	1.7
310	102195	457	35771	38	9324	132	5923	575	59953	518	58360	57	1593
91.7	93.7	70.2	65.2	86.3	88.8	80.0	64.1	88.1	88.9	89.0	89.2	80.3	78.0
27	6735	192	18983	5	1157	33	3313	72	6494	59	6079	13	415
8.0	6.2	29.5	34.6	11.4	11.0	20.0	35.9	11.0	9.6	10.1	9.3	18.3	20.3

4-YEAR LIBERAL ARTS COLLEGES				OTHER 4-YEAR COLLEGES				ALL 2-YEAR INSTITUTIONS		2-YEAR INSTITUTIONS			
PUBLIC		PRIVATE		PUBLIC		PRIVATE				PUBLIC		PRIVATE	
INSTS	EES	INSTS	EES	INSTS	EES	INSTS	EES	INSTS	EES	INSTS	EES	INSTS	EES
338	152608	637	72482	44	28760	161	14737	650	67094	581	64896	69	2198
100.0	100.0	100.0	100.0	100.0	100.0	100.0	100.0	100.0	100.0	100.0	100.0	100.0	100.0
1	58	1	3	1	48	-	-	6	656	5	645	1	11
.3	✧	.2	✧	2.3	.2	-	-	.9	1.0	.9	1.0	1.4	.5
310	144388	457	51323	38	24327	130	10705	580	59179	524	57556	56	1623
91.7	94.7	71.7	70.8	86.3	84.6	80.7	72.6	89.3	88.2	90.1	88.7	81.2	73.8
27	8162	179	21156	5	4385	31	4032	64	7259	52	6695	12	564
8.0	5.3	28.1	29.2	11.4	15.2	19.3	27.4	9.8	10.8	9.0	10.3	17.4	25.7

HEALTH INSURANCE PLAN IN EFFECT - TYPE OF INSURER

TABLE 22A

FACULTY

	ALL INSTITUTIONS		ALL 4-YEAR INSTITUTIONS		ALL 4-YEAR INSTITUTIONS: PUBLIC		ALL 4-YEAR INSTITUTIONS: PRIVATE		UNIVERSITIES: PUBLIC		UNIVERSITIES: PRIVATE	
	INSTS	EES	INSTS	EES	INSTS	EES	INSTS	EES	INSTS	EES	INSTS	EES
TOTAL	2063	431547	1390	362661	478	242041	912	120620	93	121628	61	54258
	100.0	100.0	100.0	100.0	100.0	100.0	100.0	100.0	100.0	100.0	100.0	100.0
NO RESPONSE	-	-	-	-	-	-	-	-	-	-	-	-
	-	-	-	-	-	-	-	-	-	-	-	-
BLUE CROSS	1350	307283	878	255537	328	167868	550	87669	58	80070	43	44845
	65.4	71.2	63.2	70.5	68.6	69.4	60.3	72.7	62.4	65.8	70.5	82.7
BLUE SHIELD	1184	270023	795	231460	298	152073	497	79387	53	72746	38	40012
	57.4	62.6	57.2	63.8	62.3	62.8	54.5	65.8	57.0	59.8	62.3	73.7
INSURANCE CO	970	196464	703	167993	204	102421	499	65572	47	56267	39	26357
	47.0	45.5	50.6	46.3	42.7	42.3	54.7	54.4	50.5	46.3	63.9	48.6
SELF-INSURED	102	27276	70	24452	45	21599	25	2853	6	7768	1	1155
	4.9	6.3	5.0	6.7	9.4	8.9	2.7	2.4	6.5	6.4	1.6	2.1
OTHER	293	86467	194	68763	65	47375	129	21388	15	25429	15	12070
	14.2	20.0	14.0	19.0	13.6	19.6	14.1	17.7	16.1	20.9	24.6	22.2

HEALTH INSURANCE PLAN IN EFFECT - TYPE OF INSURER

TABLE 22B

CLERICAL SERVICE

	ALL INSTITUTIONS		ALL 4-YEAR INSTITUTIONS		ALL 4-YEAR INSTITUTIONS: PUBLIC		ALL 4-YEAR INSTITUTIONS: PRIVATE		UNIVERSITIES: PUBLIC		UNIVERSITIES: PRIVATE	
	INSTS	EES	INSTS	EES	INSTS	EES	INSTS	EES	INSTS	EES	INSTS	EES
TOTAL	2061	670330	1388	601295	478	413110	910	188185	93	231299	61	94679
	100.0	100.0	100.0	100.0	100.0	100.0	100.0	100.0	100.0	100.0	100.0	100.0
NO RESPONSE	1	55	-	-	-	-	-	-	-	-	-	-
	*	*	-	-	-	-	-	-	-	-	-	-
BLUE CROSS	1361	506451	888	455351	329	311848	559	143503	59	172457	43	81417
	66.0	75.6	64.0	75.7	68.8	75.5	61.4	76.3	63.4	74.6	70.5	86.0
BLUE SHIELD	1193	455982	802	418038	299	288331	503	129707	54	158801	39	72849
	57.9	68.0	57.8	69.5	62.6	69.8	55.3	68.9	58.1	68.7	63.9	76.9
INSURANCE CO	928	302180	673	272909	201	176280	472	96629	47	103930	36	42376
	45.0	45.1	48.5	45.4	42.1	42.7	51.9	51.3	50.5	44.9	59.0	44.8
SELF-INSURED	101	38281	69	35312	45	31057	24	4255	6	15252	1	1347
	4.9	5.7	5.0	5.9	9.4	7.5	2.6	2.3	6.5	6.6	1.6	1.4
OTHER	291	153216	192	134586	64	101175	128	33411	15	54116	16	20056
	14.1	22.9	13.8	22.4	13.4	24.5	14.1	17.8	16.1	23.4	26.2	21.2

4-YEAR LIBERAL ARTS COLLEGES				OTHER 4-YEAR COLLEGES				ALL 2-YEAR INSTITUTIONS		2-YEAR INSTITUTIONS			
PUBLIC		PRIVATE		PUBLIC		PRIVATE				PUBLIC		PRIVATE	
INSTS	EES	INSTS	EES	INSTS	EES	INSTS	EES	INSTS	EES	INSTS	EES	INSTS	EES
341	109911	678	56658	44	10502	173	9704	673	68886	595	66689	78	2197
100.0	100.0	100.0	100.0	100.0	100.0	100.0	100.0	100.0	100.0	100.0	100.0	100.0	100.0
-	-	-	-	-	-	-	-	-	-	-	-	-	-
-	-	-	-	-	-	-	-	-	-	-	-	-	-
242	81290	406	35739	28	6508	101	7085	472	51746	419	50108	53	1638
71.0	74.0	59.9	63.1	63.6	62.0	58.4	73.0	70.1	75.1	70.4	75.1	67.9	74.6
221	73589	372	33589	24	5738	87	5786	389	38563	338	36982	51	1581
64.8	67.0	54.9	59.3	54.5	54.6	50.3	59.6	57.8	56.0	56.8	55.5	65.4	72.0
133	41645	381	33720	24	4509	79	5495	267	28471	238	27743	29	728
39.0	37.9	56.2	59.5	54.5	42.9	45.7	56.6	39.7	41.3	40.0	41.6	37.2	33.1
34	11550	18	1447	5	2281	6	251	32	2824	30	2798	2	26
10.0	10.5	2.7	2.6	11.4	21.7	3.5	2.6	4.8	4.1	5.0	4.2	2.6	1.2
44	20030	77	8058	6	1916	37	1260	99	17704	94	17531	5	173
12.9	18.2	11.4	14.2	13.6	18.2	21.4	13.0	14.7	25.7	15.8	26.3	6.4	7.9

4-YEAR LIBERAL ARTS COLLEGES				OTHER 4-YEAR COLLEGES				ALL 2-YEAR INSTITUTIONS		2-YEAR INSTITUTIONS			
PUBLIC		PRIVATE		PUBLIC		PRIVATE				PUBLIC		PRIVATE	
INSTS	EES	INSTS	EES	INSTS	EES	INSTS	EES	INSTS	EES	INSTS	EES	INSTS	EES
341	153051	677	76615	44	28760	172	16891	673	69035	596	66620	77	2415
100.0	100.0	100.0	100.0	100.0	100.0	100.0	100.0	100.0	100.0	100.0	100.0	100.0	100.0
-	-	-	-	-	-	-	-	1	55	-	-	1	55
-	-	-	-	-	-	-	-	.1	.1	-	-	1.3	2.3
242	118532	411	48955	28	20859	105	13131	473	51100	421	49344	52	1756
71.0	77.4	60.7	63.9	63.6	72.5	61.0	77.7	70.3	74.0	70.6	74.1	67.5	72.7
221	111324	374	45913	24	18206	90	10945	391	37944	341	36285	50	1659
64.8	72.7	55.2	59.9	54.5	63.3	52.3	64.8	58.1	55.0	57.2	54.5	64.9	68.7
130	58152	361	45102	24	14198	75	9151	255	29271	228	28377	27	894
38.1	38.0	53.3	58.9	54.5	49.4	43.6	54.2	37.9	42.4	38.3	42.6	35.1	37.0
34	13540	16	1838	5	2265	7	1070	32	2969	30	2957	2	12
10.0	8.8	2.4	2.4	11.4	7.9	4.1	6.3	4.8	4.3	5.0	4.4	2.6	.5
43	39203	80	12106	6	7856	32	1249	99	18630	94	18494	5	136
12.6	25.6	11.8	15.8	13.6	27.3	18.6	7.4	14.7	27.0	15.8	27.8	6.5	5.6

EMPLOYER-EMPLOYEE CONTRIBUTION TOWARD COST OF HEALTH INSURANCE COVERAGE OF EMPLOYEES AND DEPENDENTS

TABLE 23A

FACULTY

	ALL INSTITUTIONS		ALL 4-YEAR INSTITUTIONS		ALL 4-YEAR INSTITUTIONS PUBLIC		ALL 4-YEAR INSTITUTIONS PRIVATE		UNIVERSITIES PUBLIC		UNIVERSITIES PRIVATE	
	INSTS	EES	INSTS	EES	INSTS	EES	INSTS	EES	INSTS	EES	INSTS	EES
TOTAL	2063	431547	1390	362661	478	242041	912	120620	93	121628	61	54258
	100.0	100.0	100.0	100.0	100.0	100.0	100.0	100.0	100.0	100.0	100.0	100.0
EMPLOYEE COVERAGE												
EMPLOYER PAYS FULL COST	1126	205615	670	158920	223	110862	447	48058	47	61726	19	15820
	54.6	47.6	48.2	43.8	46.7	45.8	49.0	39.8	50.5	50.7	31.1	29.2
EMPLOYER AND EMPLOYEE SHARE COST	886	220674	680	199104	255	131179	425	67925	46	59902	39	36072
	42.9	51.1	48.9	54.9	53.3	54.2	46.6	56.3	49.5	49.3	63.9	66.5
EMPLOYEE PAYS FULL COST	45	4882	36	4376	-	-	36	4376	-	-	2	2223
	2.2	1.1	2.6	1.2	-	-	3.9	3.6	-	-	3.3	4.1
NO RESPONSE	6	376	4	261	-	-	4	261	-	-	1	143
	.3	.2	.3	.1	-	-	.5	.3	-	-	1.7	.2
DEPENDENT'S COVERAGE												
EMPLOYER PAYS FULL COST	438	84529	235	60818	76	43501	159	17317	17	26518	6	7638
	21.2	19.6	16.9	16.8	15.9	18.0	17.4	14.4	18.3	21.8	9.8	14.1
EMPLOYER AND EMPLOYEE SHARE COST	873	219231	624	195656	249	128439	375	67217	40	55835	40	36557
	42.3	50.8	44.9	54.0	52.1	53.1	41.1	55.7	43.0	45.9	65.6	67.4
EMPLOYEE PAYS FULL COST	739	126258	523	104826	151	69104	372	35722	35	38895	14	9920
	35.8	29.3	37.6	28.9	31.6	28.6	40.8	29.6	37.6	32.0	23.0	18.3
NO RESPONSE	13	1529	8	1361	2	997	6	364	1	380	1	143
	.7	.3	.6	.3	.4	.3	.7	.3	1.1	.3	1.6	.2

4-YEAR LIBERAL ARTS COLLEGES				OTHER 4-YEAR COLLEGES				ALL 2-YEAR INSTITUTIONS		2-YEAR INSTITUTIONS			
PUBLIC		PRIVATE		PUBLIC		PRIVATE				PUBLIC		PRIVATE	
INSTS	EES	INSTS	EES	INSTS	EES	INSTS	EES	INSTS	EES	INSTS	EES	INSTS	EES
341	109911	678	56658	44	10502	173	9704	673	68886	595	66689	78	2197
100.0	100.0	100.0	100.0	100.0	100.0	100.0	100.0	100.0	100.0	100.0	100.0	100.0	100.0
155	44533	324	25956	21	4603	104	6282	456	46695	415	45533	41	1162
45.5	40.5	47.8	45.8	47.7	43.8	60.1	64.7	67.8	67.8	69.7	68.3	52.6	52.9
186	65378	322	28685	23	5899	64	3168	206	21570	174	20638	32	932
54.5	59.5	47.5	50.6	52.3	56.2	37.0	32.6	30.6	31.3	29.2	30.9	41.0	42.4
-	-	30	1917	-	-	4	236	9	506	4	403	5	103
-	-	4.4	3.4	-	-	2.3	2.4	1.3	.7	.7	.6	6.4	4.7
-	-	2	100	-	-	1	18	2	115	2	115	-	-
-	-	.3	.2	-	-	.6	.3	.3	.2	.4	.2	-	-
53	15689	98	7285	6	1294	55	2394	203	23711	189	23329	14	382
15.5	14.3	14.5	12.9	13.6	12.3	31.8	24.7	30.2	34.4	31.8	35.0	17.9	17.4
182	66087	271	25929	27	6517	64	4731	249	23575	221	22810	28	765
53.4	60.1	40.0	45.8	61.4	62.1	37.0	48.8	37.0	34.2	37.1	34.2	35.9	34.8
105	27518	305	23238	11	2691	53	2564	216	21432	181	20393	35	1039
30.8	25.0	45.0	41.0	25.0	25.6	30.6	26.4	32.1	31.1	30.4	30.6	44.9	47.3
1	617	4	206	-	-	1	15	5	168	4	157	1	11
.3	.6	.5	.3	-	-	.6	.1	.7	.3	.7	.2	1.3	.5

EMPLOYER-EMPLOYEE CONTRIBUTION TOWARD COST OF HEALTH INSURANCE COVERAGE OF EMPLOYEES AND DEPENDENTS

TABLE 23B

CLERICAL SERVICE	ALL INSTITUTIONS		ALL 4-YEAR INSTITUTIONS		ALL 4-YEAR INSTITUTIONS				UNIVERSITIES			
					PUBLIC		PRIVATE		PUBLIC		PRIVATE	
	INSTS	EES	INSTS	EES	INSTS	EES	INSTS	EES	INSTS	EES	INSTS	EES
TOTAL	2061	670330	1388	601295	478	413110	910	188185	93	231299	61	94679
	100.0	100.0	100.0	100.0	100.0	100.0	100.0	100.0	100.0	100.0	100.0	100.0
EMPLOYEE COVERAGE												
EMPLOYER PAYS	1108	301271	652	253686	221	182614	431	71072	47	111578	21	24493
FULL COST	53.8	44.9	47.0	42.2	46.2	44.2	47.4	37.8	50.5	48.2	34.4	25.9
EMPLOYER AND EMPLOYEE	904	363634	697	342555	256	229655	441	112900	46	119721	39	68954
SHARE COST	43.9	54.2	50.2	57.0	53.6	55.6	48.5	60.0	49.5	51.8	63.9	72.8
EMPLOYEE PAYS	48	5398	39	5054	1	841	38	4213	-	-	1	1232
FULL COST	2.3	.8	2.8	.8	.2	.2	4.2	2.2	-	-	1.6	1.3
NO RESPONSE	1	27	-	-	-	-	-	-	-	-	-	-
	*	.1	-	-	-	-	.1	-	-	-	.1	-
DEPENDENT'S COVERAGE												
EMPLOYER PAYS	426	123667	219	98141	78	74434	141	23707	20	53028	6	8650
FULL COST	20.7	18.4	15.8	16.3	16.3	18.0	15.5	12.6	21.5	22.9	9.8	9.1
EMPLOYER AND EMPLOYEE	869	354358	628	334534	248	218828	380	115706	38	102698	40	71087
SHARE COST	42.2	52.9	45.2	55.6	51.9	53.0	41.8	61.5	40.9	44.4	65.6	75.1
EMPLOYEE PAYS	753	190269	533	166690	150	118448	383	48242	34	74393	15	14942
FULL COST	36.5	28.4	38.4	27.7	31.4	28.7	42.1	25.6	36.6	32.2	24.6	15.8
NO RESPONSE	13	2036	8	1930	2	1400	6	530	1	1180	-	-
	.6	.3	.6	.4	.4	.3	.6	.3	1.0	.5	-	-

| | 4-YEAR LIBERAL ARTS COLLEGES | | | | OTHER 4-YEAR COLLEGES | | | | ALL 2-YEAR INSTITUTIONS | | 2-YEAR INSTITUTIONS | | | |
| | PUBLIC | | PRIVATE | | PUBLIC | | PRIVATE | | | | PUBLIC | | PRIVATE | |
	INSTS	EES	INSTS	EES	INSTS	EES	INSTS	EES	INSTS	EES	INSTS	EES	INSTS	EES
	341	153051	677	76615	44	28760	172	16891	673	69035	596	66620	77	2415
	100.0	100.0	100.0	100.0	100.0	100.0	100.0	100.0	100.0	100.0	100.0	100.0	100.0	100.0
	153	53508	308	35897	21	17528	102	10682	456	47585	417	46326	39	1259
	44.9	35.0	45.5	46.9	47.7	60.9	59.3	63.2	67.8	68.9	70.0	69.5	50.6	52.1
	187	98702	334	37748	23	11232	68	6198	207	21079	175	20086	32	993
	54.8	64.5	49.3	49.3	52.3	39.1	39.5	36.7	30.8	30.5	29.4	30.2	41.6	41.1
	1	841	35	2970	-	-	2	11	9	344	3	181	6	163
	.3	.5	5.2	3.9	-	-	1.2	.1	1.3	.5	.5	.3	7.8	6.7
	-	-	-	-	-	-	-	-	1	27	1	27	-	-
	-	-	-	.1	-	-	-	-	.1	.1	.1	☆	-	.1
	52	16458	88	12340	6	4948	47	2717	207	25526	196	25234	11	292
	15.2	10.8	13.0	16.1	13.6	17.2	27.3	16.1	30.8	37.0	32.9	37.9	14.3	12.1
	183	100531	274	35303	27	15599	66	9316	241	19824	212	19122	29	702
	53.7	65.7	40.5	46.1	61.4	54.2	38.4	55.2	35.8	28.7	35.6	28.7	37.7	29.1
	105	35842	309	28442	11	8213	59	4858	220	23579	184	22163	36	1416
	30.8	23.4	45.6	37.1	25.0	28.6	34.3	28.8	32.7	34.2	30.9	33.3	46.8	58.6
	1	220	6	530	-	-	-	-	5	106	4	101	1	5
	.3	.1	.9	.7	-	-	-	.1	.7	.1	.6	.1	1.2	.2

EMPLOYER-EMPLOYEE CONTRIBUTION TOWARD COST OF HEALTH
MAINTENANCE ORGANIZATION - COVERAGE OF EMPLOYEES AND DEPENDENTS
TABLE 24A

FACULTY					ALL 4-YEAR INSTITUTIONS				UNIVERSITIES			
	ALL INSTITUTIONS		ALL 4-YEAR INSTITUTIONS		PUBLIC		PRIVATE		PUBLIC		PRIVATE	
	INSTS	EES	INSTS	EES	INSTS	EES	INSTS	EES	INSTS	EES	INSTS	EES
TOTAL	444	157574	314	134416	119	78150	195	56266	27	44171	37	39231
	100.0	100.0	100.0	100.0	100.0	100.0	100.0	100.0	100.0	100.0	100.0	100.0
EMPLOYEE COVERAGE												
EMPLOYER PAYS	145	35312	79	23988	26	17864	53	6124	5	11129	4	2065
FULL COST	32.7	22.4	25.2	17.8	21.8	22.9	27.2	10.9	18.5	25.2	10.8	5.3
EMPLOYER AND EMPLOYEE	282	117278	219	105495	90	58371	129	47124	21	32134	30	34800
SHARE COST	63.5	74.4	69.7	78.5	75.6	74.7	66.2	83.8	77.8	72.7	81.1	88.7
EMPLOYEE PAYS	10	3652	10	3652	1	908	9	2744	1	908	3	2366
FULL COST	2.3	2.3	3.2	2.7	.8	1.2	4.6	4.9	3.7	2.1	8.1	6.0
NO RESPONSE	7	1332	6	1281	2	1007	4	274	-	-	-	-
	1.5	.9	1.9	1.0	1.8	1.2	2.0	.4	-	-	-	-
DEPENDENT'S COVERAGE												
EMPLOYER PAYS	77	23548	35	16002	16	14678	19	1324	5	11129	-	-
FULL COST	17.3	14.9	11.1	11.9	13.4	18.8	9.7	2.4	18.5	25.2	-	-
EMPLOYER AND EMPLOYEE	254	101872	190	92101	88	51670	102	40431	16	25529	26	30778
SHARE COST	57.2	64.7	60.5	68.5	73.9	66.1	52.3	71.9	59.3	57.8	70.3	78.5
EMPLOYEE PAYS	105	30702	82	24912	13	10795	69	14117	6	7513	10	8310
FULL COST	23.6	19.5	26.1	18.5	10.9	13.8	35.4	25.1	22.2	17.0	27.0	21.2
NO RESPONSE	8	1452	7	1401	2	1007	5	394	-	-	1	143
	1.9	.9	2.3	1.1	1.8	1.3	2.6	.6	-	-	2.7	.3

4-YEAR LIBERAL ARTS COLLEGES				OTHER 4-YEAR COLLEGES				ALL 2-YEAR INSTITUTIONS		2-YEAR INSTITUTIONS			
PUBLIC		PRIVATE		PUBLIC		PRIVATE				PUBLIC		PRIVATE	
INSTS	EES	INSTS	EES	INSTS	EES	INSTS	EES	INSTS	EES	INSTS	EES	INSTS	EES
81	30597	110	12643	11	3382	48	4392	130	23158	128	23091	2	67
100.0	100.0	100.0	100.0	100.0	100.0	100.0	100.0	100.0	100.0	100.0	100.0	100.0	100.0
18	5563	29	2738	3	1172	20	1321	66	11324	65	11270	1	54
22.2	18.2	26.4	21.7	27.3	34.7	41.7	30.1	50.8	48.9	50.8	48.8	50.0	80.6
61	24027	74	9450	8	2210	25	2874	63	11783	62	11770	1	13
75.3	78.5	67.3	74.7	72.7	65.3	52.1	65.4	48.5	50.9	48.4	51.0	50.0	19.4
-	-	3	181	-	-	3	197	-	-	-	-	-	-
-	-	2.7	1.4	-	-	6.3	4.5	-	-	-	-	-	-
2	1007	4	274	-	-	-	-	1	51	1	51	-	-
2.5	3.3	3.6	2.2	-	-	.1	-	.7	.2	.8	.2	-	-
11	3549	8	869	-	-	11	455	42	7546	42	7546	-	-
13.6	11.6	7.3	6.9	-	-	22.9	10.4	32.3	32.6	32.8	32.7	-	-
62	23459	50	6275	10	2682	26	3378	64	9771	62	9704	2	67
76.5	76.7	45.5	49.6	90.9	79.3	54.2	76.9	49.2	42.2	48.4	42.0	100.0	100.0
6	2582	48	5248	1	700	11	559	23	5790	23	5790	-	-
7.4	8.4	43.6	41.5	9.1	20.7	22.9	12.7	17.7	25.0	18.0	25.1	-	-
2	1007	4	251	-	-	-	-	1	51	1	51	-	-
2.5	3.3	3.6	2.0	-	-	-	-	.8	.2	.8	.2	-	-

EMPLOYER-EMPLOYEE CONTRIBUTION TOWARD COST OF HEALTH MAINTENANCE ORGANIZATION - COVERAGE OF EMPLOYEES AND DEPENDENTS
TABLE 24B

CLERICAL SERVICE	ALL INSTITUTIONS		ALL 4-YEAR INSTITUTIONS		ALL 4-YEAR INSTITUTIONS				UNIVERSITIES			
					PUBLIC		PRIVATE		PUBLIC		PRIVATE	
	INSTS	EES	INSTS	EES	INSTS	EES	INSTS	EES	INSTS	EES	INSTS	EES
TOTAL	456	278514	323	253650	131	159441	192	94209	28	91245	37	65433
	100.0	100.0	100.0	100.0	100.0	100.0	100.0	100.0	100.0	100.0	100.0	100.0
EMPLOYEE COVERAGE												
EMPLOYER PAYS FULL COST	143	59033	78	46777	26	32454	52	14323	5	20135	5	4025
	31.4	21.2	24.1	18.4	19.8	20.4	27.1	15.2	17.9	22.1	13.5	6.2
EMPLOYER AND EMPLOYEE SHARE COST	300	215638	232	203030	103	125104	129	77926	22	69631	31	60176
	65.8	77.4	71.8	80.0	78.6	78.5	67.2	82.7	78.6	76.3	83.8	92.0
EMPLOYEE PAYS FULL COST	9	3110	9	3110	1	1479	8	1631	1	1479	1	1232
	2.0	1.1	2.8	1.2	.8	.9	4.2	1.7	3.6	1.6	2.7	1.9
NO RESPONSE	4	733	4	733	1	404	3	329	-	-	-	-
	.8	.3	1.3	.4	.8	.2	1.5	.4	.1	-	-	.1
DEPENDENT'S COVERAGE												
EMPLOYER PAYS FULL COST	75	37426	34	30128	16	24807	18	5321	5	20135	1	225
	16.4	13.4	10.5	11.9	12.2	15.6	9.4	5.6	17.9	22.1	2.7	.3
EMPLOYER AND EMPLOYEE SHARE COST	270	191853	202	182195	100	112531	102	69664	17	56027	25	53050
	59.2	68.9	62.5	71.8	76.3	70.6	53.1	73.9	60.7	61.4	67.6	81.1
EMPLOYEE PAYS FULL COST	106	47713	83	40473	13	21479	70	18994	6	15083	11	12158
	23.2	17.1	25.7	16.0	9.9	13.5	36.5	20.2	21.4	16.5	29.7	18.6
NO RESPONSE	5	1522	4	854	2	624	2	230	-	-	-	-
	1.2	.6	1.3	.3	1.6	.3	1.0	.3	-	-	-	-

4-YEAR LIBERAL ARTS COLLEGES				OTHER 4-YEAR COLLEGES				ALL 2-YEAR INSTITUTIONS		2-YEAR INSTITUTIONS			
PUBLIC		PRIVATE		PUBLIC		PRIVATE				PUBLIC		PRIVATE	
INSTS	EES	INSTS	EES	INSTS	EES	INSTS	EES	INSTS	EES	INSTS	EES	INSTS	EES
90	54916	108	21876	13	13280	47	6900	133	24864	131	24788	2	76
100.0	100.0	100.0	100.0	100.0	100.0	100.0	100.0	100.0	100.0	100.0	100.0	100.0	100.0
18	6606	26	6849	3	5713	21	3449	65	12256	64	12204	1	52
20.0	12.0	24.1	31.3	23.1	43.0	44.7	50.0	48.9	49.3	48.9	49.2	50.0	68.4
71	47906	74	14334	10	7567	24	3416	68	12608	67	12584	1	24
78.9	87.2	68.5	65.5	76.9	57.0	51.1	49.5	51.1	50.7	51.1	50.8	50.0	31.6
-	-	5	364	-	-	2	35	-	-	-	-	-	-
-	-	4.6	1.7	-	-	4.3	.5	-	-	-	-	-	-
1	404	3	329	-	-	-	-	-	-	-	-	-	-
1.1	.8	2.8	1.5	-	-	.1	-	-	-	-	-	-	-
11	4672	6	4602	-	-	11	494	41	7298	41	7298	-	-
12.2	8.5	5.6	21.0	-	-	23.4	7.2	30.8	29.4	31.3	29.4	-	-
71	46024	51	10774	12	10480	26	5840	68	9658	66	9582	2	76
78.9	83.8	47.2	49.3	92.3	78.9	55.3	84.6	51.1	38.8	50.4	38.7	100.0	100.0
6	3596	49	6270	1	2800	10	566	23	7240	23	7240	-	-
6.7	6.5	45.4	28.7	7.7	21.1	21.3	8.2	17.3	29.1	17.6	29.2	-	-
2	624	2	230	-	-	-	-	1	668	1	668	-	-
2.2	1.2	1.8	1.0	-	-	-	-	.8	2.7	.7	2.7	-	-

WAITING PERIOD BEFORE NEW EMPLOYEE IS COVERED UNDER HEALTH INSURANCE PLAN(S)

TABLE 25A

FACULTY

	ALL INSTITUTIONS		ALL 4-YEAR INSTITUTIONS		ALL 4-YEAR INSTITUTIONS PUBLIC		PRIVATE		UNIVERSITIES PUBLIC		PRIVATE	
	INSTS	EES	INSTS	EES	INSTS	EES	INSTS	EES	INSTS	EES	INSTS	EES
TOTAL	2063	431547	1390	362661	478	242041	912	120620	93	121628	61	54258
	100.0	100.0	100.0	100.0	100.0	100.0	100.0	100.0	100.0	100.0	100.0	100.0
NO RESPONSE	6	740	4	555	1	509	3	46	-	-	-	-
	.3	.2	.3	.2	.2	.2	.3	※	-	-	-	-
ONE MONTH OR LESS	1841	390620	1243	329135	433	223187	810	105948	87	114344	56	46787
	89.2	90.5	89.4	90.8	90.6	92.2	88.8	87.8	93.5	94.0	91.8	86.2
UNTIL STATED DATE(S) DURING FIRST YEAR EMPLOYMENT, BUT AFTER ONE MONTH OF SERVICE	67	10965	50	10011	12	5359	38	4652	4	3896	2	1116
	3.2	2.5	3.6	2.8	2.5	2.2	4.2	3.9	4.3	3.2	3.3	2.1
STATED NUMBER OF MONTHS	122	18958	71	12395	22	8386	49	4009	1	1657	1	143
	5.9	4.4	5.1	3.4	4.6	3.5	5.4	3.3	1.1	1.4	1.6	.3
OTHER	33	12301	27	11800	10	4600	17	7200	1	1731	2	6212
	1.6	2.9	1.9	3.3	2.1	1.9	1.9	6.0	1.1	1.4	3.3	11.4

WAITING PERIOD BEFORE NEW EMPLOYEE IS COVERED UNDER HEALTH INSURANCE PLAN(S)

TABLE 25B

CLERICAL SERVICE

	ALL INSTITUTIONS		ALL 4-YEAR INSTITUTIONS		ALL 4-YEAR INSTITUTIONS PUBLIC		PRIVATE		UNIVERSITIES PUBLIC		PRIVATE	
	INSTS	EES	INSTS	EES	INSTS	EES	INSTS	EES	INSTS	EES	INSTS	EES
TOTAL	2061	670330	1388	601295	478	413110	910	188185	93	231299	61	94679
	100.0	100.0	100.0	100.0	100.0	100.0	100.0	100.0	100.0	100.0	100.0	100.0
NO RESPONSE	4	77	4	77	-	-	4	77	-	-	-	-
	.2	※	.3	※	-	-	.4	※	-	-	-	-
ONE MONTH OR LESS	1705	576107	1120	515819	426	378004	694	137815	84	210595	41	74245
	82.7	85.9	80.7	85.8	89.1	91.5	76.3	73.2	90.3	91.0	67.2	78.4
UNTIL STATED DATE(S) DURING FIRST YEAR EMPLOYMENT, BUT AFTER ONE MONTH OF SERVICE	89	17387	70	16521	13	8872	57	7649	4	6797	2	1507
	4.3	2.6	5.0	2.7	2.7	2.1	6.3	4.1	4.3	2.9	3.3	1.6
STATED NUMBER OF MONTHS	232	59009	169	51538	33	18122	136	33416	5	8325	15	10815
	11.3	8.8	12.2	8.6	6.9	4.4	14.9	17.8	5.4	3.6	24.6	11.4
OTHER	42	20644	36	20234	8	9269	28	10965	1	6242	3	8112
	2.0	3.1	2.6	3.4	1.7	2.2	3.1	5.8	1.1	2.7	4.9	8.6

4-YEAR LIBERAL ARTS COLLEGES				OTHER 4-YEAR COLLEGES				ALL 2-YEAR INSTITUTIONS		2-YEAR INSTITUTIONS			
PUBLIC		PRIVATE		PUBLIC		PRIVATE				PUBLIC		PRIVATE	
INSTS	EES	INSTS	EES	INSTS	EES	INSTS	EES	INSTS	EES	INSTS	EES	INSTS	EES
341	109911	678	56658	44	10502	173	9704	673	68886	595	66689	78	2197
100.0	100.0	100.0	100.0	100.0	100.0	100.0	100.0	100.0	100.0	100.0	100.0	100.0	100.0
1	509	1	14	-	-	2	32	2	185	2	185	-	-
.3	.5	.1	⁜	-	-	1.2	.3	.3	.3	.3	.3	-	-
310	101006	610	50544	36	7837	144	8617	598	61485	530	59576	68	1909
90.9	91.8	90.0	89.2	81.8	74.6	83.2	88.8	88.9	89.3	89.1	89.3	87.2	86.9
6	1424	27	3350	2	39	9	186	17	954	12	846	5	108
1.8	1.3	4.0	5.9	4.5	.4	5.2	1.9	2.5	1.4	2.0	1.3	6.4	4.9
16	4130	35	3120	5	2599	13	746	51	6563	48	6522	3	41
4.7	3.8	5.2	5.5	11.4	24.7	7.5	7.7	7.6	9.5	8.1	9.8	3.8	1.9
8	2842	9	858	1	27	6	130	6	501	4	362	2	139
2.3	2.6	1.3	1.5	2.3	.3	3.5	1.3	.9	.7	.7	.5	2.6	6.3

4-YEAR LIBERAL ARTS COLLEGES				OTHER 4-YEAR COLLEGES				ALL 2-YEAR INSTITUTIONS		2-YEAR INSTITUTIONS			
PUBLIC		PRIVATE		PUBLIC		PRIVATE				PUBLIC		PRIVATE	
INSTS	EES	INSTS	EES	INSTS	EES	INSTS	EES	INSTS	EES	INSTS	EES	INSTS	EES
341	153051	677	76615	44	28760	172	16891	673	69035	596	66620	77	2415
100.0	100.0	100.0	100.0	100.0	100.0	100.0	100.0	100.0	100.0	100.0	100.0	100.0	100.0
-	-	1	15	-	-	3	62	-	-	-	-	-	-
-	-	.1	⁜	-	-	1.7	.4	-	-	-	-	-	-
307	143378	525	50814	35	24031	128	12756	585	60288	521	58316	64	1972
90.0	93.7	77.5	66.3	79.6	83.6	74.4	75.5	86.9	87.3	87.4	87.5	83.1	81.7
7	2008	40	5593	2	67	15	549	19	866	13	706	6	160
2.1	1.3	5.9	7.3	4.5	.2	8.7	3.3	2.8	1.3	2.2	1.1	7.8	6.6
21	5135	100	19257	7	4662	21	3344	63	7471	58	7312	5	159
6.2	3.4	14.8	25.1	15.9	16.2	12.2	19.8	9.4	10.8	9.7	11.0	6.5	6.6
7	3027	17	2598	-	-	8	255	6	410	4	286	2	124
2.1	2.0	2.5	3.4	-	-	4.7	1.5	.9	.6	.7	.4	2.6	5.1

INSTITUTIONAL PAYMENT OF MEDICARE COST (PART B) FOR RETIRED EMPLOYEE

TABLE 26A

FACULTY

	ALL INSTITUTIONS		ALL 4-YEAR INSTITUTIONS		ALL 4-YEAR INSTITUTIONS PUBLIC		PRIVATE		UNIVERSITIES PUBLIC		PRIVATE	
	INSTS	EES	INSTS	EES	INSTS	EES	INSTS	EES	INSTS	EES	INSTS	EES
TOTAL	2063	431547	1390	362661	478	242041	912	120620	93	121628	61	54258
	100.0	100.0	100.0	100.0	100.0	100.0	100.0	100.0	100.0	100.0	100.0	100.0
NO RESPONSE	12	1170	6	812	1	548	5	264	-	-	-	-
	.6	.3	.4	.2	.2	.2	.5	.2	-	-	-	-
INSTITUTION PAYS ALL	228	61169	158	52367	83	44069	75	8298	14	19439	5	3227
	11.1	14.2	11.4	14.4	17.4	18.2	8.2	6.9	15.1	16.0	8.2	5.9
INSTITUTION PAYS PART	131	31067	81	26615	52	23725	29	2890	4	4988	2	597
	6.3	7.2	5.8	7.3	10.9	9.8	3.2	2.4	4.3	4.1	3.3	1.1
INSTITUTION PAYS NONE	1692	338141	1145	282867	342	173699	803	109168	75	97201	54	50434
	82.0	78.3	82.4	78.1	71.5	71.8	88.1	90.5	80.6	79.9	88.5	93.0

INSTITUTIONAL PAYMENT OF MEDICARE COST (PART B) FOR RETIRED EMPLOYEE

TABLE 26B

CLERICAL SERVICE

	ALL INSTITUTIONS		ALL 4-YEAR INSTITUTIONS		ALL 4-YEAR INSTITUTIONS PUBLIC		PRIVATE		UNIVERSITIES PUBLIC		PRIVATE	
	INSTS	EES	INSTS	EES	INSTS	EES	INSTS	EES	INSTS	EES	INSTS	EES
TOTAL	2061	670330	1388	601295	478	413110	910	188185	93	231299	61	94679
	100.0	100.0	100.0	100.0	100.0	100.0	100.0	100.0	100.0	100.0	100.0	100.0
NO RESPONSE	11	1782	6	1406	1	930	5	476	-	-	-	-
	.5	.3	.4	.2	.2	.2	.5	.3	-	-	-	-
INSTITUTION PAYS ALL	219	116996	149	108750	83	96580	66	12170	14	47098	5	6784
	10.6	17.5	10.7	18.1	17.4	23.4	7.3	6.5	15.1	20.4	8.2	7.2
INSTITUTION PAYS PART	131	44458	83	41183	53	36950	30	4233	5	15281	2	868
	6.4	6.6	6.0	6.8	11.1	8.9	3.3	2.2	5.4	6.6	3.3	.9
INSTITUTION PAYS NONE	1700	507094	1150	449956	341	278650	809	171306	74	168920	54	87027
	82.5	75.6	82.9	74.9	71.3	67.5	88.9	91.0	79.5	73.0	88.5	91.9

| 4-YEAR LIBERAL ARTS COLLEGES | | | | OTHER 4-YEAR COLLEGES | | | | ALL 2-YEAR INSTITUTIONS | | 2-YEAR INSTITUTIONS | | | |
| PUBLIC | | PRIVATE | | PUBLIC | | PRIVATE | | | | PUBLIC | | PRIVATE | |
INSTS	EES	INSTS	EES	INSTS	EES	INSTS	EES	INSTS	EES	INSTS	EES	INSTS	EES
341	109911	678	56658	44	10502	173	9704	673	68886	595	66689	78	2197
100.0	100.0	100.0	100.0	100.0	100.0	100.0	100.0	100.0	100.0	100.0	100.0	100.0	100.0
1	548	4	254	-	-	1	10	6	358	5	353	1	5
.3	.5	.6	.4	-	-	.6	.1	.9	.5	.8	.5	1.3	.2
59	22192	55	4457	10	2438	15	614	70	8802	64	8639	6	163
17.3	20.2	8.1	7.9	22.7	23.2	8.7	6.3	10.4	12.8	10.8	13.0	7.7	7.4
43	17702	23	1974	5	1035	4	319	50	4452	46	4312	4	140
12.6	16.1	3.4	3.5	11.4	9.9	2.3	3.3	7.4	6.5	7.7	6.5	5.1	6.4
238	69469	596	49973	29	7029	153	8761	547	55274	480	53385	67	1889
69.8	63.2	87.9	88.2	65.9	66.9	88.4	90.3	81.3	80.2	80.7	80.0	85.9	86.0

| 4-YEAR LIBERAL ARTS COLLEGES | | | | OTHER 4-YEAR COLLEGES | | | | ALL 2-YEAR INSTITUTIONS | | 2-YEAR INSTITUTIONS | | | |
| PUBLIC | | PRIVATE | | PUBLIC | | PRIVATE | | | | PUBLIC | | PRIVATE | |
INSTS	EES	INSTS	EES	INSTS	EES	INSTS	EES	INSTS	EES	INSTS	EES	INSTS	EES
341	153051	677	76615	44	28760	172	16891	673	69035	596	66620	77	2415
100.0	100.0	100.0	100.0	100.0	100.0	100.0	100.0	100.0	100.0	100.0	100.0	100.0	100.0
1	930	4	468	-	-	1	8	5	376	4	372	1	4
.3	.6	.6	.6	-	-	.6	*	.7	.5	.7	.6	1.3	.2
59	41300	48	4786	10	8182	13	600	70	8246	64	8033	6	213
17.3	27.0	7.1	6.2	22.7	28.4	7.6	3.6	10.4	11.9	10.7	12.1	7.8	8.8
43	18269	26	3060	5	3400	2	305	48	3275	44	3135	4	140
12.6	11.9	3.8	4.0	11.4	11.8	1.2	1.8	7.1	4.7	7.4	4.7	5.2	5.8
238	92552	599	68301	29	17178	156	15978	550	57138	484	55080	66	2058
69.8	60.5	88.5	89.2	65.9	59.8	90.6	94.6	81.8	82.9	81.2	82.6	85.7	85.2

INSTITUTIONS PROVIDING GROUP HEALTH INSURANCE COVERAGE FOR EMPLOYEES AFTER RETIREMENT

TABLE 27A

FACULTY

| | ALL INSTITUTIONS | | ALL 4-YEAR INSTITUTIONS | | ALL 4-YEAR INSTITUTIONS | | | | UNIVERSITIES | | | |
| | | | | | PUBLIC | | PRIVATE | | PUBLIC | | PRIVATE | |
	INSTS	EES	INSTS	EES	INSTS	EES	INSTS	EES	INSTS	EES	INSTS	EES
TOTAL	2063	431547	1390	362661	478	242041	912	120620	93	121628	61	5425&
	100.0	100.0	100.0	100.0	100.0	100.0	100.0	100.0	100.0	100.0	100.0	100.0
NO RESPONSE	14	2529	6	1993	3	1694	3	299	1	1267	-	
	.7	.6	.4	.5	.6	.7	.3	.2	1.1	1.0	-	
CONTINUATION AFTER RETIREMENT	1152	336106	816	296259	399	215560	417	80699	83	111960	48	4606;
	55.8	77.9	58.7	81.7	83.5	89.1	45.7	67.0	89.2	92.1	78.7	84.9
NO CONTINUATION AFTER RETIREMENT	897	92912	568	64409	76	24787	492	39622	9	8401	13	819(
	43.5	21.5	40.9	17.8	15.9	10.2	54.0	32.8	9.7	6.9	21.3	15.1

INSTITUTIONS PROVIDING GROUP HEALTH INSURANCE COVERAGE FOR EMPLOYEES AFTER RETIREMENT

TABLE 27B

CLERICAL SERVICE

| | ALL INSTITUTIONS | | ALL 4-YEAR INSTITUTIONS | | ALL 4-YEAR INSTITUTIONS | | | | UNIVERSITIES | | | |
| | | | | | PUBLIC | | PRIVATE | | PUBLIC | | PRIVATE | |
	INSTS	EES	INSTS	EES	INSTS	EES	INSTS	EES	INSTS	EES	INSTS	EES
TOTAL	2061	670330	1388	601295	478	413110	910	188185	93	231299	61	94679
	100.0	100.0	100.0	100.0	100.0	100.0	100.0	100.0	100.0	100.0	100.0	100.0
NO RESPONSE	13	1102	5	554	2	320	3	234	-	-	-	
	.6	.2	.4	.1	.4	.1	.3	.1	-	-	-	
CONTINUATION AFTER RETIREMENT	1128	542829	796	501327	405	375142	391	126185	85	213324	46	80421
	54.8	80.9	57.3	83.4	84.7	90.8	43.0	67.1	91.4	92.2	75.4	84.9
NO CONTINUATION AFTER RETIREMENT	920	126399	587	99414	71	37648	516	61766	8	17975	15	14258
	44.6	18.9	42.3	16.5	14.9	9.1	56.7	32.8	8.6	7.8	24.6	15.1

4-YEAR LIBERAL ARTS COLLEGES				OTHER 4-YEAR COLLEGES				ALL 2-YEAR INSTITUTIONS		2-YEAR INSTITUTIONS			
PUBLIC		PRIVATE		PUBLIC		PRIVATE				PUBLIC		PRIVATE	
INSTS	EES	INSTS	EES	INSTS	EES	INSTS	EES	INSTS	EES	INSTS	EES	INSTS	EES
341	109911	678	56658	44	10502	173	9704	673	68886	595	66689	78	2197
100.0	100.0	100.0	100.0	100.0	100.0	100.0	100.0	100.0	100.0	100.0	100.0	100.0	100.0
2	427	3	299	-	-	-	-	8	536	7	484	1	52
.6	.4	.4	.5	-	-	-	-	1.2	.8	1.2	.7	1.3	2.4
282	94138	294	29825	34	9462	75	4812	336	39847	311	39062	25	785
82.7	85.6	43.4	52.7	77.3	90.1	43.4	49.6	49.9	57.8	52.2	58.6	32.1	35.7
57	15346	381	26534	10	1040	98	4892	329	28503	277	27143	52	1360
16.7	14.0	56.2	46.8	22.7	9.9	56.6	50.4	48.9	41.4	46.6	40.7	66.6	61.9

4-YEAR LIBERAL ARTS COLLEGES				OTHER 4-YEAR COLLEGES				ALL 2-YEAR INSTITUTIONS		2-YEAR INSTITUTIONS			
PUBLIC		PRIVATE		PUBLIC		PRIVATE				PUBLIC		PRIVATE	
INSTS	EES	INSTS	EES	INSTS	EES	INSTS	EES	INSTS	EES	INSTS	EES	INSTS	EES
341	153051	677	76615	44	28760	172	16891	673	69035	596	66620	77	2415
100.0	100.0	100.0	100.0	100.0	100.0	100.0	100.0	100.0	100.0	100.0	100.0	100.0	100.0
2	320	3	234	-	-	-	-	8	548	7	471	1	77
.6	.2	.4	.3	-	-	-	-	1.2	.8	1.2	.7	1.3	3.2
284	135217	278	38902	36	26601	67	6862	332	41502	308	40694	24	808
83.3	88.4	41.1	50.8	81.8	92.5	39.0	40.6	49.3	60.1	51.7	61.1	31.2	33.5
55	17514	396	37479	8	2159	105	10029	333	26985	281	25455	52	1530
16.1	11.4	58.5	48.9	18.2	7.5	61.0	59.4	49.5	39.1	47.1	38.2	67.5	63.3

SERVICE AND/OR AGE REQUIREMENTS FOR ELIGIBILITY FOR GROUP HEALTH INSURANCE COVERAGE DURING RETIREMENT

TABLE 28A

FACULTY

	ALL INSTITUTIONS		ALL 4-YEAR INSTITUTIONS		ALL 4-YEAR INSTITUTIONS PUBLIC		ALL 4-YEAR INSTITUTIONS PRIVATE		UNIVERSITIES PUBLIC		UNIVERSITIES PRIVATE	
	INSTS	EES	INSTS	EES	INSTS	EES	INSTS	EES	INSTS	EES	INSTS	EES
TOTAL	1152	336106	816	296259	399	215560	417	80699	83	111960	48	46062
	100.0	100.0	100.0	100.0	100.0	100.0	100.0	100.0	100.0	100.0	100.0	100.0
NO RESPONSE	18	5115	16	5032	13	4884	3	148	2	2131	-	
	1.6	1.5	2.0	1.7	3.3	2.3	.7	.2	2.4	1.9	-	
SERVICE AND/OR AGE REQUIREMENTS	602	186391	408	161659	217	123673	191	37986	48	69508	26	20362
	52.2	55.5	50.0	54.6	54.3	57.3	45.8	47.1	57.8	62.1	54.2	44.2
NO SERVICE AND/OR AGE REQUIREMENTS	532	144600	392	129568	169	87003	223	42565	33	40321	22	25700
	46.2	43.0	48.0	43.7	42.4	40.4	53.5	52.7	39.8	36.0	45.8	55.8

SERVICE AND/OR AGE REQUIREMENTS FOR ELIGIBILITY FOR GROUP HEALTH INSURANCE COVERAGE DURING RETIREMENT

TABLE 28B

CLERICAL SERVICE

	ALL INSTITUTIONS		ALL 4-YEAR INSTITUTIONS		ALL 4-YEAR INSTITUTIONS PUBLIC		ALL 4-YEAR INSTITUTIONS PRIVATE		UNIVERSITIES PUBLIC		UNIVERSITIES PRIVATE	
	INSTS	EES	INSTS	EES	INSTS	EES	INSTS	EES	INSTS	EES	INSTS	EES
TOTAL	1128	542829	796	501327	405	375142	391	126185	85	213324	46	80421
	100.0	100.0	100.0	100.0	100.0	100.0	100.0	100.0	100.0	100.0	100.0	100.0
NO RESPONSE	18	8233	16	8174	13	7932	3	242	2	3616	-	-
	1.6	1.5	2.0	1.6	3.2	2.1	.8	.2	2.4	1.7	-	-
SERVICE AND/OR AGE REQUIREMENTS	594	304423	401	276665	224	218843	177	57822	51	131040	26	37180
	52.7	56.1	50.4	55.2	55.3	58.4	45.3	45.8	60.0	61.4	56.5	46.2
NO SERVICE AND/OR AGE REQUIREMENTS	516	230173	379	216488	168	148367	211	68121	32	78668	20	43241
	45.7	42.4	47.6	43.2	41.5	39.5	53.9	54.0	37.6	36.9	43.5	53.8

| 4-YEAR LIBERAL ARTS COLLEGES | | | | OTHER 4-YEAR COLLEGES | | | | ALL 2-YEAR INSTITUTIONS | | 2-YEAR INSTITUTIONS | | | |
| PUBLIC | | PRIVATE | | PUBLIC | | PRIVATE | | | | PUBLIC | | PRIVATE | |
INSTS	EES	INSTS	EES	INSTS	EES	INSTS	EES	INSTS	EES	INSTS	EES	INSTS	EES
282	94138	294	29825	34	9462	75	4812	336	39847	311	39062	25	785
100.0	100.0	100.0	100.0	100.0	100.0	100.0	100.0	100.0	100.0	100.0	100.0	100.0	100.0
11	2753	3	148	-	-	-	-	2	83	2	83	-	-
3.9	2.9	1.0	.5	-	-	-	-	.6	.2	.6	.2	-	-
147	49684	140	15325	22	4481	25	2299	194	24732	183	24385	11	347
52.1	52.8	47.6	51.4	64.7	47.4	33.3	47.8	57.7	62.1	58.9	62.4	44.0	44.2
124	41701	151	14352	12	4981	50	2513	140	15032	126	14594	14	438
44.0	44.3	51.4	48.1	35.3	52.6	66.7	52.2	41.7	37.7	40.5	37.4	56.0	55.8

| 4-YEAR LIBERAL ARTS COLLEGES | | | | OTHER 4-YEAR COLLEGES | | | | ALL 2-YEAR INSTITUTIONS | | 2-YEAR INSTITUTIONS | | | |
| PUBLIC | | PRIVATE | | PUBLIC | | PRIVATE | | | | PUBLIC | | PRIVATE | |
INSTS	EES	INSTS	EES	INSTS	EES	INSTS	EES	INSTS	EES	INSTS	EES	INSTS	EES
284	135217	278	38902	36	26601	67	6862	332	41502	308	40694	24	808
100.0	100.0	100.0	100.0	100.0	100.0	100.0	100.0	100.0	100.0	100.0	100.0	100.0	100.0
11	4316	3	242	-	-	-	-	2	59	2	59	-	-
3.9	3.2	1.1	.6	-	-	-	-	.6	.1	.6	.1	-	-
149	71804	129	17219	24	15999	22	3423	193	27758	183	27448	10	310
52.4	53.1	46.4	44.3	66.7	60.1	32.8	49.9	58.1	66.9	59.5	67.5	41.7	38.4
124	59097	146	21441	12	10602	45	3439	137	13685	123	13187	14	498
43.7	43.7	52.5	55.1	33.3	39.9	67.2	50.1	41.3	33.0	39.9	32.4	58.3	61.6

EMPLOYER-EMPLOYEE CONTRIBUTIONS TOWARD COST OF RETIRED GROUP
HEALTH INSURANCE COVERAGE
FOR RETIRED EMPLOYEES AND RETIREES' DEPENDENTS

TABLE 29A

FACULTY					ALL 4-YEAR INSTITUTIONS				UNIVERSITIES			
	ALL INSTITUTIONS		ALL 4-YEAR INSTITUTIONS		PUBLIC		PRIVATE		PUBLIC		PRIVATE	
	INSTS	EES	INSTS	EES	INSTS	EES	INSTS	EES	INSTS	EES	INSTS	EE
TOTAL	1152	336106	816	296259	399	215560	417	80699	83	111960	48	4606
	100.0	100.0	100.0	100.0	100.0	100.0	100.0	100.0	100.0	100.0	100.0	100.
EMPLOYEE COVERAGE												
EMPLOYER PAYS	370	103908	246	87985	97	51375	149	36610	20	27660	18	2259
FULL COST	32.1	30.9	30.1	29.7	24.3	23.8	35.7	45.4	24.1	24.7	37.5	49.
EMPLOYER AND EMPLOYEE	277	98764	207	89413	122	66958	85	22455	19	25368	18	1485
SHARE COST	24.0	29.4	25.4	30.2	30.6	31.1	20.4	27.8	22.9	22.7	37.5	32.
EMPLOYEE PAYS	494	131837	357	117757	177	96554	180	21203	44	58932	12	861
FULL COST	42.9	39.2	43.8	39.7	44.4	44.8	43.2	26.3	53.0	52.6	25.0	18.
NO RESPONSE	11	1597	6	1104	3	673	3	431	-	-	-	
	1.0	.5	.7	.4	.7	.3	.7	.5	-	-	-	
DEPENDENT'S COVERAGE												
EMPLOYER PAYS	193	55336	117	45236	37	21200	80	24036	10	14844	10	1681
FULL COST	16.8	16.5	14.3	15.3	9.3	9.8	19.2	29.8	12.0	13.3	20.8	36.
EMPLOYER AND EMPLOYEE	304	109780	220	98960	146	80297	74	18663	21	28744	15	1147
SHARE COST	26.4	32.7	27.0	33.4	36.6	37.3	17.7	23.1	25.3	25.7	31.3	24.
EMPLOYEE PAYS	623	164865	454	146840	209	110864	245	35976	51	67363	22	1699
FULL COST	54.1	49.1	55.6	49.6	52.4	51.4	58.8	44.6	61.4	60.2	45.8	36.
NO RESPONSE	32	6125	25	5223	7	3199	18	2024	1	1009	1	77
	2.7	1.7	3.1	1.7	1.7	1.5	4.3	2.5	1.3	.8	2.1	1.

4-YEAR LIBERAL ARTS COLLEGES				OTHER 4-YEAR COLLEGES				ALL 2-YEAR INSTITUTIONS		2-YEAR INSTITUTIONS			
PUBLIC		PRIVATE		PUBLIC		PRIVATE				PUBLIC		PRIVATE	
INSTS	EES	INSTS	EES	INSTS	EES	INSTS	EES	INSTS	EES	INSTS	EES	INSTS	EES
282	94138	294	29825	34	9462	75	4812	336	39847	311	39062	25	785
100.0	100.0	100.0	100.0	100.0	100.0	100.0	100.0	100.0	100.0	100.0	100.0	100.0	100.0
68	21379	105	11339	9	2336	26	2676	124	15923	121	15788	3	135
24.1	22.7	35.7	38.0	26.5	24.7	34.7	55.6	36.9	40.0	38.9	40.4	12.0	17.2
92	38311	54	6525	11	3279	13	1076	70	9351	67	9232	3	119
32.6	40.7	18.4	21.9	32.4	34.7	17.3	22.4	20.8	23.5	21.5	23.6	12.0	15.2
119	33775	132	11530	14	3847	36	1060	137	14080	120	13587	17	493
42.2	35.9	44.9	38.7	41.2	40.7	48.0	22.0	40.8	35.3	38.6	34.8	68.0	62.8
3	673	3	431	-	-	-	-	5	493	3	455	2	38
1.1	.7	1.0	1.4	.1	.1	-	-	1.5	1.2	1.0	1.2	8.0	4.8
24	5975	51	5423	3	381	19	1795	76	10100	74	9978	2	122
8.5	6.3	17.3	18.2	8.8	4.0	25.3	37.3	22.6	25.3	23.8	25.5	8.0	15.5
111	47210	46	5617	14	4343	13	1567	84	10820	80	10688	4	132
39.4	50.1	15.6	18.8	41.2	45.9	17.3	32.6	25.0	27.2	25.7	27.4	16.0	16.8
141	38763	184	17634	17	4738	39	1352	169	18025	151	17524	18	501
50.0	41.2	62.6	59.1	50.0	50.1	52.0	28.1	50.3	45.2	48.6	44.9	72.0	63.8
6	2190	13	1151	-	-	4	98	7	902	6	872	1	30
2.1	2.4	4.5	3.9	-	-	5.4	2.0	2.1	2.3	1.9	2.2	4.0	3.9

EMPLOYER-EMPLOYEE CONTRIBUTIONS TOWARD COST OF RETIRED GROUP HEALTH INSURANCE COVERAGE FOR RETIRED EMPLOYEES AND RETIREES' DEPENDENTS

TABLE 29B

CLERICAL SERVICE	ALL INSTITUTIONS		ALL 4-YEAR INSTITUTIONS		ALL 4-YEAR INSTITUTIONS PUBLIC		ALL 4-YEAR INSTITUTIONS PRIVATE		UNIVERSITIES PUBLIC		UNIVERSITIES PRIVATE	
	INSTS	EES	INSTS	EES	INSTS	EES	INSTS	EES	INSTS	EES	INSTS	EE
TOTAL	1128	542829	796	501327	405	375142	391	126185	85	213324	46	8042
	100.0	100.0	100.0	100.0	100.0	100.0	100.0	100.0	100.0	100.0	100.0	100.
EMPLOYEE COVERAGE												
EMPLOYER PAYS FULL COST	351	151950	230	132997	97	82324	133	50673	20	47093	16	3057
	31.1	28.0	28.9	26.5	24.0	21.9	34.0	40.2	23.5	22.1	34.8	38.
EMPLOYER AND EMPLOYEE SHARE COST	274	170498	205	162213	126	120650	79	41563	20	55338	18	3299
	24.3	31.4	25.8	32.4	31.1	32.2	20.2	32.9	23.5	25.9	39.1	41.
EMPLOYEE PAYS FULL COST	493	218629	355	204776	180	171571	175	33205	45	110893	12	1685
	43.7	40.3	44.6	40.8	44.4	45.7	44.8	26.3	52.9	52.0	26.1	21.
NO RESPONSE	10	1752	6	1341	2	597	4	744	-	-	-	
	.9	.3	.7	.3	.5	.2	1.0	.6	.1	-	-	
DEPENDENT'S COVERAGE												
EMPLOYER PAYS FULL COST	181	75227	107	64174	37	32796	70	31378	10	25758	8	2077
	16.0	13.9	13.4	12.8	9.1	8.7	17.9	24.9	11.8	12.1	17.4	25.
EMPLOYER AND EMPLOYEE SHARE COST	298	184532	215	174586	147	141260	68	33326	20	58458	15	2425
	26.4	34.0	27.0	34.8	36.3	37.7	17.4	26.4	23.5	27.4	32.6	30.
EMPLOYEE PAYS FULL COST	616	272908	449	253222	214	196373	235	56849	53	126011	22	3239
	54.6	50.3	56.4	50.5	52.8	52.3	60.1	45.1	62.4	59.1	47.8	40.
NO RESPONSE	33	10162	25	9345	7	4713	18	4632	2	3097	1	300
	3.0	1.8	3.2	1.9	1.8	1.3	4.6	3.6	2.3	1.4	2.2	3.

4-YEAR LIBERAL ARTS COLLEGES				OTHER 4-YEAR COLLEGES				ALL 2-YEAR INSTITUTIONS		2-YEAR INSTITUTIONS			
PUBLIC		PRIVATE		PUBLIC		PRIVATE				PUBLIC		PRIVATE	
INSTS	EES	INSTS	EES	INSTS	EES	INSTS	EES	INSTS	EES	INSTS	EES	INSTS	EES
284	135217	278	38902	36	26601	67	6862	332	41502	308	40694	24	808
100.0	100.0	100.0	100.0	100.0	100.0	100.0	100.0	100.0	100.0	100.0	100.0	100.0	100.0
68	28050	93	14643	9	7181	24	5456	121	18953	119	18941	2	12
23.9	20.7	33.5	37.6	25.0	27.0	35.8	79.5	36.4	45.7	38.6	46.5	8.3	1.5
95	56796	52	8209	11	8516	9	359	69	8285	66	8118	3	167
33.5	42.0	18.7	21.1	30.6	32.0	13.4	5.2	20.8	20.0	21.4	19.9	12.5	20.7
119	49774	129	15306	16	10904	34	1047	138	13853	120	13277	18	576
41.9	36.8	46.4	39.3	44.4	41.0	50.7	15.3	41.6	33.4	39.0	32.6	75.0	71.3
2	597	4	744	-	-	-	-	4	411	3	358	1	53
.7	.5	1.4	2.0	-	-	.1	-	1.2	.9	1.0	1.0	4.2	6.5
24	6188	44	6731	3	850	18	3875	74	11053	73	11045	1	8
8.5	4.6	15.8	17.3	8.3	3.2	26.9	56.5	22.3	26.6	23.7	27.1	4.2	1.0
113	71051	46	7450	14	11751	7	1618	83	9946	80	9837	3	109
39.8	52.5	16.5	19.2	38.9	44.2	10.4	23.6	25.0	24.0	26.0	24.2	12.5	13.5
142	56362	174	23137	19	14000	39	1321	167	19686	148	19048	19	638
50.0	41.7	62.6	59.5	52.8	52.6	58.2	19.3	50.3	47.4	48.1	46.8	79.2	79.0
5	1616	14	1584	-	-	3	48	8	817	7	764	1	53
1.7	1.2	5.1	4.0	-	-	4.5	.6	2.4	2.0	2.2	1.9	4.1	6.5

SHORT-TERM DISABILITY INCOME PLANS IN EFFECT

TABLE 30A

FACULTY

| | ALL INSTITUTIONS | | ALL 4-YEAR INSTITUTIONS | | ALL 4-YEAR INSTITUTIONS | | | | UNIVERSITIES | | | |
| | | | | | PUBLIC | | PRIVATE | | PUBLIC | | PRIVATE | |
	INSTS	EES	INSTS	EES	INSTS	EES	INSTS	EES	INSTS	EES	INSTS	EE
TOTAL	2092	432402	1407	363203	478	242041	929	121162	93	121628	61	5425
	100.0	100.0	100.0	100.0	100.0	100.0	100.0	100.0	100.0	100.0	100.0	100
FORMAL	1438	331639	903	273210	398	196955	505	76255	73	93811	44	3499
	68.7	76.7	64.2	75.2	83.3	81.4	54.4	62.9	78.5	77.1	72.1	64
INFORMAL	464	88455	374	82009	69	41125	305	40884	19	25665	16	1888
	22.2	20.5	26.6	22.6	14.4	17.0	32.8	33.7	20.4	21.1	26.2	34
WORKMEN'S COMP.	2092	432402	1407	363203	478	242041	929	121162	93	121628	61	5425
	100.0	100.0	100.0	100.0	100.0	100.0	100.0	100.0	100.0	100.0	100.0	100
GROUP INSURANCE	300	72198	194	59434	82	48525	112	10909	13	21222	7	504
	14.3	16.7	13.8	16.4	17.2	20.0	12.1	9.0	14.0	17.4	11.5	9
OTHER	72	17657	51	13948	14	8114	37	5834	1	933	4	214
	3.4	4.1	3.6	3.8	2.9	3.4	4.0	4.8	1.1	.8	6.6	3

SHORT-TERM DISABILITY INCOME PLANS IN EFFECT

TABLE 30B

CLERICAL SERVICE

| | ALL INSTITUTIONS | | ALL 4-YEAR INSTITUTIONS | | ALL 4-YEAR INSTITUTIONS | | | | UNIVERSITIES | | | |
| | | | | | PUBLIC | | PRIVATE | | PUBLIC | | PRIVATE | |
	INSTS	EES	INSTS	EES	INSTS	EES	INSTS	EES	INSTS	EES	INSTS	EE
TOTAL	2092	670941	1407	601711	478	413110	929	188601	93	231299	61	9467
	100.0	100.0	100.0	100.0	100.0	100.0	100.0	100.0	100.0	100.0	100.0	100.
FORMAL	1596	605865	1036	546745	438	384095	598	162650	86	212764	56	9089
	76.3	90.3	73.6	90.9	91.6	93.0	64.4	86.2	92.5	92.0	91.8	96.
INFORMAL	291	37755	226	33518	24	15470	202	18048	5	10351	3	313
	13.9	5.6	16.1	5.6	5.0	3.7	21.7	9.6	5.4	4.5	4.9	3.
WORKMEN'S COMP.	2092	670941	1407	601711	478	413110	929	188601	93	231299	61	9467
	100.0	100.0	100.0	100.0	100.0	100.0	100.0	100.0	100.0	100.0	100.0	100.
GROUP INSURANCE	327	146861	220	133027	91	106856	129	26171	15	55719	9	1296
	15.6	21.9	15.6	22.1	19.0	25.9	13.9	13.9	16.1	24.1	14.8	13.
OTHER	84	27019	63	23368	14	10692	49	12676	1	1115	5	441
	4.0	4.0	4.5	3.9	2.9	2.6	5.3	6.7	1.1	.5	8.2	4.

4-YEAR LIBERAL ARTS COLLEGES				OTHER 4-YEAR COLLEGES				ALL 2-YEAR INSTITUTIONS		2-YEAR INSTITUTIONS			
PUBLIC		PRIVATE		PUBLIC		PRIVATE				PUBLIC		PRIVATE	
INSTS	EES	INSTS	EES	INSTS	EES	INSTS	EES	INSTS	EES	INSTS	EES	INSTS	EES
341	109911	686	57084	44	10502	182	9820	685	69199	600	66915	85	2284
100.0	100.0	100.0	100.0	100.0	100.0	100.0	100.0	100.0	100.0	100.0	100.0	100.0	100.0
288	94303	376	35153	37	8841	85	6105	535	58429	495	57124	40	1305
84.5	85.8	54.8	61.6	84.1	84.2	46.7	62.2	78.1	84.4	82.5	85.4	47.1	57.1
44	13770	232	19784	6	1690	57	2218	90	6446	63	5713	27	733
12.9	12.5	33.8	34.7	13.6	16.1	31.3	22.6	13.1	9.3	10.5	8.5	31.8	32.1
341	109911	686	57084	44	10502	182	9820	685	69199	600	66915	85	2284
100.0	100.0	100.0	100.0	100.0	100.0	100.0	100.0	100.0	100.0	100.0	100.0	100.0	100.0
59	24504	82	5329	10	2799	23	531	106	12764	98	12503	8	261
17.3	22.3	12.0	9.3	22.7	26.7	12.6	5.4	15.5	18.4	16.3	18.7	9.4	11.4
13	7181	28	3384	-	-	5	307	21	3709	20	3669	1	40
3.8	6.5	4.1	5.9	-	-	2.7	3.1	3.1	5.4	3.3	5.5	1.2	1.8

4-YEAR LIBERAL ARTS COLLEGES				OTHER 4-YEAR COLLEGES				ALL 2-YEAR INSTITUTIONS		2-YEAR INSTITUTIONS			
PUBLIC		PRIVATE		PUBLIC		PRIVATE				PUBLIC		PRIVATE	
INSTS	EES	INSTS	EES	INSTS	EES	INSTS	EES	INSTS	EES	INSTS	EES	INSTS	EES
341	153051	686	76960	44	28760	182	16962	685	69230	600	66748	85	2482
100.0	100.0	100.0	100.0	100.0	100.0	100.0	100.0	100.0	100.0	100.0	100.0	100.0	100.0
312	146077	445	59695	40	25254	97	12057	560	59120	521	57949	39	1171
91.5	95.4	64.9	77.6	90.9	87.8	53.3	71.1	81.8	85.4	86.8	86.8	45.9	47.2
18	3995	154	12783	1	1124	45	2135	65	4237	39	3519	26	718
5.3	2.6	22.4	16.6	2.3	3.9	24.7	12.6	9.5	6.1	6.5	5.3	30.6	28.9
341	153051	686	76960	44	28760	182	16962	685	69230	600	66748	85	2482
100.0	100.0	100.0	100.0	100.0	100.0	100.0	100.0	100.0	100.0	100.0	100.0	100.0	100.0
64	41019	95	12333	12	10118	25	870	107	13834	99	13559	8	275
18.8	26.8	13.8	16.0	27.3	35.2	13.7	5.1	15.6	20.0	16.5	20.3	9.4	11.1
13	9577	36	6911	-	-	8	1355	21	3651	20	3616	1	35
3.8	6.3	5.2	9.0	-	-	4.4	8.0	3.1	5.3	3.3	5.4	1.2	1.4

SHORT-TERM DISABILITY INCOME PLANS:
EMPLOYER-EMPLOYEE CONTRIBUTIONS TOWARD COST OF PLAN
TABLE 31A

FACULTY

	ALL INSTITUTIONS		ALL 4-YEAR INSTITUTIONS		ALL 4-YEAR INSTITUTIONS PUBLIC		PRIVATE		UNIVERSITIES PUBLIC		PRIVATE	
	INSTS	EES	INSTS	EES	INSTS	EES	INSTS	EES	INSTS	EES	INSTS	EE
TOTAL	2092	432402	1407	363203	478	242041	929	121162	93	121628	61	5425
	100.0	100.0	100.0	100.0	100.0	100.0	100.0	100.0	100.0	100.0	100.0	100.
NO RESPONSE	122	9799	81	8138	15	5473	66	2665	4	3882	-	
	5.8	2.3	5.8	2.2	3.1	2.3	7.1	2.2	4.3	3.2	-	
EMPLOYER PAYS FULL COST	1739	367512	1174	307756	399	202216	775	105540	79	103226	54	4957
	83.2	85.0	83.4	84.8	83.5	83.5	83.4	87.1	84.9	84.9	88.5	91.
EMPLOYER AND EMPLOYEE SHARE COST	231	55091	152	47309	64	34352	88	12957	10	14520	7	468.
	11.0	12.7	10.8	13.0	13.4	14.2	9.5	10.7	10.8	11.9	11.5	8.
EMPLOYEE PAYS FULL COST	-	-	-	-	-	-	-	-	-	-	-	
	-	-	-	-	-	-	-	-	-	-	-	

SHORT-TERM DISABILITY INCOME PLANS:
EMPLOYER-EMPLOYEE CONTRIBUTIONS TOWARD COST OF PLAN
TABLE 31B

CLERICAL SERVICE

	ALL INSTITUTIONS		ALL 4-YEAR INSTITUTIONS		ALL 4-YEAR INSTITUTIONS PUBLIC		PRIVATE		UNIVERSITIES PUBLIC		PRIVATE	
	INSTS	EES	INSTS	EES	INSTS	EES	INSTS	EES	INSTS	EES	INSTS	EES
TOTAL	2092	670941	1407	601711	478	413110	929	188601	93	231299	61	9467
	100.0	100.0	100.0	100.0	100.0	100.0	100.0	100.0	100.0	100.0	100.0	100.
NO RESPONSE	121	12051	80	10277	15	7647	65	2630	4	6306	-	
	5.8	1.8	5.7	1.7	3.1	1.9	7.0	1.4	4.3	2.7	-	
EMPLOYER PAYS FULL COST	1725	534655	1162	475128	400	324047	762	151081	79	185653	49	7513
	82.4	79.7	82.6	79.0	83.7	78.4	82.0	80.1	84.9	80.3	80.3	79.
EMPLOYER AND EMPLOYEE SHARE COST	246	124235	165	116306	63	81416	102	34890	10	39340	12	19549
	11.8	18.5	11.7	19.3	13.2	19.7	11.0	18.5	10.8	17.0	19.7	20.6
EMPLOYEE PAYS FULL COST	-	-	-	-	-	-	-	-	-	-	-	
	-	-	-	-	-	-	-	-	-	-	-	

4-YEAR LIBERAL ARTS COLLEGES				OTHER 4-YEAR COLLEGES				ALL 2-YEAR INSTITUTIONS		2-YEAR INSTITUTIONS			
PUBLIC		PRIVATE		PUBLIC		PRIVATE				PUBLIC		PRIVATE	
INSTS	EES	INSTS	EES	INSTS	EES	INSTS	EES	INSTS	EES	INSTS	EES	INSTS	EES
341	109911	686	57084	44	10502	182	9820	685	69199	600	66915	85	2284
100.0	100.0	100.0	100.0	100.0	100.0	100.0	100.0	100.0	100.0	100.0	100.0	100.0	100.0
11	1591	43	2076	-	-	23	589	41	1661	25	1411	16	250
3.2	1.4	6.3	3.6	-	-	12.6	6.0	6.0	2.4	4.2	2.1	18.8	10.9
282	89811	578	48746	38	9179	143	7221	565	59756	504	58029	61	1727
82.7	81.8	84.2	85.4	86.4	87.4	78.6	73.5	82.5	86.4	84.0	86.7	71.8	75.7
48	18509	65	6262	6	1323	16	2010	79	7782	71	7475	8	307
14.1	16.8	9.5	11.0	13.6	12.6	8.8	20.5	11.5	11.2	11.8	11.2	9.4	13.4
-	-	-	-	-	-	-	-	-	-	-	-	-	-
-	-	-	-	-	-	-	-	-	-	-	-	-	-

4-YEAR LIBERAL ARTS COLLEGES				OTHER 4-YEAR COLLEGES				ALL 2-YEAR INSTITUTIONS		2-YEAR INSTITUTIONS			
PUBLIC		PRIVATE		PUBLIC		PRIVATE				PUBLIC		PRIVATE	
INSTS	EES	INSTS	EES	INSTS	EES	INSTS	EES	INSTS	EES	INSTS	EES	INSTS	EES
341	153051	686	76960	44	28760	182	16962	685	69230	600	66748	85	2482
100.0	100.0	100.0	100.0	100.0	100.0	100.0	100.0	100.0	100.0	100.0	100.0	100.0	100.0
10	1145	43	2208	1	196	22	.422	41	1774	25	1331	16	443
2.9	.7	6.3	2.9	2.3	.7	12.1	2.5	6.0	2.6	4.2	2.0	18.8	17.8
284	114760	569	63445	37	23634	144	12506	563	59527	503	57777	60	1750
83.3	75.0	82.9	82.4	84.1	82.2	79.1	73.7	82.2	85.9	83.8	86.6	70.6	70.6
47	37146	74	11307	6	4930	16	4034	81	7929	72	7640	9	289
13.8	24.3	10.8	14.7	13.6	17.1	8.8	23.8	11.8	11.5	12.0	11.4	10.6	11.6
-	-	-	-	-	-	-	-	-	-	-	-	-	-
-	-	-	-	-	-	-	-	-	-	-	-	-	-

SHORT-TERM DISABILITY INCOME PLANS:
WAITING PERIOD BEFORE NEW EMPLOYEE BECOMES ELIGIBLE FOR SICK PAY
BENEFITS
TABLE 32A

FACULTY

| | ALL INSTITUTIONS | | ALL 4-YEAR INSTITUTIONS | | ALL 4-YEAR INSTITUTIONS | | | | UNIVERSITIES | | | |
| | | | | | PUBLIC | | PRIVATE | | PUBLIC | | PRIVATE | |
	INSTS	EES	INSTS	EES	INSTS	EES	INSTS	EES	INSTS	EES	INSTS	EES
TOTAL	2092	432402	1407	363203	478	242041	929	121162	93	121628	61	54258
	100.0	100.0	100.0	100.0	100.0	100.0	100.0	100.0	100.0	100.0	100.0	100.0
NO RESPONSE	165	13998	117	12029	24	7287	93	4742	3	3675	1	315
	7.9	3.2	8.3	3.3	5.0	3.0	10.0	3.9	3.2	3.0	1.6	.6
1 MONTH OR LESS	1537	352236	1006	297032	388	202097	618	94935	75	100787	53	49291
	73.5	81.5	71.5	81.8	81.2	83.5	66.5	78.4	80.7	82.9	86.9	90.8
2 TO 6 MONTHS	308	53860	222	43922	53	28069	169	15853	12	14941	5	2778
	14.7	12.5	15.8	12.1	11.1	11.6	18.2	13.1	12.9	12.3	8.2	5.1
OTHER	82	12308	62	10220	13	4588	49	5632	3	2225	2	1874
	3.9	2.8	4.4	2.8	2.7	1.9	5.3	4.6	3.2	1.8	3.3	3.5

SHORT-TERM DISABILITY INCOME PLANS:
WAITING PERIOD BEFORE NEW EMPLOYEE BECOMES ELIGIBLE FOR SICK PAY
BENEFITS
TABLE 32B

CLERICAL SERVICE

| | ALL INSTITUTIONS | | ALL 4-YEAR INSTITUTIONS | | ALL 4-YEAR INSTITUTIONS | | | | UNIVERSITIES | | | |
| | | | | | PUBLIC | | PRIVATE | | PUBLIC | | PRIVATE | |
	INSTS	EES	INSTS	EES	INSTS	EES	INSTS	EES	INSTS	EES	INSTS	EES
TOTAL	2092	670941	1407	601711	478	413110	929	188601	93	231299	61	94679
	100.0	100.0	100.0	100.0	100.0	100.0	100.0	100.0	100.0	100.0	100.0	100.0
NO RESPONSE	160	20852	114	18704	27	13517	87	5187	3	6066	1	261
	7.6	3.1	8.1	3.1	5.6	3.3	9.4	2.8	3.2	2.6	1.6	.3
1 MONTH OR LESS	1324	455359	824	407540	353	315229	471	92311	67	179916	31	54255
	63.3	67.9	58.6	67.8	73.9	76.3	50.6	48.9	72.0	77.8	50.8	57.2
2 TO 6 MONTHS	518	169252	397	151796	86	76608	311	75188	21	42386	25	35470
	24.8	25.2	28.2	25.2	18.0	18.5	33.5	39.9	22.6	18.3	41.0	37.5
OTHER	90	25478	72	23671	12	7756	60	15915	2	2931	4	4693
	4.3	3.8	5.1	3.9	2.5	1.9	6.5	8.4	2.2	1.3	6.6	5.0

| | 4-YEAR LIBERAL ARTS COLLEGES | | | | OTHER 4-YEAR COLLEGES | | | | ALL 2-YEAR INSTITUTIONS | | 2-YEAR INSTITUTIONS | | | |
| | PUBLIC | | PRIVATE | | PUBLIC | | PRIVATE | | | | PUBLIC | | PRIVATE | |
INSTS	EES	INSTS	EES	INSTS	EES	INSTS	EES	INSTS	EES	INSTS	EES	INSTS	EES
341	109911	686	57084	44	10502	182	9820	685	69199	600	66915	85	2284
100.0	100.0	100.0	100.0	100.0	100.0	100.0	100.0	100.0	100.0	100.0	100.0	100.0	100.0
19	3196	64	3652	2	416	28	775	48	1969	27	1624	21	345
5.6	2.9	9.3	6.4	4.5	4.0	15.4	7.9	7.0	2.8	4.5	2.4	24.7	15.1
278	92720	453	39621	35	8590	112	6023	531	55204	486	53760	45	1444
81.5	84.4	66.1	69.4	79.6	81.8	61.6	61.3	77.5	79.8	81.0	80.4	52.9	63.2
36	12304	129	10216	5	824	35	2859	86	9938	72	9564	14	374
10.6	11.2	18.8	17.9	11.4	7.8	19.2	29.1	12.6	14.4	12.0	14.3	16.5	16.4
8	1691	40	3595	2	672	7	163	20	2088	15	1967	5	121
2.3	1.5	5.8	6.3	4.5	6.4	3.8	1.7	2.9	3.0	2.5	2.9	5.9	5.3

| | 4-YEAR LIBERAL ARTS COLLEGES | | | | OTHER 4-YEAR COLLEGES | | | | ALL 2-YEAR INSTITUTIONS | | 2-YEAR INSTITUTIONS | | | |
| | PUBLIC | | PRIVATE | | PUBLIC | | PRIVATE | | | | PUBLIC | | PRIVATE | |
INSTS	EES	INSTS	EES	INSTS	EES	INSTS	EES	INSTS	EES	INSTS	EES	INSTS	EES
341	153051	686	76960	44	28760	182	16962	685	69230	600	66748	85	2482
100.0	100.0	100.0	100.0	100.0	100.0	100.0	100.0	100.0	100.0	100.0	100.0	100.0	100.0
21	5672	60	3692	3	1779	26	1234	46	2148	26	1616	20	532
6.2	3.7	8.7	4.8	6.8	6.2	14.3	7.3	6.7	3.1	4.3	2.4	23.5	21.4
254	114363	347	32686	32	20950	93	5370	500	47819	458	46652	42	1167
74.5	74.8	50.6	42.4	72.8	72.9	51.1	31.7	73.0	69.1	76.4	69.9	49.4	47.1
58	31110	233	31757	7	3112	53	7961	121	17456	102	16756	19	700
17.0	20.3	34.0	41.3	15.9	10.8	29.1	46.9	17.7	25.2	17.0	25.1	22.4	28.2
8	1906	46	8825	2	2919	10	2397	18	1807	14	1724	4	83
2.3	1.2	6.7	11.5	4.5	10.1	5.5	14.1	2.6	2.6	2.3	2.6	4.7	3.3

SHORT-TERM DISABILITY INCOME PLANS:
VARIATION OF LENGTH OF SICK PAY BENEFITS ACCORDING TO LENGTH OF SERVICE

TABLE 33A

FACULTY

| | | | | | ALL 4-YEAR INSTITUTIONS | | | | UNIVERSITIES | | | |
| | ALL INSTITUTIONS | | ALL 4-YEAR INSTITUTIONS | | PUBLIC | | PRIVATE | | PUBLIC | | PRIVATE | |
	INSTS	EES	INSTS	EES	INSTS	EES	INSTS	EES	INSTS	EES	INSTS	EES
TOTAL	2092	432402	1407	363203	478	242041	929	121162	93	121628	61	54258
	100.0	100.0	100.0	100.0	100.0	100.0	100.0	100.0	100.0	100.0	100.0	100.0
NO RESPONSE	135	9394	96	7904	15	4246	81	3658	1	1544	-	-
	6.5	2.2	6.8	2.2	3.1	1.8	8.7	3.0	1.1	1.3	-	-
DURATION VARIES BY LENGTH OF SERVICE	1189	269729	776	228037	332	165279	444	62758	67	82395	33	28725
	56.8	62.4	55.2	62.8	69.5	68.2	47.8	51.8	72.0	67.7	54.1	52.9
DURATION NOT RELATED TO LENGTH OF SERVICE	768	153279	535	127262	131	72516	404	54746	25	37689	28	25533
	36.7	35.4	38.0	35.0	27.4	30.0	43.5	45.2	26.9	31.0	45.9	47.1

SHORT-TERM DISABILITY INCOME PLANS:
VARIATION OF LENGTH OF SICK PAY BENEFITS ACCORDING TO LENGTH OF SERVICE

TABLE 33B

CLERICAL SERVICE

| | | | | | ALL 4-YEAR INSTITUTIONS | | | | UNIVERSITIES | | | |
| | ALL INSTITUTIONS | | ALL 4-YEAR INSTITUTIONS | | PUBLIC | | PRIVATE | | PUBLIC | | PRIVATE | |
	INSTS	EES	INSTS	EES	INSTS	EES	INSTS	EES	INSTS	EES	INSTS	EES
TOTAL	2092	670941	1407	601711	478	413110	929	188601	93	231299	61	94679
	100.0	100.0	100.0	100.0	100.0	100.0	100.0	100.0	100.0	100.0	100.0	100.0
NO RESPONSE	129	10316	90	8629	15	5316	75	3313	1	2450	-	-
	6.2	1.5	6.4	1.4	3.1	1.3	8.1	1.8	1.1	1.1	-	-
DURATION VARIES BY LENGTH OF SERVICE	1327	487488	896	442786	364	299138	532	143648	75	175177	46	80664
	63.4	72.7	63.7	73.6	76.2	72.4	57.2	76.1	80.6	75.7	75.4	85.2
DURATION NOT RELATED TO LENGTH OF SERVICE	636	173137	421	150296	99	108656	322	41640	17	53672	15	14015
	30.4	25.8	29.9	25.0	20.7	26.3	34.7	22.1	18.3	23.2	24.6	14.8

4-YEAR LIBERAL ARTS COLLEGES				OTHER 4-YEAR COLLEGES				ALL 2-YEAR INSTITUTIONS		2-YEAR INSTITUTIONS			
PUBLIC		PRIVATE		PUBLIC		PRIVATE				PUBLIC		PRIVATE	
INSTS	EES	INSTS	EES	INSTS	EES	INSTS	EES	INSTS	EES	INSTS	EES	INSTS	EES
341	109911	686	57084	44	10502	182	9820	685	69199	600	66915	85	2284
100.0	100.0	100.0	100.0	100.0	100.0	100.0	100.0	100.0	100.0	100.0	100.0	100.0	100.0
13	2605	55	2887	1	97	26	771	39	1490	22	1184	17	306
3.8	2.4	8.0	5.1	2.3	.9	14.3	7.9	5.7	2.2	3.7	1.8	20.0	13.4
232	74510	335	29250	33	8374	76	4783	413	41692	375	40552	38	1140
68.0	67.8	48.9	51.2	75.0	79.8	41.8	48.7	60.3	60.2	62.5	60.6	44.7	49.9
96	32796	296	24947	10	2031	80	4266	233	26017	203	25179	30	838
28.2	29.8	43.1	43.7	22.7	19.3	43.9	43.4	34.0	37.6	33.8	37.6	35.3	36.7

4-YEAR LIBERAL ARTS COLLEGES				OTHER 4-YEAR COLLEGES				ALL 2-YEAR INSTITUTIONS		2-YEAR INSTITUTIONS			
PUBLIC		PRIVATE		PUBLIC		PRIVATE				PUBLIC		PRIVATE	
INSTS	EES	INSTS	EES	INSTS	EES	INSTS	EES	INSTS	EES	INSTS	EES	INSTS	EES
341	153051	686	76960	44	28760	182	16962	685	69230	600	66748	85	2482
100.0	100.0	100.0	100.0	100.0	100.0	100.0	100.0	100.0	100.0	100.0	100.0	100.0	100.0
12	2559	51	2781	2	307	24	532	39	1687	22	1214	17	473
3.5	1.7	7.4	3.6	4.5	1.1	13.2	3.1	5.7	2.4	3.7	1.8	20.0	19.1
255	103187	398	53724	34	20774	88	9260	431	44702	395	43559	36	1143
74.8	67.4	58.1	69.8	77.3	72.2	48.3	54.6	62.9	64.6	65.8	65.3	42.4	46.0
74	47305	237	20455	8	7679	70	7170	215	22841	183	21975	32	866
21.7	30.9	34.5	26.6	18.2	26.7	38.5	42.3	31.4	33.0	30.5	32.9	37.6	34.9

LONG-TERM TOTAL DISABILITY INCOME PLANS IN EFFECT
TABLE 34A

FACULTY					ALL 4-YEAR INSTITUTIONS				UNIVERSITIES			
	ALL INSTITUTIONS		ALL 4-YEAR INSTITUTIONS		PUBLIC		PRIVATE		PUBLIC		PRIVATE	
	INSTS	EES	INSTS	EES	INSTS	EES	INSTS	EES	INSTS	EES	INSTS	EES
TOTAL	2092	432402	1407	363203	478	242041	929	121162	93	121628	61	54258
	100.0	100.0	100.0	100.0	100.0	100.0	100.0	100.0	100.0	100.0	100.0	100.0
NO RESPONSE	2	57	1	10	-	-	1	10	-	-	-	-
	.1	*	.1	*	-	-	.1	*	-	-	-	-
LONG-TERM PLAN IN EFFECT	1720	404744	1150	342745	441	231840	709	110905	90	118263	59	53791
	82.2	93.6	81.7	94.4	92.3	95.8	76.3	91.5	96.8	97.2	96.7	99.1
NO PLAN IN EFFECT	370	27601	256	20448	37	10201	219	10247	3	3365	2	467
	17.7	6.4	18.2	5.6	7.7	4.2	23.6	8.5	3.2	2.8	3.3	.9

LONG-TERM TOTAL DISABILITY INCOME PLANS IN EFFECT
TABLE 34B

CLERICAL SERVICE					ALL 4-YEAR INSTITUTIONS				UNIVERSITIES			
	ALL INSTITUTIONS		ALL 4-YEAR INSTITUTIONS		PUBLIC		PRIVATE		PUBLIC		PRIVATE	
	INSTS	EES	INSTS	EES	INSTS	EES	INSTS	EES	INSTS	EES	INSTS	EES
TOTAL	2092	670941	1407	601711	478	413110	929	188601	93	231299	61	94679
	100.0	100.0	100.0	100.0	100.0	100.0	100.0	100.0	100.0	100.0	100.0	100.0
NO RESPONSE	5	326	4	250	-	-	4	250	-	-	-	-
	.2	*	.3	*	-	-	.4	.1	-	-	-	-
LONG-TERM PLAN IN EFFECT	1498	578842	946	517799	425	383005	521	134794	86	219568	42	76197
	71.6	86.3	67.2	86.1	88.9	92.7	56.1	71.5	92.5	94.9	68.9	80.5
NO PLAN IN EFFECT	589	91773	457	83662	53	30105	404	53557	7	11731	19	18482
	28.2	13.7	32.5	13.9	11.1	7.3	43.5	28.4	7.5	5.1	31.1	19.5

| 4-YEAR LIBERAL ARTS COLLEGES | | | | OTHER 4-YEAR COLLEGES | | | | ALL 2-YEAR INSTITUTIONS | | 2-YEAR INSTITUTIONS | | | |
| PUBLIC | | PRIVATE | | PUBLIC | | PRIVATE | | | | PUBLIC | | PRIVATE | |
INSTS	EES	INSTS	EES	INSTS	EES	INSTS	EES	INSTS	EES	INSTS	EES	INSTS	EES
341	109911	686	57084	44	10502	182	9820	685	69199	600	66915	85	2284
100.0	100.0	100.0	100.0	100.0	100.0	100.0	100.0	100.0	100.0	100.0	100.0	100.0	100.0
-	-	-	-	-	-	1	10	1	47	1	47	-	-
-	-	-	-	-	-	.5	.1	.1	.1	.2	.1	-	-
311	103419	521	48292	40	10158	129	8822	570	61999	524	60542	46	1457
91.2	94.1	75.9	84.6	90.9	96.7	70.9	89.8	83.3	89.6	87.3	90.4	54.1	63.8
30	6492	165	8792	4	344	52	988	114	7153	75	6326	39	827
8.8	5.9	24.1	15.4	9.1	3.3	28.6	10.1	16.6	10.3	12.5	9.5	45.9	36.2

| 4-YEAR LIBERAL ARTS COLLEGES | | | | OTHER 4-YEAR COLLEGES | | | | ALL 2-YEAR INSTITUTIONS | | 2-YEAR INSTITUTIONS | | | |
| PUBLIC | | PRIVATE | | PUBLIC | | PRIVATE | | | | PUBLIC | | PRIVATE | |
INSTS	EES	INSTS	EES	INSTS	EES	INSTS	EES	INSTS	EES	INSTS	EES	INSTS	EES
341	153051	686	76960	44	28760	182	16962	685	69230	600	66748	85	2482
100.0	100.0	100.0	100.0	100.0	100.0	100.0	100.0	100.0	100.0	100.0	100.0	100.0	100.0
-	-	3	228	-	-	1	22	1	76	1	76	-	-
-	-	.4	.3	-	-	.5	.1	.1	.1	.2	.1	-	-
300	138589	378	46407	39	24848	101	12190	552	61043	516	60038	36	1005
88.0	90.6	55.1	60.3	88.6	86.4	55.5	71.9	80.6	88.2	86.0	90.0	42.4	40.5
41	14462	305	30325	5	3912	80	4750	132	8111	83	6634	49	1477
12.0	9.4	44.5	39.4	11.4	13.6	44.0	28.0	19.3	11.7	13.8	9.9	57.6	59.5

LONG-TERM TOTAL DISABILITY INCOME PLANS: TYPES IN EFFECT

TABLE 35A

FACULTY

	ALL INSTITUTIONS		ALL 4-YEAR INSTITUTIONS		ALL 4-YEAR INSTITUTIONS PUBLIC		ALL 4-YEAR INSTITUTIONS PRIVATE		UNIVERSITIES PUBLIC		UNIVERSITIES PRIVATE	
	INSTS	EES	INSTS	EES	INSTS	EES	INSTS	EES	INSTS	EES	INSTS	EES
TOTAL	1720	404744	1150	342745	441	231840	709	110905	90	118263	59	53791
	100.0	100.0	100.0	100.0	100.0	100.0	100.0	100.0	100.0	100.0	100.0	100.0
NO RESPONSE	1	55	1	55	-	-	1	55	-	-	-	-
	.1	✧	.1	✧	-	-	.1	✧	-	-	-	-
PUBLIC EMPLOYEE OR TEACHER RETIREMENT SYSTEM	681	192659	323	149027	300	147208	23	1819	53	63894	-	-
	39.6	47.6	28.1	43.5	68.0	63.5	3.2	1.6	58.9	54.0	-	-
GROUP INSURANCE PLAN	1361	311700	961	269189	312	175284	649	93905	70	96594	49	39896
	79.1	77.0	83.6	78.5	70.7	75.6	91.5	84.7	77.8	81.7	83.1	74.2
SELF-INSURED	87	47367	68	44363	49	31670	19	12693	9	13451	7	11992
	5.1	11.7	5.9	12.9	11.1	13.7	2.7	11.4	10.0	11.4	11.9	22.3
OTHER	55	20467	44	19233	20	14736	24	4497	3	6059	4	3686
	3.2	5.1	3.8	5.6	4.5	6.4	3.4	4.1	3.3	5.1	6.8	6.9
OTH PUBLIC EMPLOYEE OR TEACHER RETIREMENT SYSTEM AND GROUP INSURANCE PLAN	395	127195	191	102075	188	101979	3	96	36	47841	-	-
	23.0	31.4	16.6	29.8	42.6	44.0	.4	.1	40.0	40.5	-	-

LONG-TERM TOTAL DISABILITY INCOME PLANS: TYPES IN EFFECT

TABLE 35B

CLERICAL SERVICE

	ALL INSTITUTIONS		ALL 4-YEAR INSTITUTIONS		ALL 4-YEAR INSTITUTIONS PUBLIC		ALL 4-YEAR INSTITUTIONS PRIVATE		UNIVERSITIES PUBLIC		UNIVERSITIES PRIVATE	
	INSTS	EES	INSTS	EES	INSTS	EES	INSTS	EES	INSTS	EES	INSTS	EES
TOTAL	1498	578842	946	517799	425	383005	521	134794	86	219568	42	76197
	100.0	100.0	100.0	100.0	100.0	100.0	100.0	100.0	100.0	100.0	100.0	100.0
NO RESPONSE	1	75	1	75	-	-	1	75	-	-	-	-
	.1	✧	.1	✧	-	-	.2	.1	-	-	-	-
PUBLIC EMPLOYEE OR TEACHER RETIREMENT SYSTEM	693	332806	338	289652	323	288603	15	1049	61	154500	-	-
	46.3	57.5	35.7	55.9	76.0	75.4	2.9	.8	70.9	70.4	-	-
GROUP INSURANCE PLAN	1081	426874	729	390013	246	274356	483	115657	59	172160	36	60432
	72.2	73.7	77.1	75.3	57.9	71.6	92.7	85.8	68.6	78.4	85.8	79.3
SELF-INSURED	75	58803	56	54330	43	41506	13	12824	7	18204	3	12033
	5.0	10.2	5.9	10.5	10.1	10.8	2.5	9.5	8.1	8.3	7.1	15.8
OTHER	45	53479	33	52044	18	46405	15	5639	3	23602	3	3732
	3.0	9.2	3.5	10.1	4.2	12.1	2.9	4.2	3.5	10.7	7.1	4.9
OTH PUBLIC EMPLOYEE OR TEACHER RETIREMENT SYSTEM AND GROUP INSURANCE PLAN	325	212382	155	192538	152	192400	3	138	36	114998	-	-
	21.7	36.7	16.4	37.2	35.8	50.2	.6	.1	41.9	52.4	-	-

4-YEAR LIBERAL ARTS COLLEGES				OTHER 4-YEAR COLLEGES				ALL 2-YEAR INSTITUTIONS		2-YEAR INSTITUTIONS			
PUBLIC		PRIVATE		PUBLIC		PRIVATE				PUBLIC		PRIVATE	
INSTS	EES	INSTS	EES	INSTS	EES	INSTS	EES	INSTS	EES	INSTS	EES	INSTS	EES
311	103419	521	48292	40	10158	129	8822	.570	61999	524	60542	46	1457
100.0	100.0	100.0	100.0	100.0	100.0	100.0	100.0	100.0	100.0	100.0	100.0	100.0	100.0
-	-	1	55	-	-	-	-	-	-	-	-	-	-
-	-	.2	.1	-	-	-	-	-	-	-	-	-	-
218	76140	12	1240	29	7174	11	579	358	43632	357	43628	1	4
70.1	73.6	2.3	2.6	72.5	70.6	8.5	6.6	62.8	70.4	68.1	72.1	2.2	.3
209	68897	493	46097	33	9793	107	7912	400	42511	359	41213	41	1298
67.2	66.6	94.6	95.5	82.5	96.4	82.9	89.7	70.2	68.6	68.5	68.1	89.1	89.1
37	17462	8	496	3	757	4	205	19	3004	18	2992	1	12
11.9	16.9	1.5	1.0	7.5	7.5	3.1	2.3	3.3	4.8	3.4	4.9	2.2	.8
16	8419	10	633	1	258	10	178	11	1234	7	1087	4	147
5.1	8.1	1.9	1.3	2.5	2.5	7.8	2.0	1.9	2.0	1.3	1.8	8.7	10.1
129	47290	1	55	23	6848	2	41	204	25120	203	25116	1	4
41.5	45.7	.2	.1	57.5	67.4	1.6	.5	35.8	40.5	38.7	41.5	2.2	.3

4-YEAR LIBERAL ARTS COLLEGES				OTHER 4-YEAR COLLEGES				ALL 2-YEAR INSTITUTIONS		2-YEAR INSTITUTIONS			
PUBLIC		PRIVATE		PUBLIC		PRIVATE				PUBLIC		PRIVATE	
INSTS	EES	INSTS	EES	INSTS	EES	INSTS	EES	INSTS	EES	INSTS	EES	INSTS	EES
300	138589	378	46407	39	24848	101	12190	552	61043	516	60038	36	1005
100.0	100.0	100.0	100.0	100.0	100.0	100.0	100.0	100.0	100.0	100.0	100.0	100.0	100.0
-	-	1	75	-	-	-	-	-	-	-	-	-	-
-	-	.3	.2	-	-	-	-	-	-	-	-	-	-
233	115660	7	820	29	18443	8	229	355	43154	354	43148	1	6
77.7	83.5	1.9	1.8	74.4	74.2	7.9	1.9	64.3	70.7	68.6	71.9	2.8	.6
165	85711	358	43376	22	16485	89	11849	352	36861	321	35958	31	903
55.0	61.8	94.7	93.5	56.4	66.3	88.1	97.2	63.8	60.4	62.2	59.9	86.1	89.9
33	20052	7	676	3	3250	3	115	19	4473	18	4470	1	3
11.0	14.5	1.9	1.5	7.7	13.1	3.0	.9	3.4	7.3	3.5	7.4	2.8	.3
14	21578	9	1804	1	1225	3	103	12	1435	8	1336	4	99
4.7	15.6	2.4	3.9	2.6	4.9	3.0	.8	2.2	2.4	1.6	2.2	11.1	9.9
103	67249	1	32	13	10153	2	106	170	19844	169	19838	1	6
34.3	48.5	.3	.1	33.3	40.9	2.0	.9	30.8	32.5	32.8	33.0	2.8	.6

LONG-TERM TOTAL DISABILITY INCOME PLANS:
LENGTH OF TIME INDIVIDUAL MUST BE TOTALLY DISABLED BEFORE TOTAL DISABILITY INCOME BEGINS

TABLE 36A

FACULTY

	ALL INSTITUTIONS		ALL 4-YEAR INSTITUTIONS		ALL 4-YEAR INSTITUTIONS PUBLIC		ALL 4-YEAR INSTITUTIONS PRIVATE		UNIVERSITIES PUBLIC		UNIVERSITIES PRIVATE	
	INSTS	EES	INSTS	EES	INSTS	EES	INSTS	EES	INSTS	EES	INSTS	E
TOTAL	1720	404744	1150	342745	441	231840	709	110905	90	118263	59	537
	100.0	100.0	100.0	100.0	100.0	100.0	100.0	100.0	100.0	100.0	100.0	100
NO RESPONSE	100	26214	62	21617	37	15019	25	6598	4	4857	1	54
	5.8	6.5	5.4	6.3	8.4	6.5	3.5	5.9	4.4	4.1	1.7	10
LESS THAN 3 MONTHS	340	71536	140	49860	97	47276	43	2584	18	21031	1	3
	19.8	17.7	12.2	14.5	22.0	20.4	6.1	2.3	20.0	17.8	1.7	
3 MONTHS	343	68394	196	53212	78	38879	118	14333	10	14918	6	61
	19.9	16.9	17.0	15.5	17.7	16.8	16.6	12.9	11.1	12.6	10.2	11
6	899	230888	726	212054	218	126508	508	85546	55	75501	50	409
	52.2	57.0	63.1	62.0	49.4	54.5	71.7	77.2	61.2	63.8	84.7	76
9	1	57	1	57	-	-	1	57	-	-	-	
	.1	*	.1	*	-	-	.1	.1	-	-	-	
12 MONTHS OR MORE	37	7655	25	5945	11	4158	14	1787	3	1956	1	9
	2.2	1.9	2.2	1.7	2.5	1.8	2.0	1.6	3.3	1.7	1.7	1

LONG-TERM TOTAL DISABILITY INCOME PLANS:
LENGTH OF TIME INDIVIDUAL MUST BE TOTALLY DISABLED BEFORE TOTAL DISABILITY INCOME BEGINS

TABLE 36B

CLERICAL SERVICE

	ALL INSTITUTIONS		ALL 4-YEAR INSTITUTIONS		ALL 4-YEAR INSTITUTIONS PUBLIC		ALL 4-YEAR INSTITUTIONS PRIVATE		UNIVERSITIES PUBLIC		UNIVERSITIES PRIVATE	
	INSTS	EES	INSTS	EES	INSTS	EES	INSTS	EES	INSTS	EES	INSTS	EE
TOTAL	1498	578842	946	517799	425	383005	521	134794	86	219568	42	7619
	100.0	100.0	100.0	100.0	100.0	100.0	100.0	100.0	100.0	100.0	100.0	100.
NO RESPONSE	150	46216	91	38282	66	30652	25	7630	7	11520	1	625
	10.0	8.0	9.6	7.4	15.5	8.0	4.8	5.7	8.1	5.2	2.4	8.
LESS THAN 3 MONTHS	349	113888	151	94206	112	91121	39	3085	22	50435	1	49
	23.3	19.7	16.0	18.2	26.4	23.8	7.5	2.3	25.6	23.0	2.4	
3 MONTHS	317	99330	181	85523	77	66489	104	19034	11	31985	6	991
	21.2	17.2	19.1	16.5	18.1	17.4	20.0	14.1	12.8	14.6	14.3	13.
6	640	301444	496	284789	154	181978	342	102811	43	119641	33	5780
	42.7	52.0	52.5	55.0	36.3	47.4	65.6	76.3	50.0	54.5	78.5	75.
9	3	2024	3	2024	1	237	2	1787	-	-	1	172
	.2	.3	.3	.4	.2	.1	.4	1.3	-	-	2.4	2.
12 MONTHS OR MORE	39	15940	24	12975	15	12528	9	447	3	5987	-	
	2.6	2.8	2.5	2.5	3.5	3.3	1.7	.3	3.5	2.7	-	

4-YEAR LIBERAL ARTS COLLEGES				OTHER 4-YEAR COLLEGES				ALL 2-YEAR INSTITUTIONS		2-YEAR INSTITUTIONS			
PUBLIC		PRIVATE		PUBLIC		PRIVATE				PUBLIC		PRIVATE	
INSTS	EES	INSTS	EES	INSTS	EES	INSTS	EES	INSTS	EES	INSTS	EES	INSTS	EES
311	103419	521	48292	40	10158	129	8822	570	61999	524	60542	46	1457
100.0	100.0	100.0	100.0	100.0	100.0	100.0	100.0	100.0	100.0	100.0	100.0	100.0	100.0
30	9949	12	878	3	213	12	320	38	4597	36	4549	2	48
9.6	9.6	2.3	1.8	7.5	2.1	9.3	3.6	6.7	7.4	6.9	7.5	4.3	3.3
73	25889	32	1699	6	356	10	525	200	21676	195	21570	5	106
23.5	25.0	6.1	3.5	15.0	3.5	7.8	6.0	35.0	34.9	37.2	35.6	10.9	7.3
56	20894	86	6902	12	3067	26	1330	147	15182	138	14950	9	232
18.0	20.2	16.5	14.3	30.0	30.2	20.2	15.1	25.8	24.5	26.3	24.7	19.6	15.9
146	45065	380	38034	17	5942	78	6562	173	18834	145	17842	28	992
47.0	43.6	73.0	78.8	42.5	58.5	60.4	74.3	30.4	30.4	27.7	29.5	60.9	68.1
-	-	1	57	-	-	-	-	-	-	-	-	-	-
-	-	.2	.1	-	-	-	-	-	-	-	-	-	-
6	1622	10	722	2	580	3	85	12	1710	10	1631	2	79
1.9	1.6	1.9	1.5	5.0	5.7	2.3	1.0	2.1	2.8	1.9	2.7	4.3	5.4

4-YEAR LIBERAL ARTS COLLEGES				OTHER 4-YEAR COLLEGES				ALL 2-YEAR INSTITUTIONS		2-YEAR INSTITUTIONS			
PUBLIC		PRIVATE		PUBLIC		PRIVATE				PUBLIC		PRIVATE	
INSTS	EES	INSTS	EES	INSTS	EES	INSTS	EES	INSTS	EES	INSTS	EES	INSTS	EES
300	138589	378	46407	39	24848	101	12190	552	61043	516	60038	36	1005
100.0	100.0	100.0	100.0	100.0	100.0	100.0	100.0	100.0	100.0	100.0	100.0	100.0	100.0
52	17347	15	1226	7	1785	9	154	59	7934	57	7845	2	89
17.3	12.5	4.0	2.6	17.9	7.2	8.9	1.3	10.7	13.0	11.0	13.1	5.6	8.9
80	35155	31	2237	10	5531	7	349	198	19682	193	19570	5	112
26.7	25.4	8.2	4.8	25.6	22.3	6.9	2.9	35.9	32.2	37.5	32.6	13.9	11.1
54	29643	77	7661	12	4861	21	1455	136	13807	129	13585	7	222
18.0	21.4	20.4	16.5	30.8	19.6	20.8	11.9	24.6	22.6	25.0	22.6	19.4	22.1
102	49739	247	34845	9	12598	62	10161	144	16655	124	16134	20	521
34.0	35.8	65.2	75.2	23.1	50.6	61.4	83.3	26.1	27.3	24.0	26.9	55.5	51.8
1	237	1	62	-	-	-	-	-	-	-	-	-	-
.3	.2	.3	.1	-	-	-	-	-	-	-	-	-	-
11	6468	7	376	1	73	2	71	15	2965	13	2904	2	61
3.7	4.7	1.9	.8	2.6	.3	2.0	.6	2.7	4.9	2.5	4.8	5.6	6.1

LONG-TERM TOTAL DISABILITY INCOME PLANS:
BENEFITS PAYABLE FOR WORK-CONNECTED AND/OR NONWORK-CONNECTED DISABILITIES

TABLE 37A

FACULTY

| | ALL INSTITUTIONS | | ALL 4-YEAR INSTITUTIONS | | ALL 4-YEAR INSTITUTIONS | | | | UNIVERSITIES | | | |
| | | | | | PUBLIC | | PRIVATE | | PUBLIC | | PRIVATE | |
	INSTS	EES	INSTS	EES	INSTS	EES	INSTS	EES	INSTS	EES	INSTS	EES
TOTAL	1720	404744	1150	342745	441	231840	709	110905	90	118263	59	5379
	100.0	100:0	100.0	100.0	100.0	100.0	100.0	100.0	100.0	100.0	100.0	100.
NO RESPONSE	5	543	3	223	1	47	2	176	-	-	-	
	.3	.1	.3	.1	.2	✻	.3	.2	-	-	-	
PAYABLE FOR WORK CON-NECTED DISABILITIES ONLY	60	12342	37	9700	21	8169	16	1531	1	2023	-	
	3.5	3.0	3.2	2.8	4.8	3.5	2.3	1.4	1.1	1.7		
PAYABLE FOR NONWORK CON-NECTED DISABILITIES ONLY	164	23265	115	18032	27	7425	88	10607	1	490	5	225
	9.5	5.7	10.0	5.3	6.1	3.2	12.4	9.6	1.1	.4	8.5	4.2
PAYABLE FOR BOTH	1491	368594	995	314790	392	216199	603	98591	88	115750	54	5153
	86.7	91.2	86.5	91.8	88.9	93.3	85.0	88.8	97.8	97.9	91.5	95.8

LONG-TERM TOTAL DISABILITY INCOME PLANS:
BENEFITS PAYABLE FOR WORK-CONNECTED AND/OR NONWORK-CONNECTED DISABILITIES

TABLE 37B

CLERICAL SERVICE

| | ALL INSTITUTIONS | | ALL 4-YEAR INSTITUTIONS | | ALL 4-YEAR INSTITUTIONS | | | | UNIVERSITIES | | | |
| | | | | | PUBLIC | | PRIVATE | | PUBLIC | | PRIVATE | |
	INSTS	EES	INSTS	EES	INSTS	EES	INSTS	EES	INSTS	EES	INSTS	EES
TOTAL	1498	578842	946	517799	425	383005	521	134794	86	219568	42	76197
	100.0	100.0	100.0	100.0	100.0	100.0	100.0	100.0	100.0	100.0	100.0	100.0
NO RESPONSE	7	1060	3	208	1	21	2	187	-	-	-	-
	.5	.2	.3	✻	.2	✻	.4	.1	-	-	-	-
PAYABLE FOR WORK CON-NECTED DISABILITIES ONLY	62	15575	38	12313	22	10080	16	2233	1	3008	-	-
	4.1	2.7	4.0	2.4	5.2	2.6	3.1	1.7	1.2	1.4	-	-
PAYABLE FOR NONWORK CON-NECTED DISABILITIES ONLY	144	26609	97	21916	27	9203	70	12713	1	681	4	4206
	9.6	4.6	10.3	4.2	6.4	2.4	13.4	9.4	1.2	.3	9.5	5.5
PAYABLE FOR BOTH	1285	535598	808	483362	375	363701	433	119661	84	215879	38	71991
	85.8	92.5	85.4	93.4	88.2	95.0	83.1	88.8	97.6	98.3	90.5	94.5

4-YEAR LIBERAL ARTS COLLEGES				OTHER 4-YEAR COLLEGES				ALL 2-YEAR INSTITUTIONS		2-YEAR INSTITUTIONS			
PUBLIC		PRIVATE		PUBLIC		PRIVATE				PUBLIC		PRIVATE	
INSTS	EES	INSTS	EES	INSTS	EES	INSTS	EES	INSTS	EES	INSTS	EES	INSTS	EES
311	103419	521	48292	40	10158	129	8822	570	61999	524	60542	46	1457
100.0	100.0	100.0	100.0	100.0	100.0	100.0	100.0	100.0	100.0	100.0	100.0	100.0	100.0
-	-	2	176	1	47	-	-	2	320	2	320	-	-
-	-	.4	.4	2.5	.5	-	-	.4	.5	.4	.5	-	-
18	6065	10	1151	2	81	6	380	23	2642	22	2618	1	24
5.8	5.9	1.9	2.4	5.0	.8	4.7	4.3	4.0	4.3	4.2	4.3	2.2	1.6
24	6544	68	7084	2	391	15	1266	49	5233	44	5045	5	188
7.7	6.3	13.1	14.7	5.0	3.8	11.6	14.4	8.6	8.4	8.4	8.3	10.9	12.9
269	90810	441	39881	35	9639	108	7176	496	53804	456	52559	40	1245
86.5	87.8	84.6	82.5	87.5	94.9	83.7	81.3	87.0	86.8	87.0	86.9	86.9	85.5

4-YEAR LIBERAL ARTS COLLEGES				OTHER 4-YEAR COLLEGES				ALL 2-YEAR INSTITUTIONS		2-YEAR INSTITUTIONS			
PUBLIC		PRIVATE		PUBLIC		PRIVATE				PUBLIC		PRIVATE	
INSTS	EES	INSTS	EES	INSTS	EES	INSTS	EES	INSTS	EES	INSTS	EES	INSTS	EES
300	138589	378	46407	39	24848	101	12190	552	61043	516	60038	36	1005
100.0	100.0	100.0	100.0	100.0	100.0	100.0	100.0	100.0	100.0	100.0	100.0	100.0	100.0
-	-	2	187	1	21	-	-	4	852	4	852	-	-
-	-	.5	.4	2.6	.1	-	-	.7	1.4	.8	1.4	-	-
19	7024	10	1427	2	48	6	806	24	3262	23	3229	1	33
6.3	5.1	2.6	3.1	5.1	.2	5.9	6.6	4.3	5.3	4.5	5.4	2.8	3.3
24	6885	57	7199	2	1637	9	1308	47	4693	42	4632	5	61
8.0	5.0	15.1	15.5	5.1	6.6	8.9	10.7	8.5	7.7	8.1	7.7	13.9	6.1
257	124680	309	37594	34	23142	86	10076	477	52236	447	51325	30	911
85.7	89.9	81.8	81.0	87.2	93.1	85.2	82.7	86.5	85.6	86.6	85.5	83.3	90.6

LONG-TERM TOTAL DISABILITY INCOME PLANS:
EMPLOYER-EMPLOYEE CONTRIBUTION TOWARD COST OF PLAN
TABLE 38A

FACULTY	ALL INSTITUTIONS		ALL 4-YEAR INSTITUTIONS		ALL 4-YEAR INSTITUTIONS				UNIVERSITIES			
					PUBLIC		PRIVATE		PUBLIC		PRIVATE	
	INSTS	EES	INSTS	EES	INSTS	EES	INSTS	EES	INSTS	EES	INSTS	EE
TOTAL	1424	345392	1012	301816	345	195304	667	106512	75	105743	56	5188
	100.0	100.0	100.0	100.0	100.0	100.0	100.0	100.0	100.0	100.0	100.0	100.
NO RESPONSE	20	4079	13	3048	7	2720	6	328	-	-	-	
	1.4	1.2	1.3	1.0	2.0	1.4	.9	.3	-	-	-	
EMPLOYER PAYS FULL COST	826	173190	594	145031	141	77653	453	67378	34	46545	34	3093
	58.0	50.1	58.7	48.1	40.9	39.7	67.9	63.3	45.4	44.0	60.7	59.
EMPLOYER AND EMPLOYEE SHARE COST	353	84198	261	76708	91	48605	170	28103	22	28759	17	1257
	24.8	24.4	25.8	25.4	26.4	24.9	25.5	26.4	29.3	27.2	30.4	24
EMPLOYEE PAYS FULL COST	225	83925	144	77029	106	66326	38	10703	19	30439	5	838
	15.8	24.3	14.2	25.5	30.7	34.0	5.7	10.0	25.3	28.8	8.9	16.

LONG-TERM TOTAL DISABILITY INCOME PLANS:
EMPLOYER-EMPLOYEE CONTRIBUTION TOWARD COST OF PLAN
TABLE 38B

CLERICAL SERVICE	ALL INSTITUTIONS		ALL 4-YEAR INSTITUTIONS		ALL 4-YEAR INSTITUTIONS				UNIVERSITIES			
					PUBLIC		PRIVATE		PUBLIC		PRIVATE	
	INSTS	EES	INSTS	EES	INSTS	EES	INSTS	EES	INSTS	EES	INSTS	EE
TOTAL	1131	464135	767	426225	273	298019	494	128206	62	182654	39	7246
	100.0	100.0	100.0	100.0	100.0	100.0	100.0	100.0	100.0	100.0	100.0	100.
NO RESPONSE	19	5548	12	4148	7	3773	5	375	-	-	-	
	1.7	1.2	1.6	1.0	2.6	1.3	1.0	.3	-	-	-	
EMPLOYER PAYS FULL COST	615	183325	425	159450	80	73623	345	85827	23	50055	25	4730
	54.4	39.5	55.3	37.4	29.3	24.7	69.8	66.9	37.1	27.4	64.1	65.
EMPLOYER AND EMPLOYEE SHARE COST	282	119887	196	112882	77	81215	119	31667	19	54747	11	1638
	24.9	25.8	25.6	26.5	28.2	27.3	24.1	24.7	30.6	30.0	28.2	22.
EMPLOYEE PAYS FULL COST	215	155375	134	149745	109	139408	25	10337	20	77852	3	8776
	19.0	33.5	17.5	35.1	39.9	46.7	5.1	8.1	32.3	42.6	7.7	12.1

4-YEAR LIBERAL ARTS COLLEGES				OTHER 4-YEAR COLLEGES				ALL 2-YEAR INSTITUTIONS		2-YEAR INSTITUTIONS			
PUBLIC		PRIVATE		PUBLIC		PRIVATE				PUBLIC		PRIVATE	
INSTS	EES	INSTS	EES	INSTS	EES	INSTS	EES	INSTS	EES	INSTS	EES	INSTS	EES
236	79729	500	46507	34	9832	111	8117	412	43576	370	42266	42	1310
100.0	100.0	100.0	100.0	100.0	100.0	100.0	100.0	100.0	100.0	100.0	100.0	100.0	100.0
7	2720	5	212	-	-	1	116	7	1031	6	1019	1	12
3.0	3.4	1.0	.5	-	-	.9	1.4	1.7	2.4	1.6	2.4	2.4	.9
93	27005	342	30858	14	4103	77	5590	232	28159	202	27165	30	994
39.4	33.9	68.4	66.3	41.2	41.7	69.4	68.9	56.3	64.6	54.7	64.3	71.4	75.9
59	18236	126	13382	10	1610	27	2145	92	7490	86	7341	6	149
25.0	22.9	25.2	28.8	29.4	16.4	24.3	26.4	22.3	17.2	23.2	17.4	14.3	11.4
77	31768	27	2055	10	4119	6	266	81	6896	76	6741	5	155
32.6	39.8	5.4	4.4	29.4	41.9	5.4	3.3	19.7	15.8	20.5	15.9	11.9	11.8

4-YEAR LIBERAL ARTS COLLEGES				OTHER 4-YEAR COLLEGES				ALL 2-YEAR INSTITUTIONS		2-YEAR INSTITUTIONS			
PUBLIC		PRIVATE		PUBLIC		PRIVATE				PUBLIC		PRIVATE	
INSTS	EES	INSTS	EES	INSTS	EES	INSTS	EES	INSTS	EES	INSTS	EES	INSTS	EES
188	98807	363	43777	23	16558	92	11964	364	37910	332	37004	32	906
100.0	100.0	100.0	100.0	100.0	100.0	100.0	100.0	100.0	100.0	100.0	100.0	100.0	100.0
7	3773	4	353	-	-	1	22	7	1400	6	1371	1	29
3.7	3.8	1.1	.8	-	-	1.1	.2	1.9	3.7	1.8	3.7	3.1	3.2
53	20283	258	30274	4	3285	62	8248	190	23875	169	23312	21	563
28.2	20.5	71.1	69.2	17.4	19.8	67.4	69.0	52.2	62.9	50.9	63.0	65.6	62.1
49	23597	84	11786	9	2871	24	3497	86	7005	80	6813	6	192
26.1	23.9	23.1	26.9	39.1	17.3	26.1	29.2	23.6	18.5	24.1	18.4	18.8	21.2
79	51154	17	1364	10	10402	5	197	81	5630	77	5508	4	122
42.0	51.8	4.7	3.1	43.5	62.9	5.4	1.6	22.3	14.9	23.2	14.9	12.5	13.5

LONG-TERM TOTAL DISABILITY INCOME PLANS:
PROVISIONS FOR CONTINUATION DURING DISABILITY OF CONTRIBUTIONS OR CREDITED SERVICE TOWARD RETIREMENT ANNUITY

TABLE 39A

FACULTY

	ALL INSTITUTIONS		ALL 4-YEAR INSTITUTIONS		ALL 4-YEAR INSTITUTIONS PUBLIC		PRIVATE		UNIVERSITIES PUBLIC		PRIVATE	
	INSTS	EES	INSTS	EES	INSTS	EES	INSTS	EES	INSTS	EES	INSTS	EE
TOTAL	1424	345392	1012	301816	345	195304	667	106512	75	105743	56	5188
	100.0	100.0	100.0	100.0	100.0	100.0	100.0	100.0	100.0	100.0	100.0	100.
NO RESPONSE	66	19051	40	15372	22	14458	18	914	3	5162	-	
	4.6	5.5	4.0	5.1	6.4	7.4	2.7	.9	4.0	4.9	-	
PROVIDES FOR CONTINUA-TION DURING DISABILITY OF CREDITED SERVICE TOWARD RETIREMENT ANNUITY	829	203188	655	183589	160	93277	495	90312	40	57720	51	4687
	58.3	58.8	64.7	60.8	46.4	47.8	74.2	84.7	53.3	54.6	91.1	90.
NO PROVISIONS	529	123153	317	102855	163	87569	154	15286	32	42861	5	501
	37.1	35.7	31.3	34.1	47.2	44.8	23.1	14.4	42.7	40.5	8.9	9.7

LONG-TERM TOTAL DISABILITY INCOME PLANS:
PROVISIONS FOR CONTINUATION DURING DISABILITY OF CONTRIBUTIONS OR CREDITED SERVICE TOWARD RETIREMENT ANNUITY

TABLE 39B

CLERICAL SERVICE

	ALL INSTITUTIONS		ALL 4-YEAR INSTITUTIONS		ALL 4-YEAR INSTITUTIONS PUBLIC		PRIVATE		UNIVERSITIES PUBLIC		PRIVATE	
	INSTS	EES	INSTS	EES	INSTS	EES	INSTS	EES	INSTS	EES	INSTS	EES
TOTAL	1131	464135	767	426225	273	298019	494	128206	62	182654	39	72465
	100.0	100.0	100.0	100.0	100.0	100.0	100.0	100.0	100.0	100.0	100.0	100.0
NO RESPONSE	63	52333	38	48541	23	47785	15	756	3	22005	-	-
	5.6	11.3	5.0	11.4	8.4	16.0	3.0	.6	4.8	12.0	-	-
PROVIDES FOR CONTINUA-TION DURING DISABILITY OF CREDITED SERVICE TOWARD RETIREMENT ANNUITY	542	212593	420	198135	91	106694	329	91441	30	81634	30	55094
	47.9	45.8	54.7	46.5	33.3	35.8	66.6	71.3	48.4	44.7	76.9	76.0
NO PROVISIONS	526	199209	309	179549	159	143540	150	36009	29	79015	9	17371
	46.5	42.9	40.3	42.1	58.3	48.2	30.4	28.1	46.8	43.3	23.1	24.0

| 4-YEAR LIBERAL ARTS COLLEGES | | | | OTHER 4-YEAR COLLEGES | | | | ALL 2-YEAR INSTITUTIONS | | 2-YEAR INSTITUTIONS | | | |
| PUBLIC | | PRIVATE | | PUBLIC | | PRIVATE | | | | PUBLIC | | PRIVATE | |
INSTS	EES	INSTS	EES	INSTS	EES	INSTS	EES	INSTS	EES	INSTS	EES	INSTS	EES
236	79729	500	46507	34	9832	111	8117	412	43576	370	42266	42	1310
100.0	100.0	100.0	100.0	100.0	100.0	100.0	100.0	100.0	100.0	100.0	100.0	100.0	100.0
18	9038	12	707	1	258	6	207	26	3679	24	3651	2	28
7.6	11.3	2.4	1.5	2.9	2.6	5.4	2.6	6.3	8.4	6.5	8.6	4.8	2.1
105	30310	373	36784	15	5247	71	6657	174	19599	150	18710	24	889
44.5	38.0	74.6	79.1	44.1	53.4	64.0	82.0	42.2	45.0	40.5	44.3	57.1	67.9
113	40381	115	9016	18	4327	34	1253	212	20298	196	19905	16	393
47.9	50.7	23.0	19.4	53.0	44.0	30.6	15.4	51.5	46.6	53.0	47.1	38.1	30.0

| 4-YEAR LIBERAL ARTS COLLEGES | | | | OTHER 4-YEAR COLLEGES | | | | ALL 2-YEAR INSTITUTIONS | | 2-YEAR INSTITUTIONS | | | |
| PUBLIC | | PRIVATE | | PUBLIC | | PRIVATE | | | | PUBLIC | | PRIVATE | |
INSTS	EES	INSTS	EES	INSTS	EES	INSTS	EES	INSTS	EES	INSTS	EES	INSTS	EES
188	98807	363	43777	23	16558	92	11964	364	37910	332	37004	32	906
100.0	100.0	100.0	100.0	100.0	100.0	100.0	100.0	100.0	100.0	100.0	100.0	100.0	100.0
19	24555	9	519	1	1225	6	237	25	3792	23	3735	2	57
10.1	24.9	2.5	1.2	4.3	7.4	6.5	2.0	6.9	10.0	6.9	10.1	6.2	6.3
55	19266	249	28709	6	5794	50	7638	122	14458	108	14067	14	391
29.3	19.5	68.6	65.6	26.1	35.0	54.4	63.8	33.5	38.1	32.5	38.0	43.8	43.2
114	54986	105	14549	16	9539	36	4089	217	19660	201	19202	16	458
60.6	55.6	28.9	33.2	69.6	57.6	39.1	34.2	59.6	51.9	60.6	51.9	50.0	50.5

LONG-TERM TOTAL DISABILITY INCOME PLANS:
WAITING PERIOD BEFORE NEW EMPLOYEE IS ELIGIBLE TO PARTICIPATE IN PLAN

TABLE 40A

FACULTY

	ALL INSTITUTIONS		ALL 4-YEAR INSTITUTIONS		ALL 4-YEAR INSTITUTIONS PUBLIC		ALL 4-YEAR INSTITUTIONS PRIVATE		UNIVERSITIES PUBLIC		UNIVERSITIES PRIVATE	
	INSTS	EES	INSTS	EES	INSTS	EES	INSTS	EES	INSTS	EES	INSTS	EES
TOTAL	1424	345392	1012	301816	345	195304	667	106512	75	105743	56	51888
	100.0	100.0	100.0	100.0	100.0	100.0	100.0	100.0	100.0	100.0	100.0	100.0
NO RESPONSE	9	2862	8	2837	6	2646	2	191	-	-	-	-
	.6	.8	.8	.9	1.7	1.4	.3	.2	-	-	-	-
ONE MONTH OR LESS	669	155442	395	126507	175	102806	220	23701	36	53696	8	6140
	47.0	45.0	39.0	42.0	50.8	52.7	33.0	22.3	48.0	50.8	14.3	11.8
2 - 11 MONTHS	115	23770	77	19937	21	12008	56	7929	6	6705	7	4447
	8.1	6.9	7.6	6.6	6.1	6.1	8.4	7.4	8.0	6.3	12.5	8.6
ONE YEAR	477	102538	405	94985	77	45009	328	49976	18	27090	28	20780
	33.5	29.7	40.0	31.5	22.3	23.0	49.2	46.9	24.0	25.6	50.0	40.0
MORE THAN 1 YEAR	114	44529	93	41714	51	25947	42	15767	11	14128	9	13423
	8.0	12.9	9.2	13.8	14.8	13.3	6.3	14.8	14.7	13.4	16.1	25.9
OTHER	40	16251	34	15836	15	6888	19	8948	4	4124	4	7098
	2.8	4.7	3.4	5.2	4.3	3.5	2.8	8.4	5.3	3.9	7.1	13.7

LONG-TERM TOTAL DISABILITY INCOME PLANS:
WAITING PERIOD BEFORE NEW EMPLOYEE IS ELIGIBLE TO PARTICIPATE IN PLAN

TABLE 40B

CLERICAL SERVICE

	ALL INSTITUTIONS		ALL 4-YEAR INSTITUTIONS		ALL 4-YEAR INSTITUTIONS PUBLIC		ALL 4-YEAR INSTITUTIONS PRIVATE		UNIVERSITIES PUBLIC		UNIVERSITIES PRIVATE	
	INSTS	EES	INSTS	EES	INSTS	EES	INSTS	EES	INSTS	EES	INSTS	EES
TOTAL	1131	464135	767	426225	273	298019	494	128206	62	182654	39	72465
	100.0	100.0	100.0	100.0	100.0	100.0	100.0	100.0	100.0	100.0	100.0	100.0
NO RESPONSE	10	4090	9	4082	7	3860	2	222	-	-	-	-
	.9	.9	1.2	1.0	2.6	1.3	.4	.2	-	-	-	-
ONE MONTH OR LESS	550	193572	298	169006	162	155085	136	13921	31	88835	1	1825
	48.6	41.7	38.8	39.6	59.3	52.0	27.5	10.9	49.9	48.6	2.6	2.5
2 - 11 MONTHS	138	48825	97	42654	25	20438	72	22216	7	12544	10	11932
	12.2	10.5	12.6	10.0	9.2	6.9	14.6	17.3	11.3	6.9	25.6	16.5
ONE YEAR	319	136483	265	130401	52	82034	213	48367	13	49597	13	21591
	28.2	29.4	34.6	30.6	19.0	27.5	43.1	37.7	21.0	27.2	33.3	29.8
MORE THAN 1 YEAR	73	52815	62	52042	13	23270	49	28772	7	21227	9	24564
	6.5	11.4	8.1	12.2	4.8	7.8	9.9	22.4	11.3	11.6	23.1	33.9
OTHER	41	28350	36	28040	14	13332	22	14708	4	10451	6	12553
	3.6	6.1	4.7	6.6	5.1	4.5	4.5	11.5	6.5	5.7	15.4	17.3

4-YEAR LIBERAL ARTS COLLEGES				OTHER 4-YEAR COLLEGES				ALL 2-YEAR INSTITUTIONS		2-YEAR INSTITUTIONS			
PUBLIC		PRIVATE		PUBLIC		PRIVATE				PUBLIC		PRIVATE	
INSTS	EES	INSTS	EES	INSTS	EES	INSTS	EES	INSTS	EES	INSTS	EES	INSTS	EES
236	79729	500	46507	34	9832	111	8117	412	43576	370	42266	42	1310
100.0	100.0	100.0	100.0	100.0	100.0	100.0	100.0	100.0	100.0	100.0	100.0	100.0	100.0
6	2646	1	75	-	-	1	116	1	25	1	25	-	-
2.5	3.3	.2	.2	-	-	.9	1.4	.2	.1	.3	.1	-	-
123	43721	161	13493	16	5389	51	4068	274	28935	257	28454	17	481
52.2	54.9	32.2	29.0	47.1	54.8	46.0	50.1	66.5	66.3	69.4	67.3	40.5	36.7
12	4396	37	3052	3	907	12	430	38	3833	30	3618	8	215
5.1	5.5	7.4	6.6	8.8	9.2	10.8	5.3	9.2	8.8	8.1	8.6	19.0	16.4
52	16448	260	25977	7	1471	40	3219	72	7553	58	7114	14	439
22.0	20.6	52.0	55.8	20.6	15.0	36.0	39.7	17.5	17.3	15.7	16.8	33.3	33.5
34	9814	28	2280	6	2005	5	64	21	2815	19	2661	2	154
14.4	12.3	5.6	4.9	17.6	20.4	4.5	.8	5.1	6.5	5.1	6.3	4.8	11.8
9	2704	13	1630	2	60	2	220	6	415	5	394	1	21
3.8	3.4	2.6	3.5	5.9	.6	1.8	2.7	1.5	1.0	1.4	.9	2.4	1.6

4-YEAR LIBERAL ARTS COLLEGES				OTHER 4-YEAR COLLEGES				ALL 2-YEAR INSTITUTIONS		2-YEAR INSTITUTIONS			
PUBLIC		PRIVATE		PUBLIC		PRIVATE				PUBLIC		PRIVATE	
INSTS	EES	INSTS	EES	INSTS	EES	INSTS	EES	INSTS	EES	INSTS	EES	INSTS	EES
188	98807	363	43777	23	16558	92	11964	364	37910	332	37004	32	906
100.0	100.0	100.0	100.0	100.0	100.0	100.0	100.0	100.0	100.0	100.0	100.0	100.0	100.0
7	3860	1	200	-	-	1	22	1	8	1	8	-	-
3.7	3.9	.3	.5	-	-	1.1	.2	.3	✲	.3	✲	-	-
117	55011	98	8549	14	11239	37	3547	252	24566	240	24143	12	423
62.2	55.6	27.0	19.5	60.9	67.9	40.2	29.6	69.2	64.9	72.3	65.2	37.5	46.6
17	7862	46	7095	1	32	16	3189	41	6171	33	5925	8	246
9.0	8.0	12.7	16.2	4.3	.2	17.4	26.7	11.3	16.3	9.9	16.0	25.0	27.2
33	27254	172	21983	6	5183	28	4793	54	6082	44	5904	10	178
17.6	27.6	47.4	50.2	26.1	31.3	30.4	40.0	14.8	16.0	13.3	16.0	31.3	19.6
6	2043	31	3925	-	-	9	283	11	773	10	739	1	34
3.2	2.1	8.5	9.0	-	-	9.8	2.4	3.0	2.0	3.0	2.0	3.1	3.8
8	2777	15	2025	2	104	1	130	5	310	4	285	1	25
4.3	2.8	4.1	4.6	8.7	.6	1.1	1.1	1.4	.8	1.2	.8	3.1	2.8

LONG-TERM TOTAL DISABILITY INCOME PLANS:
MAXIMUM PERIOD DURING WHICH TOTAL DISABILITY INCOME IS PAID TO DISABLED EMPLOYEE

TABLE 41A

FACULTY

	ALL INSTITUTIONS		ALL 4-YEAR INSTITUTIONS		ALL 4-YEAR INSTITUTIONS PUBLIC		ALL 4-YEAR INSTITUTIONS PRIVATE		UNIVERSITIES PUBLIC		UNIVERSITIES PRIVATE	
	INSTS	EES	INSTS	EES	INSTS	EES	INSTS	EES	INSTS	EES	INSTS	EES
TOTAL	1424	345392	1012	301816	345	195304	667	106512	75	105743	56	51888
	100.0	100.0	100.0	100.0	100.0	100.0	100.0	100.0	100.0	100.0	100.0	100.0
NO RESPONSE	17	4335	14	3402	11	3231	3	171	-	-	-	-
	1.2	1.3	1.4	1.1	3.2	1.7	.4	.2	-	-	-	-
STATED NUMBER OF YEARS	70	11054	28	7491	13	6247	15	1244	4	4192	-	-
	4.9	3.2	2.8	2.5	3.8	3.2	2.2	1.2	5.3	4.0	-	-
TO AGE 65	1135	281080	844	248033	257	150382	587	97651	59	85910	53	48396
	79.7	81.4	83.3	82.2	74.4	77.0	88.2	91.6	78.7	81.2	94.6	93.3
FOR LIFE	129	21875	89	19274	40	16429	49	2845	6	6408	-	-
	9.1	6.3	8.8	6.4	11.6	8.4	7.3	2.7	8.0	6.1	-	-
OTHER	73	27048	37	23616	24	19015	13	4601	6	9233	3	3492
	5.1	7.8	3.7	7.8	7.0	9.7	1.9	4.3	8.0	8.7	5.4	6.7

LONG-TERM TOTAL DISABILITY INCOME PLANS:
MAXIMUM PERIOD DURING WHICH TOTAL DISABILITY INCOME IS PAID TO DISABLED EMPLOYEE

TABLE 41B

CLERICAL SERVICE

	ALL INSTITUTIONS		ALL 4-YEAR INSTITUTIONS		ALL 4-YEAR INSTITUTIONS PUBLIC		ALL 4-YEAR INSTITUTIONS PRIVATE		UNIVERSITIES PUBLIC		UNIVERSITIES PRIVATE	
	INSTS	EES	INSTS	EES	INSTS	EES	INSTS	EES	INSTS	EES	INSTS	EES
TOTAL	1131	464135	767	426225	273	298019	494	128206	62	182654	39	72465
	100.0	100.0	100.0	100.0	100.0	100.0	100.0	100.0	100.0	100.0	100.0	100.0
NO RESPONSE	19	6703	16	5377	12	4982	4	395	-	-	-	-
	1.7	1.4	2.1	1.3	4.4	1.7	.8	.3	-	-	-	-
STATED NUMBER OF YEARS	70	16726	30	13979	13	9064	17	4915	3	5444	1	2093
	6.2	3.6	3.9	3.3	4.8	3.0	3.4	3.8	4.8	3.0	2.6	2.9
TO AGE 65	871	379984	619	351534	194	236528	425	115006	50	150856	35	66118
	77.0	81.9	80.7	82.4	71.0	79.4	86.1	89.8	80.7	82.6	89.7	91.2
FOR LIFE	106	30441	73	28606	36	25737	37	2869	6	15129	-	-
	9.4	6.6	9.5	6.7	13.2	8.6	7.5	2.2	9.7	8.3	-	-
OTHER	65	30281	29	26729	18	21708	11	5021	3	11225	3	4254
	5.7	6.5	3.8	6.3	6.6	7.3	2.2	3.9	4.8	6.1	7.7	5.9

4-YEAR LIBERAL ARTS COLLEGES				OTHER 4-YEAR COLLEGES				ALL 2-YEAR INSTITUTIONS		2-YEAR INSTITUTIONS			
PUBLIC		PRIVATE		PUBLIC		PRIVATE				PUBLIC		PRIVATE	
INSTS	EES	INSTS	EES	INSTS	EES	INSTS	EES	INSTS	EES	INSTS	EES	INSTS	EES
236	79729	500	46507	34	9832	111	8117	412	43576	370	42266	42	1310
100.0	100.0	100.0	100.0	100.0	100.0	100.0	100.0	100.0	100.0	100.0	100.0	100.0	100.0
11	3231	3	171	-	-	-	-	3	933	3	933	-	-
4.7	4.1	.6	.4	-	-	-	-	.7	2.1	.8	2.2	-	-
7	1826	10	767	2	229	5	477	42	3563	41	3539	1	24
3.0	2.3	2.0	1.6	5.9	2.3	4.5	5.9	10.2	8.2	11.1	8.4	2.4	1.8
171	55833	441	42147	27	8639	93	7108	291	33047	260	31978	31	1069
72.4	70.0	88.2	90.6	79.4	87.9	83.8	87.6	70.7	75.8	70.3	75.7	73.8	81.6
33	9818	40	2583	1	203	9	262	40	2601	33	2424	7	177
14.0	12.3	8.0	5.6	2.9	2.1	8.1	3.2	9.7	6.0	8.9	5.7	16.7	13.5
14	9021	6	839	4	761	4	270	36	3432	33	3392	3	40
5.9	11.3	1.2	1.8	11.8	7.7	3.6	3.3	8.7	7.9	8.9	8.0	7.1	3.1

4-YEAR LIBERAL ARTS COLLEGES				OTHER 4-YEAR COLLEGES				ALL 2-YEAR INSTITUTIONS		2-YEAR INSTITUTIONS			
PUBLIC		PRIVATE		PUBLIC		PRIVATE				PUBLIC		PRIVATE	
INSTS	EES	INSTS	EES	INSTS	EES	INSTS	EES	INSTS	EES	INSTS	EES	INSTS	EES
188	98807	363	43777	23	16558	92	11964	364	37910	332	37004	32	906
100.0	100.0	100.0	100.0	100.0	100.0	100.0	100.0	100.0	100.0	100.0	100.0	100.0	100.0
12	4982	4	395	-	-	-	-	3	1326	3	1326	-	-
6.4	5.0	1.1	.9	-	-	-	-	.8	3.5	.9	3.6	-	-
8	2916	11	1410	2	704	5	1412	40	2747	39	2693	1	54
4.3	3.0	3.0	3.2	8.7	4.3	5.4	11.8	11.0	7.2	11.7	7.3	3.1	6.0
126	70113	314	39459	18	15559	76	9429	252	28450	230	27863	22	587
66.9	71.0	86.5	90.2	78.3	93.9	82.7	78.8	69.2	75.1	69.4	75.3	68.7	64.7
30	10608	30	1903	-	-	7	966	33	1835	27	1646	6	189
16.0	10.7	8.3	4.3	-	-	7.6	8.1	9.1	4.8	8.1	4.4	18.8	20.9
12	10188	4	610	3	295	4	157	36	3552	33	3476	3	76
6.4	10.3	1.1	1.4	13.0	1.8	4.3	1.3	9.9	9.4	9.9	9.4	9.4	8.4

OTHER EMPLOYEE BENEFIT PLANS IN EFFECT

TABLE 42A

FACULTY

	ALL INSTITUTIONS		ALL 4-YEAR INSTITUTIONS		ALL 4-YEAR INSTITUTIONS PUBLIC		PRIVATE		UNIVERSITIES PUBLIC		PRIVATE	
	INSTS	EES	INSTS	EES	INSTS	EES	INSTS	EES	INSTS	EES	INSTS	EES
TOTAL	2092	432402	1407	363203	478	242041	929	121162	93	121628	61	54258
	100.0	100.0	100.0	100.0	100.0	100.0	100.0	100.0	100.0	100.0	100.0	100.0
NO RESPONSE	1273	208671	819	164604	257	112904	562	51700	46	55626	21	16956
	60.9	48.3	58.2	45.3	53.8	46.6	60.5	42.7	49.5	45.7	34.4	31.3
LEGAL SERVICES	56	14451	31	11333	18	10438	13	895	6	5738	1	274
	2.7	3.3	2.2	3.1	3.8	4.3	1.4	.7	6.5	4.7	1.6	.5
BUSINESS TRAVEL ACCIDENT INSURANCE	528	153908	409	140178	133	79123	276	61055	26	39504	38	36190
	25.2	35.6	29.1	38.6	27.8	32.7	29.7	50.4	28.0	32.5	62.3	66.7
KEY MAN INSURANCE OR OTHER SUPPLEMENTARY LIFE INSURANCE	123	43538	103	41564	68	34787	35	6777	12	14587	3	3314
	5.9	10.1	7.3	11.4	14.2	14.4	3.8	5.6	12.9	12.0	4.9	6.1
ANNUAL PHYSICAL EXAMINATIONS	106	37309	55	31982	33	25279	22	6703	7	14135	4	5034
	5.1	8.6	3.9	8.8	6.9	10.4	2.4	5.5	7.5	11.6	6.6	9.3
OTHER	266	84078	196	78259	82	58243	114	20016	26	34892	12	9798
	12.7	19.4	13.9	21.5	17.2	24.1	12.3	16.5	28.0	28.7	19.7	18.1

OTHER EMPLOYEE BENEFIT PLANS IN EFFECT

TABLE 42B

CLERICAL SERVICE

	ALL INSTITUTIONS		ALL 4-YEAR INSTITUTIONS		ALL 4-YEAR INSTITUTIONS PUBLIC		PRIVATE		UNIVERSITIES PUBLIC		PRIVATE	
	INSTS	EES	INSTS	EES	INSTS	EES	INSTS	EES	INSTS	EES	INSTS	EES
TOTAL	2092	670941	1407	601711	478	413110	929	188601	93	231299	61	94679
	100.0	100.0	100.0	100.0	100.0	100.0	100.0	100.0	100.0	100.0	100.0	100.0
NO RESPONSE	1334	296983	877	252596	249	170293	628	82303	47	93838	27	30671
	63.8	44.3	62.3	42.0	52.1	41.2	67.6	43.6	50.5	40.6	44.3	32.4
LEGAL SERVICES	65	21863	42	18222	29	17184	13	1038	5	7273	1	392
	3.1	3.3	3.0	3.0	6.1	4.2	1.4	.6	5.4	3.1	1.6	.4
BUSINESS TRAVEL ACCIDENT INSURANCE	447	224497	334	210834	127	118809	207	92025	26	69647	32	61592
	21.4	33.5	23.7	35.0	26.6	28.8	22.3	48.8	28.0	30.1	52.5	65.1
KEY MAN INSURANCE OR OTHER SUPPLEMENTARY LIFE INSURANCE	107	74531	92	72138	68	58770	24	13368	11	29677	3	10405
	5.1	11.1	6.5	12.0	14.2	14.2	2.6	7.1	11.8	12.8	4.9	11.0
ANNUAL PHYSICAL EXAMINATIONS	94	76603	47	72197	29	61493	18	10704	6	32100	4	8544
	4.5	11.4	3.3	12.0	6.1	14.9	1.9	5.7	6.5	13.9	6.6	9.0
OTHER	258	179862	189	174902	82	137261	107	37641	26	85399	13	23202
	12.3	26.8	13.4	29.1	17.2	33.2	11.5	20.0	28.0	36.9	21.3	24.5

4-YEAR LIBERAL ARTS COLLEGES				OTHER 4-YEAR COLLEGES				ALL 2-YEAR INSTITUTIONS		2-YEAR INSTITUTIONS			
PUBLIC		PRIVATE		PUBLIC		PRIVATE				PUBLIC		PRIVATE	
INSTS	EES	INSTS	EES	INSTS	EES	INSTS	EES	INSTS	EES	INSTS	EES	INSTS	EES
341	109911	686	57084	44	10502	182	9820	685	69199	600	66915	85	2284
100.0	100.0	100.0	100.0	100.0	100.0	100.0	100.0	100.0	100.0	100.0	100.0	100.0	100.0
189	53494	417	28659	22	3784	124	6085	454	44067	383	42233	71	1834
55.4	48.7	60.8	50.2	50.0	36.0	68.1	62.0	66.3	63.7	63.8	63.1	83.5	80.3
9	2424	8	442	3	2276	4	179	25	3118	24	3099	1	19
2.6	2.2	1.2	.8	6.8	21.7	2.2	1.8	3.6	4.5	4.0	4.6	1.2	.8
97	35750	192	22054	10	3869	46	2811	119	13730	112	13431	7	299
28.4	32.5	28.0	38.6	22.7	36.8	25.3	28.6	17.4	19.8	18.7	20.1	8.2	13.1
47	18841	30	2804	9	1359	2	659	20	1974	19	1953	1	21
13.8	17.1	4.4	4.9	20.5	12.9	1.1	6.7	2.9	2.9	3.2	2.9	1.2	.9
23	9476	13	1441	3	1668	5	228	51	5327	50	5315	1	12
6.7	8.6	1.9	2.5	6.8	15.9	2.7	2.3	7.4	7.7	8.3	7.9	1.2	.5
47	19336	83	8488	9	4015	19	1730	70	5819	64	5580	6	239
13.8	17.6	12.1	14.9	20.5	38.2	10.4	17.6	10.2	8.4	10.7	8.3	7.1	10.5

4-YEAR LIBERAL ARTS COLLEGES				OTHER 4-YEAR COLLEGES				ALL 2-YEAR INSTITUTIONS		2-YEAR INSTITUTIONS			
PUBLIC		PRIVATE		PUBLIC		PRIVATE				PUBLIC		PRIVATE	
INSTS	EES	INSTS	EES	INSTS	EES	INSTS	EES	INSTS	EES	INSTS	EES	INSTS	EES
341	153051	686	76960	44	28760	182	16962	685	69230	600	66748	85	2482
100.0	100.0	100.0	100.0	100.0	100.0	100.0	100.0	100.0	100.0	100.0	100.0	100.0	100.0
180	65785	461	39698	22	10670	140	11934	457	44387	386	42264	71	2123
52.8	43.0	67.2	51.6	50.0	37.1	76.9	70.4	66.7	64.1	64.3	63.3	83.5	85.5
20	5866	8	595	4	4045	4	51	23	3641	22	3639	1	2
5.9	3.8	1.2	.8	9.1	14.1	2.2	.3	3.4	5.3	3.7	5.5	1.2	.1
93	45007	145	27943	8	4155	30	2490	113	13663	106	13481	7	182
27.3	29.4	21.1	36.3	18.2	14.4	16.5	14.7	16.5	19.7	17.7	20.2	8.2	7.3
48	25285	20	2338	9	3808	1	625	15	2393	14	2349	1	44
14.1	16.5	2.9	3.0	20.5	13.2	.5	3.7	2.2	3.5	2.3	3.5	1.2	1.8
20	23592	11	1149	3	5801	3	1011	47	4406	45	4341	2	65
5.9	15.4	1.6	1.5	6.8	20.2	1.6	6.0	6.9	6.4	7.5	6.5	2.4	2.6
47	40386	78	12431	9	11476	16	2008	69	4960	64	4829	5	131
13.8	26.4	11.4	16.2	20.5	39.9	8.8	11.8	10.1	7.2	10.7	7.2	5.9	5.3

Notes

1. INTRODUCTION AND SUMMARY

[1]Rainard B. Robbins, *College Plans for Retirement Income* (New York: Columbia University Press, 1940).

[2]William C. Greenough, *College Retirement and Insurance Plans* (New York: Columbia University Press, 1948).

[3]*Ibid.*, p. 4.

[4]*Ibid.*, p. 68.

[5]William C. Greenough and Francis P. King, *Retirement and Insurance Plans in American Colleges* (New York: Columbia University Press, 1959).

[6]William C. Greenough and Francis P. King, *Benefit Plans in American Colleges* (New York: Columbia University Press, 1969).

[7]Francis P. King, *Benefit Plans in Junior Colleges* (Washington, D.C.: American Association of Junior Colleges, 1970).

[8]The current survey of retirement and insurance plans is not duplicated by any other regular survey in higher education, including the Higher Education General Information Survey (HEGIS) of the National Center for Education Statistics, Department of Health, Education, and Welfare. HEGIS form 2300-3, "Salaries, Tenure, and Fringe Benefits of Full-Time Instructional Faculty," requests employer expenditures on behalf of faculty for retirement plans, medical/dental plans, long-term disability income payments, Social Security, and group life insurance. The expenditure data are entered separately for professors, associate professors, assistant professors, instructors, lecturers, and faculty without academic rank. The HEGIS form also collects faculty expenditure data for tuition plans, housing plans, unemployment compensation taxes, Workers' Compensation, and "other benefits in kind with cash options." No data on benefit plan provisions are collected, nor does the survey cover administrative employees, nonfaculty professionals, or the clerical and service employees in higher education, employee groups which generally account for about two-thirds of all employees. There is some question of the validity of the HEGIS data (collected on pages 9 and 10 of form 2300-3) since few institutions with defined benefit retirement plans, for example, would be in a position to obtain the actuarial cost data by rank of plan member that would enable any accurate entry of information as requested on form 2300-3. A comparable problem would face administrators seeking to enter data for group life and long-term disability insurance. Dividing the gross premium for a given coverage by the number of professors would not indicate the cost of the plan for professors. Neither would dividing by the number of participants and then multiplying by the number of professors. Nor would multiplying the plan's composite rate by the number of full professors accurately produce the requested information. Only a special actuarial analysis could produce the data asked for, and it is doubtful that any college would wish to incur the expense.

2. RETIREMENT SYSTEMS IN HIGHER EDUCATION

[1]U.S. Congress, House Committee on Education and Labor, Pension Task Force Report on Public Employee Retirement Systems, 95th Cong., 2d sess., Committee Print, March 15, 1978 (Washington, D.C.: U.S. Government Printing Office, 1978), pp. 2, 51.

[2]Paul Studenski, *Teachers' Pension Systems in the United States* (New York: Appleton, 1920), p. 16.

[3]Dorothy F. McCamman, *The Scope of Protection under State and Local Government Retirement Systems*, Report No. 12 (Washington: Social Security Board, Bureau of Research and Statistics, October 1944), p. 66.

[4]Paul Studenski, *Teachers' Pension Systems*, p. 8.

[5]Massachusetts House Document No. 1203, *Report of the Joint Special Committee on Pensions.*

[6]Paul Studenski, "Financial Aspects of New York City's Pension Systems" (New York: Citizens Budget Commission, 1933), p. 4. Mimeo.

[7]Saul Waldman, *Retirement Systems for Employees of State and Local Government*, 1966, Report No. 23 (Washington: Social Security Administration, 1968), p. 1.

[8]U.S. Congress, House Committee on Education and Labor, *Pension Task Force Report on Public Employee Retirement Systems*, 95th Cong. 2d sess., Committee Print, March 15, 1978 (Washington, D.C.: U.S. Government Printing Office, 1978), pp. 59–60.

[9]Carnegie Foundation for the Advancement of Teaching, *Bulletin*, No. 9 (1916), p. xvi.

[10]Carnegie Foundation for the Advancement of Teaching, *Annual Report*, 1917, pp. 69–74.

[11]Carnegie Foundation for the Advancement of Teaching, *Annual Report*, 1918, p. 20.

[12]For clerical-service employees, a church plan was reported by three private universities, sixty-four private four-year liberal arts colleges, twenty other private colleges, and ten private two-year colleges.

[13]Robert Tilove, *Public Employee Pension Funds* (New York: Columbia University Press, 1976), p. 205.

[14]Roger F. Murray, "Economic Aspects of Pensions: A Summary Report," in *Old Age Income Assurance: A Compendium of Papers on Problems and Policy Issues in the Public and Private Pension System. Part 5: Financial Aspects of Pension Plans*, Joint Economic Committee, Subcommittee on Fiscal Policy, 90th Cong., 1st sess. (Washington, D.C.: U.S. Government Printing Office, 1967), p. 103.

[15]U.S. Congress, House Committee on Education and Labor, *Pension Task Force Report on Public Employee Retirement Systems*, 95th Cong., 2d sess., Committee Print, March 15, 1978 (Washington, D.C.: U.S. Government Printing Office, 1978), pp. 133–34.

[16]*Ibid.*, p. 179.

[17]State Universities Retirement System, Illinois, *Annual Report for the Year Ended August 31, 1969*, p. 11.

[18]SURS, Illinois, *Annual Report for the Year Ended August 31, 1977*, p. 5–6.

[19]Teachers' Retirement Board, California State Teachers' Retirement System, *63rd Annual Report*, June 30, 1976, pp. 7, 21.

[20]New York State Employees' Retirement System, *57th Annual Report, 1977*, pp. 66–67.

[21]Pennsylvania Public School Employees' Retirement System, *Annual Report*, June 30, 1976, pp. 2, 10.

[22]New York State Teachers' Retirement System, *Annual Report*, July 1, 1973, pp. 12–13.

[23]*U.S. News and World Report*, July 25, 1977.

[24]Teachers' Retirement System of the State of Kentucky, *37th Annual Report*, 1976–1977, p. 44.

3. RETIREMENT PLAN PROVISIONS

[1]Social Security Administration, "Income of Newly Entitled Beneficiaries, 1970." *Preliminary Findings from the Survey of New Beneficiaries*, Report #10 (Washington, D.C., June 1973), p. 9.

[2]See James G. Waters, "Solving for X in the Retirement Income Formula," *Pension and Welfare News* (March 1974), pp. 45–48, 51.

[3]Report on a study by Howard Winklevoss, *Pensions and Investments*, September 12, 1977, p. 60.

[4]Janet Murray, "Homeownership and Financial Assets: Findings from the 1968 Survey of the Aged," *Social Security Bulletin* (August 1972), 35:4.

[5]David G. Brown, *The Mobile Professors* (Washington, D.C.: American Council on Education, 1967), p. 169.

[6]Bankers' Trust Company, *1975 Study of Corporate Pension Plans.* (New York: Bankers' Trust Company, 1975), p.7. Reference is to "conventional plans" in which benefits are related to both salary and years of service.

[7]Public Law 95-256, April 6, 1978.

[8]*McMann vs. United Airlines*, 98 S. Ct. 244 (1977).

[9]95th Cong., 2d Sess., House Report No. 95-950, March 14, 1978, p. 8.

[10]AARP Bulletin, June 1978, p. 4.

[11]Cf. William C. Greenough, *A New Approach to Retirement Income* (New York: TIAA, 1952). Roger G. Ibbotson and Rex A. Sinquefield, "Stocks, Bonds, Bills, and Inflation: Year-by-Year Historical Returns (1926–1974)," *The Journal of Business of the University of Chicago* (January 1976), 49(1):11–17.

4. SOCIAL SECURITY

[1]U.S. Congress, *Background Material on Social Security Coverage of Government Employees and Employees of Nonprofit Organizations*, House Subcommittee on Social Security, 94th Cong., 2d sess. (April 26, 1976).

[2]Pension Task Force, Committee on Labor-Management Relations, *New York City's Pension Systems—A Report* (New York: N.Y. Chamber of Commerce, November 1972), p. 3.

[3]Under the 1977 amendments, the taxable earnings base is the larger of: (1) the base already in effect in the year in which the determination of a base is being made; or (2) the ratio of total wages reported for the calendar year before the year in which the determination is being made to the average of total wages reported for the calendar year before the most recent calendar year in which an increase in the contribution and benefit base was made. The product determined under clause (2) is rounded to the nearest multiple of $300 or, if it is a multiple of $150 but not of $300, to the next higher multiple of $300. Social Security Act, Sec. 230.

[4]Robert J. Myers, "Summary of the Provisions of the Old-Age, Survivors and Disability Insurance System, the Hospital Insurance System" (Philadelphia: Temple University, January 1978). Mimeo., table 5.

[5]John Snee and Mary Ross, "Social Security Amendments of 1977: Legislative History and Summary of Provisions," *Social Security Bulletin* (March 1978), 41:47.

[6]Cf. William C. Greenough and Francis P. King, *Pension Plans and Public Policy* (New York: Columbia University Press, 1976), pp. 77–96, for a discussion of social adequacy and other basic principles of Social Security.

[7]Califano v. Goldfarb, U.S., 51 L.Ed. 2d 270, 97 S. Ct. [no. 75-699], March 2, 1977.

[8]Board of Trustees of the Federal Old-Age and Survivors Insurance and Disability Insurance Trust Funds, *Annual Report* (1978), p. 46, table 26.

[9]Board of Trustees of the Federal Old-Age and Survivors Insurance and Disability Insurance Trust Funds, *Annual Report* (1975), p. 47, table 15.

[10]U.S. Congress, House, *Reports of the Quadrennial Advisory Council on Social Security*, H. Doc. No. 94-75, 94th Cong., 1st sess. (March 10, 1975).

5. GROUP LIFE INSURANCE PLANS

[1]William C. Greenough and Francis P. King, *Benefit Plans in American Colleges* (New York: Columbia University Press, 1969), p. 122.

[2]Francis P. King, *Benefit Plans in Junior Colleges* (Washington, D.C.: American Association of Junior Colleges, 1971), p. 119.

[3]American Council of Life Insurance, *Life Insurance Fact Book, 1977*, p. 18. Group life insurance includes credit life insurance.

[4]*Ibid.*, p. 19.

[5]A 1967 survey of insurance coverage among a group of newly hired faculty members at the University of Iowa indicated that the faculty group did provide more adequately for their insurance needs than any similar group on which data are available, but that approximately one-half of the group was inadequately insured according to "needs" criteria supplied earlier by the survey respondents themselves. Richard E. Johnson, "The College Professor and the Adequacy of His Insurance Coverages," *The Journal of Risk and Insurance* (March 1970), 37(1):105–14.

[6]"Statement of Principles on Academic Retirement and Insurance Plans," American Association of University Professors, *Bulletin* (Autumn 1968), 44:295–297.

[7] Robert D. Eilers and Robert M. Crowe, eds., *Group Insurance Handbook* (Homewood, Ill.: Richard D. Irwin, 1965), p. 110.

[8]U.S. Bureau of the Census, *Statistical Abstract of the United States, 1977*, p. 71. (Includes total population, all ages.) American Council of Life Insurance, *Life Insurance Fact Book, 1977*, p. 94. (Includes all ordinary and term life insurance policyholders.)

[9]Greenough and King, *Benefit Plans in American Colleges*, p. 132.

[10]American Council of Life Insurance, *Group Insurance and Group Annuity Manual*, table 5, May 2, 1978. The American Council of Life Insurance has proposed that the National Association of Insurance Commissioners (NAIC) model group life insurance definition should be amended to remove the limits on group life insurance amounts.

[11]American Council of Life Insurance, *Group Insurance and Group Annuity Manual*, table 6, May 2, 1978.

[12]Twelve states do not have statutes relating to employee participation in group life insurance plans. American Council of Life Insurance, *Group Insurance and Group Annuity Manual*, table 7, January 1977. Twenty states require the excess, if any, of premium refunds, dividends or experience rating credits over the employer's contribution to the cost of the group insurance coverage, including cost of administration, to be returned or applied for the benefit of the insured employees. ACLI, *Manual*, table 10, January 1977.

6. HEALTH INSURANCE

[1]Health Insurance Institute, *Source Book of Health Insurance Data 1977–1978* (Washington, D.C.: Health Insurance Institute, 1978), pp. 8, 46.

[2]"Dental Insurance: How It Started and Where It Is Today," *Employee Benefit Plan Review* (November 1978), pp. 94–96.

[3]*An Act to Amend Title VII of the Civil Rights Act of 1964 to Prohibit Sex Discrimination on the Basis of Pregnancy*, 92 Stat. 2076 (October 31, 1978).

[4]70 S.Ct. 674, 339 U.S. 382, 94 L. Ed. 925.

[5]Health Insurance Institute, *Source Book 1977–1978*, p. 35.

[6]*Ibid.*, p. 24.

[7]"Adding Insult to Injury," *Forbes* (March 1, 1977), p. 33.

[8]*Survey of Health Maintenance Organization Growth: 1977–1978*, Interstudy, Excelsior, Minnesota.

[9]Health Insurance Institute, *Source Book 1977–1978*, p. 35.

[10]*Internal Revenue Code*, 1977, Sec. 213.

[11]The states which require the option of a terminating employee to convert to an individual basic health insurance policy are: Colorado, Illinois, Iowa, Kansas, Kentucky, Maryland, Minnesota, Missouri, New Hampshire, New York, Ohio, Pennsylvania, South Carolina, West Virginia, and Wisconsin.

[12]Health Insurance Institute, *Source Book 1977–1978*, p. 38.

[13]A. F. Ehrbar, "A Radical Prescription for Medical Care," *Fortune* (February 1977), p. 168.

7. SHORT-TERM DISABILITY INCOME AND SICK PAY PLANS

[1]*Internal Revenue Code*, 1977, Sec. 104, 105.

[2]*Internal Revenue Code*, 1977, Reg. 31.3121(a)(2)-1(a).

[3]Arthur Larson, *The Law of Workmen's Compensation* (4 vols; New York: Matthew Bender, 1978), vol. 4; section 92.10, pp. 17–1, 17–2.

8. LONG-TERM DISABILITY INCOME PLANS

[1]William C. Greenough and Francis P. King, *Benefit Plans in American Colleges* (New York: Columbia University Press, 1959), p. 184.

[2]Paula A. Franklin, "Impact of Disability on the Family Structure," *Social Security Bulletin* (May 1977), pp. 3–18.

[3]Sec. 105(d), Internal Revenue Code, effective for taxable years beginning after December 31, 1976, Public Law 95-30, sec. 301(a).

9. REGULATION AND TAXATION OF BENEFIT PLANS

[1]PL 79-15, 59 Stat. 33, USC Sec. 1011–1015 (1945).

[2]U.S. Congress, House, Committee on Education and Labor, *Pension Task Force Report on Public Employee Retirement Systems*, 95th Cong., 2d sess., Committee Print (March 15, 1978).

[3]Letter of Representatives J. Dent and J. Erlenborn to House Ways and Means Committee accompanying the *Pension Task Force Report on Public Employee Retirement Systems*, 1978.

[4]For a more complete history of the federal role in pension plan regulation, see William C. Greenough and Francis P. King, *Pension Plans and Public Policy* (New York: Columbia University Press, 1976), ch. 2, "The Beginning of American Pension Plans."

[5]U.S. Congress, House Committee on Ways and Means, *Revenue Revisions of 1942*. 77th Cong., 2d sess. (March 3, 1942), p. 87.

[6]U.S. Congress, House Committee on Ways and Means, *Revenue Revisions of 1942*. Memorandum submitted by Randolph E. Paul (March 23, 1942), pp. 1004–5.

[7]Inland Steel Company v. NLRB, affirmed 170 F 2d 247 (CCA 7, 1948), cert. den. as to the welfare fund issue, April 25, 1949, 336 US 960, pp. 251, 253.

[8]IRC Sec. 401(a)(7), later amended by PL 93-406.

[9]President's Committee on Corporate Pension Funds and Other Private Retirement and Welfare Programs, *Public Policy and Private Pension Programs: A Report to the President*

on Private Employee Retirement Plans (Washington, D.C.: U.S. Government Printing Office, 1965).

[10]Merton C. Bernstein, *The Future of Private Pensions* (New York: Free Press, 1964).

[11]Employee Retirement Income Security Act of 1974. PL 93-406, September 2, 1974.

[12]U.S. Congress, House General Subcommittee on Labor, Committee on Education and Labor, *Proposed Welfare and Pension Plan Protection Act*, H.R. 5741, 90th Cong., 2d sess. (1968), p. 465.

U.S. Congress, House General Subcommittee on Labor, Committee on Education and Labor, *Private Welfare and Pension Plan Legislation*, 92d Cong., 1st and 2d sess. (1970), p. 262.

[13]NBC, "Pensions: The Broken Promise," 12 September 1972.

[14]*Federal Register*, November 21, 1978.

[15]Age Discrimination in Employment Act of 1967, as amended (1978) by PL 95-256, April 6, 1978.

[16]The Labor Department regulations referred to in connection with the ADEA amendments of 1978 (Public Law 95-256, 92 Stat. 189, approved April 6, 1978) are from the Labor Department Interpretive Bulletin on Age Discrimination in Employee Benefit Plans, 44 FR 30647, May 25, 1979.

[17]IRC Sec. 72.

Index